PEARSON

ALWAYS LEARNING

Robin Bade • Michael Parkin

Foundations of Macroeconomics

Custom Edition for University of Toledo

Taken from:
Foundations of Macroeconomics, Seventh Edition
by Robin Bade and Michael Parkin

Pearson Learning Solutions, 501 Boylston Street, Suite 900, Boston, MA 02116
A Pearson Education Company
www.pearsoned.com

Printed in the United States of America

1 2 3 4 5 6 7 8 9 10 V092 16 15 14

000200010271910497

LA

ISBN 10: 1-269-96221-3
ISBN 13: 978-1-269-96221-6

MyEconLab® Provides the Power of Practice

Optimize your study time with **MyEconLab**, the online assessment and tutorial system. When you take a sample test online, **MyEconLab** gives you targeted feedback and a personalized Study Plan to identify the topics you need to review.

Study Plan

The Study Plan shows you the sections you should study next, gives easy access to practice problems, and provides you with an automatically generated quiz to prove mastery of the course material.

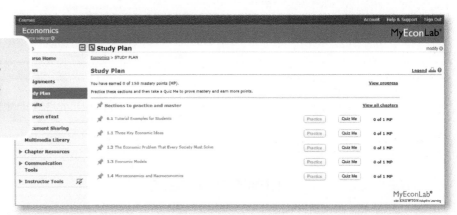

Unlimited Practice

As you work each exercise, instant feedback helps you understand and apply the concepts. Many Study Plan exercises contain algorithmically generated values to ensure that you get as much practice as you need.

Learning Resources

Study Plan problems link to learning resources that further reinforce concepts you need to master.

- **Help Me Solve This** learning aids help you break down a problem much the same way as an instructor would do during office hours. Help Me Solve This is available for select problems.

- **eText links** are specific to the problem at hand so that related concepts are easy to review just when they are needed.

- A **graphing tool** enables you to build and manipulate graphs to better understand how concepts, numbers, and graphs connect.

MyEconLab®

Find out more at www.myeconlab.com

Current News Exercises

Posted weekly, we find the latest microeconomic and macroeconomic news stories, post them, and write auto-graded multi-part exercises that illustrate the economic way of thinking about the news.

Interactive Homework Exercises

Participate in a fun and engaging activity that helps promote active learning and mastery of important economic concepts.

Pearson's experiments program is flexible and easy for instructors and students to use. For a complete list of available experiments, visit *www.myeconlab.com*.

FOUNDATIONS OF MACROECONOMICS

delivers a complete, hands-on learning system designed around active learning.

A Learning-by-Doing Approach

The **Checklist** that begins each chapter highlights the key topics covered and the chapter is divided into sections that directly correlate to the Checklist.

The **Checkpoint** that ends each section provides a full page of practice problems to encourage students to review the material while it is fresh in their minds.

Each chapter opens with a question about a central issue that sets the stage for the material.

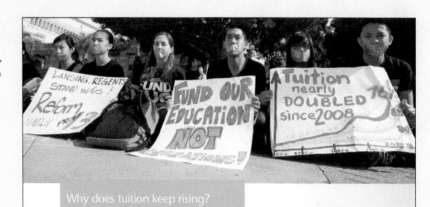

Why does tuition keep rising?

Demand and Supply

4

When you have completed your study of this chapter, you will be able to

CHAPTER CHECKLIST

1 Distinguish between quantity demanded and demand, and explain what determines demand.

2 Distinguish between quantity supplied and supply, and explain what determines supply.

3 Explain how demand and supply determine price and quantity in a market, and explain the effects of changes in demand and supply.

MyEconLab Big picture

 CHECKPOINT 4.1

Distinguish between quantity demanded and demand, and explain what determines demand.

Practice Problems

The following events occur one at a time in the market for cell phones:
- The price of a cell phone falls.
- Producers announce that cell-phone prices will fall next month.
- The price of a call made from a cell phone falls.
- The price of a call made from a land-line phone increases.
- The introduction of camera phones makes cell phones more popular.

1. Explain the effect of each event on the demand for cell phones.
2. Use a graph to illustrate the effect of each event.
3. Does any event (or events) illustrate the law of demand?

MyEconLab Study Plan 4.1
Key Terms Quiz
Solutions

 EYE on TUITION

Why Does Tuition Keep Rising?

Tuition has increased every year since 1980 and at the same time, enrollment has steadily climbed. Figure 1 shows these facts. The points tell us the levels of enrollment (x-axis) and tuition (y-axis, measured in 2010 dollars) in 1981, 1991, and each year from 2001 to 2010. We can interpret the data using the demand and supply model

In a given year, other things remain the same, but from one year to the next, some things change. The population has grown, incomes have increased, jobs that require more than a high-school diploma have expanded while jobs for high-school graduates have shrunk, and government subsidized student loans programs have expanded.

described. In 2001, demand was D_{01} and supply was S. The market was in equilibrium with 16 million students enrolled paying an average tuition of $15,000. By 2010, demand had increased to D_{10} At the tuition of 2001, there would be a severe shortage of college places, so tuition rises. In 2010, the market was in equilibrium

Eye On boxes apply theory to important issues and problems that shape our global society and individual decisions.

Confidence-Building Graphs

use color to show the direction of shifts and detailed, numbered captions guide students step-by-step through the action.

100% of the figures are animated in MyEconLab, with step-by-step audio narration.

 FIGURE 4.2

Change in Quantity Demanded Versus Change in Demand

MyEconLab Animation

1 **A decrease in the quantity demanded**
The quantity demanded decreases and there is a movement up along the demand curve D_0 if the price of the good rises and other things remain the same.

3 **A decrease in demand**
Demand decreases and the demand curve shifts leftward (from D_0 to D_1) if
- The price of a substitute falls or the price of a complement rises.
- The price of the good is expected to fall.
- Income decreases.*
- Expected future income or credit decreases.
- The number of buyers decreases.
*Bottled water is a normal good.

2 **An increase in the quantity demanded**
The quantity demanded increases and there is a movement down along the demand curve D_0 if the price of the good falls and other things remain the same.

4 **An increase in demand**
Demand increases and the demand curve shifts rightward (from D_0 to D_2) if
- The price of a substitute rises or the price of a complement falls.
- The price of the good is expected to rise.
- Income increases.
- Expected future income or credit increases.
- The number of buyers increases.

Price (dollars per bottle)
2.50
2.00
1.50
1.00
0.50

0 8 9 10 11 12 13
Quantity (millions of bottles per day)

D_2
D_0
D_1

To Erin, Tessa, Jack, Abby, and Sophie

About the Authors

Robin Bade was an undergraduate at the University of Queensland, Australia, where she earned degrees in mathematics and economics. After a spell teaching high school math and physics, she enrolled in the Ph.D. program at the Australian National University, from which she graduated in 1970. She has held faculty appointments at the University of Edinburgh in Scotland, at Bond University in Australia, and at the Universities of Manitoba, Toronto, and Western Ontario in Canada. Her research on international capital flows appears in the *International Economic Review* and the *Economic Record.*

Robin first taught the principles of economics course in 1970 and has taught it (alongside intermediate macroeconomics and international trade and finance) most years since then. She developed many of the ideas found in this text while conducting tutorials with her students at the University of Western Ontario.

Michael Parkin studied economics in England and began his university teaching career immediately after graduating with a B.A. from the University of Leicester. He learned the subject on the job at the University of Essex, England's most exciting new university of the 1960s, and at the age of 30 became one of the youngest full professors. He is a past president of the Canadian Economics Association and has served on the editorial boards of the *American Economic Review* and the *Journal of Monetary Economics.* His research on macroeconomics, monetary economics, and international economics has resulted in more than 160 publications in journals and edited volumes, including the *American Economic Review*, the *Journal of Political Economy*, the *Review of Economic Studies*, the *Journal of Monetary Economics*, and the *Journal of Money, Credit, and Banking.* He is author of the best-selling textbook, *Economics* (Addison-Wesley), now in its Eleventh Edition.

Robin and Michael are a wife-and-husband team. Their most notable joint research created the Bade-Parkin Index of central bank independence and spawned a vast amount of research on that topic. They don't claim credit for the independence of the new European Central Bank, but its constitution and the movement toward greater independence of central banks around the world were aided by their pioneering work. Their joint textbooks include *Macroeconomics* (Prentice-Hall), *Modern Macroeconomics* (Pearson Education Canada), and *Economics: Canada in the Global Environment*, the Canadian adaptation of Parkin, *Economics* (Addison-Wesley). They are dedicated to the challenge of explaining economics ever more clearly to a growing body of students.

Music, the theater, art, walking on the beach, and five grandchildren provides their relaxation and fun.

MACROECONOMICS Brief Contents

Contents

PART 2   MONITORING THE MACROECONOMY

PART 3   THE REAL ECONOMY

PART 4   THE MONEY ECONOMY

PART 5   ECONOMIC FLUCTUATIONS

PART 6   MACROECONOMIC POLICY

Preface

Students know that throughout their lives they will make economic decisions and be influenced by economic forces. They want to understand the economic principles that can help them navigate these forces and guide their decisions. *Foundations of Macroeconomics* is our attempt to satisfy this want.

The response to our earlier editions from hundreds of colleagues across the United States and throughout the world tells us that most of you agree with our view that the principles course must do four things well. It must

- Motivate with compelling issues and questions
- Focus on core ideas
- Steer a path between an overload of detail and too much left unsaid
- Encourage and aid learning by doing

The Foundations icon with its four blocks (on the cover and throughout the book) symbolizes this four-point approach that has guided all our choices in writing this text and creating its comprehensive teaching and learning supplements.

WHAT'S NEW IN THE SEVENTH EDITION

Two big stories dominate this Seventh Edition revision: A careful fine-tuning of the heavily revised and successful Sixth Edition content, and a massive investment in enhanced electronic features to bring the text to life and provide an exciting interactive experience for the student on all platforms and devices.

■ Fine-Tuning the Content

The content of this revision is driven by the drama of the extraordinary period of economic history in which we are living and its rich display of events and forces through which students can be motivated to discover the economic way of thinking. Persistent unemployment and slow growth; headwinds from Europe's unresolved debt crisis; ongoing tensions arising from offshore outsourcing; a slowing pace of China's expansion; enhanced concern about climate change; falling U.S. energy imports as fracking boosts domestic production; relentless pressure on the federal budget from the demands of an aging population and a sometimes dysfunctional Congress; the dilemma posed by slow recovery and rising government debt; the question of when and how fast to exit an era of extreme monetary stimulus; and a fluctuating dollar are just a few of these interest-arousing events. All of them feature at the appropriate points in our new edition.

Every chapter contains many small changes, all designed to enhance clarity and currency, and the text and examples are all thoroughly updated to reflect the most recently available data and events. We have also made a few carefully selected larger changes that we describe below.

■ Enhanced eText and New Interactive Electronic Features

The new enhanced Pearson eText extends the functionality of the current eText to integrate it with MyEconLab's Study Plan, now powered by Knewton Adaptive Learning, and with MyEconLab's Gradebook. The new eText also takes full advantage of available technologies to bring the student an enriched set of tools that aid comprehension and bring those moments of discovery that stick in the memory. These tools are

- A "Big Picture" video that motivates and summarizes each chapter and provides an outline answer to the chapter's motivating question.
- A series of "Snapshot" videos that illustrate and explain the key ideas in each section of a chapter. The Snapshots also contain animations and explanations of each figure, which can be played separately.
- A series of "Solutions" videos that walk the student through the solutions to the Practice Problems and In the News exercises in each Checkpoint.
- "Study Plan" links that provide opportunities for more practice with problems similar to those in the text that give targeted feedback to guide the student in answering the exercises.
- "Key Terms Quiz" links that provide opportunities for students to check their knowledge of the definitions and uses of the key terms.
- Automatic real-time updating from the St. Louis Federal Reserve data base, FRED, of all time-series figures.

■ Notable Content Changes

Because the previous edition revision was so extensive and well-received, we have limited our interventions and changes in this Seventh Edition to addressing the small number of issues raised by our reviewers and users, to ensuring that we are thoroughly up-to-date, and to focusing on the new electronic tools that we've just described. Nonetheless, some changes that we now summarize are worth noting.

We have reorganized the section in Chapter 1 on "The Economic Way of Thinking" to provide a clearer sequencing of the key ideas.

In Chapter 2, The U.S. and Global Economies, we use the new example of the complex production of the Dreamliner to motivate and illustrate what, how, and for whom in the U.S. and global economies. A new *Eye on the Past* looks at the dramatic changes in manufacturing in the U.S. economy through the example of the domestic production of shoes. Also a new photo essay highlights global differences in how goods and services are produced and the section on government has been compressed and simplified.

In Chapter 3, The Economic Problem, we illustrate economic growth and the expansion of production possibilities with the dramatic example of hydraulic fracturing—fracking—in the United States and its effects on the production and opportunity cost of energy.

Chapter 4, Demand and Supply, has a new motivating issue: "Why does tuition keep rising?" Not only is the question a deeply personal one for students but it is also a good example of how the demand-supply model enables us to isolate increasing demand as the source of a rising price. Events in the increasingly important market for solar panels provide a contrasting example of the effects of an increase in supply. We have revised the section on changes in both demand and supply to better explain the unambiguous and ambiguous cases and leave the student to pull all possible cases together.

We have added a new section to Chapter 4 on price rigidities: price floors, price ceilings, and sticky prices. The purpose of this section is to explain the features of markets that have implications for the aggregate economy. All sources of price rigidity bring an outcome that is "off" either the demand curve or the supply curve and that gives rise to search activity. Understanding persistent unemployment and the output gap is facilitated by teaching this extension of the standard demand-supply model.

In Chapter 9, Economic Growth, we have simplified the explanation of the contributions to productivity growth of capital accumulation and technological change to the fluctuating pace of productivity growth.

Topical policy issues pervade the macro chapters. These include the persistence of high unemployment in the United States, Eurozone's extreme unemployment problem, and the falling U.S. labor force participation rate in Chapter 6; the ever-widening Lucas wedge, now greater than $400,000 per person, and the persistence of U.S./E.U. productivity differences in Chapter 8; QE3 and the explosion of monetary base, the rise in bank reserves, and the collapse of the money multiplier in Chapter 11; the decrease in the demand for M1 in Chapter 12; the persistent recessionary gap in Chapter 13; the persistent federal budget deficit and rising debt to GDP ratio, and the ongoing structural deficit in Chapter 16; and the ongoing near-zero federal funds rate, an update of the contrast between monetary policy today and during the Great Depression, and nominal GDP targeting in Chapter 17.

THE FOUNDATIONS VISION

■ Focus on Core Concepts

Each chapter of *Foundations* concentrates on a manageable number of main ideas (most commonly three or four) and reinforces each idea several times throughout the chapter. This patient, confidence-building approach guides students through unfamiliar terrain and helps them to focus their efforts on the most important tools and concepts of our discipline.

■ Many Learning Tools for Many Learning Styles

Foundations' integrated print and electronic package builds on the basic fact that students have a variety of learning styles. Students have powerful tools at their fingertips: With links from eText, they can get an immediate sense of the content of a chapter by playing the Big Picture video; learn the key ideas by playing the Snapshot videos, and get a quick walkthrough of the Checkpoint Practice Problems and In the News exercises with the Solutions videos.

In MyEconLab, students can complete all Checkpoint problems and In the News exercises online and get instant feedback, work with interactive graphs and real-time data graphs, assess their skills by taking Practice Tests, receive a personalized Study Plan, and step-by-step help through the feature called "Help Me Solve This."

■ Diagrams That Tell the Whole Story

We developed the style of our diagrams with extensive feedback from faculty focus-group participants and student reviewers. All of our figures make consistent use of color to show the direction of shifts and contain detailed, numbered captions designed to direct students' attention step-by-step through the action.

Because beginning students of economics are often apprehensive about working with graphs, we have made a special effort to present material in as many as three ways—with graphs, words, and tables—in the same figure. In an innovation that seems necessary, but is to our knowledge unmatched, nearly all of the information supporting a figure appears on the same page as the figure itself. No more flipping pages back and forth!

■ Real-World Connections That Bring Theory to Life

Students learn best when they can see the purpose of what they are studying, apply it to illuminate the world around them, and use it in their lives.

Eye on boxes offer fresh new examples to help students see that economics is everywhere. Current and recent events appear in *Eye on the U.S. Economy* boxes; we place current U.S. economic events in global and historical perspectives in our *Eye on the Global Economy* and *Eye on the Past* boxes; and we show how students can use economics in day-to-day decisions in *Eye on Your Life* boxes.

The *Eye On* boxes that build off of the chapter-opening question help students see the economics behind key issues facing our world and highlight a major aspect of the chapter's story.

ORGANIZATION

We have organized the sequence of material and chapters in what we think is the most natural order in which to cover the material. But we recognize that there are alternative views on the best order. We have kept this fact and the need for flexibility firmly in mind throughout the text. Many alternative sequences work, and the Flexibility Chart on p. xxxiii explains the alternative pathways through the chapters. In using the flexibility information, keep in mind that the best sequence is the one in which we present the material. And even chapters that the flexibility chart identifies as strictly optional are better covered than omitted.

MYECONLAB

MyEconLab

MyEconLab has been designed and refined with a single purpose in mind: to create those moments of understanding that transform the difficult into the clear and obvious. With comprehensive homework, quiz, test, activity, and tutorial options, instructors can manage all their assessment needs in one program.

- All of the Checkpoint and Chapter Checkpoint Problems and Applications are assignable and automatically graded in MyEconLab.
- Extra problems and applications, including algorithmic, draw-graph, and numerical exercises are available for student practice or instructor assignment.
- Problems and applications that use real-time data continuously update.
- Test Item File questions are available for assignment as homework.
- Custom Exercise Builder gives instructors the flexibility of creating their own problems for assignment.
- Gradebook records each student's performance and time spent on the Tests and Study Plan and generates reports by student or by chapter.

New for the Seventh Edition is an enhanced Pearson eText that extends the functionality of the current eText with its embedded and auto-graded MyEconLab assessment that feeds directly into MyEconLab's Study Plan, now powered by Knewton Adaptive Learning. The enhanced eText includes video, animations, and problem-solving tools designed for student success.

The enhanced Pearson eText is available within the online course materials and offline via an iPad app. It also allows instructors and students to highlight, bookmark, and take notes.

■ Features of the Enhanced eText

Big Picture Videos   Big Picture videos, tied to the Chapter Checklist, set the stage for the main concept that will be introduced throughout the chapter. Students can use these videos to prepare for today's lecture or to help them focus on main chapter ideas.

> ### DEMAND and SUPPLY: THE BIG PICTURE
>
> Buyers like a low price, and the lower the price, the greater is the quantity they plan to buy—the law of demand.
>
> Sellers like a high price, and the higher the price, the greater is the quantity they plan to sell—the law of supply.
>
> Too high a price brings a surplus, and too low a price brings a shortage.
>
> When there is a surplus, the price falls; and when there is a shortage, the price rises—the law of market forces.

Snapshot Videos   Snapshot videos accompany every major section of each chapter and are designed to briefly present the major concepts and graphical tools covered within key sections. Using text, audio, and animation, Snapshot videos enable students with different learning styles to efficiently study and review key concepts of the chapter.

> ### 4.1 DEMAND: SNAPSHOT
>
> ■ **Law of Demand**
>
> The law of demand tells us about the relationship between the price of a good and its quantity demanded.
>
> Other things remaining the same,
>
> - If the price of a good rises, the quantity demanded of that good decreases; and
> - If the price of a good falls, the quantity demanded of that good increases.

Animations   Every textbook figure includes a step-by-step animation, with audio, to help students learn the intuition behind reading and interpreting graphs. These animations may be used for review, or as an instructional aid in the classroom. Figures labeled *MyEconLab Real-Time Data* update using the most recent data available from the Federal Reserve Bank of St. Louis's FRED site.

Embedded MyEconLab Assessment   Every Checkpoint Practice Problem, every In the News problem, and every Study Plan Problem and Application in the enhanced eText can be worked by the student directly from the eText page on which it occurs. These problems are auto-graded and feed into the MyEconLab's Study Plan, which is now powered by Knewton Adapative Learning and where students receive recommendations based upon their performance.

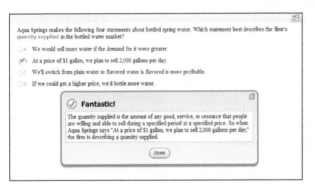

Key Terms Quiz   The Key Terms Quiz, accessible from each Checkpoint, allows students to check their understanding of key chapter concepts before moving onto the next section. The Interactive Glossary that supports the enhanced eText provides the key term definition, an example, and related terms.

Solutions Videos   Every Checkpoint Practice problem and In the News Problem is supported by a solutions video that provides a step-by-step review of the problem and its solution, including graphical analysis. Text, audio, and animation ensure that a student understands how to set-up and solve each of the problems.

■ **MyEconLab also includes:**

Economics in the News   Economics in the News is a turn-key solution to bringing daily news into the classroom. Updated daily during the academic year, we upload a relevant article and provide questions that may be assigned for homework or for classroom discussion.

Current News   Each week during the academic year, we upload multi-part exercises, with links to relevant articles, into the MyEconLab assignment manager. These enable instructors to bring current issues and events into the course with easy to assign and auto-graded exercises.

Real-Time Data Analysis Exercises (FRED)   Easy to assign and automatically graded, Real-Time Data Analysis exercises communicate directly with the Federal Reserve Bank of St. Louis's FRED site, so every time FRED posts new data, students see new data. As a result, Real-Time Data Analysis exercises offer a no-fuss solution for instructors who want to make the most recent data a central part of their macro course. End-of-chapter exercises accompanied by the Real-Time Data Analysis icon (⊕) include Real-Time Data versions in MyEconLab. Select in-text figures, labeled Real-time data, update in the eText using FRED data.

Experiments in MyEconLab   Experiments are a fun and engaging way to promote active learning and mastery of important economic concepts. Pearson's Experiments program is flexible and easy for instructors to assign and students to use.

- Single-player experiments, available to assign, allow your students to play against virtual players from anywhere at anytime so long as they have an internet connection.
- Multiplayer experiments allow you to assign and manage a real-time experiment with your class.
- Pre and post-questions for each experiment are available for assignment in MyEconLab.
- Experiments are auto-graded using algorithms that objectively evaluate a student's economic gain and performance during the experiment.

  For a complete list of available experiments, visit www.myeconlab.com.

AACSB and Learning Outcomes   All end-of-chapter and Test Item File questions are tagged in two ways: to AACSB standards and to discipline-specific Learning Outcomes. These two separate tagging systems allow professors to build assessments around desired departmental and course outcomes and track results in MyEconLab's gradebook.

■ MyEconLab and Adaptive Learning

Adaptive Study Plan   MyEconLab's Study Plan is now powered by a sophisticated adaptive learning engine that tailors learning material to meet the unique needs of each student. MyEconLab's new Adaptive Learning Study Plan monitors students' performance on homework, quizzes, and tests and continuously makes recommendations based on that performance.

   If a student is struggling with a concept such as supply and demand, or having trouble calculating a price elasticity of demand, the Study Plan provides customized remediation activities—a pathway based on personal proficiencies, number of attempts, or difficulty of questions—to get the student back on track. Students will also receive recommendations for additional practice in the form of rich multi-media learning aids such as videos, an interactive eText, Help Me Solve This tutorials, and graphing tools.

   The Study Plan can extrapolate a student's future trouble spots and provide learning material and practice to avoid pitfalls. In addition, students who are showing a high degree of success with the assessment material are offered a chance to work on future topics based on the professor's course coverage preferences. This personalized and adaptive feedback and support ensures that your students are optimizing their current and future course work and mastering the concepts, rather than just memorizing and guessing answers.

You can learn more about adaptive learning at http://www.myeconlab .com/product-info/adaptive.

Dynamic Study Modules   Dynamic Study Modules, which focus on key topic areas and are available from within MyEconLab, are an additional way for students to obtain tailored help. These modules work by continuously assessing student performance and activity on discrete topics and provide personalized content in real time to reinforce concepts that target each student's particular strengths and weaknesses.

Each Dynamic Study Module, accessed by computer, smartphone, or tablet, promotes fast learning and long-term retention. Because MyEconLab and Dynamic Study Modules help students stay on track and achieve a higher level of subject-matter mastery, more class time is available for interaction, discussion, collaboration, and exploring applications to current news and events.

Instructors can register, create, and access all of their MyEconLab courses at www.pearsonmylab.com.

SUPPORT MATERIALS FOR INSTRUCTORS AND STUDENTS

Foundations of Macroeconomics is accompanied by the most comprehensive set of teaching and learning tools ever assembled. Each component of our package is organized by Checkpoint topic for a tight, seamless integration with both the textbook and the other components. In addition to authoring the MyEconLab and PowerPoint content, we have helped in the reviewing and revising of the Study Guide, Solutions Manual, Instructor's Manual, and Test Item Files to ensure that every element of the package achieves the consistency that students and teachers need.

■ PowerPoint Resources

We have created the PowerPoint resources based on our 20 years of experience using this tool in our own classrooms. We have created five sets of PowerPoint presentations for instructors.
They are:

* Lecture notes with full-color, animated figures, and tables from the textbook
* Figures and tables from the textbook, animated with step-by-step walk-through for instructors to use in their own personal slides
* *Eye On* features
* Checkpoint Practice Problems and solutions

A student version of the lecture notes is also available on MyEconLab.

■ Instructor's Manual

The Instructor's Manual, written by Luke Armstrong and reviewed by Mark Rush, contains chapter outlines and road maps, additional exercises with solutions, a comprehensive Chapter Lecture resource, and a virtual encyclopedia of suggestions on how to enrich class presentation and use class time efficiently. The Instructor's Manual has been updated to reflect changes in the main text as well as infused with a fresh and intuitive approach to teaching this course. The Instructor's Manual is available for download in Word and PDF formats.

■ Solutions Manual

The Solutions Manual, written by Mark Rush and checked for accuracy by Jeannie Gillmore, contains the solutions to all Checkpoint Practice Problems, In the News exercises, and Chapter Checkpoint Problems and Applications. The Solutions Manual is available for download in Word and PDF formats.

■ Three Test Item Files and TestGen

More than 5,000 multiple-choice, numerical, fill-in-the-blank, short answer, essay, and integrative questions make up the three Test Item Files that support *Foundations of Macroeconomics*. Mark Rush reviewed and edited questions from three dedicated principles instructors to form one of the most comprehensive testing systems on the market. Our authors are Gregory E. Givens (University of Alabama), Buffie Schmidt (Augusta State University), and Rolando Sanchez (Northwest Vista College).The entire set of questions is available for download in Word, PDF, and TestGen formats.

All three Test Item Files are available in test generator software (TestGen with QuizMaster). TestGen's graphical interface enables instructors to view, edit, and add questions; transfer questions to tests; and print different forms of tests. Instructors also have the option to reformat tests with varying fonts and styles, margins, and headers and footers, as in any word-processing document. Search and sort features let the instructor quickly locate questions and arrange them in a preferred order. QuizMaster, working with your school's computer network, automatically grades the exams, stores the results on disk, and allows the instructor to view and print a variety of reports.

■ Instructor's Resource Disk

This Disk contains the Instructor's Manual, Solutions Manual, and Test Item Files in Word and PDF formats. It also contains the Computerized Test Item Files (with a TestGen program installer) and PowerPoint resources. It is compatible with both Windows and Macintosh operating systems.

For your convenience, all instructor resources are also available online via our centralized supplements Web site, the Instructor Resource Center (www .pearsonhighered.com/irc). For access or more information, contact your local Pearson representative or request access online at the Instructor Resource Center.

■ Study Guide for Students

Mark Rush of the University of Florida has prepared the Study Guide, which is available in both print and electronic formats in MyEconLab. It provides an expanded Chapter Checklist that enables the student to break the learning tasks down into smaller, bite-sized pieces; self-test materials; and additional practice problems. The Study Guide has been carefully coordinated with the text, MyEconLab, and the Test Item Files.

ACKNOWLEDGMENTS

Working on a project such as this one generates many debts that can never be repaid. But they can be acknowledged, and it is a special pleasure to be able to do so here and to express our heartfelt thanks to each and every one of the following long list, without whose contributions we could not have produced *Foundations*.

Mark Rush again coordinated, managed, and contributed to our Study Guide, Solutions Manual, Instructor's Manual, and Test Item Files. He assembled, polished, wrote, and rewrote these materials to ensure their close consistency with the text. He and we were in constant contact as all the elements of our text and package came together. Mark also made many valuable suggestions for improving the text and the Checkpoint Problems. His contribution went well beyond that of a reviewer, and his effervescent sense of humor kept us all in good spirits along the way.

Working closely with Mark, Luke Armstrong wrote content for the Instructor's Manual. Buffie Schmidt, Greg Givens, and Rolando Sanchez authored new questions for the Test Item Files.

Michelle Sheran (University of North Carolina, Greensboro) and Carol Dole (Jacksonville University) recorded the narrations that accompany the Big Picture, Snapshot, and Solutions videos in the eText. The engaging style and clarity of these outstanding teachers makes these videos a powerful learning tool. Fred Bounds (Georgia Perimeter College), Carol Dole, Trevor Collier (University of Dayton), and Paul Lande (Loyola University Maryland) provided outstanding reviews of the Study Plan and Assessment problems in MyEconLab and helped us to make these autograded exercises and their feedback messages as effective as possible.

The ideas from which *Foundations* grew began to form over dinner at the Andover Inn in Andover, Massachusetts, with Denise Clinton and Sylvia Mallory. We gratefully acknowledge Sylvia's role not only at the birth of this project but also in managing its initial development team. Denise has been an ongoing inspiration for 15 years, and we are privileged to have the benefit of her enormous experience.

The success of *Foundations* owes much to its outstanding Executive Acquisitions Editor, Adrienne D'Ambrosio. Adrienne's acute intelligence and sensitive understanding of the market have helped sharpen our vision of this text and package. Her value-added on this project is huge. It has been, and we hope it will for many future editions remain, a joy to work with her.

Sarah Dumouchelle, Editorial Project Manager, ensured that we were provided with outstanding and timely reviews and managed the photo research and our supplements. Elissa Senra-Sargent, Editorial Assistant, helped us in many ways, particularly in envisioning the new cover design.

Jonathan Boylan created the new impressive cover design and converted the raw ideas of our brainstorms into an outstandingly designed text.

Susan Schoenberg, Media Director, Denise Clinton, Media Publisher, Melissa Honig, Senior Media Producer, and Noel Lotz, Content Product Manager have set a new standard for online learning and teaching resources. Building on the pioneering work of Michelle Neil, Susan worked creatively to improve our technology systems. Melissa managed the building of MyEconLab, and Noel managed reviews of the content. They have all been sources of high energy, good sense, and level-headed advice and quickly found creative solutions to all our technology problems.

Nancy Freihofer, our outstanding, ever calm, Senior Production Project Manager, worked with a talented team at Integra, Project Editor, Heather Johnson, and designer, art coordinator, and typesetter. Our copy editor, Catherine Baum, gave our work a thorough review and helpful polish, and our proofreader ensured the most error-free text we have yet produced.

Our Executive Marketing Manager, Lori DeShazo, has been a constant source of good judgment and sound advice on content and design issues, ranging over the entire package from text to print and electronic supplements.

Richard Parkin, our technical illustrator, created the figures in the text, the dynamic figures in the eText, the animated figures in the PowerPoint presentations, created the animations for and assembled the enhanced eText videos, and contributed many ideas to improving the clarity of our illustrations in all media.

Jeannie Gillmore, our long-standing personal assistant, worked closely with us to create MyEconLab exercises and guided solutions.

Don Davison of Galvaston College found an embarrassing error that has been present in the previous editions and that we are pleased to have been able to correct.

Sharmistha Nag, our new personal assistant, worked with us to create the Key Terms Quizzes and to make daily news problems available in the MyEconLab assignment manager for easy assignment and auto-grading.

Finally, our reviewers, whose names appear on the following pages, have made an enormous contribution to this text and MyEconLab resources. Once again we find ourselves using superlatives, but they are called for. In the many texts that we've written, we've not seen reviewing of the quality that we enjoyed on this revision. It has been a pleasure (if at times a challenge) to respond constructively to their many excellent suggestions.

Robin Bade
Michael Parkin
London, Ontario, Canada
robin@econ100.com
michael.parkin@uwo.ca

FOUNDATIONS OF MACROECONOMICS: FLEXIBILITY CHART

Flexibility

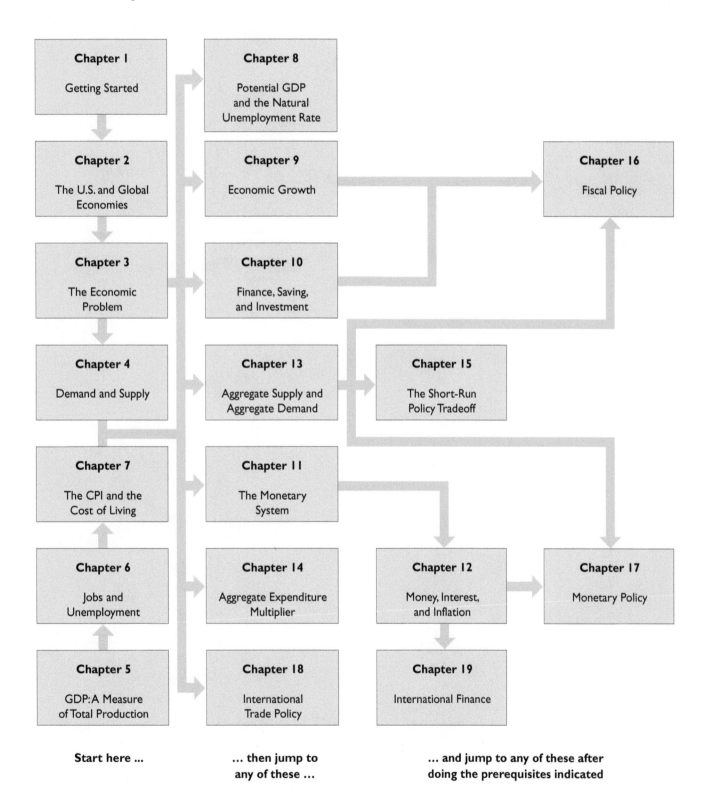

Start here ...   **... then jump to any of these ...**   **... and jump to any of these after doing the prerequisites indicated**

Reviewers

Alfredo A. Romero Aguirre, North Carolina A&T State University

Seemi Ahmad, Dutchess Community College

William Aldridge, Shelton State Community College

Rashid B. Al-Hmoud, Texas Tech University

Neil Alper, Northeastern University

Nejat Anbarci, Deakin University

J.J. Arias, Georgia College & State University

Luke A. Armstrong, Lee College

Leland Ash, Skagit Valley College

Ali Ataiifar, Delaware County Community College

John Baffoe-Bonnie, Pennsylvania State University, Delaware County Campus

A. Paul Ballantyne, University of Colorado

Tyra D. Barrett, Pellissippi State Community College

Sue Bartlett, University of South Florida

Gerald Baumgardner, Penn College

Klaus Becker, Texas Tech University

Clive Belfield, Queen's College, City University of New York

William K. Bellinger, Dickinson College

John Bethune, Barton College

Prasun Bhattacharjee, East Tennessee State University

Gautam Bhattacharya, University of Kansas

Gerald W. Bialka, University of North Florida

David Bivin, Indiana University–Purdue University at Indianapolis

Geoffrey Black, Boise State University

Carey Anne Borkoski, Arundel Community College

Jurgen Brauer, Augusta State University

Greg Brock, Georgia Southern University

Barbara Brogan, Northern Virginia Community College

Bruce C. Brown, California State Polytechnic University, Pomona

Christopher Brown, Arkansas State University

James O. Brown, Delta State University

Brian Buckley, Clemson University

Donald Bumpass, Sam Houston State University

Seewoonundun Bunjun, East Stroudsburg University

Nancy Burnett, University of Wisconsin at Oshkosh

James L. Butkiewicz, University of Delaware

Barbara Caldwell, Saint Leo University

Bruce Caldwell, University of North Carolina, Greensboro

Joseph Calhoun, Florida State University

Robert Carlsson, University of South Carolina

Shawn Carter, Jacksonville State University

Regina Cassady, Valencia Community College

Jack Chambless, Valencia Community College

Joni Charles, Southwest Texas State University

Anoshua Chaudhuri, San Francisco State University

Robert Cherry, Brooklyn College

Chi-Young Choi, University of New Hampshire

Paul Cichello, Xavier University

Quentin Ciolfi, Brevard Community College

Victor V. Claar, Henderson State University

Jane L. Cline, Forsyth Technical Community College

Jim Cobbe, Florida State University

John Cochran, University of Chicago

Mike Cohick, Collin County Community College

Ludovic Comeau, De Paul University

Carol Conrad, Cerro Coso Community College

Christopher Cornell, Vassar College

Richard Cornwall, University of California, Davis

Kevin Cotter, Wayne State University

Erik Craft, University of Richmond

Tom Creahan, Morehead State University

Elizabeth Crowell, University of Michigan at Dearborn

Susan Dadres, Southern Methodist University

David Davenport, McLennan Community College

Troy Davig, College of William and Mary

Jeffrey Davis, ITT Technical Institute (Utah)

Lewis Davis, Union College

Dennis Debrecht, Carroll College

Al DeCooke, Broward Community College

Jason J. Delaney, Georgia Gwinnett College

Vince DiMartino, University of Texas at San Antonio

Vernon J. Dobis, Minnesota State University–Moorhead

Carol Dole, Jacksonville University

Kathleen Dorsainvil, American University

John Dorsey, University of Maryland, College Park

Amrik Singh Dua, Mt. San Antonio College

Marie Duggan, Keene State College

Allen Dupont, North Carolina State University

David Eaton, Murray State University

Kevin J. Egan, University of Toledo

Harold W. Elder, University of Alabama

Harry Ellis, University of North Texas

Stephen Ellis, North Central Texas College

Carl Enomoto, New Mexico State University

Chuen-mei Fan, Colorado State University

Chris Fant, Spartanburg Community College

Elena Ermolenko Fein, Oakton Community College

Gary Ferrier, University of Arkansas

Rudy Fichtenbaum, Wright State University

Donna K. Fisher, Georgia Southern University

Kaya Ford, Northern Virginia Community College

Robert Francis, Shoreline Community College

Roger Frantz, San Diego State University

Amanda S. Freeman, Kansas State University

Marc Fusaro, East Carolina University
Arthur Friedberg, Mohawk Valley Community College
Julie Gallaway, Southwest Missouri State University
Byron Gangnes, University of Hawaii
Gay Gareschè, Glendale Community College
Neil Garston, California State University, Los Angeles
Lisa Geib-Gunderson, University of Maryland
Lisa M. George, City University of New York
Linda Ghent, Eastern Illinois University
Soma Ghosh, Bridgewater State College
Kirk Gifford, Ricks College
Scott Gilbert, Southern Illinois University
Maria Giuili, Diablo Valley Community College
Mark Gius, Quinnipiac College
Gregory E. Givens, University of Alabama
Randall Glover, Brevard Community College
Stephan Gohmann, University of Louisville
Richard Gosselin, Houston Community College
John Graham, Rutgers University
Patricia E. Graham, University of Northern Colorado
Warren Graham, Tulsa Community College
Homer Guevara, Jr., Northwest Vista College
Osman Gulseven, North Carolina State University
Jang-Ting Guo, University of California, Riverside
Dennis Hammett, University of Texas at El Paso
Leo Hardwick, Macomb Community College
Mehdi Haririan, Bloomsburg University
Paul Harris, Camden County Community College
Mark Healy, William Rainey Harper College
Rey Hernandez-Julian, Metropolitan State College of Denver
Gus Herring, Brookhaven College
Michael Heslop, Northern Virginia Community College
Steven Hickerson, Mankato State University

Frederick Steb Hipple, East Tennessee State University
Lee Hoke, University of Tampa
Andy Howard, Rio Hondo College
Yu Hsing, Southeastern Louisiana University
Greg Hunter, California State Polytechnic University, Pomona
Matthew Hyle, Winona State University
Todd Idson, Boston University
Harvey James, University of Hartford
Russell Janis, University of Massachusetts at Amherst
Ricot Jean, Valencia College
Jay A. Johnson, Southeastern Louisiana University
Ted Joyce, City University of New York, Baruch College
Ahmad A. Kader, University of Nevada, Las Vegas
Jonathan D. Kaplan, California State University, Sacramento
Arthur Kartman, San Diego State University
Chris Kauffman, University of Tennessee
Diane Keenan, Cerritos College
Brian Kench, University of Tampa
John Keith, Utah State University
Kristen Keith, University of Toledo
Joe Kerkvliet, Oregon State University
Randall Kesselring, Arkansas State University
Gary Kikuchi, University of Hawaii at Manoa
Douglas Kinnear, Colorado State University
Morris Knapp, Miami Dade Community College
Steven Koch, Georgia Southern University
Kate Krause, University of New Mexico
Stephan Kroll, California State University, Sacramento
Joyce Lapping, University of Southern Maine
Tom Larson, California State University, Los Angeles
Robert Lemke, Florida International University
J. Mark Leonard, University of Nebraska at Omaha
Tony Lima, California State University, Hayward
Joshua Long, Ivy Tech Community College

Kenneth Long, New River Community College
Noel Lotz, Middle Tennessee State University
Marty Ludlum, Oklahoma City Community College
Brian Lynch, Lake Land College
Michael Machiorlatti, Oklahoma City Community College
Roger Mack, De Anza College
Michael Magura, University of Toledo
Mark Maier, Glendale College
Svitlana Maksymenko, University of Pittsburgh
Paula Manns, Atlantic Cape Community College
Dan Marburger, Arkansas State University
Kathryn Marshall, Ohio State University
John V. Martin, Boise State University
Drew E. Mattson, Anoka-Ramsey Community College
Stephen McCafferty, Ohio State University
Thomas S. McCaleb, Florida State University
Katherine S. McCann, University of Delaware
William McLean, Oklahoma State University
Diego Mendez-Carbajo, Illinois Wesleyan University
Evelina Mengova, California State University, Fullerton
Thomas Meyer, Patrick Henry Community College
Meghan Millea, Mississippi State University
Michael Milligan, Front Range Community College
Jenny Minier, University of Miami
David Mitchell, Valdosta State University
Dr. Carl B. Montano, Lamar University
Christine Moser, Western Michigan University
William Mosher, Clark University
Mike Munoz, Northwest Vista College
John R. Mundy, St. Johns River State College
Kevin Murphy, Oakland University
Ronald Nate, Brigham Young University, Idaho
Nasrin Nazemzadeh, Rowan Cabarrus Community College
Michael Nelson, Texas A&M University

Rebecca Neumann, University of Wisconsin—Milwaukee

Charles Newton, Houston Community College Southwest

Melinda Nish, Salt Lake Community College

Lee Nordgren, Indiana University at Bloomington

Norman P. Obst, Michigan State University

Inge O'Connor, Syracuse University

William C. O'Connor, Western Montana College–University of Montana

Fola Odebunmi, Cypress College

Victor I. Oguledo, Florida A&M University

Charles Okeke, College of Southern Nevada

Lydia M. Ortega, St. Philip's College

P. Marcelo Oviedo, Iowa State University

Jennifer Pate, Ph.D., Loyola Marymount University

Sanjay Paul, Elizabethtown College

Ken Peterson, Furman University

Tim Petry, North Dakota State University

Charles Pflanz, Scottsdale Community College

Jonathon Phillips, North Carolina State University

Basharat Pitafi, Southern Illinois University

Anthony Plunkett, Harrison College

Paul Poast, Ohio State University

Greg Pratt, Mesa Community College

Fernando Quijano, Dickinson State University

Andy Radler, Butte Community College

Ratha Ramoo, Diablo Valley College

Karen Reid, University of Wisconsin, Parkside

Mary Rigdon, University of Texas, Austin

Helen Roberts, University of Illinois at Chicago

Greg Rose, Sacramento City College

Barbara Ross, Kapi'olani Community College

Elham Rouhani, Gwinnett Technical College

Jeffrey Rous, University of North Texas

June Roux, Salem Community College

Udayan Roy, Long Island University

Nancy C. Rumore, University of Louisiana–Lafayette

Mark Rush, University of Florida

Rolando Sanchez, Northwest Vista College

Joseph Santos, South Dakota State University

Roland Santos, Lakeland Community College

Mark Scanlan, Stephen F. Austin State University

Ted Scheinman, Mount Hood Community College

Buffie Schmidt, Augusta State University

Jerry Schwartz, Broward Community College

Gautam Sethi, Bard College

Margaret Anne Shannon, Georgia Southern University

Mushtaq Sheikh, Union County College

Michelle Sheran-Andrews, University of North Carolina at Greensboro

Virginia Shingleton, Valparaiso University

Steven S. Shwiff, Texas A & M University—Commerce

Charles Sicotte, Rock Valley College

Issoufou Soumaila, Texas Tech University

Martin Spechler, Indiana University

Leticia Starkov, Elgin Community College

Stela Stefanova, University of Delaware

John Stiver, University of Connecticut

Richard W. Stratton, The University of Akron

Abdulhamid Sukar, Cameron University

Terry Sutton, Southeast Missouri State University

Janet M. Thomas, Bentley College

Donna Thompson, Brookdale Community College

Deborah Thorsen, Palm Beach State College

James Thorson, Southern Connecticut State University

Marc Tomljanovich, Colgate University

Cynthia Royal Tori, Valdosta State University

Ngoc-Bich Tran, San Jacinto College South

Nora Underwood, University of California, Davis

Jogindar S. Uppal, State University of New York

Va Nee L. Van Vleck, California State University, Fresno

Victoria Vernon, Empire State College / SUNY

Christian Weber, Seattle University

Ethel Weeks, Nassau Community College

Jack Wegman, Santa Rosa Junior College

Jason White, Northwest Missouri State University

Benjamin Widner, Colorado State University

Barbara Wiens-Tuers, Pennsylvania State University, Altoona

Katherine Wolfe, University of Pittsburgh

Kristen Wolfe, St. Johns River State College

You're in school!
Did you make the right decision?

Getting Started

When you have completed your study of this chapter, you will be able to

1 Define economics and explain the kinds of questions that economists try to answer.

2 Explain the ideas that define the economic way of thinking.

MyEconLab Big Picture

1.1 DEFINITION AND QUESTIONS

We want more than we can get. We want good health and long lives. We want spacious and comfortable homes. We want sports shoes and jet skis. We want the time to enjoy our favorite sports, video games, novels, music, and movies; to travel to exotic places; and just to hang out with friends. Wants exceed the resources available to satisfy them, and this fundamental fact is the source of all economic questions and problems.

■ Scarcity

Scarcity
The condition that arises because wants exceed the ability of resources to satisfy them.

Our inability to satisfy all our wants is called **scarcity**. The ability of each of us to satisfy our wants is limited by the time we have, the incomes we earn, and the prices we pay for the things we buy. These limits mean that everyone has unsatisfied wants. The ability of all of us as a society to satisfy our wants is limited by the productive resources that exist. These resources include the gifts of nature, our labor and ingenuity, and the tools and equipment that we have made.

Everyone, poor and rich alike, faces scarcity. A student wants Beyonce's latest album and a paperback but has only $10.00 in his pocket. He faces scarcity. Brad Pitt wants to spend a week in New Orleans discussing plans for his new eco-friendly housing and he also wants to spend the week promoting his new movie. He faces scarcity. The U.S. government wants to increase spending on homeland security and cut taxes. It faces scarcity. An entire society wants improved health care, an Internet connection in every classroom, clean lakes and rivers, and so on. Society faces scarcity. Scarcity is everywhere: Even parrots face scarcity!

Faced with scarcity, we must make choices. We must choose among the available alternatives. The student must choose the album or the paperback. Brad Pitt must choose New Orleans or promoting his new movie. The government must choose greater security or tax cuts. And society must choose among health care, computers, the environment, and so on.

Not only do I want a cracker—we all want a cracker!

© The New Yorker Collection 1985 Frank Modell from cartoonbank.com. All Rights Reserved.

■ Economics Defined

Economics
The social science that studies the choices that individuals, businesses, governments, and entire societies make as they cope with *scarcity*, the influences on those choices, and the arrangements that coordinate them.

Economics is the social science that studies the choices that individuals, businesses, governments, and entire societies make as they cope with *scarcity*, the influences on those choices, and the arrangements that coordinate them.

The subject has two broad parts:

- Microeconomics, and
- Macroeconomics

Microeconomics

Microeconomics
The study of the choices that individuals and businesses make and the way these choices interact and are influenced by governments.

Microeconomics is the study of the choices that individuals and businesses make and the way these choices interact and are influenced by governments. Some examples of microeconomic questions are: Will you buy a 3-D TV or a standard one? Will Nintendo sell more units of Wii if it cuts the price? Will a cut in the income tax rate encourage people to work longer hours? Will a hike in the gas tax encourage more people to drive hybrid or smaller automobiles? Are song downloads killing CDs?

Macroeconomics

Macroeconomics is the study of the aggregate (or total) effects on the national economy and the global economy of the choices that individuals, businesses, and governments make. Some examples of macroeconomic questions are: Why did production and jobs expand slowly in the United States during 2012 and 2013? Why are incomes growing much faster in China and India than in the United States? Why is unemployment in Europe so high? Why are Americans borrowing more than $1 billion a day from the rest of the world?

Two big questions define the scope of economics:

* How do choices end up determining *what, how,* and *for whom* goods and services get produced?
* When do choices made in the pursuit of *self-interest* also promote the *social interest*?

■ What, How, and For Whom?

Goods and services are the objects and actions that people value and produce to satisfy human wants. Goods are *objects* that satisfy wants. Sports shoes and ketchup are examples. Services are *actions* that satisfy wants. Haircuts and rock concerts are examples. We produce a dazzling array of goods and services that range from necessities such as food, houses, and health care to leisure items such as Blu-ray players and roller coaster rides.

What?

What determines the quantities of corn we grow, homes we build, and health-care services we produce? Sixty years ago, farm output was 5 percent of total U.S. production. Today, it is 1 percent. Over the same period, the output of mines, construction, and utilities slipped from 9 percent to 7 percent of total production and manufacturing fell from 28 percent to 12 percent. These decreases in output are matched by increases in the production of a wide range of services, up from 58 percent of total production 60 years ago to 80 percent today. How will these quantities change in the future as ongoing changes in technology make an ever-wider array of goods and services available to us?

How?

How are goods and services produced? In a vineyard in France, a hundred basket-carrying workers pick the annual grape crop by hand. In a vineyard in California, a huge machine and a few workers do the same job. Look around and you will see many examples of this phenomenon—the same job being done in different ways. In some stores, checkout clerks key in prices. In others, they use a laser scanner. One farmer keeps track of his livestock feeding schedules and inventories by using paper-and-pencil records, while another uses a computer. In some plants, GM hires workers to weld auto bodies and in others it uses robots to do the job.

Why do we use machines in some cases and people in others? Do mechanization and technological change destroy more jobs than they create? Do they make us better off or worse off?

In a California vineyard a machine and a few workers do the same job as a hundred grape pickers in France.

For Whom?

For whom are goods and services produced? The answer to this question depends on the incomes that people earn and the prices they pay for the goods and services they buy. At given prices, a person who has a high income is able to buy more goods and services than a person who has a low income. Doctors earn much higher incomes than do nurses and medical assistants, so doctors get more of the goods and services produced than nurses and medical assistants get.

You probably know about many other persistent differences in incomes. Men, on average, earn more than women. Whites, on average, earn more than minorities. College graduates, on average, earn more than high school graduates. Americans, on average, earn more than Europeans, who in turn earn more, on average, than Asians and Africans. But there are some significant exceptions. The people of Japan and Hong Kong now earn an average income similar to that of Americans. And there is a lot of income inequality throughout the world.

What determines the incomes we earn? Why do doctors earn larger incomes than nurses? Why do men earn more, on average, than women? Why do college graduates earn more, on average, than high school graduates? Why do Americans earn more, on average, than Africans?

Economics explains how the choices that individuals, businesses, and governments make and the interactions of those choices end up determining *what, how,* and *for whom* goods and services are produced. In answering these questions, we have a deeper agenda in mind. We're not interested in just knowing how many Blu-ray players are produced, how they are produced, and who gets to enjoy them. We ultimately want to know the answer to the second big economic question that we'll now explore.

A doctor gets more of the goods and services produced than a nurse or a medical assistant gets.

■ Can the Pursuit of Self-Interest Be in the Social Interest?

Every day, you and 316 million other Americans, along with 7.1 billion people in the rest of the world, make economic choices that result in *"what," "how,"* and *"for whom"* goods and services are produced.

Are the goods and services produced, and the quantities in which they are produced, the right ones? Do the scarce resources get used in the best possible way? Do the goods and services that we produce go to the people who benefit most from them?

Self-Interest and the Social Interest

Choices that are the best for the individual who makes them are choices made in the pursuit of **self-interest**. Choices that are the best for society as a whole are said to be in the **social interest**. The social interest has two dimensions: *efficiency* and *equity*. We'll explore these concepts in later chapters. For now, think of efficiency as being achieved by baking the biggest possible pie, and think of equity as being achieved by sharing the pie in the fairest possible way.

You know that your own choices are the best ones for you—or at least you *think* they're the best at the time that you make them. You use your time and other resources in the way that you think is best. You might consider how your choices affect other people, but you order a home delivery pizza because you're hungry and want to eat, not because you're concerned that the delivery person or the cook needs an income. You make choices that are in your self-interest—choices that you think are best for you.

Self-interest
The choices that are best for the individual who makes them.

Social interest
The choices that are best for society as a whole.

When you act on your economic decisions, you come into contact with thousands of other people who produce and deliver the goods and services that you decide to buy or who buy the things that you sell. These people have made their own decisions—what to produce and how to produce it, whom to hire or whom to work for, and so on. Like you, all these people make choices that they think are best for them. When the pizza delivery person shows up at your home, he's not doing you a favor. He's earning his income and hoping for a good tip.

Can it be possible that when each one of us makes choices that are in our own best interest—in our self-interest—it turns out that these choices are also the best choices for society as a whole—in the social interest?

Adam Smith, regarded as the founder of economic science, (see *Eye on the Past* on p. 13) said the answer is *yes*. He believed that when we pursue our self-interest, we are led by an *invisible hand* to promote the social interest.

Is Adam Smith correct? Can it really be possible that the pursuit of self-interest promotes the social interest? Much of the rest of this book helps you to learn what economists know about this question and its answer. To help you start thinking about the question, we're going to illustrate it with four topics that generate heated discussion in today's world. You're already at least a little bit familiar with each one of them. They are

- Globalization
- The "Information Age"
- Climate change
- Government budget deficit and debt

Globalization

Globalization—the expansion of international trade and the production of components and services by firms in other countries—has been going on for centuries. But in recent years, its pace has accelerated. Microchips, satellites, and fiber-optic cables have lowered the cost of communication and globalized production decisions. When Nike produces more sports shoes, people in Malaysia get more work. When Steven Spielberg makes a new movie, programmers in New Zealand write the code that makes magical animations. And when China Airlines wants a new airplane, Americans who work for Boeing build it.

Workers in Asia make our shoes.

Globalization is bringing rapid income growth, especially in Asia. But globalization is leaving some people behind. Jobs in manufacturing and routine services are shrinking in the United States, and some nations of Africa and South America are not sharing in the prosperity enjoyed in other parts of the world.

The owners of multinational firms benefit from lower production costs and consumers benefit from low-cost imported goods. But don't displaced American workers lose? And doesn't even the worker in Malaysia, who sews your new shoes for a few cents an hour, also lose? Is globalization in the social interest, or does globalization benefit just some at the expense of others?

The "Information Age"

We are living at a time of extraordinary economic change that has been called the *Information Revolution*. This name suggests a parallel with the *Industrial Revolution* that occurred around 1800 and the *Agricultural Revolution* of 12,000 years ago.

The changes that occurred during the last 30 years were based on one major technology: the microprocessor or computer chip. The spin-offs from faster and

The computer chip has transformed our lives.

cheaper computing have been widespread in telecommunications, music, and movie recording, and the automation of millions of routine tasks that previously required human decision and action. You encounter these automated tasks every day when you check out at the grocery store, use an ATM, or call a government department or large business. All the new products and processes and the low-cost computing power that made them possible resulted from people pursuing their self-interest. They did not result from any grand design or government plan.

When Gordon Moore set up Intel and started making chips, and Bill Gates quit Harvard to set up Microsoft, they weren't thinking how much easier it would be for you to turn in your essay on time if you had a better computer. Moore and Gates and thousands of other entrepreneurs were in hot pursuit of the big payoffs that many of them achieved. Yet their actions made many other people better off. They advanced the social interest.

But were resources used in the best possible way? Or did Intel and Microsoft set their prices too high and put their products out of reach for too many people? And did they really need to be rewarded with billions of dollars?

Climate Change

The Earth is getting hotter and the ice at the two poles is melting. Since the late nineteenth century, the Earth's surface temperature has increased about 1 degree Fahrenheit, and close to a half of that increase occurred over the past 25 years.

Most climate scientists believe that the current warming has come at least in part from human economic activity—from self-interested choices—and that, if left unchecked, the warming will bring large future economic costs.

Are the choices that each of us makes to use energy damaging the social interest? What needs to be done to make our choices serve the social interest? Would the United States joining with other nations to limit carbon emissions serve the social interest? What other measures might be introduced?

Human activity is raising the Earth's temperature.

A government budget time bomb is ticking as spending grows faster than tax revenues.

Government Budget Deficit and Debt

Every year since 2001, the U.S. government has run a budget deficit. On average, the government has spent $1.6 billion a day more than it has received in taxes. The government's debt has increased each day by that amount. Over the 12 year period from 2002 to 2013, government debt increased by $6.85 trillion. Your personal share of this debt is $22,000.

This large deficit and debt is just the beginning of an even bigger problem. From about 2020 onwards, the retirement and health-care benefits to which older Americans are entitled are going to cost increasingly more than current taxes can cover. With no changes in tax or benefit rates, the budget deficit will increase and the debt will swell ever higher.

Deficits and the debts they create cannot persist indefinitely, and debts must somehow be repaid. They will most likely be repaid by you, not by your parents. When we make our voter choices, we pursue our self-interest. Do our choices serve the social interest? Do the choices made by politicians and bureaucrats in Washington and the state capitals promote the social interest, or do they only serve their self-interests?

The four issues we've just reviewed raise questions that are hard to answer. We'll return to each of them at various points throughout this text and explain when the social interest is served and when there remain problems to be solved.

CHECKPOINT 1.1

MyEconLab Study Plan 1.1
Key Terms Quiz
Solutions

Define economics and explain the kinds of questions that economists try to answer.

Practice Problems

1. Economics studies choices that arise from one fact. What is that fact?
2. Provide three examples of wants in the United States today that are especially pressing but not satisfied.
3. In the following three news items, find examples of the *what, how,* and *for whom* questions: "With more research, we will cure cancer"; "A good education is the right of every child"; "Congress raises taxes to curb the deficit."
4. How does a new Starbucks in Beijing, China, influence self-interest and the social interest?
5. How does Facebook influence self-interest and the social interest?

In the News

1. According to the Bureau of Labor Statistics (BLS), high-paying jobs in health care and jobs in leisure, hospitality, and education will expand quickly over the next five years. How does the BLS expect *what* and *for whom* goods and services are produced to change in the next five years?
2. In May 2011, businesses cut hiring because the higher price of gas pushed up costs and higher food prices forced consumers to cut spending.

   Source: CNNMoney, June 4, 2011

   Did businesses and consumers act in their self-interest or the social interest?

Solutions to Practice Problems

1. The fact is scarcity—human wants exceed the resources available.
2. Examples would include security from terrorism, cleaner air in our cities, better public schools, and better public infrastructure. (Think of others.)
3. More research is a *how* question, and a cure for cancer is a *what* question. Good education is a *what* question, and every child is a *for whom* question. Raising taxes is a *for whom* question.
4. Decisions made by Starbucks are in Starbucks' self-interest but they also serve the self-interest of its customers and so contribute to the social interest.
5. Facebook serves the self-interest of its investors, users, and advertisers. It also serves the social interest by enabling people to share information.

Solutions to In the News

1. The BLS expects the quantities of goods and services produced by workers in health care, leisure, hospitality, and education to increase. For whom they are produced depends on how people's incomes and the prices of goods and services will change in the next five years. The BLS expects workers in these high-paying jobs and expanding industries will get more of them.
2. Businesses made their decisions on the basis of their costs, so they acted in their self-interest. Consumers' decisions to cut spending were made on the basis of the prices they face, so they acted in their self-interest.

1.2 THE ECONOMIC WAY OF THINKING

The definition of economics and the kinds of questions that economists try to answer give you a flavor of the scope of economics. But they don't tell you how economists *think* about these questions and how they go about seeking answers to them. You're now going to see how economists approach their work.

We'll break this task into two parts. First, we'll explain the ideas that economists use to frame their view of the world. These ideas will soon have you thinking like an economist. Second, we'll look at economics both as a social science and as a policy tool that governments, businesses, and *you* can use.

■ Economic Ideas

Six ideas define the *economic way of thinking*:

- A choice is a *tradeoff*
- *Cost* is what you *must give up* to get something.
- *Benefit* is what you gain from something.
- People make *rational choices* by comparing benefits and costs.
- Most choices are "*how much*" choices made at the *margin*.
- Choices respond to *incentives*.

■ A Choice Is a Tradeoff

Tradeoff
An exchange—giving up one thing to get something else.

A **tradeoff** is an exchange—giving up one thing to get something else. Because we face scarcity, we must make choices. And when we make a choice, we select from the available alternatives. You can think about choices as tradeoffs. When you choose one thing, you give up something else that you could have chosen.

Think about what you will do on Saturday night. You can spend the night studying for your next economics test or having fun with your friends, but you can't do both of these activities at the same time. You must choose how much time to devote to each. Whatever choice you make, you could have chosen something else. When you choose how to spend your Saturday night, you face a tradeoff between studying and hanging out with your friends. To get more study time, you must give up some time with your friends.

■ Cost: What You *Must* Give Up

Opportunity cost
The opportunity cost of something is the best thing you must give up to get it.

The **opportunity cost** of something is the best thing you must give up to get it. You most likely think about the cost of something as the money you must spend to get it. But dig a bit deeper. If you spend $10 on a movie ticket, you can't spend it on a sandwich. The movie ticket really costs a sandwich. The *cost* of something is what must be given up to get it, not the money spent on it. Economists use the term *opportunity cost* to emphasize this view of cost.

The biggest opportunity cost you face is that of being in school. This opportunity cost has two components: things you can't afford to buy and things you can't do with your time.

Start with the things you can't afford to buy. You've spent all your income on tuition, residence fees, books, and a laptop. If you weren't in school, you would have spent this money on tickets to ball games and movies and all the other things that you enjoy. But that's only the start of the things you can't afford to buy

The opportunity cost of being in school: things you can't buy and do.

because you're in school. You've also given up the opportunity to get a job and buy the things that you could afford with your higher income. Suppose that the best job you could get if you weren't in school is working at Citibank as a teller earning $24,000 a year. Another part of your opportunity cost of being in school is all the things that you would buy with that extra $24,000.

Now think about the time that being a student eats up. You spend many hours each week in class, doing homework assignments, preparing for tests, and so on. To do all these school activities, you must give up what would otherwise be leisure time spent with your friends.

The opportunity cost of being in school is the best alternative things that you can't afford and that you don't have the time to enjoy. You might put a dollar value on this cost but the cost is the things you give up, not dollars.

The opportunity cost of being in school includes forgone earnings.

■ Benefit: What You Gain

The **benefit** from something is the gain or pleasure that it brings, measured by what you are *willing to give up* to get it. Benefit is determined by personal *preferences*—by what a person likes and dislikes and the intensity of those feelings. If you get a huge kick out of *Madden Football* that video game brings you a large benefit. And if you have little interest in listening to Yo Yo Ma playing a Vivaldi cello concerto, that activity brings you a small benefit.

Some benefits are large and easy to identify, such as the benefit that you get from being in school. A big piece of that benefit is the goods and services that you will be able to enjoy with the boost to your earning power when you graduate. Some benefits are small, such as the benefit you receive from a slice of pizza.

Economists measure benefit as the most that a person is *willing to give up* to get something. You are willing to give up a lot for something that brings a large benefit. For example, because being in school brings a large benefit, you're *willing to give up* a lot of time and goods and services to get that benefit. But you're willing to give up very little for something that brings a small benefit. For example, you might be willing to give up one iTunes download to get a slice of pizza.

Benefit
The benefit from something is the gain or pleasure that it brings, measured by what you are *willing to give up* to get it.

■ Rational Choice

A basic idea of economics is that in making choices, people act rationally. A **rational choice** is one that uses the available resources to best achieve the objective of the person making the choice.

But how do people choose rationally? The answer is by comparing the *benefits* and *costs* of the alternative choices and choosing the alternative that makes *net benefit*—benefit minus cost—as large as possible.

You have chosen to be a student. If that choice is rational, as economists assume, your benefit from being in school exceeds the cost, so your net benefit is maximized by being in school. For an outstanding baseball player, a high earning potential makes the opportunity cost of school higher than the benefit from school, so for that person, net benefit is maxmized by choosing full-time sport. (*Eye on the Benefit and Cost of School* on p. 15 explores these examples more closely.)

The preferences of the person making a choice determine its benefit, so two people can make different rational choices even if they face the same cost. For example, you might like chocolate ice cream more than vanilla ice cream, but your friend prefers vanilla. So it is rational for you to choose chocolate and for your friend to choose vanilla.

Rational choice
A choice that uses the available resources to best achieve the objective of the person making the choice.

A rational choice might turn out not to have been the best choice after the event. For example, a farmer might decide to plant wheat rather than soybeans. Then, when the crop comes to market, the price of soybeans might be much higher than the price of wheat. The farmer's choice was rational when it was made, but subsequent events made it less profitable than the alternative choice.

All the rational choices we've just considered (school or not, chocolate or vanilla ice cream, soybeans or wheat) involve choosing between two things. One or the other is chosen. We call such choices *all-or-nothing* choices. Many choices are of this type, but most choices involve *how much* of an activity to do.

■ How Much? Choosing at the Margin

You can allocate the next hour between studying and instant messaging your friends, but the choice is not all or nothing. You must decide how many minutes to allocate to each activity. To make this decision, you compare the benefit of a little bit more study time with its cost—you make your choice *at the margin*.

Other words for "margin" are "border" or "edge." You can think of a choice at the margin as one that adjusts the border or edge of a plan to determine the best course of action. Making a choice at the **margin** means comparing the relevant alternatives systematically and incrementally.

Marginal Cost

The opportunity cost of a one-unit increase in an activity is called **marginal cost**. The marginal cost of something is what you *must* give up to get *one additional* unit of it. Think about your marginal cost of going to the movies for a third time in a week. Your marginal cost of seeing the movie is what you must give up to see that one additional movie. It is *not* what you give up to see all three movies. The reason is that you've already given up something for two movies, so you don't count that cost as resulting from the decision to see the third movie.

The marginal cost of any activity increases as you do more of it. You know that going to the movies decreases your study time and lowers your grade. Suppose that seeing a second movie in a week lowers your grade by five percentage points. Seeing a third movie will lower your grade by more than five percentage points. Your marginal cost of moviegoing is increasing as you see more movies.

Marginal Benefit

The benefit of a one-unit increase in an activity is called **marginal benefit**. Marginal benefit is what you gain from having *one more* unit of something. But the marginal benefit from something is *measured* by what you *are willing* to give up to get that *one additional* unit of it.

A fundamental feature of marginal benefit is that it diminishes. Think about your marginal benefit from movies. If you've been studying hard and haven't seen a movie this week, your marginal benefit from seeing your next movie is large. But if you've been on a movie binge this week, you now want a break and your marginal benefit from seeing your next movie is small.

Because the marginal benefit from a movie decreases as you see more movies, you are willing to give up less to see one additional movie. For example, you know that going to the movies decreases your study time and lowers your grade. You pay for seeing a movie with a lower grade. You might be willing to give up ten percentage points to see your first movie in a week, but you won't be willing to take such a big hit on your grade to see a second movie in a week. Your willingness to pay to see a movie decreases as the number of movies increases.

Margin
A choice on the margin is a choice that is made by comparing *all* the relevant alternatives systematically and incrementally.

Marginal cost
The opportunity cost that arises from a one-unit increase in an activity. The marginal cost of something is what you *must* give up to get *one additional* unit of it.

Marginal benefit
The benefit that arises from a one-unit increase in an activity. The marginal benefit of something is *measured* by what you *are willing* to give up to get *one additional* unit of it.

Making a Rational Choice

So, will you go to the movies for that third time in a week? The answer is found by comparing marginal benefit and marginal cost.

If the marginal cost of the movie is less than the marginal benefit from it, seeing the third movie adds more to benefit than to cost. Your net benefit increases, so your rational choice is to see the third movie.

If the marginal cost of the movie exceeds the marginal benefit from it, seeing the third movie adds more to cost than to benefit. Your net benefit decreases, so your rational choice is to spend the evening studying.

When the marginal benefit from something equals its marginal cost, the choice is rational and it is not possible to make a better choice. Scarce resources are being used in the best possible way.

■ Choices Respond to Incentives

The choices we make depend on the incentives we face. An **incentive** is a reward or a penalty—a "carrot" or a "stick"—that encourages or discourages an action. We respond positively to "carrots" and negatively to "sticks." The carrots are marginal benefits; the sticks are marginal costs. A change in marginal benefit or a change in marginal cost changes the incentives that we face and leads us to change our actions.

Most students believe that the payoff from studying just before a test is greater than the payoff from studying a month before a test. In other words, as a test date approaches, the marginal benefit from studying increases and the incentive to study becomes stronger. For this reason, we observe an increase in study time and a decrease in leisure pursuits during the last few days before a test. And the more important the test, the greater is this effect.

A change in marginal cost also changes incentives. For example, suppose that last week, you found your course work easy and you scored 100 percent on your practice quizzes. You figured that the marginal cost of taking an evening off to enjoy a movie was low and that your grade on the next test would not suffer, so you had a movie feast. But this week the going has gotten tough. You're just not getting it, and your practice test scores are low. If you take off even one evening this week, your grade on the next test will suffer. The marginal cost of seeing a movie is now high, so you decide to give the movies a miss.

A central idea of economics is that by observing *changes in incentives*, we can predict how *choices change*.

Incentive
A reward or a penalty—a "carrot" or a "stick"—that encourages or discourages an action.

Changes in marginal benefit and marginal cost change the incentive to study or to enjoy a movie.

■ Economics as Social Science

Economists try to understand and predict the effects of economic forces by using the *scientific method* first developed by physicists. The scientific method is a commonsense way of systematically checking what works and what doesn't work.

A scientist begins with a question or a puzzle about cause and effect arising from some observed facts. An economist might wonder why computers are getting cheaper and more computers are being used. Are computers getting cheaper because more people are buying them? Or are more people buying computers because they are getting cheaper? Or is some third factor causing both the price of a computer to fall and the quantity of computers bought to increase?

Economic Models

A scientist's second step is to build a model that provides a possible answer to the question of interest. All sciences use models. An **economic model** is a description of the economy or a part of the economy that includes only those features assumed necessary to explain the observed facts.

Economic model
A description of the economy or a part of the economy that includes only those features assumed necessary to explain the observed facts.

A model is analogous to a map. If you want to know about valleys and mountains, you use a physical map; if you're studying nations, you use a political map; if you want to drive from *A* to *B* in an unfamiliar city, you use a street map; and if you're a telephone engineer who is wanting to fix a broken connection, you use a map of the cables and conduit under the streets.

Sometimes, in the natural sciences, models are physical objects such as a plastic model of an atom or DNA. But models are also mathematical and often can be visualized in graphs. You can imagine a Lego model of an economy, but you can also see that such a model wouldn't be very revealing. So in economics we use mathematical and graph-based models.

The questions we posed about the price and quantity of computers bought are answered by an economic model called the "demand and supply model" that you will study in Chapter 4.

Check Models Against Facts

A scientist's third step is to check the proposed model against the facts. Physicists can check whether their models correspond to the facts by doing experiments. For example, with a particle accelerator, a physicist can test a model of the structure of an atom.

Economists have a harder time than physicists, but they still approach the task in a scientific manner. To check an economic model against the facts, economists use natural experiments, statistical investigations, and laboratory experiments.

A natural experiment is a situation that arises in the ordinary course of economic life in which the one factor of interest is different and other things are equal (or similar). For example, Canada has higher unemployment benefits than the United States, but the people in the two nations are similar. So to study the effect of unemployment benefits on the unemployment rate, economists might compare the United States with Canada.

A statistical investigation looks for a *correlation*—a tendency for the values of two variables to move together (either in the same direction or in opposite directions) in a predictable and related way. For example, cigarette smoking and lung cancer are correlated. Sometimes a correlation shows a causal influence of one variable on the other. Smoking does cause lung cancer. But sometimes the direction of causation is hard to determine.

EYE on the PAST
Adam Smith and the Birth of Economics as a Social Science

Many people had written about economics before Adam Smith did, but he made economics a social science.

Born in 1723 in Kirkcaldy, a small fishing town near Edinburgh, Scotland, Smith was the only child of the town's customs officer. Lured from his professorship (he was a full professor at 28) by a wealthy Scottish duke who gave him a pension of £300 a year—ten times the average income at that time—Smith devoted ten years to writing his masterpiece, *An Inquiry into the Nature and Causes of the Wealth of Nations,* published in 1776.

Why, Adam Smith asked in that book, are some nations wealthy while others are poor? He was pondering these questions at the height of the Industrial Revolution. During these years, new technologies were applied to the manufacture of textiles, iron, transportation, and agriculture.

Adam Smith answered his questions by emphasizing the role of the division of labor and free markets. To illustrate his argument, he used the example of a pin factory. He guessed that one person, using the hand tools available in the 1770s, might make 20 pins a day. Yet, he observed, by using those same hand tools but breaking the process into a number of individually small operations in which people specialize—by the division of labor—ten people could make a staggering 48,000 pins a day.

But a large market is needed to support the division of labor: One factory employing ten workers would need to sell more than 15 million pins a year to stay in business!

Smith saw free competitive markets as another source of wealth. The self-interested pursuit of profit, led by an invisible hand, resulted in resources being used in ways that created the greatest possible value and wealth.

A laboratory experiment puts people in a decision-making situation and varies the influence of one factor at a time to discover how they respond.

Disagreement: Normative versus Positive

Economists sometimes disagree about assumptions and models. They also sometimes disagree about what policy should be followed. Some disagreements can be settled by appealing to further facts, but others cannot.

Disagreements that can't be settled by facts are *normative statements*—statements about what *ought to be.* These statements depend on values and cannot be tested. The statement "We *ought* to cut back on our use of coal" is a normative statement. You may agree or disagree with it, but you can't test it. It doesn't assert a fact that can be checked. Economists as social scientists try to steer clear of normative statements.

Disagreements that *can* be settled by facts are *positive statements*—statements about *what is.* A positive statement might be right or wrong and we can discover which by careful observation of facts. "Our planet is warming because of the quantity of coal that we're burning" is a positive statement. It could be right or wrong, and it can be tested.

■ Economics as Policy Tool

Economics is useful, and you don't have to be an economist to think like one and to use the insights of economics as a policy tool. The subject provides a way of approaching problems in all aspects of our lives:

- Personal
- Business
- Government

Personal Economic Policy

Should you take out a student loan? Should you get a weekend job? Should you buy a used car or a new one? Should you rent an apartment or take out a loan and buy a condominium? Should you pay off your credit card balance or make just the minimum payment? How should you allocate your time between study, working for a wage, caring for family members, and having fun? How should you allocate your time between studying economics and your other subjects? Should you leave school after getting a bachelor's degree or should you go for a master's or a professional qualification?

All these questions involve a marginal benefit and a marginal cost. Although some of the numbers might be hard to pin down, you will make more solid decisions if you approach these questions with the tools of economics.

Business Economic Policy

Should Sony make only flat panel televisions and stop making conventional ones? Should Texaco get more oil and gas from the Gulf of Mexico or from Alaska? Should Palm outsource its online customer services to India or run the operation from California? Should Marvel Studios produce *Spider-Man 4,* a sequel to *Spider-Man 3*? Can Microsoft compete with Google in the search engine business? Can eBay compete with the surge of new Internet auction services? Is Alex Rodriguez really worth $32,000,000 to the New York Yankees?

Like personal economic questions, these business questions involve the evaluation of a marginal benefit and a marginal cost. Some of the questions require a broader investigation of the interactions of individuals and businesses. But again, by approaching these questions with the tools of economics and by hiring economists as advisers, businesses can make better decisions.

Government Economic Policy

How can California balance its budget? Should the federal government cut taxes or raise them? How can the tax system be simplified? Should people be permitted to invest their Social Security money in stocks that they pick themselves? Should Medicaid and Medicare be extended to the entire population? Should there be a special tax to penalize corporations that send jobs overseas? Should cheap foreign imports of furniture and textiles be limited? Should the farms that grow tomatoes and sugar beets receive a subsidy? Should water be transported from Washington and Oregon to California?

These government policy questions call for decisions that involve the evaluation of a marginal benefit and a marginal cost and an investigation of the interactions of individuals and businesses. Yet again, by approaching these questions with the tools of economics, governments can make better decisions.

Notice that all the policy questions we've just posed involve a blend of the positive and the normative. Economics can't help with the normative part—the objective. But for a given objective, economics provides a method of evaluating alternative solutions. That method is to evaluate the marginal benefits and marginal costs and to find the solution that brings the greatest available gain.

EYE on the BENEFIT AND COST OF SCHOOL

Did You Make the Right Decision?

Did you make the right decision when you chose school over looking for a full-time job? Or, if you have a full-time job and you're studying in what would be your leisure time, did you make the right choice? Does school provide a big enough benefit to justify its cost?

The Benefits of School

Being in school has many benefits for which people are willing to pay. They fall into two broad categories: present enjoyment and a higher future income.

You can easily make a list of all the fun things you do with your friends in school that would be harder to do if you didn't have these friends and opportunities for social interaction that school provides.

Putting a dollar value on the items in your list would be hard but it is possible to put a dollar value, or rather an expected dollar value, on the other benefit—a higher future income.

On average, a high-school graduate earns $40,000 a year. A graduate with a bachelor's degree earns, on average, $76,000 a year.

So by being in school, you can expect (on average) to increase your annual earnings by $36,000 a year.

This number is likely to grow as the economy becomes more productive and prices and earnings rise.

The Costs of School

The opportunity cost of being in school for a full-time student includes:

- Tuition
- Books
- Other study costs
- Forgone earnings

For a student attending a state university in her or his home state, tuition is around $10,000 per year.

Books and other study aids cost around $1,000 per year.

Forgone earnings are the wage of a high-school graduate in a starter job, which is around $24,000 a year.

So the total annual cost is about $35,000 or $105,000 for a 3-year degree and $140,000 for a 4-year degree.

Net Benefit

The benefit of extra earnings alone brings in $36,000 a year or $360,000 in 10 years and $1,440,000 in a working life of 40 years.

The costs are incurred in the present and the benefits accrue in the future, so we need to lower the benefits to be able to compare them properly with the costs. You'll learn how to do that later in your economics course. But even allowing for the fact that the costs are now and the benefits in the future, net benefit is big!

Is School Always Best?

At the age of 18, Clayton Kershaw was considered the top high-schooler available entering the 2006 MLB Draft. He signed with the Los Angeles Dodgers with a bonus said to be $2.3 million, and turned down a baseball scholarship at Texas A & M.

As the Dodgers starting pitcher, Clayton's value to the team is high and earned him a salary of $11 million in 2013.

Clayton Kershaw's opportunity cost of a college education vastly exceeded the benefit he could expect to get from it. So Clayton, like you, maximized his net benefit and made the right decision.

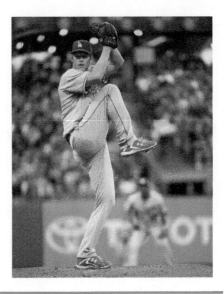

MyEconLab Study Plan 1.2
Key Terms Quiz
Solutions

CHECKPOINT 1.2

Explain the ideas that define the economic way of thinking.

Practice Problems

Every week, Kate plays tennis for two hours, and her grade on each math test is 70 percent. Last week, after playing for two hours, Kate considered playing for another hour. She decided to play for another hour and cut her study time by one hour. But last week, her math grade fell to 60 percent. Use this information to work Problems **1** to **4**.

1. What was Kate's opportunity cost of the third hour of tennis?
2. Given that Kate played the third hour, what can you conclude about her marginal benefit and marginal cost of the second hour of tennis?
3. Was Kate's decision to play the third hour of tennis rational?
4. Did Kate make her decision on the margin?

In the News

The *New York Times* reports that cruise lines have been slashing prices and cruise sales are up. It says this surge of interest tells us that despite the uncertain economic climate, people clearly need more fun in their lives and view their vacations as a valuable and necessary part of it.

1. In deciding whether to take a cruise, would you face a tradeoff?
2. How would you make a rational choice about taking a cruise?
3. What would be the marginal benefit from a cruise? What would be the marginal cost of a cruise?
4. Why would you expect a lower price to increase the number of people who decide to take a cruise?

Solutions to Practice Problems

1. Kate's opportunity cost of the third hour of tennis was the drop in her grade of ten percentage points.
2. The marginal benefit from the second hour of tennis must have exceeded the marginal cost of the second hour because Kate chose to play the third hour.
3. If marginal benefit exceeded marginal cost, Kate's decision was rational.
4. Kate made her decision on the margin because she compared the benefit and cost of one more hour (marginal benefit and marginal cost).

Solutions to In the News

1. You would face a tradeoff because you would have to forgo something else that you might otherwise do with your resources (time and budget).
2. You would make a rational choice by comparing the marginal benefit from a cruise and the marginal cost of taking one.
3. The marginal benefit from a cruise is the most you are willing to pay for one. The marginal cost is what you would have to pay to take a cruise.
4. With a lower price, more people will have a marginal benefit that exceeds the price and they will choose to take a cruise.

CHAPTER SUMMARY

Key Points

1. **Define economics and explain the kinds of questions that economists try to answer.**

   * Economics is the social science that studies the choices that we make as we cope with scarcity and the incentives that influence and reconcile our choices.
   * Microeconomics is the study of individual choices and interactions, and macroeconomics is the study of the national economy and global economy.
   * The first big question of economics is: How do the choices that people make end up determining *what, how,* and *for whom* goods and services are produced?
   * The second big question is: When do choices made in the pursuit of *self-interest* also promote the *social interest*?

2. **Explain the ideas that define the economic way of thinking.**

   * Six ideas define the economic way of thinking:
     1. A choice is a *tradeoff.*
     2. *Cost* is what you *must* give up to get something.
     3. *Benefit* is what you gain when you get something (measured by what you *are willing to* give up to get it).
     4. People make *rational* choices by comparing benefits and costs.
     5. A "how much" choice is made on the *margin* by comparing *marginal benefit* and *marginal cost.*
     6. Choices respond to *incentives.*
   * Economists use the *scientific method* to try to understand how the economic world works. They create economic models and test them using natural experiments, statistical investigations, and laboratory experiments.
   * Economics is a tool for personal, business, and government decisions.

Key Terms

MyEconLab Key Terms Quiz

Benefit, 9	Margin, 10	Scarcity, 2
Economic model, 12	Marginal benefit, 10	Self-interest, 4
Economics, 2	Marginal cost, 10	Social interest, 4
Goods and services, 3	Microeconomics, 2	Tradeoff, 8
Incentive, 11	Opportunity cost, 8	
Macroeconomics, 3	Rational choice, 9	

CHAPTER CHECKPOINT

Study Plan Problems and Applications

1. Provide three examples of scarcity that illustrate why even the 1,210 billionaires in the world face scarcity.

2. Label each entry in List 1 as dealing with a microeconomic topic or a macroeconomic topic. Explain your answer.

Use the following information to work Problems 3 to 6.

The Social Network had world-wide box office receipts of $225 million. The movie had a production budget of about $70 million and additional marketing costs of about $50 million. Creating a successful movie brings pleasure to millions, generates work for thousands, and makes a few people rich.

3. What contribution does a movie like *The Social Network* make to coping with scarcity? When you buy a movie ticket, are you buying a good or a service?

4. Who decides whether a movie is going to be a blockbuster? How do you think the creation of a blockbuster movie influences *what*, *how*, and *for whom* goods and services are produced?

5. What are some of the components of marginal cost and marginal benefit that the producer of a movie faces?

6. Suppose that Jesse Eisenberg had been offered a bigger and better part in another movie and that to hire him for *The Social Network,* the producer had to double Jesse's pay. What incentives would have changed? How might the changed incentives have changed the choices that people made?

7. What is the social interest? Distinguish it from self-interest. In your answer give an example of self-interest and an example of social interest.

8. Pam, Pru, and Pat are deciding how they will celebrate the New Year. Pam prefers to take a cruise, is happy to go to Hawaii, but does not want to go skiing. Pru prefers to go skiing, is happy to go to Hawaii, but does not want to take a cruise. Pat prefers to go to Hawaii or to take a cruise but does not want to go skiing. Their decision is to go to Hawaii. Is this decision rational? What is the opportunity cost of the trip to Hawaii for each of them? What is the benefit that each gets?

9. Label each of the entries in List 2 as a positive or a normative statement.

Use the following information to work Problems 10 to 12.

Hundreds line up for 5 p.m. Eminem ticket giveaway

Eminem fans lined up all day to get a free ticket to his secret concert at which he will release his new album *Relapse* (his first in 5 years).

Source: *Detroit Free Press*, May 18, 2009

10. With tickets free and the show to be held in a 1,500-seat Detroit theater, what is free and what is scarce? Explain your answer.

11. What do you think Eminem's incentive is to give a free show? Was his decision made in self-interest or in the social interest? Explain your answer.

12. Is the marginal benefit from the concert zero? Explain your answer.

 13. Read *Eye on the Benefit and Cost of School* on p. 15 and explain why both you and Alex Rodriguez made the right decision.

LIST 1

- Motor vehicles production in China is growing by 10 percent a year.
- Coffee prices rocket.
- Globalization has reduced African poverty.
- The government must cut its budget deficit.
- Apple sells 3 million iPhones a month.

LIST 2

- Low-income people pay too much for housing.
- The number of U.S. farms has decreased over the past 50 years.
- Toyota expands parts production in the United States.
- Imports from China are swamping U.S. department stores.
- The population of rural United States is declining.

Instructor Assignable Problems and Applications

MyEconLab Homework, Quiz, or Test if assigned by instructor

1. Which of the following are components of the opportunity cost of being a full-time student? The cost of
   - Tuition and books
   - Residence and a meal plan
   - A subscription to the *New Yorker* magazine
   - The income a student will earn after graduating

2. Think about the following news items and label each as involving a *what, how,* or *for whom* question:
   - Today, most stores use computers to keep their inventory records, whereas 20 years ago most stores used paper records.
   - Health-care professionals and drug companies recommend that Medicaid drug rebates be made available to everyone in need.
   - A doubling of the gas tax might lead to a better public transit system.

3. On May 3, 2013, the headlines in List 1 appeared in *The Wall Street Journal*. Classify each headline as a signal that the news article is about a microeconomic topic or a macroeconomic topic. Explain your answers.

4. Your school decides to increase the intake of new students next year. To make its decision, what economic concepts would it have considered? Would the school have used the "economic way of thinking" in reaching its decision? Would the school have made its decision on the margin?

5. Provide two examples of a monetary incentive and two examples of a non-monetary incentive, a carrot and a stick of each, that government policies use to influence behavior.

6. Think about each of the items in List 2 and explain how they affect incentives and might change the choices that people make.

7. Does the decision to make a blockbuster movie mean that some other more desirable activities get fewer resources than they deserve? Is your answer positive or normative? Explain your answer.

8. Provide two examples of economics being used as a tool by each of a student, a business, and a government. Classify your examples as dealing with microeconomic topics and macroeconomic topics.

Use the following news clip to work Problems 9 to 12.

Obama will drive up miles-per-gallon requirements

Obama's revision of auto-emission and fuel-economy standards will require automakers to boost fuel economy to 35.5 miles per gallon by 2016, notching up 5% each year from 2012, to limit the amount of carbon dioxide cars can emit.

Source: *USA Today*, May 18, 2009

9. What are two benefits of the new miles-per-gallon requirements? Are these benefits in someone's self-interest or in the social interest?

10. What are two benefits of the new auto-emission standards?

11. What costs associated with the new miles-per-gallon requirements arise from decisions made in self-interest and in the social interest?

12. What costs associated with the new auto-emission standards arise from decisions made in self-interest and in the social interest?

LIST 1

- Job Gains Calm Slump Worries
- Washington Post's Profit Falls
- Overcapacity, Fuel Costs Hit Shipping
- Green Shoots in Greece?

LIST 2

- A hurricane hits Central Florida.
- The World Series begins tonight but a storm warning is in effect for the area around the stadium.
- The price of a personal computer falls to $50.
- Unrest in the Middle East sends the price of gas to $5 a gallon.

Multiple Choice Quiz

1. Which of the following describes the reason why scarcity exists?

   A. Governments make bad economic decisions.
   B. The gap between the rich and the poor is too wide.
   C. Wants exceed the resources available to satisfy them.
   D. There is too much unemployment.

2. Which of the following defines economics?
   Economics is the social science that studies _____.

   A. the best way of eliminating scarcity
   B. the choices made to cope with scarcity, how incentives influence those choices, and how the choices are coordinated
   C. how money is created and used
   D. the inevitable conflict between self-interest and the social interest

3. Of the three big questions, *what*, *how*, and *for whom*, which of the following is an example of a *how* question?

   A. Why do doctors and lawyers earn high incomes?
   B. Why don't we produce more small cars and fewer gas guzzlers?
   C. Why do we use machines rather than migrant workers to pick grapes?
   D. Why do college football coaches earn more than professors?

4. Which of the following is not a key idea in the economic way of thinking?

   A. People make rational choices by comparing costs and benefits.
   B. Poor people are discriminated against and should be treated more fairly.
   C. A rational choice is made at the margin.
   D. Choices respond to incentives.

5. A rational choice is _____.

   A. the best thing you must forgo to get something
   B. what you are willing to forgo to get something
   C. made by comparing marginal benefit and marginal cost
   D. the best for society

6. Which of the following best illustrates your marginal benefit from studying?

   A. The knowledge you gain from studying 2 hours a night for a month
   B. The best things forgone by studying 2 hours a night for a month
   C. What you are willing to give up to study for one additional hour
   D. What you must give up to be able to study for one additional hour

7. The scientific method uses models to _____.

   A. clarify normative disagreements
   B. avoid the need to study real questions
   C. replicate all the features of the real world
   D. focus on those features of reality assumed relevant for understanding a cause and effect relationship

8. Which of the following is a positive statement?

   A. We should stop using corn to make ethanol because it is raising the cost of food.
   B. You will get the most out of college life if you play a sport once a week.
   C. Competition among cell-phone providers across the borders of Canada, Mexico, and the United States has driven roaming rates down.
   D. Bill Gates ought to spend more helping to eradicate malaria in Africa.

APPENDIX: MAKING AND USING GRAPHS

When you have completed your study of this appendix, you will be able to

1   Interpret graphs that display data.

2   Interpret the graphs used in economic models.

3   Define and calculate slope.

4   Graph relationships among more than two variables.

Basic Idea

A graph represents a quantity as a distance and enables us to visualize the relationship between two variables. To make a graph, we set two lines called *axes* perpendicular to each other, like those in Figure A1.1. The vertical line is called the *y*-axis, and the horizontal line is called the *x*-axis. The common zero point is called the *origin.* In Figure A1.1, the *x*-axis measures temperature in degrees Fahrenheit. A movement to the right shows an increase in temperature, and a movement to the left shows a decrease in temperature. The *y*-axis represents ice cream consumption, measured in gallons per day.

To make a graph, we need a value of the variable on the *x*-axis and a corresponding value of the variable on the *y*-axis. For example, if the temperature is 40°F, ice cream consumption is 5 gallons a day at point *A* in Figure A1.1. If the temperature is 80°F, ice cream consumption is 20 gallons a day at point *B* in Figure A1.1. Graphs like that in Figure A1.1 can be used to show any type of quantitative data on two variables.

FIGURE A1.1

Making a Graph   MyEconLab Animation

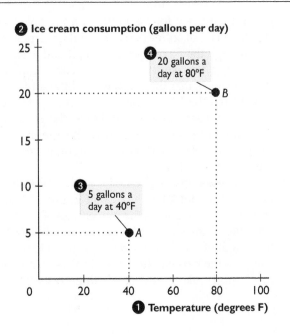

All graphs have axes that measure quantities as distances.

❶   The horizontal axis (*x*-axis) measures temperature in degrees Fahrenheit. A movement to the right shows an increase in temperature.

❷   The vertical axis (*y*-axis) measures ice cream consumption in gallons per day. A movement upward shows an increase in ice cream consumption.

❸   Point *A* shows that 5 gallons of ice cream are consumed on a day when the temperature is 40°F.

❹   Point *B* shows that 20 gallons of ice cream are consumed on a day when the temperature is 80°F.

■ Interpreting Data Graphs

Scatter diagram
A graph of the value of one variable against the value of another variable.

A **scatter diagram** is a graph of the value of one variable against the value of another variable. It is used to reveal whether a relationship exists between two variables and to describe the relationship. Figure A1.2 shows two examples.

Figure A1.2(a) shows the relationship between expenditure and income. Each point shows expenditure per person and income per person in the United States in a given year from 2000 to 2012. The points are "scattered" within the graph. The label on each point shows its year. The point marked 10 shows that in 2010, income per person was $32,335 and expenditure per person was $29,686. This scatter diagram reveals that as income increases, expenditure also increases.

Figure A1.2(b) shows the relationship during the 1990s between the percentage of Americans who own a cell phone and the average monthly cell-phone bill. This scatter diagram reveals that as the cost of using a cell phone falls, the number of cell-phone subscribers increases.

Time-series graph
A graph that measures time on the x-axis and the variable or variables in which we are interested on the y-axis.

A **time-series graph** measures time (for example, months or years) on the x-axis and the variable or variables in which we are interested on the y-axis. Figure A1.2(c) shows an example. In this graph, time (on the x-axis) is measured in years, which run from 1980 to 2012. The variable that we are interested in is the price of coffee, and it is measured on the y-axis.

A time-series graph conveys an enormous amount of information quickly and easily, as this example illustrates. It shows when the value is

1. High or low. When the line is a long way from the x-axis, the price is high, as it was in 1986. When the line is close to the x-axis, the price is low, as it was in 2001.

2. Rising or falling. When the line slopes upward, as in 1994, the price is rising. When the line slopes downward, as in 1996, the price is falling.

3. Rising or falling quickly or slowly. If the line is steep, then the price is rising or falling quickly. If the line is not steep, the price is rising or falling slowly. For example, the price rose quickly in 1994 and slowly in 1995. The price fell quickly in 1996 and slowly in 2003.

Trend
A general tendency for the value of a variable to rise or fall over time.

A time-series graph also reveals whether the variable has a trend. A **trend** is a general tendency for the value of a variable to rise or fall over time. You can see that the price of coffee had a general tendency to fall from 1980 to late in 2000. That is, although the price rose and fell, it had a general tendency to fall.

With a time-series graph, we can compare different periods quickly. Figure A1.2(c) shows that the 2000s were different from the 1990s, which in turn were different from the 1980s. The price of coffee started the 1980s high and then fell for a number of years. During the 1990s, the price was on a roller coaster. And during the 2000s, the price rose steadily. This graph conveys a wealth of information about the price of coffee, and it does so in much less space than we have used to describe only some of its features.

Cross-section graph
A graph that shows the values of an economic variable for different groups in a population at a point in time.

A **cross-section graph** shows the values of an economic variable for different groups in a population at a point in time. Figure A1.2(d) is an example of a cross-section graph. It shows the percentage of people who participate in selected sports activities in the United States. This graph uses bars rather than dots and lines, and the length of each bar indicates the participation rate. Figure A1.2(d) enables you to compare the participation rates in these ten sporting activities. And you can do so much more quickly and clearly than by looking at a list of numbers.

■ **FIGURE A1.2**

Data Graphs   MyEconLab Animation

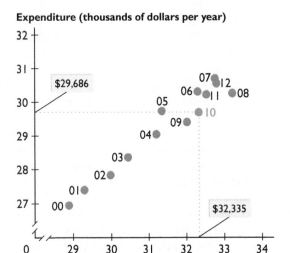

(a) **Scatter Diagram: Expenditure and income**

(b) **Scatter Diagram: Subscribers and cost**

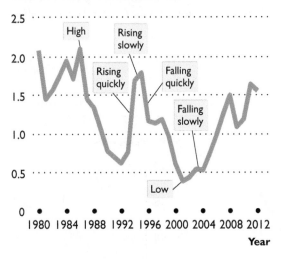

(c) **Time Series: The price of coffee**

(d) **Cross Section: Participation in selected sports activities**

A scatter diagram reveals the relationship between two variables. In part (a), as income increases, expenditure almost always increases. In part (b), as the monthly cell-phone bill falls, the percentage of people who own a cell phone increases.

A time-series graph plots the value of a variable on the *y*-axis against time on the *x*-axis. Part (c) plots the price of coffee each year from 1980 to 2012. The graph shows when the price of coffee was high and low, when it increased and decreased, and when it changed quickly and changed slowly.

A cross-section graph shows the value of a variable across the members of a population. Part (d) shows the participation rate in the United States in each of ten sporting activities.

◾ Interpreting Graphs Used in Economic Models

We use graphs to show the relationships among the variables in an economic model. An *economic model* is a simplified description of the economy or of a component of the economy such as a business or a household. It consists of statements about economic behavior that can be expressed as equations or as curves in a graph. Economists use models to explore the effects of different policies or other influences on the economy in ways similar to those used to test model airplanes in wind tunnels and models of the climate.

Figure A1.3 shows graphs of the relationships between two variables that move in the same direction. Such a relationship is called a **positive relationship** or **direct relationship**.

Part (a) shows a straight-line relationship, which is called a **linear relationship**. The distance traveled in 5 hours increases as the speed increases. For example, point *A* shows that 200 miles are traveled in 5 hours at a speed of 40 miles an hour. And point *B* shows that the distance traveled in 5 hours increases to 300 miles if the speed increases to 60 miles an hour.

Part (b) shows the relationship between distance sprinted and recovery time (the time it takes the heart rate to return to its normal resting rate). An upward-sloping curved line that starts out quite flat but then becomes steeper as we move along the curve away from the origin describes this relationship. The curve slopes upward and becomes steeper because the extra recovery time needed from sprinting another 100 yards increases. It takes 5 minutes to recover from sprinting 100 yards but 15 minutes to recover from sprinting 200 yards.

Part (c) shows the relationship between the number of problems worked by a student and the amount of study time. An upward-sloping curved line that starts out quite steep and becomes flatter as we move away from the origin shows this

Positive relationship or direct relationship
A relationship between two variables that move in the same direction.

Linear relationship
A relationship that graphs as a straight line.

◾ **FIGURE A1.3**

Positive (Direct) Relationships   MyEconLab Animation

(a) Positive linear relationship

Part (a) shows that as speed increases, the distance traveled in a given number of hours increases along a straight line.

(b) Positive becoming steeper

Part (b) shows that as the distance sprinted increases, recovery time increases along a curve that becomes steeper.

(c) Positive becoming less steep

Part (c) shows that as study time increases, the number of problems worked increases along a curve that becomes less steep.

relationship. Study time becomes less effective as you increase the hours worked and become more tired.

Figure A1.4 shows relationships between two variables that move in opposite directions. Such a relationship is called a **negative relationship** or **inverse relationship**.

Part (a) shows the relationship between the number of hours spent playing squash and the number of hours spent playing tennis when the total number of hours available is five. One extra hour spent playing tennis means one hour less playing squash and vice versa. This relationship is negative and linear.

Part (b) shows the relationship between the cost per mile traveled and the length of a journey. The longer the journey, the lower is the cost per mile. But as the journey length increases, the fall in the cost per mile becomes smaller. This feature of the relationship is shown by the fact that the curve slopes downward, starting out steep at a short journey length and then becoming flatter as the journey length increases. This relationship arises because some of the costs, such as auto insurance, are fixed, and as the journey length increases, the fixed costs are spread over more miles.

Part (c) shows the relationship between the amount of leisure time and the number of problems worked by a student. Increasing leisure time produces an increasingly large reduction in the number of problems worked. This relationship is a negative one that starts out with a gentle slope at a small number of leisure hours and becomes steeper as the number of leisure hours increases. This relationship is a different view of the idea shown in Figure A1.3(c).

Many relationships in economic models have a maximum or a minimum. For example, firms try to make the largest possible profit and to produce at the lowest possible cost. Figure A1.5 shows relationships that have a maximum or a minimum.

Negative relationship or inverse relationship
A relationship between two variables that move in opposite directions.

▮ **FIGURE A1.4**

Negative (Inverse) Relationships

MyEconLab Animation

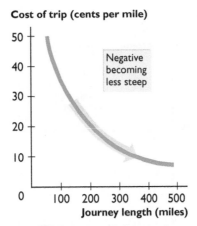

(a) **Negative linear relationship**

Part (a) shows that as the time playing tennis increases, the time playing squash decreases along a straight line.

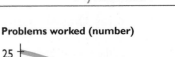

(b) **Negative becoming less steep**

Part (b) shows that as the journey length increases, the cost of the trip falls along a curve that becomes less steep.

(c) **Negative becoming steeper**

Part (c) shows that as leisure time increases, the number of problems worked decreases along a curve that becomes steeper.

■ **FIGURE A1.5**

Maximum and Minimum Points

In part (a), as the rainfall increases, the curve ❶ slopes upward as the yield per acre rises, ❷ is flat at point A, the maximum yield, and then ❸ slopes downward as the yield per acre falls.

In part (b), as the speed increases, the curve ❶ slopes downward as the cost per mile falls, ❷ is flat at the minimum point B, and then ❸ slopes upward as the cost per mile rises.

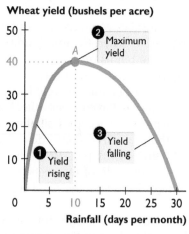

(a) Relationship with a maximum

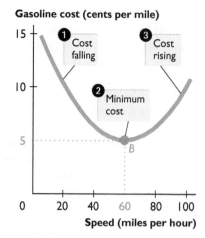

(b) Relationship with a minimum

Part (a) shows a relationship that starts out sloping upward, reaches a maximum, and then slopes downward. Part (b) shows a relationship that begins sloping downward, falls to a minimum, and then slopes upward.

Finally, there are many situations in which, no matter what happens to the value of one variable, the other variable remains constant. Sometimes we want to show two variables that are unrelated in a graph. Figure A1.6 shows two graphs in which the variables are unrelated.

■ **FIGURE A1.6**

Variables That Are Unrelated

In part (a), as the price of bananas increases, the student's grade in economics remains at 75 percent. These variables are unrelated, and the curve is horizontal.

In part (b), the vineyards of France produce 3 billion gallons of wine no matter what the rainfall is in California. These variables are unrelated, and the curve is vertical.

(a) Unrelated: y constant

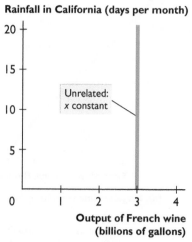

(b) Unrelated: x constant

The Slope of a Relationship

We can measure the influence of one variable on another by the slope of the relationship. The **slope** of a relationship is the change in the value of the variable measured on the y-axis divided by the change in the value of the variable measured on the x-axis. We use the Greek letter Δ (delta) to represent "change in." So Δy means the change in the value of y, and Δx means the change in the value of x. The slope of the relationship is

$$\Delta y \div \Delta x.$$

If a large change in y is associated with a small change in x, the slope is large and the curve is steep. If a small change in y is associated with a large change in x, the slope is small and the curve is flat.

Figure A1.7 shows you how to calculate slope. The slope of a straight line is the same regardless of where on the line you calculate it—the slope is constant. In part (a), when x increases from 2 to 6, y increases from 3 to 6. The change in x is 4—that is, Δx is 4. The change in y is 3—that is, Δy is 3. The slope of that line is 3/4. In part (b), when x increases from 2 to 6, y *decreases* from 6 to 3. The change in y is *minus* 3—that is, Δy is -3. The change in x is plus 4—that is, Δx is 4. The slope of the curve is $-3/4$.

In part (c), we calculate the slope at a point on a curve. To do so, place a ruler on the graph so that it touches point A and no other point on the curve, then draw a straight line along the edge of the ruler. The slope of this straight line is the slope of the curve at point A. This slope is 3/4.

Slope
The change in the value of the variable measured on the y-axis divided by the change in the value of the variable measured on the x-axis.

FIGURE A1.7

Calculating Slope

MyEconLab Animation

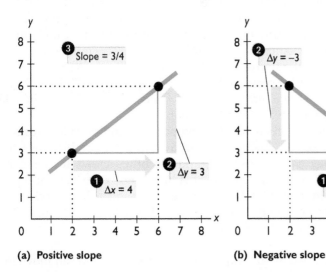

(a) Positive slope

(b) Negative slope

(c) Slope at a point

In part (a), ❶ when Δx is 4, ❷ Δy is 3, so ❸ the slope ($\Delta y \div \Delta x$) is 3/4.

In part (b), ❶ when Δx is 4, ❷ Δy is -3, so ❸ the slope ($\Delta y \div \Delta x$) is $-3/4$.

In part (c), the slope of the curve at point A equals the slope of the red line. ❶ When Δx is 4, ❷ Δy is 3, so ❸ the slope ($\Delta y \div \Delta x$) is 3/4.

■ Relationships Among More Than Two Variables

All the graphs that you have studied so far plot the relationship between two variables as a point formed by the x and y values. But most of the relationships in economics involve relationships among many variables, not just two. For example, the amount of ice cream consumed depends on the price of ice cream and the temperature. If ice cream is expensive and the temperature is low, people eat much less ice cream than when ice cream is inexpensive and the temperature is high. For any given price of ice cream, the quantity consumed varies with the temperature; and for any given temperature, the quantity of ice cream consumed varies with its price.

Figure A1.8 shows a relationship among three variables. The table shows the number of gallons of ice cream consumed per day at various temperatures and ice cream prices. How can we graph these numbers?

To graph a relationship that involves more than two variables, we use the *ceteris paribus* assumption.

Ceteris Paribus

The Latin phrase *ceteris paribus* means "other things remaining the same." Every laboratory experiment is an attempt to create *ceteris paribus* and isolate the relationship of interest. We use the same method to make a graph.

Figure A1.8(a) shows an example. This graph shows what happens to the quantity of ice cream consumed when the price of ice cream varies while the temperature remains constant. The curve labeled 70°F shows the relationship between ice cream consumption and the price of ice cream if the temperature is 70°F. The numbers used to plot that curve are those in the first and fourth columns of the table in Figure A1.8. For example, if the temperature is 70°F, 10 gallons are consumed when the price is $2.75 a scoop and 18 gallons are consumed when the price is $2.25 a scoop. The curve labeled 90°F shows the relationship between consumption and the price when the temperature is 90°F.

We can also show the relationship between ice cream consumption and temperature while the price of ice cream remains constant, as shown in Figure A1.8(b). The curve labeled $2.75 shows how the consumption of ice cream varies with the temperature when the price of ice cream is $2.75 a scoop. The numbers used to plot that curve are those in the fourth row of the table in Figure A1.8. For example, at $2.75 a scoop, 10 gallons are consumed when the temperature is 70°F and 20 gallons are consumed when the temperature is 90°F. A second curve shows the relationship when the price of ice cream is $2.00 a scoop.

Figure A1.8(c) shows the combinations of temperature and price that result in a constant consumption of ice cream. One curve shows the combinations that result in 10 gallons a day being consumed, and the other shows the combinations that result in 7 gallons a day being consumed. A high temperature and a high price lead to the same consumption as a lower temperature and a lower price. For example, 10 gallons of ice cream are consumed at 90°F and $3.25 a scoop, at 70°F and $2.75 a scoop, and at 50°F and $2.50 a scoop.

With what you've learned about graphs in this Appendix, you can move forward with your study of economics. There are no graphs in this textbook that are more complicated than the ones you've studied here.

FIGURE A1.8

Graphing a Relationship Among Three Variables

MyEconLab Animation

Price (dollars per scoop)	Ice cream consumption (gallons per day)			
	30°F	50°F	70°F	90°F
2.00	12	18	25	50
2.25	10	12	18	37
2.50	7	10	13	27
2.75	5	7	10	20
3.00	3	5	7	14
3.25	2	3	5	10
3.50	1	2	3	6

(a) Price and consumption at a given temperature

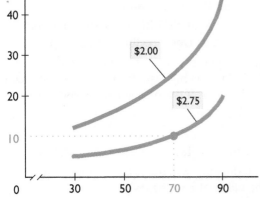

(b) Temperature and consumption at a given price

(c) Temperature and price at a given consumption

The table tells us how many gallons of ice cream are consumed at different prices and different temperatures. For example, if the price is $2.75 a scoop and the temperature is 70°F, 10 gallons of ice cream are consumed. This set of values is highlighted in the table and each part of the figure.

Part (a) shows the relationship between price and consumption when temperature is held constant. One curve holds temperature at 90°F, and the other at 70°F.

Part (b) shows the relationship between temperature and consumption when price is held constant. One curve holds the price at

$2.75 a scoop, and the other at $2.00 a scoop.

Part (c) shows the relationship between temperature and price when consumption is held constant. One curve holds consumption at 10 gallons a day, and the other at 7 gallons a day.

MyEconLab Chapter 1 Study Plan

APPENDIX CHECKPOINT

Study Plan Problems

The spreadsheet in Table 1 provides data on the U.S. economy: Column A is the year; the other columns are quantities sold in millions per year of compact discs (column B), music videos (column C), and singles downloads (column D). Use this spreadsheet to work Problems 1 and 2.

TABLE 1

	A	B	C	D
1	2002	803	15	51
2	2004	767	33	139
3	2006	620	23	586
4	2008	385	13	1,033
5	2010	226	9	1,162
6	2012	211	11	1,392

1. Draw a scatter diagram to show the relationship between the quantities sold of compact discs and music videos. Describe the relationship.

2. Draw a time-series graph of the quantity of compact discs sold. Say in which year or years the quantity sold (a) was highest, (b) was lowest, (c) increased the most, and (d) decreased the most. If the data show a trend, describe it.

TABLE 2

x	0	1	2	3	4	5
y	32	31	28	23	16	7

3. Is the relationship between x and y in Table 2 positive or negative? Calculate the slope of the relationship when x equals 2 and when x equals 4. How does the slope change as the value of x increases?

TABLE 3

Price (dollars per ride)	Balloon rides (number per day)		
	50°F	70°F	90°F
5	32	50	40
10	27	40	32
15	18	32	27
20	10	27	18

4. Table 3 provides data on the price of a balloon ride, the temperature, and the number of rides a day. Draw graphs to show the relationship between
   - The price and the number of rides, when the temperature is 70°F.
   - The number of rides and the temperature, when the price is $15 a ride.

MyEconLab Homework, Quiz, or Test if assigned by instructor

Instructor Assignable Problems

Use the information in Table 1 to work Problems 1 and 2.

1. Draw a scatter diagram to show the relationship between quantities sold of music videos and singles downloads. Describe the relationship.

2. Draw a time-series graph of the quantity of music videos sold. Say in which year or years the quantity sold (a) was highest, (b) was lowest, (c) decreased the most, and (d) decreased the least. If the data show a trend, describe it.

Use the information in Table 4 on the relationship between two variables x and y to work Problems 3 and 4.

TABLE 4

x	0	1	2	3	4	5
y	0	1	4	9	16	25

3. Is the relationship between x and y in Table 4 positive or negative? Explain.

4. Calculate the slope of the relationship when x equals 2 and x equals 4. How does the slope change as the value of x increases?

TABLE 5

Price (dollars per cup)	Hot chocolate (number per week)		
	50°F	70°F	90°F
2.00	40	30	20
2.50	30	20	10
3.00	20	10	0
3.50	10	0	0

5. Table 5 provides data on the price of hot chocolate, the temperature, and the number of cups a week. Draw graphs to show the relationship between
   - The price and the number of cups of hot chocolate, when the temperature is constant.
   - The temperature and the number of cups of hot chocolate, when the price is constant.

MyEconLab Key Terms Quiz

Key Terms

Cross-section graph, 22
Direct relationship, 24
Inverse relationship, 25
Linear relationship, 24

Negative relationship, 25
Positive relationship, 24
Scatter diagram, 22
Slope, 27

Time-series graph, 22
Trend, 22

Who makes the Dreamliner?

The U.S. and Global Economies

2

When you have completed your study of this chapter, you will be able to

1 Describe what, how, and for whom goods and services are produced in the United States.

2 Describe what, how, and for whom goods and services are produced in the global economy.

3 Explain the circular flow model of the U.S. economy and of the global economy.

MyEconLab Big Picture

MyEconLab Snapshot

2.1 WHAT, HOW, AND FOR WHOM?

Walk around a shopping mall and pay close attention to the range of goods and services that are being offered for sale. Go inside some of the shops and look at the labels to see where various items are manufactured. The next time you travel on an interstate highway, look at the large trucks and pay attention to the names and products printed on their sides and the places in which the trucks are registered. Open the Yellow Pages and flip through a few sections. Notice the huge range of goods and services that businesses are offering.

You've just done a sampling of *what* goods and services are produced and consumed in the United States today.

■ What Do We Produce?

We place the goods and services produced into two large groups:

- Consumption goods and services
- Capital goods

Consumption Goods and Services

Consumption goods and services
Goods and services that individuals and governments buy and use in the current period.

Consumption goods and services are items that individuals and governments buy and use up in the current period. Consumption goods and services bought by households include items such as housing, automobiles, bottled water, ramen noodles, chocolate bars, Po' Boy sandwiches, movies, downhill skiing lessons, and doctor and dental services. Consumption goods and services bought by governments include items such as police and fire services, garbage collection, and education.

Capital Goods

Capital goods
Goods bought by businesses and governments to increase productive resources and to use over future periods to produce other goods and services.

Capital goods are goods that businesses and governments buy to increase productive resources to use over future periods to produce other goods and services. Capital goods bought by businesses include items such as auto assembly lines, shopping malls, airplanes, and oil tankers. Capital goods bought by governments include missiles and weapons systems for national security, public schools and universities, and interstate highways.

Consumption goods and services represent 85 percent of U.S. production by value and that percentage doesn't fluctuate much. *Eye on the U.S. Economy* opposite breaks the goods and services down into smaller categories.

Health services is the largest category, with 17.6 percent of the value of total production. Real estate services come next at 12.6 percent. The main components of this item are the services of rental and owner-occupied housing. Professional and business services, which include the services of accountants and lawyers, are 12.5 percent of total production. Other large components of services are education and retail and wholesale trades.

The manufacture of goods represents only 11.5 percent of total production and the largest category of goods produced, chemicals, accounts for less than 2 percent of total production.

Construction accounts for 3.5 percent of production, and utilities, mining, and agriculture together make up only 5 percent. The nation's farms produce only a bit more than 1 percent of total production.

EYE on the U.S. ECONOMY
What We Produce

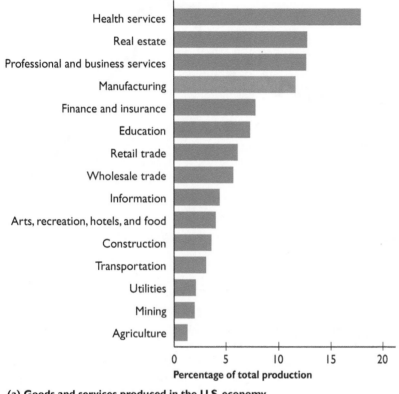

(a) Goods and services produced in the U.S. economy

Percentage of total production

Health services
Real estate
Professional and business services
Manufacturing
Finance and insurance
Education
Retail trade
Wholesale trade
Information
Arts, recreation, hotels, and food
Construction
Transportation
Utilities
Mining
Agriculture

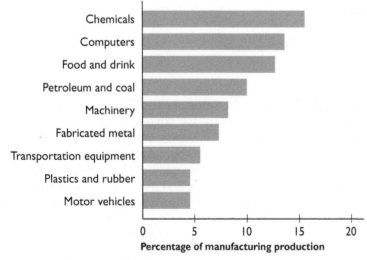

(b) U.S. Manufacturing: Some details

Percentage of manufacturing production

Chemicals
Computers
Food and drink
Petroleum and coal
Machinery
Fabricated metal
Transportation equipment
Plastics and rubber
Motor vehicles

SOURCE OF DATA: Bureau of Economic Analysis.

Health-care services ...

education services ...

and retail trades are among the largest categories of services produced.

The largest category of goods produced is chemicals.

EYE on the PAST
Changes in What We Produce

Freeport, Maine, became a shoemaking center in 1881 when the H.E. Davis Shoe Company opened its steam-powered factory in the town. Over the following years, many other shoe-makers set up in Freeport and produc-tion steadily expanded. The town's shoe production peaked in 1968 after which it shrank rapidly. When the Freeport Shoe Company closed its factory in 1972, it became the fifteenth shoe factory to close in Freeport in four years. Today, the Freeport econ-omy is based on shopping, not shoes.

Freeport's story of shoemaking was repeated across America and the graph tells this broader story. And as manu-facturing has shrunk, retail and other services have expanded.

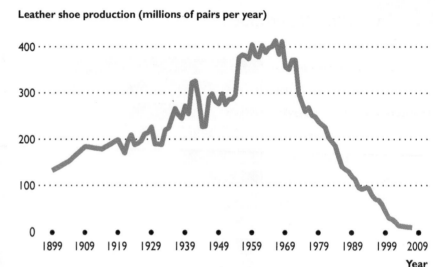

SOURCES OF DATA: *Historical Statistics of the United States Millennial Edition Online* and *Statistical Abstract of the United States, 2012.*

■ How Do We Produce?

Goods and services are produced by using productive resources. Economists call the productive resources **factors of production**. Factors of production are grouped into four categories:

- Land
- Labor
- Capital
- Entrepreneurship

Factors of production
The productive resources that are used to produce goods and services—land, labor, capital, and entrepreneurship.

Land

In economics, **land** includes all the "gifts of nature" that we use to produce goods and services. Land is what, in everyday language, we call *natural resources*. It includes land in the everyday sense, minerals, energy, water, air, and wild plants, animals, birds, and fish. Some of these resources are renewable, and some are non-renewable. The U.S. Geological Survey maintains a national inventory of the quantity and quality of natural resources and monitors changes to that inventory.

The United States covers almost 2 billion acres. About 45 percent of the land is forest, lakes, and national parks. In 2009, almost 50 percent of the land was used for agriculture and 5 percent was urban, but urban land use is growing and agri-cultural land use is shrinking.

Our land surface and water resources are renewable, and some of our mineral resources can be recycled. But many mineral resources can be used only once. They are nonrenewable resources. Of these, the United States has vast known reserves of coal, oil, and natural gas.

Land
The "gifts of nature," or *natural resources,* that we use to produce goods and services.

Labor

Labor is the work time and work effort that people devote to producing goods and services. Labor includes the physical and mental efforts of all the people who work on farms and construction sites and in factories, shops, and offices. The Census Bureau and Bureau of Labor Statistics measure the quantity of labor at work every month.

In the United States in April 2013, 155 million people had jobs or were available for work. Some worked full time, some worked part time, and some were unemployed but looking for an acceptable vacant job. The total amount of time worked during 2011 was about 275 billion hours.

The quantity of labor increases as the adult population increases. The quantity of labor also increases if a larger percentage of the population takes jobs. During the past 50 years, a larger proportion of women have taken paid work and this trend has increased the quantity of labor. At the same time, a slightly smaller proportion of men have taken paid work and this trend has decreased the quantity of labor.

The *quality* of labor depends on how skilled people are. A laborer who can push a hand cart but can't drive a truck is much less productive than one who can drive. An office worker who can use a computer is much more productive than one who can't. Economists use a special name for human skill: human capital. **Human capital** is the knowledge and skill that people obtain from education, on-the-job training, and work experience.

You are building your own human capital right now as you work on your economics course and other subjects. Your human capital will continue to grow when you get a full-time job and become better at it. Human capital improves the *quality* of labor and increases the quantity of goods and services that labor can produce.

Capital

Capital consists of the tools, instruments, machines, buildings, and other items that have been produced in the past and that businesses now use to produce goods and services. Capital includes hammers and screwdrivers, computers, auto assembly lines, office towers and warehouses, dams and power plants, airplanes, shirt factories, and shopping malls.

Capital also includes inventories of unsold goods or of partly finished goods on a production line. And capital includes what is sometimes called *infrastructure capital*, such as highways and airports.

Capital, like human capital, makes labor more productive. A truck driver can produce vastly more transportation services than someone pushing a hand cart; the Interstate highway system enables us to produce vastly more transportation services than was possible on the old highway system that preceded it.

The Bureau of Economic Analysis in the U.S. Department of Commerce keeps track of the total value of capital in the United States and how it grows over time. Today, the value of capital in the U.S. economy is around $50 trillion.

Financial Capital Is Not Capital

In everyday language, we talk about money, stocks, and bonds as being capital. These items are *financial capital,* and they are not productive resources. They enable people to provide businesses with financial resources, but they are *not* used to produce goods and services. They are not capital.

Labor
The work time and work effort that people devote to producing goods and services.

Human capital
The knowledge and skill that people obtain from education, on-the-job training, and work experience.

Capital
Tools, instruments, machines, buildings, and other items that have been produced in the past and that businesses now use to produce goods and services.

The information economy consists of the jobs and businesses that produce and use computers and equipment powered by computer chips. This information economy is highly visible in your daily life.

The pairs of images here illustrate two examples. In each pair, a new technology enables capital to replace labor.

The top pair of pictures illustrate the replacement of bank tellers (labor) with ATMs (capital). Although the ATM was invented almost 40 years ago, when it made its first appearance, it was located only inside banks and was not able to update customers' accounts. It is only in the last decade that ATMs have spread to corner stores and enable us to get cash and check our bank balance from almost anywhere in the world.

The bottom pair of pictures illustrate a more recent replacement of labor with capital: self-check-in. Air passengers today issue their own boarding pass, often at their own computer before leaving home. For international

flights, some of these machines now even check passport details.

The number of bank teller and airport check-in clerk jobs is shrinking,

but these new technologies are creating a whole range of new jobs for people who make, program, install, and repair the vast number of machines.

Entrepreneurship

Entrepreneurship is the human resource that organizes land, labor, and capital to produce goods and services. Entrepreneurs are creative and imaginative. They come up with new ideas about what and how to produce, make business decisions, and bear the risks that arise from these decisions. If their ideas work out, they earn a profit. If their ideas turn out to be wrong, they bear the loss.

The quantity of entrepreneurship is hard to describe or measure. During some periods, there appears to be a great deal of imaginative entrepreneurship around. People such as Sam Walton, who created Wal-Mart, one of the world's largest retailers; Bill Gates, who founded the Microsoft empire; and Mark Zuckerberg, who founded Facebook, are examples of extraordinary entrepreneurial talent. But these highly visible entrepreneurs are just the tip of an iceberg that consists of hundreds of thousands of people who run businesses, large and small.

For Whom Do We Produce?

Who gets the goods and services depends on the incomes that people earn. A large income enables a person to buy large quantities of goods and services. A small income leaves a person with a small quantity of goods and services.

People earn their incomes by selling the services of the factors of production they own. **Rent** is paid for the use of land, **wages** are paid for the services of labor, **interest** is paid for the use of capital, and entrepreneurs receive a **profit** (or incur a **loss**) for running their businesses. What are the shares of these four factor incomes in the United States? Which factor receives the largest share?

Figure 2.1(a) answers these questions. It shows that wages were 69 percent of total income in 2011 and rent, interest, and profit were 31 percent of total income. These percentages remain remarkably constant over time. We call the distribution of income among the factors of production the *functional distribution of income*.

Figure 2.1(b) shows the *personal distribution of income*—the distribution of income among households—in 2011. Some households, like that of Alex Rodriguez, earn many millions of dollars a year. These households are in the richest 20 percent who earn 50 percent of total income. Households at the other end of the scale, like those of fast-food servers, are in the poorest 20 percent who earn only 3 percent of total income. The distribution of income has been changing and becoming more unequal. The rich have become richer. But it isn't the case, on the whole, that the poor have become poorer. They just haven't become richer as fast as the rich have.

Rent
Income paid for the use of land.

Wages
Income paid for the services of labor.

Interest
Income paid for the use of capital.

Profit (or loss)
Income earned by an entrepreneur for running a business.

■ FIGURE 2.1

For Whom in 2011

MyEconLab Animation

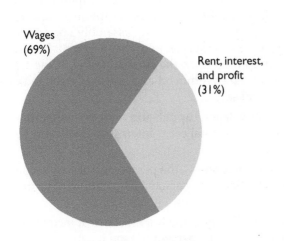

(a) Functional distribution of income

(b) Personal distribution of income

SOURCES OF DATA: Bureau of Economic Analysis, *National Income and Product Accounts*, Table 1.10 and U.S. Census Bureau, *Income, Poverty, and Health Insurance Coverage in the United States*: 2011, Current Population Reports P60-243, 2012.

In 2011, wages (the income from labor) were 69 percent of total income. Rent, interest, and profit (the income from the services of land, capital, and entrepreneurship) totaled the remaining 31 percent.

In 2011, the 20 percent of the population with the highest incomes received 50 percent of total income. The 20 percent with the lowest incomes received only 3 percent of total income.

MyEconLab Study Plan 2.1
                Key Terms Quiz
                Solutions

 CHECKPOINT 2.1

Describe what, how, and for whom goods and services are produced in the United States.

Practice Problems

1. What are the types of goods and services produced? Give an example of each (different from those in the chapter) and distinguish between them.
2. Name the four factors of production and the incomes they earn.
3. Distinguish between the functional distribution of income and the personal distribution of income.
4. In the United States, which factor of production earned the largest share of income in 2011 and what percentage did it earn?

In the News

What microloans miss
The 2006 Nobel Peace Prize winner Muhammad Yunus has said that "all people are entrepreneurs" and that microloans will pull poor people out of poverty. Only 14 percent of Americans are entrepreneurs while almost 40 percent of Peruvians are.

Source: James Surowiecki, *The New Yorker*, March 17, 2008

With only 14 percent of Americans earning their income from entrepreneurship, from what factor of production do most Americans earn their income? What is that income called? Why might so many people in Peru be entrepreneurs?

Solutions to Practice Problems

1. The goods and services produced fall into two types: consumption goods and services and capital goods. A hamburger is a consumption good and a haircut is a consumption service. An oil rig and auto assembly line are capital goods. A consumption good or service is an item that is bought by individuals or the government and is used up in the current period. A capital good is bought by businesses or the government and it is used over and over again to produce other goods and services.
2. The factors of production are land, labor, capital, and entrepreneurship. Land earns rent; labor earns wages; capital earns interest; and entrepreneurship earns profit or incurs a loss.
3. The functional distribution of income shows the percentage of total income received by each factor of production. The personal distribution of income shows how total income is shared among households.
4. Labor is the factor of production that earns the largest share of income. In 2011, labor in the United States earned 69 percent of total income.

Solution to In the News

Most Americans earn their income from supplying labor services and the income they earn is called a wage. Peru is a poor country in which jobs are more limited than in the United States. So to earn an income, many Peruvians are self-employed and work as small entrepreneurs.

2.2   THE GLOBAL ECONOMY

We're now going to look at *what, how,* and *for whom* goods and services get produced in the global economy. We'll begin with a brief overview of the people and countries that form the global economy.

■ The People

Visit the Web site of the U.S. Census Bureau and go to the population clocks to find out how many people there are today in both the United States and the entire world. On the day these words were written, May 9, 2013, the U.S. clock recorded a population of 315,824,000. The world clock recorded a global population of 7,084,065,000. The U.S. clock ticks along showing a population increase of one person every 15 seconds. The world clock spins faster, adding 30 people in the same 15 seconds.

■ The Economies

The world's 7.1 billion (and rising) population lives in 176 economies, which the International Monetary Fund classifies into two broad groups:

- Advanced economies
- Emerging market and developing economies

Advanced Economies

Advanced economies are the richest 29 countries (or areas). The United States, Japan, Italy, Germany, France, the United Kingdom, and Canada belong to this group. So do four new industrial Asian economies: Hong Kong, South Korea, Singapore, and Taiwan. The other advanced economies include Australia, New Zealand, and most of the rest of Western Europe. Almost 1 billion people (15 percent of the world's population) live in the advanced economies.

Emerging Market and Developing Economies

Emerging market economies are 28 countries in Central and Eastern Europe and Asia. Almost 500 million people live in these countries—about half of the number in the advanced economies. These countries are important because they are emerging (hence the name) from a system of state-owned production, central economic planning, and heavily regulated markets moving toward a system of free enterprise and unregulated markets.

Developing economies are the 119 countries in Africa, Asia, the Middle East, Europe, and Central and South America. More than 5.5 billion people—almost four out of every five people—live in the developing economies.

Developing economies vary enormously in size, in the level of average income, and the rate of growth of production and incomes. But in all the developing economies, average incomes are much lower than those in the advanced economies, and in some cases, they are extremely low.

Five emerging market and developing economies, representing 3 billion people or 42 percent of the world's population and known as BRICS (Brazil, Russia, India, China, and South Africa), hold regular meetings to advance the interests of these nations and draw attention to their development problems.

■ *What* in the Global Economy?

First, let's look at the big picture. Imagine that each year the global economy produces an enormous pie. In 2013, the pie was worth about $87 trillion! To give this number some meaning, if the pie were shared equally among the world's 7.1 billion people, each of us would get a slice worth a bit more than $12,254.

Where Is the Global Pie Baked?

Figure 2.2 shows us where in the world the pie is baked. The advanced economies produce 50 percent—19 percent in the United States, 14 percent in the Euro area, and 17 percent in the other advanced economies. This 50 percent of global output (by value) is produced by 15 percent of the world's population.

The BRICS economies, highlighted in the figure, together produce 28 percent of the world's output. China, with 15 percent of world production, dominates this group and South Africa, the group's smallest member, produces barely 1 percent of global output. This 28 percent of the global pie is baked by 42 percent of the world's population.

The remaining 22 percent of the global pie comes from other emerging market and developing economies and is baked by 43 percent of the world's people.

Unlike the slices of an apple pie, those of the global pie have different fillings. Some slices have more oil, some more food, some more clothing, some more housing services, some more autos, and so on. Let's look at some of these different fillings and at some similarities too.

■ FIGURE 2.2

What in the Global Economy in 2013   MyEconLab Animation

If we show the value of production in the world economy as a pie, the United States produces a slice that is 19 percent of the total. The Euro area produces 14 percent and other advanced economies 17 percent, so together, the advanced economies produce 50 percent of global output.

Another 28 percent of the global pie comes from the BRICS economies, and China, with 15 percent of world output, dominates this group.

The remaining 22 percent of world output comes from emerging market and developing economies in Africa, Asia, the Middle East, and the Western Hemisphere.

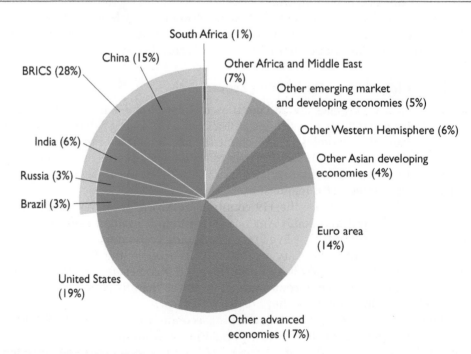

SOURCE OF DATA: International Monetary Fund, World Economic Outlook Database, April 2013.

EYE on the DREAMLINER

Who Makes the Dreamliner?

Boeing designed, assembles, and markets the Dreamliner, but the airplane is made by more than 400 firms on four continents that employ thousands of workers and millions of dollars' worth of specialized capital equipment. The graphic identifies some of the firms and the components they make.

Boeing and these firms make decisions and pay their workers, investors, and raw material suppliers to influence *what*, *how*, and *for whom* goods and services are produced. All these decisions are made in self-interest, and produce an airplane at the lowest possible cost.

Rudder, Chengdu Aircraft, China

Tail fin, Boeing, US

Wing, Mitsubishi, Japan

Wing tips, Korean Air, Korea

Horizontal stabilizer, Alenia, Italy

Fuselage, Alenia, Italy

Leading edge, Spirit Aerosystems, US

Fuselage, Kawasaki, Japan

Rear fuselage, Vaught, US

Forward fuselage, Spirit Aerosystems, US

Trailing edge, Hawker de Havilland, Australia

Engine, Rolls-Royce, UK

Cargo doors, Saab, Sweden

Landing gear, Messier-Dowty, UK

Passenger doors, Latecoere, France

Some Differences in What Is Produced

What is produced in the developing economies contrasts sharply with that of the advanced economies. Manufacturing is the big story. Developing economies have large and growing industries, which produce textiles, footwear, sports gear, toys, electronic goods, furniture, steel, and even automobiles and airplanes.

Food production is a small part of the U.S. and other advanced economies and a large part of the developing economies such as Brazil, China, and India. But the advanced economies produce about one third of the world's food. How come? *Total* production is much larger in the advanced economies than in the developing economies, but a small percentage of a big number can be *greater* than a large percentage of a small number!

Some Similarities in What Is Produced

If you were to visit a shopping mall in Canada, England, Australia, Japan, or any of the other advanced economies, you would wonder whether you had left the United States. You would see Starbucks, Burger King, Pizza Hut, Domino's Pizza, KFC, Kmart, Wal-Mart, Target, Gap, Tommy Hilfiger, Lululemon, Banana Republic, the upscale Louis Vuitton and Burberry, and a host of other familiar names. And, of course, you would see McDonald's golden arches. You would see them in any of the 119 countries in which one or more of McDonald's 30,000 restaurants are located.

The similarities among the advanced economies go beyond the view from main street and the shopping mall. The structure of *what* is produced is similar in these economies. As percentages of the total economy, agriculture and manufacturing are small and shrinking whereas services are large and expanding.

McDonald's in Shanghai.

■ *How* in the Global Economy?

Goods and services are produced using land, labor, capital, and entrepreneurial resources, and the combinations of these resources used are chosen to produce at the lowest possible cost. Each country or region has its own blend of factors of production, but there are some interesting common patterns and crucial differences between the advanced and developing economies that we'll now examine.

Human Capital Differences

One of the biggest distinguishing features of an advanced economy from an emerging market or developing economy is its quantity of *human capital*. Advanced economies have much higher levels of human capital.

Education levels are the handiest measure of human capital. In an advanced economy such as the United States, almost everyone has completed high school. And 30 percent of the U.S. population has completed 4 years or more of college.

In contrast, in developing economies, the proportion of the population who has completed high school or has a college degree is small. In the poorest of the developing economies, many children even miss out on basic primary education—they just don't go to school at all.

On-the-job training and experience are also much less extensive in the developing economies than in the advanced economies.

Physical Capital Differences

Another major feature of an advanced economy that differentiates it from a developing economy is the amount of capital available for producing goods and services. The differences begin with the basic transportation system. In the advanced economies, a well-developed highway system connects all the major cities and points of production. You can see this difference vividly if you open a road atlas of North America: Contrast the U.S. interstate highway system with the sparse highways of Mexico. You would see a similar contrast if you flipped through a road atlas of Western Europe and Africa.

But it isn't the case that the developing economies have no highways and no modern trucks and cars. In fact, some of them have the newest and the best. But the new and best are usually inside and around the major cities—see *Eye on the Global Economy* opposite.

The contrasts in the transportation system are matched by those on farms and in factories. In general, the more advanced the economy, the greater are the amount and sophistication of the capital equipment used in production. But again, the contrast is not all or nothing. Some factories in India, China, and other parts of Asia use the very latest technologies. Furniture manufacturing is an example. To make furniture of a quality that Americans are willing to buy, firms in Asia use machines like those in the furniture factories of North Carolina.

The differences in human capital and physical capital between advanced and developing economies have a big effect on *who* gets the goods and services, which we'll now examine.

■ *For Whom* in the Global Economy?

Who gets the world's goods and services depends on the incomes that people earn. We're now going to see how incomes are distributed within economies and across the world.

EYE on the GLOBAL ECONOMY
Differences in How We Produce

Big differences exist in how goods and services are produced and the images here illustrate three examples.

Laundry services (top), transportation services (center), and highway systems (bottom) can use a large amount of capital and almost no labor (left) or use almost no capital and a large amount of labor (right).

Capital-intensive automatic laundry equipment, big trucks, and multi-lane paved freeways are common in advanced economies but rare in poorer developing economies.

Riverside clothes washing, human pedal power, and unsealed dirt tracks are seen only in developing economies.

But we also see huge differences even within a developing economy. The bottom pictures contrast Beijing's capital-intensive highway system with the unpaved and sometimes hazardous roads of rural China.

Personal Distribution of Income

You saw earlier (on p. 37) that in the United States, the lowest-paid 20 percent of the population receives 3 percent of total income and the highest-paid 20 percent receives 50 percent of total income. The personal distribution of income in the world economy is much more unequal. According to World Bank data, the lowest-paid 20 percent of the world's population receives 2 percent of world income and the highest-paid 20 percent receives about 70 percent of world income.

International Distribution

Much of the greater inequality at the global level arises from differences in average incomes among countries. Figure 2.3 shows some of these differences. It shows the dollar value of what people can afford each day on average. You can see that in the United States, that number is $137 a day—an average person in the United States can buy goods and services that cost $137. This amount is around five times the world average. The Euro area has an average income of around two thirds that of the United States at $93 per day. Income levels fall off quickly as we move farther down the graph, with Russia at $49 a day, China $25 a day, India $10 a day, and Africa only $7 a day.

As people have lost well-paid manufacturing jobs and found lower-paid service jobs, inequality has increased in the United States and in most other advanced economies. Inequality is also increasing in the developing economies. People with skills enjoy rapidly rising incomes but the incomes of the unskilled are falling.

A Happy Paradox and a Huge Challenge

Despite the increase in inequality inside most countries, inequality across the entire world has decreased during the past 20 years. And most important, according to Xavier Sala-i-Martin, an economics professor at Columbia University, extreme poverty has declined. Professor Sala-i-Martin estimates that between 1976 and 1998, the number of people who earn $1 a day or less fell by 235 million and the number who earn $2 a day or less fell by 450 million. This positive situation arises because in China, the largest nation, incomes have increased rapidly and lifted millions from extreme poverty. Incomes are growing quickly in India too.

Lifting Africa from poverty is today's big challenge. In 1960, 11 percent of the world's poor lived in Africa, but in 1998, 66 percent did. Between 1976 and 1998, the number of people in Africa who earn $1 a day or less rose by 175 million, and the number who earn $2 a day or less rose by 227 million.

■ **FIGURE 2.3**

For Whom in the Global Economy in 2012   MyEconLab Animation

In 2012, the average income per person per day in the United States was $137. It was $93 in the Euro area and $49 in Russia. The number falls to $25 in China, $10 in India, and $7 in Africa.

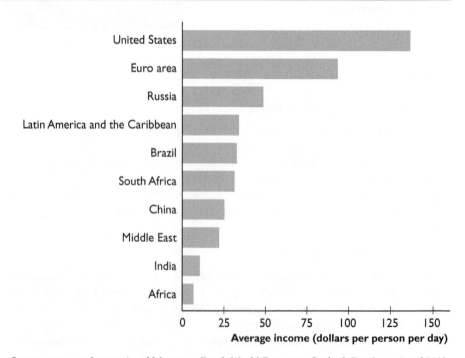

SOURCE OF DATA: International Monetary Fund, World Economic Outlook Database, April 2013.

EYE on YOUR LIFE
The U.S. and Global Economies in Your Life

You've encountered a lot of facts and trends about what, how, and for whom goods and services are produced in the U.S. economy and the global economy. How can you use this information? You can use it in two ways:

1. To inform your choice of career
2. To inform your stand on the politics of protecting U.S. jobs

Career Choices

As you think about your future career, you are now better informed about some of the key trends. You know that manufacturing is shrinking. The U.S. economy is what is sometimes called a *post-industrial economy.* Industries that provided the backbone of the economy in previous generations have fallen to barely a fifth of

the economy today, and the trend continues. It is possible that by the middle of the current century, manufacturing will be as small a source of jobs as agriculture is today.

So, a job in a manufacturing business is likely to lead to some tough situations and possibly the need for several job changes over a working life.

As manufacturing shrinks, so services expand, and this expansion will continue. The provision of health care, education, communication, wholesale and retail trades, and entertainment are all likely to expand in the future and be sources of increasing employment and rising wages. A job in a service-oriented business is more likely to lead to steady advances in income.

Political Stand on Job Protection

As you think about the stand you will take on the political question of protecting U.S. jobs, you are better informed about the basic facts and trends.

When you hear that manufacturing jobs are disappearing to China, you will be able to place that news in historical perspective. You might reasonably be concerned, especially if you or a member of your family has lost a job. But you know that trying to reverse or even halt this process is flying in the face of stubborn historical trends.

In later chapters, you will learn that there are good economic reasons to be skeptical about any form of protection and placing limits on competition.

CHECKPOINT 2.2

MyEconLab Study Plan 2.2
Solutions

Describe what, how, and for whom goods and services are produced in the global economy.

Practice Problems

1. Describe what, how, and for whom goods and services are produced in developing economies.
2. A Clinton Foundation success story is that it loaned $23,000 to Rwandan coffee growers to support improvements to coffee washing stations and provided technical support. What was the source of the success?

Solutions to Practice Problems

1. In developing countries, agriculture is the largest percentage, manufacturing is an increasing percentage, and services are a small percentage of total production. Most production does not use modern capital-intensive technologies, but some industries do. People who work in factories have rising incomes while those who work in rural industries are left behind.
2. The technical support allowed Rwandan coffee growers to improve their knowledge of coffee farming, which increased their human capital. The improvements to washing stations was a change in physical capital that allowed farmers to increase the quan-tity of washed coffee.

MyEconLab Snapshot

Circular flow model
A model of the economy that shows the circular flow of expenditures and incomes that result from decision makers' choices and the way those choices interact to determine what, how, and for whom goods and services are produced.

Households
Individuals or groups of people living together.

Firms
The institutions that organize the production of goods and services.

Market
Any arrangement that brings buyers and sellers together and enables them to get information and do business with each other.

Goods markets
Markets in which goods and services are bought and sold.

Factor markets
Markets in which the services of factors of production are bought and sold.

2.3 THE CIRCULAR FLOWS

We can organize the data you've just studied using the **circular flow model**—a model of the economy that shows the circular flow of expenditures and incomes that result from decision makers' choices and the way those choices interact to determine what, how, and for whom goods and services are produced. Figure 2.4 shows the circular flow model.

■ Households and Firms

Households are individuals or groups of people living together. The 121 million households in the United States own the factors of production—land, labor, capital, and entrepreneurship—and choose the quantities of these resources to provide to firms. Households also choose the quantities of goods and services to buy.

Firms are the institutions that organize the production of goods and services. The 28 million firms in the United States choose the quantities of the factors of production to hire and the quantities of goods and services to produce.

■ Markets

Households choose the quantities of the factors of production to provide to firms, and firms choose the quantities of the services of the factors of production to hire. Firms choose the quantities of goods and services to produce, and households choose the quantities of goods and services to buy. How are these choices coordinated and made compatible? The answer is: by markets.

A **market** is any arrangement that brings buyers and sellers together and enables them to get information and do business with each other. An example is the market in which oil is bought and sold—the world oil market. The world oil market is not a place. It is the network of oil producers, oil users, wholesalers, and brokers who buy and sell oil. In the world oil market, decision makers do not meet physically. They make deals by telephone, fax, and the Internet.

Figure 2.4 identifies two types of markets: goods markets and factor markets. Goods and services are bought and sold in **goods markets;** and the services of factors of production are bought and sold in **factor markets.**

■ Real Flows and Money Flows

When households choose the quantities of services of land, labor, capital, and entrepreneurship to offer in factor markets, they respond to the incomes they receive—rent for land, wages for labor, interest for capital, and profit for entrepreneurship. When firms choose the quantities of factor services to hire, they respond to the rent, wages, interest, and profits they must pay to households.

Similarly, when firms choose the quantities of goods and services to produce and offer for sale in goods markets, they respond to the amounts that they receive from the expenditures that households make. And when households choose the quantities of goods and services to buy, they respond to the amounts they must pay to firms.

Figure 2.4 shows the flows that result from these choices made by households and firms. The flows shown in orange are *real flows:* the flows of the factors of production that go from households through factor markets to firms and of the goods and services that go from firms through goods markets to households. The flows in the opposite direction are *money flows:* the flows of payments made in exchange for the services of factors of production (shown in blue) and of expenditures on goods and services (shown in red).

Lying behind these real flows and money flows are millions of individual choices about what to consume and what and how to produce. These choices result in buying plans by households and selling plans by firms in goods markets. And the choices result in selling plans by households and buying plans by firms in factor markets that interact to determine the prices that people pay and the incomes they earn, and so determine for whom goods and services are produced. You'll learn in Chapter 4 how markets coordinate the buying plans and selling plans of households and firms and make them compatible.

Firms produce most of the goods and services that we consume, but governments provide some of the services that we enjoy. Governments also play a big role in modifying for whom goods and services are produced by changing the personal distribution of income. We're now going to look at the role of governments in the U.S. economy and add them to the circular flow model.

FIGURE 2.4

The Circular Flow Model   MyEconLab Animation

Rent, wages, interest, and profit

Expenditures on goods and services

HOUSEHOLDS

Land, labor, capital, and entrepreneurship services supplied

Goods and services bought

FACTOR MARKETS

GOODS MARKETS

Land, labor, capital, and entrepreneurship services hired

Goods and services supplied

FIRMS

Rent, wages, interest, and profit

Expenditures on goods and services

The orange flows are the services of factors of production that go from households through factor markets to firms and the goods and services that go from firms through goods markets to households. These flows are *real* flows.

The blue flow is the income earned by the factors of production, and the red flow is the expenditures on goods and services. These flows are *money* flows.

The choices that generate these real and money flows determine *what*, *how*, and *for whom* goods and services are produced.

■ Governments

More than 86,000 organizations operate as governments in the United States. Some are tiny like the Yuma, Arizona, school district and some are enormous like the U.S. federal government. We divide governments into two levels:

- Federal government
- State and local government

Federal Government

The federal government's major expenditures provide

1. Goods and services
2. Social Security and welfare payments
3. Transfers to state and local governments

The goods and services provided by the federal government include the legal system, which protects property and enforces contracts, and national defense. Social Security and welfare benefits, which include income for retired people and programs such as Medicare and Medicaid, are transfers from the federal government to households. Federal government transfers to state and local governments are payments designed to provide more equality across the states and regions.

The federal government finances its expenditures by collecting a variety of taxes. The main taxes paid to the federal government are

1. Personal income taxes
2. Corporate (business) income taxes
3. Social Security taxes

In 2012, the federal government spent $3 trillion—about 19 percent of the total value of all the goods and services produced in the United States in that year. The taxes they raised were less than this amount—the government had a deficit.

State and Local Government

The state and local governments' major expenditures are to provide

1. Goods and services
2. Welfare benefits

The goods and services provided by state and local governments include the state courts and police, schools, roads, garbage collection and disposal, water supplies, and sewage management. Welfare benefits provided by state governments include unemployment benefits and other aid to low-income families.

State and local governments finance these expenditures by collecting taxes and receiving transfers from the federal government. The main taxes paid to state and local governments are

1. Sales taxes
2. Property taxes
3. State income taxes

In 2012, state and local governments spent $2.2 trillion or 14 percent of the total value of all the goods and services produced in the United States.

■ Governments in the Circular Flow

Figure 2.5 adds governments to the circular flow model. As you study this figure, first notice that the outer circle is the same as in Figure 2.4. In addition to these flows, governments buy goods and services from firms. The red arrows that run from governments through the goods markets to firms show this expenditure.

Households and firms pay taxes to governments. The green arrows running directly from households and firms to governments show these flows. Also, governments make money payments to households and firms. The green arrows running directly from governments to households and firms show these flows. Taxes and transfers are direct transactions with governments and do not go through the goods markets and factor markets.

Not part of the circular flow and not visible in Figure 2.5, governments provide the legal framework within which all transactions occur. For example, governments operate the courts and legal system that enable contracts to be written and enforced.

■ FIGURE 2.5

Governments in the Circular Flow

MyEconLab Animation

The green flows from households and firms to governments are taxes, and the green flows from governments to households and firms are money transfers.

The red flow from governments through the goods markets to firms is the expenditure on goods and services by governments.

EYE on the PAST
Growing Government

One hundred years ago, the federal government spent 2 cents out of each dollar earned. Today, the federal government spends 23 cents. Government grew during the two world wars and during the 1960s and 1970s as social programs expanded.

Only during the 1980s and 1990s did big government begin to shrink in a process begun by Ronald Reagan and continued by Bill Clinton. But 9-11 saw the start of a new era of growing government, and fiscal stimulus and bailouts to cope with the global financial crisis sent spending soaring.

SOURCE OF DATA: Budget of the United States Government, Historical Tables, Table 1.1.

■ Circular Flows in the Global Economy

Households and firms in the U.S. economy interact with households and firms in other economies in two main ways: They buy and sell goods and services and they borrow and lend. We call these two activities:

*   International trade
*   International finance

International Trade

Many of the goods that you buy were not made in the United States. Your iPod, Wii games, Nike shoes, cell phone, T-shirt, and bike were made somewhere in Asia or possibly Europe or South or Central America. The goods and services that we buy from firms in other countries are U.S. *imports*.

Much of what is produced in the United States doesn't end up being bought by Americans. Boeing, for example, sells most of the airplanes it makes to foreign airlines. The banks of Wall Street sell banking services to Europeans and Asians. The goods and services that we sell to households and firms in other countries are U.S. *exports*.

International Finance

When firms or governments want to borrow, they look for the lowest interest rate available. Sometimes, that is outside the United States. Also, when the value of our imports exceeds the value of our exports, we must borrow from the rest of the world.

Firms and governments in the rest of the world behave in the same way. They look for the lowest interest rate at which to borrow and the highest at which to lend. They might borrow from or lend to Americans.

Figure 2.6 shows the flows through goods markets and financial markets in the global economy. Households and firms in the U.S. economy interact with those in the rest of the world (other economies) in goods markets and financial markets.

The red flow shows the expenditure by Americans on imports of goods and services, and the blue flow shows the expenditure by the rest of the world on U.S. exports (other countries' imports). The green flow shows U.S. lending to the rest of the world, and the orange flow shows U.S. borrowing from the rest of the world.

It is these international trade and international finance flows that tie nations together in the global economy and through which global booms and slumps are transmitted.

FIGURE 2.6

Circular Flows in the Global Economy

MyEconLab Animation

Households and firms in the U.S. economy interact with those in the rest of the world (other economies) in goods markets and financial markets.

The red flow shows the expenditure by Americans on imports of goods and services, and the blue flow shows the expenditure by the rest of the world on U.S. exports (other countries' imports).

The green flow shows U.S. lending to the rest of the world, and the orange flow shows U.S. borrowing from the rest of the world.

EYE on the GLOBAL ECONOMY
The Ups and Downs in International Trade

International trade expanded rapidly after China became a powerful player in the global economy.

At an average growth rate of close to 7 percent a year, world trade has doubled every decade and increased as a percentage of world production.

A mini-recession in 2001 slowed the growth in world trade to a crawl and the 2009 global economic slump reduced world trade.

After the slump of 2009, world trade bounced back to more than 30 percent of global production in 2011 and 2012.

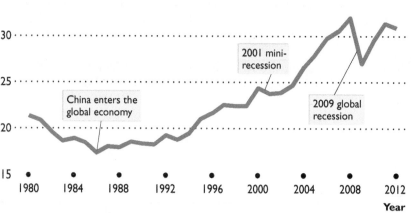

SOURCE OF DATA: International Monetary Fund, World Economic Outlook Database, April 2013.

MyEconLab Study Plan 2.3
Key Terms Quiz
Solutions

CHECKPOINT 2.3

Explain the circular flow model of the U.S. economy and of the global economy.

Practice Problems

1. Describe the flows in the circular flow model in which consumption expenditure, purchases of new national defense equipment, and payments for labor services appear. Through which market does each of these flows pass?
2. Of the flows that run between households, firms, and governments in the circular flow model, which ones are real flows and which are money flows?

Solutions to Practice Problems

1. Consumption expenditure flows from households to firms through the goods market. Purchases of national defense flow from governments to firms through the goods market. Payments for labor services flow from firms to households through the factor market.
2. The real flows are the flows of services of factors of production that go from households to firms through factor markets and the goods and services that go from firms to households and from firms to governments through goods markets. The money flows are the flows of factor incomes, household and government expenditures on goods and services, taxes, and transfers.

CHAPTER SUMMARY

Key Points

1. **Describe what, how, and for whom goods and services are produced in the United States.**

   - Consumption goods and services represent 85 percent of total production; capital goods represent 15 percent.
   - Goods and services are produced by using the four factors of production: land, labor, capital, and entrepreneurship.
   - The incomes people earn (rent for land, wages for labor, interest for capital, and profit for entrepreneurship) determine who gets the goods and services produced.

2. **Describe what, how, and for whom goods and services are produced in the global economy.**

   - Sixty-one percent of the world's production (by value) comes from the advanced industrial countries and the emerging market economies.
   - Production in the advanced economies uses more capital (both machines and human), but some developing economies use the latest capital and technologies.
   - The global distribution of income is more unequal than the U.S. distribution. Poverty has fallen in Asia, but it has increased in Africa.

3. **Explain the circular flow model of the U.S. economy and of the global economy.**

   - The circular flow model of the U.S. economy shows the real flows of factors of production and goods and the corresponding money flows of incomes and expenditures.
   - Governments in the circular flow receive taxes, make transfers, and buy goods and services.
   - The circular flow model of the global economy shows the flows of U.S. exports and imports and the international financial flows that result from lending to and borrowing from other countries.

Key Terms

MyEconLab Key Terms Quiz

Capital, 35
Capital goods, 32
Circular flow model, 46
Consumption goods and services, 32
Entrepreneurship, 36
Factor markets, 46

Factors of production, 34
Firms, 46
Goods markets, 46
Households, 46
Human capital, 35
Interest, 37

Labor, 35
Land, 34
Market, 46
Profit (or loss), 37
Rent, 37
Wages, 37

CHAPTER CHECKPOINT

Study Plan Problems and Applications

1. Explain which of the following items are *not* consumption goods and services:
   • A chocolate bar   • A ski lift   • A golf ball

2. Explain which of the following items are *not* capital goods:
   • An auto assembly line   • A shopping mall   • A golf ball

3. Explain which of the following items are *not* factors of production:
   • Vans used by a baker to deliver bread
   • 1,000 shares of Amazon.com stock
   • Undiscovered oil in the Arctic Ocean

4. Which factor of production earns the highest percentage of total U.S. income? Define that factor of production. What is the income earned by this factor of production called?

5. With more job training and more scholarships to poor American students, which special factor of production is likely to grow faster than in the past?

6. Define the factor of production called capital. Give three examples of capital, different from those in the chapter. Distinguish between the factor of production capital and financial capital.

7. A Job Creation through Entrepreneurship Act, debated in the House of Representatives in 2009, would award grants to small business owners, some of which would be aimed at women, Native Americans, and veterans. The Act would provide $189 million in 2010 and $531 million between 2010 and 2014. Explain how you would expect this Act to influence *what, how,* and *for whom* goods and services are produced in the United States.

8. In the circular flow model, explain the real flow and/or the money flow in which each item in List 1 belongs. Show your answers on a graph.

9. **For-profit colleges may face aid cuts**

   The Obama Administration proposes a new rule: Federal aid to for-profit colleges will be cut if students in vocational programs graduate without a degree. Millions of low-income students are borrowing heavily to attend colleges and too many of them are dropping out, and failing to get a job.

   Source: *USA Today,* June 2, 2011

   How do you think the personal distribution of income would change if all graduates could obtain a well-paying job that uses their knowledge gained in college?

10. Read *Eye on the Dreamliner* on p. 41 and then answer the following questions:
    • How many firms are involved in the production of the Dreamliner and how many are identified in the figure on p. 41?
    • Is the Dreamliner a capital good or a consumption good? Explain why.
    • State the factors of production that make the Dreamliner and provide an example of each.
    • Explain how the production of the Dreamliner influences *what, how,* and *for whom,* goods and services are produced.
    • Use a graph to show where in the circular flow model of the global economy the flows of the components listed on p. 41 appear and where the sales of Dreamliners appear.

LIST 1

• You buy a coffee at Starbucks.
• The government buys some Dell computers.
• A student works at Kinko.
• Donald Trump rents a building to Marriot hotels.
• You pay your income tax.

Instructor Assignable Problems and Applications

MyEconLab Homework, Quiz, or Test if assigned by instructor

1. Boeing's Dreamliner has had a rocky start.
   - Why doesn't Boeing manufacture all the components of the Dreamliner at its own factory in the United States?
   - Describe some of the changes in *what, how,* and *for whom,* that would occur if Boeing manufactured all the components of the Dreamliner at its own factories in the United States.
   - State some of the tradeoffs that Boeing faces in making the Dreamliner.
   - Why might Boeing's decisions in making the Dreamliner be in the social interest?

2. The global economy has three cell-phone users for every fixed line user. Two in every three cell-phone users live in a developing nation and the growth rate is fastest in Africa. In 2000, 1 African in 50 had a cell phone; in 2009, it was 14 in 50. Describe the changes in *what, how,* and *for whom* telecommunication services are produced in the global economy.

3. Which of the entries in List 1 are consumption goods and services and which are government goods? Explain your choice.

4. Which of the entries in List 1 are capital goods? Explain your choice.

5. Which of the entries in List 1 are factors of production? Explain your choice.

6. In the African nation of Senegal, to enroll in school a child needs a birth certificate that costs $25. This price is several weeks' income for many families. Explain how this requirement is likely to affect the growth of human capital in Senegal.

7. **China's prosperity brings income gap**

   The Asian Development Bank [ADB] reports that China has the largest gap between the rich and the poor in Asia. Ifzal Ali, the ADB's chief economist, claims it is not that the rich are getting richer and the poor are getting poorer, but that the rich are getting richer faster than the poor.

   Source: *Financial Times,* August 9, 2007

   Explain how the distribution of personal income in China can be getting more unequal even though the poorest 20 percent are getting richer.

8. Compare the scale of agricultural production in the advanced and developing economies. In which is the percentage higher? In which is the total amount produced greater?

9. On a graph of the circular flow model, indicate in which real or money flow each entry in List 2 belongs.

Use the following information to work Problems 10 and 11.

Poor India makes millionaires at fastest pace

India, with the world's largest population of poor people, also paradoxically created millionaires at the fastest pace in the world. Millionaires increased by 22.7 percent to 123,000. In contrast, the number of Indians living on less than a dollar a day is 350 million and those living on less than $2 a day is 700 million. In other words, there are 7,000 very poor Indians for every millionaire.

Source: *The Times of India,* June 25, 2008

10. How is the personal distribution of income in India changing?

11. Why might incomes of $1 a day and $2 a day underestimate the value of the goods and services that these households actually consume?

LIST 1

- An interstate highway
- An airplane
- A school teacher
- A stealth bomber
- A garbage truck
- A pack of bubble gum
- President of the United States
- A strawberry field
- A movie
- An ATM

LIST 2

- General Motors pays its workers wages.
- IBM pays a dividend to its stockholders.
- You buy your groceries.
- Chrysler buys robots.
- Southwest rents some aircraft.
- Nike pays Roger Federer for promoting its sports shoes.

Multiple Choice Quiz

1. Which of the following classifications is correct?
   A. City streets are consumption goods because they wear out with use.
   B. Stocks are capital goods because when people buy and sell them they make a profit.
   C. The coffee maker in the coffee shop at an airport is a consumption good because people buy the coffee it produces.
   D. White House security is a government service because it is paid for by the government.

2. Which of the following statements about U.S. production is correct?
   A. Construction accounts for a larger percentage of total production than does manufacturing.
   B. Real estate services account for 12.6 percent of the value of total production, larger than any other item of services or goods.
   C. Consumption goods and services represent 85 percent of U.S. production by value and that percentage doesn't fluctuate much.
   D. The manufacture of goods represents more than 50 percent of total production.

3. Which of the following items is *not* a factor of production?
   A. An oil rig in the Gulf of Mexico
   B. A ski jump in Utah
   C. A bank loan to a farmer
   D. An orange grove in Florida

4. What is human capital?
   A. Immigrant labor
   B. Someone who operates heavy equipment
   C. Your professor's knowledge of the economy
   D. A car assembly line robot

5. Which of the following statements is correct?
   A. Labor earns wages and entrepreneurship earns bonuses.
   B. Land earns interest and capital earns rent.
   C. Entrepreneurship earns interest and capital earns profit.
   D. Capital earns interest and labor earns wages.

6. How are goods and services produced in the global economy?
   A. Developing countries use less human capital but just as much physical capital as advanced economies.
   B. Emerging economies use more capital-intensive technology than do developing economies.
   C. Human capital in all economies is similar.
   D. Advanced economies use less capital than developing economies.

7. In the circular flow model, which of the following items is a real flow?
   A. The flow of government expenditures to firms for the goods bought
   B. The flow of income from firms to households for the services of the factors of production hired
   C. The flow of U.S. borrowing from the rest of the world
   D. The flow of labor services from households to firms

Is wind power free?

The Economic Problem

3

When you have completed your study of this chapter, you will be able to

1 Explain and illustrate the concepts of scarcity, production efficiency, and tradeoff using the production possibilities frontier.

2 Calculate opportunity cost.

3 Explain what makes production possibilities expand.

4 Explain how people gain from specialization and trade.

MyEconLab Big Picture

MyEconLab Snapshot

3.1 PRODUCTION POSSIBILITIES

Every working day in mines, factories, shops, and offices and on farms and construction sites across the United States, we produce a vast array of goods and services. In the United States in 2011, 250 billion hours of labor equipped with $50 trillion worth of capital produced $15 trillion worth of goods and services.

Although our production capability is enormous, it is limited by our available resources and by technology. At any given time, we have fixed quantities of the factors of production and a fixed state of technology. Because our wants exceed our resources, we must make choices. We must rank our wants and decide which to satisfy and which to leave unsatisfied. In using our scarce resources, we make rational choices. And to make a rational choice, we must determine the costs and benefits of the alternatives.

Your first task in this chapter is to learn about an economic model of scarcity, choice, and opportunity cost—a model called the production possibilities frontier.

■ Production Possibilities Frontier

Production possibilities frontier
The boundary between the combinations of goods and services that can be produced and the combinations that cannot be produced, given the available factors of production and the state of technology.

The **production possibilities frontier** is the boundary between the combinations of goods and services that can be produced and the combinations that cannot be produced, given the available factors of production—land, labor, capital, and entrepreneurship—and the state of technology.

Although we produce millions of different goods and services, we can visualize the limits to production most easily if we imagine a simpler world that produces just two goods. Imagine an economy that produces only DVDs and cell phones. All the land, labor, capital, and entrepreneurship available gets used to produce these two goods.

Land can be used for movie studios and DVD factories or cell-phone factories. Labor can be trained to work as movie actors, camera and sound crews, movie producers, and DVD makers or as cell-phone makers. Capital can be used for making movies, making and coating disks, and transferring images to disks, or for the equipment that makes cell phones. Entrepreneurs can put their creative talents to managing movie studios and running electronics businesses that make DVDs or to running cell-phone businesses. In every case, the more resources that are used to produce DVDs, the fewer are left to produce cell phones.

Suppose that if no factors of production are allocated to producing cell phones, the maximum number of DVDs that can be produced is 15 million a year. So one production possibility is no cell phones and 15 million DVDs. Another possibility is to allocate sufficient resources to produce 1 million cell phones a year. But these resources must be taken from DVD factories. Suppose that the economy can now produce only 14 million DVDs a year. As resources are moved from producing DVDs to producing cell phones, the economy produces more cell phones but fewer DVDs.

The table in Figure 3.1 illustrates these two combinations of cell phones and DVDs as possibilities A and B. Suppose that C, D, E, and F are other combinations of the quantities of these two goods that the economy can produce. Possibility F uses all the resources to produce 5 million cell phones a year and allocates no resources to producing DVDs. These six possibilities are alternative combinations of the quantities of the two goods that the economy can produce by *using all of its resources, given the technology.*

The graph in Figure 3.1 illustrates the production possibilities frontier, *PPF*, for cell phones and DVDs. Each point on the graph labeled *A* through *F* represents the possibility in the table identified by the same letter. For example, point *B* represents the production of 1 million cell phones and 14 million DVDs. These quantities also appear in the table as possibility *B*.

The *PPF* shows the limits to production *with the available resources and technology*. If either resources or technology change, the *PPF* shifts. More resources or better technology shift it outward and a loss of resources shifts it inward.

The *PPF* is a valuable tool for illustrating the effects of scarcity and its consequences. The *PPF* puts three features of production possibilities in sharp focus. They are the distinctions between

- Attainable and unattainable combinations
- Efficient and inefficient production
- Tradeoffs and free lunches

FIGURE 3.1

The Production Possibilities Frontier

MyEconLab Animation

The table and the graph show the production possibilities frontier for cell phones and DVDs.

Point *A* tells us that if the economy produces no cell phones, the maximum quantity of DVDs it can produce is 15 million a year. Each point *A*, *B*, *C*, *D*, *E*, and *F* on the graph represents the possibility in the table identified by the same letter. The line passing through these points is the production possibilities frontier.

Cell phones (millions)	0	1	2	3	4	5
DVDs (millions)	15	14	12	9	5	0
Possibility	*A*	*B*	*C*	*D*	*E*	*F*

Attainable and Unattainable Combinations

Because the *PPF* shows the *limits* to production, it separates attainable combinations from unattainable ones. The economy can produce combinations of cell phones and DVDs that are smaller than those on the *PPF,* and it can produce any of the combinations *on* the *PPF.* These combinations of cell phones and DVDs are attainable. But it is impossible to produce combinations that are larger than those on the *PPF.* These combinations are unattainable.

Figure 3.2 emphasizes the attainable and unattainable combinations. Only the points on the *PPF* and inside it (in the orange area) are attainable. The combinations of cell phones and DVDs beyond the *PPF* (in the white area), such as the combination at point *G,* are unattainable. These points illustrate combinations that cannot be produced with the current resources and technology. The *PPF* tells us that the economy can produce 4 million cell phones and 5 million DVDs at point *E or* 2 million cell phones and 12 million DVDs at point *C.* But the economy cannot produce 4 million cell phones and 12 million DVDs at point *G.*

Efficient and Inefficient Production

Production efficiency
A situation in which the economy is getting all that it can from its resources and cannot produce more of one good or service without producing less of something else.

Production efficiency occurs when the economy is getting all that it can from its resources. When production is efficient it is not possible to produce more of one good or service without producing less of something else. For production to be efficient, there must be full employment—not just of labor but of all the available factors of production—and each resource must be assigned to the task that it performs comparatively better than other resources can.

FIGURE 3.2

Attainable and Unattainable Combinations   MyEconLab Animation

---

The production possibilities frontier, *PPF,* separates attainable combinations from unattainable ones. The economy can produce at any point *inside* the *PPF* (the orange area) or at any point *on* the frontier. Any point outside the production possibilities frontier, such as point *G,* is unattainable.

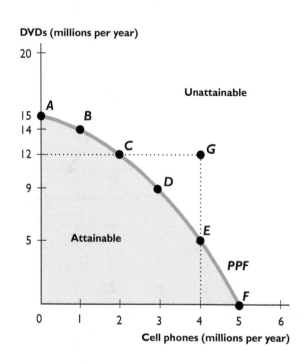

Figure 3.3 illustrates the distinction between efficient and inefficient production. With *inefficient* production, the economy might be producing 3 million cell phones and 5 million DVDs at point *H*. With an *efficient* use of the economy's resources, it is possible to produce at a point on the *PPF* such as point *D* or *E*. At point *D*, there are more DVDs and the same quantity of cell phones as at point *H*. And at point *E*, there are more cell phones and the same quantity of DVDs as at point *H*. At points *D* and *E*, production is efficient.

Tradeoffs and Free Lunches

A **tradeoff** is an exchange—giving up one thing to get something else. You trade off income for a better grade when you decide to cut back on the hours you spend on your weekend job and allocate the time to extra study. The Ford Motor Company faces a tradeoff when it cuts the production of trucks and uses the resources saved to produce more hybrid SUVs. The federal government faces a tradeoff when it cuts NASA's space exploration program and allocates more resources to homeland security. As a society, we face a tradeoff when we decide to cut down a forest and destroy the habitat of the spotted owl.

The production possibilities frontier illustrates the idea of a tradeoff. The *PPF* in Figure 3.3 shows how. If the economy produces at point *E* and people want to produce more DVDs, they must forgo some cell phones. In the move from point *E* to point *D*, people trade off cell phones for DVDs.

Economists often express the central idea of economics—that choices involve tradeoff—with the saying "There is no such thing as a free lunch." A *free lunch* is a gift—getting something without giving up something else. What does the

Tradeoff
An exchange—giving up one thing to get something else.

FIGURE 3.3

Efficient and Inefficient Production, Tradeoffs, and Free Lunches

MyEconLab Animation

❶ When production occurs at a point on the *PPF*, such as point *E*, resources are used efficiently.

❷ When production occurs at a point inside the *PPF*, such as point *H*, resources are used inefficiently.

❸ When production is efficient—on the *PPF*—the economy faces a tradeoff. To move from point *E* to point *D* requires that some cell phones be given up for more DVDs.

❹ When production is inefficient—inside the *PPF*—there is a free lunch. To move from point *H* to point *D* does not involve a tradeoff.

famous saying mean? Suppose some resources are not being used or are not being used efficiently. Isn't it then possible to avoid a tradeoff and get a free lunch?

The answer is yes. You can see why in Figure 3.3. If production is taking place *inside* the *PPF* at point *H,* then it is possible to move to point *D* and increase the production of DVDs by using currently unused resources or by using resources in their most productive way. Nothing is forgone to increase production—there is a free lunch.

When production is efficient—at a point on the *PPF*—choosing to produce more of one good involves a tradeoff. But if production is inefficient—at a point inside the *PPF*—there is a free lunch. More of some goods and services can be produced without producing less of any others.

So "there is no such thing as a free lunch" means that when resources are used efficiently, every choice involves a tradeoff. Because economists view people as making rational choices, they expect that resources will be used efficiently. That is why they emphasize the tradeoff idea and deny the existence of free lunches. We might *sometimes* get a free lunch, but we *almost always* face a tradeoff.

EYE on YOUR LIFE
Your Production Possibilities Frontier

Two "goods" that concern you a great deal are your grade point average (GPA) and the amount of time you have available for leisure or earning an income. You face a tradeoff. To get a higher GPA you must give up leisure or income. Your forgone leisure or forgone income is the opportunity cost of a higher GPA. Similarly, to get more leisure or more income, you must accept a lower grade. A lower grade is the opportunity cost of increased leisure or increased income.

The figure illustrates a student's *PPF.* Any point on or beneath the *PPF* is attainable and any point above the *PPF* is unattainable. A student who wastes time or doesn't study efficiently ends up with a lower GPA than the highest attainable from the time spent studying. But a student who works efficiently achieves a point *on* the *PPF* and achieves production efficiency.

The student in the figure allocates the scarce 168 hours a week between studying (class and study hours) and other activities (work, leisure, and sleep hours). The student attends class and studies for 48 hours each week and works or has fun (and sleeps) for the other 120 hours. With this allocation of time, and studying efficiently, the student's GPA is 3.

CHECKPOINT 3.1

MyEconLab Study Plan 3.1

Key Terms Quiz

Solutions

Explain and illustrate the concepts of scarcity, production efficiency, and tradeoff using the production possibilities frontier.

Practice Problems

1. Table 1 sets out the production possibilities of a small Pacific island economy. Draw the economy's *PPF*.

Figure 1 shows an economy's *PPF* and identifies some production points. Use this figure to work Problems **2** to **4**.

2. Which points are attainable? Explain why.

3. Which points are efficient and which points are inefficient? Explain why.

4. Which points illustrate a tradeoff? Explain why.

In the News

Loss of honeybees is less but still a threat

Honeybees are crucial for the pollination of almonds in California's Central Valley. During 2008, 30 percent of U.S. honeybees died.

Source: *USA Today*, May 20, 2009

Explain how this loss of honeybees affected the Central Valley's *PPF*.

Solutions to Practice Problems

1. The *PPF* is the boundary between attainable and unattainable combinations of goods. Figure 2 shows the economy's *PPF*. The graph plots each row of the table as a point with the corresponding letter.

2. Attainable points: Any point on the *PPF* is attainable and any point below (inside) the *PPF* is attainable. Points outside the *PPF* (F and G) are unattainable. In Figure 1, the attainable points are *A, B, C, D*, and *E*.

3. Efficient points: Production is efficient when it is not possible to produce more of one good without producing less of another good. To be efficient, a point must be attainable, so points *F* and *G* can't be efficient. Points inside the *PPF* can't be efficient because more goods can be produced, so *D* and *E* are not efficient. The only efficient points are those *on* the *PPF*—*A, B*, and *C*.

    Inefficient points: Inefficiency occurs when resources are misallocated or unemployed. Such points are *inside* the *PPF*. These points are *D* and *E*.

4. Tradeoff: Begin by recalling that a tradeoff is an exchange—giving up something to get something else. A tradeoff occurs when moving along the *PPF* from one point to another point. So moving from any point *on* the *PPF*, point *A, B*, or *C*, to another point *on* the *PPF* illustrates a tradeoff.

Solution to In the News

Honeybees are a resource used in the production of almonds. At the start of 2008, Central Valley farmers were at a point on their *PPF*. A 30 percent drop in honeybees reduced the quantity of almonds produced by about 30 percent. With no change in the quantity of other resources and technology, the quantity of other crops produced remained the same and the Central Valley *PPF* shifted inward.

TABLE 1

Possibility	Fish (pounds)		Berries (pounds)
A	0	and	20
B	1	and	18
C	2	and	15
D	3	and	11
E	4	and	6
F	5	and	0

FIGURE 1

3.2   OPPORTUNITY COST

You've seen that moving from one point to another on the *PPF* involves a trade-off. But what are the terms of the tradeoff? *How much* of one item must be forgone to obtain an additional unit of another item—a large amount or a small amount? The answer is given by opportunity cost—the best thing you must give up to get something (see p. 8). We can use the *PPF* to calculate opportunity cost.

■ The Opportunity Cost of a Cell Phone

The opportunity cost of a cell phone is the number of DVDs forgone to get an additional cell phone. It is calculated as the number of DVDs forgone divided by the number of cell phones gained.

Figure 3.4 illustrates the calculation. At point *A,* the quantities produced are zero cell phones and 15 million DVDs; and at point *B,* the quantities produced are 1 million cell phones and 14 million DVDs. To gain 1 million cell phones by moving from point *A* to point *B,* 1 million DVDs are forgone, so the opportunity cost of 1 cell phone is 1 DVD.

At point *C,* the quantities produced are 2 million cell phones and 12 million DVDs. To gain 1 million cell phones by moving from point *B* to point *C,* 2 million DVDs are forgone. Now the opportunity cost of 1 cell phone is 2 DVDs.

If you repeat these calculations, moving from *C* to *D, D* to *E,* and *E* to *F,* you will obtain the opportunity costs shown in the table and the graph.

■ FIGURE 3.4

Calculating the Opportunity Cost of a Cell Phone   MyEconLab Animation

Movement along *PPF*	Decrease in quantity of DVDs	Increase in quantity of cell phones	Decrease in DVDs divided by increase in cell phones
A to *B*	1 million	1 million	1 DVD per phone
B to *C*	2 million	1 million	2 DVDs per phone
C to *D*	3 million	1 million	3 DVDs per phone
D to *E*	4 million	1 million	4 DVDs per phone
E to *F*	5 million	1 million	5 DVDs per phone

Along the *PPF* from *A* to *F,* the opportunity cost of a cell phone increases as the quantity of cell phones produced increases.

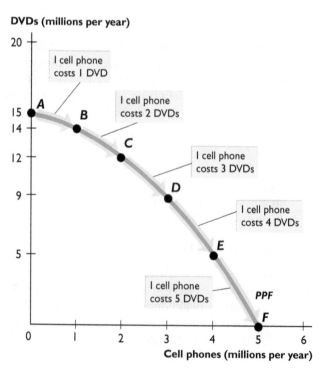

■ Opportunity Cost and the Slope of the *PPF*

Look at the numbers that we've just calculated for the opportunity cost of a cell phone and notice that they follow a striking pattern. The opportunity cost of a cell phone increases as the quantity of cell phones produced increases.

The magnitude of the *slope* of the *PPF* measures the opportunity cost. Because the *PPF* in Figure 3.4 is bowed outward, its slope changes and gets steeper as the quantity of cell phones produced increases.

When a small quantity of cell phones is produced—between points *A* and *B*—the *PPF* has a gentle slope and the opportunity cost of a cell phone is low. A given increase in the quantity of cell phones costs a small decrease in the quantity of DVDs. When a large quantity of cell phones is produced—between points *E* and *F*—the *PPF* is steep and the opportunity cost of a cell phone is high. A given increase in the quantity of cell phones costs a large decrease in the quantity of DVDs. Figure 3.5 shows the increasing opportunity cost of a cell phone.

■ Opportunity Cost Is a Ratio

The opportunity cost of a cell phone is the *ratio* of DVDs forgone to cell phones gained. Similarly, the opportunity cost of a DVD is the *ratio* of cell phones forgone to DVDs gained. So the opportunity cost of a DVD is equal to the inverse of the opportunity cost of a cell phone. For example, moving along the *PPF* in Figure 3.4 from *C* to *D* the opportunity cost of a cell phone is 3 DVDs. Moving along the *PPF* in the opposite direction, from *D* to *C*, the opportunity cost of a DVD is 1/3 of a cell phone.

■ FIGURE 3.5

The Opportunity Cost of a Cell Phone

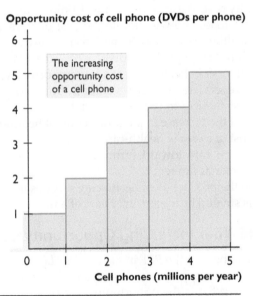

Because the *PPF* in Figure 3.4 is bowed outward, the opportunity cost of a cell phone increases as the quantity of cell phones produced increases.

Cell phones (millions)	0 to 1	1 to 2	2 to 3	3 to 4	4 to 5
Opportunity cost (DVDs per phone)	1	2	3	4	5

EYE on the ENVIRONMENT

Is Wind Power Free?

Wind power is not free. To use it, we must give up huge amounts of other goods and services to build wind turbines and transmission lines.

Wind turbines can produce electricity only when there is wind, which turns out, at best, to be 40 percent of the time and, on average, about 25 percent of the time. Also some of the best wind farm locations are a long way from major population centers, so transmission lines would be long and power transmission losses large.

If we produced 55 percent of our electricity using South Dakota wind power, we would be operating inside the *PPF* at a point such as Z.

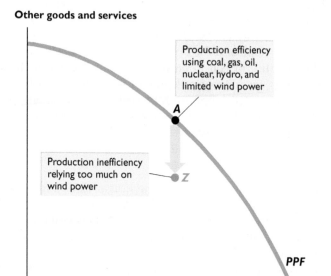

Increasing Opportunity Costs Are Everywhere

Just about every production activity that you can think of has increasing opportunity cost. We allocate the most skillful farmers and the most fertile land to producing food, and we allocate the best doctors and the least fertile land to producing health-care services. Some resources are equally productive in both activities. If we shift these equally productive resources away from farming to hospitals, we get an increase in health care at a low opportunity cost. But if we keep increasing health-care services, we must eventually build hospitals on the most fertile land and get the best farmers to become hospital porters. The production of food drops drastically and the increase in the production of health-care services is small. The opportunity cost of a unit of health-care services rises. Similarly, if we shift resources away from health care toward farming, we must eventually use more skilled doctors and nurses as farmers and more hospitals as hydroponic tomato factories. The decrease in the production of health-care services is large, but the increase in food production is small. The opportunity cost of a unit of food rises.

Your Increasing Opportunity Cost

Flip back to the *PPF* in *Eye on Your Life* on page 62 and think about its implications for your opportunity cost of a higher grade.

What is the opportunity cost of spending time with your friends in terms of the grade you might receive on your exam? What is the opportunity cost of a higher grade in terms of the activities you give up to study? Do you face increasing opportunity costs in these activities?

CHECKPOINT 3.2

MyEconLab Study Plan 3.2
Key Terms Quiz
Solutions

Calculate opportunity cost.

Practice Problems

Table 1 shows Robinson Crusoe's production possibilities.

1. What is his opportunity cost of a pound of berries when Crusoe increases the quantity of berries from 21 pounds to 26 pounds and production is efficient? Does this opportunity cost increase as he produces more berries?

2. If Crusoe is producing 10 pounds of fish and 21 pounds of berries, what is his opportunity cost of an extra pound of berries? And what is his opportunity cost of an extra pound of fish? Explain your answers.

In the News

Obama drives up miles-per-gallon requirements
Emissions from all new vehicles must be cut from 354 grams to 250 grams. To meet this new standard, the price of a new vehicle will rise by $1,300.
Source: *USA Today*, May 20, 2009

Calculate the opportunity cost of reducing the emission level by 1 gram.

Solutions to Practice Problems

1. If Crusoe's production is efficient, he is producing at a point *on* his *PPF*. His opportunity cost of an extra pound of berries is the quantity of fish he must give up to get the berries. It is calculated as the decrease in the quantity of fish divided by the increase in the quantity of berries as he moves along his *PPF*.

    To increase the quantity of berries from 21 pounds to 26 pounds (from row *F* to row *E* of Table 1), production of fish decreases from 15 pounds to 13 pounds. To gain 5 pounds of berries, Crusoe must forgo 2 pounds of fish. The opportunity cost of 1 pound of berries is the 2 pounds of fish forgone divided by 5 pounds of berries gained—2/5 of a pound of fish.

    Crusoe's opportunity cost of berries increases as he produces more berries. To see why, move Crusoe from row *E* to row *D* in Table 1. His production of berries increases by 4 pounds and his production of fish falls by 2.5 pounds. His opportunity cost of 1 pound of berries increases to 5/8 of a pound of fish.

2. Figure 1 graphs the data in Table 1 and shows Crusoe's *PPF*. If Crusoe is producing 10 pounds of fish and 21 pounds of berries, he is producing at point *Z*. Point *Z* is a point *inside* Crusoe's *PPF*. When Crusoe produces 21 pounds of berries, he has enough time available to produce 15 pounds of fish at point *F* on his *PPF*. To produce more fish, Crusoe can move from *Z* toward *F* on his *PPF* and forgo no berries. His opportunity cost of a pound of fish is zero. Similiarly, his opportunity cost of a pound of berries is zero.

Solution to In the News

By spending $1,300 extra on a new car, you forgo $1,300 of other goods. With a new car, your emissions fall from 354 grams to 250 grams, a reduction of 104 grams. The opportunity cost of a 1-gram reduction in emissions is $1,300 of other goods divided by 104 grams, or $12.50 of other goods.

TABLE 1

Possibility	Fish (pounds)		Berries (pounds)
A	0	and	36
B	4.0	and	35
C	7.5	and	33
D	10.5	and	30
E	13.0	and	26
F	15.0	and	21
G	16.5	and	15
H	17.5	and	8
I	18.0	and	0

FIGURE 1

Economic growth
The sustained expansion of production possibilities.

3.3 ECONOMIC GROWTH

Economic growth is the sustained expansion of production possibilities. Our economy grows when we develop better technologies for producing goods and services; improve the quality of labor by education, on-the-job training, and work experience; and acquire more machines to help us produce.

To study economic growth, we must change the two goods and look at the production possibilities for a consumption good and a capital good. A cell phone is a consumption good and a cell-phone factory is a capital good. By using today's resources to produce cell-phone factories, the economy can expand its future production possibilities. The greater the production of new capital—the number of new cell-phone factories—the faster is the expansion of production possibilities.

Figure 3.6 shows how the *PPF* can expand. If no new factories are produced (at point *L*), production possibilities do not expand and the *PPF* stays at its original position. By producing fewer cell phones and using resources to produce 2 new cell-phone factories (at point *K*), production possibilities expand and the *PPF* rotates outward to the new *PPF*.

But economic growth is *not* free. To make it happen, consumption must decrease. The move from *L* to *K* in Figure 3.6 means forgoing 2 million cell phones now. The opportunity cost of producing more cell-phone factories is producing fewer cell phones today.

Also, economic growth is no magic formula for abolishing scarcity. Economic growth shifts the *PPF* outward, but on the new *PPF* we continue to face opportunity costs. To keep producing capital, current consumption must be less than its maximum possible level.

FIGURE 3.6

Expanding Production Possibilities

❶ If firms allocate no resources to producing cell-phone factories and produce 5 million cell phones a year at point *L*, the *PPF* doesn't change.

❷ If firms decrease cell-phone production to 3 million a year and produce 2 cell-phone factories, at point *K*, production possibilities will expand. After a year, the *PPF* shifts outward to the new *PPF* and production can move to point *K'*.

EYE on the U.S. ECONOMY
Expanding Our Production Possibilities

Horizontal drilling and hydraulic fracturing—fracking—combined with recent advances in remote sensing technology have made it possible to extract a large quantity of gas trapped in shale at low cost. The United States has an estimated 750 trillion cubic feet of this gas, enough for more than 90 years at today's extraction rate. The map below shows the locations of these gas deposits.

Figure 1 shows two recent years of shale gas production, which in January 2012 was double its rate just two years earlier.

Was this increase in gas production achieved by sliding along the *PPF* and producing less of other goods and servces? No! It was the result of advances in technology and opening up additional gas wells.

Figure 2 illustrates how these changes shifted the *PPF* from PPF_{10} in 2010 to PPF_{12} in 2012. Point *J* is the same on both curves because if we produced at that point (only other goods and services and no gas), we would not get the benefits of the technological advances in gas production. In 2010 we produced at point *K*, and in 2012 at point *K'*. Along PPF_{12} the opportunity cost of gas is lower than along PPF_{10}.

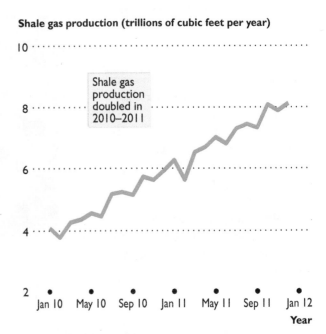

Figure 1 Shale Gas Production

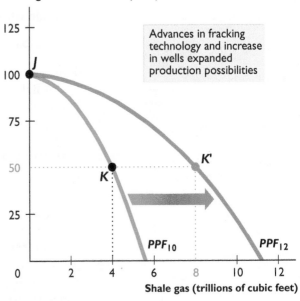

Figure 2 Shale Gas Versus Other Goods and Services

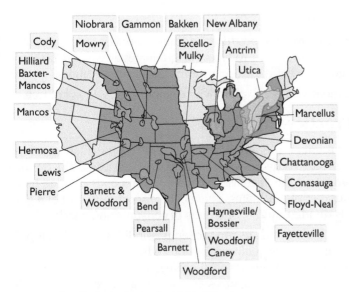

Natural Gas Shale Basins in the United States

SOURCE OF DATA: Energy Information Administration.

EYE on the GLOBAL ECONOMY
Hong Kong's Rapid Economic Growth

Hong Kong's production possibilities per person were 25 percent of those of the United States in 1960. By 2012, they had grown to become equal to U.S. production possibilities per person. Hong Kong grew faster than the United States because it allocated more of its resources to accumulating capital and less to consumption than did the United States.

In 1960, the United States and Hong Kong produced at point *A* on their respective *PPFs*. In 2012, Hong Kong was at point *B* and the United States was at point *C*.

If Hong Kong continues to produce at a point such as *B*, it will grow more rapidly than the United States and its *PPF* will eventually shift out

beyond the *PPF* of the United States. But if Hong Kong produces at a point such as *D*, the pace of expansion of its *PPF* will slow.

Capital goods (per person)

United States and Hong Kong in 2012

Hong Kong in 1960

United States in 1960

B

D

C

A *A*

0

Consumption goods (per person)

TABLE 1

Possibility	Education services (graduates)	Consumption goods (units)
A	1,000	0
B	750	1,000
C	500	2,000
D	0	3,000

CHECKPOINT 3.3

Explain what makes production possibilities expand.

Practice Problems

1. Table 1 shows an economy that produces education services and consumption goods. If the economy currently produces 500 graduates a year and 2,000 units of consumption goods, what is the opportunity cost of one additional graduate?

2. How does an economy grow? Explain why economic growth is not free.

Solutions to Practice Problems

1. By increasing the number of graduates from 500 to 750, the quantity of consumption goods produced decreases from 2,000 to 1,000 units. The opportunity cost of a graduate is the decrease in consumption goods divided by the increase in the number of graduates. That is, the opportunity cost of a graduate is 1,000 units divided by 250, or 4 units of consumption goods.

2. An economy grows if it expands its production possibilities—if it develops better technologies; improves the quality of labor by education, on-the-job training, and work experience; and acquires more machines to use in production. Economic growth occurs when resources are used today to produce better technologies, better quality labor, or more machines. Those resources cannot be used to produce goods and services today, so the cost of economic growth is the goods and services forgone today. Economic growth is not free.

3.4 SPECIALIZATION AND TRADE

MyEconLab Snapshot

The next time you visit your favorite fast-food restaurant, watch what the workers are doing. You might see one person re-stocking the bread, salad materials, meat, sauces, boxes, and wrappers; another working the grill and another the fry maker; another assembling meals; and yet another taking orders and payments. Imagine how long you would wait for your burger if each worker performed all the tasks needed to fill each customer's not-so-fast-food order.

Specialization makes people more productive in two ways: It brings absolute advantage and comparative advantage.

Specialization boosts productivity in a fast-food kitchen

■ Absolute Advantage and Comparative Advantage

A person has an **absolute advantage** if that person is more productive than another. Being more productive means using fewer inputs or taking less time to produce a good or perform a production task. Being more productive also means being able to produce more with given inputs in a given amount of time.

The specialized workers at McDonald's have an *absolute advantage* over the same number of workers each performing all the tasks needed to make a burger.

A person has a **comparative advantage** in an activity if that person can perform the activity at a lower opportunity cost than anyone else. Recall that the opportunity cost of something is what you must give up to get it.

Notice the contrast between *absolute advantage* and *comparative advantage*. Absolute advantage is about *productivity*—how long does it take to produce a unit of a good. Comparative advantage is about *opportunity cost*—how much of some other good must be forgone to produce a unit of a good.

Absolute advantage
When one person (or nation) is more productive than another—needs fewer inputs or takes less time to produce a good or perform a production task.

Comparative advantage
The ability of a person to perform an activity or produce a good or service at a lower opportunity cost than anyone else.

EYE on the U.S. ECONOMY
No One Knows How to Make a Pencil

Not many products in today's world are as simple as a pencil. Yet the story of how the pencil in your hand got there illustrates the astonishing power of specialization and trade.

When you hold a pencil, you're holding cedar grown in Oregon, graphite mined in Sri Lanka, clay from Mississippi, wax from Mexico, rapeseed oil grown in the Dutch East Indies, pumice from Italy, copper from Arizona, and zinc from Alaska.

These materials were harvested and mined by thousands of workers

equipped with hundreds of specialized tools, all of which were manufactured by thousands of other workers using hundreds more specialized tools. These tools were in turn made of steel, itself made from iron ore, and from other minerals and materials.

Rail, road, and ocean transportation systems moved all these things to custom-built factories that made graphite "leads," erasers, brass to hold the erasers, paint, and glue.

Finally, all these components were bought by a pencil factory, which, with

its millions of dollars' worth of custom machinery, put them all together.

Millions of people contributed to making that pencil, many of whom don't even know what a pencil is and *not one of whom knows how to make a pencil*. No one directed all these people. Each worker and business went about its self-interested specialized task trading with each other in markets.

Adapted from *I Pencil*, by Leonard Read, Foundation for Economic Education, 1958.

■ Comparative Advantage: An Example

We're going to explore the idea of comparative advantage and make it concrete by looking at production in two smoothie bars: one operated by Liz and the other operated by Joe. You will see how we identify comparative advantage and how it creates an opportunity for Liz and Joe to gain from specialization and trade.

Liz's Smoothie Bar

Liz produces smoothies and salads in a high-tech bar. She can turn out *either* a smoothie *or* a salad every 2 minutes. If she spends all her time making smoothies, she produces 30 an hour. If she spends all her time making salads, she also produces 30 an hour. If she splits her time equally between the two, she can produce 15 smoothies *and* 15 salads an hour. For each additional smoothie Liz produces, she must decrease her production of salads by one, and for each additional salad Liz produces, she must decrease her production of smoothies by one. So

TABLE 3.1   LIZ'S PRODUCTION POSSIBILITIES

Item	Minutes to produce 1	Quantity per hour
Smoothies	2	30
Salads	2	30

> Liz's opportunity cost of producing 1 smoothie is 1 salad,

and

> Liz's opportunity cost of producing 1 salad is 1 smoothie.

Liz's customers buy smoothies and salads in equal quantities, so Liz splits her time equally between the items and produces 15 smoothies and 15 salads an hour.

Joe's Smoothie Bar

Joe also produces both smoothies and salads. Joe's bar is smaller than Liz's, and he has only one blender—a slow, old machine. Even if Joe uses all his resources to produce smoothies, he can produce only 6 an hour. But Joe is pretty good in the salad department, so if he uses all his resources to make salads, he can produce 30 an hour. Joe's ability to make smoothies and salads is the same regardless of how he splits an hour between the two tasks. He can make a salad in 2 minutes or a smoothie in 10 minutes. For each additional smoothie Joe produces, he must decrease his production of salads by 5. And for each additional salad Joe produces, he must decrease his production of smoothies by 1/5 of a smoothie. So

TABLE 3.2   JOE'S PRODUCTION POSSIBILITIES

Item	Minutes to produce 1	Quantity per hour
Smoothies	10	6
Salads	2	30

> Joe's opportunity cost of producing 1 smoothie is 5 salads,

and

> Joe's opportunity cost of producing 1 salad is 1/5 of a smoothie.

Joe's customers, like Liz's, buy smoothies and salads in equal quantities. Joe spends 50 minutes of each hour making smoothies and 10 minutes of each hour making salads. With this division of his time, Joe produces 5 smoothies and 5 salads an hour.

Liz's and Joe's *PPFs*

The *PPF*s in Figure 3.7 illustrate the situation we've just described. In part (a), Liz faces a *PPF* that enables her to produce 15 smoothies and 15 salads. In part (b), Joe faces a *PPF* that enables him to produce 5 smoothies and 5 salads. On Liz's *PPF*, one smoothie costs one salad. On Joe's *PPF*, one smoothie costs 5 salads.

The *PPF*s in Figure 3.7 contrast with the outward-bowed *PPF*s that you've seen earlier in this chapter, which capture the general rule that the opportunity cost of a good increases as we increase its rate of production. It is easier to identify comparative advantage and see the gains from trade when individuals have

FIGURE 3.7

Production Possibilities Frontiers

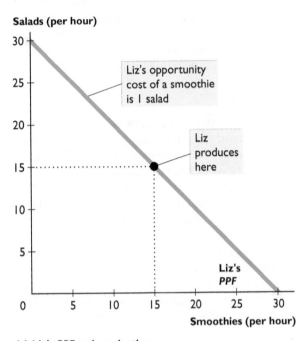

(a) Liz's PPF and production

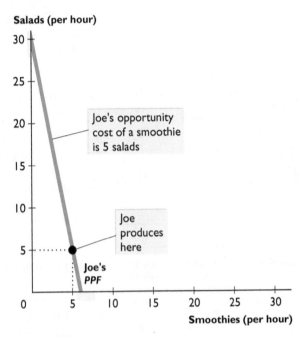

(b) Joe's PPF and production

Liz can produce 30 smoothies per hour or 30 salads per hour or any other combination along her PPF in part (a). Liz chooses to produce 15 smoothies and 15 salads per hour.

Joe can produce 6 smoothies per hour or 30 salads per hour or any other combination along his PPF in part (b). Joe chooses to produce 5 smoothies and 5 salads per hour.

constant opportunity cost. And as you will soon see, the social PPF is outward-bowed even when individuals have constant opportunity cost and linear PPFs.

Liz's Greater Productivity

You can see from the production numbers that Liz is three times as productive as Joe—her 15 smoothies and 15 salads an hour are three times Joe's 5 smoothies and 5 salads. Liz is more productive than Joe in producing both smoothies and salads, but Liz has a comparative advantage in only one of the activities.

Liz's Comparative Advantage

In which of the two activities does Liz have a *comparative* advantage? Recall that comparative advantage is a situation in which one person's opportunity cost of producing a good is lower than another person's opportunity cost of producing that same good.

You've seen that Liz's opportunity cost of a smoothie is 1 salad, whereas Joe's opportunity cost of a smoothie is 5 salads. To produce 1 smoothie, Liz must forgo 1 salad while Joe must forgo 5 salads. So, because Liz forgoes fewer salads to make a smoothie, she has a comparative advantage in producing smoothies.

What about Joe? Doesn't he have a comparative advantage at anything? He does as you're about to see.

Joe's Comparative Advantage

Look at the opportunity costs of producing salads. For Liz, that opportunity cost is 1 smoothie. But for Joe, a salad costs only 1/5 of a smoothie. Because Joe's opportunity cost of a salad is less than Liz's, Joe has a comparative advantage in producing salads.

It is always true that if one person has a comparative advantage in producing a good, others have a comparative advantage in producing some other good.

■ Achieving Gains from Trade

Liz and Joe run into each other one evening in a singles bar. After a few minutes of getting acquainted, Liz tells Joe about her amazingly profitable smoothie business. Her only problem, she tells Joe, is that she wishes she could produce more because potential customers leave when her lines get too long.

Joe isn't sure whether to risk spoiling his chances with Liz by telling her about his own struggling business, but he takes the risk. When he explains to Liz that he spends 50 minutes of every hour making 5 smoothies and 10 minutes making 5 salads, Liz's eyes pop. "Have I got a deal for you!" she exclaims.

Here's the deal that Liz sketches on a paper napkin. Joe stops making smoothies and allocates all his time to producing salads. Liz stops making salads and allocates all her time to producing smoothies. That is, they both specialize in producing the good in which they have a comparative advantage—see Table 3.3(b). They then trade: Liz sells Joe 10 smoothies and Joe sells Liz 20 salads—the price of a smoothie is 2 salads—see Table 3.3(c).

After the trade, Joe has 10 salads (the 30 he produces minus the 20 he sells to Liz) and the 10 smoothies that he buys from Liz. So Joe doubles the quantities of smoothies and salads he can sell. Liz has 20 smoothies (the 30 she produces minus the 10 she sells to Joe) and the 20 salads she buys from Joe. See Table 3.3(d). From specialization and trade, each gains 5 smoothies and 5 salads—see Table 3.3(e).

TABLE 3.3   LIZ AND JOE GAIN FROM TRADE

(a) Before Trade	Liz	Joe
Smoothies	15	5
Salads	15	5
(b) Specialization	**Liz**	**Joe**
Smoothies	30	0
Salads	0	30
(c) Trade	**Liz**	**Joe**
Smoothies	sell 10	buy 10
Salads	buy 20	sell 20
(d) After Trade	**Liz**	**Joe**
Smoothies	20	10
Salads	20	10
(e) Gains from Trade	**Liz**	**Joe**
Smoothies	+5	+5
Salads	+5	+5

EYE on YOUR LIFE
Your Comparative Advantage

What you have learned in this chapter has huge implications for the way you organize your life. It also has implications for the position that you take on the controversial issue of offshore outsourcing.

Just as an economy expands its production possibilities by accumulating capital, so also will you expand your production possibilities by accumulating human capital. That is what you're doing right now in school.

By discovering your comparative advantage, you will be able to focus on producing the items that make you as well off as possible. Think hard about what you enjoy doing, and that you do comparatively better than others. That, most likely, is where your comparative advantage lies.

In today's world, it is a good idea to try to remain flexible so that you can switch jobs if you discover that your comparative advantage has changed.

Looking beyond your own self-interest, are you going to be a voice that supports or opposes offshore outsourcing?

You've learned in this chapter that regardless of whether outsourcing remains inside the United States, as it does with Liz and Joe at their smoothie bars, or is global like the outsourcing of jobs by U. S. producers to India, both parties gain from trade.

Americans pay less for goods and services and Indians earn higher incomes. But some Americans lose, at least in the short run.

Liz draws a figure (Figure 3.8) to illustrate her idea. The blue *PPF* is Liz's and the red *PPF* is Joe's. They are each producing at the points marked *A*. Liz's proposal is that they each produce at the points marked *B*. They then trade smoothies and salads.

Liz suggests that they trade at a price of 2 salads per smoothie (1/2 a smoothie per salad). This price turns out to give each of them equal gains.

Liz gets salads for 1/2 a smoothie each, which is less than the 1 smoothie that it costs her to produce them. Joe gets smoothies for 2 salads each, which is less than the 5 salads it costs him to produce them. Each moves to the points marked *C* where Liz has 20 smoothies and 20 salads, 5 of each more than she has producing only for herself. And Joe has 10 smoothies and 10 salads, also 5 more of each than he has producing only for himself. Because of the gains from trade, total production increases by 10 smoothies and 10 salads.

Notice that the points *C* are *outside* Liz's and Joe's *PPFs*. This is the magic of the gains from trade. Everyone gains and everyone can enjoy quantities of goods and services that exceed their own ability to produce them.

Notice finally, that for the Liz-Joe society, despite the fact that they each have constant opportunity costs, the society's opportunity cost is increasing. The first 30 smoothies can be produced (by Liz) for 1 salad per smoothie, but the 31st smoothie produced (by Joe) costs 5 salads.

FIGURE 3.8

The Gains from Specialization and Trade   MyEconLab Animation

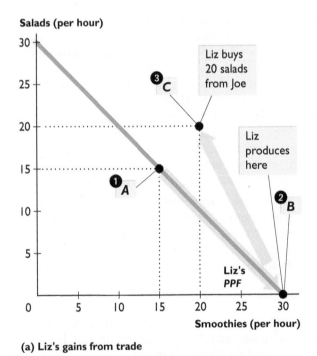

(a) Liz's gains from trade

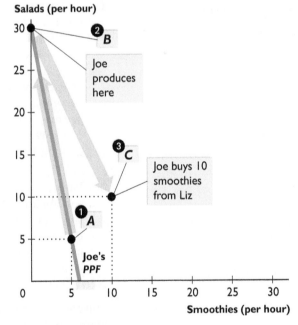

(b) Joe's gains from trade

❶ Liz and Joe each produce at point *A* on their respective *PPFs*. Liz has a comparative advantage in producing smoothies, and Joe has a comparative advantage in producing salads.

❷ Joe specializes in salads and Liz specializes in smoothies, so they each produce at point *B* on their respective *PPFs*.

❸ They exchange smoothies for salads at a price of 2 salads per smoothie. Each goes to point *C*—a point *outside* their individual *PPFs*. They each gain 5 salads and 5 smoothies—the quantities at point *C* minus the quantities at point *A*.

MyEconLab Study Plan 3.4
Key Terms Quiz
Solutions

TABLE 1 TONY'S PRODUCTION POSSIBILITIES

Snowboards (per week)		Skis (per week)
25	and	0
20	and	10
15	and	20
10	and	30
5	and	40
0	and	50

TABLE 2 PATTY'S PRODUCTION POSSIBILITIES

Snowboards (per week)		Skis (per week)
20	and	0
10	and	5
0	and	10

CHECKPOINT 3.4

Explain how people gain from specialization and trade.

Practice Problems

Tony and Patty produce skis and snowboards. Tables 1 and 2 show their production possibilities. Each week, Tony produces 5 snowboards and 40 skis and Patty produces 10 snowboards and 5 skis.

1. Who has a comparative advantage in producing snowboards? Who has a comparative advantage in producing skis?

2. If Tony and Patty specialize and trade, what are the gains from trade?

In the News

With big boost from sugar cane, Brazil is satisfying its fuel needs
Brazil is almost self-sufficient in ethanol. Brazilian ethanol is made from sugar and costs 83¢ per gallon whereas U.S. ethanol, made from corn, costs $1.14 per gallon. The United States does not import ethanol.

Source: *The New York Times*, April 12, 2006

Which country has a comparative advantage in producing ethanol? Explain why both the United States and Brazil can gain from specialization and trade.

Solutions to Practice Problems

1. The person with a comparative advantage in snowboards is the one who has the lower opportunity cost of producing a snowboard. Tony's production possibilities show that to produce 5 more snowboards he must produce 10 fewer skis. So Tony's opportunity cost of a snowboard is 2 skis.

   Patty's production possibilities show that to produce 10 more snowboards, she must produce 5 fewer skis. So Patty's opportunity cost of a snowboard is 1/2 a ski. Patty has a comparative advantage in snowboards because her opportunity cost of a snowboard is less than Tony's. Tony's comparative advantage is in skis. For each ski produced, Tony must forgo making 1/2 a snowboard, whereas Patty must forgo making 2 snowboards for a ski. So Tony's opportunity cost of a ski is lower than Patty's.

2. Patty has a comparative advantage in snowboards, so she specializes in snowboards. Tony has a comparative advantage in skis, so he specializes in skis. Patty makes 20 snowboards and Tony makes 50 skis. Before specializing, they made 15 snowboards and 45 skis. By specializing, total output increases by 5 snowboards and 5 skis. They share this gain by trading.

Solution to In the News

The cost of producing a gallon of ethanol is less in Brazil than in the United States, so Brazil has a comparative advantage in producing ethanol. If Brazil specializes in producing ethanol and the United States specializes in producing other goods (for example, movies or food) and the two countries engage in free trade, each country can gain because it will get to a point outside its own *PPF*.

CHAPTER SUMMARY

Key Points

1. **Explain and illustrate the concepts of scarcity, production efficiency, and tradeoff using the production possibilities frontier.**

   - The production possibilities frontier, *PPF*, describes the limits to what can be produced by using all the available resources efficiently.
   - Points inside and on the *PPF* are attainable. Points outside the *PPF* are unattainable.
   - Production at any point on the *PPF* achieves production efficiency. Production at a point inside the *PPF* is inefficient.
   - When production is efficient—on the *PPF*—people face a tradeoff. If production is at a point inside the *PPF*, there is a free lunch to be had.

2. **Calculate opportunity cost.**

   - Along the *PPF*, the opportunity cost of *X* (the item measured on the *x*-axis) is the decrease in *Y* (the item measured on the *y*-axis) divided by the increase in *X*.
   - The opportunity cost of *Y* is the inverse of the opportunity cost of *X*.
   - The opportunity cost of producing a good increases as the quantity of the good produced increases.

3. **Explain what makes production possibilities expand.**

   - Technological change and increases in capital and human capital expand production possibilities.
   - The opportunity cost of economic growth is the decrease in current consumption.

4. **Explain how people gain from specialization and trade.**

   - A person has a comparative advantage in an activity if he or she can perform that activity at a lower opportunity cost than someone else.
   - People gain by increasing the production of the item in which they have a comparative advantage and trading.

Key Terms

MyEconLab Key Terms Quiz

Absolute advantage, 71
Comparative advantage, 71
Economic growth, 68

Production efficiency, 60
Production possibilities frontier, 58
Tradeoff, 61

CHAPTER CHECKPOINT

Study Plan Problems and Applications

1. Table 1 shows the quantities of corn and beef that a farm can produce in a year. Draw a graph of the farm's *PPF*. Mark on the graph:
   - An inefficient combination of corn and beef—label this point *A*.
   - An unattainable combination of corn and beef—label this point *B*.
   - An efficient combination of corn and beef—label this point *C*.

Use the following information to work Problems **2** and **3**.

The people of Leisure Island have 50 hours of labor a day that can be used to produce entertainment and good food. Table 2 shows the maximum quantity of *either* entertainment *or* good food that Leisure Island can produce with different quantities of labor.

2. Is an output of 50 units of entertainment and 50 units of good food attainable and efficient? With a production of 50 units of entertainment and 50 units of good food, do the people of Leisure Island face a tradeoff?

3. What is the opportunity cost of producing an additional unit of entertainment? Explain how the opportunity cost of producing a unit of entertainment changes as more entertainment is produced.

Use the following information to work Problems **4** and **5**.

Malaria can be controlled

The World Health Organization's malaria chief says that it is too costly to try to fully eradicate the disease. He says that by using nets, medicine, and DDT it is possible to eliminate 90 percent of malaria cases. But to eliminate 100 percent of cases would be extremely costly.

Source: *The New York Times*, March 4, 2008

4. Make a graph of the production possibilities frontier with malaria control on the *x*-axis and other goods and services on the *y*-axis.

5. Describe how the opportunity cost of controlling malaria changes as more resources are used to reduce the number of malaria cases.

6. Explain how the following events influence U.S. production possibilities:
   - Some retail workers are re-employed building dams and wind farms.
   - More people take early retirement.
   - Drought devastates California's economy.

Use the following information to work Problems **7** and **8**.

Figure 1 shows Tom's production possibilities and Figure 2 shows Abby's production possibilities. Tom uses all his resources and produces 2 rackets and 20 balls an hour. Abby uses all her resources and produces 2 rackets and 40 balls an hour.

7. What is Tom's opportunity cost of producing a racket? What is Abby's opportunity cost of a racket? Who has a comparative advantage in producing rackets? Who has a comparative advantage in producing balls?

8. If Tom and Abby specialize and trade 15 balls for 1 racket, what are the gains from trade?

9. Read *Eye on the Environment* on p. 66 and describe a tradeoff faced when deciding how to generate electricity and whether to use wind power.

TABLE 1

Corn (bushels)		Beef (pounds)
250	and	0
200	and	300
100	and	500
0	and	600

TABLE 2

Labor (hours)	Entertainment (units)		Good food (units)
0	0	or	0
10	20	or	30
20	40	or	50
30	60	or	60
40	80	or	65
50	100	or	67

FIGURE 1

FIGURE 2

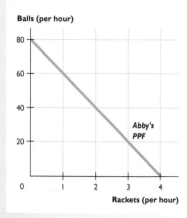

Instructor Assignable Problems and Applications

MyEconLab Homework, Quiz, or Test if assigned by instructor

Use the following information to work Problems **1** to **4**.

Representatives Waxman of California and Markey of Massachusetts proposed a law to limit greenhouse gas emissions from electricity generation and require electricity producers to generate a minimum percentage of power using renewable fuels, with some emission rights to be auctioned. The Congressional Budget Office estimated that the government would receive $846 billion from auctions and would spend $821 billion on incentive programs and compensation for higher energy prices. Electricity producers would spend $208 million a year to comply with the new rules. (Think of these dollar amounts as dollars' worth of other goods and services.)

1. Would the Waxman-Markey law achieve production efficiency?

2. Is the $846 billion that electricity producers would pay for the right to emit greenhouse gasses part of the opportunity cost of producing electricity?

3. Is the $821 billion that the government would spend on incentive programs and compensation for higher energy prices part of the opportunity cost of producing electricity?

4. Is the $208 million that electricity producers will spend to comply with the new rules part of the opportunity cost of producing electricity?

5. The people of Foodland have 40 hours of labor a day to bake pizza and bread. Table 1 shows the maximum quantity of *either* pizza *or* bread that Foodland can bake with different quantities of labor. Can Foodland produce 30 pizzas and 30 loaves of bread a day? If it can, is this output efficient, do the people of Foodland face a tradeoff, and what is the opportunity cost of producing an additional pizza?

TABLE 1

Labor (hours)	Pizzas		Bread (loaves)
0	0	or	0
10	30	or	10
20	50	or	20
30	60	or	30
40	65	or	40

Use Table 2, which shows a farm's production possibilities, to work Problems **6** and **7**.

6. If the farm uses its resources efficiently, what is the opportunity cost of an increase in chicken production from 300 pounds to 500 pounds a year? Explain your answer.

7. If the farm adopted a new technology, which allows it to use fewer resources to fatten chickens, explain how the farm's production possibilities will change. Explain how the opportunity cost of producing a bushel of soybean will be affected.

TABLE 2

Soybean (bushels per year)		Chicken (pounds per year)
500	and	0
400	and	300
200	and	500
0	and	600

8. In an hour, Sue can produce 40 caps or 4 jackets and Tessa can produce 80 caps or 4 jackets. Who has a comparative advantage in producing caps? If Sue and Tessa specialize and trade, who will gain?

Use the following information to work Problems **9** to **11**.

Cheap broadband's a winner

Inexpensive broadband access has created a new generation of television producers and the Internet is their native medium.

Source: *The New York Times*, December 2, 2007

9. How has inexpensive broadband changed the production possibilities of video entertainment and other goods and services?

10. Sketch a *PPF* for video entertainment and other goods and services before broadband.

11. Explain how the arrival of inexpensive broadband has changed the *PPF*.

Multiple Choice Quiz

TABLE 1

Possibility	Fish (pounds)		Berries (pounds)
A	0	and	40
B	1	and	36
C	2	and	30
D	3	and	22
E	4	and	12
F	5	and	0

1. Table 1 shows the *PPF* of an island community. Choose the best statement.
   A. This community has enough resources to produce 2 pounds of fish and 36 pounds of berries.
   B. This community cannot produce 2 pounds of fish and 36 pounds of berries because this combination is inefficient.
   C. This community will waste resources if it produces 2 pounds of fish and 22 pounds of berries.
   D. This community can produce 2 pounds of fish and 30 pounds of berries but this combination is inefficient.

2. Table 1 shows the *PPF* of an island community. Choose the best statement.
   A. Suppose that this community produces 3 pounds of fish and 20 pounds of berries. If it decides to gather more berries, it faces a tradeoff.
   B. When this community produces 4 pounds of fish and 12 pounds of berries it faces a tradeoff, but it is inefficient.
   C. Suppose that this community produces 5 pounds of fish and 0 pounds of berries. If it decides to gather some berries, it will get a free lunch.
   D. If this community produces 3 pounds of fish and 22 pounds of berries, production is efficient but to produce more fish it faces a tradeoff.

3. Table 1 shows the *PPF* of an island community. This community's opportunity cost of producing 1 pound of fish _____.
   A. is the increase in the quantity of berries gathered as the quantity of fish increases by 1 pound
   B. increases as the quantity of berries gathered increases
   C. is 10 pounds of berries if the quantity of fish increases from 2 to 3 pounds
   D. increases as the quantity of fish caught increases

4. Table 1 shows the *PPF* of an island community. Choose the best statement.
   A. When a drought hits the island, its *PPF* rotates outward.
   B. When the islanders discover a better way of catching fish, the island's *PPF* rotates outward.
   C. When islanders reduce the time they spend gathering berries, the *PPF* rotates inward.
   D. If the islanders decide to spend more time gathering berries but continue to spend the same amount of time fishing, they face a tradeoff.

5. Mary makes 10 pies and 20 cakes a day and her opportunity cost of producing a cake is 2 pies. Tim makes 20 pies and 10 cakes a day and his opportunity cost of producing a cake is 4 pies. If Mary and Tim specialize in producing the good in which they have a comparative advantage, _____.
   A. Mary produces only pies
   B. Tim produces both pies and cakes
   C. Mary produces only cakes while Tim produces only pies
   D. Tim produces only cakes while Mary produces only pies

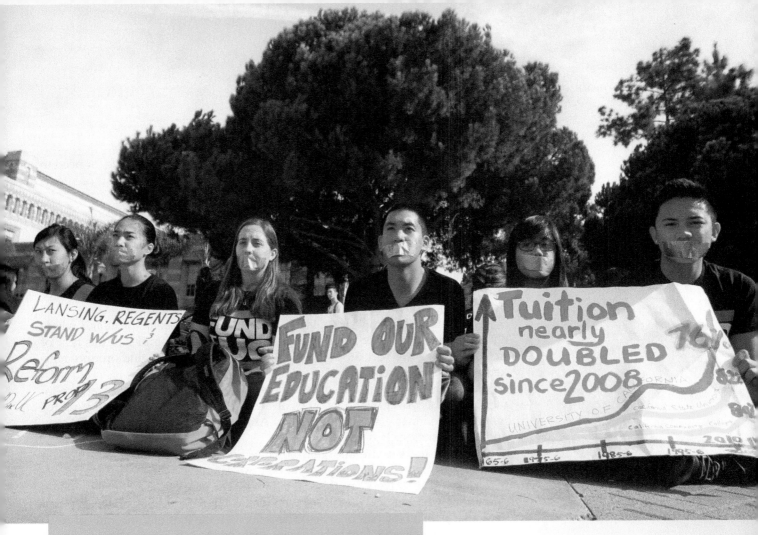

Why does tuition keep rising?

Demand and Supply

4

When you have completed your study of this chapter, you will be able to

1 Distinguish between quantity demanded and demand, and explain what determines demand.

2 Distinguish between quantity supplied and supply, and explain what determines supply.

3 Explain how demand and supply determine price and quantity in a market, and explain the effects of changes in demand and supply.

4 Explain how price floors, price ceilings, and sticky prices create surpluses, unemployment, and shortages.

MyEconLab Big Picture

81

COMPETITIVE MARKETS

When you need a new pair of running shoes, want a bagel and a latte, or need to fly home for Thanksgiving, you must find a place where people sell those items or offer those services. The place where you find them is a *market*.

You learned in Chapter 2 that a market is any arrangement that brings buyers and sellers together. A market has two sides: demand (buyers) and supply (sellers). There are markets for *goods* such as apples and hiking boots, for *services* such as haircuts and tennis lessons, for *resources* such as computer programmers and tractors, and for other manufactured *inputs* such as memory chips and auto parts. There are also markets for money such as Japanese yen and for financial securities such as Yahoo! stock. Only imagination limits what can be traded in markets.

Some markets are physical places where buyers and sellers meet and where an auctioneer or a broker helps to determine the prices. Examples of this type of market are the New York Stock Exchange; wholesale fish, meat, and produce markets; and used car auctions.

Some markets are virtual spaces where buyers and sellers never meet face-to-face but connect over telephone lines or the Internet. Examples include currency markets, e-commerce Web sites such as Amazon.com and bananarepublic.com, and auction sites such as eBay.

But most markets are unorganized collections of buyers and sellers. You do most of your trading in this type of market. An example is the market for basketball shoes. The buyers in this $3-billion-a-year market are the 45 million Americans who play basketball (or who want to make a fashion statement) and are looking for a new pair of shoes. The sellers are the tens of thousands of retail sports equipment and footwear stores. Each buyer can visit several different stores, and each seller knows that the buyer has a choice of stores.

Markets vary in the intensity of competition that buyers and sellers face. In this chapter, we're going to study a *competitive market* that has so many buyers and so many sellers that no single buyer or seller can influence the price.

Markets for running shoes ...   *coffee and bagel ...*   *and airline travel.*

4.1   DEMAND

MyEconLab Snapshot

First, we'll study the behavior of buyers in a competitive market. The **quantity demanded** of any good, service, or resource is the amount that people are willing and able to buy during a specified period at a specified price. For example, when spring water costs $1 a bottle, you decide to buy 2 bottles a day. The 2 bottles a day is your quantity demanded of spring water.

The quantity demanded is measured as an amount *per unit of time*. For example, your quantity demanded of water is 2 bottles *per day*. We could express this quantity as 14 bottles per week, or some other number per month or per year. A particular number of bottles without a time dimension has no meaning.

Many things influence buying plans, and one of them is price. We look first at the relationship between quantity demanded and price. To study this relationship, we keep all other influences on buying plans the same and we ask: How, other things remaining the same, does the quantity demanded of a good change as its price varies? The law of demand provides the answer.

Quantity demanded
The amount of any good, service, or resource that people are willing and able to buy during a specified period at a specified price.

■ The Law of Demand

The **law of demand** states

> Other things remaining the same, if the price of a good rises, the quantity demanded of that good decreases; and if the price of a good falls, the quantity demanded of that good increases.

So the law of demand states that when all other things remain the same, if the price of an iPhone falls, people will buy more iPhones; or if the price of a baseball ticket rises, people will buy fewer baseball tickets.

Why does the quantity demanded increase if the price falls, all other things remaining the same?

The answer is that, faced with a limited budget, people always have an incentive to find the best deals available. If the price of one item falls and the prices of all other items remain the same, the item with the lower price is a better deal than it was before, so some people buy more of this item. Suppose, for example, that the price of bottled water fell from $1 a bottle to 25 cents a bottle while the price of Gatorade remained at $1 a bottle. Wouldn't some people switch from Gatorade to water? By doing so, they save 75 cents a bottle, which they can spend on other things they previously couldn't afford.

Think about the things that you buy and ask yourself: Which of these items does *not* obey the law of demand? If the price of a new textbook were lower, other things remaining the same (including the price of a used textbook), would you buy more new textbooks? Then think about all the things that you do not now buy but would if you could afford them. How cheap would a PC have to be for you to buy *both* a desktop and a laptop? There is a price that is low enough to entice you!

■ Demand Schedule and Demand Curve

Demand is the relationship between the quantity demanded and the price of a good when all other influences on buying plans remain the same. The quantity demanded is *one* quantity at *one* price. *Demand is a list of quantities at different prices* illustrated by a demand schedule and a demand curve.

Demand
The relationship between the quantity demanded and the price of a good when all other influences on buying plans remain the same.

Demand schedule

A list of the quantities demanded at each different price when all the other influences on buying plans remain the same.

Demand curve

A graph of the relationship between the quantity demanded of a good and its price when all the other influences on buying plans remain the same.

A **demand schedule** is a list of the quantities demanded at each different price when *all the other influences on buying plans remain the same*. The table in Figure 4.1 is a demand schedule for bottled water. It tells us that if the price of water is $2.00 a bottle, the quantity demanded is 8.5 million bottles a day. If the price of water is $1.50 a bottle, the quantity demanded is 9 million bottles a day. The quantity demanded increases to 10 million bottles a day at a price of $1.00 a bottle and to 12 million bottles a day at a price of 50 cents a bottle.

A **demand curve** is a graph of the relationship between the quantity demanded of a good and its price when all the other influences on buying plans remain the same. The points on the demand curve labeled A through D represent the rows A through D of the demand schedule. For example, point B on the graph represents row B of the demand schedule and shows that the quantity demanded is 9 million bottles a day when the price is $1.50 a bottle. Point C on the demand curve represents row C of the demand schedule and shows that the quantity demanded is 10 million bottles a day when the price is $1.00 a bottle.

The downward slope of the demand curve illustrates the law of demand. Along the demand curve, when the price of the good *falls*, the quantity demanded *increases*. For example, in Figure 4.1, when the price of a bottle of water falls from $1.00 to 50 cents, the quantity demanded increases from 10 million bottles a day to 12 million bottles a day. Conversely, when the price *rises*, the quantity demanded *decreases*. For example, when the price rises from $1.00 to $1.50 a bottle, the quantity demanded decreases from 10 million bottles a day to 9 million bottles a day.

■ **FIGURE 4.1**

Demand Schedule and Demand Curve   MyEconLab Animation

The table shows a demand schedule that lists the quantity of water demanded at each price if all other influences on buying plans remain the same. At a price of $1.50 a bottle, the quantity demanded is 9 million bottles a day.

The demand curve shows the relationship between the quantity demanded and price, other things remaining the same. The downward-sloping demand curve illustrates the law of demand. When the price falls, the quantity demanded increases; and when the price rises, the quantity demanded decreases.

	Price (dollars per bottle)	Quantity demanded (millions of bottles per day)
A	2.00	8.5
B	1.50	9.0
C	1.00	10.0
D	0.50	12.0

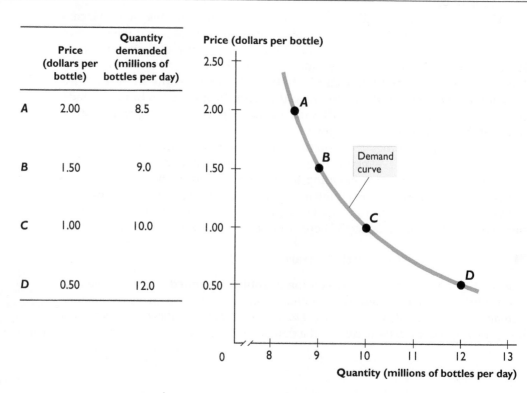

■ Changes in Demand

The demand curve shows how the quantity demanded changes when the price of the good changes but *all other influences on buying plans remain the same*. When the price of a good changes, we call the resulting change in buying plans a **change in the quantity demanded.** When any influence on buying plans other than the price of the good changes, there is a **change in demand.**

The main influences on buying plans that change demand are

- Prices of related goods
- Expected Future Prices
- Income
- Expectations
- Number of buyers
- Preferences

Prices of Related Goods

Goods have substitutes and complements. A **substitute** for a good is another good that can be consumed in its place. Chocolate cake is a substitute for cheesecake, and bottled water is a substitute for Gatorade. The demand for a good and the price of one of its substitutes move in the *same direction*. The demand for a good *increases* if the price of one of its substitutes *rises* and *decreases* if the price of one of its substitutes *falls*. For example, the demand for cheesecake increases when the price of chocolate cake rises.

A **complement** of a good is another good that is consumed with it. Wrist guards are a complement of in-line skates, and bottled water is a complement of fitness center services. The demand for a good and the price of one of its complements move in *opposite directions*. The demand for a good *decreases* if the price of one of its complements *rises* and *increases* if the price of one of its complements *falls*. For example, the demand for wrist guards decreases when the price of in-line skates rises.

Expected Future Prices

A rise in the expected *future* price of a good increases the *current* demand for that good and a fall in the expected *future* price decreases *current* demand. If you expect the price of noodles to rise next week, you buy a big enough stockpile to get you through the next few weeks. Your demand for noodles today has increased. If you expect the price of noodles to fall next week, you buy none now and plan to buy next week. Your demand for noodles today has decreased.

Income

A rise in income brings an increase in demand and a fall in income brings a decrease in demand for a **normal good**. A rise in income brings a *decrease* in demand and a fall in income brings an *increase* in demand for an **inferior good**. For example, if your income increases and you decide to buy more chicken and less pasta, for you, chicken is a normal good and pasta is an inferior good.

Expectations

When income is expected to increase in the future, or when credit is easy to get and the cost of borrowing is low, the demand for some goods increases. And when income is expected to decrease in the future, or when credit is hard to get and the cost of borrowing is high, the demand for some goods decreases.

Change in the quantity demanded
A change in the quantity of a good that people plan to buy that results from a change in the price of the good with all other influences on buying plans remaining the same.

Change in demand
A change in the quantity that people plan to buy when any influence on buying plans other than the price of the good changes.

Substitute
A good that can be consumed in place of another good.

Complement
A good that is consumed with another good.

Normal good
A good for which demand increases when income increases and demand decreases when income decreases.

Inferior good
A good for which demand decreases when income increases and demand increases when income decreases.

Number of Buyers

The greater the number of buyers in a market, the larger is demand. For example, the demand for parking spaces, movies, bottled water, or just about anything is greater in New York City than it is in Boise, Idaho.

Preferences

Tastes or *preferences*, as economists call them, influence demand. When preferences change, the demand for one item increases and the demand for another item (or items) decreases. For example, preferences have changed as people have become better informed about the health hazards of tobacco. This change in preferences has decreased the demand for cigarettes and has increased the demand for nicotine patches. Preferences also change when new goods become available. For example, the development of MP3 technology has decreased the demand for CDs and has increased the demand for Internet service and MP3 players.

◼ Illustrating Changes in Buying Plans

Figure 4.2 illustrates and summarizes the distinction between a change in the quantity demanded and a change in demand. When the price of a good changes, there is a *change in the quantity demanded* shown by a *movement along the demand curve*. When any other influence on buying plans changes, there is a *change in demand*, which is shown by a *shift of the demand curve*. When demand *decreases*, the demand curve *shifts leftward* to D_1, and when demand *increases*, the demand curve *shifts rightward* to D_2.

◼ **FIGURE 4.2**

Change in Quantity Demanded Versus Change in Demand

MyEconLab Animation

❶ A decrease in the quantity demanded

The quantity demanded decreases and there is a movement up along the demand curve D_0 if the price of the good rises and other things remain the same.

❸ A decrease in demand

Demand decreases and the demand curve shifts leftward (from D_0 to D_1) if

- The price of a substitute falls or the price of a complement rises.
- The price of the good is expected to fall.
- Income decreases.*
- Expected future income or credit decreases.
- The number of buyers decreases.

  * Bottled water is a normal good.

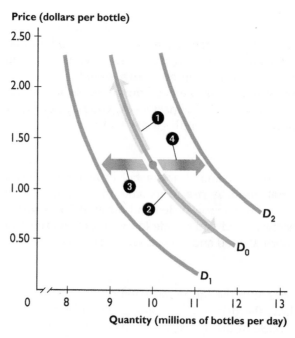

❷ An increase in the quantity demanded

The quantity demanded increases and there is a movement down along the demand curve D_0 if the price of the good falls and other things remain the same.

❹ An increase in demand

Demand increases and the demand curve shifts rightward (from D_0 to D_2) if

- The price of a substitute rises or the price of a complement falls.
- The price of the good is expected to rise.
- Income increases.
- Expected future income or credit increases.
- The number of buyers increases.

CHECKPOINT 4.1

MyEconLab Study Plan 4.1
Key Terms Quiz
Solutions

Distinguish between quantity demanded and demand, and explain what determines demand.

Practice Problems

The following events occur one at a time in the market for cell phones:
- The price of a cell phone falls.
- Producers announce that cell-phone prices will fall next month.
- The price of a call made from a cell phone falls.
- The price of a call made from a land-line phone increases.
- The introduction of camera phones makes cell phones more popular.

1. Explain the effect of each event on the demand for cell phones.

2. Use a graph to illustrate the effect of each event.

3. Does any event (or events) illustrate the law of demand?

In the News

Airlines, now flush, fear a downturn
So far this year, airlines have been able to raise fares but still fill their planes.

Source: *The New York Times*, June 10, 2011

Does this news clip imply that the law of demand doesn't work in the real world? Explain why or why not.

Solutions to Practice Problems

1. A fall in the price of a cell phone increases the quantity of cell phones demanded but has no effect on the demand for cell phones.
   With the producers' announcement, the expected future price of a cell phone falls, which decreases the demand for cell phones today.
   A fall in the price of a call from a cell phone increases the demand for cell phones because a cell-phone call and a cell phone are complements.
   A rise in the price of a call from a land-line phone increases the demand for cell phones because a land-line phone and a cell phone are substitutes.
   With cell phones more popular, the demand for cell phones increases.

2. Figure 1 illustrates the effect of a fall in the price of a cell phone as a movement along the demand curve D.
   Figure 2 illustrates the effect of an increase in the demand for cell phones as the shift of the demand curve from D_0 to D_1 and a decrease in the demand for cell phones as the shift of the demand curve from D_0 to D_2.

3. A fall in the price of a cell phone (other things remaining the same) illustrates the law of demand. Figure 1 illustrates the law of demand. The other events change demand and do not illustrate the law of demand.

Solution to In the News

The law of demand states: If the price of an airline ticket rises, other things remaining the same, the quantity demanded of airline tickets will decrease. The demand curve for airline tickets slopes downward. The law of demand does work in the real world. Airlines can still fill their planes because "other things" did not remain the same. Some event increased the demand for airline tickets.

FIGURE 1

FIGURE 2

4.2 SUPPLY

A market has two sides. On one side are the buyers, or demanders, that we've just studied. On the other side of the market are the sellers, or suppliers. We now study the forces that determine suppliers' plans.

The **quantity supplied** of a good, service, or resource is the amount that people are willing and able to sell during a specified period at a specified price. For example, when the price of spring water is $1.50 a bottle, a spring owner decides to sell 2,000 bottles a day. The 2,000 bottles a day is the quantity supplied of spring water by this individual producer. (As in the case of demand, the quantity supplied is measured as an amount *per unit of time*.)

Many things influence selling plans, and one of them is the price. We look first at the relationship between quantity supplied of a good and its price. To study this relationship, we keep all other influences on selling plans the same, and we ask: Other things remaining the same, how does the quantity supplied of a good change as its price varies? The law of supply provides the answer.

Quantity supplied
The amount of any good, service, or resource that people are willing and able to sell during a specified period at a specified price.

■ The Law of Supply

The **law of supply** states

> Other things remaining the same, if the price of a good rises, the quantity supplied of that good increases; and if the price of a good falls, the quantity supplied of that good decreases.

So the law of supply states that when all other things remain the same, if the price of bottled water rises, spring owners will offer more water for sale; if the price of a flat screen TV falls, Sony Corp. will offer fewer flat screen TVs for sale.

Why, other things remaining the same, does the quantity supplied increase if the price rises and decrease if the price falls? Part of the answer lies in the principle of increasing opportunity cost (see p. 68). Because factors of production are not equally productive in all activities, as more of a good is produced, the opportunity cost of producing it increases. A higher price provides the incentive to bear the higher opportunity cost of increased production. Another part of the answer is that for a given cost, the higher price brings a larger profit, so sellers have greater incentive to increase production.

Think about the resources that you own and can offer for sale to others and ask yourself: Which of these items does *not* obey the law of supply? If the wage rate for summer jobs increased, would you have an incentive to work longer hours and bear the higher opportunity cost of forgone leisure? If the bank offered a higher interest rate on deposits, would you have an incentive to save more and bear the higher opportunity cost of forgone consumption? If the used book dealer offered a higher price for last year's textbooks, would you have an incentive to sell that handy math text and bear the higher opportunity cost of visiting the library (or finding a friend) whenever you needed the book?

■ Supply Schedule and Supply Curve

Supply is the relationship between the quantity supplied and the price of a good when all other influences on selling plans remain the same. The quantity supplied is *one* quantity at *one* price. *Supply* is a *list of quantities at different prices* illustrated by a supply schedule and a supply curve.

Supply
The relationship between the quantity supplied and the price of a good when all other influences on selling plans remain the same.

A **supply schedule** lists the quantities supplied at each different price when all the other influences on selling plans remain the same. The table in Figure 4.3 is a supply schedule for bottled water. It tells us that if the price of water is 50 cents a bottle, the quantity supplied is 8 million bottles a day. If the price of water is $1.00 a bottle, the quantity supplied is 10 million bottles a day. The quantity supplied increases to 11 million bottles a day at a price of $1.50 a bottle and to 11.5 million bottles a day at a price of $2.00 a bottle.

A **supply curve** is a graph of the relationship between the quantity supplied of a good and its price when all the other influences on selling plans remain the same. The points on the supply curve labeled A through D represent the rows A through D of the supply schedule. For example, point C on the supply curve represents row C of the supply schedule and shows that the quantity supplied is 10 million bottles a day when the price is $1.00 a bottle. Point B on the supply curve represents row B of the supply schedule and shows that the quantity supplied is 11 million bottles a day when the price is $1.50 a bottle.

The upward slope of the supply curve illustrates the law of supply. Along the supply curve, when the price of the good *rises*, the quantity supplied *increases*. For example, in Figure 4.3, when the price of a bottle of water rises from $1.50 to $2.00, the quantity supplied increases from 11 million bottles a day to 11.5 million bottles a day. And when the price *falls*, the quantity supplied *decreases*. For example, when the price falls from $1.50 to $1.00 a bottle, the quantity supplied decreases from 11 million bottles a day to 10 million bottles a day.

Supply schedule
A list of the quantities supplied at each different price when all the other influences on selling plans remain the same.

Supply curve
A graph of the relationship between the quantity supplied of a good and its price when all the other influences on selling plans remain the same.

FIGURE 4.3

Supply Schedule and Supply Curve

MyEconLab Animation

	Price (dollars per bottle)	Quantity supplied (millions of bottles per day)
A	2.00	11.5
B	1.50	11.0
C	1.00	10.0
D	0.50	8.0

The table shows a supply schedule that lists the quantity of water supplied at each price if all other influences on selling plans remain the same. At a price of $1.50 a bottle, the quantity supplied is 11 million bottles a day.

The supply curve shows the relationship between the quantity supplied and price, other things remaining the same. The upward-sloping supply curve illustrates the law of supply. When the price rises, the quantity supplied increases; and when the price falls, the quantity supplied decreases.

MyEconLab Snapshot

Change in the quantity supplied
A change in the quantity of a good that suppliers plan to sell that results from a change in the price of the good.

Change in supply
A change in the quantity that suppliers plan to sell when any influence on selling plans other than the price of the good changes.

Substitute in production
A good that can be produced in place of another good.

Complement in production
A good that is produced along with another good.

■ Changes in Supply

The supply curve shows how the quantity supplied changes when the price of the good changes but *all other influences on selling plans remain the same*. When the price of the good changes, we call the resulting influence on selling plans a **change in the quantity supplied.** When any other influence on selling plans changes, there is a **change in supply.**

The main influences on selling plans that change supply are

- Prices of related goods
- Prices of resources and other inputs
- Expectations
- Number of sellers
- Productivity

Prices of Related Goods

Related goods are either substitutes *in production* or complements *in production*. A **substitute in production** for a good is another good that can be produced in its place. Skinny jeans are substitutes in production for boot cut jeans in a clothing factory. The supply of a good *decreases* if the price of one of its substitutes in production *rises;* and the supply of a good *increases* if the price of one of its substitutes in production *falls*. That is, the supply of a good and the price of one of its substitutes in production move in *opposite directions*. For example, a clothing factory can produce cargo pants or button-fly jeans, so these goods are substitutes in production. When the price of button-fly jeans rises, the clothing factory switches production from cargo pants to button-fly jeans, so the supply of cargo pants decreases.

A **complement in production** of a good is another good that is produced along with it. Cream is a complement in production of skim milk in a dairy. The supply of a good *increases* if the price of one of its complements in production *rises;* and the supply of a good *decreases* if the price of one of its complements in production *falls*. That is, the supply of a good and the price of one of its complements in production move in the *same direction*. For example, when a dairy produces skim milk, it also produces cream, so these goods are complements in production. When the price of skim milk rises, the dairy produces more skim milk, so the supply of cream increases.

Prices of Resources and Other Inputs

Supply changes when the price of a resource or other input used to produce the good changes. The reason is that resource and input prices influence the cost of production. The more it costs to produce a good, the smaller is the quantity supplied of that good at each price (other things remaining the same). For example, if the wage rate of bottling-plant workers rises, it costs more to produce a bottle of water, so the supply of bottled water decreases.

Expected Future Prices

Expectations about future prices influence supply. For example, a severe frost that wipes out Florida's citrus crop doesn't change the production of orange juice today, but it does decrease production later in the year when the current crop would normally have been harvested. Sellers of orange juice will expect the price to rise in the future. To get the higher future price, some sellers will increase their inventory of frozen juice, and this action decreases the supply of juice today.

Number of Sellers

The greater the number of sellers in a market, the larger is the supply. For example, many new sellers have developed springs and water-bottling plants in the United States, and the supply of bottled water has increased.

Productivity

Productivity is output per unit of input. An increase in productivity lowers the cost of producing the good and increases its supply. A decrease in productivity has the opposite effect and decreases supply.

Technological change and the increased use of capital increase productivity. For example, advances in electronic technology have lowered the cost of producing a computer and increased the supply of computers. Technological change brings new goods such as the iPad, the supply of which was previously zero.

Natural events such as severe weather and earthquakes decrease productivity and decrease supply. For example, the tsunami of 2004 decreased the supply of agricultural products and seafood in many places surrounding the Indian Ocean.

■ Illustrating a Change in Selling Plans

Figure 4.4 illustrates and summarizes the distinction between a change in the quantity supplied and a change in supply. When the price of a good changes, there is a *change in the quantity supplied* shown by a *movement along the supply curve*. When any other influence on buying plans changes, there is a *change in supply*, which is shown by a *shift of the supply curve*. When supply *decreases*, the supply curve *shifts leftward* to S_1 and when supply *increases*, the supply curve *shifts rightward* to S_2.

■ FIGURE 4.4

Change in Quantity Supplied Versus Change in Supply

MyEconLab Animation

❶ A decrease in the quantity supplied

The quantity supplied decreases and there is a movement down along the supply curve S_0 if the price of the good falls and other things remain the same.

❸ A decrease in supply

Supply decreases and the supply curve shifts leftward (from S_0 to S_1) if

- The price of a substitute in production rises.
- The price of a complement in production falls.
- A resource price or other input price rises.
- The price of the good is expected to rise.
- The number of sellers decreases.
- Productivity decreases.

❷ An increase in the quantity supplied

The quantity supplied increases and there is a movement up along the supply curve S_0 if the price of the good rises and other things remain the same.

❹ An increase in supply

Supply increases and the supply curve shifts rightward (from S_0 to S_2) if

- The price of a substitute in production falls.
- The price of a complement in production rises.
- A resource price or other input price falls.
- The price of the good is expected to fall.
- The number of sellers increases.
- Productivity increases.

EYE on YOUR LIFE
Understanding and Using Demand and Supply

To truly understand the demand and supply model, it is a good idea to go beyond just memorizing the key terms and definitions and lists of factors that change demand or change supply. Take ownership of the model by seeing how it explains your buying plans and your selling plans.

Your Buying Plans

Think about the things you buy: the quantities you buy and the prices you pay. These quantities and prices are points on your demand curves.

Now think about how some price changes would change your buying plans. How would your buying plans change if prices at the campus coffee shop increased? For which items would you change your quantity demanded? And for which items would you change your demand?

How would your buying plans change if you started a new job with a higher wage? What would you buy more of? What would you buy less of?

Suppose that you were just about to get a new smart phone when Apple and Samsung announce plans to launch new phones next month. You figure that the prices of the older models will fall. How will this fall in the expected future price of a smart phone influence your buying plans?

For each thought experiment we've just described, think about whether you are sliding along a demand curve or shifting a demand curve.

Your Selling Plans

Most likely, you don't sell much stuff, but you own one precious resource that you might sell: your time.

If you have a job, think about the number of hours you work and the wage rate you earn. Are you working as many hours as you want to? If you are, you're at a point on the supply curve of your labor services.

How would you respond to a rise in the wage rate? Would you plan to work more hours or fewer hours?

Another thing you own is a pile of textbooks. Think about your selling plan for when your courses are over at the end of the semester. What is the lowest price at which you will sell this textbook? That price is a point on your supply curve of this book to the used book market.

You might also have a few old things that you'd like to sell on eBay. Again, think about your minimum supply-price—the point on your supply curve of these items.

By doing these thought experiments about your selling plans, you can make the idea of supply and the supply curve more concrete.

From Plans to Actions

Your demand and supply curves and the *market* demand and supply curves describe *plans*. They are statements about "what-if." They describe the buying plans and the selling plans at different possible prices. But when you act on your plan and buy something, someone else must have a plan to sell that item. Your buying plan must match someone else's selling plan.

Neither demand nor supply on its own tells us what actually happens in a market. To find buying plans and selling plans that match, we must look at demand and supply together. That's what you will do in the final section of this chapter. You will see how prices adjust to balance the opposing forces of demand and supply.

The Rest of Your Life

The demand and supply model is going to be a big part of the rest of your life! You will use it again and again during your economics course, so having a firm grasp of it will bring an immediate payoff.

But much more important, by understanding the laws of demand and supply and being aware of how prices adjust to balance these two opposing forces, you will have a much better appreciation of how your economic world works.

Every time you hear someone complaining about a price hike and blaming it on someone's greed, think about the market forces and how demand and supply determine that price.

As you shop for your favorite clothing, music, and food items, try to describe how supply and demand influence the prices of these goods.

CHECKPOINT 4.2

MyEconLab Study Plan 4.2
Key Terms Quiz
Solutions

Distinguish between quantity supplied and supply, and explain what determines supply.

Practice Problems

Lumber companies make timber beams from logs. In the process of making beams, the mill produces sawdust, which is made into pressed wood. In the market for timber beams, the following events occur one at a time:
- The wage rate of sawmill workers rises.
- The price of sawdust rises.
- The price of a timber beam rises.
- The price of a timber beam is expected to rise next year.
- A new law reduces the amount of forest that can be cut for timber.
- A new technology lowers the cost of producing timber beams.

1. Explain the effect of each event on the supply of timber beams.
2. Use a graph to illustrate the effect of each event.
3. Does any event (or events) illustrate the law of supply?

In the News

Rising wages pose dilemma for China
Chinese private-sector wages rose 14 percent in 2012. This trend in rapidly rising wage rates might hurt its manufacturing dominance.
                    Source: *The Wall Street Journal*, May 17, 2013
Explain the effect of the rising wage rates on the supply of manufactured goods.

Solutions to Practice Problems

1. A rise in workers' wage rates increases the cost of producing a timber beam and decreases the supply of timber beams. A rise in the price of sawdust increases the supply of timber beams because sawdust and timber beams are complements in production. A rise in the price of a timber beam increases the quantity of timber beams supplied but has no effect on the supply of timber beams. An expected rise in the price of a timber beam decreases the supply of timber beams today as producers hold back and wait for the higher price. The new law decreases the supply of timber beams. The new technology increases the supply of timber beams.

2. In Figure 1, an increase in the supply shifts the supply curve from S_0 to S_1, and a decrease in the supply shifts the supply curve from S_0 to S_2. In Figure 2, the rise in the price of a beam creates a movement along the supply curve.

3. A rise in the price of a beam, other things remaining the same, is the only event that illustrates the law of supply—see Figure 2.

Solution to In the News

Rising wage rates increase the cost of production and with no change in productivity will decrease China's supply of manufactured goods.

FIGURE 1

FIGURE 2

Market equilibrium
When the quantity demanded equals the quantity supplied—buyers' and sellers' plans are in balance.

Equilibrium price
The price at which the quantity demanded equals the quantity supplied.

Equilibrium quantity
The quantity bought and sold at the equilibrium price.

4.3 MARKET EQUILIBRIUM

In everyday language, "equilibrium" means "opposing forces are in balance." In a market, demand and supply are the opposing forces. **Market equilibrium** occurs when the quantity demanded equals the quantity supplied—when buyers' and sellers' plans are in balance. At the **equilibrium price,** the quantity demanded equals the quantity supplied. The **equilibrium quantity** is the quantity bought and sold at the equilibrium price.

In the market for bottled water in Figure 4.5, equilibrium occurs where the demand curve and the supply curve intersect. The equilibrium price is $1.00 a bottle, and the equilibrium quantity is 10 million bottles a day.

■ Price: A Market's Automatic Regulator

When equilibrium is disturbed, market forces restore it. The **law of market forces** states

> When there is a surplus, the price falls; and when there is a shortage, the price rises.

A *surplus* is the amount by which the quantity supplied exceeds the quantity demanded. If there is a surplus, suppliers must cut the price to sell more. Buyers are pleased to take the lower price, so the price falls. Because a surplus arises when the price is above the equilibrium price, a falling price is exactly what the market needs to restore equilibrium.

A *shortage* is the amount by which the quantity demanded exceeds the quantity supplied. If there is a shortage, buyers must pay a higher price to get more. Sellers are pleased to take the higher price, so the price rises. Because a shortage arises when the price is below the equilibrium price, a rising price is exactly what is needed to restore equilibrium.

■ **FIGURE 4.5**

Equilibrium Price and Equilibrium Quantity

❶ Market equilibrium occurs at the intersection of the demand curve and the supply curve.

❷ The equilibrium price is $1.00 a bottle.

❸ At the equilibrium price, the quantity demanded and the quantity supplied are 10 million bottles a day, which is the equilibrium quantity.

FIGURE 4.6

The Forces That Achieve Equilibrium

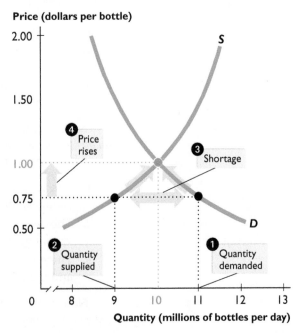

(a) Surplus and price falls

(b) Shortage and price rises

At $1.50 a bottle, ❶ the quantity supplied is 11 million bottles of water, ❷ the quantity demanded is 9 million bottles, ❸ the surplus is 2 million bottles of water, and ❹ the price falls.

At 75 cents a bottle, ❶ the quantity demanded is 11 million bottles of water, ❷ the quantity supplied is 9 million bottles, ❸ the shortage is 2 million bottles of water, and ❹ the price rises.

In Figure 4.6(a), at $1.50 a bottle, there is a surplus: The price falls, the quantity demanded increases, the quantity supplied decreases, and the surplus is eliminated at $1.00 a bottle.

In Figure 4.6(b), at 75 cents a bottle, there is a shortage of water: The price rises, the quantity demanded decreases, the quantity supplied increases, and the shortage is eliminated at $1.00 a bottle.

Predicting Price Changes: Three Questions

Because price adjustments eliminate shortages and surpluses, markets are normally in equilibrium. When an event disturbs an equilibrium, a new equilibrium soon emerges. To explain and predict changes in prices and quantities, we need to consider only changes in the *equilibrium* price and the *equilibrium* quantity. We can work out the effects of an event on a market by answering three questions:

1. Does the event influence demand or supply?

2. Does the event *increase* or *decrease* demand or supply—shift the demand curve or the supply curve *rightward* or *leftward*?

3. What are the new *equilibrium* price and *equilibrium* quantity and how have they changed?

■ Effects of Changes in Demand

Let's practice answering the three questions by working out the effects of an event in the market for bottled water: A new study says that tap water is unsafe.

1. With tap water unsafe, the demand for bottled water changes.
2. The demand for bottled water *increases*, and the demand curve *shifts rightward*. Figure 4.7(a) shows the shift from D_0 to D_1.
3. There is now a *shortage* at $1.00 a bottle. The *price rises* to $1.50 a bottle, and the quantity increases to 11 million bottles.

Note that there is *no change in supply*; the rise in price brings an *increase in the quantity supplied*—a movement along the supply curve.

Let's work out what happens if the price of a zero-calorie sports drink falls.

1. The sports drink is a substitute for bottled water, so when its price changes, the demand for bottled water changes.
2. The demand for bottled water *decreases*, and the demand curve *shifts leftward*. Figure 4.7(b) shows the shift from D_0 to D_2.
3. There is now a *surplus* at $1.00 a bottle. The price *falls* to 75 cents a bottle, and the quantity decreases to 9 million bottles.

Note again that there is *no change in supply*; the fall in price brings a *decrease in the quantity supplied*—a movement along the supply curve.

■ **FIGURE 4.7**

The Effects of a Change in Demand

(a) An increase in demand

❶ An increase in demand shifts the demand curve rightward to D_1 and creates a shortage of water. ❷ The price rises, ❸ the quantity supplied increases, and ❹ the equilibrium quantity increases.

(b) A decrease in demand

❶ A decrease in demand shifts the demand curve leftward to D_2 and creates a surplus of water. ❷ The price falls, ❸ the quantity supplied decreases, and ❹ the equilibrium quantity decreases.

EYE on TUITION

Why Does Tuition Keep Rising?

Tuition has increased every year since 1980 and at the same time, enrollment has steadily climbed. Figure 1 shows these facts. The points tell us the levels of enrollment (*x*-axis) and tuition (*y*-axis, measured in 2010 dollars) in 1981, 1991, and each year from 2001 to 2010. We can interpret the data using the demand and supply model

More than 4,500 public and private, 2-year and 4-year schools supply college education services and more than 20 million people demand these services.

The law of demand says: Other things remaining the same, if tuition rises, the quantity of college places demanded decreases. The law of supply says: Other things remaining the same, if tuition rises, the quantity of college places supplied increases. Tuition is determined at the level that makes the quantity of college places demanded equal the quantity supplied.

In a given year, other things remain the same, but from one year to the next, some things change. First, the population grows. Second, the number of jobs that require more than a high-school diploma expands and the number of jobs for high-school graduates shrinks. These changes increase the demand for college education.

Figure 2 illustrates the market for college education that we've just described. In 2001, demand was D_{01} and

supply was S. The market was in equilibrium with 16 million students enrolled paying an average tuition of $15,000. By 2010, demand had increased to D_{10}. At the tuition of 2001, there would be a severe shortage of college places, so tuition rises. In 2010, the market was in equilibrium at a tuition of $21,000 with 21 million students enrolled.

Demand for college places will keep increasing and tuition will keep rising.

**Tuition
(thousands of 2010 dollars per year)**

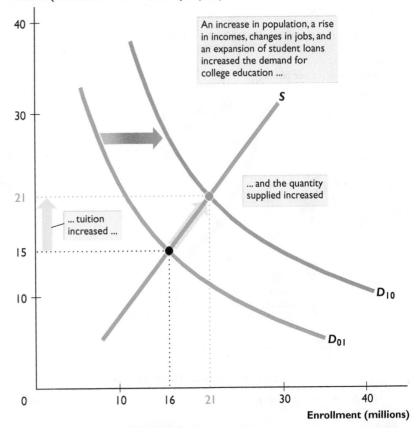

Figure 1 The Data: A Scatter Diagram

Figure 2 The Market for College Education

■ **Effects of Changes in Supply**

You can get more practice working out the effects of another event in the market for bottled water: European water bottlers buy springs and open new plants in the United States.

1. With more suppliers of bottled water, the supply changes.
2. The supply of bottled water *increases*, and the supply curve *shifts rightward*. Figure 4.8(a) shows the shift from S_0 to S_1.
3. There is now a *surplus* at $1.00 a bottle. The *price falls* to 75 cents a bottle, and the quantity increases to 11 million bottles.

Note that there is *no change in demand*; the fall in price brings an *increase in the quantity demanded*—a movement along the demand curve.
What happens if a drought dries up some springs?

1. The drought is a change in productivity, so the supply of water changes.
2. With fewer springs, the supply of bottled water *decreases*, and the supply curve *shifts leftward*. Figure 4.8(b) shows the shift from S_0 to S_2.
3. There is now a *shortage* at $1.00 a bottle. The *price rises* to $1.50 a bottle, and the quantity decreases to 9 million bottles.

Again, there is *no change in demand*; the rise in price brings a *decrease in the quantity demanded*—a movement along the demand curve.

■ **FIGURE 4.8**

The Effects of a Change in Supply

(a) An increase in supply

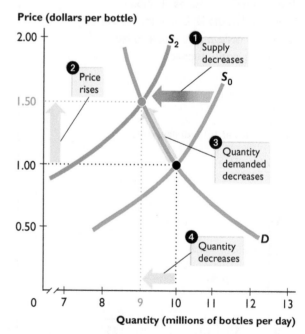

(b) A decrease in supply

❶ An increase in supply shifts the supply curve rightward to S_1 and creates a surplus of water. ❷ The price falls, ❸ the quantity demanded increases, and ❹ the equilibrium quantity increases.

❶ A decrease in supply shifts the supply curve leftward to S_2 and creates a shortage of water. ❷ The price rises, ❸ the quantity demanded decreases, and ❹ the equilibrium quantity decreases.

EYE on the GLOBAL ECONOMY
The Market for Solar Panels

Solar panels are produced in the United States, China, Japan, Korea, and Norway and used all over the world. The market for solar panels is a global market.

Figure 1 shows that the price of a solar panel has fallen and the quantity installed each year has increased. We can interpret these facts by using the demand and supply model of the market for solar panels.

The law of demand says: Other things remaining the same, if the price of a solar panel falls, the quantity of

solar panels demanded increases. The law of supply says: Other things remaining the same, if the price of a solar panel falls, the quantity of solar panels supplied decreases. The price of a solar panel is determined at the level that makes the quantity demanded equal the quantity supplied.

In Figure 2, the demand for solar panels is D and in 2009, supply was S_{09}. The market was in equilibrium with 11 gigawatts (GW) of units installed at a price of $2 per unit.

Two things are changing in the market for solar panels: The price of silicon from which the panels are made is falling and solar panel technology is getting better. These changes lower the cost of producing solar panels and increase the supply. But they have no effect on the demand.

In Figure 2, supply increased to S_{11} in 2011 and to S_{13} in 2013. The price fell and the quantity of solar panels demanded has increased. The price will keep falling as technology advances.

Installing solar panels on a home in California

Figure 1 The Data: A Scatter Diagram

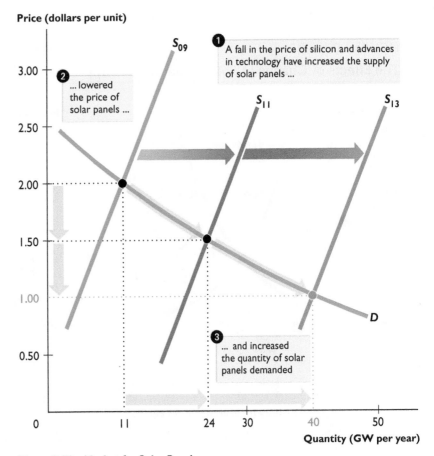

Figure 2 The Market for Solar Panels

■ Effects of Changes in Both Demand and Supply

When events occur that change *both* demand and supply, you can find the resulting change in the equilibrium price and equilibrium quantity by combining the cases you've just studied.

Both Demand and Supply Change in the Same Direction

When demand and supply change in the same direction, the equilibrium quantity changes in that same direction, but we need to know the magnitudes of the changes in demand and supply to predict whether the price rises or falls. If demand increases by more than supply increases, the price rises. But if supply increases by more than demand increases, the price falls.

Figure 4.9(a) shows the case when both demand and supply increase and by the same amount. The equilibrium quantity increases. But because the increase in demand equals the increase in supply, neither a shortage nor a surplus arises so the price doesn't change. A bigger increase in demand would have created a shortage and a rise in the price; a bigger increase in supply would have created a surplus and a fall in the price.

Figure 4.9(b) shows the case when both demand and supply decrease by the same amount. Here the equilibrium quantity decreases and again the price might either rise or fall.

■ FIGURE 4.9

The Effects of Change in *Both* Demand and Supply in the *Same Direction*

(a) Increase in both demand and supply

(b) Decrease in both demand and supply

❶ An increase in demand shifts the demand curve rightward to D_1 and an increase in supply shifts the supply curve rightward to S_1.
❷ The price might rise or fall, but ❸ the quantity increases.

❶ A decrease in demand shifts the demand curve leftward to D_1 and a decrease in supply shifts the supply curve leftward to S_1.
❷ The price might rise or fall, but ❸ the quantity decreases.

Both Demand and Supply Change in Opposite Directions

When demand and supply change in opposite directions, we can predict how the price changes, but we need to know the magnitudes of the changes in demand and supply to say whether the equilibrium quantity increases or decreases. If demand changes by more than supply, the equilibrium quantity changes in the same direction as the change in demand. But if supply changes by more than demand, the equilibrium quantity changes in the same direction as the change in supply.

Figure 4.10(a) illustrates what happens when demand decreases and supply increases by the same amount. At the initial price, there is a surplus, so the price falls. A decrease in demand decreases the quantity and an increase in supply increases the quantity, so when these changes occur together, we can't say what happens to the quantity unless we know the magnitudes of the changes.

Figure 4.10(b) illustrates what happens when demand increases and supply decreases by the same amount. In this case, at the initial price, there is a shortage, so the price rises. An increase in demand increases the quantity and a decrease in supply decreases the quantity, so again, when these changes occur together, we can't say what happens to the quantity unless we know the magnitudes of the changes in demand and supply.

For all the cases in Figures 4.9 and 4.10 where you "can't say" what happens to price or quantity, draw some examples that go in each direction.

■ **FIGURE 4.10**

The Effects of Change in *Both* Demand and Supply in *Opposite Directions*   MyEconLab Animation

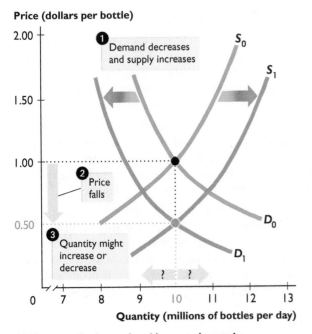

(a) Decrease in demand and increase in supply

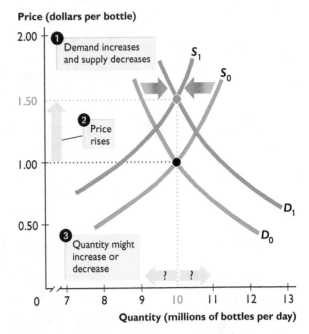

(b) Increase in demand and decrease in supply

1 A decrease in demand shifts the demand curve leftward to D_1 and an increase in supply shifts the supply curve rightward to S_1.
2 The price falls, but **3** the quantity might increase or decrease.

1 An increase in demand shifts the demand curve rightward to D_1 and a decrease in supply shifts the supply curve leftward to S_1.
2 The price rises, but **3** the quantity might increase or decrease.

MyEconLab Study Plan 4.3
Key Terms Quiz
Solutions

CHECKPOINT 4.3

Explain how demand and supply determine price and quantity in a market, and explain the effects of changes in demand and supply.

Practice Problems

TABLE 1

Price (dollars per carton)	Quantity demanded	Quantity supplied
	(cartons per day)	
1.00	200	110
1.25	175	130
1.50	150	150
1.75	125	170
2.00	100	190

Table 1 sets out the demand and supply schedules for milk.

1. What is the equilibrium price and equilibrium quantity of milk?
2. Describe the situation in the milk market if the price were $1.75 a carton and explain how the market reaches equilibrium.
3. A drought decreases the quantity supplied by 45 cartons a day at each price. What is the new equilibrium and how does the market adjust to it?
4. If milk becomes more popular and better feeds increase milk production, describe how the equilibrium price and quantity of milk will change.

In the News

After wild weather, higher food prices on horizon
After heavy rain this year, the corn harvest will be less than expected while the demand for corn will continue to increase. Food prices will continue to rise.

Source: npr, June 9, 2011

Using the demand and supply model, explain why food prices are expected to rise.

Solutions to Practice Problems

1. Equilibrium price is $1.50 a carton; equilibrium quantity is 150 cartons a day.
2. At $1.75 a carton, the quantity demanded (125 cartons) is less than the quantity supplied (170 cartons), so there is a surplus of 45 cartons a day. The price begins to fall, and as it does, the quantity demanded increases, the quantity supplied decreases, and the surplus decreases. The price will fall until the surplus is eliminated. The price falls to $1.50 a carton.
3. The supply decreases by 45 cartons a day so at $1.50 a carton there is a shortage of milk. The price begins to rise, and as it does, the quantity demanded decreases, the quantity supplied increases, and the shortage decreases. The price will rise until the shortage is eliminated. The new equilibrium occurs at $1.75 a carton and 125 cartons a day (Figure 1).
4. With milk more popular, demand increases. With better feeds, supply increases. If supply increases by more than demand, a surplus arises. The price falls, and the quantity increases (Figure 2). If demand increases by more than supply, a shortage arises. The price rises, and the quantity increases. If demand and supply increase by the same amount, there is no shortage or surplus, so the price does not change, but the quantity increases.

Solution to In the News

A fall in the corn harvest will decrease the supply of corn and shift the supply curve of corn leftward. The increase in the demand for corn will shift the demand curve rightward. The price of corn will rise. The higher price of corn will decrease the supply of food made from corn and raise the price of this food.

FIGURE 1

FIGURE 2

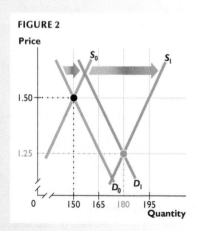

4.4 PRICE RIGIDITIES

You've seen that price adjustments bring market equilibrium. But suppose that for some reason, the price in a market does not adjust. What happens then? The answer depends on why the price doesn't adjust. There are three possibilities:

- Price floor
- Price ceiling or price cap
- Sticky price

■ Price Floor

A **price floor** is a government regulation that places a lower limit on the price at which a particular good, service, or factor of production may be traded. A **minimum wage law**—a government regulation that makes hiring labor for less than a specified wage illegal—is an example of a price floor. Firms are free to pay a wage rate that exceeds the minimum but may not pay less than the minimum. What are the effects of a minimum wage?

Firms hire labor, so they decide how much labor to demand. The lower the wage rate, the greater is the quantity of labor that firms demand. Households decide how much labor to supply. The higher the wage rate, the greater is the quantity of labor households are willing to supply. The wage rate adjusts to make the quantity of labor demanded equal to the quantity supplied.

Figure 4.11 shows the market for fast-food servers in Yuma, Arizona. In this market, the demand for labor curve is *D* and the supply of labor curve is *S*. Equilibrium occurs at a wage rate of $5 an hour with 5,000 people employed as servers.

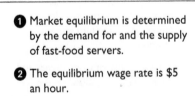

Price floor
A government regulation that places a lower limit on the price at which a particular good, service, or factor of production may be traded.

Minimum wage law
A government regulation that makes hiring labor for less than a specified wage illegal.

■ FIGURE 4.11

A Market for Fast-Food Servers

MyEconLab Animation

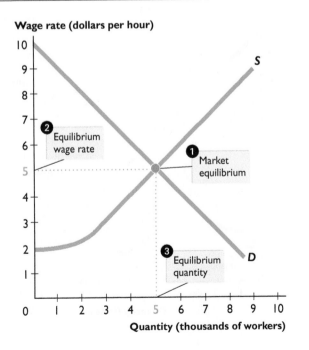

Wage rate (dollars per hour)

Quantity (thousands of workers)

1 Market equilibrium is determined by the demand for and the supply of fast-food servers.

2 The equilibrium wage rate is $5 an hour.

3 At the equilibrium wage rate, the equilibrium quantity of fast-food servers is 5,000.

Suppose that the government thinks that no one should have to work for a wage rate as low as $5 an hour and introduces a minimum wage. The effect of a minimum wage depends on whether it is set below or above the equilibrium wage. In Figure 4.11, the equilibrium wage rate is $5 an hour, and at this wage rate, firms hire 5,000 workers. If the government introduced a minimum wage below $5 an hour, nothing would change. The reason is that firms are already paying $5 an hour, and because this wage exceeds the minimum wage, the wage rate paid doesn't change. Firms continue to hire 5,000 workers.

Now suppose that the government introduces a minimum wage of $7 an hour. Figure 4.12 shows the effects of this law. Wage rates below $7 an hour are illegal, so we've shaded the illegal region below the minimum wage. Firms and workers are no longer permitted to operate at the equilibrium point in this market because it is in the illegal region. Market forces and the law are in conflict.

The government can set a minimum wage, but it can't tell employers how many workers to hire. If firms must pay $7 an hour for labor, they will hire only 3,000 workers. At the equilibrium wage rate of $5 an hour, firms hired 5,000 workers. So when the minimum wage is introduced, firms fire 2,000 workers.

But at $7 an hour, another 2,000 people who didn't want to work for $5 an hour now try to find work as servers, so at $7 an hour, the quantity supplied is 7,000 workers. With 2,000 workers fired and another 2,000 looking for work at the higher wage rate, 4,000 people who would like to work as servers are unemployed.

Somehow, the 3,000 jobs available must be allocated among the 7,000 people who would like them. How is this allocation achieved? The answer is some combination of first-come, first-served and discrimination. When price doesn't allocate scarce resources, waiting lines and personal characteristics take over.

FIGURE 4.12

A Minimum Wage Creates Unemployment

MyEconLab Animation

A minimum wage is introduced above the equilibrium wage rate. In this example, the minimum wage is $7 an hour.

❶ The quantity of labor demanded decreases to 3,000 workers.

❷ The quantity of labor supplied increases to 7,000 workers.

❸ 4,000 people are unemployed.

EYE on the U.S. ECONOMY
The Federal Minimum Wage

The *Fair Labor Standards Act* sets the federal minimum wage, but most states set their own minimum at a higher level than the federal minimum.

The minimum wage creates unemployment. But how much? Until recently, most economists believed that a 10 percent increase in the minimum wage decreased teenage employment by between 1 and 3 percent.

David Card of the University of California at Berkeley and Alan Krueger of Princeton University have challenged this view. They say that following a rise in the minimum wage in California, New Jersey, and Texas, the employment rate of low-income workers *increased*, and they suggest three reasons why:

(1) Workers become more conscientious and productive.

(2) Workers are less likely to quit, so costly labor turnover is reduced.

(3) Managers make a firm's operations more efficient.

Most economists are skeptical about these ideas. They say that if higher wages make workers more productive and reduce labor turnover, firms will freely pay workers a higher wage. And they argue that there are other explanations for the employment increase that Card and Krueger found.

Daniel Hamermesh of the University of Texas at Austin says that they got the timing wrong. Firms anticipated the minimum wage rise and so cut employment before it occurred. Looking at employment changes after the minimum wage increased missed its main effect. Finis Welch of Texas A&M University and Kevin Murphy of the University of Chicago say the employment effects that Card and Krueger found are caused by regional differences in economic growth, not changes in the minimum wage.

Also, looking only at employment misses the supply-side effect of the minimum wage. It brings an increase in the number of people who drop out of high school to look for work.

■ Price Ceiling or Price Cap

A **price ceiling** or **price cap** is a government regulation that places an *upper* limit on the price at which a particular good, service, or factor of production may be traded. You've probably encountered several price ceilings or price caps. One example is a ceiling on apartment rents—a rent ceiling. New York City has some notable rent ceilings that limit the rent that landlords can charge. Another example is a cap on college tuition. Student groups often lobby for tuition caps, and state legislatures sometimes deliver. A further example is a price cap on campus parking. College administrators think that parking must not be too expensive for students, so they keep the price low. A final example is a price cap—a zero price—on freeways.

To see how a price cap works, first imagine an unrestricted market in student parking. College administrators decide the quantity of parking spaces to make available, and the higher the price of a parking permit, the greater is the quantity of parking that the college is willing to supply.

Students decide the quantity of parking spaces to demand, and the lower the price of a permit, the greater is the quantity of parking spaces demanded. If the price of parking on campus is $100 a month, few students would drive to school. There would be a big increase in car-pooling, riding the bus, walking, and cycling.

Figure 4.13 illustrates a market for campus parking. The demand curve is *D*, and the supply curve is *S*. The price adjusts to an equilibrium of $80 a month, at which 2,000 parking spaces are demanded and supplied.

The effect of a price cap depends on whether it is imposed at a level above or below the equilibrium price. With a price cap *above* the equilibrium price, nothing would change. The reason is that people are already paying the equilibrium price, and because this price is below the price cap, the price paid doesn't change.

Price ceiling or price cap
A government regulation that places an *upper* limit on the price at which a particular good, service, or factor of production may be traded.

■ **FIGURE 4.13**

An Unregulated Market in Campus Parking Spaces

1 Market equilibrium is determined by the demand for parking spaces and the supply of parking spaces.

2 The equilibrium price is $80 a month.

3 At the equilibrium price, 2,000 parking spaces are demanded and supplied.

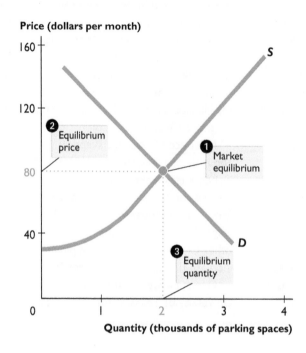

But a price cap set *below* the equilibrium price has powerful effects on the market. The reason is that it attempts to prevent the price from rising by enough to bring equality of the quantity demanded and the quantity supplied. The regulation and the market are in conflict, and one (or both) of them must yield.

Figure 4.14 shows the effects of a price cap that is set *below* the equilibrium price. The price cap is $40 a month. We've shaded the area above the price cap because any price in this region is unavailable. At a price of $40 a month, the quantity of parking supplied is 1,000 spaces and the quantity demanded is 3,000 spaces, so the price cap creates a shortage of 2,000 parking spaces.

The first effect, then, of a price cap is a shortage. People are seeking a larger amount of parking than the college has an incentive to make available.

But the story does not end here. Somehow the 1,000 spaces that the college is willing to make available must be allocated among students who are seeking 3,000 spaces. Blocking price adjustments that bring the number of spaces demanded into equality with the number supplied doesn't end scarcity. When the college is unwilling to permit the price to rise and allocate scarce parking spaces, some other allocation mechanism must be used.

Some possibilities are a parking permit lottery; a first-come, first-served rule; a senior student priority rule; and issuing so many permits that students end up spending a large amount of time hunting for a space and sometimes end up missing class because they couldn't find a parking place.

Note that all of these alternative ways of rationing parking spaces impose costs on the students. When students don't pay the equilibrium price for parking, they pay in other ways—with their time or by being denied parking altogether.

FIGURE 4.14

A Price Cap in a Market for Campus Parking Spaces

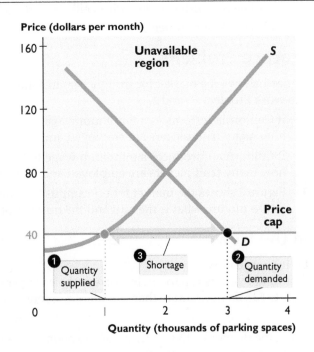

The college administration caps the price of parking at $40 a month.

❶ The number of parking spaces supplied is 1,000 spaces.

❷ The number of parking spaces demanded is 3,000.

❸ There is a shortage of 2,000 parking spaces.

Sticky Price

In most markets, a law or regulation does not restrict the price. But in some markets, the buyer and seller agree on a price for a fixed period; and in others, the seller sets a price that changes infrequently. For example, in some labor markets, firms enter into long-term contracts with labor unions that fix wage rates for at least one year and often for as many as three years. Borrowers and lenders often agree on an interest rate that is fixed for the term of a loan, which could be for as long as 30 years. And many commodities such as sugar, oil, and coal are traded on long-term contracts.

In these markets, the price adjustment process that is described in Figure 4.6 on p. 95 is slowed down. Prices do adjust, but not quickly enough to avoid shortages or surpluses.

If demand increases or if supply decreases after a price (or wage) contract is struck, a shortage arises. The quantity supplied is less than the quantity demanded, so the quantity supplied determines the quantity that is actually traded. Buyers' plans are frustrated. The price gradually rises as contracts come up for renewal, but in the intervening period, a shortage persists.

Similarly, if demand decreases or if supply increases after a price (or wage) contract is struck, a surplus arises. The quantity demanded is less than the quantity supplied, so the quantity demanded determines the quantity that is actually traded. Sellers' plans are frustrated. In the labor market, the sellers are workers, and some of them become unemployed. The price (or wage rate) gradually falls as contracts come up for renewal, but in the intervening period, a surplus and above-normal unemployment persist.

MyEconLab Study Plan 4.4
Key Terms Quiz
Solutions

FIGURE 1

FIGURE 2

FIGURE 3

CHECKPOINT 4.4

Explain how price floors, price ceilings, and sticky prices create surpluses, unemployment, and shortages.

Practice Problems

Figure 1 shows the market for fruit pickers in southern California. Use Figure 1 to work Problems **1** and **2**.

1. If California introduces a minimum wage for fruit pickers of $5 an hour, how many fruit pickers are employed and how many are unemployed?
2. If California introduces a minimum wage for fruit pickers of $8 an hour, how many fruit pickers are employed and how many are unemployed?
3. Figure 2 shows the market for on-campus housing. If a price cap is set at $600 a month, what is the rent and the number of apartments rented?

In the News

Living wage now
Fast-food workers call for an increase in their wage rate from about $8 an hour to $15 an hour, more than double the federal minimum wage.

Source: *The Age*, August 31, 2013

Using the demand and supply model, explain how a doubling of the current minimum wage rate will influence employment in the fast-food industry.

Solutions to Practice Problems

1. A minimum wage of $5 an hour is *below* the market equilibrium wage of $6 an hour, so pickers are paid $6 an hour. 4,000 fruit pickers are employed and there are no unemployed fruit pickers.
2. A minimum wage rate of $8 an hour is *above* the market equilibrium wage rate of $6 an hour (Figure 3). At $8 an hour, 3,000 fruit pickers are demanded and 5,000 pickers would like jobs, so there is a surplus of pickers. 3,000 pickers are employed at $8 an hour and 2,000 fruit pickers are unemployed.

FIGURE 4

3. The equilibrium rent is $800 a month. A price cap of $600 a month is *below* the equilibrium rent, so a shortage of apartments arises—1,000 apartments are supplied and 4,000 are demanded. The rent is $600 a month and 1,000 apartments are rented (Figure 4).

Solution to In the News

The current wage rate of fast-food workers is above the federal minimum wage and is the market equilibrium wage rate. The introduction of a $15 an hour minimum wage will decrease the quantity of fast-food workers demanded and increase the quantity supplied. Fast food outlets will employ fewer workers.

CHAPTER SUMMARY

Key Points

1. **Distinguish between quantity demanded and demand, and explain what determines demand.**

   - Other things remaining the same, the quantity demanded increases as the price falls and decreases as the price rises—the law of demand.
   - Changes in the prices of related goods, income, expectations about future prices and income, the number of buyers, and preferences change demand.

2. **Distinguish between quantity supplied and supply, and explain what determines supply.**

   - Other things remaining the same, the quantity supplied increases as the price rises and decreases as the price falls—the law of supply.
   - Changes in the prices of related goods, prices of resources and other inputs, expected future prices, the number of sellers, and productivity change supply.

3. **Explain how demand and supply determine price and quantity in a market, and explain the effects of changes in demand and supply.**

   - The price adjusts to maintain market equilibrium—to keep the quantity demanded equal to the quantity supplied. A surplus brings a fall in the price; a shortage brings a rise in the price.
   - An increase in demand increases both the price and the quantity; a decrease in demand decreases both the price and the quantity. An increase in supply increases the quantity but decreases the price; and a decrease in supply decreases the quantity but increases the price.

4. **Explain how price floors, price ceilings, and sticky prices cause surpluses, unemployment, and shortages.**

   - A price floor above the equilibrium price creates a surplus (unemployment in the labor market).
   - A price ceiling below the equilibrium price creates a shortage.
   - A sticky price brings a temporary shortage or surplus.

Key Terms

MyEconLab Key Terms Quiz

CHAPTER CHECKPOINT

Study Plan Problems and Applications

1. Explain how each of the following events changes the demand for or supply of air travel.
   - Airfares tumble, while long-distance bus fares don't change.
   - The price of jet fuel rises.
   - Airlines reduce the number of flights each day.
   - People expect airfares to increase next summer.
   - The price of train travel falls.
   - The price of a pound of air cargo increases.

Use the laws of demand and supply to explain whether the statements in Problems 2 and 3 are true or false. In your explanation, distinguish between a change in demand and a change in the quantity demanded and between a change in supply and a change in the quantity supplied.

2. The United States does not allow oranges from Brazil (the world's largest producer of oranges) to enter the United States. If Brazilian oranges were sold in the United States, oranges and orange juice would be cheaper.

3. If the price of frozen yogurt falls, the quantity of ice cream consumed will decrease and the price of ice cream will rise.

4. Table 1 shows the demand and supply schedules for running shoes. What is the market equilibrium? If the price is $70 a pair, describe the situation in the market. Explain how market equilibrium is restored. If a rise in income increases the demand for running shoes by 100 pairs a day at each price, explain how the market adjusts to its new equilibrium.

5. "As more people buy fuel-efficient hybrid cars, the demand for gasoline will decrease and the price of gasoline will fall. The fall in the price of gasoline will decrease the supply of gasoline." Is this statement true? Explain.

6. Table 2 shows the demand and supply schedules for student workers at campus venues. If the college introduces a minimum wage of $11.50 an hour, how many students are employed and how many students want work at a campus venue but can't find a job?

Use the following information to work Problems 7 and 8.

Pricier bread and cereal. Coming soon?
Wheat and corn prices surged last week and could hit the items in your grocery basket by mid-summer. It's a case of two extremes: drought in parts of the United States and in Europe have sparked fears of a supply crunch of wheat, while supplies of corn are being threatened by flooding and heavy rain in the Midwest.

Source: CNN Money, May 19, 2011

7. Explain why the drought will lead to a rise in the price of bread.

8. Use graphs to show why the price of corn has risen and show its effect on the price of cereals.

9. Read *Eye on Tuition* on p. 97 and explain how we know that tuition has risen because the demand for college places has increased and not because the supply has decreased.

TABLE 1

Price (dollars per pair)	Quantity demanded	Quantity supplied
	(pairs per day)	
60	1,000	400
70	900	500
80	800	600
90	700	700
100	600	800
110	500	900

TABLE 2

Wage rate (dollars per hour)	Quantity demanded	Quantity supplied
	(student workers)	
10.00	600	300
10.50	500	350
11.00	400	400
11.50	300	450
12.00	200	500
12.50	100	550

Instructor Assignable Problems and Applications

MyEconLab Homework, Quiz, or Test if assigned by instructor

1. Why can we be confident that the market for college education is competitive and that an increase in demand rather than the greed of college administrators is the reason for the ongoing rise in tuition?

2. What is the effect on the equilibrium price and equilibrium quantity of orange juice if the price of apple juice decreases and the wage rate paid to orange grove workers increases?

3. What is the effect on the equilibrium in the orange juice market if orange juice becomes more popular and a cheaper robot is used to pick oranges?

4. **Rain falls on wheat parade**
   The price of wheat has fallen from $9 a bushel to $7 a bushel in the past seven months as rain and snow fell on the southern states.

   Source: *The Wall Street Journal*, February 12, 2013

   Explain the effect of the fall in the wheat price on the market for cereals.

Table 1 shows the demand and supply schedules for boxes of chocolates in an average week. Use this information to work Problems 5 and 6.

5. If the price of chocolates is $17.00 a box, describe the situation in the market. Explain how market equilibrium is restored.

6. During Valentine's week, more people buy chocolates and chocolatiers offer their chocolates in special red boxes, which cost more to produce than the everyday box. Set out the three-step process of analysis and show on a graph the adjustment process to the new equilibrium. Describe the changes in the equilibrium price and the equilibrium quantity.

7. After a severe bout of foreclosures and defaults on home loans, banks made it harder for people to borrow. How does this change influence
   - The demand for new homes?
   - The supply of new homes?
   - The price of new homes?

   Illustrate your answer with a graphical analysis.

8. **Hong Kong introduces minimum wage**
   Hong Kong's first minimum wage is set at $HK28 an hour—$HK5 less than labor unions wanted, but $HK5 more than the employers had offered. About 315,000 people will be affected by the new wage.

   Source: *The Economist*, January 11, 2011

   What will be the effects of the minimum wage if the employers' offer is equal to the equilibrium wage? What will be the effects of the minimum wage if the labor unions' demand is equal to the equilibrium wage?

9. "As more people buy cell phones, the demand for cell-phone service increases and the price of cell-service falls, which decreases the supply of cell-phone service." Is this statement true or false? Explain.

10. **Steel output set for historic drop**
    Steel producers expect to cut output by 10 percent in response to cancelled orders from construction companies and car and appliance producers.

    Source: *The Financial Times*, December 28, 2008

    Explain how the cancellation of orders change the market for steel. What happens to the equilibrium price of steel?

TABLE 1

Price (dollars per box)	Quantity demanded	Quantity supplied
	(boxes per day)	
13.00	1,600	1,200
14.00	1,500	1,300
15.00	1,400	1,400
16.00	1,300	1,500
17.00	1,200	1,600
18.00	1,100	1,700

Multiple Choice Quiz

1. Which of the following events illustrates the law of demand? Other things remaining the same, a rise in the price of a good will _____.
   A. decrease the quantity demanded of that good
   B. increase the demand for a substitute of that good
   C. decrease the demand for the good
   D. increase the demand for a complement of that good

2. In the market for jeans, which of the following events increases the demand for a pair of jeans?
   A. The wage rate paid to garment workers rises.
   B. The price of a denim skirt (a substitute for jeans) rises.
   C. The price of denim cloth falls.
   D. New technology reduces the time it takes to make a pair of jeans.

3. Other things remaining the same, a fall in the price of peanuts will _____.
   A. increase the supply of peanuts
   B. decrease the supply of peanut butter
   C. decrease the quantity supplied of peanuts
   D. decrease the supply of peanuts

4. In the market for cell phones, which of the following events increases the supply of cell phones?
   A. New technology lowers the cost of making a cell phone
   B. A rise in the price of an e-book reader (a substitute in production)
   C. An increase in people's incomes
   D. A rise in the wage rate paid to electronics workers

5. When floods wiped out the banana crop in Central America, the equilibrium price of bananas _____ and the equilibrium quantity of bananas _____.
   A. rose; increased
   B. rose; decreased
   C. fell; increased
   D. fell; decreased

6. A decrease in the demand for chocolate with no change in supply will create a _____ of chocolate at today's price, but gradually the price will _____.
   A. surplus; fall
   B. shortage; fall
   C. surplus; rise
   D. shortage; rise

7. A minimum wage set above the market equilibrium wage rate _____.
   A. increases both employment and the quantity of labor supplied
   B. decreases unemployment and raises the wage rate of those employed
   C. raises the wage rate of those employed and increases the supply of jobs
   D. increases unemployment and decreases employment

8. A rent ceiling creates a _____ of housing if it _____ the equilibrium rent.
   A. surplus; is less than
   B. shortage; is less than
   C. surplus; exceeds
   D. shortage; exceeds

How do we track the booms and busts in our economy?

GDP: A Measure of Total Production and Income

5

CHAPTER CHECKLIST

When you have completed your study of this chapter, you will be able to

1 Define GDP and explain why the value of production, income, and expenditure are the same for an economy.

2 Describe how economic statisticians measure GDP and distinguish between nominal GDP and real GDP.

3 Describe the uses of real GDP and explain its limitations as a measure of the standard of living.

MyEconLab *Big Picture*

5.1 GDP, INCOME, AND EXPENDITURE

Where is the U.S. economy heading? Will it remain weak, begin to expand more rapidly, or sink into a deeper recession?

Everyone wants to know the answers to these questions. The people who make business decisions—homebuilders, auto producers, cell-phone service providers, airlines, oil producers, airplane makers, farmers, and retailers—want to know the answers so they can plan their production to align with demand. Governments want the answers because the amount of tax revenue that they collect depends on how much people earn and spend, which in turn depends on the state of the economy. Governments and the Federal Reserve want to know because they might be able to take actions that avoid excessive bust or boom. Ordinary citizens want the answers to plan their big decisions such as how long to remain in school, whether to rent or buy a new home, and how much to save toward retirement.

To assess the state of the economy we measure gross domestic product, or GDP. You're about to discover that GDP measures the value of total production, total income, and total expenditure.

■ GDP Defined

Gross domestic product (GDP)
The market value of all the final goods and services produced within a country in a given time period.

We measure total production as **gross domestic product,** or **GDP,** which is the market value of all the final goods and services produced within a country in a given time period. This definition has four parts, which we'll examine in turn.

Value Produced

To measure total production, we must add together the production of apples and oranges, bats and balls. Just counting the items doesn't get us very far. Which is the greater total production: 100 apples and 50 oranges or 50 apples and 100 oranges?

GDP answers this question by valuing items at their *market value*—at the prices at which the items are traded in markets. If the price of an apple is 10 cents and the price of an orange is 20 cents, the market value of 100 apples plus 50 oranges is $20 and the market value of 50 apples and 100 oranges is $25. By using market prices to value production, we can add the apples and oranges together.

What Produced

Final good or service
A good or service that is produced for its final user and not as a component of another good or service.

Intermediate good or service
A good or service that is used as a component of a final good or service.

A **final good or service** is something that is produced for its final user and not as a component of another good or service. A final good or service contrasts with an **intermediate good or service,** which is used as a component of a final good or service. For example, a Ford car is a final good, but a Firestone tire that Ford buys and installs on the car is an intermediate good. In contrast, if you buy a replacement Firestone tire for your car, then that tire is a final good. The same good can be either final or intermediate depending on how it is used.

GDP does not count the value of everything that is produced. With one exception, it includes only those items that are traded in markets and does not include the value of goods and services that people produce for their own use. For example, if you buy a car wash, the value produced is included in GDP. But if you wash your own car, your production is not counted as part of GDP. The exception is the market value of homes that people own. GDP puts a rental value on these homes and pretends that the owners rent their homes to themselves.

Where Produced

Only goods and services that are produced *within a country* count as part of that country's GDP. Nike Corporation, a U.S. firm, produces sneakers in Vietnam, and the market value of those shoes is part of Vietnam's GDP, not part of U.S. GDP. Toyota, a Japanese firm, produces automobiles in Georgetown, Kentucky, and the value of this production is part of U.S. GDP, not part of Japan's GDP.

When Produced

GDP measures the value of production *during a given time period.* This time period is either a quarter of a year—called the quarterly GDP data—or a year—called the annual GDP data. The Federal Reserve and others use the quarterly GDP data to keep track of the short-term evolution of the economy, and economists use the annual GDP data to examine long-term trends.

GDP measures not only the value of total production but also total income and total expenditure. The circular flow model that you studied in Chapter 2 explains why.

◼ Circular Flows in the U.S. Economy

Four groups buy the final goods and services produced: households, firms, governments, and the rest of the world. Four types of expenditure correspond to these groups:

- Consumption expenditure
- Investment
- Government expenditure on goods and services
- Net exports of goods and services

Consumption Expenditure

Consumption expenditure is the expenditure by households on consumption goods and services. It includes expenditures on *nondurable goods* such as orange juice and pizza, *durable goods* such as televisions and DVD players, and *services* such as rock concerts and haircuts. Consumption expenditure also includes house and apartment rents, including the rental value of owner-occupied housing.

Consumption expenditure
The expenditure by households on consumption goods and services.

Investment

Investment is the purchase of new *capital goods* (tools, instruments, machines, and buildings) and additions to inventories. Capital goods are *durable goods* produced by one firm and bought by another. Examples are PCs produced by Dell and bought by Ford Motor Company, and airplanes produced by Boeing and bought by United Airlines. Investment also includes the purchase of new homes by households.

Investment
The purchase of new *capital goods* (tools, instruments, machines, buildings) and additions to inventories.

At the end of a year, some of a firm's output might remain unsold. For example, if Ford produces 4 million cars and sells 3.9 million of them, the other 0.1 million (100,000) cars remain unsold. In this case, Ford's inventory of cars increases by 100,000. When a firm adds unsold output to inventory, we count those items as part of investment.

It is important to note that investment does *not* include the purchase of stocks and bonds. In macroeconomics, we reserve the term "investment" for the purchase of new capital goods and the additions to inventories.

Government Expenditure on Goods and Services

Government expenditure on goods and services
The expenditure by all levels of government on goods and services.

Government expenditure on goods and services is expenditure by all levels of government on goods and services. For example, the U.S. Defense Department buys missiles and other weapons systems, the State Department buys travel services, the White House buys Internet services, and state and local governments buy cruisers for law enforcement officers.

Net Exports of Goods and Services

Net exports of goods and services
The value of exports of goods and services minus the value of imports of goods and services.

Exports of goods and services
Items that firms in the United States produce and sell to the rest of the world.

Imports of goods and services
Items that households, firms, and governments in the United States buy from the rest of the world.

Net exports of goods and services is the value of exports of goods and services minus the value of imports of goods and services. **Exports of goods and services** are items that firms in the United States produce and sell to the rest of the world. **Imports of goods and services** are items that households, firms, and governments in the United States buy from the rest of the world. Imports are produced in other countries, so expenditure on imports is not included in expenditure on U.S.-produced goods and services. If exports exceed imports, net exports are positive and expenditure on U.S.-produced goods and services increases. If imports exceed exports, net exports are negative and expenditure on U.S.-produced goods and services decreases.

Total Expenditure

Total expenditure on goods and services produced in the United States is the sum of the four items that you've just examined. We call consumption expenditure C, investment I, government expenditure on goods and services G, and net exports of goods and services NX. So total expenditure, which is also the total amount received by the producers of final goods and services, is

$$\text{Total expenditure} = C + I + G + NX.$$

Income

Labor earns wages, capital earns interest, land earns rent, and entrepreneurship earns profits. Households receive these incomes. Some part of total income, called *undistributed profit,* is a combination of interest and profit that firms retain and do not pay to households. But from an economic viewpoint, undistributed profit is income paid to households and then loaned to firms.

■ Expenditure Equals Income

Figure 5.1 shows the circular flows of income and expenditure that we've just described. The figure is based on Figures 2.4 and 2.5 (on p. 47 and p. 49), but it includes some more details and additional flows.

    We call total income Y and show it by the blue flow from firms to households. When households receive their incomes, they pay some in taxes and save some. Some households receive benefits from governments. **Net taxes** equal taxes paid minus cash benefits received and are the green flow from households to governments labeled NT. **Saving** is the amount of income that is not paid in net taxes or spent on consumption goods and services. Saving flows from households to financial markets and is the green flow labeled S. These two green flows are not expenditures on goods and services. They are just flows of money. Because households allocate all their incomes after paying net taxes to consumption and saving,

Net taxes
Taxes paid minus cash benefits received from governments.

Saving
The amount of income that is not paid in net taxes or spent on consumption goods and services.

$$Y = C + S + NT.$$

The red flows show the four expenditure flows: consumption expenditure from households to firms, government expenditure from governments to firms, and net exports from the rest of the world to firms. Investment flows from the financial markets, where firms borrow, to the firms that produce capital goods.

Because firms pay out everything they receive as incomes to the factors of production, total expenditure equals total income. That is,

$$Y = C + I + G + NX.$$

From the viewpoint of firms, the value of production is the cost of production, which equals income. From the viewpoint of purchasers of goods and services, the value of production is the cost of buying it, which equals expenditure. So

The value of production equals income equals expenditure.

The circular flow and the equality of income and expenditure provide two approaches to measuring GDP that we'll study in the next section.

FIGURE 5.1

The Circular Flow of Income and Expenditure   MyEconLab Animation

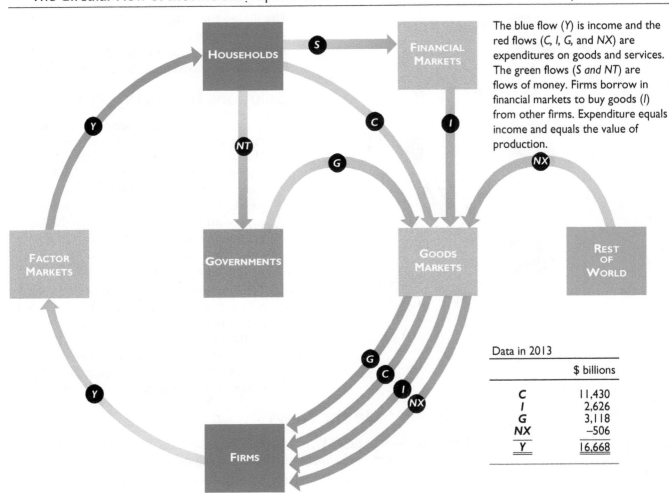

The blue flow (*Y*) is income and the red flows (*C, I, G,* and *NX*) are expenditures on goods and services. The green flows (*S and NT*) are flows of money. Firms borrow in financial markets to buy goods (*I*) from other firms. Expenditure equals income and equals the value of production.

Data in 2013

	$ billions
C	11,430
I	2,626
G	3,118
NX	−506
Y	16,668

MyEconLab Study Plan 5.1
Key Terms Quiz
Solutions

CHECKPOINT 5.1

Define GDP and explain why the value of production, income, and expenditure are the same for an economy.

Practice Problems

LIST 1

- Banking services bought by a student
- New cars bought by Hertz, the car rental firm
- Newsprint bought by *USA Today* from International Paper
- The purchase of a new aircraft for the vice president
- New house bought by Beyoncé

1. Classify each of the items in List 1 as a final good or service or as an intermediate good or service and identify which is a component of consumption expenditure, investment, or government expenditure on goods and services.

2. Figure 1 shows the flows of expenditure and income on Lotus Island. In 2013, *R* was $10 billion; *W* was $30 billion; *U* was $12 billion; *X* was $15 billion; and *Z* was $3 billion. Calculate total expenditure and total income.

In the News

U.S. economy grew slower in spring than previously reported
Real GDP increased at an annual rate of 1.0 percent in the second quarter of 2011. Investment, exports, consumption expenditure, and government expenditure increased faster than 1.0 percent.

Source: BEA News Release, August 26, 2011

Use Figure 1 to indicate the flows in which the items in the news clip occur. How can GDP increase by 1.0 percent if the other items in the news clip increased faster than 1.0 percent?

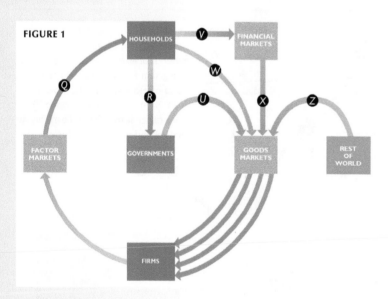

FIGURE 1

Solutions to Practice Problems

1. The student's banking service is a final service and part of consumption expenditure. Hertz's new cars are additions to capital, so they are part of investment and final goods. Newsprint is an input into the newspaper, so it is an intermediate good and not a final expenditure. The new aircraft for the vice president is a final good and part of government expenditure. The new house is a final good and part of investment.

2. Total expenditure is the sum of *C*, *I*, *G*, and *NX*. In Figure 1, *C* is the flow *W*; *I* is the flow *X*; *G* is the flow *U*; and *NX* is the flow *Z*. So total expenditure equals $W + X + U + Z$, which is $60 billion. Total income is the blue flow, *Q*. But total income equals total expenditure, so total income is $60 billion.

Solution to In the News

GDP is the sum of flows *W*, *X*, *U*, and *Z*. Investment is *X*, consumption expenditure is *W*, government expenditure is *U*, and exports are part of *Z*.

$GDP = C + I + G + X - M$, so if $C + I + G + X$ grew faster than 1 percent, then *M* must have grown faster than $C + I + G + X$.

5.2   MEASURING U.S. GDP

MyEconLab Snapshot

U.S. GDP is the market value of all the final goods and services produced within the United States during a year. In 2013, U.S. GDP was $16.7 trillion. The Bureau of Economic Analysis in the U.S. Department of Commerce measures GDP by using two approaches:

- Expenditure approach
- Income approach

■ The Expenditure Approach

The expenditure approach measures GDP by using data on consumption expenditure, investment, government expenditure on goods and services, and net exports. This approach is like attaching a meter to the circular flow diagram on all the flows running through the goods markets to firms and measuring the magnitudes of those flows. Table 5.1 shows this approach. The first column gives the terms used in the U.S. National Income and Product Accounts. The next column gives the symbols we used in the previous section.

Using the expenditure approach, GDP is the sum of consumption expenditure on goods and services (C), investment (I), government expenditure on goods and services (G), and net exports of goods and services (NX). The third column gives the expenditures in 2013. GDP measured by the expenditure approach was $16,668 billion (the data are for the second quarter of 2013).

Net exports were negative in 2013 because imports exceeded exports. Imports were $2,748 billion and exports were $2,242 billion, so net exports—exports minus imports—were −$506 billion as shown in the table.

The fourth column in Table 5.1 shows the relative magnitudes of the expenditures. Consumption expenditure is by far the largest component of total expenditure; government expenditure is the next largest. Investment and exports are a similar size; and net exports is the smallest component. In 2013, consumption expenditure was 68.6 percent, investment was 15.8 percent, government expenditure was 18.7 percent, and net exports were a negative 3.0 percent of GDP.

■ **TABLE 5.1**

GDP: The Expenditure Approach

MyEconLab Real-time data

Item	Symbol	Amount in 2013 (second quarter) (billions of dollars)	Percentage of GDP
Consumption expenditure	C	11,430	68.6
Investment	I	2,626	15.8
Government expenditure	G	3,118	18.7
Net exports	NX	−506	−3.0
GDP	Y	16,668	100.0

The expenditure approach measures GDP by adding together consumption expenditure (C), investment (I), government expenditure (G), and net exports (NX).

In 2013, GDP measured by the expenditure approach was $16,668 billion.

SOURCE OF DATA: U.S. Department of Commerce, Bureau of Economic Analysis.

Expenditures Not in GDP

Total expenditure (and GDP) does not include all the things that people and businesses buy. GDP is the value of *final goods and services,* so spending that is *not* on final goods and services is not part of GDP. Spending on intermediate goods and services is not part of GDP, although it is not always obvious whether an item is an intermediate good or a final good (see *Eye on the U.S. Economy* below). Also, we do not count as part of GDP spending on

- Used goods
- Financial assets

Used Goods   Expenditure on used goods is not part of GDP because these goods were part of GDP in the period in which they were produced and during which time they were new goods. For example, a 2010 automobile was part of GDP in 2010. If the car is traded on the used car market in 2014, the amount paid for the car is not part of GDP in 2014.

Financial Assets   When households buy financial assets such as bonds and stocks, they are making loans, not buying goods and services. The expenditure on newly produced capital goods is part of GDP, but the purchase of financial assets is not.

EYE on the U.S. ECONOMY
Is a Computer Program an Intermediate Good or a Final Good?

When American Airlines buys a new reservations software package, is that like General Motors buying tires? If it is, then software is an *intermediate good* and it is not counted as part of GDP. Airline ticket sales, like GM cars, are part of GDP, but the intermediate goods that are used to produce air transportation or cars are *not* part of GDP.

Or when American Airlines buys new software, is that like General Motors buying a new assembly-line robot? If it is, then the software is a capital good and its purchase is the purchase of a final good. In this case, the software purchase is an *investment* and it *is* counted as part of GDP.

Brent Moulton worked as a government economist in the Bureau of Economic Analysis (BEA). Moulton's job was to oversee periodic adjustments to the GDP estimates to incorporate new data and new ideas about the economy.

The biggest change made was in how the purchase of computer software by firms is classified. Before 1999, it was regarded as an *intermediate good.* But since 1999, it has been treated as an *investment.*

How big a deal is this? When the BEA recalculated the 1996 GDP, the change increased the estimate of the 1996 GDP by $115 billion. That is a lot of money. To put it in perspective: GDP

in 1996 was $7,662 billion. So the adjustment was 1.5 percent of GDP.

This change is a good example of the ongoing effort by the BEA to keep the GDP measure as accurate as possible.

■ The Income Approach

To measure GDP using the income approach, the Bureau of Economic Analysis uses income data collected by the Internal Revenue Service and other agencies. The BEA takes the incomes that firms pay households for the services of the factors of production they hire—wages for labor services, interest for the use of capital, rent for the use of land, and profits for entrepreneurship—and sums those incomes. This approach is like attaching a meter to the circular flow diagram on all the flows running through factor markets from firms to households and measuring the magnitudes of those flows. Let's see how the income approach works.

The U.S. National Income and Product Accounts divide incomes into two big categories:

- Wage income
- Interest, rent, and profit income

Wage Income

Wage income, called *compensation of employees* in the national accounts, is the total payment for labor services. It includes net wages and salaries plus fringe benefits paid by employers such as health-care insurance, Social Security contributions, and pension fund contributions.

Interest, Rent, and Profit Income

Interest, rent, and profit income, called *net operating surplus* in the national accounts, is the total income earned by capital, land, and entrepreneurship.

Interest income is the interest that households receive on capital. A household's capital is equal to its net worth—its assets minus its borrowing.

Rent includes payments for the use of land and other rented factors of production. It includes payments for rented housing and imputed rent for owner-occupied housing. (Imputed rent is an estimate of what homeowners would pay to rent the housing they own and use themselves. By including this item in the national accounts, we measure the total value of housing services, whether they are owned or rented.)

Profit includes the profits of corporations and the incomes of proprietors who run their own businesses. These incomes are a mixture of interest and profit.

Table 5.2 shows the relative magnitudes of these components of incomes.

Net Domestic Product at Factor Cost

The sum of wages, interest, rent, and profit is *net domestic product at factor cost*. Net domestic product at factor cost is not GDP, and we must make two further adjustments to get to GDP: one from factor cost to market prices and another from net product to gross product.

From Factor Cost to Market Price

The expenditure approach values goods and services at market prices, and the income approach values them at factor cost—the cost of the factors of production used to produce them. Indirect taxes (such as sales taxes) and subsidies (payments by government to firms) make these two values differ. Sales taxes make market prices exceed factor cost, and subsidies make factor cost exceed market prices. To convert the value at factor cost to the value at market prices, we must add indirect taxes and subtract subsidies.

TABLE 5.2

GDP: The Income Approach

The sum of all incomes equals net domestic product at factor cost. The income approach measure of GDP equals net domestic product at factor cost plus indirect taxes less subsidies plus depreciation (capital consumption).

In 2013, GDP measured by the income approach was $16,668 billion. This amount is $154 billion more than GDP measured by the expenditure approach—a statistical discrepancy of −$154 billion.

Wages are by far the largest part of total income.

Item	Amount in 2013 (second quarter) (billions of dollars)	Percentage of GDP
Wages (compensation of employees)	8,820	52.9
Interest, rent, and profit (net operating surplus)	4,290	25.7
Net domestic product at factor cost	13,110	78.7
Indirect taxes less subsidies	1,080	6.5
Depreciation (capital consumption)	2,632	15.8
GDP (income approach)	16,822	100.9
Statistical discrepancy	−154	−0.9
GDP (expenditure approach)	16,668	100.0

SOURCE OF DATA: U.S. Department of Commerce, Bureau of Economic Analysis.

Depreciation
The decrease in the value of capital that results from its use and from obsolescence.

From Net Product to Gross Product

The income approach measures *net* product and the expenditure approach measures *gross* product. The difference is **depreciation,** which is the decrease in the value of capital that results from its use and from obsolescence. Firms' profits, which are included in the income approach, are net of depreciation, so the income approach gives a *net* measure. Investment, which is included in the expenditure approach, includes the purchase of capital to replace worn out or obsolete capital, so the expenditure approach gives a *gross* measure. To get *gross* domestic product from the income approach, we must *add* depreciation to total income.

Statistical Discrepancy

The expenditure approach and income approach do not deliver exactly the same estimate of GDP. If a taxi driver doesn't report all his tips, they get missed in the income approach, but they get caught by the expenditure approach when he spends his income. So the sum of expenditures might exceed the sum of incomes. But most income gets reported to the Internal Revenue Service on tax returns while many items of expenditure are not recorded and must be estimated. So the sum of incomes might exceed the sum of estimated expenditures.

The discrepancy between the expenditure approach and the income approach estimates of GDP is called the *statistical discrepancy,* and it is calculated as the GDP expenditure total minus the GDP income total.

The two measures of GDP provide a check on the accuracy of the numbers. If the two are wildly different, we will want to know what mistakes we've made. Have we omitted some item? Have we counted something twice? The fact that the two estimates are close gives some confidence that they are reasonably accurate. But the expenditure total is regarded as the more reliable estimate of GDP, so the discrepancy is added to or subtracted from income to reconcile the two estimates.

Table 5.2 summarizes the calculation of GDP using the income approach and its reconcilation with GDP using the expenditure approach. The table also shows the relative magnitudes of the components of the income measure.

■ GDP and Related Measures of Production and Income

Although GDP is the main measure of total production, you will sometimes encounter another: gross *national* product or GNP.

Gross National Product

A country's *gross national product*, or *GNP*, is the market value of all the final goods and services produced anywhere in the world in a given time period by the factors of production supplied by the residents of that country. For example, Nike's income from the capital that it supplies to its Vietnam shoe factory is part of U.S. GNP but not part of U.S. GDP. It is part of Vietnam's GDP. Similarly, Toyota's income on the capital it supplies to its Kentucky auto plant is part of U.S. GDP but not part of U.S. GNP. It is part of Japan's GNP.

GNP equals GDP plus net factor income received from or paid to other countries. The difference between U.S. GDP and GNP is small. But in an oil-rich Middle Eastern country such as Bahrain, where a large amount of capital is owned by foreigners, GNP is much smaller than GDP; and in a poor country such as Bangladesh, whose people work abroad and send income home, GNP is much larger than GDP.

Disposable Personal Income

You've seen that consumption expenditure is the largest component of aggregate expenditure. The main influence on consumption expenditure is *disposable personal income*, which is the income received by households minus personal income taxes paid. Because disposable personal income plays an important role in influencing spending, the national accounts measure this item along with a number of intermediate totals that you can see in Figure 5.2. This figure shows how disposable personal income is calculated and how it relates to GDP and GNP.

FIGURE 5.2

GDP and Related Product and Income Measures

MyEconLab Animation

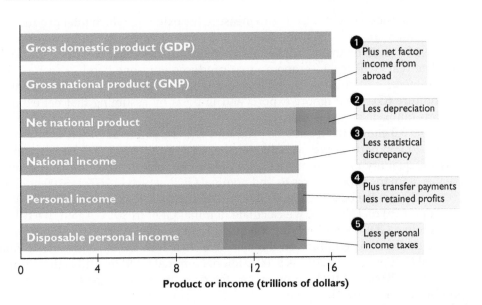

Product or income (trillions of dollars)

The bars show six related product and income measures and the relationship among them.

❶ Add net factor income from abroad to GDP to get GNP.

❷ Subtract depreciation from GNP to get net national product.

❸ Subtract the statistical discrepancy between the expenditure and income measures (almost invisible in the figure because it is tiny) to get national income.

❹ Add transfer payments by governments less profits retained by firms to get personal income.

❺ Finally, subtract personal income taxes to get disposable personal income.

SOURCE OF DATA: U.S. Department of Commerce, Bureau of Economic Analysis.

Real GDP and Nominal GDP

You've seen that GDP measures total expenditure on final goods and services in a given period. Suppose that we want to compare GDP in two periods, say 2009 and 2013. In 2009, GDP was $14,418 billion and by 2013, it was $16,668 billion—14 percent higher than in 2009. What does this 14 percent increase mean?

The answer is a combination of two things:

* We produced more goods and services.
* We paid higher prices for our goods and services.

Producing more goods and services contributes to an improvement in our standard of living. Paying higher prices means that our *cost of living* has increased but our standard of living has not. So it matters a great deal why GDP has increased. If the 14 percent increase is accounted for mainly by higher prices, our standard of living hasn't changed much. But if the 14 percent increase is accounted for mainly by the production of more goods and services, our standard of living might have increased a lot.

You're now going to see how economists at the Bureau of Economic Analysis isolate the effects on GDP of an increase in production. Their first step is to distinguish between two GDP concepts: real GDP and nominal GDP.

Real GDP is the value of the final goods and services produced in a given year expressed in terms of the prices in a *reference base year*. The *reference base year* is the year we choose against which to compare all other years. In the United States today, the *reference base year* is 2009.

Real GDP contrasts with **nominal GDP,** which is the value of the final goods and services produced in a given year expressed in terms of the prices of that same year. Nominal GDP is just a more precise name for GDP.

The method used to calculate real GDP has changed in recent years and is now a bit technical, but the essence of the calculation hasn't changed. Here, we describe the essence of the calculation. An appendix to this chapter describes the technical details of the method used by the Bureau of Economic Analysis.

Calculating Real GDP

The goal of calculating *real GDP* is to measure the extent to which total production has increased and remove from the nominal GDP numbers the influence of price changes. To focus on the principles and keep the numbers easy to work with, we'll calculate real GDP for an economy that produces only one good in each of the GDP categories: consumption expenditure (C), investment (I), and government expenditure (G). We'll ignore exports and imports by assuming that net exports (exports minus imports) is zero.

Table 5.3 shows the quantities produced and the prices in 2009 (the *base year*) and in 2013. In part (a), we calculate nominal GDP in 2009. For each item, we multiply the quantity produced by its price to find the total expenditure on the item. We then sum the expenditures to find nominal GDP, which in 2009 is $100 million. Because 2009 is the base year, real GDP and nominal GDP are equal in 2009.

In part (b) of Table 5.3, we calculate nominal GDP in 2013. Again, we calculate nominal GDP by multiplying the quantity of each item produced by its price to find the total expenditure on the item. We then sum the expenditures to find nominal GDP, which in 2013 is $300 million. Nominal GDP in 2013 is three times its value in 2009. But by how much has the quantity of final goods and services produced increased? That's what real GDP will tell us.

Real GDP
The value of the final goods and services produced in a given year expressed in terms of the prices in a base year.

Nominal GDP
The value of the final goods and services produced in a given year expressed in terms of the prices of that same year.

TABLE 5.3

Calculating Nominal GDP and Real GDP in 2009 and 2013

	Item	Quantity (millions of units)	Price (dollars per unit)	Expenditure (millions of dollars)
(a) In 2009				
C	T-shirts	10	5	50
I	Computer chips	3	10	30
G	Security services	1	20	20
Y	Real GDP and Nominal GDP in 2009			100
(b) In 2013				
C	T-shirts	4	5	20
I	Computer chips	2	20	40
G	Security services	6	40	240
Y	Nominal GDP in 2013			300
(c) Quantities of 2013 valued at prices of 2009				
C	T-shirts	4	5	20
I	Computer chips	2	10	20
G	Security services	6	20	120
Y	Real GDP in 2013			160

The base year is 2009, so real GDP and nominal GDP are equal in that year.

Between 2009 and 2013, the production of security services (G) increased, but the production of T-shirts (C) and computer chips (I) decreased. In the same period, the price of a T-shirt remained constant, but the other two prices doubled.

Nominal GDP increased from $100 million in 2009 in part (a) to $300 million in 2013 in part (b).

Real GDP in part (c), which is calculated by using the quantities of 2013 in part (b) and the prices of 2009 in part (a), increased from $100 million in 2009 to $160 million in 2013, a 60 percent increase.

In part (c) of Table 5.3, we calculate real GDP in 2013. You can see that the quantity of each good and service produced in part (c) is the same as that in part (b). They are the quantities of 2013. You can also see that the prices in part (c) are the same as those in part (a). They are the prices of the base year—2009.

For each item, we now multiply the quantity produced in 2013 by its price in 2009 to find what the total expenditure would have been in 2013 if prices had remained the same as they were in 2009. We then sum these expenditures to find real GDP in 2013, which is $160 million.

Nominal GDP in 2013 is three times its value in 2009, but real GDP in 2013 is only 1.6 times its 2009 value—a 60 percent increase in *real* GDP.

Using the Real GDP Numbers

In the example that we've just worked through, we found the value of real GDP in 2013 based on the prices of 2009. This number alone enables us to compare production in two years only. By repeating the calculation that we have done for 2013 using the data for each year between 2009 and 2013, we can calculate the *annual percentage change* of real GDP—the annual growth rate of real GDP. This is the most common use of the real GDP numbers. Also, by calculating real GDP every three months—known as *quarterly real GDP*—the Bureau of Economic Analysis is able to provide valuable information that is used to interpret the current state of the economy. This information is used to guide both government macroeconomic policy and business production and investment decisions.

MyEconLab Study Plan 5.2
Key Terms Quiz
Solutions

CHECKPOINT 5.2

Describe how economic statisticians measure GDP and distinguish between nominal GDP and real GDP.

Practice Problems

Table 1 shows some of the items in the U.S. National Income and Product Accounts in 2010. Use Table 1 to work Problems 1 to 3.

1. Use the expenditure approach to calculate U.S. GDP in 2010.
2. What was U.S. GDP as measured by the income approach in 2010? By how much did gross domestic product and net domestic product differ in 2010?
3. Calculate U.S. GNP and U.S. national income in 2010.
4. Table 2 shows some data for an economy. If the base year is 2013, calculate the economy's nominal GDP and real GDP in 2014.

TABLE 1

Item	Amount (trillions of dollars)
Consumption expenditure	10.2
Government expenditure	3.1
Indirect taxes less subsidies	1.0
Depreciation	1.9
Net factor income from abroad	0.2
Investment	1.7
Net exports	−0.5
Statistical discrepancy	0

TABLE 2

(a) In 2013:

Item	Quantity	Price
Apples	60	$0.50
Oranges	80	$0.25

(b) In 2014:

Item	Quantity	Price
Apples	160	$1.00
Oranges	220	$2.00

In the News

Factory orders fell 4 percent in March

The Commerce Department reported orders for manufactured goods decreased 4 percent, with nondurable goods falling 2.4 percent and durable goods falling 5.8 percent, while business inventories of durable goods increased 0.9 percent.

Source: *The Wall Street Journal*, May 3, 2013

Which component of GDP changes when sales of (i) nondurable goods fall and (ii) durable goods fall, and (iii) inventories of durable goods increase? Provide an example of each item of expenditure.

Solutions to Practice Problems

1. GDP was $14.5 trillion. The expenditure approach sums the expenditure on final goods and services. That is, GDP = $C + I + G + NX$.
   In 2010, U.S. GDP = ($10.2 + $1.7 + $3.1 − $0.5) trillion = $14.5 trillion.

2. GDP as measured by the income approach was $14.5 trillion. With the statistical discrepancy zero, GDP (expenditure approach) = GDP (income approach). Gross domestic product minus net domestic product equals depreciation, which was $1.9 trillion.

3. GNP = GDP + Net factor income from abroad. In 2010, GNP was $14.7 trillion ($14.5 trillion + $0.2 trillion). National income = GNP − Depreciation, which equals $14.7 trillion − $1.9 trillion = $12.8 trillion.

4. Nominal GDP in 2014 equals (160 apples × $1) + (220 oranges × $2) = $600. Real GDP in 2014 at 2013 prices equals (160 apples × $0.50 per apple) + (220 oranges × $0.25 per orange) = $135.

Solution to In the News

(i) Nondurable goods, such as gasoline and coffee bought by households, are part of consumption expenditure, C. (ii) Durable goods, such as iPhones bought by households, are part of consumption expenditure, C, and durable goods, such as aircraft bought by firms, are part of investment, I. (iii) An inventory of durable goods, such as the auto parts at a Ford plant, is part of investment, I.

5.3   THE USES AND LIMITATIONS OF REAL GDP

We use estimates of real GDP for three main purposes:

- To compare the standard of living over time
- To track the course of the business cycle
- To compare the standard of living among countries

■ The Standard of Living Over Time

A nation's *standard of living* is measured by the value of goods and services that its people enjoy, *on average*. Income per person determines what people can afford to buy and real GDP is a measure of real income. So *real GDP per person*—real GDP divided by the population—is a commonly used measure for comparing the standard of living over time.

Real GDP per person tells us the value of goods and services that the average person can enjoy. By using *real* GDP, we remove any influence that rising prices and a rising cost of living might have had on our comparison.

A handy way of comparing real GDP per person over time is to express it as a ratio of its value in some reference year. Table 5.4 provides the numbers for the United States that compare 2013 with 53 years earlier, 1960. In 1960, real GDP per person was $17,212 and in 2013 it was $49,636, or 2.9 times its 1960 level. To the extent that real GDP per person measures the standard of living, people were 2.9 times as well off in 2013 as their grandparents had been in 1960.

Figure 5.3 shows the entire 53 years of real GDP per person from 1960 to 2013 and displays two features of our changing standard of living:

1. The growth of potential GDP per person
2. Fluctuations of real GDP per person around potential GDP

Potential GDP is the level of real GDP when all the economy's factors of production—labor, capital, land, and entrepreneurial ability—are fully employed. When some factors of production are *unemployed*, real GDP is *below* potential GDP. And when some factors of production are *over-employed* and working harder and for longer hours than can be maintained in the long run, real GDP *exceeds* potential GDP.

You've seen that real GDP per person in 2013 was 2.9 times that of 1960. But in 2013, some labor and other factors of production were unemployed and the economy was producing less than potential GDP. To measure the trend in the standard of living, we must remove the influence of short-term fluctuations and focus on the path of potential GDP.

The growth rate of potential GDP fluctuates less than the growth rate of real GDP. During the 1960s, potential GDP per person grew at an average rate of 2.8 percent a year, but since 1970, its growth rate has slowed to 1.9 percent a year. This growth slowdown means that potential GDP is lower today (and lower by a large amount) than it would have been if the 1960s growth rate could have been maintained. If potential GDP had kept growing at the 1960s pace, potential GDP per person in 2013 would have been $30,000 more than it actually was. The cumulatively lost income from the growth slowdown of the 1970s is a staggering $406,000 per person. Understanding the reasons for the growth slowdown is one of the major tasks of macroeconomists.

TABLE 5.4   REAL GDP PER PERSON IN 1960 AND 2013

Year	1960	2013
Real GDP (billions)	$3,106	$15,680
Population (millions)	180.4	315.9
Real GDP per person	$17,212	$49,636

Potential GDP
The value of real GDP when all the economy's factors of production—labor, capital, land, and entrepreneurial ability—are fully employed.

■ **FIGURE 5.3**

Real GDP and Potential GDP Per Person in the United States: 1960–2013   MyEconLab Animation

Real GDP grows and fluctuates around the growth path of potential GDP. Potential GDP per person grew at an annual rate of 2.8 percent during the 1960s and slowed to 1.9 percent after 1970.

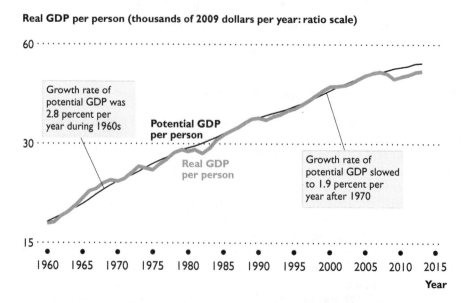

SOURCES OF DATA: Bureau of Economic Analysis and the Congressional Budget Office.

■ Tracking the Course of the Business Cycle

Business cycle
A periodic but irregular up-and-down movement of total production and other measures of economic activity.

We call the fluctuations in the pace of economic activity the business cycle. A **business cycle** is a periodic but irregular up-and-down movement of total production and other measures of economic activity such as employment and income. The business cycle isn't a regular, predictable, and repeating cycle like the phases of the moon. The timing and the intensity of the business cycle vary a lot, but every cycle has two phases:

1. Expansion
2. Recession

and two turning points:

1. Peak
2. Trough

Recession
A period during which real GDP decreases for at least two successive quarters; or defined by the NBER as "a period of significant decline in total output, income, employment, and trade, usually lasting from six months to a year, and marked by contractions in many sectors of the economy."

Figure 5.4 shows these features of the most recent U.S. business cycle using real GDP as the measure of economic activity. An *expansion* is a period during which real GDP increases. In the early stage of an expansion, real GDP remains below potential GDP and as the expansion progresses, real GDP eventually exceeds potential GDP.

A common definition of **recession** is a period during which real GDP decreases—its growth rate is negative—for at least two successive quarters. The National Bureau of Economic Research (NBER), which dates the U.S. business cycle phases and turning points, defines a recession more broadly as "a significant decline in economic activity spread across the economy, lasting more than a few

FIGURE 5.4

The Most Recent U.S. Business Cycle   MyEconLab Real-time data

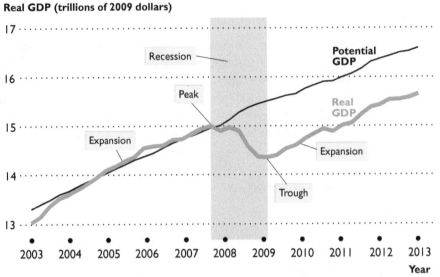

SOURCES OF DATA: Bureau of Economic Analysis, the Congressional Budget Office, and the National Bureau of Economic Research.

The most recent business cycle peak was in the fourth quarter of 2007 and the trough was in the second quarter of 2009 after which a new expansion began. Between the peak and the trough, the economy was in a recession. The recession was extremely deep and the expansion that followed was extremely weak—real GDP has remained a long way below potential GDP.

months, normally visible in real GDP, real income, employment, industrial production, and wholesale-retail sales." This definition means that sometimes the NBER declares a recession even though real GDP has not decreased for two successive quarters. A recession in 2001 was such a recession. An expansion ends and a recession begins at a business cycle peak. A peak is the highest level of real GDP that has been attained up to that time. A recession ends at a trough when real GDP reaches a low point and from which a new expansion begins.

The shaded bar in Figure 5.4 highlights the 2008–2009 recession. This recession was unusually severe. It lowered real GDP to its 2005 level. The end of a recession isn't the end of pain. When an expansion begins, real GDP is below potential GDP. And even after two years into the expansion that followed the 2008–2009 recession, real GDP had not returned to its previous peak level and the gap between real GDP and potential GDP was wide.

The period that began in 1991 following a severe recession and that ended with the global financial crisis of 2008 was so free from serious downturns in real GDP and other indicators of economic activity that it was called the *Great Moderation*, a name that contrasts it with the Great Depression. Some starry-eyed optimists even began to declare that the business cycle was dead. This long period of expansion also turned the attention of macroeconomists away from the business cycle and toward a focus on economic growth and the possibility of achieving faster growth.

But the 2008–2009 recession put the business cycle back on the agenda. Economists were criticized for not predicting it, and old divisions among economists that many thought were healed erupted in the pages of *The Economist* and *The New York Times* and online on a host of blogs.

We'll be examining the causes of recession and the alternative views among economists in greater detail as you progress through the rest of your study of macroeconomics.

EYE on the BOOMS AND BUSTS

How Do We Track the Booms and Busts of our Economy?

The National Bureau of Economic Research (NBER) Business Cycle Dating Committee determines the dates of U.S. business cycle turning points.

To identify the date of a business cycle peak, the NBER committee looks at data on industrial production, total employment, real GDP, and wholesale and retail sales.

Of these variables, real GDP is the most reliable measure of aggregate domestic production.

But when the NBER committee met in November 2008 to determine when the economy went into recession, the two measures of real GDP—the expenditure approach and the income approach—told conflicting stories.

For a few quarters in 2007 and 2008, because of the statistical discrepancy, the two estimates of real GDP did "not speak clearly about the date of a peak in activity."

So the NBER committee looked closely at the data on real personal income, real manufacturing, wholesale and retail sales, industrial production, and employment. All of these data peaked between November 2007 and June 2008. Weighing all the evidence, the committee decided that November 2007 was the peak.

But as the figure shows, real GDP didn't begin a sustained fall until the second quarter of 2008.

In contrast to the difficult task of dating the cycle peak, the trough was clear. It occured in the second quarter of 2009.

Real GDP (trillions of 2009 dollars)

SOURCES OF DATA: Bureau of Economic Analysis and the National Bureau of Economic Research.

Let's now leave comparisons of the standard of living over time and business cycles and briefly see how we compare the standard of living among countries.

■ The Standard of Living Among Countries

To use real GDP per person to compare the standard of living among countries, we must convert the numbers for other countries into U.S. dollars. To calculate real GDP, we must also use a common set of prices—called *purchasing power parity prices*—for all countries. The International Monetary Fund performs these calculations and if you turn back to Figure 2.3 on p. 44 you can see some comparisons based on these data. They tell, for example, that an average American has a standard of living (income per person) almost 6 times that of an average person in China.

Real GDP provides an easy way of comparing living standards. But real GDP doesn't include *all* the goods and services produced. Also, real GDP has nothing to say about factors other than the goods and services that affect the standard of living. Let's explore these limitations of real GDP.

■ Goods and Services Omitted from GDP

GDP measures the value of goods and services that are bought in markets. GDP excludes

- Household production
- Underground production
- Leisure time
- Environment quality

Household Production

Household production is the production of goods and services (mainly services) in the home. Examples of this production are preparing meals, changing a light bulb, cutting grass, washing a car, and helping a student with homework. Because we don't buy these services in markets, they are not counted as part of GDP. The result is that GDP *underestimates* the value of the production.

Many items that were traditionally produced at home are now bought in the market. For example, more families now eat in fast-food restaurants—one of the fastest-growing industries in the United States—and use day-care services. These trends mean that food preparation and child-care services that were once part of household production are now measured as part of GDP. So real GDP grows more rapidly than does real GDP plus home production.

Underground Production

Underground production is the production of goods and services hidden from the view of government because people want to avoid taxes and regulations or their actions are illegal. Because underground production is unreported, it is omitted from GDP.

Examples of underground production are the distribution of illegal drugs, farm work that uses illegal workers who are paid less than the minimum wage, and jobs that are done for cash to avoid paying income taxes. This last category might be quite large and includes tips earned by cab drivers, hairdressers, and hotel and restaurant workers.

Edgar L. Feige, an economist at the University of Wisconsin, estimates that U.S. underground production was about 16 percent of GDP during the early 1990s. Underground production in many countries, especially in most developing countries, is estimated to be larger than that in the United States.

Leisure Time

Leisure time is an economic good that is not valued as part of GDP. Yet the marginal hour of leisure time must be at least as valuable to us as the wage we earn for working. If it were not, we would work instead. Over the years, leisure time has steadily increased as the workweek gets shorter, more people take early retirement, and the number of vacation days increases. These improvements in our standard of living are not measured in real GDP.

Environment Quality

Pollution is an economic *bad* (the opposite of a *good*). The more we pollute our environment, other things remaining the same, the lower is our standard of living. This lowering of our standard of living is not measured by real GDP.

■ Other Influences on the Standard of Living

The quantity of goods and services consumed is a major influence on the standard of living. But other influences are

- Health and life expectancy
- Political freedom and social justice

Health and Life Expectancy

Good health and a long life—the hopes of everyone—do not show up directly in real GDP. A higher real GDP enables us to spend more on medical research, health care, a good diet, and exercise equipment. As real GDP has increased, our life expectancy has lengthened. But we face new health and life expectancy problems every year. Diseases, such as AIDS, and drug abuse are taking young lives at a rate that causes serious concern. When we take these negative influences into account, real GDP growth might overstate the improvements in the standard of living.

Political Freedom and Social Justice

A country might have a very large real GDP per person but have limited political freedom and social justice. For example, a small elite might enjoy political liberty and extreme wealth while the majority of people have limited freedom and live in poverty. Such an economy would generally be regarded as having a lower standard of living than one that had the same amount of real GDP but in which everyone enjoyed political freedom.

EYE on YOUR LIFE
Making GDP Personal

As you read a newspaper or business magazine, watch a TV news show, or browse a news Web site, you often come across reports about GDP.

What do these reports mean for you? Where in the National Income and Product Accounts do *your* transactions appear? How can you use information about GDP in your life?

Your Contribution to GDP

Your own economic transactions show up in the National Income and Product Accounts on both the expenditure side and the income side—as part of the expenditure approach and part of the income approach to measuring GDP.

Most of your expenditure is part of Consumption Expenditure. If you were to buy a new home, that item would appear as part of Investment. Because much of what you buy is produced in another country, expenditure on these goods shows up as part of Imports.

If you have a job, your income appears in Compensation of Employees.

Because the GDP measure of the value of production includes only market transactions, some of your own production of goods and services is most likely not counted in GDP.

What are the nonmarket goods and services that you produce? How would you go about valuing them?

Making Sense of the Numbers

To use the GDP numbers in a news report, you must first check whether the reporter is referring to *nominal* GDP or *real* GDP.

Using U.S. real GDP per person, check how your income compares with the average income in the United States. When you see GDP numbers for other countries, compare your income with that of a person in France, or Canada, or China.

EYE on the GLOBAL ECONOMY
Which Country Has the Highest Standard of Living?

You've seen that as a measure of the standard of living, GDP has limitations. To compare the standard of living across countries, we must consider other factors in addition to GDP.

GDP measures only the market value of all the final goods and services produced and bought in markets. GDP omits some goods and services (those produced in the home and in the hidden economy). It omits the value of leisure time, of good health and long life expectancy, as well as of political freedom and social justice. It also omits the damage (negative value) that pollution does to the environment.

These limitations of GDP as a measure of the standard of living apply in every country. So to make international comparisons of the standard of living, we must look at real GDP and other indicators. Nonetheless, real GDP per person is a major component of international comparisons.

Many alternatives to GDP have been proposed. One, called Green GDP, subtracts from GDP an estimate of the cost of greenhouse gas emissions and other negative influences on the environment. Another measure, called the Happy Planet Index, or HPI, goes further and subtracts from GDP an estimate of the cost of depleting nonrenewable resources.

Neither the Green GDP nor the HPI are reliable measures because they rely on guesses about the costs of pollution and resource depletion that are subjective and unreliable.

Taking an approach that focuses on the quality of life factors, the United Nations (UN) has constructed a Human Development Index (HDI), which combines real GDP, life expectancy and health, and education.

The figure shows the relationship between the HDI and GDP in 2012. (In the figure, each dot represents a country.) These two measures of the standard of living tell a similar but not identical story.

The United States has the third highest HDI in the figure, lower than Norway and Australia. Why does the United States not have a higher HDI?

The UN says that the people who live in the two countries with higher HDIs live longer, have access to universal health care, and have better schools than do people in the United States. The HDI emphasized equality of access to these services.

The HDI doesn't include political freedom and social justice. If it did, the United States would score highly on that component of the index.

The bottom line is that we don't know which country has the highest standard of living. But we do know that GDP per person alone does not provide the complete answer.

SOURCE OF DATA: *United Nations Human Development Report*, 2011, http://hdr.undp.org/.

MyEconLab Study Plan 5.3

Key Terms Quiz

Solutions

 CHECKPOINT 5.3

Describe the uses of real GDP and explain its limitations as a measure of the standard of living.

Practice Problems

The United Nations Human Development Report gives the data for 2011 in Table 1. Other information suggests that household production is similar in Canada and the United States and smaller than in China and Russia. The underground economy is larger in Russia and China and a similar proportion of each of these economies. Canadians and Americans enjoy more leisure hours than do the Chinese and Russians. Canada and the United States spend significantly more on the environment than do China and Russia. Use this information and ignore any other influences to work Problems **1** and **2**.

TABLE 1

Country	Real GDP per person
China	$4,833
Russia	$13,543
United States	$48,666
Canada	$50,265

1. In which pair (or pairs) of countries is it easiest to compare the standard of living? And in which pair (or pairs) is it most difficult? Explain why.

2. Do the differences in real GDP per person correctly rank the standard of living in these four countries? What additional information would we need to be able to make an accurate assessment of the relative standard of living in these four countries?

In the News

Economists look to expand GDP to include the quality of life
Robert Kennedy, when seeking the Democratic presidential nomination in 1968, remarked that GDP measures everything except that which makes life worthwhile.

Source: *The New York Times*, September 1, 2008

Which items did Robert Kennedy probably think were missing?

Solutions to Practice Problems

1. Two pairs—Canada and the United States, and China and Russia—are easy to compare because household production, the underground economy, leisure hours, and the environment are similar in the countries in each pair. The most difficult comparison is Canada and the United States with either China or Russia. Household production and the underground economy narrow the differences but leisure hours and the environment widen them.

2. Differences in real GDP per person probably correctly rank the standard of living because where the gap is small (Canada and the United States), other factors are similar, and where other factors differ, the gaps are huge. More information on the value of household production, the underground economy, the value of leisure, and the value of environmental differences is required to make an accurate assessment of relative living standards.

Solution to In the News

GDP measures production that is traded in markets. GDP does not include household production, leisure time, health and life expectancy, political freedom, and social justice. These items are probably the ones that Kennedy believed were missing from GDP as a measure of the quality of life.

CHAPTER SUMMARY

Key Points

1. **Define GDP and explain why the value of production, income, and expenditure are the same for an economy.**

   - GDP is the market value of all final goods and services produced within a country in a given time period.
   - We can value goods and services either by what they cost to produce (incomes) or by what people are willing to pay (expenditures).
   - The value of production equals income equals expenditure.

2. **Describe how economic statisticians measure GDP and distinguish between nominal GDP and real GDP.**

   - BEA measures GDP by summing expenditures and by summing incomes. With no errors of measurement the two totals are the same, but in practice, a small statistical discrepancy arises.
   - A country's GNP is similar to its GDP, but GNP is the value of production by factors of production supplied by the residents of a country.
   - Nominal GDP is the value of production using the prices of the current year and the quantities produced in the current year.
   - Real GDP is the value of production using the prices of a base year and the quantities produced in the current year.

3. **Describe the uses of real GDP and explain its limitations as a measure of the standard of living.**

   - We use real GDP per person to compare the standard of living over time.
   - We use real GDP to determine when the economy has reached a business cycle peak or trough.
   - We use real GDP per person expressed in purchasing power parity dollars to compare the standard of living among countries.
   - Real GDP omits some goods and services and ignores some factors that influence the standard of living.
   - The Human Development Index takes some other factors into account.

Key Terms

MyEconLab Key Terms Quiz

Business cycle, 128
Consumption expenditure, 115
Depreciation, 122
Exports of goods and services, 116
Final good or service, 114
Government expenditure on goods and services, 116

Gross domestic product (GDP), 114
Imports of goods and services, 116
Intermediate good or service, 114
Investment, 115
Net exports of goods and services, 116
Net taxes, 116

Nominal GDP, 124
Potential GDP, 127
Real GDP, 124
Recession, 128
Saving, 116

Study Plan Problems and Applications

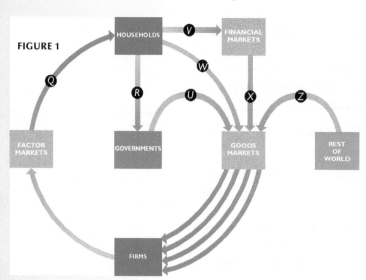

FIGURE 1

1. Figure 1 shows the flows of income and expenditure in an economy. In 2013, U was $2 trillion, V was $1.5 trillion, W was $7 trillion, X was $1.5 trillion, and Z was zero. Calculate total income, net taxes, and GDP.

Use the following data to work Problems **2** and **3**.

The national accounts of Parchment Paradise are kept on (you guessed it) parchment. A fire in the statistics office destroys some accounts, leaving only the following data:

- GDP (income approach) $2,900
- Consumption expenditure $2,000
- Indirect taxes less subsidies $100
- Interest, rent, and profit $500
- Investment $800
- Government expenditure $400
- Wages $2,000
- Net factor income from abroad $50
- Net exports −$200

2. Calculate GDP (expenditure approach) and depreciation.

3. Calculate net domestic product at factor cost, the statistical discrepancy, and GNP.

Use the following information to work Problems **4** to **6**.

An economy produces only fun and food. Table 1 shows the prices and the quantities of fun and food produced in 2013 and 2014. The base year is 2013.

4. Calculate nominal GDP in 2013 and 2014.

5. Calculate the percentage increase in production in 2014.

6. If potential GDP was $270 in 2013 and it grew by 1 percent in 2014, in which phase of the business cycle is the economy? Explain.

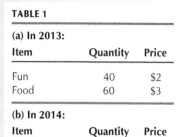

TABLE 1

(a) In 2013:

Item	Quantity	Price
Fun	40	$2
Food	60	$3

(b) In 2014:

Item	Quantity	Price
Fun	35	$3
Food	65	$2

Use the following information to work Problems **7** to **9**.

Expansion remains slow

The Commerce Department reported that retail sales increased 1.3 percent in June. Net exports were up 0.8 percent in the first quarter and inventories held by businesses rose by 0.3 percent in June. Total sales by businesses rose 0.3 percent.

Source: Commerce Department, 2013

7. Which component of GDP changed because retail sales increased? Which component of GDP changed because inventories held by businesses fell?

8. Explain the effect of the rise in net exports on GDP.

9. Does the statement that total sales by businesses were up 0.3 percent mean that GDP increased by 0.3 percent? Explain your answer.

 10. Read *Eye on the Booms and Busts* on p. 130 and explain why the NBER reported that the 2008 recession began before real GDP had fallen for two successive quarters.

Instructor Assignable Problems and Applications

MyEconLab Homework, Quiz, or Test if assigned by instructor

1. In France, real GDP was the same in 2012 as it had been in 2011, but in the last quarter of 2012 and the first quarter of 2013, France's real GDP decreased. In the United States, real GDP increased in 2012, and in the first quarter of 2013, it was higher than in the last quarter of 2012.

   Based on this information, which country was in a recession at the beginning of 2013? What features of the information provided led you to your conclusion?

2. Classify each of the items in List 1 as a final good or service or an intermediate good or service and identify it as a component of consumption expenditure, investment, or government expenditure on goods and services.

Use the following information to work Problems 3 and 4.

Mitsubishi Heavy Industries makes the wings of the new Boeing 787 Dreamliner in Japan. Toyota assembles cars for the U.S. market in Kentucky.

3. Explain where these activities appear in the National Income and Product Accounts of the United States.

4. Explain where these activities appear in the National Income and Product Accounts of Japan.

Use the data on the economy of Iberia in Table 1 to work Problems 5 and 6.

5. Calculate Iberia's GDP.

6. Calculate Iberia's imports of goods and services.

Use Table 2, which shows an economy's total production and the prices of the final goods it produced in 2013 and 2014, to work Problems 7 to 9.

7. Calculate nominal GDP in 2013 and 2014.

8. The base year is 2013. Calculate real GDP in 2013 and 2014.

9. Calculate the percentage increase in production in 2014.

Use the following information to work Problems 10 and 11.

Cash-paying vultures pick bones of U.S. housing market as mortgages dry up
New-home sales fell to an annual pace of 250,000 in February, an all-time low in records dating to 1963, the Commerce Department reported March 23. Existing-home sales dropped to a 4.88 million annualized pace in February, down 2.8 percent from a year earlier, the National Association of Realtors said, while the median price of existing homes fell to $156,100, the lowest since February 2002.

Source: Bloomberg, March 29, 2011

10. Where do new-home sales appear in the circular flow of expenditure and income? Explain how a fall in new home sales affects real GDP.

11. Where do sales of previously owned homes appear in the circular flow of expenditure and income? Explain how a fall in sales of previously owned homes affects real GDP.

12. **The road less traveled**
   If we are right, this year is different and global growth will rise to an above-trend pace during the second half of 2013.

Source: J.P. Morgan Global Data Watch, May, 2013

   Does this news mean that the 2008–2009 recession was expected to end in the second half of 2013? Does recession end only when real GDP growth rises above trend??

LIST 1

- Banking services bought by Target
- Security system bought by the White House
- Coffee beans bought by Starbucks
- New coffee machines bought by Starbucks
- Starbucks grande mocha frappuccino bought by a student
- New battle ship bought by the U.S. navy

TABLE 1

Item	Amount
Net taxes	$18 billion
Government expenditure	$20 billion
Saving	$15 billion
Consumption expenditure	$67 billion
Investment	$21 billion
Exports	$30 billion.

TABLE 2

(a) In 2013:

Item	Quantity	Price
Fish	100	$2
Berries	50	$6

(b) In 2014:

Item	Quantity	Price
Fish	75	$5
Berries	65	$10

Multiple Choice Quiz

1. Gross domestic product is the market value of all the _____ in a given time period.

   A. goods and services bought by Americans
   B. goods and services produced by American companies in all countries
   C. final goods and services produced by all firms located in the United States
   D. U.S.-produced goods and services bought in the United States

2. A _____ is a final good and _____ is an intermediate good.

   A. new car bought by a student; a used SUV bought by a dealer
   B. new textbook; a used textbook
   C. new iPhone bought by a student; a new computer bought by Wal-Mart
   D. tank of gasoline bought by you; jet fuel bought by Southwest Airlines

3. Saving equals _____.

   A. income minus consumption expenditure minus net taxes
   B. income minus net taxes
   C. total income minus total expenditure
   D. net taxes minus government expenditure

4. The expenditure approach to measuring U.S. GDP equals _____.

   A. the sum of U.S. consumption expenditure and U.S. investment
   B. U.S. government expenditure minus taxes paid by Americans
   C. all expenditure on final goods and services produced in the United States in a given time period
   D. all expenditure by Americans on goods and services produced in the United States in a given time period

5. When using the income approach to measure GDP at market prices, in addition to summing all factor incomes it is necessary to _____.

   A. subtract depreciation because profit is not reported as net profit
   B. add depreciation because capital depreciates when goods are manufactured
   C. add indirect taxes less subsidies to convert aggregate income from factor cost to market prices
   D. add a statistical discrepancy which is the sum of depreciation and indirect taxes less subsidies

6. The following statements about the business cycle are correct *except* _____.

   A. it is a regular predictable cycle in real GDP around potential GDP
   B. from the peak to the trough, the economy is in a recession
   C. from the trough to the peak, the economy is in an expansion
   D. it is a periodic movement in economic activity including employment

7. Real GDP per person is not an accurate measure of the standard of living because it _____.

   A. includes the goods and services that governments buy
   B. omits the goods and services that people produce for themselves
   C. includes goods and services bought by firms
   D. omits the goods and services imported from other countries

APPENDIX: MEASURING REAL GDP

This appendix explains the method used by the Bureau of Economic Analysis (BEA) to calculate real GDP using a measure called **chained-dollar real GDP**. We begin by explaining the problem that arises from using the prices of the base year (the method on pp. 124–125) and how the problem can be overcome.

Chained-dollar real GDP
The measure of real GDP calculated by the Bureau of Economic Analysis.

■ The Problem With Base-Year Prices

When we calculated real GDP on pp. 124–125, we found that real GDP in 2013 was 60 percent greater than it was in 2009. But instead of using the prices of 2009 as the constant prices, we could have used the prices of 2013. In this case, we would have valued the quantities produced in 2009 at the prices of 2013. By comparing the values of real GDP in 2009 and 2013 at the constant prices of 2013, we get a different number for the percentage increase in production. If you use the numbers in Table 5.3 on p. 125 to value 2009 production at 2013 prices, you will get a real GDP in 2009 of $150 million (2013 dollars). Real GDP in 2013 at 2013 prices is $300 million. So by using the prices of 2013, production doubled—a 100 percent increase—from 2009 to 2013. Did production in fact increase by 60 percent or 100 percent?

The problem arises because to calculate real GDP, we weight the quantity of each item produced by its price. If all prices change by the same percentage, then the *relative* weight on each good or service doesn't change and the percentage change in real GDP from the first year to the second is the same regardless of which year's prices we use. But if prices change by different percentages, then the *relative* weight on each good or service *does* change and the percentage change in real GDP from the first year to the second depends on which prices we use. So which year's prices should we use: those of the first year or those of the second?

The answer given by the BEA method is to use the prices of both years. If we calculate the percentage change in real GDP twice, once using the prices of the first year and again using the prices of the second year, and then take the average of those two percentage changes, we get a unique measure of the change in real GDP and one that gives equal importance to the *relative* prices of both years.

To illustrate the calculation of the BEA measure of real GDP, we'll work through an example. The method has three steps:

- Value production in the prices of adjacent years.
- Find the average of two percentage changes.
- Link (chain) to the base year.

■ Value Production in the Prices of Adjacent Years

The first step is to value production in *adjacent* years at the prices of both years. We'll make these calculations for 2013, and its preceding year, 2012.

Table A5.1 shows the quantities produced and prices in the two years. Part (a) shows the nominal GDP calculation for 2012—the quantities produced in 2012 valued at the prices of 2012. Nominal GDP in 2012 is $145 million. Part (b) shows the nominal GDP calculation for 2013—the quantities produced in 2013 valued at the prices of 2013. Nominal GDP in 2013 is $172 million. Part (c) shows the value of the quantities produced in 2013 at the prices of 2012. This total is $160 million. Finally, part (d) shows the value of the quantities produced in 2012 at the prices of 2013. This total is $158 million.

■ **TABLE A5.1**

Real GDP Calculation Step 1: Value Production in Adjacent Years at Prices of Both Years

	Item	Quantity (millions of units)	Price (dollars per unit)	Expenditure (millions of dollars)
(a) In 2012				
C	T-shirts	3	5	15
I	Computer chips	3	10	30
G	Security services	5	20	100
Y	Nominal GDP in 2012			145
(b) In 2013				
C	T-shirts	4	4	16
I	Computer chips	2	12	24
G	Security services	6	22	132
Y	Nominal GDP in 2013			172
(c) Quantities of 2013 valued at prices of 2012				
C	T-shirts	4	5	20
I	Computer chips	2	10	20
G	Security services	6	20	120
Y	2013 production at 2012 prices			160
(d) Quantities of 2012 valued at prices of 2013				
C	T-shirts	3	4	12
I	Computer chips	3	12	36
G	Security services	5	22	110
Y	2012 production at 2013 prices			158

Step 1 is to value the production of adjacent years at the prices of both years.

Here, we value the production of 2012 and 2013 at the prices of both 2012 and 2013.

The value of 2012 production at 2012 prices, in part (a), is nominal GDP in 2012.

The value of 2013 production at 2013 prices, in part (b), is nominal GDP in 2013.

Part (c) calculates the value of 2013 production at 2012 prices, and part (d) calculates the value of 2012 production at 2013 prices.

We use these numbers in Step 2.

Find the Average of Two Percentage Changes

The second step is to find the percentage change in the value of production based on the prices in the two adjacent years. Table A5.2 summarizes these calculations.

Valued at the prices of 2012, production increased from $145 million in 2012 to $160 million in 2013, an increase of 10.3 percent. Valued at the prices of 2013, production increased from $158 million in 2012 to $172 million in 2013, an increase of 8.9 percent. The average of these two percentage changes in the value of production is 9.6. That is, $(10.3 + 8.9) \div 2 = 9.6$.

We've now found the *growth rate* of real GDP in 2013. But we also want to calculate the *level* of real GDP. This level depends on the *reference base year*. The simplest example is when the previous year (2012 in this case) is the base year. In 2012, real GDP equals nominal GDP, which is $145 million. Real GDP in 2013, valued in 2012 dollars is 9.6 percent higher, which equals $159 million.

Although the real GDP of $159 million is expressed in 2012 dollars, the calculation uses the average of the *relative prices* of the final goods and services that make up GDP in 2012 and 2013.

When the base year is not the previous year, we need to link or chain the current year to the base year. Let's see how we do this linking.

■ **TABLE A5.2**

Real GDP Calculation Step 2: Find Average of Two Percentage Changes

Value of Production in Adjacent Years		Millions of dollars
2012 production at 2012 prices		145
2013 production at 2012 prices		160
Percentage change in production at 2012 prices	10.3	
2012 production at 2013 prices		158
2013 production at 2013 prices		172
Percentage change in production at 2013 prices	8.9	
Average of two percentage changes in production	9.6	

Using the numbers calculated in Step 1, we find the percentage change in production from 2012 to 2013 valued at 2012 prices, which is 10.3 percent.

We also find the percentage change in production from 2012 to 2013 valued at 2013 prices, which is 8.9 percent.

We then find the average of these two percentage changes, which is 9.6 percent.

Link (Chain) to the Base Year

To link to the base year, we repeat the calculation that we've just described to obtain the real GDP growth rate each year. Real GDP equals nominal GDP in the base year, which currently is 2009. By applying the calculated growth rates to each successive year, we can obtain *chained-dollar real GDP* in 2009 dollars.

Figure A5.1 shows an example with real GDP equal to nominal GDP at $75 million in the base year, 2009, and assumed growth rates of real GDP for each year between 2006 and 2013. The 2013 growth rate is the 9.6 percent that we calculated in Table A5.2 above.

Starting with real GDP in the base year, we apply the calculated percentage change of 2.7 percent, so real GDP in 2010 was 2.7 percent higher than $75 million, which is $77 million. Repeating the calculation, real GDP in 2011 is 3.5 percent higher, which is $80 million, and in 2012, real GDP is 4.6 percent higher, which is $83 million. In 2013, real GDP is 9.6 percent higher than $83 million, which is $91 million.

The same method is used to chain-link the years before the base year. For example, real GDP in 2008 is 8.2 percent lower than in 2009 at $69 million.

■ **FIGURE A5.1**

Real GDP Calculation Step 3: Link (Chain) to the Base Year   MyEconLab Animation

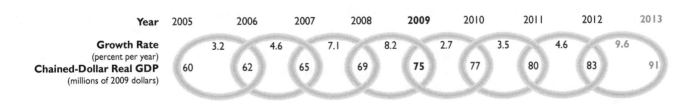

The growth rate of real GDP from one year to the next is calculated for every pair of years and then linked to the base year. Suppose that real GDP was $75 million in the base year, 2009. By applying the growth rate between each pair of years, we find the chained-dollar real GDP for each year, expressed in terms of the value of the dollar in the base year. Here, the percentages for 2007 through to 2013 are assumed. By 2013, the chained-dollar real GDP has increased to $91 million in 2009 dollars.

MyEconLab Chapter 5 Study Plan

APPENDIX CHECKPOINT

Study Plan Problems

An island economy produces only bananas and coconuts. Table 1 gives the quantities produced and prices in 2012 and in 2013. The base year is 2012.

1. Calculate nominal GDP in 2012 and nominal GDP in 2013.

2. Calculate the value of 2013 production in 2012 prices and the percentage increase in production when valued at 2012 prices.

3. Calculate the value of 2012 production in 2013 prices and the percentage increase in production when valued at 2013 prices.

4. Use the chained-dollar method to calculate real GDP in 2012 and 2013. In terms of what dollars is each of these two real GDPs measured?

5. Using the chained-dollar method, compare the growth rates of nominal GDP and real GDP in 2013.

6. If the base year is 2013, use the chained-dollar method to calculate real GDP in 2012 and 2013. In terms of what dollars is each of these two real GDPs measured?

7. If the base year is 2013, compare the growth rates of nominal GDP and real GDP in 2013.

TABLE 1

(a) In 2012:

Item	Quantity	Price
Bananas	100	$10
Coconuts	50	$12

(b) In 2013:

Item	Quantity	Price
Bananas	110	$15
Coconuts	60	$10

MyEconLab Homework, Quiz, or Test if assigned by instructor

Instructor Assignable Problems

An economy produces only food and fun. Table 2 shows the quantities produced and prices in 2012 and 2013. The base year is 2013.

1. Calculate nominal GDP in 2012 and nominal GDP in 2013.

2. Calculate the value of 2013 production in 2012 prices and the percentage increase in production when valued at 2012 prices.

3. Calculate the value of 2012 production in 2013 prices and the percentage increase in production when valued at 2013 prices.

4. Using the chained-dollar method, calculate real GDP in 2012 and 2013. In terms of what dollars is each of these two real GDPs measured?

5. Using the chained-dollar method, compare the growth rates of nominal GDP and real GDP in 2013.

6. If the base year is 2012, use the chained-dollar method to calculate real GDP in 2012 and 2013. In terms of what dollars is each of these two real GDPs measured?

7. If the base year is 2012, compare the growth rates of nominal GDP and real GDP in 2013.

TABLE 2

(a) In 2012:

Item	Quantity	Price
Food	100	$2
Fun	50	$6

(b) In 2013:

Item	Quantity	Price
Food	75	$5
Fun	65	$10

MyEconLab Key Terms Quiz

Key Term

Chained-dollar real GDP, 139

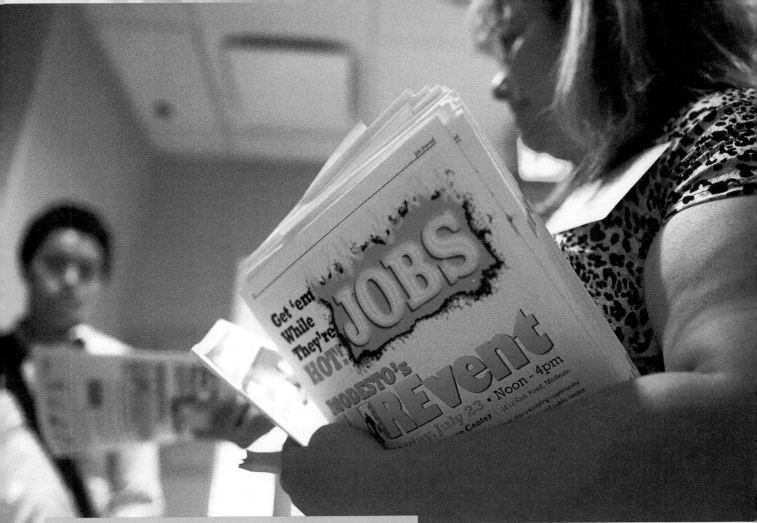

How long does it take
to find a job?

Jobs and Unemployment

6

**When you have completed your study of this chapter,
you will be able to**

1 Define the unemployment rate and other labor market indicators.

2 Describe the trends and fluctuations in the indicators of labor market
performance in the United States.

3 Describe the types of unemployment, define full employment, and
explain the link between unemployment and real GDP.

MyEconLab Big Picture

6.1   LABOR MARKET INDICATORS

Every month, 1,600 field interviewers and supervisors working on a joint project between the Bureau of Labor Statistics (or BLS) and the Bureau of the Census survey 60,000 households and ask a series of questions about the age and labor market status of their members. This survey is called the *Current Population Survey*. Let's look at the types of data collected by this survey.

■ Current Population Survey

Figure 6.1 shows the categories into which the BLS divides the population. It also shows the relationships among the categories. The first category divides the population into two groups: the working-age civilian population and others. The **working-age population** is the total number of people aged 16 years and over who are not in jail, hospital, or some other form of institutional care or in the U.S. Armed Forces. In May 2013, the estimated population of the United States was 316.1 million, the working-age population was 245.6 million, and 70.5 million people were under 16 years of age, in the military, or living in institutions.

The second category divides the working-age population into two groups: those in the labor force and those not in the labor force. The **labor force** is the number of people employed plus the number unemployed. In May 2013, the U.S. labor force was 155.7 million and 89.9 million people were not in the labor force. Most of those not in the labor force were in school full time or had retired from work.

The third category divides the labor force into two groups: the employed and the unemployed. In May 2013 in the United States, 143.9 million people were employed and 11.8 million people were unemployed.

■ Population Survey Criteria

The survey counts as *employed* all persons who, during the week before the survey, either

1. Worked at least 1 hour as paid employees or worked 15 hours or more as unpaid workers in their family business or
2. Were not working but had jobs or businesses from which they were temporarily absent.

The survey counts as *unemployed* all persons who, during the week before the survey,

1. Had no employment,
2. Were available for work,

and either

1. Had made specific efforts to find employment during the previous four weeks or
2. Were waiting to be recalled to a job from which they had been laid off.

People in the working-age population who by the above criteria are neither employed nor unemployed are classified as not in the labor force.

Working-age population
The total number of people aged 16 years and over who are not in jail, hospital, or some other form of institutional care or in the U.S. Armed Forces.

Labor force
The number of people employed plus the number unemployed.

To be counted as unemployed, a person must not only want a job but also have tried to find one.

FIGURE 6.1

Population Labor Force Categories

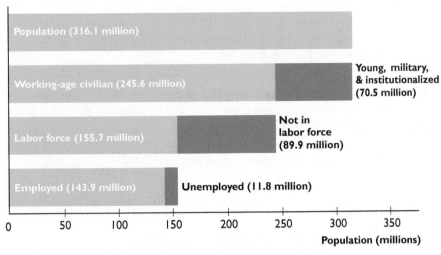

SOURCE OF DATA: Bureau of Labor Statistics.

The U.S. population is divided into the working-age population and the young, military, and institutionalized. The working-age population is divided into the labor force and those not in the labor force. The labor force is divided into those employed and those unemployed. The figure shows the data for May 2013.

■ Two Main Labor Market Indicators

Using the numbers from the Current Population Survey, the BLS calculates several indicators of the state of the labor market. The two main labor market indicators are

- The unemployment rate
- The labor force participation rate

The Unemployment Rate

The amount of unemployment is an indicator of the extent to which people who want jobs can't find them. It tells us the amount of slack in the labor market. The **unemployment rate** is the percentage of the people in the labor force who are unemployed. That is,

$$\text{Unemployment rate} = \frac{\text{Number of people unemployed}}{\text{Labor force}} \times 100.$$

Unemployment rate
The percentage of the people in the labor force who are unemployed.

In May 2013, the number of people unemployed was 11.8 million and the labor force was 155.7 million. We can use these numbers to calculate the unemployment rate in May 2013, which is

$$\text{Unemployment rate} = \frac{11.8 \text{ million}}{155.7 \text{ million}} \times 100$$

$$= 7.6 \text{ percent.}$$

The Labor Force Participation Rate

The number of people in the labor force is an indicator of the willingness of people of working age to take jobs. The **labor force participation rate** is the percentage of the working-age population who are members of the labor force. That is,

$$\text{Labor force participation rate} = \frac{\text{Labor force}}{\text{Working-age population}} \times 100.$$

In May 2013, the labor force was 155.7 million and the working-age population was 245.6 million. We can use these numbers to calculate the labor force participation rate in May 2013, which is

$$\text{Labor force participation rate} = \frac{155.7 \text{ million}}{245.6 \text{ million}} \times 100.$$

$$= 63.4 \text{ percent.}$$

■ Alternative Measures of Unemployment

The unemployment rate based on the official definition of unemployment omits some types of underutilization of labor. The omissions are

- Marginally attached workers
- Part-time workers

Marginally Attached Workers

Some people who think of themselves as being in the labor force and unemployed are not counted in the official labor force numbers. They are marginally attached workers. A **marginally attached worker** is a person who does not have a job, is available and willing to work, has not made specific efforts to find a job within the previous four weeks, but has looked for work sometime in the recent past. A **discouraged worker** is a marginally attached worker who has not made specific efforts to find a job within the previous four weeks because previous unsuccessful attempts were discouraging.

Other marginally attached workers differ from discouraged workers only in their reasons for not having looked for a job during the previous four weeks. For example, Martin doesn't have a job and is available for work, but he has not looked for work in the past four weeks because he was busy cleaning his home after a flood. He is a marginally attached worker but not a discouraged worker. Lena, Martin's wife, doesn't have a job and is available for work, but she hasn't looked for work in the past four weeks because she's been looking for six months and hasn't had a single job offer. She is a discouraged worker.

Neither the unemployment rate nor the labor force participation rate includes marginally attached workers. In May 2013, 753,000 people were discouraged workers. If we add them to both the number unemployed and the labor force, the unemployment rate becomes 8.0 percent—only slightly higher than the standard definition of the unemployment rate. Also in May 2013, 1,372,000 people were other marginally attached workers. If we add them and the discouraged workers to both the number unemployed and the labor force, the unemployment rate becomes 8.8 percent—1.2 percentage points higher than the standard definition.

EYE on the U.S. ECONOMY
The Current Population Survey

The Bureau of Labor Statistics and the Bureau of the Census go to great lengths to collect accurate labor force data. They constantly train and retrain around 1,600 field interviewers and supervisors. Each month, each field interviewer contacts 37 households and asks basic demographic questions about everyone living at the address and detailed labor force questions about those aged 16 or over.

Once a household has been selected for the survey, it is questioned for four consecutive months and then again for the same four months a year later. Each month, the addresses that have been in the panel eight times are removed and 6,250 new addresses are added. The rotation and overlap of households provide

very reliable information about month-to-month and year-to-year changes in the labor market.

The first time that a household is in the panel, an interviewer, armed with a hand-held computer, visits it. If the household has a telephone, most of the subsequent interviews are

conducted by phone, many of them from one of the three telephone interviewing centers in Hagerstown, Maryland; Jeffersonville, Indiana; and Tucson, Arizona.

For more information about the Current Population Survey, visit www.bls.gov/cps/cps_faq.htm.

Part-Time Workers

The Current Population Survey measures the number of full-time workers and part-time workers. **Full-time workers** are those who usually work 35 hours or more a week. **Part-time workers** are those who usually work less than 35 hours a week. Part-time workers are divided into two groups: part time for economic reasons and part time for noneconomic reasons.

People who work **part time for economic reasons** (also called *involuntary part-time workers*) are people who work 1 to 34 hours but are looking for full-time work. These people are unable to find full-time work because of unfavorable business conditions or seasonal decreases in the availability of full-time work.

People who work part time for noneconomic reasons do not want full-time work and are not available for such work. This group includes people with health problems, family or personal responsibilities, or education commitments that limit their availability for work.

The Bureau of Labor Statistics uses the data on full-time and part-time status to measure the slack in the labor market that results from people being underemployed—employed but not able to find as much employment as they would like.

In May 2013, when employment was 143.9 million, full-time employment was 117.1 million and part-time employment was 26.8 million. An estimated 7.9 million people worked part time for economic reasons. When this number, along with marginally attached workers, is added to the number unemployed, the unemployment rate becomes 13.8 percent.

Full-time workers
People who usually work 35 hours or more a week.

Part-time workers
People who usually work less than 35 hours a week.

Part time for economic reasons
People who work 1 to 34 hours per week but are looking for full-time work and cannot find it because of unfavorable business conditions.

MyEconLab Study Plan 6.1
Key Terms Quiz
Solutions
Real-Time Data

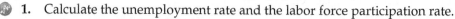

CHECKPOINT 6.1

Define the unemployment rate and other labor market indicators.

Practice Problems

The BLS reported that in July 2009, the labor force was 154.5 million, employment was 140.0 million, and the working-age population was 235.9 million.

1. Calculate the unemployment rate and the labor force participation rate.
2. The BLS also reported that 24 percent of all employment in July 2009 was part time and that 9.1 million people worked part time for economic reasons. How many people worked part time for noneconomic reasons?

In the News

Summer 2012 youth labor market

From April to July 2012, the number of employed youth 16- to 24-years old rose by 2.1 million to 19.5 million. Unemployment of youth increased from 3.2 million to 4.0 million. In July, the youth labor force grew by 2.9 million to a total of 23.5 million and the youth population was 38 million.

Source: BLS Press Release, August 12, 2012

How did the youth unemployment rate change from April to July? Calculate the youth labor force participation rate in July.

Solutions to Practice Problems

1. The unemployment rate is 9.4 percent. The labor force is the sum of the number employed plus the number unemployed. So the number unemployed equals the labor force minus the number employed, which equals 154.5 million minus 140.0 million, or 14.5 million. The unemployment rate is the number unemployed as a percentage of the labor force. The Unemployment rate = (14.5 million ÷ 154.5 million) × 100 or 9.4 percent. The labor force participation rate is 65.5 percent. The labor force participation rate is the percentage of the working-age population who are in the labor force. Labor force participation rate = (154.5 ÷ 235.9) × 100, or 65.5 percent.

2. 24.5 million people worked part time for noneconomic reasons. Employment was 140 million. Part-time employment was 24 percent of 140 million, which equals 33.6 million. Given that 9.1 million worked part time for economic reasons, 33.6 million minus 9.1 million, or 24.5 million worked part time for noneconomic reasons.

Solution to In the News

The unemployment rate is the number unemployed as a percentage of the labor force. The April labor force equals the July labor force (23.5 million) minus the increase of 2.9 million from April to July. That is, the April labor force was 20.6 million. In April, 3.2 million youths were unemployed, so the April unemployment rate was (3.2 ÷ 20.6) × 100, or 15.5 percent. In July, 4.0 million youths were unemployed and the labor force was 23.5 million, so the unemployment rate was 17 percent. From April to July, the unemployment rate fell from 15.5 percent to 17 percent. The labor force participation rate equals the labor force (23.5 million) as a percentage of the population (38 million), which was 61.8 percent.

6.2 LABOR MARKET TRENDS AND FLUCTUATIONS

MyEconLab Snapshot

What do we learn about the U.S. labor market from changes in the unemployment rate, the labor force participation rate, and the alternative measures of unemployment? Let's explore the trends and fluctuations in these indicators.

■ Unemployment Rate

Figure 6.2 shows the U.S. unemployment rate over the 84 years from 1929 to 2013. Over these years, the average U.S. unemployment rate was 7.2 percent, but from 1948 to 2013, the long-term average was 5.8 percent. The unemployment rate was below this long-term average during the 1940s through the 1960s and during the late 1990s and early 2000s. It was above the long-term average during the 1970s to the mid-1990s and 2009–2013.

During the 1960s, the unemployment rate gradually fell to 3.5 percent. These years saw a rapid rate of job creation, partly from the demands placed on the economy by the growth of defense production during the Vietnam War and partly from an expansion of consumer spending encouraged by an expansion of social programs. Another burst of rapid job creation driven by the "new economy"—the high-technology sector driven by the expansion of the Internet—lowered the unemployment rate to below average from 1995 through the early 2000s.

The most striking event visible in Figure 6.2 is the **Great Depression,** a period of high unemployment, low incomes, and extreme economic hardship that lasted from 1929 to 1939. By 1933, the worst of the Great Depression years, real GDP had fallen by a huge 30 percent and as the figure shows, one in four of the people who wanted jobs couldn't find them. The horrors of the Great Depression led to the New Deal and shaped political attitudes that persist today.

Great Depression
A period of high unemployment, low incomes, and extreme economic hardship that lasted from 1929 to 1939.

■ FIGURE 6.2

The U.S. Unemployment Rate: 1929–2013

MyEconLab Real-time data

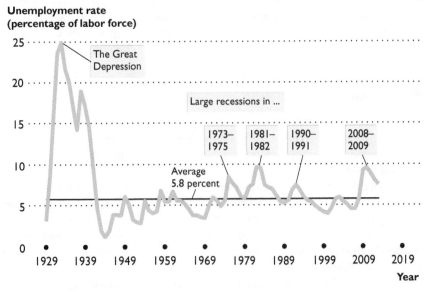

The average unemployment rate from 1948 to 2013 was 5.8 percent. The unemployment rate increases in recessions and decreases in expansions. Unemployment was at its lowest during World War II and the expansions of the 1950s, 1960s, and the 1990s and at its highest during the Great Depression and the recessions of 1981–1982 and 2008–2009.

Source of data: Bureau of Labor Statistics.

EYE on the GLOBAL ECONOMY
Unemployment Around the World

U.S. unemployment falls inside the range experienced by other countries. The highest unemployment rates have been in the United Kingdom, Canada, and the Eurozone; and the lowest have been in Japan and the newly industrializing Asian economies.

Differences in unemployment rates were large during the early 1980s, narrowed through the 1990s and early 2000s and widened after the 2008 recession.

The Eurozone, with a higher average unemployment rate than the United States, also has higher unemployment benefits and more regulated labor markets.

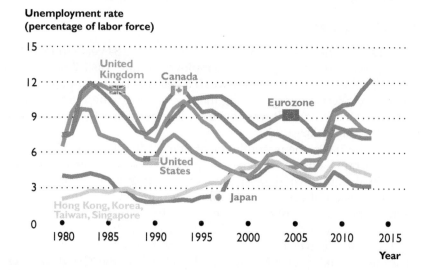

SOURCE OF DATA: International Monetary Fund, *World Economic Outlook,* April 2013.

During the recessions of 1973–1975, 1981–1982, 1990–1991, and 2008–2009, the unemployment rate increased. During the post-war years, the unemployment rate peaked in November–December 1982, when 10.8 percent of the labor force were unemployed. By mid-2011, although the economy had come out of recession and entered into a slow expansion, the unemployment rate stood at 9.1 percent. While the popular representation of the 2008–2009 recession compares it with the Great Depression, you can see in Figure 6.2 that 2010 is strikingly different from 1933, the year in which the unemployment rate peaked during the Great Depression.

■ The Participation Rate

Figure 6.3 shows the labor force participation rate, which increased from 59 percent in 1960 to 67 percent at its peak in 1999. Why did the labor force participation rate increase? The main reason is an increase in the number of women who have entered the labor force.

Figure 6.3 shows that from 1960 to 1999, the participation rate of women increased from 37 percent to 60 percent. This increase is spread across women of all age groups and occurred for four main reasons. First, more women pursued a college education and so increased their earning power. Second, technological change in the workplace created a large number of white-collar jobs with flexible work hours that many women found attractive. Third, technological change in the home increased the time available for paid employment. And fourth, families looked increasingly to a second income to balance tight budgets.

FIGURE 6.3

The Changing Face of the Labor Market: 1960–2013

MyEconLab Real-time data

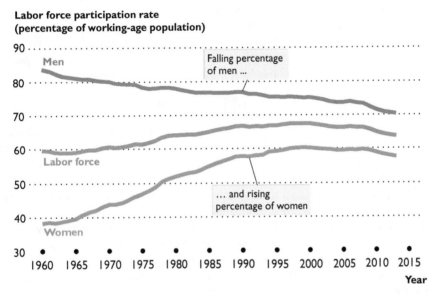

The labor force participation rate increased from 1960 to 1999 but then decreased slightly.

The labor force participation rate of women has driven these trends, increasing strongly from 37 percent in 1960 to 60 percent in 1999.

The labor force participation rate of men has decreased steadily through the past 53 years.

SOURCE OF DATA: Bureau of Labor Statistics.

EYE on the GLOBAL ECONOMY
Women in the Labor Force

The labor force participation rate of women has increased in most advanced nations. But the participation rate of women in the labor force varies a great deal around the world. The figure compares eight other countries with the United States.

The U.S. rank is surprisingly low and economists Francine D. Blau and Lawrence M. Kahn who have studied these data say that other countries have more "family-friendly" labor market policies. But they say these policies encourage part-time work and U.S. women are more likely than women in other countries to have good full-time jobs as managers or professionals.

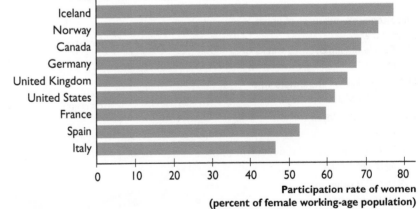

SOURCE OF DATA: OECD.

Cultural factors play a central role in influencing national differences in women's work choices. But education, and particularly the percentage of

women with a college degree, is the dominant source of international differences in women's and men's job market prospects.

Figure 6.3 also shows another remarkable trend in the U.S. labor force: The participation rate of men *decreased* from 83 percent in 1960 to 70 percent in 2013. As in the case of women, this decrease is spread across all age groups. Some of the decrease occurred because older men chose to retire earlier. During the 1990s, some of this earlier retirement was made possible by an increase in wealth. But some arose from job loss at an age at which finding a new job is difficult. For other men, mainly those in their teens and twenties, decreased labor force participation occurred because more chose to remain in full-time education.

■ Alternative Measures of Unemployment

You've seen that the official measure of unemployment does not include marginally attached workers and people who work part time for economic reasons. The Bureau of Labor Statistics (BLS) now provides three broader measures of the unemployment rate, known as U-4, U-5, and U-6, that include these wider groups of the jobless. The official unemployment rate (based on the standard definition of unemployment) is called U-3 and as these names imply, there is also a U-1 and U-2 measure. The U-1 and U-2 measures of the unemployment rate are narrower than the official measure. U-1 is the percentage of the labor force that has been unemployed for 15 weeks or more and is a measure of long-term involuntary unemployment. U-2 is the percentage of the labor force that has been laid off and is another measure of involuntary unemployment.

Figure 6.4 shows the history of these six measures of unemployment since 1994 (the year in which the BLS started to measure them). The relative magnitudes of the six measures are explained by what they include—the broader the measure, the higher the average. The six measures follow similar but not identical tracks,

■ FIGURE 6.4

Alternative Measures of Unemployment: 1994–2013   MyEconLab Real-time data

The alternative measures of unemployment are:

U-1 People unemployed 15 weeks or longer

U-2 People laid off and others who completed a temporary job

U-3 Total unemployed (official measure)

U-4 Total unemployed plus discouraged workers

U-5 U-4 plus other marginally attached workers

U-6 U-5 plus employed part time for economic reasons

U-1, U-2, and U-3 are percentages of the labor force.

U-4, U-5, and U-6 are percentages of the labor force plus the unemployed in the added category.

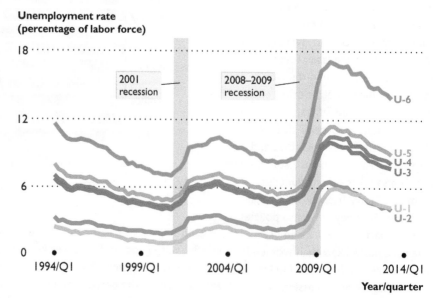

SOURCE OF DATA: Bureau of Labor Statistics.

rising during the recessions and falling in the expansions between the recessions. But during the 2001 recession, U-1 barely changed while during the 2008–2009 recession, it more than doubled in less than a year.

■ A Closer Look at Part-Time Employment

The broadest measure of the unemployment rate, U-6, includes people who work part time for economic reasons. Let's take a closer look at part-time employment.

A part-time job is attractive to many workers because it enables them to balance family and other commitments with work. Part-time jobs are attractive to employers because they don't have to pay benefits to part-time workers and are less constrained by government regulations. People who choose part-time jobs are part time for noneconomic reasons. People who take a part-time job because they can't find a full-time job are part time for economic reasons. The BLS measures these two groups and Figure 6.5 shows the data since 1980 (but with a change in the definitions in 1994).

The number of people who work part time for noneconomic reasons is double the number who work part time for economic reasons. Also, the percentage of the labor force who are part time for noneconomic reasons is remarkably steady at an average of 13 percent (old definition) and 14 percent (new definition) of the labor force, and that percentage barely fluctuates with the business cycle.

The percentage of the labor force who work part-time for economic reasons experiences large swings. In the 1981–1982 recession, it climbed to 6.2 percent and in the 2008–2009 recession, it climbed to 6.4 percent.

■ FIGURE 6.5

Part-Time Workers: 1980–2013

MyEconLab Real-time data

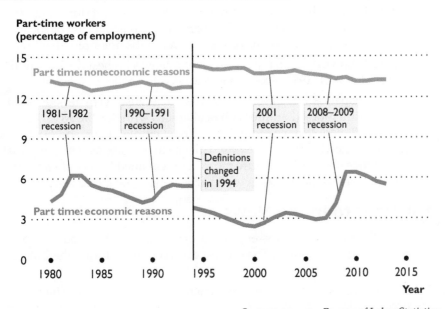

The annual average percentage of all employed workers who are part time for noneconomic reasons is a steady 13 percent (old definition) and 14 percent (new definition) and this percentage barely fluctuates with the business cycle.

But the percentage of all employed workers who are part time for economic reasons fluctuates with the business cycle. It increases in a recession and decreases in an expansion.

SOURCE OF DATA: Bureau of Labor Statistics.

MyEconLab Study Plan 6.2

Key Terms Quiz

Solutions

CHECKPOINT 6.2

Describe the trends and fluctuations in the indicators of labor market performance in the United States.

Practice Problems

FIGURE 1

Unemployment rate
(percentage of labor force)

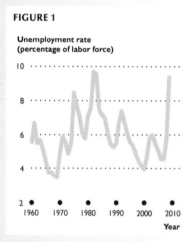

1. Figure 1 shows the unemployment rate in the United States from 1960 to 2010. In which decade—the 1960s, 1970s, 1980s, 1990s, or 2000s—was the average unemployment rate the lowest and what brought low unemployment in that decade? In which decade was the average unemployment rate the highest and what brought high unemployment in that decade?

2. Describe the trends in the participation rates of men and women and of all workers.

In the News

For young people, a jobless summer

In July 2009, the youth unemployment rate hit 18.5 percent—the highest level since the BLS started recording youth labor statistics. The proportion of young people working was 51.4 percent, another historic low for the month of July.

Source: *The Wall Street Journal*, August 27, 2009

In addition, Table 1 sets out data for the youth labor force participation rate and unemployment rate during four major recent U.S. recessions.

1. Compare the changes in the labor force participation rate during the recessions in Table 1. During which recession did the labor force participation rate drop the most?

2. Compare the changes in the unemployment rate during the recessions in Table 1. During which recession did the unemployment rate rise the most?

TABLE 1

Recession years	Participation rate	Unemployment rate
	(percent in July)	
1973	71.9	11.1
1974	73.2	12.4
1975	73.0	16.3
1981	75.3	16.2
1982	74.7	18.6
1990	75.1	10.9
1991	73.6	13.7
2008	65.1	14.0
2009	63.0	18.5

Solutions to Practice Problems

1. Figure 1 shows that the unemployment rate was lowest during the 1960s when defense spending on the Vietnam War and expansion of social programs brought rapid expansions and lowered the unemployment rate.

   Figure 1 shows that the unemployment rate was highest during the 1980s. During the 1981–1982 recession it increased to almost 10 percent.

2. The participation rate of women increased because (1) better-educated women earn more, (2) more white-collar jobs with flexible work hours were created, (3) people have more time for paid employment, and (4) families increasingly needed two incomes to balance their budgets. The participation rate of men decreased because more men remained in school and some men took early retirement. The overall participation rate increased.

Solutions to In the News

1. As each recession progressed, the participation rate dropped, except during the 1973–1975 recession. The biggest drop occurred during the 2008–2009 recession.

2. As each recession progressed, the unemployment rate rose. The biggest rise occurred during the 1973–1975 recession when it rose from 11.1 percent to 16.3 percent—a 5.2 percentage point rise.

6.3 UNEMPLOYMENT AND FULL EMPLOYMENT

MyEconLab Snapshot

There is always someone without a job who is searching for one, so there is always some unemployment. The key reason is that the labor market is constantly churning. New jobs are created and old jobs die; and some people move into the labor force and some move out of it. This churning creates unemployment.

We distinguish among three types of unemployment:

- Frictional unemployment
- Structural unemployment
- Cyclical unemployment

■ Frictional Unemployment

Frictional unemployment is the unemployment that arises from people entering and leaving the labor force, from quitting jobs to find better ones, and from the ongoing creation and destruction of jobs—from normal labor turnover. Frictional unemployment is a permanent and healthy phenomenon in a dynamic, growing economy.

There is an unending flow of people into and out of the labor force as people move through the stages of life—from being in school to finding a job, to working, perhaps to becoming unhappy with a job and looking for a new one, and finally, to retiring from full-time work.

There is also an unending process of job creation and job destruction as new firms are born, firms expand or contract, and some firms fail and go out of business.

The flows into and out of the labor force and the processes of job creation and job destruction create the need for people to search for jobs and for businesses to search for workers. Businesses don't usually hire the first person who applies for a job, and unemployed people don't usually take the first job that comes their way. Instead, both firms and workers spend time searching for what they believe will be the best available match. By this process of search, people can match their own skills and interests with the available jobs and find a satisfying job and a good income.

Frictional unemployment
The unemployment that arises from people entering and leaving the labor force, from quitting jobs to find better ones, and from the ongoing creation and destruction of jobs—from normal labor turnover.

A new graduate interviews for a job.

■ Structural Unemployment

Structural unemployment is the unemployment that arises when changes in technology or international competition change the skills needed to perform jobs or change the locations of jobs. Structural unemployment usually lasts longer than frictional unemployment because workers must retrain and possibly relocate to find a job. For example, when banks introduced the automatic teller machine in the 1970s, many bank-teller jobs were destroyed. Meanwhile, new jobs for life-insurance salespeople and retail clerks were created. The former bank tellers remained unemployed for several months until they moved, retrained, and got one of these new jobs. Structural unemployment is painful, especially for older workers for whom the best available option might be to retire early but with a lower income than they had expected.

Sometimes, the amount of structural unemployment is small. At other times, it is large, and at such times, structural unemployment can become a serious long-term problem. It was especially large during the late 1970s and early 1980s.

Structural unemployment
The unemployment that arises when changes in technology or international competition change the skills needed to perform jobs or change the locations of jobs.

Jobs lost to computer technology.

■ Cyclical Unemployment

Cyclical unemployment
The fluctuating unemployment over the business cycle that increases during a recession and decreases during an expansion.

The fluctuating unemployment over the business cycle—higher than normal unemployment at a business cycle trough and the lower than normal unemployment at a business cycle peak—is called **cyclical unemployment.** A worker who is laid off because the economy is in a recession and who gets rehired some months later when the expansion begins has experienced cyclical unemployment.

■ "Natural" Unemployment

Natural unemployment rate
The unemployment rate when the economy is at full employment.

Full employment
When there is no cyclical unemployment or, equivalently, when *all* the unemployment is frictional or structural.

Natural unemployment is the unemployment that arises from frictions and structural change when there is no cyclical unemployment—when all the unemployment is frictional and structural. Natural unemployment as a percentage of the labor force is called the **natural unemployment rate.**

Full employment is defined as a situation in which the unemployment rate equals the natural unemployment rate.

What determines the natural unemployment rate? Is it constant or does it change over time?

The natural unemployment rate is influenced by many factors but the most important ones are

- The age distribution of the population
- The pace of structural change
- The real wage rate
- Unemployment benefits

EYE on the UNEMPLOYED

How Long Does it Take to Find a Job?

The average duration of unemployment spells varies over the business cycle. In 2000, at a cycle peak when the unemployment rate was below the natural rate at 4 percent, the median time to find a job was 6 weeks. In 2013, in a slow expansion when the unemployment rate was above the natural rate at 7.5 percent, the median time to find a job was 16 weeks.

The figure provides more information: It shows the percentage of the unemployed at four unemployment durations. You can see that long-term unemployment (27 weeks and over) was much greater in 2013 than it was at the cycle peak in 2000.

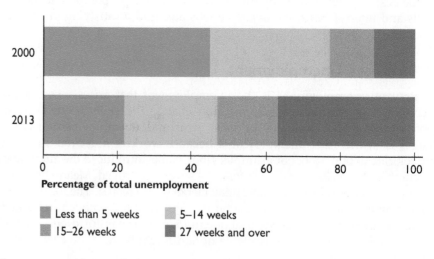

SOURCE OF DATA: Bureau of Labor Statistics.

The Age Distribution of the Population

An economy with a young population has lots of new job seekers every year and has a high level of frictional unemployment. An economy with an aging population has fewer new job seekers and a low level of frictional unemployment.

The Pace of Structural Change

The pace of structural change is sometimes low. The same jobs using the same machines remain in place for many years. But sometimes a technological upheaval sweeps aside the old ways, wipes out millions of jobs, and makes the skills once used to perform these jobs obsolete. The amount of structural unemployment fluctuates with the pace of technological change. The change is driven by fierce international competition, especially from fast-changing Asian economies. A high level of structural unemployment is present in many parts of the United States today.

The Real Wage Rate

The natural unemployment rate is influenced by the level of the real wage rate. Anything that raises the real wage rate above the market equilibrium level creates a surplus of labor and increases the natural unemployment rate. The real wage rate might exceed the market equilibrium level for two reasons: a minimum wage and an efficiency wage. The federal minimum wage creates unemployment because it is set above the equilibrium wage rate of low-skilled young workers. An efficiency wage is a wage set above the going market wage to enable firms to attract the most productive workers, get them to work hard, and discourage them from quitting. When firms set their wage above the going market wage, some workers would like to work for these firms but can't get jobs.

Unemployment Benefits

Unemployment benefits increase the natural unemployment rate by lowering the opportunity cost of job search. European countries have more generous unemployment benefits and higher natural unemployment rates than the United States. Extending unemployment benefits raises the natural unemployment rate.

There is no controversy about the existence of a natural unemployment rate. Nor is there disagreement that the natural unemployment rate changes. But economists don't know its exact size or the extent to which it fluctuates. The Congressional Budget Office estimates the natural unemployment rate and its estimate for 2013 was 6 percent—about 80 percent of the actual unemployment rate in that year.

■ Unemployment and Real GDP

Cyclical unemployment is the fluctuating unemployment over the business cycle—unemployment that increases during a recession and decreases during an expansion. At full employment, there is *no* cyclical unemployment. At a business cycle trough, cyclical unemployment is *positive* and at a business cycle peak, cyclical unemployment is *negative*.

Figure 6.6(a) shows the unemployment rate in the United States between 1980 and 2013. It also shows the natural unemployment rate and cyclical unemployment. The natural unemployment rate in this figure was estimated by the Congressional Budget Office (CBO).

In Figure 6.6(a), you can see that during most of the 1980s, the early 1990s, early 2000s, and during 2008–2009, unemployment was above the natural unemployment rate, so cyclical unemployment was positive (the red sections of the line). You can also see that during the late 1980s, from 1997 to 2001, and during 2005–2008 unemployment was below the natural unemployment rate, so cyclical unemployment was negative (the blue sections of the line).

As the unemployment rate fluctuates around the natural unemployment rate, real GDP fluctuates around potential GDP. **Potential GDP** is the value of real GDP when the economy is at full employment—all the economy's factors of production (labor, capital, land, and entrepreneurial ability) are employed. Real GDP equals potential GDP when the economy is at full employment. Real GDP minus potential GDP expressed as a percentage of potential GDP is called the **output gap.**

Figure 6.6(b) shows the U.S. *output gap* from 1980 to 2013. You can see that as the unemployment rate fluctuates around the natural unemployment rate, the output gap also fluctuates. When the unemployment rate is above the natural unemployment rate, in part (a), the output gap is negative (real GDP is below potential GDP), in part (b); when the unemployment rate is below the natural unemployment rate, the output gap is positive (real GDP is above potential GDP); and when the unemployment rate equals the natural unemployment rate, the output gap is zero (real GDP equals potential GDP).

You can also see in Figure 6.6 that the unemployment rate is a lagging indicator of the business cycle. Long after a recession is over, the unemployment rate is still rising.

Potential GDP
The value of real GDP when the economy is at full employment— all the economy's factors of production (labor, capital, land, and entrepreneurial ability) are employed.

Output gap
Real GDP minus potential GDP expressed as a percentage of potential GDP.

EYE on YOUR LIFE
Your Labor Market Status and Activity

You are going to spend a lot of your life in the labor market. Most of the time, you'll be supplying labor services. But first, you must find a job. Most likely, one job will not last your entire working life. You will want to find a new job when you decide to quit or when changing economic conditions destroy your current job.

As you look for a job, get a job, quit a job, or get laid off and look for a new job, you will pass through many and possibly all of the population categories used in the Current Population Survey that you've learned about in this chapter.

Think about your current labor market status while you are studying economics.

• Are you in the labor force or not?
• If you are in the labor force, are you employed or unemployed?
• If you are employed, are you a part-time or a full-time worker?

Now think about someone you know who is unemployed or has been unemployed. Classify the unemployment experienced by this person as

• frictional,
• structural, or
• cyclical.

How can you tell the type of unemployment experienced by this person?

The labor market conditions that you face today or when you graduate and look for a job depend partly on general national economic conditions—on whether the economy is in recession or booming.

Labor market conditions also depend on where you live. Visit the Bureau of Labor Statistics' Web site at www.bls.gov/sae/sm_mrs.htm. There you can find information on employment and unemployment for your state and metropolitan area or county. By comparing the labor market conditions in your own region with those in other areas, you can figure out where it might be easier to find work.

FIGURE 6.6

The Relationship Between Unemployment and the Output Gap

MyEconLab Real-time data

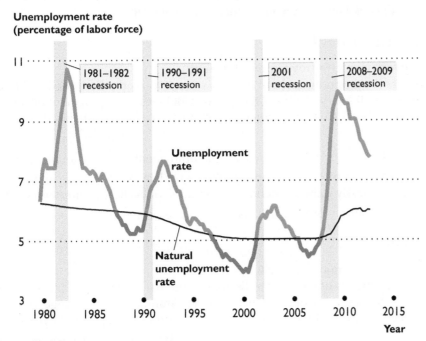

(a) Cyclical and natural unemployment

As the unemployment rate fluctuates around the natural unemployment rate in part (a), the output gap—real GDP minus potential GDP expressed as a percentage of potential GDP—fluctuates around a zero output gap in part (b).

When the unemployment rate *exceeds* the natural unemployment rate, real GDP is below potential GDP and the output gap is negative (red sections in both parts).

When the unemployment rate is *below* the natural unemployment rate, real GDP is above potential GDP and the output gap is positive (blue sections in both parts).

The natural unemployment rate shown in the graph is the Congressional Budget Office's estimate. It might turn out to be a substantial underestimate for the years since 2008.

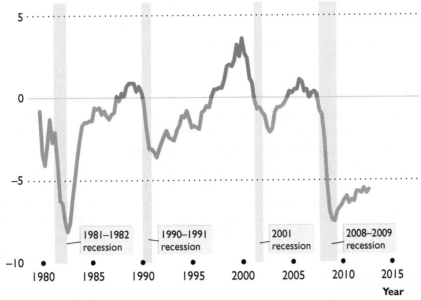

(b) The output gap

SOURCES OF DATA: Bureau of Economic Analysis, Bureau of Labor Statistics, and Congressional Budget Office.

MyEconLab Study Plan 6.3
Key Terms Quiz
Solutions

CHECKPOINT 6.3

Describe the types of unemployment, define full employment, and explain the link between unemployment and real GDP.

Practice Problems

Recovery won't improve unemployment
Despite some optimism about the seeds of recovery, the Congressional Budget Office (CBO) sees joblessness rising. The CBO sees unemployment peaking at 10.4% next year from an average of 9.3% this year, before it falls to 9.1% in 2011.

Source: *Fortune*, August 25, 2009

Before the recession began, the U.S. unemployment rate was about 6 percent.

1. As a recession begins, firms quickly make layoffs. Is this rise in unemployment mostly a rise in frictional, structural, or cyclical unemployment?
2. Why does unemployment continue to rise as an expansion begins?

In the News

BofA cutbacks may hit 40,000
Bank of America officials have discussed eliminating about 40,000 positions during the first wave of a restructuring. The numbers could change, but the restructuring would reduce the bank's workforce over a period of years.

Source: *The Wall Street Journal*, September 9, 2011

Postal Service targets 220,000 job cuts
The U.S. Postal Service plans to reduce its workforce by 220,000 jobs to remedy its dire financial situation. The Postal Service, financed mostly by postage, has been struggling as a result of the economic slowdown.

Source: *The Wall Street Journal*, August 12, 2011

What type of unemployment will arise from the cut in employment in each of these cases? Explain your answer.

Solutions to Practice Problems

1. When a recession starts, firms are quick to lay off workers. Most of the rise in unemployment is cyclical—related to the state of the economy. The unemployment rate rises quickly as the number of layoffs increases.
2. The unemployment rate is a lagging indicator of the business cycle. When an expansion begins, firms start hiring. Unemployed workers get jobs, but the labor force increases as marginally attached workers start to look for jobs. In the early stages of an expansion, the number of marginally attached workers looking for jobs exceeds the number of people hired and unemployment increases.

Solution to In the News

Bank of America is reducing its workforce as it restructures its organization in response to changing technology. Because online banking has grown, the bank will close many branches. Cuts in its workforce will create structural unemployment. The U.S. Postal Service is cutting its workforce in response to a downturn in economic activity. Cuts in its workforce will create cyclical unemployment.

CHAPTER SUMMARY

Key Points

1. **Define the unemployment rate and other labor market indicators.**

   - The unemployment rate is the number of people unemployed as a percentage of the labor force, and the labor force is the sum of the number of people employed and the number unemployed.
   - The labor force participation rate is the labor force as a percentage of the working-age population.

2. **Describe the trends and fluctuations in the indicators of labor market performance in the United States.**

   - The unemployment rate fluctuates with the business cycle, increasing in recessions and decreasing in expansions.
   - The labor force participation rate of women has increased, and the labor force participation rate of men has decreased.

3. **Describe the types of unemployment, define full employment, and explain the link between unemployment and real GDP.**

   - Unemployment can be frictional, structural, or cyclical.
   - Full employment occurs when there is no cyclical unemployment and at full employment, the unemployment rate equals the natural unemployment rate.
   - Potential GDP is the real GDP produced when the economy is at full employment.
   - As the unemployment rate fluctuates around the natural unemployment rate, real GDP fluctuates around potential GDP and the output gap fluctuates between negative and positive values.

Key Terms

MyEconLab Key Terms Quiz

CHAPTER CHECKPOINT

Study Plan Problems and Applications

Use the following information gathered by a BLS labor market survey of four households to work Problems 1 and 2.

- Household 1: Candy worked 20 hours last week setting up her Internet shopping business. The rest of the week, she completed application forms and attended two job interviews. Husband Jerry worked 40 hours at his job at GM. Daughter Meg, a student, worked 10 hours at her weekend job at Starbucks.
- Household 2: Joey, a full-time bank clerk, was on vacation. Wife, Serena, who wants a full-time job, worked 10 hours as a part-time checkout clerk.
- Household 3: Ari had no work last week but was going to be recalled to his regular job in two weeks. Partner Kosta, after months of searching for a job and not being able to find one, has stopped looking and will go back to school.
- Household 4: Mimi and Henry are retired. Son Hank is a professional artist, who painted for 12 hours last week and sold one picture.

1. Classify each of the 10 people into the labor market category used by the BLS. Who are part-time workers and who are full-time workers? Of the part-time workers, who works part time for economic reasons?

2. Calculate the unemployment rate and the labor force participation rate, and compare these rates with those in the United States in 2013.

3. Describe two examples of people who work part time for economic reasons and two examples of people who work part time for noneconomic reasons.

4. Explain the relationship between the percentage of employed workers who have part-time jobs and the business cycle.

5. Distinguish among the three types of unemployment: frictional, structural, and cyclical. Provide an example of each type of unemployment in the United States today.

6. Describe the relationship between the unemployment rate and the natural unemployment rate as the output gap fluctuates between being positive and being negative.

Use the following information to work Problems 7 and 8.

U.S. unemployment rate lowest since 2008
The Labor Department said that the economy added 146,000 jobs in November, and the unemployment rate fell to 7.7% from 7.9% in October. But it fell mainly because workers dropped out of the labor force.

Source: CNN Money, December 7, 2012

7. Explain how the new jobs change the labor force and the unemployment rate.

8. Explain why workers dropping out of the labor force lowers the unemployment rate and why by more than new jobs do.

9. Read *Eye on the Unemployed* on p. 156. In which year, 2000 or 2013, was real GDP below potential GDP? How can you tell from the graph on p. 156?

Instructor Assignable Problems and Applications

MyEconLab Homework, Quiz, or
Test if assigned by instructor

Real-Time Data

1. In the United States,
   * Compare the duration of unemployment in 2013 with that in 2000 and explain whether the difference was most likely the result of frictions, structural change, or the business cycle.
   * How does the unemployment of marginally attached workers influence the duration of unemployment in 2013 compared with that in 2000?

2. The Bureau of Labor Statistics reported that in the second quarter of 2008 the working-age population was 233,410,000, the labor force was 154,294,000, and employment was 146,089,000. Calculate for that quarter the labor force participation rate and the unemployment rate.

3. In July 2011, in the economy of Sandy Island, 10,000 people were employed and 1,000 were unemployed. During August 2011, 80 people lost their jobs and didn't look for new ones, 20 people quit their jobs and retired, 150 people who had looked for work were hired, 50 people became discouraged workers, and 40 new graduates looked for work. Calculate the change in the unemployment rate from July 2011 to August 2011.

4. The BLS survey reported the following data in a community of 320 people: 200 worked at least 1 hour as paid employees; 20 did not work but were temporarily absent from their jobs; 40 did not have jobs and didn't want to work; 10 were available for work and last week they had looked for work; and 6 were available for work and were waiting to be recalled to their previous job. Calculate the unemployment rate and the labor force participation rate.

5. Describe the trends and fluctuations in the unemployment rate in the United States from 1949 through 2013. In which periods was the unemployment rate above average and in which periods was it below average?

6. Describe how the labor force participation rate in the United States changed between 1960 and 2013. Contrast and explain the different trends in the labor force participation rates of women and men.

7. Explain why the natural unemployment rate is not zero and why the unemployment rate fluctuates around the natural unemployment rate.

Use the following information to work Problems 8 and 9.

Michigan unemployment tops 15%
The U.S. Department of Labor reported that Michigan's unemployment rate in June 2009 rose to 15.2%, becoming the first state in 25 years to suffer an unemployment rate exceeding 15%. Michigan has been battered by the collapse of the auto industry and the housing crisis and has had the highest unemployment rate in the nation for the past 12 months.

Source: CNN Money, July 17, 2009

8. Why is the reality of the unemployment problem in Michigan actually worse than the unemployment rate statistic of 15.2 percent?

9. Is this increased unemployment frictional, structural, or cyclical? Explain.

Multiple Choice Quiz

1. The BLS counts Jody as being unemployed if she _____.
   - A. had a job last month but not this month
   - B. doesn't have a job because the U.S. factory where she worked cannot compete with cheap Chinese imports
   - C. wants a job and looked for a job last year but has now stopped looking
   - D. wants a job and is willing to take a job but after searching last week cannot find a job

2. A marginally attached worker is a person who _____.
   - A. works part time for economic reasons
   - B. works part time for noneconomic reasons
   - C. doesn't work, is available and willing to work, but hasn't looked for a job recently
   - D. has no job but would like one and has gone back to school to retrain

3. If the BLS included all marginally attached workers as being unemployed, the _____ would be _____.
   - A. unemployment rate; higher
   - B. labor force; unchanged
   - C. labor force participation rate; lower
   - D. unemployment rate; lower

4. When the economy goes into recession, the biggest increase in unemployment is _____.
   - A. structural because jobs are lost in most states
   - B. cyclical because jobs are lost in many industries as they cut production
   - C. frictional because the creation of jobs slows
   - D. the combination of structural and frictional as few new jobs are created

5. The economy is at full employment when all unemployment is _____.
   - A. structural
   - B. cyclical
   - C. structural and cyclical
   - D. structural and frictional

6. Potential GDP is the value of real GDP when _____.
   - A. the unemployment rate equals the natural unemployment rate
   - B. there is no frictional unemployment
   - C. there is no structural unemployment
   - D. the unemployment rate is zero

7. When the unemployment rate_____ the natural unemployment rate, real GDP is _____ potential GDP and the output gap is _____.
   - A. exceeds; below; negative
   - B. is below; below; negative
   - C. exceeds; above; positive
   - D. is below; above; negative

MyEconLab Big Picture

Which movie *really* was
the biggest box office hit?

The CPI and the Cost of Living

7

**When you have completed your study of this chapter,
you will be able to**

1 Explain what the Consumer Price Index (CPI) is and how it is calculated.

2 Explain the limitations of the CPI and describe other measures of the price level.

3 Adjust money values for inflation and calculate real wage rates and real interest rates.

7.1 THE CONSUMER PRICE INDEX

The **Consumer Price Index** (CPI) is a measure of the average of the prices paid by urban consumers for a fixed market basket of consumption goods and services. The Bureau of Labor Statistics (BLS) calculates the CPI every month, and we can use these numbers to compare what the fixed market basket costs this month with what it cost in some previous month or other period.

■ Reading the CPI Numbers

The CPI is defined to equal 100 for a period called the **reference base period.** Currently, the reference base period is 1982–1984. That is, the CPI equals 100 on the average over the 36 months from January 1982 through December 1984.

In May 2013, the CPI was 232.9. This number tells us that the average of the prices paid by urban consumers for a fixed market basket of consumption goods and services was 132.9 percent higher in May 2013 than it was on the average during 1982–1984.

In April 2013, the CPI was 232.5. Comparing the CPI in May 2013 with the CPI in April 2013 tells us that the average of the prices paid by urban consumers for a fixed market basket of consumption goods and services *increased* by 0.4 percentage points in May 2013.

■ Constructing the CPI

Constructing the CPI is a huge operation that costs millions of dollars and involves three stages:

- Selecting the CPI market basket
- Conducting the monthly price survey
- Calculating the CPI

■ The CPI Market Basket

The first stage in constructing the CPI is to determine the *CPI market basket.* This "basket" contains the goods and services represented in the index and the relative importance, or weight, attached to each of them. The idea is to make the weight of the items in the CPI basket the same as in the budget of an average urban household. For example, if the average household spends 2 percent of its income on public transportation, then the CPI places a weight of 2 percent on the prices of bus, subway, and other transit system rides.

Although the CPI is calculated every month, the CPI market basket isn't updated every month. The information used to determine the CPI market basket comes from a survey, called the *Consumer Expenditure Survey,* that discovers what people actually buy. This survey is an ongoing activity, and the CPI market basket in 2013 was based on a survey conducted during 2011. An astonishing 88,000 individuals and families contributed information. Some of them were interviewed every three months, and others kept detailed diaries for two weeks in which they listed absolutely everything they bought. (Before 1999, the Consumer Expenditure Survey was conducted less frequently.)

The reference base period for the CPI has been fixed at 1982–1984 for more than 20 years and doesn't change when a new Consumer Expenditure Survey is used to update the market basket.

Figure 7.1 shows the CPI market basket in May 2013. The basket contains around 80,000 goods and services arranged in the eight large groups shown in the figure. The most important item in a household's budget is housing, which accounts for 40.9 percent of total expenditure. Transportation comes next at 17.2 percent. Third in relative importance is food and beverages at 15.2 percent. These three groups account for almost three quarters of the average household budget. Medical care takes 7.0 percent, education and communication takes 6.7 percent, recreation takes 6 percent, and apparel (clothing and footwear) takes 3.6 percent. Another 3.4 percent is spent on other goods and services.

The BLS breaks down each of these categories into smaller ones. For example, education and communication breaks down into textbooks and supplies, tuition, telephone services, and personal computer services.

As you look at these numbers, remember that they apply to the average household. Each individual household is spread around the average. Think about your own expenditure and compare it with the average.

■ The Monthly Price Survey

Each month, BLS employees check the prices of the 80,000 goods and services in the CPI market basket in 30 metropolitan areas. Because the CPI aims to measure price changes, it is important that the prices recorded each month refer to exactly the same items. For example, suppose the price of a box of jelly beans has increased but a box now contains more beans. Has the price of a jelly bean increased? The BLS employee must record the details of changes in quality, size, weight, or packaging so that price changes can be isolated from other changes.

Once the raw price data are in hand, the next task is to calculate the CPI.

■ FIGURE 7.1

The CPI Market Basket

MyEconLab Animation

CPI weights

Other goods and services (3.4 percent)
Apparel (3.6 percent)
Recreation (6.0 percent)
Education and communication (6.7 percent)
Medical care (7.0 percent)
Food and beverages (15.2 percent)

Transportation (17.2 percent)

Housing (40.9 percent)

This shopping cart is filled with the items that an average urban household buys. Housing (40.9 percent), transportation (17.2 percent), and food and beverages (15.2 percent) take almost three quarters of household income.

SOURCE OF DATA: Bureau of Labor Statistics.

■ Calculating the CPI

The CPI calculation has three steps:

- Find the cost of the CPI market basket at base period prices.
- Find the cost of the CPI market basket at current period prices.
- Calculate the CPI for the base period and the current period.

We'll work through these three steps for a simple example. Suppose the CPI market basket contains only two goods and services: oranges and haircuts. We'll construct an annual CPI rather than a monthly CPI with the reference base period 2010 and the current period 2014.

Table 7.1 shows the quantities in the CPI market basket and the prices in the base period and the current period. Part (a) contains the data for the base period. In that period, consumers bought 10 oranges at $1 each and 5 haircuts at $8 each. To find the cost of the CPI market basket in the base period prices, multiply the quantities in the CPI market basket by the base period prices. The cost of oranges is $10 (10 at $1 each), and the cost of haircuts is $40 (5 at $8 each). So total expenditure in the base period on the CPI market basket is $50 ($10 + $40).

Part (b) contains the price data for the current period. The price of an orange increased from $1 to $2, which is a 100 percent increase ($1 ÷ $1 × 100 = 100 percent). The price of a haircut increased from $8 to $10, which is a 25 percent increase ($2 ÷ $8 × 100 = 25 percent).

The CPI provides a way of averaging these price increases by comparing the cost of the basket rather than the price of each item. To find the cost of the CPI market basket in the current period, 2014, multiply the quantities in the basket by their 2014 prices. The cost of oranges is $20 (10 at $2 each), and the cost of haircuts is $50 (5 at $10 each). So total expenditure on the fixed CPI market basket at current period prices is $70 ($20 + $50).

TABLE 7.1

The Consumer Price Index: A Simplified CPI Calculation

(a) The cost of the CPI basket at base period prices: 2010

Item	CPI market basket Quantity	CPI market basket Price	Cost of CPI basket
Oranges	10	$1 each	$10
Haircuts	5	$8 each	$40
		Cost of CPI market basket at base period prices	$50

(b) The cost of the CPI basket at current period prices: 2014

Item	CPI market basket Quantity	CPI market basket Price	Cost of CPI basket
Oranges	10	$2 each	$20
Haircuts	5	$10 each	$50
		Cost of CPI market basket at current period prices	$70

You've now taken the first two steps toward calculating the CPI. The third step uses the numbers you've just calculated to find the CPI for 2010 and 2014. The formula for the CPI is

$$\text{CPI} = \frac{\text{Cost of CPI basket at current period prices}}{\text{Cost of CPI basket at base period prices}} \times 100.$$

In Table 7.1, you established that in 2010, the cost of the CPI market basket was $50 and in 2014, it was $70. If we use these numbers in the CPI formula, we can find the CPI for 2010 and 2014. The base period is 2010, so

$$\text{CPI in 2010} = \frac{\$50}{\$50} \times 100 = 100.$$

$$\text{CPI in 2014} = \frac{\$70}{\$50} \times 100 = 140.$$

The principles that you've applied in this simplified CPI calculation apply to the more complex calculations performed every month by the BLS.

Figure 7.2(a) shows the CPI in the United States during the 40 years between 1973 and 2013. The CPI increased every year during this period until 2009 when it fell slightly. During the late 1970s and in 1980, the CPI was increasing rapidly, but since the early 1980s, the rate of increase has slowed.

■ Measuring Inflation and Deflation

A major purpose of the CPI is to measure *changes* in the cost of living and in the value of money. To measure these changes, we calculate the **inflation rate,** which is the percentage change in the price level from one year to the next. To calculate the inflation rate, we use the formula

Inflation rate
The percentage change in the price level from one year to the next.

$$\text{Inflation rate} = \frac{(\text{CPI in current year} - \text{CPI in previous year})}{\text{CPI in previous year}} \times 100.$$

Suppose that the current year is 2014 and the CPI for 2014 is 140. And suppose that in the previous year, 2013, the CPI was 120. Then in 2014,

$$\text{Inflation rate} = \frac{(140 - 120)}{120} \times 100 = 16.7 \text{ percent}.$$

If the inflation rate is *negative*, the price level is *falling* and we have **deflation.** The United States has rarely experienced deflation, but 2009 was one of those rare years. You can check the latest data by visiting the BLS Web site. In July 2009, the CPI was 215.4, and in July 2008, it was 220.0. So during the year to July 2009,

Deflation
A situation in which the price level is *falling* and the inflation rate is *negative*.

$$\text{Inflation rate} = \frac{(215.4 - 220.0)}{220.0} \times 100 = -2.1 \text{ percent}.$$

Figure 7.2(b) shows the inflation rate in the United States between 1973 and 2013. The change in the price level in part (a) and the inflation rate in part (b) are related. When the price *level* rises rapidly, the inflation rate is high; when the price *level* rises slowly, the inflation rate is low; and when the price level is falling, the inflation rate is negative.

EYE on the PAST
700 Years of Inflation and Deflation

These extraordinary data show that inflation became a persistent problem only after 1900. During the preceding 600 years, inflation was almost unknown. Inflation increased slightly during the sixteenth century after Europeans discovered gold in America. But this inflation barely reached 2 percent a year—less than we have today—and eventually subsided. The Industrial Revolution saw a temporary burst of inflation followed by a period of deflation.

SOURCES OF DATA: E.H. Phelps Brown and Sheila V. Hopkins, *Economica*, 1955, and Robert Sahr, http://oregonstate.edu/dept/pol_sci/fac/sahr/sahr.htm.

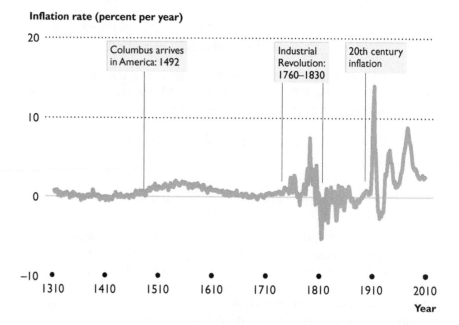

FIGURE 7.2

The CPI and the Inflation Rate: 1973–2013

MyEconLab Real-time data

(a) CPI: 1973–2013

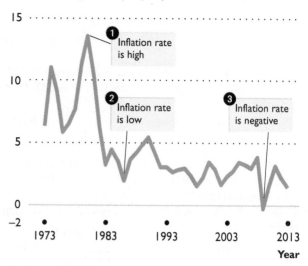

(b) CPI inflation rate: 1973–2013

SOURCE OF DATA: Bureau of Labor Statistics.

❶ The price level in part (a) was rising rapidly during the 1970s and 1980s and the inflation rate in part (b) was high.

❷ The price level was rising slowly during the 1990s and 2000s and the inflation rate was low.

❸ In 2009, the price level fell and the inflation rate was negative.

CHECKPOINT 7.1

MyEconLab Study Plan 7.1
Key Terms Quiz
Solutions

Explain what the Consumer Price Index (CPI) is and how it is calculated.

Practice Problems

A Consumer Expenditure Survey in Sparta shows that people buy only juice and cloth. In 2012, the year of the Consumer Expenditure Survey and also the reference base year, the average household spent $40 on juice and $25 on cloth. Table 1 sets out the prices of juice and cloth in 2012 and 2014.

1. Calculate the CPI market basket and the percentage of the average household budget spent on juice in the reference base year.

2. Calculate the CPI in 2014 and the inflation rate between 2012 and 2014.

3. Table 2 shows the CPI in Sparta. Calculate the inflation rates in 2010 and 2011. Did the price level rise in 2011? Did the inflation rate increase in 2011?

TABLE 1 PRICES

	2012	2014
Juice	$4 a bottle	$4 a bottle
Cloth	$5 a yard	$6 a yard

In the News

Consumer price index falls 0.4% in April
The CPI in April 2013 was 233 and 0.4% lower than in March. In April, food prices rose 0.2% while energy prices fell 4.3%.

Source: BLS, April, 2013

Distinguish between the price level and the inflation rate and explain why the CPI fell by only 0.4 percent when energy fell by 4.3 percent.

TABLE 2

Year	CPI
2009	200
2010	219
2011	237

Solutions to Practice Problems

1. The CPI market basket is the quantities bought during the Consumer Expenditure Survey year, 2012. The average household spent $40 on juice at $4 a bottle, so it bought 10 bottles of juice. The average household spent $25 on cloth at $5 a yard, so it bought 5 yards of cloth. The CPI market basket is made up of 10 bottles of juice and 5 yards of cloth.
   In the reference base year, the average household spent $40 on juice and $25 on cloth, so the household budget was $65. Expenditure on juice was 61.5 percent of the household budget: ($40 ÷ $65) × 100 = 61.5 percent.

2. To calculate the CPI in 2014, find the cost of the CPI market basket in 2012 and 2014. In 2012, the CPI basket costs $65 ($40 for juice + $25 for cloth). In 2014, the CPI market basket costs $70 (10 bottles of juice at $4 a bottle + 5 yards of cloth at $6 a yard). The CPI in 2014 is ($70 ÷ $65) × 100 = 107.7. The inflation rate is [(107.7 − 100) ÷ 100] × 100 = 7.7 percent.

3. The inflation rate in 2010 is [(219 − 200) ÷ 200] × 100 = 9.5 percent. The inflation rate in 2011 is [(237 − 219) ÷ 219] × 100 = 8.2 percent. In 2011, the price level increased, but the inflation rate decreased.

Solution to In the News

The CPI is the price level. The percentage change in the CPI is the inflation rate. Food and beverage is 15.2 percent of the CPI basket. Energy is included in transportation and housing. For the CPI to have fallen by 0.4 percent when energy prices fell 4.3 percent, other prices must have risen by more than 0.4 percent.

Cost of living index
A measure of the change in the amount of money that people need to spend to achieve a given standard of living.

7.2 THE CPI AND OTHER PRICE LEVEL MEASURES

The purpose of the CPI is to measure the cost of living or what amounts to the same thing, the *value of money*. The CPI is sometimes called a **cost of living index** —a measure of the change in the amount of money that people need to spend to achieve a given standard of living. The CPI is not a perfect measure of the cost of living (value of money) for two broad reasons.

First, the CPI does not try to measure all the changes in the cost of living. For example, the cost of living rises in a severe winter as people buy more natural gas and electricity to heat their homes. A rise in the prices of these items increases the CPI. But the increased quantities of natural gas and electricity bought don't change the CPI because the CPI market basket is fixed. So part of this increase in spending—the increase in the cost of maintaining a given standard of living—doesn't show up as an increase in the CPI.

Second, even those components of the cost of living that are measured by the CPI are not always measured accurately. The result is that the CPI is possibly a biased measure of changes in the cost of living.

Let's look at some of the sources of bias in the CPI and the ways the BLS tries to overcome them.

■ Sources of Bias in the CPI

The potential sources of bias in the CPI are

- New goods bias
- Quality change bias
- Commodity substitution bias
- Outlet substitution bias

New Goods Bias

Every year, some new goods become available and some old goods disappear. Make a short list of items that you take for granted today that were not available 10 or 20 years ago. This list includes cell phones, tablet computers, and flat-panel, large-screen television sets. A list of items no longer available or rarely bought includes audiocassette players, vinyl records, photographic film, and typewriters.

When we want to compare the price level in 2014 with that in 2004, 1994, or 1984, we must do so by comparing the prices of different baskets of goods. We can't compare the same baskets because today's basket wasn't available 10 years ago and the basket of 10 years ago isn't available today.

To make comparisons, the BLS tries to measure the price of the service performed by yesterday's goods and today's goods. It tries to compare, for example, the price of listening to recorded music, regardless of the technology that delivers that service. But the comparison is hard to make. Today's smart phone delivers an improved quality of sound and level of convenience compared to yesterday's Walkman and Discman.

How much of a new product represents an increase in quantity and quality and how much represents a higher price? The BLS does its best to answer this question, but there is no sure way of making the necessary adjustment. It is believed that the arrival of new goods puts an upward bias into the CPI and its measure of the inflation rate.

To measure the CPI, the BLS must compare the price of today's smart phone with that of the 1970s Walkman and 1980s Discman.

Quality Change Bias

Cars, cell phones, laptops, and many other items get better every year. For example, central locking, airbags, and antilock braking systems all add to the quality of a car. But they also add to the cost. Is the improvement in quality greater than the increase in cost? Or do car prices rise by more than can be accounted for by quality improvements? To the extent that a price rise is a payment for improved quality, it is not inflation. Again, the BLS does the best job it can to estimate the effects of quality improvements on price changes. But the CPI probably counts too much of any price rise as inflation and so overstates inflation.

To compare the price of today's cars with those of earlier years, the BLS must value the improvements in features and quality.

Commodity Substitution Bias

Changes in relative prices lead consumers to change the items they buy. People cut back on items that become relatively more costly and increase their consumption of items that become relatively less costly. For example, suppose the price of carrots rises while the price of broccoli remains constant. Now that carrots are more costly relative to broccoli, you might decide to buy more broccoli and fewer carrots. Suppose that you switch from carrots to broccoli, spend the same amount on vegetables as before, and get the same enjoyment as before. Your cost of vegetables has not changed. The CPI says that the price of vegetables has increased because it ignores your substitution between goods in the CPI market basket.

When consumers substitute lower priced broccoli for higher priced carrots, the CPI overstates the rise in the price of vegetables.

Outlet Substitution Bias

When confronted with higher prices, people use discount stores more frequently and convenience stores less frequently. This phenomenon is called *outlet substitution*. Suppose, for example, that gas prices rise by 10¢ a gallon. Instead of buying from your nearby gas station for $4.599 a gallon, you now drive farther to a gas station that charges $4.499 a gallon. Your cost of gas has increased because you must factor in the cost of your time and the gas that you use driving several blocks down the road. But your cost has not increased by as much as the 10¢ a gallon increase in the pump price. However, the CPI says that the price of gas has increased by 10¢ a gallon because the CPI does not measure outlet substitution.

The growth of online shopping in recent years has provided an alternative to discount stores that makes outlet substitution even easier and potentially makes this source of bias more serious.

As consumers shop around for the lowest prices, outlet substitution occurs and the CPI overstates the rise in prices actually paid.

■ The Magnitude of the Bias

You have reviewed the sources of bias in the CPI. But how big is the bias? When this question was tackled in 1996 by a Congressional Advisory Commission chaired by Michael Boskin, an economics professor at Stanford University, the answer was that the CPI overstated inflation by 1.1 percentage points a year. That is, if the CPI reports that inflation is 3.1 percent a year, most likely inflation is actually 2 percent a year.

In the period since the Boskin Commission reported, the BLS has taken steps to reduce the CPI bias. The more frequent Consumer Expenditure Survey that we described earlier in this chapter is one of these steps. Beyond that, the BLS uses ever more sophisticated models and methods to try to eliminate the sources of bias and make the CPI as accurate as possible.

■ Two Consequences of the CPI Bias

Avoiding bias in the CPI is important for two main reasons. Bias leads to

- Distortion of private contracts
- Increases in government outlays and decreases in taxes

Distortion of Private Contracts

Many wage contracts contain a cost of living adjustment. For example, the United Auto Workers Union (UAW) and Ford Motor Company might agree on a wage rate of $30 an hour initially that increases over three years at the same rate as the cost of living increases. The idea is that both the union and the employer want a contract in "real" terms. As the cost of living rises, the firm wants to pay the workers the number of dollars per hour that buys a given market basket of goods and services. And the firm is happy to pay the higher wage because it can sell its output for a higher price.

Suppose that over the three years of a UAW and Ford contract, the CPI increases by 5 percent each year. The wage rate paid by Ford will increase to $31.50 in the second year and $33.08 in the third year.

But suppose that the CPI is biased and the true price increase is 3 percent a year. The workers' cost of living increases by this amount, so in the second year, $30.90 rather than $31.50 is the intended wage. In the third year, a wage rate of $31.83 and not $33.08 compensates for the higher cost of living. So in the second year, the workers gain 60¢ an hour, or $21 for a 35-hour workweek. And in the third year, they gain $1.25 an hour, or $43.75 for a 35-hour workweek.

The workers' gain is Ford's loss. With a work force of a few thousand, the loss amounts to several thousand dollars a week and a few million dollars over the life of a 3-year wage contract.

If the CPI bias was common knowledge and large, the CPI would not be used without some adjustment in contracts. Unions and employers would seek agreement on the extent of the bias and make an appropriate adjustment to their contract. But for a small bias, the cost of negotiating a more complicated agreement might be too large.

Increases in Government Outlays and Decreases in Taxes

Because rising prices decrease the buying power of the dollar, the CPI is used to adjust the incomes of the 55 million Social Security beneficiaries, 45 million food stamp recipients, and 4 million retired former military personnel and federal civil servants (and their surviving spouses). The CPI is also used to adjust the budget for 3 million school lunches.

Close to a third of federal government outlays are linked directly to the CPI. If the CPI has a 1.1 percentage point bias, all of these expenditures increase by more than required to compensate for the fall in the buying power of the dollar and, although a bias of 1.1 percent a year seems small, accumulated over a decade, it adds up to almost a trillion dollars of additional government outlays.

The CPI is also used to adjust the income levels at which higher tax rates apply. The tax rates on large incomes are higher than those on small incomes so, as incomes rise, if these adjustments were not made, the burden of taxes would rise relentlessly. To the extent that the CPI is biased upward, the tax adjustments over-compensate for rising prices and decrease the amount paid in taxes.

■ Alternative Measures of the Price Level and Inflation Rate

Several alternative measures of the price level and inflation rate are available. One based on wholesale prices and another based on producers' prices are similar to the CPI, both in the way they are constructed and their potential for bias. But three other price indexes that we'll briefly describe here are less biased. These indexes are the

- GDP price index
- Personal consumption expenditures (PCE) price index
- PCE price index excluding food and energy

GDP Price Index

The **GDP price index** (also called the *GDP deflator*) is an average of the current prices of all the goods and services included in GDP expressed as a percentage of base year prices. Two key differences between the GDP price index and the CPI result in different estimates of the price level and inflation rate.

First, the GDP price index uses the prices of all the goods and services in GDP—consumption goods and services, capital goods, government goods and services, and export goods and services—while the CPI uses prices of consumption goods and services only. For example, the GDP price index includes the prices of paper mills bought by 3M to make Post-it® Notes, nuclear submarines bought by the Defense Department, and Boeing 747s bought by British Airways.

Second, the GDP price index weights each item using information about current quantities. In contrast, the CPI weights each item using information from a *past* Consumer Expenditure Survey. But because of the breadth of the items that the GDP price index includes, it is not an alternative to the CPI as a measure of the cost of living.

GDP price index
An average of the current prices of all the goods and services included in GDP expressed as a percentage of base year prices.

Personal Consumption Expenditures (PCE) Price Index

The **Personal Consumption Expenditures price index** (or **PCE price index**) is an average of the current prices of the goods and services included in the consumption expenditure component of GDP expressed as a percentage of base year prices. The PCE price index has the same advantages as the GDP price index—it uses current information on quantities and to some degree overcomes the sources of bias in the CPI. It also has an advantage shared by the CPI of focusing on consumption expenditure and therefore being a possible measure of the cost of living.

A weakness of the PCE price index is that it is based on data that become known after the lapse of several months. So the CPI provides more current information about the inflation rate than what the PCE price index provides.

PCE price index
An average of the current prices of the goods and services included in the consumption expenditure component of GDP expressed as a percentage of base year prices.

PCE Price Index Excluding Food and Energy

Food and energy prices fluctuate much more than other prices and their changes can obscure the underlying trends in prices. By excluding these highly variable items, the underlying price level and inflation trends can be seen more clearly. The percentage change in the PCE price index excluding food and energy is called the **core inflation rate.**

Figure 7.3(a) shows the three *price levels* measured by the CPI, the PCE price index, and PCE price index excluding food and energy. The two measures based on the PCE price index are very similar but the CPI measure rises above the other two and the gap widens to 100 percentage points over the 40 years shown here.

Core inflation rate
The annual percentage change in the PCE price index excluding the prices of food and energy.

Figure 7.3(b) shows the three consumer price *inflation rates*. These measures move up and down in similar ways, but the CPI measure exceeds the PCE price index measures. The average difference between the CPI and PCE measures is about a half a percentage point. The core inflation rate has almost the same average as the PCE inflation rate, but it fluctuates less. You can see why this measure provides a better indication of the inflation trend than the index that includes food and energy prices.

This higher CPI is a reflection of its bias and a confirmation that the PCE price index, which is based on current period actual expenditures, avoids most of the sources of bias in the CPI.

◼ FIGURE 7.3

Three Measures of Consumer Prices

MyEconLab Real-time data

The three measures of the *price level* in part (a) rise together, but the CPI rises above the two PCE measures reflecting the bias in the CPI.

The three measures of the *inflation rate* in part (b) fluctuate together, but the CPI inflation rate is higher than the PCE price index inflation rate or the core inflation rate. The core inflation rate fluctuates less than the other two measures.

(a) Three measures of price level

(b) Three measures of inflation

SOURCES OF DATA: Bureau of Labor Statistics and Bureau of Economic Analysis.

CHECKPOINT 7.2

Explain the limitations of the CPI and describe other measures of the price level.

Practice Problems

Economists in the Statistics Bureau decide to check the CPI substitution bias. To do so, they conduct a Consumer Expenditure Survey in both 2012 and 2013. Table 1 shows the results of the survey. It shows the items that consumers buy and their prices. The Statistics Bureau fixes the reference base year as 2012.

1. Calculate the CPI in 2013 if the CPI basket contains the 2012 quantities.
2. Calculate the CPI in 2013 if the CPI basket contains the 2013 quantities.
3. Is there any substitution bias in the CPI that uses the 2012 basket? Explain.

TABLE 1

	2012		2013	
Item	Quantity	Price	Quantity	Price
Broccoli	10	$3.00	15	$3.00
Carrots	15	$2.00	10	$4.00

In the News

News releases

In 2011, the CPI increased by 1.4 percent, the GDP price index increased by 1.2 percent, and the PCE price index increased by 1.8 percent.

Source: Bureau of Economic Analysis, August 29, 2011

Why do these three measures of the price level give different inflation rates?

Solutions to Practice Problems

1. Table 2 shows the calculation of the CPI in 2013 when the CPI basket is made of the 2012 quantities. The cost of the 2012 basket at 2012 prices is $60 and the cost of the 2012 basket at 2013 prices is $90. So the CPI in 2013 using the 2012 basket is ($90 ÷ $60) × 100 = 150.

2. Table 3 shows the calculation of the CPI in 2013 when the CPI basket is made of the 2013 quantities. The cost of the 2013 basket at 2012 prices is $65, and the cost of the 2013 basket at 2013 prices is $85. So the CPI in 2013 using the 2013 basket is ($85 ÷ $65) × 100 = 131.

3. The CPI that uses the 2012 basket displays some bias. With the price of broccoli constant and the price of carrots rising, consumers buy fewer carrots and more broccoli and they spend $85 on vegetables. But they would have spent $90 if they had not substituted broccoli for some carrots. The price of vegetables does not rise by 50 percent as shown by the CPI. Because of substitution, the price of vegetables rises by only 42 percent ($85 is 42 percent greater than $60). Using the 2013 basket, the price of vegetables rises by only 31 percent ($85 compared with $65). A CPI substitution bias exists.

TABLE 2

Item	2012 basket at 2012 prices	2012 basket at 2013 prices
Broccoli	$30	$30
Carrots	$30	$60
Total	$60	$90

TABLE 3

Item	2013 basket at 2012 prices	2013 basket at 2013 prices
Broccoli	$45	$45
Carrots	$20	$40
Total	$65	$85

Solution to In the News

These three measures of the price level are based on the prices of different baskets of goods and services. The GDP price index is the broadest measure and its basket contains all the goods and services that are counted in GDP—U.S.-produced goods and services that households, firms, governments, and foreigners buy in the current year. The basket of the PCE price index contains the goods and services in GDP that households buy in the current year. The CPI basket contains only the goods and services that urban consumers buy in the base year.

Which postage stamp has the higher real price: the 2¢ stamp of 1913 or today's 46¢ stamp?

7.3   NOMINAL AND REAL VALUES

In 2013, it cost 46 cents to mail a first-class letter. One hundred years earlier, in 1913, that same letter would have cost 2 cents to mail. Does it *really* cost you 23 times the amount that it cost your great-great-grandmother to mail a letter?

You know that it does not. You know that a dollar today buys less than what a dollar bought in 1913, so the cost of a stamp has not really increased to 23 times its 1913 level. But has it increased at all? Did it really cost you any more to mail a letter in 2013 than it cost your great-great-grandmother in 1913?

The CPI can be used to answer questions like these. In fact, that is one of the main reasons for constructing a price index. Let's see how we can compare the price of a stamp in 1913 and the price of a stamp in 2013.

■ Dollars and Cents at Different Dates

To compare dollar amounts at different dates, we need to know the CPI at those dates. Currently, the CPI has a base of 100 for 1982–1984. That is, the average of the CPI in 1982, 1983, and 1984 is 100. (The numbers for the three years are 96.4, 99.6, and 103.9, respectively. Calculate the average of these numbers and check that it is indeed 100.)

In 2013, the CPI was 232.1, and in 1913, it was 9.9. By using these two numbers, we can calculate the relative value of the dollar in 1913 and 2013. To do so, we divide the 2013 CPI by the 1913 CPI. That ratio is 232.1 ÷ 9.9 = 23.4. That is, prices on average were 23.4 times higher in 2013 than in 1913.

We can use this ratio to convert the price of a 2-cent stamp in 1913 into its 2013 equivalent. The formula for this calculation is

$$\text{Price of stamp in 2013 dollars} = \text{Price of stamp in 1913 dollars} \times \frac{\text{CPI in 2013}}{\text{CPI in 1913}}$$

$$= 2 \text{ cents} \times \frac{232.1}{9.9} = 46.9 \text{ cents}.$$

So your great-great-grandmother paid a bit more than you pay! It really cost her almost 1 cent more to mail that first-class letter than it cost you in 2013. She paid the equivalent of 46.9 cents in 2013 money, and you paid 46 cents.

We've just converted the 1913 price of a stamp to its 2013 equivalent. We can do a similar calculation the other way around—converting the 2013 price to its 1913 equivalent. The formula for this alternative calculation is

$$\text{Price of stamp in 1913 dollars} = \text{Price of stamp in 2013 dollars} \times \frac{\text{CPI in 1913}}{\text{CPI in 2013}}$$

$$= 46 \text{ cents} \times \frac{9.9}{232.1} = 1.96 \text{ cents}.$$

The interpretation of this number is that you pay the *equivalent* of 1.96 cents in 1913 dollars. Your *real* price of a stamp is 1.96 cents expressed in 1913 dollars.

The calculations that we've just done are examples of converting a *nominal* value into a *real* value. A nominal value is one that is expressed in current dollars. A real value is one that is expressed in the dollars of a given year. We're now going to see how we convert other nominal macroeconomic variables into real variables using a similar method.

Nominal and Real Values in Macroeconomics

Macroeconomics makes a big issue of the distinction between the nominal value and the real value of a variable. Three nominal and real variables occupy a central position in macroeconomics. They are

- Nominal GDP and real GDP
- The nominal wage rate and the real wage rate
- The nominal interest rate and the real interest rate

We begin our examination of real and nominal variables in macroeconomics by reviewing what you've already learned about the distinction between nominal GDP and real GDP and interpreting that distinction in a new way.

Nominal GDP and Real GDP

When we calculated the 1913 value of a 46-cent 2013 postage stamp, we multiplied the 2013 price by the ratio of the CPI in 1913 to the CPI in 2013. By this calculation, we found the "real" value of a 2013 stamp in 1913 dollars.

But when we calculated the real GDP of 2013 in 2009 dollars in Chapter 5 (pp. 124–125), we didn't multiply nominal GDP in 2013 by the ratio of a price index in the two years. Instead, we expressed the values of the goods and services produced in 2013 in terms of the prices that prevailed in 2009. We calculated real GDP directly.

But we can *interpret* real GDP in 2013 as nominal GDP in 2013 multiplied by the ratio of the GDP price index in 2009 to the GDP price index in 2013. The GDP price

EYE on the U.S. ECONOMY
Deflating the GDP Balloon

Nominal GDP increased every year between 1980 and 2013 except for 2009. Part of the increase reflects increased production, and part of it reflects rising prices.

You can think of GDP as a balloon that is blown up by growing production and rising prices. In the figure, the GDP price index or *GDP deflator* lets the inflation air—the contribution of rising prices—out of the nominal GDP balloon so that we can see what has happened to real GDP.

The small red balloon for 1980 shows real GDP in that year. The green balloon shows nominal GDP in 2013. The red balloon for 2013 shows real GDP for that year.

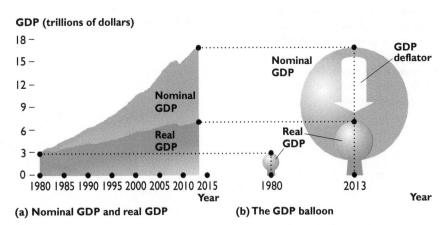

(a) Nominal GDP and real GDP

(b) The GDP balloon

SOURCE OF DATA: Bureau of Economic Analysis.

To see real GDP in 2013, we use the GDP price index to deflate nominal GDP. With the inflation air removed, we can see by how much real GDP grew from 1980 to 2013.

index in 2009 (the base year) is defined to be 100, so we can interpret real GDP in any year as nominal GDP divided by the GDP price index in that year multiplied by 100. We don't calculate real GDP this way, but we can interpret it this way.

The GDP price index, or the CPI, or some other price index might be used to convert a nominal variable to a real variable.

■ Nominal Wage Rate and Real Wage Rate

The price of labor services is the wage rate—the income that an hour of labor earns. In macroeconomics, we are interested in economy-wide performance, so we focus on the *average* hourly wage rate. The **nominal wage rate** is the average hourly wage rate measured in *current* dollars. The **real wage rate** is the average hourly wage rate measured in the dollars of a given reference base year.

To calculate the real wage rate relevant to a consumer, we divide the nominal wage rate by the CPI and multiply by 100. That is,

$$\text{Real wage rate in 2013} = \frac{\text{Nominal wage rate in 2013}}{\text{CPI in 2013}} \times 100.$$

In 2013, the nominal wage rate (average hourly wage rate) of production workers was \$20.10 and the CPI was 232.1, so

$$\text{Real wage rate in 2013} = \frac{\$20.10}{232.1} \times 100 = \$8.66.$$

Because we measure the real wage rate in constant base period dollars, a change in the real wage rate measures the change in the quantity of goods and

Nominal wage rate
The average hourly wage rate measured in current dollars.

Real wage rate
The average hourly wage rate measured in the dollars of a given reference base year.

■ FIGURE 7.4

Nominal and Real Wage Rates: 1980–2013   MyEconLab Real-time data

The nominal wage rate has increased every year since 1980. The real wage rate decreased slightly from 1982 through the mid-1990s, after which it increased slightly again. Over the entire 33-year period, the real wage rate remained steady.

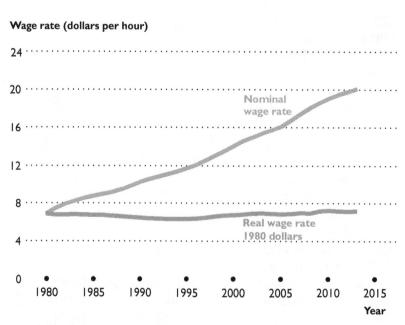

SOURCE OF DATA: Bureau of Labor Statistics.

services that an hour's work can buy. In contrast, a change in the nominal wage rate measures a combination of a change in the quantity of goods and services that an hour's work can buy and a change in the price level. So the real wage rate removes the effects of inflation from the changes in the nominal wage rate.

The real wage rate is a significant economic variable because it measures the real reward for labor, which is a major determinant of the standard of living. The real wage rate is also significant because it measures the real cost of labor services, which influences the quantity of labor that firms are willing to hire.

Figure 7.4 shows what has happened to the nominal wage rate and the real wage rate in the United States between 1980 and 2013. The nominal wage rate is the average hourly earnings of production workers. This measure is just one of several different measures of average hourly earnings that we might have used.

The nominal wage rate increased from $6.85 an hour in 1980 to $20.10 an hour in 2013, but the real wage rate barely changed. In 1980 dollars, the real wage rate in 2013 was only $7.13 an hour.

The real wage rate barely changed as the nominal wage rate increased because the nominal wage rate grew at a rate almost equal to the inflation rate. When the effects of inflation are removed from the nominal wage rate, we can see what is happening to the buying power of the average wage rate.

You can also see that the real wage rate has fluctuated a little. It decreased slightly until the mid-1990s, after which it increased slightly.

EYE on the PAST
The Nominal and Real Wage Rates of Presidents of the United States

Who earned more, Barack Obama in 2013, or George Washington in 1788? George Washington's pay was $25,000 (on the green line) but in 2013 dollars it was $619,000 (on the red line). Barack Obama was paid $400,000 in 2013.

But presidential accommodations are more comfortable today, and presidential travel arrangements are a breeze compared to earlier times. So adding in the perks of the job, Barack Obama doesn't get such a raw deal.

SOURCE OF DATA:
Robert Sahr, Oregon State University, http://oregonstate.edu/cla/polisci/sahr/sahr

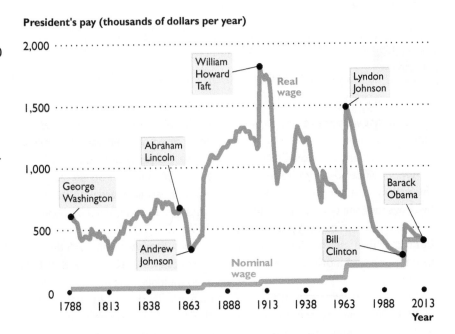

■ Nominal Interest Rate and Real Interest Rate

Nominal interest rate
The dollar amount of interest expressed as a percentage of the amount loaned.

Real interest rate
The goods and services forgone in interest expressed as a percentage of the amount loaned and calculated as the nominal interest rate minus the inflation rate.

You've just seen that we can calculate real values from nominal values by deflating them using the CPI. And you've seen that to make this calculation, we *divide* the nominal value by a price index. Converting a nominal interest rate to a real interest rate is a bit different. To see why, we'll start with their definitions.

A **nominal interest rate** is the dollar amount of interest expressed as a percentage of the amount loaned. For example, suppose that you have $1,000 in a bank deposit—a loan by you to a bank—on which you receive interest of $50 a year. The nominal interest rate is $50 as a percentage of $1,000, which is 5 percent a year.

A **real interest rate** is the goods and services forgone in interest expressed as a percentage of the amount loaned. Continuing with the above example, at the end of one year your bank deposit has increased to $1,050—the original $1,000 plus the $50 interest. Suppose that prices have increased by 3 percent, so now you need $1,030 to buy what $1,000 would have bought a year earlier. How much interest have you *really* received? The answer is $20, or a real interest rate of 2 percent a year.

To convert a nominal interest rate to a real interest rate, we *subtract* the *inflation rate*. That is,

$$\text{Real interest rate} = \text{Nominal interest rate} - \text{Inflation rate}.$$

Plug your numbers into this formula. Your nominal interest rate is 5 percent a year, and the inflation rate is 3 percent a year. Your real interest rate is 5 percent minus 3 percent, which equals 2 percent a year.

Figure 7.5 shows the nominal and the real interest rates in the United States between 1972 and 2012. When the inflation rate is high, the gap between the real interest rate and nominal interest rate is large. Sometimes, the real interest rate is negative (as it was in the mid-1970s) and the lender pays the borrower!

EYE on BOX OFFICE HITS

Which Movie *Really* Was the Biggest Box Office Hit?

Gone with the Wind is the answer to the question that we posed at the beginning of this chapter.

To get this answer, Box-Office Mojo (www.boxofficemojo.com) calculates the amount that a movie *really* earns by converting the dollars earned to their equivalent in current year dollars. But rather than use the CPI, it uses the average prices of movie tickets as its price index.

Gone with the Wind was made in 1939. Looking only at its performance in the United States, the movie was rereleased in nine subsequent years and by 2012 it had earned a total box office revenue of almost $200 million.

The Avengers, released in 2012, earned $623 million. So the 2012 *The Avengers* earned more than three times the dollars earned by *Gone with the Wind*.

To convert the *Gone with the Wind* revenues into 2012 dollars, Box-Office Mojo multiplies the dollars received each year by the 2012 ticket price and divides by the ticket price for the year in which the dollars were earned.

Valuing the tickets for *Gone with the Wind* at 2012 movie-ticket prices, it has earned $1,604 million, about 2.6 times *The Avengers* revenue.

Because Box-Office Mojo uses average ticket prices, the real variable that it compares is the number of tickets sold. The average ticket price in 2012 was $7.96, which means 202 million have seen *Gone with the Wind* and 78 million have seen *The Avengers*. *Gone with the Wind* was the biggest hit because it was seen by the greatest number of people.

FIGURE 7.5

Nominal and Real Interest Rates: 1973–2013

MyEconLab Real-time data

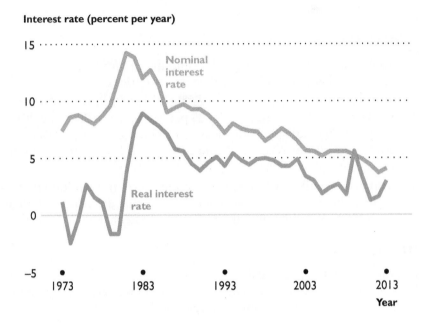

The interest rate shown here is that paid by the safest large corporations on long-term bonds (known as Moody's AAA). The real interest rate equals the nominal interest rate minus the inflation rate. The vertical gap between the nominal interest rate and the real interest rate is the inflation rate. The real interest rate is usually positive, but during the 1970s, it became negative.

SOURCES OF DATA: Federal Reserve and Bureau of Labor Statistics

EYE on YOUR LIFE
A Student's CPI

The CPI measures the percentage change in the average prices paid for the basket of goods and services bought by a typical urban household.

A student is not a typical household. How have the prices of a student's basket of goods and services changed? The answer is by a lot more than those of an average household.

Suppose that a student spends 25 percent of her income on rent, 25 percent on tuition, 25 percent on books and study supplies, 10 percent on food, 10 percent on transportation, and 5 percent on clothing.

We can use these weights and the data collected by the BLS on individual

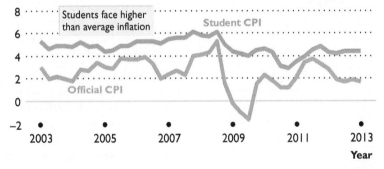

SOURCE OF DATA: Bureau of Labor Statistics.

price categories to find the student's CPI and the inflation rate that it implies.

The graph shows this student's inflation rate compared to that of the

official CPI. Between 2003 and 2013, a student's CPI rose 32 percent above the official CPI. Rent, textbooks, and tuition are the main items whose prices rose faster than average.

MyEconLab Study Plan 7.3
Key Terms Quiz
Solutions

CHECKPOINT 7.3

Adjust money values for inflation and calculate real wage rates and real interest rates.

Practice Problems

TABLE 1

Year	Price of gasoline (cents per gallon)	CPI
1981	138	90.9
1991	114	136.2
2001	146	176.6
2011	358	224.9

1. Table 1 shows the price of gasoline and the CPI for four years. The reference base period is 1982–1984. Calculate the real price of gasoline each year. In which year was this real price highest and in which year was it lowest?

2. Ford says it cut its labor costs by 35 percent between 2006 and 2011. Ford's wage rate, including benefits, was $80 an hour in 2006 and $58 an hour in 2011. The CPI was 202 in 2006 and 218 in 2011. Did the real wage rate fall by more or less than 35 percent?

3. Sally worked all year and put her savings into a mutual fund that paid a nominal interest rate of 7 percent a year. During the year, the CPI increased from 165 to 177. What was the real interest rate that Sally earned?

In the News

Inflation can act as a safety valve
Workers will more readily accept a real wage cut that arises from an increase in the CPI than a cut in their nominal wage rate.

Source: FT.com, May 28, 2009

Explain why inflation influences a worker's real wage rate. Why might this observation be true?

Solutions to Practice Problems

TABLE 2

Year	Price of gasoline (cents per gallon)	CPI	Price of gasoline (1982–1984 cents per gallon)
1981	136	90.9	152
1991	114	136.2	84
2001	146	176.6	83
2011	358	224.9	159

1. To calculate the real price, divide the nominal price by the CPI and multiply by 100. Table 2 shows the calculations. The real price was highest in 2011, when it was 159 cents (1982–1984 cents) per gallon. The real price was lowest in 2001, when it was 83 cents (1982–1984 cents) per gallon.

2. The real wage rate in 2006, expressed in dollars of the reference base year, equals ($80 ÷ 202) × 100, or $39.60 an hour. The real wage rate in 2011, expressed in dollars of the reference base year, equals ($58 ÷ 218) × 100, or $26.61 an hour. The real wage rate of these workers fell by 32.8 percent.

3. The inflation rate during the year equals (177 − 165) ÷ 165 × 100 = 7.3 percent. The real interest rate that Sally earned equals the nominal interest rate minus the inflation rate, which is 7.0 − 7.3 = −0.3 percent. Sally's real interest rate was negative. (If Sally had kept her savings in cash, her nominal interest rate would have been zero, and her real interest rate would have been −7.3 percent. She would have been worse off.)

Solution to In the News

The real wage rate equals the (Nominal wage rate ÷ CPI) × 100. Two reasons why a real wage cut from inflation is more acceptable are: A rising CPI *gradually* lowers the real wage rate, while a cut in the nominal wage rate *suddenly* lowers the real wage rate. Inflation lowers everyone's real wage rate but a cut in one worker's nominal wage rate lowers only that worker's real wage rate.

CHAPTER SUMMARY

Key Points

1. **Explain what the Consumer Price Index (CPI) is and how it is calculated.**

   - The Consumer Price Index (CPI) is a measure of the average of the prices of the goods and services that an average urban household buys.
   - The CPI is calculated by dividing the cost of the CPI market basket in the current period by its cost in the base period and then multiplying by 100.

2. **Explain the limitations of the CPI and describe other measures of the price level.**

   - The CPI does not include all the items that contribute to the cost of living.
   - The CPI cannot provide an accurate measure of price changes because of new goods, quality improvements, and substitutions that consumers make when relative prices change.
   - Other measures of the price level include the GDP price index, the PCE price index, and the PCE price index excluding food and energy.
   - Both the GDP price index and the PCE price index use current information on quantities and to some degree overcome the sources of bias in the CPI.
   - The PCE price index excluding food and energy is used to calculate the core inflation rate, which shows the inflation trend.

3. **Adjust money values for inflation and calculate real wage rates and real interest rates.**

   - To adjust a money value (also called a nominal value) for inflation, we express the value in terms of the dollars of a given year.
   - To convert a dollar value of year B to the dollars of year A, multiply the value in year B by the price level in year A and divide by the price level in year B.
   - The real wage rate equals the nominal wage rate divided by the CPI and multiplied by 100.
   - The real interest rate equals the nominal interest rate minus the inflation rate.

Key Terms

MyEconLab Key Terms Quiz

Consumer Price Index, 166
Core inflation rate, 175
Cost of living index, 172
Deflation, 169
GDP price index, 175
Inflation rate, 169

Nominal interest rate, 182
Nominal wage rate, 180
PCE price index, 175
Real interest rate, 182
Real wage rate, 180
Reference base period, 166

CHAPTER CHECKPOINT

Study Plan Problems and Applications

1. In Canada, the reference base period for the CPI is 2002. By 2012, prices had risen by 21.6 percent since the base period. The inflation rate in Canada in 2013 was 1.1 percent. Calculate the CPI in Canada in 2013.

2. In Brazil, the reference base period for the CPI is 2000. By 2005, prices had risen by 51 percent since the base period. The inflation rate in Brazil in 2006 was 10 percent, and in 2007, the inflation rate was 9 percent. Calculate the CPI in Brazil in 2006 and 2007. Brazil's CPI in 2008 was 173. Did Brazil's inflation rate increase or decrease in 2008?

3. Tables 1 and 2 show the quantities of the goods that Suzie bought and the prices she paid during two consecutive weeks. Suzie's CPI market basket contains the goods she bought in Week 1. Calculate the cost of Suzie's CPI market basket in Week 1 and in Week 2. What percentage of the CPI market basket is gasoline? Calculate the value of Suzie's CPI in Week 2 and her inflation rate in Week 2.

Use the following information to work Problems 4 and 5.

The GDP price index in the United States in 2000 was about 90, and real GDP in 2000 was $11 trillion (2005 dollars). The GDP price index in 2010 was about 111, and real GDP in 2010 was $13.1 trillion (2005 dollars).

4. Calculate nominal GDP in 2000 and in 2010 and the percentage increase in nominal GDP between 2000 and 2010.

5. What was the percentage increase in production between 2000 and 2010, and by what percentage did the cost of living rise between 2000 and 2010?

6. Table 3 shows the prices that Terry paid for some of his expenditures in June and July 2013. Explain and discuss why these prices might have led to commodity substitution or outlet substitution.

7. In 2013, Annie, an 80-year-old, is telling her granddaughter Mary about the good old days. Annie says that in 1933, you could buy a nice house for $15,000 and a jacket for $5. Mary says that in 2013 such a house costs $220,000 and such a jacket costs $70. The CPI in 1933 was 16.7 and in 2013 it was 218.1. Which house and which jacket have the lower prices?

Use the following information to work Problems 8 and 9.

CPI: Inflation rate picks up in August

The CPI rose 3.8% in August compared to a year earlier. Food prices rose 4.6% and clothing prices were up 4.2%, while new car prices rose 3.8% and medical care was up 3.2%.

Source: CNN Money, September 15, 2011

8. What percentage change in the CPI during the year to August 2011 is accounted for by the changes in the prices of food, clothing, and medical care?

9. Given the changes in the prices of food, clothing, and medical care, by what percentage did the prices of the other items in the CPI basket change?

 10. Read *Eye on Box Office Hits* on p. 182 and using BLS data for the CPI in 1982 and 1997, determine which movie had the greater *real* box office revenues, *E.T.: The Extra-Terrestrial,* which earned $435 million in 1982 or *Titanic,* which earned $601 million in 1997.

TABLE 1 DATA FOR WEEK 1

Item	Quantity	Price (per unit)
Coffee	11 cups	$3.25
DVDs	1	$25.00
Gasoline	15 gallons	$2.50

TABLE 2 DATA FOR WEEK 2

Item	Quantity	Price (per unit)
Coffee	11 cups	$3.25
DVDs	3	$12.50
Gasoline	5 gallons	$3.00
Concert	1 ticket	$95.00

TABLE 3

Item	Price in June	Price in July
	(dollars per unit)	
Steak	4.11	4.01
Bread	3.25	3.12
Bacon	3.62	3.64
Milk	2.62	2.62
Tomatoes	1.60	1.62
Apples	1.18	1.19
Bananas	0.62	0.66
Chicken	1.28	1.26
Lettuce	1.64	1.68

Instructor Assignable Problems and Applications

MyEconLab Homework, Quiz, or Test if assigned by instructor

1. Compare the method used by Box-Office Mojo to calculate real box-office receipts with the method used on p. 178 to calculate the real price of a postage stamp. Compare and contrast the real variables that each method calculates.

2. Pete is a student who spends 10 percent of his expenditure on books and supplies, 30 percent on tuition, 30 percent on rent, 10 percent on food and drink, 10 percent on transportation, and the rest on clothing. The price index for each item was 100 in 2000. Table 1 shows the prices in 2011.
   What is Pete's CPI in 2011? (Hint: The contribution of each item to the CPI is its price weighted by its share of total expenditure.) Did Pete experience a higher or lower inflation rate between 2000 and 2011 than the student whose CPI is shown on p. 183?

3. The people on Coral Island buy only juice and cloth. The CPI market basket contains the quantities bought in 2010. The average household spent $60 on juice and $30 on cloth in 2010 when the price of juice was $2 a bottle and the price of cloth was $5 a yard. In the current year, 2011, juice is $4 a bottle and cloth is $6 a yard. Calculate the CPI and the inflation rate in 2011.

4. Tables 2 and 3 show the quantities of the goods that Harry bought and the prices he paid during two consecutive weeks. Harry's CPI market basket contains the goods he bought in Week 1. Calculate Harry's CPI in Week 2. What was his inflation rate in Week 2?

Use the following information to work Problems 5 and 6.

The base year is 2009. Real GDP in 2009 was $10 trillion (2009 dollars). The GDP price index in 2009 was 112, and real GDP in 2013 was $11 trillion (2009 dollars).

5. Calculate nominal GDP in 2009 and in 2013 and the percentage increase in nominal GDP from 2009 to 2013.

6. What was the percentage increase in production from 2009 to 2013, and by what percentage did the cost of living rise from 2009 to 2013?

7. In 1988, the average wage rate was $9.45 an hour and in 2008 the average wage rate was $18.00 an hour. The CPI in 1988 was 118.3 and in 2008 it was 215.3. Which real wage rate is higher?

8. Imagine that you are given $1,000 to spend and told that you must spend it all buying items from a Sears catalog. But you do have a choice of catalog. You may select from the 1903 catalog or from Sears.com today. You will pay the prices quoted in the catalog that you choose.

   Which catalog will you choose and why? Refer to any biases in the CPI that might be relevant to your choice.

Use the following information to work Problems 9 and 10.

Money market funds are yielding almost nothing
Last month, the interest rate on a money market fund averaged 0.08% a year and on 5-year CDs it was 2.6% a year. The inflation rate was 0.1% a year.

Source: *USA Today*, August 12, 2009

9. Calculate the real interest rate on each of these financial assets.

10. To maintain these real interest rates in the coming months, how will these nominal rates change if the inflation rate increases to 0.2 percent a year?

TABLE 1

Item	Price in 2011
Books and supplies	172.6
Tuition	169.0
Rent	159.0
Food and drink	129.8
Transportation	115.4
Clothing	92.9

TABLE 2 DATA FOR WEEK 1

Item	Quantity	Price (per unit)
Coffee	5 cups	$3.00
iTunes songs	5	$1.00
Gasoline	10 gallons	$2.00

TABLE 3 DATA FOR WEEK 2

Item	Quantity	Price (per unit)
Coffee	4 cups	$3.25
iTunes songs	10	$1.00
Gasoline	10 gallons	$3.00

Multiple Choice Quiz

1. The CPI measures the average prices paid by _____ for _____.
   - A. urban consumers; a fixed basket of consumption goods and services
   - B. urban consumers; the average basket of goods and services they buy
   - C. all consumers; housing, transportation, and food
   - D. everyone who earns an income; the necessities of life

2. The BLS reported that the CPI in July 2010 was 226. This news tells you that _____.
   - A. consumer prices during July were 226 percent higher than they were during the base year
   - B. the CPI inflation rate in July was 26 percent a year
   - C. consumer prices rose by 26 percent during the month of July
   - D. the prices of consumption goods and services have risen, on average, by 126 percent since the base year

3. When the price level _____ the inflation rate _____.
   - A. rises rapidly; increases
   - B. rises rapidly; is high
   - C. falls; is zero
   - D. rises slowly; falls

4. The CPI bias arises from all of the following items *except* _____.
   - A. the introduction of new goods and services
   - B. the improved quality of goods
   - C. the goods and services bought by poor people
   - D. consumers' responses to price changes

5. Of the alternative measures of the price level, the _____ overcomes the bias of the CPI and is a better measure of the cost of living because it _____.
   - A. GDP price index; uses a current basket
   - B. PCE price index; uses a current basket of all consumption goods
   - C. PCE price index excluding food and energy; is less volatile
   - D. GDP price index; includes all goods and services bought by Americans

6. If nominal GDP increases by 5 percent a year and the GDP price index rises by 2 percent a year, then real GDP increases by _____.
   - A. 7 percent a year
   - B. 3 percent a year
   - C. 2.5 percent a year
   - D. 10 percent a year

7. When the CPI increases from 200 in 2010 to 210 in 2011 and the nominal wage rate is constant at $10 an hour, the real wage rate _____.
   - A. increases by 10 percent
   - B. increases to $15 an hour
   - C. decreases by 5 percent
   - D. is $10 an hour

8. When the price level is rising at _____ and the real interest rate is 1 percent a year, the nominal interest rate is 3 percent a year.
   - A. 4 percent a year
   - B. 3 percent a year
   - C. 2 percent a year
   - D. 1 percent a year

Why do Americans earn more and produce more than Europeans?

Potential GDP and the Natural Unemployment Rate

8

CHAPTER CHECKLIST

When you have completed your study of this chapter, you will be able to

1 Explain what determines potential GDP.

2 Explain what determines the natural unemployment rate.

MyEconLab Big Picture

MyEconLab Snapshot

MACROECONOMIC APPROACHES AND PATHWAYS

In the three previous chapters, you learned how economists define and measure real GDP, employment and unemployment, the price level, and the inflation rate—the key variables that *describe* macroeconomic performance. Your task in this chapter and those that follow is to learn the *macroeconomic theory* that *explains* macroeconomic performance and provides the basis for *policies* that might improve it.

The macroeconomic theory that we present is today's consensus view on how the economy works. But it isn't the view of all macroeconomists. Today's consensus is a merger of three earlier schools of thought that have sharply contrasting views about the causes of recessions and the best policies for dealing with them. Some economists continue to identify with these schools of thought, and the severity of the 2008–2009 recession and slow recovery intensified debate and gave economists of all shades of opinion a platform from which to present their views.

We begin with an overview of the three schools of thought from which today's consensus has emerged.

■ The Three Main Schools of Thought

The three main schools of macroeconomic thought are

- Classical macroeconomics
- Keynesian macroeconomics
- Monetarist macroeconomics

Classical Macroeconomics

Classical macroeconomics
The view that the market economy works well, that aggregate fluctuations are a natural consequence of an expanding economy, and that government intervention cannot improve the efficiency of the market economy.

According to **classical macroeconomics,** markets work well and deliver the best available macroeconomic performance. Aggregate fluctuations are a natural consequence of an expanding economy with rising living standards, and government intervention can only hinder the ability of the market to allocate resources efficiently. The first classical macroeconomists included Adam Smith, David Ricardo, and John Stuart Mill, all of whom worked in the 18th and 19th centuries. Modern day classical economists include the 2004 Nobel Laureates Edward C. Prescott of the University of Arizona and Finn E. Kydland of Carnegie-Mellon University and the University of California at Santa Barbara.

Classical macroeconomics fell into disrepute during the Great Depression of the 1930s, a time when many people believed that *capitalism*, the political system of private ownership, free markets, and democratic political institutions, could not survive and began to advocate *socialism*, a political system based on state ownership of capital and central economic planning.

Classical macroeconomics predicted that the Great Depression would eventually end but offered no method for ending it more quickly.

Keynesian Macroeconomics

Keynesian macroeconomics
The view that the market economy is inherently unstable and needs active government intervention to achieve full employment and sustained economic growth.

According to **Keynesian macroeconomics,** the market economy is inherently unstable and requires active government intervention to achieve full employment and sustained economic growth. One person, John Maynard Keynes, and his book *The General Theory of Employment, Interest, and Money,* published in 1936, began this school of thought. Keynes' theory was that depression and high unemployment occur when households don't spend enough on consumption goods and services and businesses don't spend enough investing in new capital. That is, too little *private* spending is the cause of depression (and recession). To counter the problem of too little private spending, *government* spending must rise.

This Keynesian view picked up many followers and by the 1950s it was the mainstream, but it lost popularity during the inflationary 1970s when it seemed ever more remote from the problems of that decade. The global recession of 2008–2009 and the fear of another great depression revived interest in Keynesian ideas and brought a new wave of attacks on classical macroeconomics with Nobel Laureate Paul Krugman leading the charge in the columns of the *New York Times*.

Monetarist Macroeconomics

According to **monetarist macroeconomics,** the *classical* view of the world is broadly correct but in addition to fluctuations that arise from the normal functioning of an expanding economy, fluctuations in the quantity of money generate the business cycle. A slowdown in the growth rate of money brings recession and a large decrease in the quantity of money brought the Great Depression.

Milton Friedman, intellectual leader of the Chicago School of economists during the 1960s and 1970s, was the most prominent monetarist. The view that monetary contractions are the sole source of recessions and depressions is held by few economists today. But the view that the quantity of money plays a role in economic fluctuations is accepted by all economists and is part of today's consensus.

Monetarist macroeconomics The view that the market economy works well, that aggregate fluctuations are a natural consequence of an expanding economy, but that fluctuations in the quantity of money generate the business cycle.

■ Today's Consensus

Each of the earlier schools provides insights and ingredients that survive in today's consensus. *Classical* macroeconomics provides the story of the economy at or close to full employment. But the classical approach doesn't explain how the economy performs in the face of a major slump in spending.

Keynesian macroeconomics takes up the story in a recession or depression. When spending is cut and the demand for most goods and services and the demand for labor all decrease, prices and wage rates don't fall but the quantity of goods and services sold and the quantity of labor employed do fall and the economy goes into recession. In a recession, an increase in spending by governments, or a tax cut that leaves people with more of their earnings to spend, can help to restore full employment.

Monetarist macroeconomics elaborates the Keynesian story by emphasizing that a contraction in the quantity of money brings higher interest rates and borrowing costs, which are a major source of cuts in spending that bring recession. Increasing the quantity of money and lowering the interest rate in a recession can help to restore full employment. And keeping the quantity of money growing steadily in line with the expansion of the economy's production possibilities can help to keep inflation in check and can also help to moderate the severity of a recession.

Another component of today's consensus is the view that the *long-term* problem of economic growth is more important than the *short-term* problem of recessions. Take a look at *Eye on the U.S. Economy,* on p. 192, and you will see why. Even a small slowdown in economic growth brings a huge cost in terms of a permanently lower level of income per person. This cost is much larger than that arising from the income lost during recessions. But the costs of recessions are serious because they are concentrated on those who are unemployed.

■ The Road Ahead

This book bases your tour of macroeconomics on the new consensus. We begin in this chapter and the two that follow by explaining what determines potential GDP and the pace at which it grows. We then study money and explain what brings inflation. Finally, we explain how real and monetary forces interact to bring about the business cycle. We also explain the policy tools available to governments and central banks to improve macroeconomic performance.

EYE on the U.S. ECONOMY
The Lucas Wedge and the Okun Gap

During the 1960s, U.S. real GDP per person grew at a rate of 2.8 percent a year. The black line in part (a) shows the path that would have been followed if this growth rate had been maintained. After 1970, growth slowed to 2.0 percent per year and the blue line shows the path that real GDP per person followed. University of Chicago economist Robert E. Lucas, Jr. pointed out the large output loss that resulted from this growth slowdown. Part (a) shows this loss as the *Lucas wedge*, which is equivalent to a staggering $406,000 per person or 8.2 years' income.

Real GDP fluctuates around potential GDP and when the output gap is negative, output is lost. Brookings Institution economist Arthur B. Okun drew attention to this loss. Part (b) shows this loss as the *Okun gap*, which is equivalent to $27,000 per person or about 7 months' income.

Smoothing the business cycle and eliminating the Okun gap has a big payoff. But finding ways of restoring real GDP growth to its 1960s rate has a vastly bigger payoff.

SOURCES OF DATA: Bureau of Economic Analysis and the Congressional Budget Office.

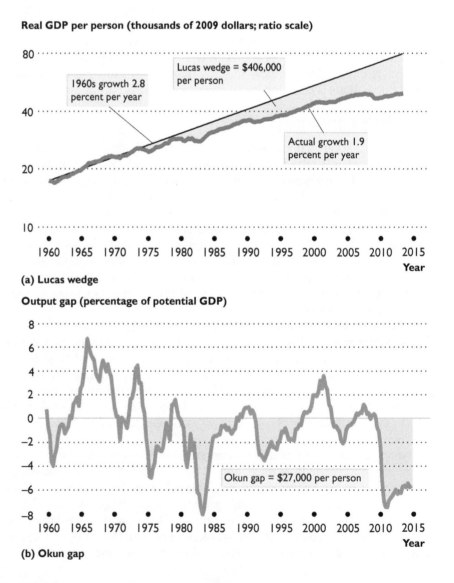

Real GDP per person (thousands of 2009 dollars; ratio scale)

1960s growth 2.8 percent per year

Lucas wedge = $406,000 per person

Actual growth 1.9 percent per year

(a) Lucas wedge

Output gap (percentage of potential GDP)

Okun gap = $27,000 per person

(b) Okun gap

8.1 POTENTIAL GDP

MyEconLab Snapshot

Potential GDP is the value of real GDP when all the economy's factors of production—labor, capital, land, and entrepreneurial ability—are fully employed. It is vital to understand the forces that determine potential GDP for three reasons. First, when the economy is *at* full employment, real GDP equals potential GDP; so actual real GDP is determined by the same factors that determine potential GDP. Second, real GDP can exceed potential GDP only temporarily as it approaches and then recedes from a business cycle peak. So potential GDP is the *sustainable* upper limit of production. Third, real GDP fluctuates around potential GDP, which means that on the average over the business cycle, real GDP equals potential GDP.

We produce the goods and services that make up real GDP by using the *factors of production*: labor and human capital, physical capital, land (and natural resources), and entrepreneurship. At any given time, the quantities of capital, land, and entrepreneurship and the state of technology are fixed. But the quantity of labor is not fixed. It depends on the choices that people make about the allocation of time between work and leisure. So with fixed quantities of capital, land, and entrepreneurship and fixed technology, real GDP depends on the quantity of labor employed. To describe this relationship between real GDP and the quantity of labor employed, we use a relationship that is similar to the production possibilities frontier, which is called the production function.

Potential GDP
The value of real GDP when all the economy's factors of production—labor, capital, land, and entrepreneurial ability—are fully employed.

EYE on the GLOBAL ECONOMY
Potential GDP in the United States and European Union

In 2011, real GDP in the United States was $60 per hour worked. In 14 major European economies, real GDP averaged only $48 per hour worked—a gap of 25 percent. (Both numbers are measured in 2011 U.S. dollars.) Part (a) of the figure shows this difference.

Not only do Americans produce more per hour than Europeans, they work longer hours too. In 2011, Americans worked an average of 33 hours per week while Europeans worked only an average of 31 hours per week—a difference of more than 5 percent. Part (b) of the figure shows this difference.

Europeans achieve their shorter work hours by taking longer vacations

and having more sick days than Americans.

The combination of greater production per hour and longer work hours translates into a substantially larger real GDP per worker in the United States than in Europe.

In 2011, real GDP per worker in the United States was $103,000 while in Europe it was only $74,000—a gap of almost 40 percent.

This chapter enables you to understand the sources of these differences in wage rates, work hours, and production.

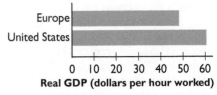
(a) Real GDP per hour worked

(b) Average weekly hours

(c) Real GDP per worker

SOURCE OF DATA: Organization for Economic Cooperation and Development

■ The Production Function

Production function
A relationship that shows the maximum quantity of real GDP that can be produced as the quantity of labor employed changes and all other influences on production remain the same.

The **production function** is a relationship that shows the maximum quantity of real GDP that can be produced as the quantity of labor employed changes and all other influences on production remain the same. Figure 8.1 shows a production function, which is the curve labeled *PF*.

In Figure 8.1, 100 billion labor hours can produce a real GDP of $11 trillion (at point *A*); 200 billion hours can produce a real GDP of $16 trillion (at point *B*); and 300 billion hours can produce a real GDP of $20 trillion (at point *C*).

The production function shares a feature of the *production possibilities frontier* that you studied in Chapter 3 (p. 60). Like the *PPF*, the production function is a boundary between the attainable and the unattainable. It is possible to produce at any point along the production function and beneath it in the shaded area. But it is not possible to produce at points above the production function. Those points are unattainable.

Diminishing returns
The tendency for each additional hour of labor employed to produce a successively smaller additional amount of real GDP.

The production function displays **diminishing returns**—each additional hour of labor employed produces a successively smaller additional amount of real GDP. The first 100 billion hours of labor produces $11 trillion of real GDP. The second 100 billion hours of labor increases real GDP from $11 trillion to $16 trillion, so the

■ **FIGURE 8.1**

The Production Function

MyEconLab Animation

The production function shows the maximum quantity of real GDP that can be produced as the quantity of labor employed changes and all other influences on production remain the same. In this example, 100 billion hours of labor can produce $11 trillion of real GDP at point A, 200 billion hours of labor can produce $16 trillion of real GDP at point B, and 300 billion hours of labor can produce $20 trillion of real GDP at point C.

The production function separates attainable combinations of labor hours and real GDP from unattainable combinations and displays diminishing returns: Each additional hour of labor produces a successively smaller additional amount of real GDP.

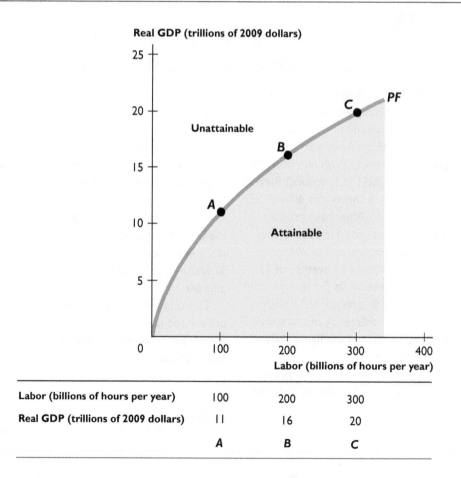

Labor (billions of hours per year)	100	200	300
Real GDP (trillions of 2009 dollars)	11	16	20
	A	*B*	*C*

second 100 billion hours produces only an additional $5 trillion of real GDP. The third 100 billion hours of labor increases real GDP from $16 trillion to $20 trillion, so the third 100 billion hours produces only an additional $4 trillion of real GDP.

Diminishing returns arise because the quantity of capital (and other factors of production) is fixed. As more labor is hired, the additional output produced decreases because the extra workers have less capital with which to work. For example, a forest service has three chain saws and an axe and hires three workers to clear roads and trails of fallen trees and debris during the spring thaw. Hiring a fourth worker will contribute less to the amount cleared than the amount that the third worker added, and hiring a fifth worker will add even less.

Because real GDP depends on the quantity of labor employed, potential GDP depends on the production function and the quantity of labor employed. To find potential GDP, we must understand what determines the quantity of labor employed.

■ The Labor Market

You've already studied the tool that we use to determine the quantity of labor employed: demand and supply. In macroeconomics, we apply the concepts of demand, supply, and market equilibrium to the economy-wide labor market.

The quantity of labor employed depends on firms' decisions about how much labor to hire (the demand for labor). It also depends on households' decisions about how to allocate time between employment and other activities (the supply of labor). And it depends on how the labor market coordinates the decisions of firms and households (labor market equilibrium). So we will study

- The demand for labor
- The supply of labor
- Labor market equilibrium

The Demand for Labor

The **quantity of labor demanded** is the total labor hours that all the firms in the economy plan to hire during a given time period at a given real wage rate. The **demand for labor** is the relationship between the quantity of labor demanded and the real wage rate when all other influences on firms' hiring plans remain the same. The lower the real wage rate, the greater is the quantity of labor demanded.

The real wage rate is the *nominal wage rate* (the dollars per hour that people earn on average) divided by the price level (see Chapter 7, p. 180). We express the real wage rate in constant dollars—today in 2009 dollars. Think of the real wage rate as the quantity of real GDP that an hour of labor earns.

The lower the real wage rate, the greater is the quantity of labor that firms find it profitable to hire. The real wage rate influences the quantity of labor demanded because what matters to firms is not the number of dollars they pay for an hour of labor (the nominal wage rate) but how much output they must sell to earn those dollars. So firms compare the extra output that an hour of labor can produce with the real wage rate.

If an additional hour of labor produces at least as much additional output as the real wage rate, a firm hires that labor. At a small quantity of labor, an extra hour of labor produces more output than the real wage rate. But each additional hour of labor produces less additional output than the previous hour. As a firm hires more labor, eventually the extra output from an extra hour of labor equals the real wage rate. This equality determines the quantity of labor demanded at the real wage rate.

Quantity of labor demanded
The total labor hours that all the firms in the economy plan to hire during a given time period at a given real wage rate.

Demand for labor
The relationship between the quantity of labor demanded and the real wage rate when all other influences on firms' hiring plans remain the same.

The Demand for Labor in a Soda Factory You might understand the demand for labor better by thinking about a single firm rather than the economy as a whole. Suppose that the money wage rate is $15 an hour and that the price of a bottle of soda is $1.50. For the soda factory, the real wage rate is a number of bottles of soda. To find the soda factory's real wage rate, divide the money wage rate by the price of its output—$15 an hour ÷ $1.50 a bottle. The real wage rate is 10 bottles of soda an hour. It costs the soda factory 10 bottles of soda to hire an hour of labor. As long as the soda factory can hire labor that produces more than 10 additional bottles of soda an hour, it is profitable to hire more labor. Only when the extra output produced by an extra hour of labor falls to 10 bottles an hour has the factory reached the profit-maximizing quantity of labor.

Labor Demand Schedule and Labor Demand Curve We can represent the demand for labor as either a demand schedule or a demand curve. The table in Figure 8.2 shows part of a demand for labor schedule. It tells us the quantity of labor demanded at three different real wage rates. For example, if the real wage rate is $50 an hour (row *B*), the quantity of labor demanded is 200 billion hours a year. If the real wage rate rises to $80 an hour (row *A*), the quantity of labor demanded decreases to 100 billion hours a year. And if the real wage rate falls to $25 an hour (row *C*), the quantity of labor demanded increases to 300 billion hours a year.

Figure 8.2 shows the demand for labor curve. Points *A*, *B*, and *C* on the demand curve correspond to rows *A*, *B*, and *C* of the demand schedule.

■ FIGURE 8.2

The Demand for Labor   MyEconLab Animation

Firms are willing to hire labor only if the labor produces more than its real wage rate. So the lower the real wage rate, the more labor firms can profitably hire and the greater is the quantity of labor demanded.

At a real wage rate of $50 an hour, the quantity of labor demanded is 200 billion hours at point *B*.

❶ If the real wage rate rises to $80 an hour, the quantity of labor demanded decreases to 100 billion hours at point *A*.

❷ If the real wage rate falls to $25 an hour, the quantity of labor demanded increases to 300 billion hours at point *C*.

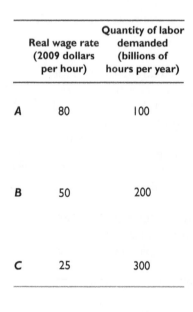

	Real wage rate (2009 dollars per hour)	Quantity of labor demanded (billions of hours per year)
A	80	100
B	50	200
C	25	300

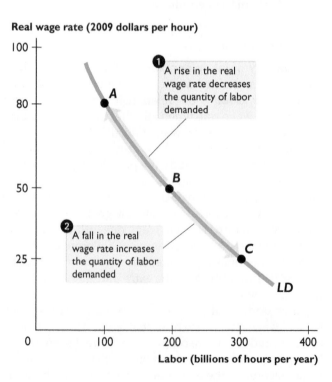

The Supply of Labor

The **quantity of labor supplied** is the number of labor hours that all the households in the economy plan to work during a given time period at a given real wage rate. The **supply of labor** is the relationship between the quantity of labor supplied and the real wage rate when all other influences on work plans remain the same.

We can represent the supply of labor as either a supply schedule or a supply curve. The table in Figure 8.3 shows a supply of labor schedule. It tells us the quantity of labor supplied at three different real wage rates. For example, if the real wage rate is $50 an hour (row *B*), the quantity of labor supplied is 200 billion hours a year. If the real wage rate falls to $25 an hour (row *A*), the quantity of labor supplied decreases to 100 billion hours a year. And if the real wage rate rises to $75 an hour (row *C*), the quantity of labor supplied increases to 300 billion hours a year.

Figure 8.3 shows the supply of labor curve. It corresponds to the supply schedule, and the points *A*, *B*, and *C* on the supply curve correspond to the rows *A*, *B*, and *C* of the supply schedule.

The real wage rate influences the quantity of labor supplied because what matters to people is not the number of dollars they earn but what those dollars will buy. The quantity of labor supplied increases as the real wage rate increases for two reasons:

- Hours per person increase.
- Labor force participation increases.

Quantity of labor supplied
The number of labor hours that all the households in the economy plan to work during a given time period at a given real wage rate.

Supply of labor
The relationship between the quantity of labor supplied and the real wage rate when all other influences on work plans remain the same.

FIGURE 8.3

The Supply of Labor

MyEconLab Animation

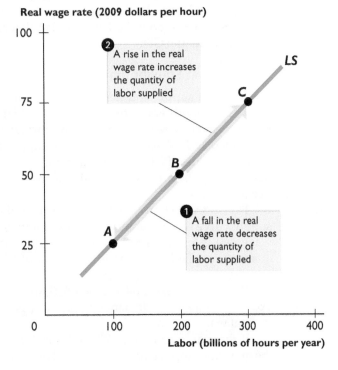

	Real wage rate (2009 dollars per hour)	Quantity of labor supplied (billions of hours per year)
C	75	300
B	50	200
A	25	100

Households are willing to supply labor only if the real wage rate is high enough to attract them from other activities. The higher the real wage rate, the greater is the quantity of labor supplied.

At a real wage rate of $50 an hour, the quantity of labor supplied is 200 billion hours at point *B*.

❶ If the real wage rate falls to $25 an hour, the quantity of labor supplied decreases to 100 billion hours at point *A*.

❷ If the real wage rate rises to $75 an hour, the quantity of labor supplied increases to 300 billion hours at point *C*.

Hours per Person The real wage rate is the opportunity cost of taking leisure and not working. As the opportunity cost of taking leisure rises, other things remaining the same, households choose to work more. But other things don't remain the same. A higher real wage rate brings a higher income, which increases the demand for leisure and encourages less work.

So a rise in the real wage rate has two opposing effects. But for most households, the opportunity cost effect is stronger than the income effect, so a rise in the real wage rate brings an increase in the quantity of labor supplied.

Labor Force Participation Most people have productive opportunities outside the labor force and choose to work only if the real wage rate exceeds the value of other productive activities. For example, a parent might spend time caring for her or his child. The alternative is day care. The parent will choose to work only if he or she can earn enough per hour to pay the cost of day care and have enough left to make the work effort worthwhile. The higher the real wage rate, the more likely it is that a parent will choose to work and so the greater is the labor force participation rate.

Other Influences on Labor Supply Decisions Many factors other than the real wage rate influence labor supply decisions and influence the position of the labor supply curve. Income taxes and unemployment benefits are two of these factors.

The work-leisure decision depends on the *after-tax* wage rate—the wage rate actually received by the household. So, for a given wage rate, the income tax decreases the after-tax wage rate and the quantity of labor supplied decreases. The result is a decrease in the supply of labor. (The income tax rate doesn't change the demand for labor because for the employer, the cost of labor is the before-tax wage rate.)

Unemployment benefits lower the cost of searching for a job and encourage unemployed workers to take longer to find the best job available. The result is a decrease in the supply of labor.

Higher income tax rates and more generous unemployment benefits decrease the supply of labor—the labor supply curve lies farther to the left.

Let's now see how the labor market determines employment, the real wage rate, and potential GDP.

Labor Market Equilibrium

The forces of supply and demand operate in labor markets just as they do in the markets for goods and services. The price of labor services is the real wage rate. A rise in the real wage rate eliminates a shortage of labor by decreasing the quantity demanded and increasing the quantity supplied. A fall in the real wage rate eliminates a surplus of labor by increasing the quantity demanded and decreasing the quantity supplied. If there is neither a shortage nor a surplus, the labor market is in equilibrium.

Figure 8.4(a) shows the labor market equilibrium. The demand curve and the supply curve are the same as those in Figures 8.2 and 8.3. In part (a), if the real wage rate is less than $50 an hour, the quantity of labor demanded exceeds the quantity supplied and there is a shortage of labor. In this situation, the real wage rate rises.

If the real wage rate exceeds $50 an hour, the quantity of labor supplied exceeds the quantity demanded and there is a surplus of labor. In this situation, the real wage rate falls.

If the real wage rate is $50 an hour, the quantity of labor demanded equals the quantity supplied and there is neither a shortage nor a surplus of labor. In this

FIGURE 8.4

Labor Market Equilibrium and Potential GDP

MyEconLab Animation

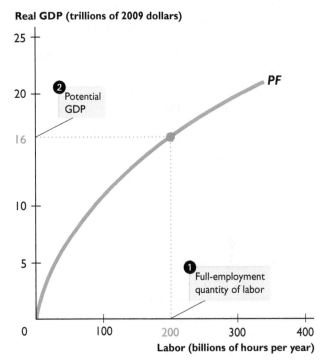

(a) The labor market

(b) Potential GDP

❶ Full employment occurs when the quantity of labor demanded equals the quantity of labor supplied. ❷ The equilibrium real wage rate is $50 an hour, and ❸ the equilibrium quantity of labor employed is 200 billion hours a year.

Potential GDP is the real GDP produced on the production function by the full-employment quantity of labor. ❶ The full-employment quantity of labor, 200 billion hours a year, produces a ❷ potential GDP of $16 trillion.

situation, the labor market is in equilibrium and the real wage rate remains constant. The equilibrium quantity of labor is 200 billion hours a year. When the equilibrium quantity of labor is employed, the economy is at full employment. So the full-employment quantity of labor is 200 billion hours a year.

Full Employment and Potential GDP

When the labor market is in equilibrium, the economy is at full employment and real GDP equals potential GDP.

You've seen that the quantity of real GDP depends on the quantity of labor employed. The production function tells us how much real GDP a given amount of employment can produce. Now that we've determined the full-employment quantity of labor, we can find potential GDP.

Figure 8.4(b) shows the relationship between labor market equilibrium and potential GDP. The equilibrium quantity of labor employed in Figure 8.4(a) is 200 billion hours. The production function in Figure 8.4(b) tells us that 200 billion hours of labor produces $16 trillion of real GDP. This quantity of real GDP is potential GDP.

EYE on U.S. POTENTIAL GDP

Why Do Americans Earn More and Produce More Than Europeans?

The quantity of capital per worker is greater in the United States than in Europe, and U.S. technology, on the average, is more productive than European technology.

These differences between the United States and Europe mean that U.S. labor is more productive than European labor.

Because U.S. labor is more productive than European labor, U.S. employers are willing to pay more for a given quantity of labor than European employers are. So the demand for labor curve in the United States, LD_{US}, lies to the right of the European demand for labor curve, LD_{EU}, in part (a) of the figure.

This difference in the productivity of labor also means that the U.S. production function, PF_{US}, lies above the European production function, PF_{EU}, in part (b) of the figure.

Higher income taxes and unemployment benefits in Europe mean that to induce a person to take a job, a firm in Europe must offer a higher wage rate than a firm in the United States has to offer. So the European labor supply curve, LS_{EU}, lies to the left of the U.S. labor supply curve, LS_{US}.

Equilibrium employment is higher in the United States than in Europe— Americans work longer hours—and the equilibrium real wage rate is higher in the United States than in Europe.

Potential GDP is higher in the United States than in Europe for two reasons: U.S. workers are more productive per hour of work and they work longer hours than Europeans.

Real wage rate (2011 dollars per hour)

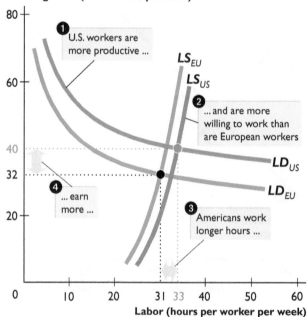

(a) Labor market in Europe and the United States

Real GDP (2011 dollars per hour of work)

(b) Production function in Europe and the United States

CHECKPOINT 8.1

Explain what determines potential GDP.

MyEconLab Study Plan 8.1
Key Terms Quiz
Solutions

Practice Problem

1. Table 1 describes an economy's production function and demand for labor.

TABLE 1

Quantity of labor demanded (billions of hours per year)	0	1	2	3	4
Real GDP (billions of 2009 dollars)		0	40	70	90	100
Real wage rate (2009 dollars per hour)		50	40	30	20	10

Table 2 describes the supply of labor in this economy.

TABLE 2

Quantity of labor supplied (billions of hours per year)	0	1	2	3	4
Real wage rate (2009 dollars per hour)		10	20	30	40	50

Use the data in Tables 1 and 2 to make graphs of the labor market and production function. What are the equilibrium real wage rate and employment? What is potential GDP?

In the News

NITC bridge project

Canada is the United State's largest trading partner and 25 percent of the goods trade crosses the Detroit River. The NITC bridge, costing $1 billion, will increase capacity, reduce traffic bottlenecks and improve opportunities for businesses in both countries by providing a state-of-the-art, publicly operated border crossing.

Source: CNN, June 18, 2013

Explain how this huge project will influence potential GDP in Canada and the United States.

Solution to Practice Problem

1. The demand for labor is a graph of the first and last row of Table 1 and the supply of labor is a graph of the data in Table 2 (Figure 1). The production function is a graph of the first two rows of Table 1 (Figure 2).
    Labor market equilibrium occurs when the real wage rate is $30 an hour and 2 billion hours of labor are employed (Figure 1). Potential GDP is the real GDP produced by the equilibrium quantity of labor (2 billion hours in Figure 1). Potential GDP is $70 billion (Figure 2).

Solution to In the News

Potential GDP will increase, in both Canada and the United States. With increased border efficiency, the production function in both countries will shift upward. With no change in employment, real GDP would increase. But the construction project will increase the demand for U.S. and Canadian labor, increase the full-employment quantity of labor, and increase potential GDP. This project is likely to bring a boost to trade between Canada and the United States.

FIGURE 1

FIGURE 2

8.2 THE NATURAL UNEMPLOYMENT RATE

So far, we've focused on the forces that determine the real wage rate, the quantity of labor employed, and real GDP at full employment. We're now going to bring unemployment into the picture.

You learned in Chapter 6 that the BLS measures the amount of unemployment by counting the number of people who do not have a job, are willing to work, and have looked for work in the past 4 weeks. And you learned how we classify unemployment as frictional, structural, or cyclical. Finally, you learned that when the economy is at full employment, all the unemployment is frictional or structural and the unemployment rate is called the *natural unemployment rate*.

Measuring, describing, and classifying unemployment tell us a lot about it. But these activities do not *explain* the amount of unemployment that exists or why the unemployment rate changes over time and varies across economies.

Many forces interact to determine the unemployment rate. Understanding these forces is a challenging task. Economists approach this task in two steps. The first step is to understand what determines the natural unemployment rate—the unemployment rate when the economy is at full employment. The second step is to understand what makes unemployment fluctuate around the natural unemployment rate. In this chapter, we take the first of these steps. We take the second step in Chapters 13–15 when we study economic fluctuations.

EYE on the PAST
Average Unemployment Rates over Six Decades

If we look back at the U.S. economy decade by decade, we can see through some of the ups and downs of the business cycle and reveal the broad trends. By looking at the average unemployment rates across the decades, we get an estimate of movements in the natural unemployment rate.

The figure shows these averages. During the 1950s and 1960s, the unemployment rate averaged less than 5 percent. During the 1970s, the average unemployment rate climbed to 6 percent, and in the 1980s, it climbed to more than 7 percent. The 1990s and 2000s saw the average unemployment rate fall but not quite back to the rate of the 1950s and 1960s.

High cyclical unemployment since 2008 swells the 2010s average.

You will be a member of the labor force of the late 2010s. The average unemployment rate of the second decade of the 2000s will have a big effect on your job market success.

Unemployment rate (percentage of labor force)

SOURCE OF DATA: Bureau of Labor Statistics.

To understand the amount of frictional and structural unemployment that exists at the natural unemployment rate, economists focus on two fundamental causes of unemployment that cut across the frictional-structural classification. These two fundamental causes of unemployment are

- Job search
- Job rationing

■ Job Search

Job search is the activity of looking for an acceptable vacant job. Because the labor market is in a constant state of change, there are always some people who have not yet found suitable jobs and who are actively searching. The failure of businesses destroys jobs. The expansion of businesses and the startup of new businesses create jobs. As people pass through different stages of life, some enter or reenter the labor market, others leave their jobs to look for better ones, and others retire. This constant churning in the labor market means that there are always some people looking for jobs, and these people are part of the unemployed.

The amount of job search depends on a number of factors that change over time. The main ones are

- Demographic change
- Unemployment benefits
- Structural change

Job search
The activity of looking for an acceptable vacant job.

Demographic Change

An increase in the proportion of the population that is of working age brings an increase in the entry rate into the labor force and an increase in the unemployment rate. This factor was important in the U.S. labor market during the 1970s. The bulge in the birth rate that occurred in the late 1940s and early 1950s increased the proportion of new entrants into the labor force during the 1970s and brought an increase in the unemployment rate.

As the birth rate declined, the bulge moved into higher age groups and the proportion of new entrants declined during the 1990s. During this period, the unemployment rate decreased.

Another source of demographic change has been an increase in the number of households with two incomes. When unemployment comes to one of these workers, it is possible, with income still flowing in, to take longer to find a new job. This factor might have increased frictional unemployment.

Unemployment Benefits

The opportunity cost of job search influences the length of time that an unemployed person spends searching for a job. With no unemployment benefits, the opportunity cost of job search is high, and a person is likely to accept a job that is found quickly. With generous unemployment benefits, the opportunity cost of job search is low, and a person is likely to spend a considerable time searching for the ideal job.

Generous unemployment benefits are a large part of the story of high unemployment rates in Europe and some other countries such as Canada—see *Eye on the Global Economy* on p. 204.

EYE on the GLOBAL ECONOMY
Unemployment Benefits and the Natural Unemployment Rate

The gap between U.S. and Canadian unemployment rates provides information about the influence of unemployment benefits. The two unemployment rates followed similar cycles, but the Canadian unemployment rate exceeded the U.S. rate, which suggests that the natural unemployment rate was higher in Canada than in the United States.

Why? In 1980, Canadian unemployment benefits increased and are available to all the unemployed. In the United States only **38** percent of the unemployed receive benefits.

U.S. unemployment benefits were extended to provide a further 20 weeks of income to the unemployed during the last recession and this change contributed to narrowing the

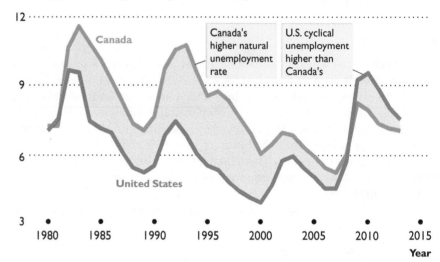

SOURCE OF DATA: Bureau of Labor Statistics and Statistics Canada.

Canada–U.S. unemployment gap. But cyclical unemployment increased in the United States by more than in Canada and was the main source of the reversal of the gap between the two unemployment rates.

Structural Change

Technological change influences unemployment. Sometimes it brings a structural slump, a condition in which some industries and even regions contract while other industries and regions flourish. When these events occur, labor turnover is high, job search increases, and the natural unemployment rate rises.

At other times, technological change brings a structural boom. It creates new jobs that are a good match for the people who are losing their jobs. When these events occur, labor turnover might be high, but job search decreases because new jobs are found quickly, and the natural unemployment rate falls. The Internet economy of the 1990s is an example of a structural boom. Lots of new jobs were created in every major population center, and those jobs were a good match for the skills available, so the natural unemployment rate decreased.

■ Job Rationing

Job rationing
A situation that arises when the real wage rate is above the full-employment equilibrium level.

Job rationing occurs when the real wage rate is above the full-employment equilibrium level. You have learned that markets allocate scarce resources by adjusting the market price to bring buying plans and selling plans into balance. You can think of the market as *rationing* scarce resources. In the labor market, the real wage rate rations employment and therefore rations jobs. Changes in the real wage rate keep the number of people seeking work and the number of jobs available in balance. But the real wage rate is not the only possible instrument for rationing jobs.

In some industries, the real wage rate is set above the full-employment equilibrium level, which brings a surplus of labor. In these labor markets, jobs are rationed by some other means.

The real wage rate might be set above the full-employment equilibrium level for three reasons:

- Efficiency wage
- Minimum wage
- Union wage

Efficiency Wage

An **efficiency wage** is a real wage rate that is set above the full-employment equilibrium wage rate to induce a greater work effort. The idea is that if a firm pays only the going market average wage, employees have no incentive to work hard because they know that even if they are fired for slacking off, they can find a job with another firm at a similar wage rate. But if a firm pays *more* than the going market average wage, employees have an incentive to work hard because they know that if they are fired, they *cannot* expect to find a job with another firm at a similar wage rate.

Efficiency wage
A real wage rate that is set above the full-employment equilibrium wage rate to induce greater work effort.

Further, by paying an efficiency wage, a firm can attract the most productive workers. Also, its workers are less likely to quit their jobs, so the firm faces a lower rate of labor turnover and lower training costs. Finally, the firm's recruiting costs are lower because it always faces a steady stream of available new workers.

Paying an efficiency wage is costly, so only those firms that can't directly monitor the work effort of their employees use this device. For example, truck drivers and plant maintenance workers might receive efficiency wages. If enough firms pay an efficiency wage, the average real wage rate will exceed the full-employment equilibrium level.

The Minimum Wage

A **minimum wage law** is a government regulation that makes hiring labor for less than a specified wage illegal. If the minimum wage is set below the equilibrium wage, the minimum wage has no effect. The minimum wage law and market forces are not in conflict. But if a minimum wage is set above the equilibrium wage, the minimum wage is in conflict with market forces and unemployment arises.

Minimum wage law
A government regulation that makes hiring labor for less than a specified wage illegal.

The current federal minimum wage is $7.25 an hour, and the minimum wage has a major effect in the markets for low-skilled labor. Because skill grows with work experience, teenage labor is particularly affected by the minimum wage.

Union Wage

A **union wage** is a wage rate that results from collective bargaining between a labor union and a firm. Because a union represents a group of workers, it can usually achieve a wage rate that exceeds the level that would prevail in a competitive labor market.

Union wage
A wage rate that results from collective bargaining between a labor union and a firm.

For the United States, it is estimated that, on average, union wage rates are 30 percent higher than nonunion wage rates. But this estimate probably overstates the true effects of labor unions on the wage rate. In some industries, union wages are higher than nonunion wages because union members do jobs that require greater skill than nonunion jobs. In these cases, even without a union, those workers would earn a higher wage.

One way to calculate the effects of unions is to examine the wages of union and nonunion workers who do nearly identical work. For workers with similar skill levels, the union-nonunion wage difference is between 10 and 25 percent. For example, pilots who are members of the Air Line Pilots Association earn about 25 percent more than nonunion pilots with the same level of skill.

Labor unions are much more influential in Europe than in the United States. In Europe, unions not only achieve wage rates above those of a competitive market but also have broad political influence on labor market conditions.

Job Rationing and Unemployment

Whether because of efficiency wages, a minimum wage law, or the actions of labor unions, if the real wage rate is above the full-employment equilibrium level, the natural unemployment rate increases. The above-equilibrium real wage rate decreases the quantity of labor demanded and increases the quantity of labor supplied.

Figure 8.5 illustrates job rationing and the frictional and structural unemployment it creates. The full-employment equilibrium real wage rate is $50 an hour, and the equilibrium quantity of labor is 200 billion hours a year. The existence of efficiency wages, the minimum wage, and union wages raises the economy's average real wage rate to $60 an hour. At this wage rate, the quantity of labor demanded decreases to 175 billion hours and the quantity of labor supplied increases to 240 billion hours. Firms ration jobs and choose the workers to hire on the basis of criteria such as education and previous job experience. The labor market is like a game of musical chairs in which a large number of chairs have been removed. So the quantity of labor supplied persistently exceeds the quantity demanded, and additional unemployment arises from job rationing.

▨ FIGURE 8.5

Job Rationing Increases the Natural Unemployment Rate   MyEconLab Animation

The full-employment equilibrium real wage rate is $50 an hour. Efficiency wages, the minimum wage, and union wages put the average real wage rate above the full-employment equilibrium level—at $60 an hour.

❶ The quantity of labor demanded decreases to 175 billion hours.

❷ The quantity of labor supplied increases to 240 billion hours.

❸ A surplus of labor arises and increases the natural unemployment rate.

EYE on the U.S. ECONOMY
The Federal Minimum Wage

The Fair Labor Standards Act of 1938 set the federal minimum wage in the United States at 25¢ an hour. Over the years, the minimum wage has increased, and in 2013 it was $7.25 an hour. Although the minimum wage has increased, it hasn't kept up with the rising cost of living.

The figure shows the real minimum wage rate in 2009 dollars. You can see that during the late 1960s, the real minimum wage in 2009 dollars was almost $10 an hour. It decreased during the 1970s and 1980s and has fluctuated around an average of about $6.50 an hour since the mid-1980s.

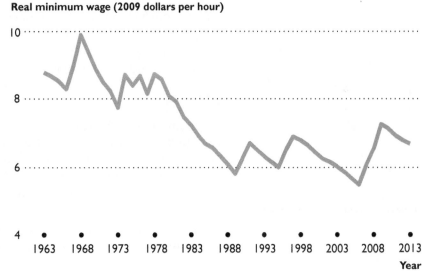

SOURCE OF DATA: Bureau of Labor Statistics.

EYE on YOUR LIFE
Natural Unemployment

You will encounter natural unemployment at many points in your life.

If you now have a job, you probably went through a spell of natural unemployment as you searched for it.

When you graduate and look for a full-time job, you will most likely spend some more time searching for the best match for your skills and location preferences.

In today's world of rapid technological change, most of us must retool and change our jobs at least once and for many of us, more than once.

You might know an older worker who has recently lost a job and is going through the agony of figuring out what to do next.

Although natural unemployment can be painful for people who experience it, from a social perspective, it is productive. It enables scarce labor resources to be re-allocated to their most valuable uses.

MyEconLab Study Plan 8.2
Key Terms Quiz
Solutions

CHECKPOINT 8.2

Explain what determines the natural unemployment rate.

Practice Problems

During the past 50 years, Singapore has seen huge changes: rapid population growth and the introduction of newer and newer technologies. Singapore has modest unemployment benefits, no minimum wage, and weak labor unions.

1. Does Singapore's unemployment arise mainly from job search or job rationing?
2. Which of the factors listed above suggest that Singapore has a higher natural unemployment rate than the United States and which suggest that Singapore has a lower natural unemployment rate?
3. Figure 1 illustrates the labor market in an economy in which at full employment, 1,000 people a day job search. What is the equilibrium real wage rate and employment? Calculate the natural unemployment rate.

FIGURE 1

Real wage rate (2009 dollars per hour)

Labor (thousands of workers per day)

In the News

The minimum wage increases again

A minimum wage increase provides a silver lining for part-time workers, as employers choose to promote more from within the firm than from outside. Low-skilled and youth workers who are employed gain, but for unemployed teenage workers, job prospects look grim.

Source: laborlawcenter.com

Explain why some part-time workers, low-skilled workers, and youth workers gain and why unemployed teenagers find it hard to get jobs.

Solutions to Practice Problems

1. Singapore's unemployment arises mainly from job search. Of the sources of job rationing (efficiency wages, minimum wages, and union wages) only efficiency wages applies.
2. Singapore's rapid population growth and the introduction of new technologies increase the amount of job search —factors that increase the natural unemployment rate.

   Singapore has modest unemployment benefits, which limit the amount of job search, and no minimum wage and weak labor unions, which limit the amount of job rationing—factors that lower the natural unemployment rate
3. Labor market equilibrium determines the equilibrium real wage rate at $3 an hour and full employment at 3,000 workers. Unemployment is 1,000, so the labor force is 4,000 and the natural unemployment rate equals $(1,000 \div 4,000) \times 100$, or 25 percent.

Solution to In the News

When the government raises the minimum wage, firms retain those workers who produce at least as much output per hour as the minimum wage rate. Job experience helps part-time and low-skilled employees retain their jobs, but teenagers with no experience will find it hard to get jobs.

CHAPTER SUMMARY

Key Points

1. **Explain what determines potential GDP.**

   - Potential GDP is the quantity of real GDP that the full-employment quantity of labor produces.
   - The production function describes the relationship between real GDP and the quantity of labor employed when all other influences on production remain the same. As the quantity of labor increases, real GDP increases.
   - The quantity of labor demanded increases as the real wage rate falls, other things remaining the same.
   - The quantity of labor supplied increases as the real wage rate rises, other things remaining the same.
   - At full-employment equilibrium, the real wage rate makes the quantity of labor demanded equal the quantity of labor supplied.

2. **Explain what determines the natural unemployment rate.**

   - The unemployment rate at full employment is the natural unemployment rate.
   - Unemployment is always present because of job search and job rationing.
   - Job search is influenced by demographic change, unemployment benefits, and structural change.
   - Job rationing arises from an efficiency wage, the minimum wage, and a union wage.

Key Terms

MyEconLab Key Terms Quiz

Classical macroeconomics, 190
Demand for labor, 195
Diminishing returns, 194
Efficiency wage, 205
Job rationing, 204
Job search, 203
Keynesian macroeconomics, 190
Minimum wage law, 205

Monetarist macroeconomics, 191
Potential GDP, 193
Production function, 194
Quantity of labor demanded, 195
Quantity of labor supplied, 197
Supply of labor, 197
Union wage, 205

CHAPTER CHECKPOINT

Study Plan Problems and Applications

Use the events in List 1, which occur in the United States one at a time, to work Problems 1 to 4.

LIST 1

- Dell introduces a new supercomputer that everyone can afford.
- A major hurricane hits Florida.
- More high school graduates go to college.
- The CPI rises.
- An economic slump in the rest of the world decreases U.S. exports.

1. Sort the items into four groups: those that change the production function, those that change the demand for labor, those that change the supply of labor, and those that do not change the production function, the demand for labor, or the supply of labor. Say in which direction any changes occur.

2. Which of the events increase the equilibrium quantity of labor and which decrease it?

3. Which of the events raise the real wage rate and which lower it?

4. Which of the events increase potential GDP and which decrease it?

Use the information set out in Table 1 and Table 2 about the economy of Athabasca to work Problems 5 and 6.

5. Calculate the quantity of labor employed, the real wage rate, and potential GDP.

6. If the labor force participation increases, explain how employment, the real wage rate, and potential GDP change.

Use the following information to work Problems 7 and 8.

Suppose that the United States cracks down on illegal immigrants and returns millions of workers to their home countries.

7. Explain how the U.S. real wage rate, U.S. employment, and U.S. potential GDP would change.

8. In the countries to which the immigrants return, explain how employment, the real wage rate, and potential GDP would change.

9. Two island economies, Cocoa Island and Plantation Island, are identical in every respect except one. A survey tells us that at full employment, people on Cocoa Island spend 1,000 hours a day on job search, while the people on Plantation Island spend 2,000 hours a day on job search. Which economy has the greater potential GDP? Which has the higher real wage rate? And which has the higher natural unemployment rate?

10. **Decoding 'natural' rate of unemployment**
    Unemployment is a normal feature of our economy and the Congressional Budget Office believes the "natural" unemployment rate increased from 5 percent in 2007 to 6 percent in 2012.

    Source: The Wall Street Journal, September 7, 2012

    Provide some reasons why the natural unemployment rate might have increased.

11. Read *Eye on U.S. Potential GDP* on p. 200 and then explain why U.S. potential GDP per worker per week is greater than that in Europe. What could induce Europeans to work the same hours as Americans and would that close the gap between potential GPD per worker in the two economies?

TABLE 1 PRODUCTION FUNCTION

Labor hours (millions)	Real GDP (millions of 2009 dollars)
0	0
1	10
2	19
3	27
4	34
5	40

TABLE 2 LABOR MARKET

Real wage rate (2009 dollars per hour)	Quantity of labor demanded	Quantity of labor supplied
	(millions of hours per year)	
10	1	5
9	2	4
8	3	3
7	4	2
6	5	1

Instructor Assignable Problems and Applications

MyEconLab Homework, Quiz, or Test if assigned by instructor

Use the following information to work Problems **1** and **2**.

In Korea, real GDP per hour of labor is $22, the real wage rate is $15 per hour, and people work an average of 46 hours per week.

1. Draw a graph of the demand for and supply of labor in Korea and the United States. Mark a point at the equilibrium quantity of labor per person per week and the real wage rate in each economy. Explain the difference in the two labor markets.

2. Draw a graph of the production functions in Korea and the United States. Mark a point on each production function that shows potential GDP per hour of work in each economy. Explain the difference in the two production functions.

Use the following list of events that occur one at a time to work Problems **3** to **6**.

- The Middle East cuts supplies of oil to the United States.
- The New York Yankees win the World Series.
- U.S. labor unions negotiate wage hikes that affect all workers.
- A huge scientific breakthrough doubles the output that an additional hour of U.S. labor can produce.
- Migration to the United States increases the working-age population.

3. Sort the items into four groups: those that change the production function, those that change the demand for labor, those that change the supply of labor, and those that do not change the production function, the demand for labor, or the supply of labor. Say in which direction each change occurs.

4. Which of the events increase the equilibrium quantity of labor and which decrease the equilibrium quantity of labor?

5. Which of the events raise the real wage rate and which of the events lower the real wage rate?

6. Which of the events increase potential GDP and which decrease potential GDP?

Use the information set out in Table 1 and Table 2 about the economy of Nautica to work Problems **7** and **8**.

7. What is the quantity of labor employed, potential GDP, the real wage rate, and total labor income?

8. Suppose that the government introduces a minimum wage of $0.80 an hour. What is the real wage rate, the quantity of labor employed, potential GDP, and unemployment? Does the unemployment arise from job search or job rationing? Is the unemployment cyclical? Explain.

9. **Fixing up for the fall show**
   Businesses damaged by flooding from Tropical Storm Irene are under pressure to rebuild and reopen this week as Vermont's peak leaf-peeping season begins. Not everyone is cheering. Vermont's recovery hasn't reached every road, and the rebuilding work will persist long after the maple leaves fall.

   Source: *The Wall Street Journal*, September 21, 2011

   Explain the effect of Tropical Storm Irene on employment across Vermont. Did Vermont move along its production function or did its production function shift? How did Vermont's potential GDP change?

TABLE 1 PRODUCTION FUNCTION

Labor hours (per day)	Real GDP (2009 dollars per year)
0	0
10	100
20	180
30	240
40	280

TABLE 2 LABOR MARKET

Real wage rate (2009 dollars per hour)	Quantity of labor demanded	Quantity of labor supplied
	(hours per day)	
1.00	10	50
0.80	20	40
0.60	30	30
0.40	40	20

Multiple Choice Quiz

1. U.S. potential GDP is the value of the goods and services produced in the United States _____.

   A. in the reference base year
   B. when the U.S. unemployment rate is zero
   C. when the U.S. economy is at full employment
   D. when the U.S. inflation rate is zero

2. The demand for labor curve shows the relationship between _____.

   A. the quantity of labor employed and firms' profits
   B. all households' willingness to work and the real wage rate
   C. the quantity of labor businesses are willing to hire and the real wage rate
   D. the labor force and the real wage rate

3. The supply of labor is the relationship between _____.

   A. the quantity of labor supplied and leisure time forgone
   B. the real wage rate and the quantity of labor supplied
   C. firms' willingness to supply jobs and the real wage rate
   D. the labor force participation rate and the real wage rate

4. Households' labor supply decisions are influenced by all of the following *except* _____.

   A. the opportunity cost of taking leisure and not working
   B. the after-tax wage rate
   C. unemployment benefits
   D. the number of full-time jobs available

5. The full-employment quantity of labor _____.

   A. increases if labor becomes more productive
   B. cannot increase because everyone who wants a job has one
   C. increases as the economy moves along its production function
   D. decreases if the income tax rate decreases

6. The natural unemployment rate _____.

   A. increases if unemployment benefits become more generous
   B. increases in a recession
   C. increases as the average age of the labor force rises
   D. decreases as firms outsource manufacturing jobs

7. Job rationing _____.

   A. increases the natural unemployment rate
   B. has no effect on the natural unemployment rate
   C. increases labor turnover as firms compete for high quality labor
   D. decreases the demand for labor, which lowers the real wage rate

8. An efficiency wage results in all of the following *except* _____.

   A. a decrease in the rate of labor turnover
   B. an increase in the full-employment quantity of labor
   C. greater work effort
   D. an increase in the cost of monitoring work effort

Why are some nations rich
and others poor?

Economic Growth

**When you have completed your study of this chapter,
you will be able to**

1 Define and calculate the economic growth rate, and explain the
  implications of sustained growth.

2 Explain the sources of labor productivity growth.

3 Review the theories of economic growth.

4 Describe policies that speed economic growth.

MyEconLab Big Picture

Economic growth
A sustained expansion of production possibilities.

9.1 THE BASICS OF ECONOMIC GROWTH

Economic growth is a sustained expansion of production possibilities. Maintained over decades, rapid economic growth can transform a poor nation into a rich one. Such has been the experience of Hong Kong, South Korea, Taiwan, and some other Asian economies. Slow economic growth or the absence of growth can condemn a nation to devastating poverty. Such has been the fate of Sierra Leone, Somalia, Zambia, and much of the rest of Africa.

Economic growth is different from the rise in incomes that occurs during the recovery from a recession. Economic growth is a sustained trend, not a temporary cyclical expansion.

■ Calculating Growth Rates

Economic growth rate
The annual percentage change of real GDP.

We express the **economic growth rate** as the annual percentage change of real GDP. To calculate this growth rate, we use the formula:

$$\text{Growth rate of real GDP} = \frac{\substack{\text{Real GDP} \\ \text{in current year}} - \substack{\text{Real GDP} \\ \text{in previous year}}}{\text{Real GDP in previous year}} \times 100.$$

For example, if real GDP in the current year is \$8.4 trillion and if real GDP in the previous year was \$8.0 trillion, then

$$\text{Growth rate of real GDP} = \frac{\$8.4 \text{ trillion} - \$8.0 \text{ trillion}}{\$8.0 \text{ trillion}} \times 100 = 5 \text{ percent.}$$

The growth rate of real GDP tells us how rapidly the total economy is expanding. This measure is useful for telling us about potential changes in the balance of economic power among nations, but it does not tell us about changes in the standard of living.

The standard of living depends on real GDP per person (also called *per capita real GDP*), which is real GDP divided by the population. So the contribution of real GDP growth to the change in the *standard of living* depends on the growth rate of real GDP per person. We use the above formula to calculate this growth rate, replacing real GDP with real GDP per person.

Suppose, for example, that in the current year, when real GDP is \$8.4 trillion, the population is 202 million. Then real GDP per person in the current year is \$8.4 trillion divided by 202 million, which equals \$41,584. And suppose that in the previous year, when real GDP was \$8.0 trillion, the population was 200 million. Then real GDP per person in that year was \$8.0 trillion divided by 200 million, which equals \$40,000.

Use these two values of real GDP per person with the growth formula to calculate the growth rate of real GDP per person. That is,

$$\text{Growth rate of real GDP per person} = \frac{\$41,584 - \$40,000}{\$40,000} \times 100 = 4 \text{ percent.}$$

We can also calculate the growth rate of real GDP per person by using the formula:

$$\text{Growth rate of real GDP per person} = \text{Growth rate of real GDP} - \text{Growth rate of population.}$$

In the example you've just worked through, the growth rate of real GDP is 5 percent. The population changes from 200 million to 202 million, so

$$\text{Growth rate of population} = \frac{202 \text{ million} - 200 \text{ million}}{200 \text{ million}} \times 100 = 1 \text{ percent}$$

and

Growth rate of real GDP per person = 5 percent − 1 percent = 4 percent.

This formula makes it clear that real GDP per person grows only if real GDP grows faster than the population grows. If the growth rate of the population exceeds the growth of real GDP, then real GDP per person falls.

■ The Magic of Sustained Growth

Sustained growth of real GDP per person can transform a poor society into a wealthy one. The reason is that economic growth is like compound interest. Suppose that you put $100 in the bank and earn 5 percent a year interest on it. After one year, you have $105. If you leave that money in the bank for another year, you earn 5 percent interest on the original $100 and on the $5 interest that you earned last year. You are now earning interest on interest! The next year, things get even better. Then you earn 5 percent on the original $100 and on the interest earned in the first year and the second year. Your money in the bank is *growing* at a rate of 5 percent a year. Before too many years have passed, you'll have $200 in the bank. But after *how many* years?

The answer is provided by a formula known as the **Rule of 70**, which states that the number of years it takes for the level of any variable to double is approximately 70 divided by the annual percentage growth rate of the variable. Using the Rule of 70, you can now calculate how many years it takes your $100 to become $200. It is 70 divided by 5, which is 14 years.

The Rule of 70 applies to any variable, so it applies to real GDP per person. Table 9.1 shows the doubling time for a selection of other growth rates. You can see that real GDP per person doubles in 70 years (70 divided by 1)—an average human life span—if the growth rate is 1 percent a year. It doubles in 35 years if the growth rate is 2 percent a year and in just 10 years if the growth rate is 7 percent a year.

We can use the Rule of 70 to answer other questions about economic growth. For example, in 2010, U.S. real GDP per person was approximately 4 times that of China. China's recent growth rate of real GDP per person was 7 percent a year. If this growth rate were to be maintained, how long would it take China's real GDP per person to reach that of the United States in 2010?

The answer, provided by the Rule of 70, is 20 years. China's real GDP per person doubles in 10 (70 divided by 7) years. It doubles again to 4 times its current level in another 10 years. So after 20 years of growth at 7 percent a year—that is by 2030—China's real GDP per person would be 4 times its current level and equal to that of the United States in 2010.

Rule of 70
The number of years it takes for the level of any variable to double is approximately 70 divided by the annual percentage growth rate of the variable.

TABLE 9.1 GROWTH RATES

Growth rate (percent per year)	Years for level to double
1	70
2	35
3	23
4	18
5	14
6	12
7	10
8	9
9	8
10	7

EYE on the PAST

How Fast Has Real GDP per Person Grown?

Professor Michael Kremer of Harvard University and Professor J. Bradford DeLong of the University of California, Berkeley, have constructed an extraordinary picture of real GDP in the global economy going back one million years. According to their numbers, human societies lived for a million years with no economic growth.

The top figure shows the numbers using the value of the dollar in 2009 as the measuring rod. Real GDP per person averaged $150 a year from 1,000,000 BC until 1620! It rose to $190 when Aristotle and Plato were teaching in Athens, around 500 BC, but slipped back over the next thousand years to $140 as the Roman Empire collapsed around 400 AD. When the Black Death gripped Europe in the 1340s, incomes fell to a 1-million-year low and even when the Pilgrim Fathers began to arrive in America in the 1620s, incomes were still the same as those of Ancient Greece!

Then, beginning around 1750, first in England and then in Europe and the United States, an astonishing change known as the Industrial Revolution occurred. Real GDP per person began to increase, apparently without limit. By 1850, real GDP per person was twice its 1650 level. By 1950, it was more than five times its 1850 level, and by 2000, it was four times its 1950 level.

The lower figure gives you a close-up view of U.S. real GDP per person over the past 110 years. Part (a) shows that in 2013, real GDP per person was almost eight times its level in 1903. It has grown by 2 percent a year, but the growth rate has been uneven: Almost no growth in the 1930s and the fastest growth in the 1940s.

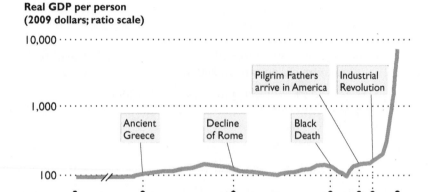

**Real GDP per person
(2009 dollars; ratio scale)**

SOURCE OF DATA: J. Bradford DeLong, *"Estimating World GDP, One Million B.C.—Present."*

Part (b) shows that growth, measured decade by decade, has slowed since the 1960s and the growth rate between 2000 and 2010 was lower than that in any decade except the 1930s. But the reason is not that potential GDP growth slowed. Rather, it is because there was a deep recession in 2008 and 2009.

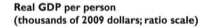

**Real GDP per person
(thousands of 2009 dollars; ratio scale)**

(a) Real GDP per person

(b) Growth rate of real GDP per person

SOURCES OF DATA: Bureau of Economic Analysis and the Bureau of Labor Statistics.

CHECKPOINT 9.1

Define and calculate the economic growth rate, and explain the implications of sustained growth.

Practice Problems

1. Mexico's real GDP was 8,762 billion pesos in 2010 and 9,105 billion pesos in 2011. Mexico's population growth rate in 2011 was 1 percent. Calculate Mexico's economic growth rate in 2011 and the growth rate of real GDP per person in Mexico in 2011.

2. Calculate the approximate number of years it will take for real GDP per person to double if an economy maintains an economic growth rate of 12 percent a year and a population growth rate of 2 percent a year.

3. Calculate the change in the number of years it will take for real GDP per person in India to double if the growth rate of real GDP per person increases from 8 percent a year to 10 percent a year.

In the News

ADB reduces China growth estimate
Since 1980 China's real GDP per person has grown at 10 percent a year. The Asian Development Bank (ADB) cut its estimate for China's growth to 9.3 percent this year.

Source: Bloomberg, September 13, 2011

If China's growth rate remains at 9.3 percent a year, how many additional years will it take for China to double its real GDP per person?

Solutions to Practice Problems

1. Mexico's economic growth rate in 2011 was 3.9 percent. The economic growth rate equals the percentage change in real GDP:
   [(Real GDP in 2011 − Real GDP in 2010) ÷ Real GDP in 2010] × 100, which is
   [(9,105 billion − 8,762 billion) ÷ 8,762 billion] × 100, or 3.9 percent.
   The growth rate of real GDP per person equals 2.9 percent.
   Growth rate of real GDP per person equals (Growth rate of real GDP − Population growth rate), which is (3.9 percent − 1 percent), or 2.9 percent.

2. It will take 7 years for real GDP per person to double. The growth rate of real GDP per person equals the economic growth rate minus the population growth rate. Real GDP per person grows at 12 percent minus 2 percent, which is 10 percent a year. The Rule of 70 tells us that the level of a variable that grows at 10 percent a year will double in 70 ÷ 10 years, or 7 years.

3. Two years. The Rule of 70 tells us that a variable that grows at 8 percent a year will double in 70 ÷ 8 years, which is approximately 9 years. By increasing its growth rate to 10 percent a year, the variable will double in 7 years.

Solution to In the News

With a growth rate of 10 percent a year, real GDP per person will double in 7 years (70 ÷ 10). If the growth rate is maintained at 9.3 per cent a year, real GDP per person will double in 7.5 years (70 ÷ 9.3)—taking an additional 0.5 year.

9.2 LABOR PRODUCTIVITY GROWTH

Real GDP grows when the quantities of the factors of production grow or when persistent advances in technology make them increasingly productive. To understand what determines the growth rate of real GDP, we must understand what determines the growth rates of the factors of production and the rate of increase in their productivity. You're going to see how saving and investment determine the growth rate of physical capital and how the growth of physical capital and human capital and advances in technology interact to determine the economic growth rate.

We are interested in real GDP growth because it contributes to improvements in our standard of living. But our standard of living improves only if we produce more goods and services with each hour of labor. So our main concern is to understand the forces that make our labor more productive. Let's start by defining labor productivity.

■ Labor Productivity

Labor productivity
The quantity of real GDP produced by one hour of labor.

Labor productivity is the quantity of real GDP produced by one hour of labor. It is calculated by using the formula:

$$\text{Labor productivity} = \frac{\text{Real GDP}}{\text{Aggregate hours}}.$$

For example, if real GDP is $8,000 billion and if aggregate hours are 200 billion, then we can calculate labor productivity as

$$\text{Labor productivity} = \frac{\$8,000\ \text{billion}}{200\ \text{billion hours}} = \$40\ \text{per hour}.$$

When labor productivity grows, real GDP per person grows. So the growth in labor productivity is the basis of the rising standard of living. What makes labor productivity grow? We'll answer this question by considering the influences on labor productivity growth under two broad headings:

- Saving and investment in physical capital
- Expansion of human capital and discovery of new technologies

These two broad influences on labor productivity growth interact and are the sources of the extraordinary growth in productivity during the past 200 years. Although they interact, we'll begin by looking at each on its own.

■ Saving and Investment in Physical Capital

Saving and investment in physical capital increase the amount of capital per worker and increase labor productivity. Labor productivity took a dramatic upturn when the amount of capital per worker increased during the Industrial Revolution. Production processes that use hand tools can create beautiful objects, but production methods that use large amounts of capital per worker, such as auto plant assembly lines, enable workers to be much more productive. The accumulation of capital on farms and building sites; in textile factories, iron foundries and steel mills, coal mines, chemical plants, and auto plants; and at banks and insurance companies added incredibly to the productivity of our labor.

A strong and experienced farm worker of 1830, using a scythe, could harvest 3 acres of wheat a day. A farm worker of 1831, using a mechanical reaper, could harvest 15 acres a day. And a farm worker of today, using a combine harvester, can harvest and thresh hundreds of acres a day.

The next time you see a movie set in the old West, look carefully at how little capital there is. Try to imagine how productive you would be in such circumstances compared with your productivity today.

Capital Accumulation and Diminishing Marginal Returns

Although saving and investment in additional capital is a source of labor productivity growth, without the expansion of human capital and technological change, it would not bring sustained economic growth. Eventually growth would slow and most likely stop. The reason is a fundamental fact about capital known as the **law of diminishing marginal returns**, which states that:

> If the quantity of capital is small, an increase in capital brings a large increase in production; and if the quantity of capital is large, an increase in capital brings a small increase in production.

This law applies to all factors of production, not only to capital, and is the reason why the demand for labor curve slopes downward (see Chapter 8, p. 196).

You can see why the law of diminishing marginal returns applies to capital by thinking about how your own productivity is influenced by the capital you own. When you got your first computer your small quantity of capital increased and your productivity increased enormously. You most likely don't have two computers, but if you do, the productivity boost from your second computer was much smaller than that from the first. If you don't have two computers, one of the reasons is that you doubt it would be worth the expense because it would contribute such a small amount to your labor productivity.

Farm labor productivity increased from harvesting 3 acres per day in 1830...

to harvesting hundreds of acres per day in the twenty-first century.

Illustrating the Law of Diminishing Marginal Returns

Figure 9.1 illustrates the relationship between capital and productivity. The curve *PC* is a **productivity curve,** which shows how real GDP per hour of labor changes as the quantity of capital per hour of labor changes.

In Figure 9.1, when the quantity of capital (measured in real dollars) increases from $40 to $80 per hour of labor, real GDP per hour of labor increases from $30 to $50, a $20 or 67 percent increase. But when the quantity of capital increases from $180 to $220 per hour of labor, the same $40 increase as before, real GDP per hour of labor increases from $80 to $84, only a $4 or 5 percent increase. If capital per hour of labor keeps increasing, labor productivity increases by ever smaller amounts and eventually stops rising.

■ Expansion of Human Capital and Discovery of New Technologies

The expansion of human capital and the discovery of new technologies have a profoundly different effect on labor productivity than capital accumulation has. They don't display diminishing marginal returns.

Expansion of Human Capital Human capital—the accumulated skill and knowledge of people—comes from three sources:

1. Education and training
2. Job experience
3. Health and diet

Productivity curve
The relationship that shows how real GDP per hour of labor changes as the quantity of capital per hour of labor changes.

■ FIGURE 9.1

The Effects of an Increase in Capital

MyEconLab Animation

When workers are equipped with more capital, they become more productive. The productivity curve *PC* shows how an increase in capital per hour of labor increases real GDP per hour of labor.

❶ When the quantity of capital per hour of labor increases from a low $40 to $80, real GDP per hour of labor increases by $20.

❷ When the quantity of capital per hour of labor increases from a high $180 to $220, real GDP per hour of labor increases by $4.

An equal-size increase in capital per hour of labor brings a diminishing increase in output, the greater is the quantity of capital.

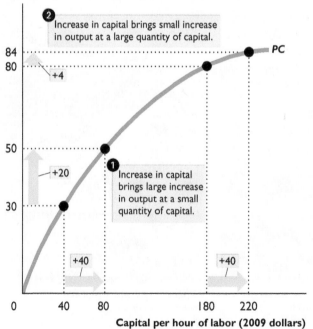

A hundred years ago, most people attended school for around eight years. A hundred years before that, most people had no formal education at all. Today, 90 percent of Americans complete high school and more than 60 percent go to college or university. Our ability to read, write, and communicate effectively contributes enormously to our productivity.

The education of thousands of scientists, engineers, mathematicians, biologists, computer programmers, and people equipped with a host of other specialist skills has made huge contributions to labor productivity and to the advance in technology.

While formal education is productive, school is not the only place where people acquire human capital. We also learn from on-the-job experience—from *learning by doing*. One carefully studied example illustrates the importance of learning by doing. Between 1941 and 1944 (during World War II), U.S. shipyards produced 2,500 Liberty Ships—cargo ships built to a standardized design. In 1941, it took 1.2 million person-hours to build a ship. By 1942, it took 600,000, and by 1943, it took only 500,000. Not much change occurred in the physical capital employed during these years, but an enormous amount of human capital was accumulated. Thousands of workers and managers learned from experience and their productivity more than doubled in two years.

Strong, healthy, well-nourished workers are much more productive than those who lack good nutrition, health care, and opportunties to exercise. This fact creates a virtuous circle. Improved health care, diet, and exercise increase labor productivity; and increased labor productivity brings the increased incomes that make these health improvements possible.

The expansion of human capital is the most fundamental source of economic growth because it directly increases labor productivity and is the source of the discovery of new technologies.

Discovery of New Technologies The growth of physical capital and the expansion of human capital have made large contributions to economic growth, but the discovery of new technologies has made an even greater contribution.

The development of writing, one of the most basic human skills, was the source of some of the earliest productivity gains. The ability to keep written records made it possible to reap ever-larger gains from specialization and trade. Imagine how hard it would be to do any kind of business if all the accounts, invoices, and agreements existed only in people's memories.

Production using 1950s technology.

Later, the development of mathematics laid the foundation for the eventual extension of knowledge in physics, chemistry, and biology. This base of scientific knowledge was the foundation for the technological advances of the Industrial Revolution 200 years ago and of today's Information Revolution.

Since the Industrial Revolution, technological change has become a part of everyday life. Firms routinely conduct research to develop technologies that are more productive, and partnerships between business and the universities are commonplace in fields such as biotechnology and electronics.

Illustrating the Effects of Human Capital and Technological Change

Figure 9.2 illustrates the effects of the expansion of human capital and the discovery of new technologies and labor productivity: They shift the *productivity curve* upward. In the figure, these influences shift the productivity curve from PC_0 to PC_1. Imagine that PC_0 is the productivity curve in 1960 and PC_1 is the productivity curve for 2010. With capital of $180 per hour of labor, workers could

Production using 2000s technology.

produce $80 of real GDP per hour of labor in 2010. If workers had been equipped with the same amount of capital but with the technology of 1960, they would have produced only $40 of real GDP per hour of labor. The upward shift of the productivity curve illustrates the fact that labor and capital become more productive at each quantity of capital per hour of labor. Capital is still subject to diminishing marginal returns but the overall level of productivity is higher with expanded human capital and more productive technologies.

■ Combined Influences Bring Labor Productivity Growth

To reap the benefits of technological change—to use new technologies to make labor productivity grow—capital must increase. Some of the most powerful and far-reaching technologies are embodied in human capital—for example, language, writing, mathematics, physics, biology, and engineering. But most technologies are embodied in physical capital. For example, to increase the productivity of transportation workers by using the discovery of the internal combustion engine, millions of horse-drawn carriages had to be replaced by automobiles and trucks; more recently, to increase the labor productivity of office workers by using the discovery of computerized word processing, millions of typewriters had to be replaced by computers and printers.

Figure 9.3 shows how the combined effects of capital accumulation, the expansion of human capital, and the discovery of new technologies bring labor productivity growth. In 1960, the productivity curve is PC_0, workers have $80 of capital per hour and produce $25 of real GDP per hour. By 2010, capital has increased to $180 per hour. With no expansion of human capital or technological

---

■ FIGURE 9.2

The Effects of Human Capital and Technological Change   MyEconLab Animation

When human capital expands or technology advances, labor becomes more productive—a given amount of capital per hour of labor can produce more real GDP per hour of labor.

Here, with 1960's technology on PC_0, $180 of capital per hour of labor can produce $40 of goods and services—real GDP per hour of labor.

With 2010's technology on PC_1, the same $180 of capital per hour of labor can produce $80 of goods and services—real GDP per hour of labor.

The expansion of human capital and the discovery of new technologies shift the productivity curve upward and are not subject to diminishing marginal returns.

FIGURE 9.3

How Labor Productivity Grows

In 1960, workers had $80 of capital per hour of labor and produced real GDP per hour of $25 on PC_0.

❶ When the quantity of capital increased from $80 per hour of labor in 1960 to $180 per hour of labor in 2010, real GDP per hour of labor increased from $25 to $40 along PC_0.

❷ The expansion of human capital and discovery of new technologies shifted the productivity curve upward and increased real GDP per hour of labor from $40 to $80.

advance, real GDP per hour of labor would have increased to $40. But with the human capital and technology of 2010, output per hour increases to $80.

You've now seen what makes labor productivity grow. *Eye on the U.S. Economy* on p. 224 looks at the quantitative importance of the sources of growth since 1960. Real GDP grows because labor becomes more productive and also because the *quantity of labor* increases. Figure 9.4 summarizes the sources of economic growth and shows how the growth in labor productivity together with the growth in the quantity of labor bring real GDP growth.

FIGURE 9.4

The Sources of Economic Growth

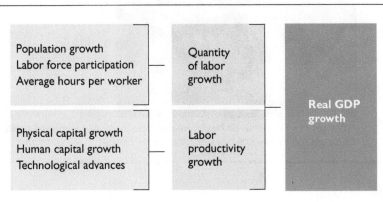

Real GDP depends on the quantity of labor and labor productivity.

The quantity of labor depends on the population, the labor force participation rate, and the average hours per worker.

Labor productivity depends on the amounts of physical capital and human capital and the state of technology.

Growth in quantity of labor and growth in labor productivity bring real GDP growth.

EYE on the U.S. ECONOMY
U.S. Labor Productivity Growth Since 1960

The figure shows how labor productivity growth has fluctuated over the past 50 years. It also shows the contributions to productivity growth of increases in capital per worker (the green bars) and advances in technology and the growth of human capital (the blue bars).

You can see that most of the fluctuations in productivity growth arise from changes in the pace of technological change and human capital accumulation.

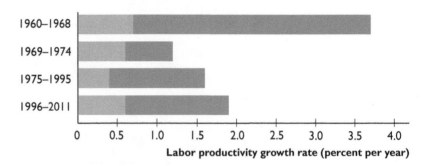

Capital growth per hour of labor

Human capital growth and technological change

SOURCES OF DATA: Bureau of Economic Analysis, Bureau of Labor Statistics, and authors' calculations.

The Booming Sixties

Plastics, the laser, the computer, the transistor, the space race, the interstate highway system, the shopping mall, and passenger jet were among the technological advances that brought extraordinary labor productivity growth during the 1960s.

Passenger jets and the construction of thousands of miles of interstate highways were among the technological advances that increased labor productivity during the 1960s.

The Stagnant Seventies

An oil price hike and oil embargo as well as higher taxes and expanded regulation slowed productivity growth during the 1970s and the higher cost of energy diverted the focus of technological change toward saving energy rather than increasing labor productivity.

An embargo on oil exports to the United States and a higher cost of energy as well as tax hikes contributed to the productivity growth slowdown of the 1970s.

The Information Age

The Internet has transformed our lives and unlocking the human genome has opened the possibility of dramatic advances in health care. But the information age increase in labor productivity is lower than that of the 1960s.

Advances in information technologies and biotechnologies increased productivity during the 1990s and 2000s but not by as much as the technological advances of the 1960s did.

CHECKPOINT 9.2

Explain the sources of labor productivity growth.

Practice Problems

Use the data in Table 1 to work Problems 1 and 2.

TABLE 1

Item	2012	2013
Aggregate labor hours (billions)	25.0	25.6
Real GDP (billions of 2009 dollars)	1,000	1,050

1. Calculate the growth rate of real GDP in 2013.
2. Calculate labor productivity in 2012 and 2013, and the growth rate of labor productivity in 2013.

In the News

Labor productivity on the rise
The BLS reported the following data for the year to March 2013: In the nonfarm sector, output increased 2.4 percent as aggregate hours increased 1.5 percent; in the manufacturing sector, output increased 2.5 percent as aggregate hours increased by 0.9 percent.

Source: bls.gov/news.release

As aggregate hours increased, output increased but did labor productivity in each sector increase? In which sector was growth in labor productivity greater?

Solutions to Practice Problems

1. The growth rate of real GDP in 2013 was 5 percent. The growth rate equals [($1,050 billion − $1,000 billion) ÷ $1,000 billion] × 100 = 5 percent.
2. Labor productivity is $40.00 an hour in 2012 and $41.02 an hour in 2013.
   Labor productivity equals real GDP divided by aggregate labor hours.
   In 2012, labor productivity was ($1,000 billion ÷ 25 billion) or $40.00 per hour of labor. In 2013, labor productivity was ($1,050 billion ÷ 25.6 billion) or $41.02 per hour of labor.
   The growth rate of labor productivity in 2013 was 2.55 percent.
   Labor productivity growth rate was [($41.02 − $40.00) ÷ $40.00] × 100 or 2.55 percent.

Solution to In the News

Output = Aggregate hours × Labor productivity. In each sector, output increased by more than the increase in aggregate hours, so labor productivity must have increased. Output growth in manufacturing was almost the same as that in the nonfarm sector while growth in aggregate hours was much slower in manufacturing, so labor productivity must have increased by a larger percentage in the manufacturing sector than in the nonfarm sector.

9.3 ECONOMIC GROWTH THEORIES: OLD AND NEW

You've seen that real GDP grows when labor productivity and the quantity of labor grow. You've also seen that labor productivity grows when saving and investment increase physical capital, when education and on-the-job training expand human capital, and when research leads to the discovery of new technologies. But what *causes* saving and investment in new capital, the expansion of human capital, the discovery of new technologies, and population growth? Economists have been trying to answer this question and understand why and how poor countries become rich and rich countries become richer since the time of Adam Smith in the eighteenth century. We'll look at two sets of ideas: old and new.

■ Old Growth Theory

Classical growth theory
The theory that the clash between an exploding population and limited resources will eventually bring economic growth to an end.

An old growth theory remains relevant today because some people believe that it might turn out to be correct. It is called **classical growth theory,** and it predicts that a clash between an exploding population and limited resources will eventually bring economic growth to an end. According to classical growth theory, labor productivity growth is temporary. When labor productivity rises and lifts real GDP per person above the subsistence level, which is the minimum real income needed to maintain life, a population explosion occurs. Eventually, the population grows so large that capital per worker and labor productivity fall and real GDP per person returns to the subsistence level.

Adam Smith, Thomas Robert Malthus, and David Ricardo, the leading economists of the late eighteenth and early nineteenth centuries, proposed this theory, but the view is most closely associated with Malthus and is sometimes called the *Malthusian theory.* It is also sometimes called the Doomsday theory.

Many people today are Malthusians. They say that if today's global population of 7 billion explodes to 11 billion by 2200, we will run out of many natural resources and the population will grow faster than the quantity of capital so labor productivity will fall and we will return to the primitive standard of living that was experienced before the Industrial Revolution. (You can see in *Eye on the Past* on p. 216 that for most of human history, people did live on the brink of subsistence.) We must act, say the Malthusians, to contain the population growth. This dismal implication led to economics being called the *dismal science.*

■ New Growth Theory

New growth theory
The theory that our unlimited wants will lead us to ever greater productivity and perpetual economic growth.

New growth theory predicts that our unlimited wants will lead us to ever greater productivity and perpetual economic growth. According to new growth theory, real GDP per person grows because of the choices people make in the pursuit of profit. Paul Romer of Stanford University developed this theory during the 1980s, building on ideas developed by Joseph Schumpeter during the 1930s and 1940s.

Choices and Innovation

The new growth theory emphasizes three facts about market economies:

- Human capital expands because of choices.
- Discoveries result from choices.
- Discoveries bring profit, and competition destroys profit.

Human Capital Expansion and Choices People decide how long to remain in school, what to study, and how hard to study. And when they graduate from school, people make more choices about job training and on-the-job learning. All these choices govern the speed at which human capital expands.

Discoveries and Choices When people discover a new product or technique, they consider themselves lucky. They are right, but chance does not determine the pace at which new discoveries are made—and at which technology advances. It depends on how many people are looking for a new technology and how intensively they are looking.

Discoveries and Profits Profit is the spur to technological change. The forces of competition squeeze profits, so to increase profit, people constantly seek either lower-cost methods of production or new and better products for which people are willing to pay a higher price. Inventors can maintain a profit for several years by taking out a patent or copyright, but eventually a new discovery is copied and profits disappear.

Two other facts play a key role in the new growth theory:

- Many people can use discoveries at the same time.
- Physical activities can be replicated.

Discoveries Used by All Once a profitable new discovery has been made, everyone can use it. For example, when Marc Andreeson created Mosaic, the Web browser that led to the creation of Netscape Navigator and Microsoft's Internet Explorer, everyone who was interested in navigating the Internet had access to a new and more efficient tool. One person's use of a Web browser does not prevent others from using it. This fact means that as the benefits of a new discovery spread, free resources become available. These resources are free because nothing is given up when an additional person uses them. They have a zero opportunity cost.

Replicating Activities Production activities can be replicated. For example, there might be 2, 3, or 53 identical firms making fiber-optic cable by using an identical assembly line and production technique. If one firm increases its capital and output, that *firm* experiences diminishing returns. But the economy can increase its capital and output by adding another identical fiber cable factory, and the *economy* does not experience diminishing returns.

The assumption that capital does not experience diminishing returns is the central novel proposition of the new growth theory. The implication of this simple and appealing idea is astonishing. As capital accumulates, labor productivity grows indefinitely as long as people devote resources to expanding human capital and introducing new technologies.

Perpetual Motion

Economic growth is like the perpetual motion machine in Figure 9.5. Growth is driven by insatiable wants that lead us to pursue profit and innovate. New and better products result from this process; new firms start up, and old firms go out of business. As firms start up and die, jobs are created and destroyed. New and better jobs lead to more leisure and more consumption. But our insatiable wants are still there, so the process continues—wants, profit incentives, innovation, and new products. The economic growth rate depends on the ability and the incentive to innovate.

FIGURE 9.5

A Perpetual Motion Machine

MyEconLab Animation

❶ People want a higher standard of living and are spurred by ❷ profit incentives to make the ❸ innovations that lead to ❹ new and better techniques and new and better products, which in turn lead to ❺ the birth of new firms and the death of some old firms, ❻ new and better jobs, and ❼ more leisure and more consumption goods and services. The result is ❽ a higher standard of living. But people want a yet higher standard of living, and the growth process continues.

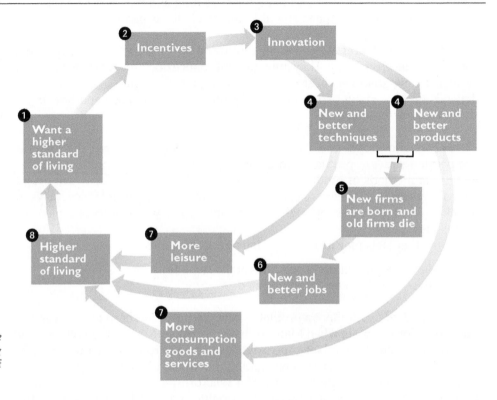

Based on a similar figure in *These Are the Good Old Days: A Report on U.S. Living Standards*, Federal Reserve Bank of Dallas 1993 Annual Report.

EYE on YOUR LIFE

How You Influence and Are Influenced by Economic Growth

Many of the choices that you make affect your personal economic growth rate—the pace of expansion of your own standard of living. And these same choices, in combination with similar choices made by millions of other people, have a profound effect on the economic growth of the nation and the world.

The most important of these choices right now is your choice to increase your human capital. By being in school, you have decided to expand your human capital.

You will continue to expand your human capital long after you finish school as your earning power rises with on-the-job experience. You might even decide to return to school at a later stage in your life.

A choice that will become increasingly important later in your life is to accumulate a retirement fund. This choice provides not only a source of income for you when you eventually retire but also financial resources that firms can use to finance the expansion of physical capital.

Not only do your choices influence economic growth; economic growth also has a big influence on you—on how you earn your income and on the standard of living that your income makes possible.

Because of economic growth, the jobs available today are more interesting and less dangerous and strenuous than those of 100 years ago; and jobs are hugely better paid. But for many of us, economic growth means that we must accept change and be ready to learn new skills and get new jobs.

CHECKPOINT 9.3

Review the theories of economic growth.

MyEconLab Study Plan 9.3
Key Terms Quiz
Solutions

Practice Problems

1. What is the classical growth theory and why does it predict that economic growth will eventually end?

2. What is the driving force of economic growth according to new growth theory? Why does it predict that economic growth will never end?

In the News

The productivity watch

Former Federal Reserve chairman Alan Greenspan attributes the growth of labor productivity to IT investments that boosted labor productivity, which boosted company profits, which led to more IT investments, and so on, leading to a nirvana of high growth.

Source: *Fortune* Magazine, September 4, 2006

Which of the growth theories that you've studied in this chapter best corresponds to the explanation given by Mr. Greenspan?

Solutions to Practice Problems

1. The classical growth theory predicts that labor productivity growth is temporary: When labor productivity increases, real GDP per person increases and because it exceeds the real income needed to maintain life, a population explosion occurs. The population becomes so large that capital per worker and labor productivity decrease and real GDP per person returns to its subsistence level.

2. The driving force of economic growth according to new growth theory is a persistent pursuit of profit that is the incentive to innovate along with an absence of diminishing returns. New growth theory predicts that economic growth will never end because our unlimited wants will lead us to make choices that will bring ever-greater productivity and perpetual economic growth.

Solution to In the News

Mr. Greenspan is describing the new growth theory. According to this theory, real GDP per person grows because of the choices people make in the pursuit of profit. The perpetual pursuit of profit leads to innovations (IT innovations in the period described here) that increase labor productivity and increase profit. The perpetual pursuit of profit will bring persistent economic growth.

9.4 ACHIEVING FASTER GROWTH

Why did it take more than a million years of human life before economic growth began? Why are some countries even today still barely growing? Why don't all societies save and invest in new capital, expand human capital, and discover and apply new technologies on a scale that brings rapid economic growth? What actions can governments take to encourage growth?

■ Preconditions for Economic Growth

The main reason economic growth is either absent or slow is that some societies lack the incentive system that encourages growth-producing activities. One of the fundamental preconditions for creating the incentives that lead to economic growth is economic freedom.

Economic Freedom

Economic freedom is present when people are able to make personal choices, their private property is protected by the rule of law, and they are free to buy and sell in markets. The rule of law, an efficient legal system, and the ability to enforce contracts are essential foundations for creating economic freedom. Impediments to economic freedom are corruption in the courts and government bureaucracy; barriers to trade, such as import bans; high tax rates; stringent regulations on business, such as health, safety, and environmental regulation; restrictions on banks; labor market regulations that limit a firm's ability to hire and lay off workers; and illegal markets, such as those that violate intellectual property rights.

No unique political system is necessary to deliver economic freedom. Democratic systems do a good job, but the rule of law, not democracy, is the key requirement for creating economic freedom. Nondemocratic political systems that respect the rule of law can also work well. Hong Kong is the best example of a place with little democracy but a lot of economic freedom—and a lot of economic growth. No country with a high level of economic freedom is economically poor, but many countries with low levels of economic freedom stagnate.

Property Rights

Economic freedom requires the protection of private property—the factors of production and goods that people own. The social arrangements that govern the protection of private property are called **property rights.** They include the rights to physical property (land, buildings, and capital equipment), to financial property (claims by one person against another), and to intellectual property (such as inventions). Clearly established and enforced property rights provide people with the incentive to work and save. If someone attempts to steal their property, a legal system will protect them. Such property rights also assure people that government itself will not confiscate their income or savings.

Markets

Economic freedom also requires free markets. Buyers and sellers get information and do business with each other in *markets*. Market prices send signals to buyers and sellers that create incentives to increase or decrease the quantities demanded and supplied. Markets enable people to trade and to save and invest. But markets cannot operate without property rights.

Economic freedom
A condition in which people are able to make personal choices, their private property is protected by the rule of law, and they are free to buy and sell in markets.

Property rights
The social arrangements that govern the protection of private property.

Property rights and markets create incentives for people to specialize and trade, to save and invest, to expand their human capital, and to discover and apply new technologies. Early human societies based on hunting and gathering did not experience economic growth because they lacked property rights and markets. Economic growth began when societies evolved the institutions that create incentives. But the presence of an incentive system and the institutions that create it do not guarantee that economic growth will occur. They permit economic growth but do not make it inevitable.

Growth begins when the appropriate incentive system exists because people can specialize in the activities at which they have a comparative advantage and trade with each other. You saw in Chapter 3 how everyone gains from such activity. By specializing and trading, everyone can acquire goods and services at the lowest possible cost. Consequently, people can obtain a greater volume of goods and services from their labor.

As an economy moves from one with little specialization to one that reaps the gains from specialization and trade, its production and consumption grow. Real GDP per person increases, and the standard of living rises.

But for growth to be persistent, people must face incentives that encourage them to pursue the three activities that generate *ongoing* economic growth: saving and investment, expansion of human capital, and the discovery and application of new technologies.

■ Policies to Achieve Faster Growth

To achieve faster economic growth, we must increase the growth rate of capital per hour of labor, increase the growth rate of human capital, or increase the pace of technological advance. The main actions that governments can take to achieve these objectives are

- Create incentive mechanisms.
- Encourage saving.
- Encourage research and development.
- Encourage international trade.
- Improve the quality of education.

Create Incentive Mechanisms

Economic growth occurs when the incentives to save, invest, and innovate are strong enough. These incentives require property rights enforced by a well-functioning legal system. Property rights and a legal system are the key ingredients that are missing in many societies. For example, they are absent throughout much of Africa. The first priority for growth policy is to establish these institutions so that incentives to save, invest, and innovate exist. Russia is a leading example of a country that is striving to take this step toward establishing the conditions in which economic growth can occur.

Encourage Saving

Saving finances investment, which brings capital accumulation. So encouraging saving can increase the growth of capital and stimulate economic growth. The East Asian economies have the highest saving rates and the highest growth rates. Some African economies have the lowest saving rates and the lowest growth rates.

Tax incentives can increase saving. Individual Retirement Accounts (IRAs) are an example of a tax incentive to save. Economists claim that a tax on consumption rather than on income provides the best incentive to save.

Encourage Research and Development

Everyone can use the fruits of basic research and development efforts. For example, all biotechnology firms can use advances in gene-splicing technology. Because basic inventions can be copied, the inventor's profit is limited and so the market allocates too few resources to this activity.

Governments can direct public funds toward financing basic research, but this solution is not foolproof. It requires a mechanism for allocating public funds to their highest-valued use. The National Science Foundation is one possibly efficient channel for allocating public funds to universities and public research facilities to finance and encourage basic research. Government programs such as national defense and space exploration also lead to innovations that have wide use. Laptop computers and nonstick coatings are two prominent examples of innovations that came from the U.S. space program.

Encourage International Trade

Free international trade stimulates economic growth by extracting all the available gains from specialization and trade. The fastest-growing nations today are those with the fastest-growing exports and imports. The creation of the North American Free Trade Agreement and the integration of the economies of Europe through the formation of the European Union are examples of successful actions that governments have taken to stimulate economic growth through trade.

Improve the Quality of Education

The free market would produce too little education because it brings social benefits beyond the benefits to the people who receive the education. By funding basic education and by ensuring high standards in skills such as language, mathematics, and science, governments can contribute enormously to a nation's growth potential. Education can also be expanded and improved by using tax incentives to encourage improved private provision. Singapore's Information Technology in Education program is one of the best examples of a successful attempt to stimulate growth through education.

■ How Much Difference Can Policy Make?

It is easy to make a list of policy actions that could increase a nation's economic growth rate. It is hard to convert that list into acceptable actions that make a big difference.

Political equilibrium arises from the balance of the interests of one group against the interests of another group. Change brings gains for some and losses for others, so change is slow. And even when change occurs, if the economic growth rate can be increased by even as much as half a percentage point, it takes many years for the full benefits to accrue.

A well-intentioned government cannot dial up a big increase in the economic growth rate, but it can pursue policies that will nudge the economic growth rate upward. Over time, the benefits from these policies will be large.

EYE on RICH AND POOR NATIONS

Why Are Some Nations Rich and Others Poor?

Political stability, property rights protected by the rule of law, and limited government intervention in markets: These are key features of the economies that enjoy high or rapidly rising incomes and they are the features missing in economies that remain poor. All the rich nations have possessed these growth-inducing characteristics for the many decades during which their labor productivity and standard of living have been rising.

The United States started to grow rapidly 150 years ago and overtook Europe in the early 20th century. In the past 50 years, the gaps between these countries haven't changed much. (See part (a) of the figure.)

In a transition from Communism to a market economy, Eastern Europe is now growing faster.

Tribal conflict in Africa and bureaucratic overload in Central and South America have kept growth slow and the gap between the United States and these regions has widened.

Real GDP per person in East Asian economies, in part (b), has converged toward that in the United States. These economies are like fast trains running on the same track at similar speeds with roughly constant gaps between them. Hong Kong and Singapore are the lead trains and run about 15 years in front of Taiwan, 20 years in front of South Korea, and almost 40 years in front of China.

Between 1960 and 2010, Hong Kong and Singapore transformed themselves from poor developing economies to take their places among the world's richest economies.

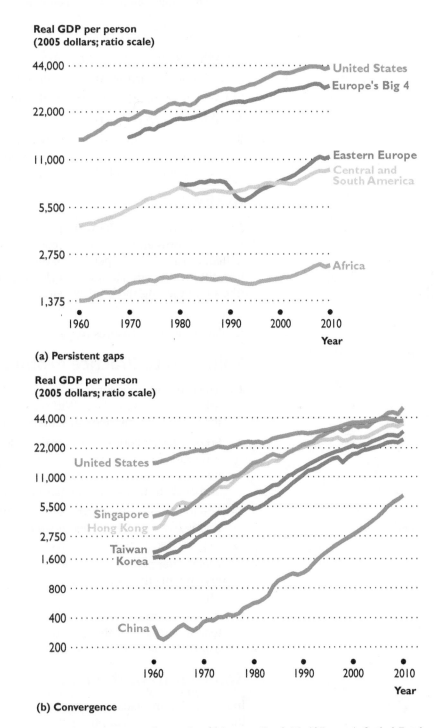

Real GDP per person
(2005 dollars; ratio scale)

(a) Persistent gaps

Real GDP per person
(2005 dollars; ratio scale)

(b) Convergence

SOURCE OF DATA: International Monetary Fund, *World Economic Outlook Database*.

MyEconLab Study Plan 9.4
Key Terms Quiz
Solutions

 CHECKPOINT 9.4

Describe policies that speed economic growth.

Practice Problems

1. What are the preconditions for economic growth?
2. Why does much of Africa experience slow economic growth?
3. Why is economic freedom crucial for achieving economic growth?
4. What role do property rights play in encouraging economic growth?
5. Explain why, other things remaining the same, a country with a well-educated population has a faster economic growth rate than a country that has a poorly educated population.

In the News

India's economy hits the wall

Just six months ago, the Indian economy was growing rapidly; now growth has halted. India needs to spend $500 billion upgrading its infrastructure and education and health-care facilities. Agriculture remains unproductive; and reforms, like strengthening the legal system, have been ignored.

Source: *BusinessWeek*, July 1, 2008

Explain how the measures reported in the news clip could lead to faster growth.

Solutions to Practice Problems

1. The preconditions for economic growth are economic freedom, private property rights, and markets. Without these preconditions, people have little incentive to undertake the actions that lead to economic growth.
2. Some African countries experience slow economic growth because they lack economic freedom, private property rights are not enforced, and markets do not function well. People in these countries have little incentive to specialize and trade or to accumulate both physical and human capital.
3. Economic freedom is crucial for achieving economic growth because economic freedom allows people to make choices and gives them the incentives to pursue growth-producing activities.
4. Clearly defined private property rights and a legal system to enforce them give people the incentive to work, save, invest, and accumulate human capital.
5. A well-educated population has more skills and greater labor productivity than a poorly educated population. A well-educated population can contribute to the research and development that create new technology.

Solution to In the News

Investment in infrastructure and education and heath-care facilities would increase India's stock of physical capital, which would increase labor productivity. Better education and heath care would increase human capital and again increase labor productivity. With better technology and more capital used on farms, productivity of farm workers would increase. Strengthening the legal system could better enforce property rights. Each of these measures could lead to faster growth in labor productivity and faster growth in real GDP per person in India.

CHAPTER SUMMARY

Key Points

MyEconLab Key Terms Quiz

1. **Define and calculate the economic growth rate, and explain the implications of sustained growth.**

   - Economic growth is the sustained expansion of production possibilities. The annual percentage change in real GDP measures the economic growth rate.
   - Real GDP per person must grow if the standard of living is to rise.
   - Sustained economic growth transforms poor nations into rich ones.
   - The Rule of 70 tells us the number of years in which real GDP doubles— 70 divided by the percentage growth rate of real GDP.

2. **Explain the sources of labor productivity growth.**

   - Real GDP grows when aggregate hours and labor productivity grow.
   - Real GDP per person grows when labor productivity grows.
   - The interaction of saving and investment in physical capital, expansion of human capital, and technological advances bring labor productivity growth.
   - Saving and investment in physical capital alone cannot bring sustained steady growth because of diminishing marginal returns to capital.

3. **Review the theories of economic growth.**

   - Classical growth theory predicts that economic growth will end because a population explosion will lower real GDP per person to its subsistence level.
   - New growth theory predicts that capital accumulation, human capital growth, and technological change respond to incentives and can bring persistent growth in labor productivity.

4. **Describe policies that speed economic growth.**

   - Economic growth requires an incentive system created by economic freedom, property rights, and markets.
   - It might be possible to achieve faster growth by encouraging saving, subsidizing research and education, and encouraging international trade.

Key Terms

MyEconLab Key Terms Quiz

CHAPTER CHECKPOINT

Study Plan Problems and Applications

1. Explain why sustained growth of real GDP per person can transform a poor country into a wealthy one.

2. In 2005 and 2006, India's real GDP grew by 9.2 percent a year and its population grew by 1.6 percent a year. If these growth rates are sustained, in what years would
   - Real GDP be twice what it was in 2006?
   - Real GDP per person be twice what it was in 2006?

3. Describe how U.S. real GDP per person has changed over the last 100 years.

4. Explain the link between labor hours, labor productivity, and real GDP.

5. Explain how saving and investment in capital change labor productivity. Why do diminishing returns arise? Provide an example of diminishing returns. Use a graph of the productivity curve to illustrate your answer.

6. Explain how advances in technology change labor productivity. Do diminishing returns arise? Provide an example of an advance in technology. Use a graph of the productivity curve to illustrate your answer.

7. Explain how an increase in human capital changes labor productivity. Do diminishing returns arise? Provide an example of an increase in human capital. Use a graph of the productivity curve to illustrate your answer.

8. What were the sources of labor productivity growth in the U.S. economy during the fifty years since 1960? How did the 1960s differ from the more recent decades?

9. Draw productivity curves to illustrate the changes in labor productivity that occured in the U.S. economy in the 1960s and the years since 1996. Can you think of some of the new technologies that arrived in these two periods?

10. What can governments in Africa do to encourage economic growth and raise the standard of living in their countries?

11. **Slowing down growth**
    China's GDP growth target for the 12th Five-Year-Plan period 2011–2015 is 7 percent a year. This largely symbolic goal (China's average growth rate for the past five years was a whopping 11 percent a year) shows that the central government wants to fundamentally restructure the economy.

    Source: *The Daily Telegraph*, September 25, 2011

    If China reduces its economic growth rate from 11 percent a year to 7 percent a year, how many additional years will it take for GDP to double? In what year will China's GDP quadruple?

 12. Read *Eye on Rich and Poor Nations* on p. 233. Which nations are the richest and which are growing the fastest? What are the conditions that lead to higher incomes and faster growing incomes?

Instructor Assignable Problems and Applications

MyEconLab Homework, Quiz, or Test if assigned by instructor

1. Distinguish between a low and high income and a low and high economic growth rate. What are the key features of an economy that are present when incomes are high or fast growing and absent when incomes are low and stagnating or growing slowly? Provide an example of an economy with a low income and slow growth rate, a low income and rapid growth rate, and a high income with sustained growth over many decades.

Use the following information to work Problems 2 and 3.

China's growth rate of real GDP in 2005 and 2006 was 10.5 percent a year and its population growth rate was 0.5 percent a year.

2. If these growth rates continue, in what year would real GDP be twice what it was in 2006?

3. If these growth rates continue, in what year would real GDP per person be twice what it was in 2006?

4. Explain how an increase in physical capital and an increase in human capital change labor productivity. Use a graph to illustrate your answer.

5. Table 1 describes labor productivity in an economy. What must have occured in this economy during year 1?

6. Describe and illustrate in a graph what happened in the economy in Table 1 if in year 1, capital per hour of labor was 30 and in year 2 it was 40.

7. China invests almost 50 percent of its annual production in new capital compared to 15 percent in the United States. Capital per hour of labor in China is about 25 percent of that in the United States. Explain which economy has the higher real GDP per hour of labor, the faster growth rate of labor productivity, and which experiences the more severe diminishing returns.

8. **China's growth slows as government changes gears**
China's economy grew 7.5 percent in the second quarter of this year. For the past 30 years, China has relied on cheap credit, heavy manufacturing, infrastructure investment, and exports as the source of double-digit growth. But with the population aging and its labor force shrinking, China will need to increase labor productivity if it is to return to double-digit growth.

Source: *The New York Times*, July 14, 2013

Suggest changes in government policies that might increase labor productivity and return China to double-digit growth.

9. **India's growth could be even better, says OECD**
India's current growth averaged 8.5 percent a year over the past four years. This growth rate is sustainable, but a rate of 10 percent was possible if reforms were introduced. The OECD suggests that ongoing economic liberalization could help the country double its real GDP per person in 10 years.

Source: *The Independent*, October 10, 2007

By raising the real GDP growth rate from 8.5 percent a year to 10 percent a year and maintaining a constant population growth rate, how many years earlier will real GDP per person be doubled?

TABLE 1 LABOR PRODUCTIVITY

Capital per hour of labor	Real GDP per hour of labor	
	in year 1	in year 2
10	7	9
20	13	17
30	18	24
40	22	30
50	25	35
60	27	39
70	28	42

Multiple Choice Quiz

1. If real GDP increases from $5 billion to $5.25 billion and the population increases from 2 million to 2.02 million, real GDP per person increases by _____ percent.
   A. 5.0
   B. 1.0
   C. 2.5
   D. 4.0

2. If the population growth rate is 2 percent, real GDP per person will double in 7 years if real GDP grows by _____ percent per year.
   A. 7
   B. 10
   C. 12
   D. 14

3. All of the following increase labor productivity *except* _____.
   A. the accumulation of skill and knowledge
   B. an increase in capital per hour of labor
   C. an increase in consumption
   D. the employment of a new technology

4. The increase in real GDP per hour of labor that results from an increase in capital per hour of labor _____.
   A. is constant and independent of the quantity of capital
   B. is larger at a small quantity of capital than at a large quantity of capital
   C. is smaller at a small quantity of capital than at a large quantity of capital
   D. decreases as technology advances

5. The increase in real GDP per hour of labor that results from an advance in technology makes labor _____ productive _____.
   A. more; at all quantities of capital
   B. less; and capital more productive
   C. more; only at a large quantity of capital
   D. more; and capital less productive

6. The classical growth theory is that real GDP per person _____.
   A. only temporarily rises and then returns to the subsistence level
   B. grows forever
   C. is constant and does not change
   D. increases as the population grows

7. In new growth theory, the source of economic growth is _____.
   A. more leisure
   B. new and better jobs
   C. the persistent want for a higher standard of living
   D. an ever increasing growth rate of capital per hour of labor

8. An economy can achieve faster economic growth *without* _____.
   A. markets and property rights
   B. people being willing to save and invest
   C. incentives to encourage the research for new technologies
   D. an increase in the population growth rate

RATES
Mortgage and
Home Equity

Home Lending

Fixed
Interest Rate
3.500%
APR
3.579%

Adjustable (ARM)
Interest Rate
2.625%
APR
3.092%

Jumbo Fixed
Interest Rate
3.750%
APR
3.807%

**Home Equity
Line of Credit**
Crista® Rate of
4.240%
Variable APR
(Prime + 0.990% Variable APR
or lower)*

Why have interest rates
been so low?

Finance, Saving, and Investment

10

When you have completed your study of this chapter,
you will be able to

1 Describe the financial markets and the key financial institutions.

2 Explain how borrowing and lending decisions are made and how these decisions interact in the loanable funds market.

3 Explain how a government budget surplus or deficit influences the real interest rate, investment, and saving.

MyEconLab Big Picture

10.1 FINANCIAL INSTITUTIONS AND MARKETS

Financial institutions and markets provide the channels through which saving flows to finance the investment in capital that makes our economy grow. The health of these institutions and markets spreads to affect the performance of every other market—of the labor market and the markets for goods and services.

When financial institutions are in good health and financial markets are working well, a high level of investment brings a rapidly growing economy and rising living standards. When financial institutions get sick and financial markets dry up, a low level of investment slows economic growth and sometimes puts the economy in recession with falling living standards.

■ Some Finance Definitions

Finance, money, and capital are three terms that we use in our everyday lives almost interchangeably. Yet these terms have distinctly different meanings in the study of financial markets. Let's examine their differences.

Finance and Money

Finance is the lending and borrowing that moves funds from savers to spenders. *Money* is the object (or objects) that people use to make payments. You might say "I'm going to borrow some money to buy a car." Your borrowing and someone else's lending is a financial transaction—*finance*. You pay for the new car using *money*. By distinguishing between finance and money and studying them separately, we can better understand their roles and effects on the economy. For the rest of this chapter, we study finance; in Chapters 11 and 12, we study money.

Capital: Physical and Financial

Capital or physical capital
The tools, instruments, machines, buildings, and other items that have been produced in the past and that are used to produce goods and services.

Capital—also called **physical capital**—is the tools, instruments, machines, buildings, and other items that have been produced in the past and that are used to produce goods and services. Inventories of raw materials, semifinished goods, and components are part of physical capital. *Financial capital* is the funds used to buy physical capital. You're going to see how decisions about investment and saving, along with borrowing and lending, influence the quantity of physical capital.

Investment, Capital, Wealth, and Saving

Gross investment
The total amount spent on new capital.

Net investment
The change in the quantity of capital—equals gross investment minus depreciation.

Wealth
The value of all the things that people own.

Investment (Chapter 5, p. 115) increases the quantity of capital and *depreciation* (Chapter 5, p. 122) decreases it. The total amount spent on new capital is called **gross investment**. The change in the quantity of capital is called **net investment**. Net investment equals gross investment minus depreciation. Figure 10.1 illustrates these concepts. Tom's end-of-year capital of $40,000 equals his initial capital of $30,000 plus net investment of $10,000; and net investment equals gross investment of $30,000 minus depreciation of $20,000.

Wealth is the value of all the things that people own. What people own is related to what they earn, but it is not the same thing. People earn an income, which is the amount they receive during a given time period from supplying the services of the resources they own. *Saving* (Chapter 5, p. 116), the amount of income that is not paid in taxes or spent on consumption, adds to wealth. Wealth also increases when the market value of assets rises—called *capital gains*.

FIGURE 10.1

Capital and Investment

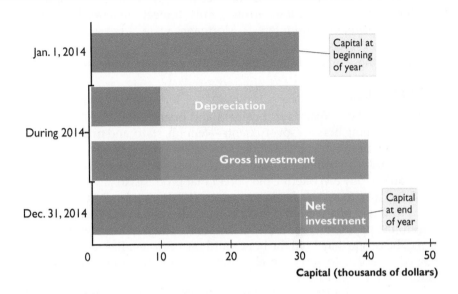

On January 1, 2014, Tom's DVD Burning, Inc. had DVD-recording machines valued at $30,000. During 2014, the value of Tom's machines fell by $20,000—depreciation—and he spent $30,000 on new machines—gross investment. Tom's net investment was $10,000, so at the end of 2014, Tom had capital valued at $40,000.

If at the end of the school year, you have $250 in the bank and textbooks worth $300 and that's all that you own, your wealth is $550. If during the summer, you earn $5,000 (after-tax income) and spend $1,000 on consumption, your bank account increases to $4,250 and your wealth becomes $4,550. Your wealth has increased by $4,000, which equals your saving—your income of $5,000 minus your consumption expenditure of $1,000.

National wealth and national saving work like this personal example. The wealth of a nation at the end of a year equals its wealth at the start of the year plus its saving during the year, which equals income minus consumption expenditure.

To make real GDP grow, saving and wealth must be transformed into investment and capital. This transformation takes place in the markets for financial capital and through the activities of financial institutions that we now describe.

Markets for Financial Capital

Saving is the source of the funds that are used to finance investment, and these funds are supplied and demanded in three types of financial markets:

- Loan markets
- Bond markets
- Stock markets

Loan Markets

Businesses often want short-term loans to buy inventories or to extend credit to their customers. Sometimes they get these funds in the form of a loan from a bank. Households often want funds to purchase big-ticket items, such as automobiles or household furnishings and appliances. They get these funds as bank loans, often in the form of outstanding credit card balances.

Households also get funds to buy new homes. (Expenditure on new homes is counted as part of investment.) These funds are usually obtained as a loan that is secured by a *mortgage*—a legal contract that gives ownership of a home to the lender in the event that the borrower fails to meet the agreed payment schedule (of loan repayments and interest). Mortgages were at the center of the U.S. credit crisis of 2007–2008.

All of these types of financing take place in loan markets.

Bond Markets

When Wal-Mart expands its business and opens new stores, it gets the funds it needs by selling bonds. Governments—federal, state, and municipal—also get the funds they need to finance a budget deficit by issuing bonds.

Bond
A promise to pay specified sums of money on specified dates.

A **bond** is a promise to make specified payments on specified dates. For example, you can buy a Western Union bond that promises to pay $6.20 every year until 2035 and then to make a final payment of $100 in October 2036.

The buyer of a Western Union bond makes a loan to the company and is entitled to the payments promised by the bond. When a person buys a newly issued bond, he or she may hold the bond until the borrower has repaid the amount borrowed or sell it to someone else. Bonds issued by firms and governments are traded in the *bond market*.

The term of a bond might be long (decades) or short (just a month or two). Firms often issue very short-term bonds as a way of getting paid for their sales before the buyer is able to pay. For example, when GM sells $100 million of railway locomotives to Union Pacific, GM wants to be paid when the items are shipped. But Union Pacific doesn't want to pay until the locomotives are earning an income. In this situation, Union Pacific might promise to pay GM $101 million three months in the future. A bank would be willing to buy this promise for (say) $100 million. GM gets $100 million immediately and the bank gets $101 million in three months when Union Pacific honors its promise. The U.S. Treasury issues promises of this type, called *Treasury bills*.

Another type of bond is a *mortgage-backed security*, which entitles its holder to the income from a package of mortgages. Mortgage lenders create mortgage-backed securities. They make mortgage loans to home buyers and then create securities that they sell to obtain more funds to make more mortgage loans. The holder of a mortgage-backed security is entitled to receive payments that derive from the payments received by the mortgage lender from the homebuyer–borrower.

Mortgage-backed securities were at the center of the storm in the financial markets in 2007–2008.

Stock Markets

When Boeing wants to raise funds to expand its airplane-building business, it issues stock. A **stock** is a certificate of ownership and claim to a firm's profits. Boeing has issued about 900 million shares of its stock. If you owned 900 Boeing shares, you would own one millionth of Boeing and be entitled to receive one millionth of its profits.

Stock
A certificate of ownership and claim to the profits that a firm makes.

A *stock market* is a financial market in which shares in corporations' stocks are traded. The New York Stock Exchange, the London Stock Exchange (in England), the Frankfurt Stock Exchange (in Germany), and the Tokyo Stock Exchange are all examples of stock markets.

Financial Institutions

Financial markets are highly competitive because of the role played by financial institutions in those markets. A **financial institution** is a firm that operates on both sides of the markets for financial capital: It borrows in one market and lends in another. The key financial institutions are

Financial institution
A firm that operates on both sides of the markets for financial capital: It borrows in one market and lends in another.

- Investment banks
- Commercial banks
- Government-sponsored mortgage lenders
- Pension funds
- Insurance companies

Investment Banks

Investment banks are firms that help other financial institutions and governments raise funds by issuing and selling bonds and stocks, as well as providing advice on transactions such as mergers and acquisitions. Until the late 1980s, the United States maintained a sharp separation between investment banking and commercial banking—a separation that was imposed by the Glass-Steagall Act of 1933. Until 2008, four big Wall Street firms—Goldman Sachs, Lehman Brothers, Merrill Lynch, and Morgan Stanley—provided investment banking services. But in the financial meltdown of 2008, Lehman disappeared and Merrill Lynch was taken over by the Bank of America, a commercial bank.

Commercial Banks

The bank that you use for your own banking services and that issues your credit card is a commercial bank. We'll explain their role in Chapter 11 where we study the role of money in our economy.

Government-Sponsored Mortgage Lenders

Two large financial institutions, the Federal National Mortgage Association, or Fannie Mae, and the Federal Home Loan Mortgage Corporation, or Freddie Mac, are government-sponsored enterprises that buy mortgages from banks, package them into *mortgage-backed securities*, and sell them. In September 2008, Fannie Mae and Freddie Mac owned or guaranteed $6 trillion worth of mortgages (half of the U.S. total of $12 trillion) and were taken over by the federal government.

Pension Funds

Pension funds are financial institutions that use the pension contributions of firms and workers to buy bonds and stocks. The mortgage-backed securities of Fannie Mae and Freddie Mac are among the assets of pension funds. Some pension funds are very large and play an active role in the firms whose stock they hold.

Insurance Companies

Insurance companies enter into agreements with households and firms to provide compensation in the event of accident, theft, fire, ill health, and a host of other misfortunes. Some companies, for example, provide insurance that pays out if a firm fails and cannot meet its bond obligations; and some insure other insurers in a complex network of reinsurance.

Insurance companies receive premiums from their customers, make payments against claims, and use the funds they have received but not paid out as claims to buy bonds and stocks on which they earn interest.

In normal times, insurance companies have a steady flow of funds coming in from premiums and interest on the financial assets they hold and a steady, but smaller, flow of funds paying claims. Their profit is the gap between the two flows. But in unusual times, when large and widespread losses are being incurred, insurance companies can run into difficulty in meeting their obligations. Such a situation arose in 2008 for one of the biggest insurers, AIG, and the firm was taken into public ownership.

■ Insolvency and Illiquidity

Net worth

The total market value of what a financial institution has lent minus the market value of what it has borrowed.

A financial institution's **net worth** is the total market value of what it has lent minus the market value of what it has borrowed. If net worth is positive, the institution is *solvent* and can remain in business. But if net worth is negative, the institution is *insolvent* and must stop trading. The owners of an insolvent financial institution—usually its stockholders—bear the loss when the assets are sold and debts paid.

A financial institution both borrows and lends, so it is exposed to the risk that its net worth might become negative. To limit that risk, institutions are regulated and a minimum amount of their lending must be backed by their net worth.

Sometimes, a financial institution is solvent but illiquid. A firm is *illiquid* if it has made long-term loans with borrowed funds and is faced with a sudden demand to repay more of what it has borrowed than it has in available cash. In normal times, a financial institution that is illiquid can borrow from another institution. But if all financial institutions are short of cash, the market for loans among financial institutions dries up.

Insolvency and illiquidity were at the core of the financial meltdown of 2007–2008.

■ Interest Rates and Asset Prices

Stocks, bonds, short-term securities, and loans are collectively called *financial assets*. The *interest rate* on a financial asset is a percentage of the price of the asset.

Because the interest rate is a percentage of the price of an asset, if the asset price rises, other things remaining the same, the interest rate falls. And conversely, if the asset price falls, other things remaining the same, the interest rate rises.

To see this *inverse relationship* between an asset price and interest rate, look at the example of a Microsoft share. In September 2009, the price of a Microsoft share was $25 and each share entitled its owner to 50 cents of Microsoft profit. The interest rate on a Microsoft share as a percentage was

$$\text{Interest rate} = (\$0.50 \div \$25) \times 100 = 2 \text{ percent.}$$

If the price of a Microsoft share increased to $50 and each share still entitled its owner to 50 cents of Microsoft profit, the interest rate on a Microsoft share as a percentage would become

$$\text{Interest rate} = (\$0.50 \div \$50) \times 100 = 1 \text{ percent.}$$

This relationship means that an asset price and interest rate are determined simultaneously—one implies the other. In the next part of this chapter, we learn how asset prices and interest rates are determined in the financial markets.

CHECKPOINT 10.1

Describe the financial markets and the key financial institutions.

Practice Problems

1. Michael is an Internet service provider. On December 31, 2011, he bought an existing business with servers and a building worth $400,000. During 2012, he bought new servers for $500,000. The market value of his older servers fell by $100,000. What was Michael's gross investment, depreciation, and net investment during 2012? What is Michael's capital at the end of 2012?

2. Lori is a student who teaches golf on the weekend and in a year earns $20,000 after paying her taxes. At the beginning of 2011, Lori owned $1,000 worth of books, DVDs, and golf clubs and she had $5,000 in a savings account at the bank. During 2011, the interest on her savings account was $300 and she spent a total of $15,300 on consumption goods and services. The market value of her books, DVDs, and golf clubs did not change. How much did Lori save in 2011? What was her wealth at the end of 2011?

In the News

IMF urges EU banks to raise capital
European banks face $400 billion in potential losses from the euro-zone debt crisis, the International Monetary Fund said as it urged banks to raise capital.
Source: *The Wall Street Journal*, September 22, 2011

What are the financial institutions that the IMF urges to raise more capital? What exactly is the "capital" referred to in the news clip? How might raising more capital make financial institutions safer?

Solutions to Practice Problems

1. Michael's gross investment during 2012 was $500,000—the market value of the new servers he bought.

   Michael's depreciation during 2012 was $100,000—the fall in the market value of his older servers.

   Michael's net investment during 2012 was $400,000. Net investment equals gross investment minus depreciation, which is ($500,000 − $100,000).

   At the end of 2012, Michael's capital was $800,000. The capital grew during 2012 by the amount of net investment, so at the end of 2012 capital was $400,000 + $400,000, which equals $800,000.

2. Lori saved $5,000. Saving equals income (after tax) minus the amount spent. That is, Lori's saving was $20,300 minus $15,300, or $5,000.

   Lori's wealth at the end of 2011 was $11,000—the sum of her wealth at the start of 2011 ($6,000) plus her saving during 2011 ($5,000).

Solution to In the News

The institutions are some European banks. "Capital" in the news clip is the banks' own funds. By using more of its own funds and less borrowed funds, a financial institution decreases its risk of insolvency in the event that its assets lose value.

MyEconLab Snapshot

Loanable funds market
The aggregate of all the individual financial markets.

10.2   THE LOANABLE FUNDS MARKET

In macroeconomics, we group all the individual financial markets into a single loanable funds market. The **loanable funds market** is the aggregate of the markets for loans, bonds, and stocks. In the loanable funds market, there is just one average interest rate that we refer to as *the* interest rate.

Thinking about financial markets as a single loanable funds market makes sense because the individual markets are highly interconnected with many common influences that move the interest rates on individual assets up and down together.

■ Flows in the Loanable Funds Market

The circular flow model (see Chapter 5, pp. 116–117) provides the accounting framework that describes the flows in the loanable funds market.

Loanable funds are used for three purposes:

1. Business investment
2. Government budget deficit
3. International investment or lending

And loanable funds come from three sources:

1. Private saving
2. Government budget surplus
3. International borrowing

Firms often use *retained earnings*—profits not distributed to stockholders—to finance business investment. These earnings belong to the firm's stockholders and are borrowed from the stockholders rather than being paid to them as dividends. To keep the accounts in the clearest possible way, we think of these retained earnings as being both a use and a source of loanable funds. They are part of business investment on the uses side and part of private saving on the sources side.

We measure all the flows of loanable funds in real terms—in constant 2009 dollars.

You're now going to see how these real flows and the real interest rate are determined in the loanable funds market by studying

- The demand for loanable funds
- The supply of loanable funds
- Equilibrium in the loanable funds market

■ The Demand for Loanable Funds

The *quantity of loanable funds demanded* is the total quantity of funds demanded to finance investment, the government budget deficit, and international investment or lending during a given period. Investment is the major item and the focus of our explanation of the forces that influence the demand side of the loanable funds market. The other two items—the government budget deficit and international investment and lending—can be thought of as amounts to be added to investment. (We study the effects of the government budget later in this chapter on pp. 256–259 and international borrowing and lending in Chapter 19.)

What determines investment and the demand for loanable funds? How does Amazon.com decide how much to borrow to build some new warehouses? Many details influence such a decision, but we can summarize them in two factors:

1. The real interest rate
2. Expected profit

The real interest rate is the opportunity cost of the funds used to finance the purchase of capital, and firms compare the real interest rate with the rate of profit they expect to earn on their new capital. Firms invest only when they expect to earn a rate of profit that exceeds the real interest rate. Fewer projects are profitable at a high real interest rate than at a low real interest rate, so:

> Other things remaining the same, the higher the real interest rate, the smaller is the quantity of loanable funds demanded; and the lower the real interest rate, the greater is the quantity of loanable funds demanded.

Demand for Loanable Funds Curve

The **demand for loanable funds** is the relationship between the quantity of loanable funds demanded and the real interest rate when all other influences on borrowing plans remain the same. Figure 10.2 illustrates the demand for loanable funds as a schedule and as a curve.

Demand for loanable funds
The relationship between the quantity of loanable funds demanded and the real interest rate when all other influences on borrowing plans remain the same.

FIGURE 10.2

The Demand for Loanable Funds   MyEconLab Animation

	Real interest rate (percent per year)	Loanable funds demanded (trillions of 2009 dollars)
A	10	1.0
B	8	1.5
C	6	2.0
D	4	2.5
E	2	3.0

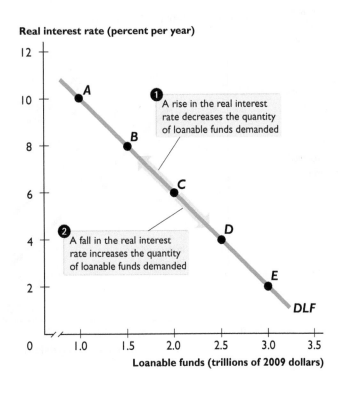

The table shows the quantity of loanable funds demanded at five real interest rates. The graph shows the demand for loanable funds curve, DLF. Points A through E correspond to the rows of the table.

1 If the real interest rate rises, the quantity of loanable funds demanded decreases.

2 If the real interest rate falls, the quantity of loanable funds demanded increases.

To understand the demand for loanable funds, think about Amazon.com's decision to borrow $100 million to build some new warehouses. Suppose that Amazon expects to get a return of $5 million a year from this investment before paying interest costs. If the interest rate is less than 5 percent a year, Amazon expects to make a profit, so it builds the warehouses. If the interest rate is more than 5 percent a year, Amazon expects to incur a loss, so it doesn't build the warehouses. The quantity of loanable funds demanded is greater, the lower is the interest rate.

Changes in the Demand for Loanable Funds

When the expected profit changes, the demand for loanable funds changes. Other things remaining the same, the greater the expected profit from new capital, the greater is the amount of investment and the greater is the demand for loanable funds.

The expected profit rises during a business cycle expansion and falls during a recession; rises when technological change creates profitable new products; rises as a growing population brings increased demand; and fluctuates with contagious swings of optimism and pessimism, called "animal spirits" by Keynes and "irrational exuberance" by Alan Greenspan.

Figure 10.3 shows how the demand for loanable funds curve shifts when the expected profit changes. With average profit expectations, the demand for loanable funds curve is DLF_0. A rise in expected profit shifts the demand curve rightward to DLF_1; a fall in expected profit shifts the demand curve leftward to DLF_2.

FIGURE 10.3

Changes in the Demand for Loanable Funds

MyEconLab Animation

A change in expected profit changes the demand for loanable funds and shifts the demand for loanable funds curve.

❶ An increase in expected profit increases the demand for loanable funds and shifts the demand curve rightward to DLF_1.

❷ A decrease in expected profit decreases the demand for loanable funds and shifts the demand curve leftward to DLF_2.

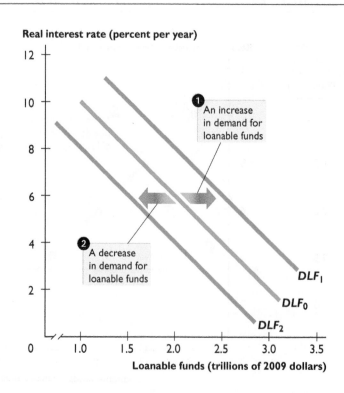

■ The Supply of Loanable Funds

The *quantity of loanable funds supplied* is the total funds available from private saving, the government budget surplus, and international borrowing during a given period. Saving is the main source of supply of loanable funds. A government budget surplus and international borrowing are other sources.

Saving and the supply of loanable funds are determined by decisions by people like you. Suppose that you've graduated and landed a great job that pays you $50,000 a year. How do you decide how much of your income to spend on consumption goods and how much to save and supply in the loanable funds market? Your decision will be influenced by many factors, but chief among them are

1. The real interest rate
2. Disposable income
3. Wealth
4. Expected future income
5. Default risk

We begin by focusing on the real interest rate.

> Other things remaining the same, the higher the real interest rate, the greater is the quantity of loanable funds supplied; and the lower the real interest rate, the smaller is the quantity of loanable funds supplied.

The Supply of Loanable Funds Curve

The **supply of loanable funds** is the relationship between the quantity of loanable funds supplied and the real interest rate when all other influences on lending plans remain the same. Figure 10.4 illustrates the supply of loanable funds.

The key reason the supply of loanable funds curve slopes upward is that the real interest rate is the *opportunity cost* of consumption expenditure. A dollar spent is a dollar not saved, so the interest that could have been earned on that saving is forgone. Forgone interest is the opportunity cost of consumption regardless of whether a person is a lender or a borrower. For a lender, saving less means receiving less interest. For a borrower, saving less means paying less off a loan (or increasing a loan) and paying more interest.

By thinking about student loans, you can see why the real interest rate influences saving and the supply of loanable funds. If the real interest rate on student loans jumped to 20 percent a year, graduates would save more (buying cheaper food and finding lower-rent accommodations) to pay off their loans as quickly as possible and avoid, as much as possible, paying the higher interest cost of their loan. If the real interest rate on student loans fell to 1 percent a year, graduates would save less and take longer to pay off their loans because the interest burden would be easier to bear.

Changes in the Supply of Loanable Funds

A change in any influence on saving, other than the real interest rate, changes the supply of loanable funds. The other four factors listed above—disposable income, wealth, expected future income, and default risk—are the main things that change the supply of loanable funds.

Supply of loanable funds
The relationship between the quantity of loanable funds supplied and the real interest rate when all other influences on lending plans remain the same.

FIGURE 10.4

The Supply of Loanable Funds

The table shows the quantity of loanable funds supplied at five real interest rates. The graph shows the supply of loanable funds curve, *SLF*. Points *A* through *E* correspond to the rows of the table.

❶ If the real interest rate rises, the quantity of loanable funds supplied increases.

❷ If the real interest rate falls, the quantity of loanable funds supplied decreases.

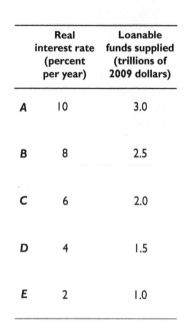

	Real interest rate (percent per year)	Loanable funds supplied (trillions of 2009 dollars)
A	10	3.0
B	8	2.5
C	6	2.0
D	4	1.5
E	2	1.0

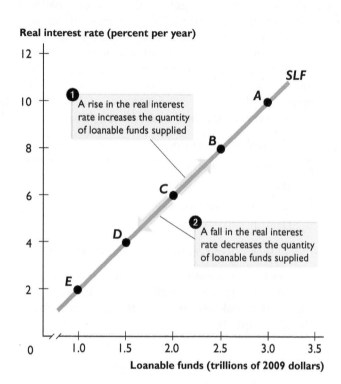

Disposable Income A household's *disposable income* is the income earned minus net taxes. The greater a household's disposable income, other things remaining the same, the greater is its saving. For example, a student whose disposable income is $10,000 a year spends the entire $10,000 and saves nothing. An economics graduate whose disposable income is $50,000 a year spends $40,000 and saves $10,000.

Wealth A household's wealth is what it owns. The greater a household's wealth, other things remaining the same, the less it will save.

Patty is a department store executive who has $15,000 in the bank and no debts: She decides to spend $5,000 on a vacation and save nothing this year. Tony, another department store executive, has nothing in the bank and owes $10,000 on his credit card: He decides to cut consumption and start saving.

Expected Future Income The higher a household's expected future income, other things remaining the same, the smaller is its saving today: If two households have the same current disposable income, the household with the larger expected future disposable income will spend a larger portion of its current disposable income on consumption goods and services and so save less today.

Look at Patty and Tony again. Patty has just been promoted and will receive a $10,000 pay raise next year. Tony has just been told that he will be laid off at the end of the year. On receiving this news, Patty buys a new car—increases her consumption expenditure and cuts her saving—and Tony sells his car and takes the bus—decreases his consumption expenditure and increases his saving.

Most young households expect to have a higher future income for some years and then to have a lower income during retirement. Because of this pattern of income over the life cycle, young people save a small amount, middle-aged people save a lot, and retired people gradually spend their accumulated savings.

Default Risk Default risk is the risk that a loan will not be repaid, or not repaid in full. The greater that risk, the higher is the interest rate needed to induce a person to lend and the smaller is the supply of loanable funds. In normal times, default risk is low but in times of financial crisis when asset prices tumble, default can become widespread as financial institutions become *illiquid* or *insolvent*.

Shifts of the Supply of Loanable Funds Curve

When any of the four influences we've just described changes, the supply of loanable funds changes and the supply of loanable funds curve shifts. An increase in disposable income, or a decrease in wealth, expected future income, or default risk increases the supply of loanable funds.

Figure 10.5 shows how the supply of loanable funds curve shifts. Initially, the supply of loanable funds curve is SLF_0. Then disposable income increases or wealth, expected future income, or default risk decreases. The supply of loanable funds curve shifts rightward from SLF_0 to SLF_1. Changes in these factors in the opposite direction shift the supply curve leftward from SLF_0 to SLF_2.

◾ FIGURE 10.5

Changes in the Supply of Loanable Funds   MyEconLab Animation

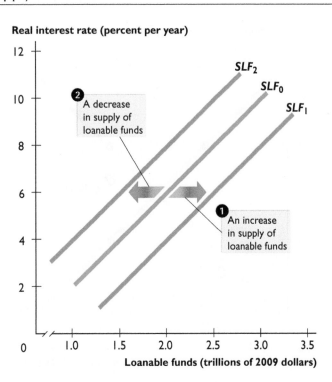

Real interest rate (percent per year)

Loanable funds (trillions of 2009 dollars)

❶ An increase in disposable income or a decrease in wealth, expected future income, or default risk increases the supply of loanable funds and shifts the supply of loanable funds curve rightward from SLF_0 to SLF_1.

❷ A decrease in disposable income or an increase in wealth, expected future income, or default risk decreases the supply of loanable funds and shifts the supply of loanable funds curve leftward from SLF_0 to SLF_2.

■ Equilibrium in the Loanable Funds Market

You've seen that, other things remaining the same, the quantities of loanable funds demanded and supplied depend on the real interest rate. The higher the real interest rate, the greater is the amount of saving and the larger is the quantity of loanable funds supplied. But the higher the real interest rate, the smaller is the amount of investment and the smaller is the quantity of loanable funds demanded. There is one interest rate at which the quantities of loanable funds demanded and supplied are equal, and that interest rate is the equilibrium real interest rate.

Figure 10.6 shows how the demand for and supply of loanable funds determine the real interest rate. The *DLF* curve is the demand curve and the *SLF* curve is the supply curve. When the real interest rate exceeds 6 percent a year, the quantity of loanable funds supplied exceeds the quantity demanded. Borrowers have an easy time finding the funds they want, but lenders are unable to lend all the funds they have available. The real interest rate falls and continues to fall until the quantity of funds supplied equals the quantity of funds demanded.

Alternatively, when the interest rate is less than 6 percent a year, the quantity of loanable funds supplied is less than the quantity demanded. Borrowers can't find the funds they want, but lenders are able to lend all the funds they have available. So the real interest rate rises and continues to rise until the quantity of funds supplied equals the quantity demanded.

Regardless of whether there is a surplus or a shortage of loanable funds, the real interest rate changes and is pulled toward an equilibrium level. In Figure 10.6,

■ FIGURE 10.6

Equilibrium in the Loanable Funds Market

MyEconLab Animation

① If the real interest rate is 8 percent a year, the quantity of loanable funds demanded is less than the quantity supplied. There is a surplus of funds, and the real interest rate falls.

② If the real interest rate is 4 percent a year, the quantity of loanable funds demanded exceeds the quantity supplied. There is a shortage of funds, and the real interest rate rises.

③ When the real interest rate is 6 percent a year, the quantity of loanable funds demanded equals the quantity supplied. There is neither a shortage nor a surplus of funds, and the real interest rate is at its equilibrium level.

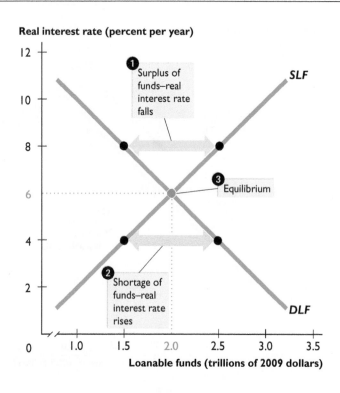

the equilibrium real interest rate is 6 percent a year. At this interest rate, there is neither a surplus nor a shortage of funds. Borrowers can get the funds they want, and lenders can lend all the funds they have available. The plans of borrowers (investors) and lenders (savers) are consistent with each other.

■ Changes in Demand and Supply

Fluctuations in either the demand for loanable funds or the supply of loanable funds bring fluctuations in the real interest rate and in the equilibrium quantity of funds lent and borrowed. Here we'll illustrate the effects of an increase in each.

An increase in expected profit increases the demand for loanable funds. With no change in supply, there is a shortage of funds and the interest rate rises until the equilibrium is restored. In Figure 10.7(a), the increase in the demand for loanable funds shifts the demand for loanable funds curve rightward from DLF_0 to DLF_1. At a real interest rate of 6 percent a year, there is a shortage of funds. The real interest rate rises to 8 percent a year, and the equilibrium quantity of funds increases.

If one of the influences on saving plans changes and increases saving, the supply of loanable funds increases. With no change in demand, there is a surplus of funds and the interest rate falls until the equilibrium is restored. In Figure 10.7(b), the increase in the supply of loanable funds shifts the supply of loanable funds curve rightward from SLF_0 to SLF_1. At a real interest rate of 6 percent a year, there is a surplus of funds. The real interest rate falls to 4 percent a year, and the equilibrium quantity of funds increases.

Over time, both demand and supply in the loanable funds market fluctuate and the real interest rate rises and falls. Both the supply of loanable funds and the demand for loanable funds tend to increase over time. On the average, they increase at a similar pace, so although demand and supply trend upward, the real interest rate has no trend. It fluctuates around a constant average level.

■ FIGURE 10.7

Changes in Demand and Supply in the Loanable Funds Market   MyEconLab Animation

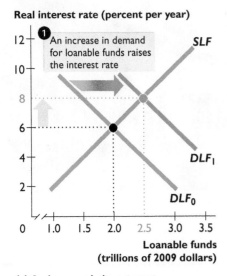

(a) An increase in investment

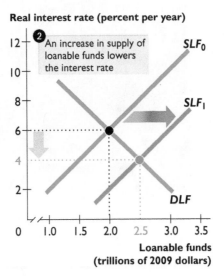

(b) An increase in saving

1 If the demand for loanable funds increases and the supply of loanable funds remains the same, the real interest rate rises and the equilibrium quantity of funds increases.

2 If the supply of loanable funds increases and the demand for loanable funds remains the same, the real interest rate falls and the equilibrium quantity of funds increases.

EYE on the U.S. ECONOMY
The Loanable Funds Market in a Financial Crisis

Financial markets can be turbulent and in 2007 and 2008, events in the loanable funds market created a financial crisis, the effects of which are still with us today.

An increase in default risk decreased supply; and the disappearance of some major Wall Street institutions and lowered profit expectations decreased demand.

Bear Stearns was absorbed by JP Morgan with help from the Federal Reserve; Lehman Brothers' assets were taken over by Barclays; Fannie Mae and Freddie Mac went into government oversight with U.S. taxpayer guarantees; Merrill Lynch became part of the Bank of America; AIG received an $85 billion lifeline from the Federal Reserve and sold off parcels of its business to financial institutions around the world; Wachovia was taken over by Wells Fargo and Washington Mutual by JP Morgan Chase.

But what caused the increase in default risk and the failure of so many financial institutions?

Between 2002 and 2005, interest rates were low. There were plenty of willing borrowers and plenty of willing lenders. Fueled by easy loans, home prices rose rapidly. Lenders bundled their loans into mortgage-backed securities and sold them to eager buyers around the world.

Then, in 2006, interest rates began to rise and home prices began to fall. People defaulted on mortgages; banks took losses and some became insolvent. A downward spiral of lending was under way.

CHECKPOINT 10.2

Explain how borrowing and lending decisions are made and how these decisions interact in the loanable funds market.

Practice Problem

First Call, Inc. is a cellular phone company. It plans to build an assembly plant that costs $10 million if the real interest rate is 6 percent a year. If the real interest rate is 5 percent a year, First Call will build a larger plant that costs $12 million. And if the real interest rate is 7 percent a year, First Call will build a smaller plant that costs $8 million. Use this information to work Problems 1 and 2.

1. Draw a graph of First Call's demand for loanable funds curve.

2. First Call expects its profit from the sale of cellular phones to double next year. If other things remain the same, explain how this increase in expected profit influences First Call's demand for loanable funds.

3. Draw graphs that illustrate how an increase in the supply of loanable funds and a decrease in the demand for loanable funds can lower the real interest rate and leave the equilibrium quantity of loanable funds unchanged.

In the News

Poof! How home loans transform
Banks make a profit by transforming home loans into mortgage-backed securities and trading them on financial loans markets. Banks then use this profit to issue more home loans. During the credit crisis, the market for mortgage-backed securities issued by banks almost stopped functioning.
Source: The New York Times, September 18, 2009
Explain why the market for mortgage-backed securities almost stopped functioning during the credit crisis of 2007–2008.

Solutions to Practice Problems

1. The demand for loanable funds curve is the downward-sloping curve DLF_0 and passes through the points highlighted in Figure 1.

2. An increase in the expected profit increases investment today, which increases the quantity of loanable funds demanded at each real interest rate. The demand for loanable funds curve shifts rightward to DLF_1 (Figure 1).

3. The increase in the supply of loanable funds shifts the supply curve rightward. The decrease in the demand for loanable funds shifts the demand curve leftward. The real interest rate falls. If the shifts are of the same magnitude, the equilibrium quantity of funds remains unchanged (Figure 2). If the shift of the supply curve is greater (less) than that of the demand curve, then the equilibrium quantity of funds increases (decreases).

Solution to In the News

The banks that create and sell mortgage-backed securities demand loanable funds and the banks that buy these securities supply loanable funds. When home prices started to fall and home owners defaulted, banks made fewer home loans and the demand for mortgage-backed securities decreased. These securities also became riskier, so the supply of loanable funds to buy them dried up.

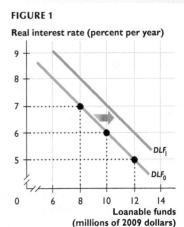

FIGURE 1
Real interest rate (percent per year)
Loanable funds (millions of 2009 dollars)

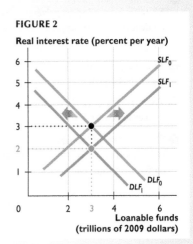

FIGURE 2
Real interest rate (percent per year)
Loanable funds (trillions of 2009 dollars)

10.3 GOVERNMENT IN LOANABLE FUNDS MARKET

The government enters the loanable funds market when it has a budget surplus or budget deficit. So actions that change the government's budget balance influence the loanable funds market and the real interest rate. A change in the real interest rate influences both saving and investment. To complete our study of the forces that determine the quantity of investment and the real interest rate, we investigate the role played by the government's budget balance.

■ A Government Budget Surplus

A government budget surplus increases the supply of loanable funds. The real interest rate falls, which decreases private saving and decreases the quantity of private funds supplied. The lower real interest rate increases the quantity of loanable funds demanded and increases investment.

Figure 10.8 shows these effects of a government budget surplus. The private supply of loanable funds curve is *PSLF*. The supply of loanable funds curve, *SLF*, shows the sum of the private supply and the government budget surplus. Here, the government budget surplus is $1 trillion, so at each real interest rate the *SLF* curve lies $1 trillion to the right of the *PSLF* curve. That is, the horizontal distance between the *PSLF* curve and the *SLF* curve is the government budget surplus.

■ FIGURE 10.8

Government Budget Surplus

MyEconLab Animation

The demand for loanable funds curve is *DLF*, and the private supply of loanable funds curve is *PSLF*. With a balanced government budget, the real interest rate is 6 percent a year and investment is $2 trillion a year. Private saving and investment are $2 trillion a year.

❶ A government budget surplus of $1 trillion is added to private saving to determine the supply of loanable funds curve *SLF*.

❷ The real interest rate falls to 4 percent a year.

❸ The quantity of private saving decreases to $1.5 trillion.

❹ The quantity of loanable funds demanded and investment increase to $2.5 trillion.

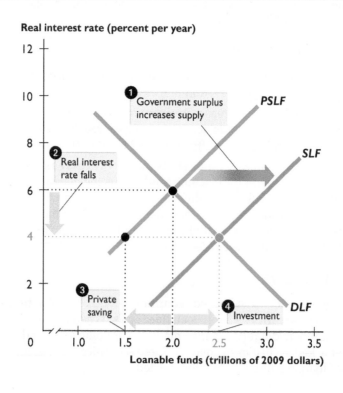

With no government budget surplus, the real interest rate is 6 percent a year, the quantity of loanable funds is $2 trillion a year and investment is $2 trillion a year. But with the government budget surplus of $1 trillion a year, the equilibrium real interest rate falls to 4 percent a year and the quantity of loanable funds increases to $2.5 trillion a year.

The fall in the real interest rate decreases private saving to $1.5 trillion, but investment increases to $2.5 trillion, which is financed by private saving and the government budget surplus (government saving).

■ A Government Budget Deficit

A government budget deficit increases the demand for loanable funds. The real interest rate rises, which increases private saving and increases the quantity of private funds supplied. But the higher real interest rate decreases investment and the quantity of loanable funds demanded by firms to finance investment.

Figure 10.9 shows these effects of a government budget deficit. The private demand for loanable funds curve is *PDLF*. The demand for loanable funds curve, *DLF*, shows the sum of the private demand and the government budget deficit. Here, the government budget deficit is $1 trillion, so at each real interest rate the *DLF* curve lies $1 trillion to the right of the *PDLF* curve. That is, the horizontal distance between the *PDLF* curve and the *DLF* curve equals the government budget deficit.

With no government budget deficit, the real interest rate is 6 percent a year, the quantity of loanable funds is $2 trillion a year and investment is $2 trillion a

FIGURE 10.9

Government Budget Deficit

MyEconLab Animation

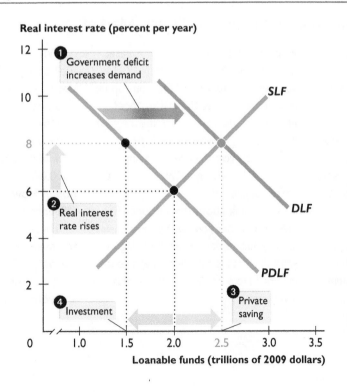

The supply of loanable funds curve is *SLF* and the private demand for loanable funds curve is *PDLF*. With a balanced government budget, the real interest rate is 6 percent a year and the quantity of loanable funds is $2 trillion a year. Private saving and investment are $2 trillion a year.

❶ A government budget deficit of $1 trillion is added to the private demand for funds to determine the demand for loanable funds curve *DLF*.

❷ The real interest rate rises to 8 percent a year.

❸ The quantity of private funds supplied and the quantity of loanable funds increase to $2.5 trillion.

❹ Investment decreases to $1.5 trillion. Investment is crowded out.

year. But with the government budget deficit of $1 trillion, the real interest rate rises from 6 percent a year to 8 percent a year and the quantity of loanable funds increases from $2 trillion to $2.5 trillion.

The rise in the real interest rate increases private saving to $2.5 trillion, but investment decreases to $1.5 trillion. The tendency for a government budget deficit to raise the real interest rate and decrease investment is called the **crowding-out effect**. Investment does not decrease by the full amount of the government budget deficit because private saving increases. In this example, private saving increases by $0.5 trillion to $2.5 trillion.

Crowding-out effect
The tendency for a government budget deficit to raise the real interest rate and decrease investment.

The Ricardo-Barro Effect

First suggested by the English economist David Ricardo in the eighteenth century and refined by Robert J. Barro of Harvard University during the 1980s, the Ricardo-Barro effect holds that the effects we've just shown are wrong and that the government budget deficit has no effect on the real interest rate or investment. Barro says that rational taxpayers can see that a deficit today means that future taxes will be higher and future disposable incomes will be smaller. With smaller expected future disposable incomes, saving increases. The increase in saving increases the supply of loanable funds—shifts the *SLF* curve rightward—by an amount equal to the government budget deficit. The supply of loanable funds might increase and lessen the influence of the government budget deficit on the real interest rate and investment, but most economists regard the full Ricardo-Barro effect as unlikely.

EYE on YOUR LIFE
Your Participation in the Loanable Funds Market

Think about the amount of saving that you do. How much of your disposable income do you save? Is it a positive amount or a negative amount?

If you save a positive amount, what do you do with your savings? Do you put them in a bank, in the stock market, in bonds, or just keep money at home? What is the interest rate you earn on your savings?

If you save a negative amount, just what does that mean? It means that you have a deficit (like a government deficit). You're spending more than

your disposable income. In this case, how do you finance your deficit? Do you get a student loan? Do you run up an outstanding credit card balance? How much do you pay to finance your negative saving (your *dissaving*)?

How do you think your saving will change when you graduate and get a better-paying job?

Also think about the amount of investment that you do. You are investing in your human capital by being in school. What is this investment costing you? How are you financing this investment?

When you graduate and start a well-paying job, you will need to decide whether to buy an apartment or a house or to rent your home.

How would you make a decision whether to buy or rent a home? Would it be smart to borrow $300,000 to finance the purchase of a home? How would the interest rate influence your decision?

These examples show just some of the many decisions and transactions you will make in the loanable funds market—the link between your saving and your investment.

EYE on FINANCIAL MARKETS

Why Have Interest Rates Been So Low?

Interest rates have been at a record low level since 2008 and with what you have learned in this chapter, you can explain why.

The most recent normal year in the U.S. economy is 2007, the eve of the onset of a global financial crisis.

In 2007, the total amount borrowed in the U.S. loanable funds market was $51 trillion, and the real interest rate was 2 percent a year.

The figure illustrates this situation. The supply of loanable funds curve was SLF_{07} and the demand for loanable funds curve was DLF_{07}. Both the demand curve and the supply curve include borrowing and lending decisions by households, firms, governments, the rest of the world, and financial institutions,

including the Federal Reserve (or Fed). Loanable funds market equilibrium occurred at a real interest rate of 2 percent a year and a total quantity of loanable funds of $51 trillion.

Interest rates fell to a record low because the demand for loanable funds decreased and the supply increased.

On the demand side of the market, by mid-2009, expected profit had fallen, which decreased investment from $2.2 trillion in 2007 to $1.5 trillion and the demand for loanable funds by households and businesses had decreased sharply. But the federal government launched a massive rescue plan that increased its outlays and demand for loanable funds.

Despite the large increase in government demand, the overall demand for loanable funds decreased: The demand by households, businesses, and financial institutions decreased by more than the demand by the federal government increased.

By 2013, the demand for loanable funds had decreased to DLF_{13}.

On the supply side of the market, the Fed continued to supply large quantities of funds. The Fed's goal was to lower the interest rate and stimulate investment. (You will study the actions that enable the Fed to increase the supply of loanable funds in Chapter 11, and the effects of those actions in Ch17.)

By 2013, the supply of loanable funds had increased to SLF_{13}.

The equilibrium real interest rate was 0.5 percent per year, and the equilibrium quantity of loanable funds was $55 trillion.

Even without the increase in supply, the real interest rate would have fallen, but the equilibrium quantity of loanable funds would also have fallen.

The increase in the supply of loanable funds limited the decrease in investment and lessened the severity of the recession triggered by the financial crisis.

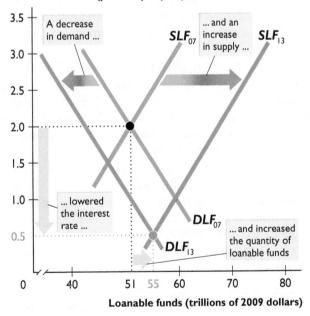

SOURCES OF DATA: Bureau of Economic Analysis and Federal Reserve. The interest rate is the average of the yield on Aaa equities, government bonds, mortages, and federal funds, adjusted for inflation measured by the consumer price index.

MyEconLab Study Plan 10.3

Key Terms Quiz

Solutions

TABLE 1

Real interest rate (percent per year)	Loanable funds demanded	Loanable funds supplied
	(trillions of 2009 dollars per year)	
4	3.5	0.5
5	3.0	1.0
6	2.5	1.5
7	2.0	2.0
8	1.5	2.5
9	1.0	3.0
10	0.5	3.5

FIGURE 1

Real interest rate (percent per year)

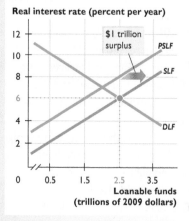

Loanable funds
(trillions of 2009 dollars)

FIGURE 2

Real interest rate (percent per year)

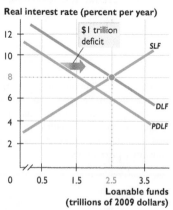

Loanable funds
(trillions of 2009 dollars)

CHECKPOINT 10.3

Explain how a government budget surplus or deficit influences the real interest rate, investment, and saving.

Practice Problems

Table 1 shows the demand for loanable funds schedule and the supply of loanable funds schedule when the government budget is balanced.

1. If the government budget surplus is $1 trillion, what are the real interest rate, the quantity of investment, and the quantity of private saving?

2. If the government budget deficit is $1 trillion, what are the real interest rate, the quantity of investment, and the quantity of private saving? Is there any crowding out in this situation?

3. If the government budget deficit is $1 trillion and the Ricardo-Barro effect occurs, what are the real interest rate and the quantity of investment?

In the News

U.S. budget deficit shrinks as revenues rise

With revenues up 14% from a year earlier and government spending falling slightly, the budget deficit remains large but it is the smallest in 5 years.

Source: *The Wall Street Journal*, August 12, 2013

Explain the effect of a large federal deficit and debt on economic growth.

Solutions to Practice Problems

1. If the government budget surplus is $1 trillion, the supply of loanable funds increases. Figure 1 shows the supply of loanable funds *SLF*. The equilibrium real interest rate falls from 7 percent to 6 percent a year and the quantity of loanable funds increases to $2.5 trillion. Investment is $2.5 trillion and private saving is $1.5 trillion.

2. If the government budget deficit is $1 trillion, the demand for loanable funds increases. Figure 2 shows the demand for loanable funds curve *DLF*. The equilibrium real interest rate rises from 7 percent to 8 percent a year and the quantity of loanable funds increases to $2.5 trillion. Investment decreases to $1.5 trillion. Crowding out occurs because the deficit increases the real interest rate, which decreases investment.

3. If the Ricardo-Barro effect occurs, private saving adjusts to offset the budget deficit of $1 trillion. The supply of loanable funds increases by $1 trillion and the equilibrium real interest rate remains at 7 percent a year. The quantity of loanable funds is $3 trillion and it finances investment of $2 trillion and the budget deficit of $1 trillion. Crowding out does not occur.

Solution to In the News

Compared to a balanced budget, a large federal deficit and debt increases the demand for loanable funds. It raises the real interest rate and lowers private investment. Investment increases the capital stock, which increases labor productivity and real GDP. The higher real interest rate slows the growth of the capital stock, slows labor productivity growth, and slows real GDP growth.

CHAPTER SUMMARY

Key Points

1. Describe the financial markets and the key financial institutions.

- Firms use financial capital to buy and operate physical capital.
- Gross investment is the total amount spent on physical capital in a given period. Net investment equals gross investment minus depreciation.
- Wealth is the value of what people own; saving is the amount of disposable income that is not spent, and it adds to wealth.
- The market for financial capital is a market made up of the markets for loans, bonds, and stocks.

2. Explain how borrowing and lending decisions are made and how these decisions interact in the loanable funds market.

- Other things remaining the same, the lower the real interest rate or the higher the expected profit rate, the greater is the quantity of loanable funds demanded.
- The demand for loanable funds changes when the expected profit rate changes.
- Other things remaining the same, the higher the real interest rate, the greater is the quantity of loanable funds supplied.
- The supply of loanable funds changes when disposable income, wealth, expected future income, or default risk changes.
- Equilibrium in the loanable funds market determines the real interest rate.
- At the equilibrium real interest rate, the quantity of loanable funds demanded equals the quantity of loanable funds supplied.

3. Explain how a government budget surplus or deficit influences the real interest rate, investment, and saving.

- A government budget surplus increases the supply of loanable funds and a government budget deficit increases the demand for loanable funds.
- With no change in private saving, an increase in the government budget deficit raises the real interest rate and crowds out investment.
- A government budget deficit might increase private saving because it decreases expected future disposable income.

Key Terms

MyEconLab Key Terms Quiz

Bond, 242
Capital or physical capital, 240
Crowding-out effect, 258
Demand for loanable funds, 247
Financial institution, 243
Gross investment, 240

Loanable funds market, 246
Net investment, 240
Net worth, 244
Stock, 242
Supply of loanable funds, 249
Wealth, 240

CHAPTER CHECKPOINT

Study Plan Problems and Applications

1. On January 1, 2013, Terry's Towing Service owned 4 tow trucks valued at $300,000. During 2013, Terry's bought 2 new trucks for a total of $180,000. At the end of 2013, the market value of all of the firm's trucks was $400,000. What was Terry's gross investment? Calculate Terry's depreciation and net investment.

Use the following information to work Problems 2 and 3.

The Bureau of Economic Analysis reported that the U.S. capital stock was $44.1 trillion at the end of 2009, $45.0 trillion at the end of 2010, and $46.4 trillion at the end of 2011. Depreciation in 2010 was $2.4 trillion, and gross investment during 2011 was $2.9 trillion (all in 2009 dollars).

2. Calculate U.S. net investment and gross investment during 2010.

3. Calculate U.S. depreciation and net investment during 2011.

4. Mike takes a summer job washing cars. During the summer, he earns an after-tax income of $3,000 and he spends $1,000 on goods and services. What was Mike's saving during the summer and the change, if any, in his wealth?

5. What is the market for financial capital? What is financial capital? Explain why, when the real interest rate rises, the demand for loanable funds does not change but the quantity of funds demanded decreases.

6. With an increase in global tension during 2005 and 2006, many governments increased defense spending, which decreased government budget surpluses. Show, on a graph, the effects of a decrease in government budget surpluses if there is no Ricardo-Barro effect. Explain how the effects differ if there is a partial Ricardo-Barro effect.

7. **Brazil's high-speed train project**
   Brazil's bullet-train project is one of the most ambitious parts of the government's plan to invest $235 billion over the next decade in transportation networks and energy projects—part of its effort to reduce costs and boost economic growth.

   Source: *The Wall Street Journal*, August 12, 2013

   Draw a graph of the loanable funds market. Suppose that the Brazilian government borrows the required funds in the loanable funds market. How will this borrowing change the real interest rate and the quantity of saving?

8. **Celtic Tiger purrs**
   A banking crisis forced Ireland to seek a $91.61 billion bailout from the EU and the IMF. Under the terms of its bailout, the government must reduce its budget deficit from 10% of GDP to 8.6% in 2012. Ireland's economic growth started to pick up despite the cutbacks in government spending.

   Source: *The Wall Street Journal*, September 22, 2011

   Explain the effect of the cut in the budget deficit on the loanable funds market in Ireland. Why might the economy have grown strongly?

9. Read *Eye on Financial Markets* on p. 259. What would the real interest rate and quantity of loanable funds have been in 2013 if the supply of loanable funds had been at its 2007 level? Explain your answer.

Instructor Assignable Problems and Applications

MyEconLab Homework, Quiz, or Test if assigned by instructor

1. Explain why the supply of loanable funds and the demand for loanable funds decreased during the global financial crisis of 2007–2008. Draw a graph of the loanable funds market before the crisis and use your graph to illustrate the source and effects of the crisis on saving, investment, and the real interest rate.

2. On January 1, 2011, Sophie's Internet Cafe owned 10 computer terminals valued at $8,000. During 2011, Sophie's bought 5 new computer terminals at a cost of $1,000 each, and at the end of the year, the market value of all of Sophie's computer terminals was $11,000. What was Sophie's gross investment, depreciation, and net investment?

3. The numbers in the second column of Table 1 are the Federal Reserve's estimates of personal wealth at the end of each year. The numbers in the third column are the Bureau of Economic Analysis's estimates of personal saving each year. In which years did the change in wealth exceed saving? In which years did saving exceed the change in wealth? Given the definitions of saving and wealth, how can the change in wealth differ from saving?

4. Cindy takes a summer job and earns an after-tax income of $8,000. Her living expenses during the summer were $2,000. What was Cindy's saving during the summer and the change, if any, in her wealth?

5. The stock market boom of 2002–2007 increased wealth by trillions of dollars. Explain the effect of this increase in wealth on the equilibrium real interest rate, investment, and saving.

TABLE 1

Year	Wealth	Saving
	(billions of dollars)	
2007	64,266	249
2008	51,476	592
2009	54,239	553
2010	57,578	593

Use the following information to work Problems 6 and 7.

The U.S. saving rate increased from –0.2 percent in 2006 to 4.8 percent in 2007 to 8.7 percent in 2008, and then decreased to 5.3 percent in 2010.

6. How can the saving rate be negative? Why might a negative saving rate be something to worry about? How might U.S. saving be increased?

7. Explain why the U.S. saving rate might have increased and its effect on the supply of loanable funds.

Use the following information to work Problems 8 to 10.

IMF says it battled crisis well

The International Monetary Fund (IMF) reported that it acted effectively in combating the global recession, especially in Eastern Europe. The IMF made $163 billion available to developing countries. The IMF required countries with large deficits to cut spending or not increase it, but it urged the United States, Western European countries, and China to run deficits to stimulate their economies.

Source: *The Wall Street Journal*, September 29, 2009

8. Explain how an increase in government expenditure will change the government's budget balance and the loanable funds market.

9. Why do you think the IMF required countries with large deficits, like those in Eastern Europe, to cut spending rather than increase it?

10. The Center for Economic and Policy Research in Washington, D.C., claims that the IMF didn't allow developing countries that were looking for loans to expand their deficits sufficiently. Would these countries have weathered the global recession better if they had obtained larger loans from the IMF?

Multiple Choice Quiz

1. Financial capital is the _____.

    A. money used to buy stocks and bonds
    B. money used to buy physical capital
    C. funds that savers supply and buyers of physical capital borrow
    D. money in the bank

2. If the price of a U.S. government bond is $50 and the owner of the bond is entitled to $2.50 income each year, then the interest rate on the bond is _____.

    A. 0.2 percent
    B. 5 percent
    C. 10 percent
    D. 20 percent

3. In the loanable funds market, an increase in _____.

    A. the real interest rate increases the demand for loanable funds
    B. expected profit increases the demand for loanable funds
    C. expected profit doesn't change the demand for loanable funds, but the quantity of loanable funds demanded increases
    D. the real interest rate doesn't change the demand for loanable funds, but the quantity of loanable funds demanded increases

4. The supply of loanable funds increases _____.

    A. when the demand for loanable funds increases
    B. when people increase saving as the real interest rate rises
    C. when disposable income increases or wealth decreases
    D. if net taxes decrease or expected future income increases

5. An increase in expected profit _____ the real interest rate and _____ the quantity of loanable funds.

    A. decreases; decreases
    B. increases; decreases
    C. decreases; increases
    D. increases; increases

6. A government budget surplus _____.

    A. increases the supply of loanable funds
    B. raises the real interest rate
    C. decreases the demand for loanable funds and lowers the real interest rate
    D. decreases net taxes, increases disposable income, and increases saving

7. Crowding out occurs when _____.

    A. households' budgets are in deficit and saving decreases
    B. the government budget is in surplus, so people have paid too much tax
    C. the government budget is in deficit and the real interest rate rises
    D. the government budget is in deficit but taxpayers are rational and the Ricardo-Barro effect operates

8. An increase in the government budget deficit _____.

    A. increases private saving and investment
    B. increases private saving and decreases investment
    C. increases the supply of private saving and decreases investment
    D. decreases private saving and investment

How does the Fed create money
and regulate its quantity?

The Monetary System

**When you have completed your study of this chapter,
you will be able to**

1   Define money and describe its functions.

2   Describe the functions of banks.

3   Describe the functions of the Federal Reserve System (the Fed).

4   Explain how the banking system creates money and how the Fed
    controls the quantity of money.

MyEconLab Big Picture

11.1 WHAT IS MONEY?

Money, like fire and the wheel, has been around for a very long time. An incredible array of items has served as money. North American Indians used wampum (beads made from shells), Fijians used whales' teeth, and early American colonists used tobacco. Cakes of salt served as money in Ethiopia and Tibet. What do wampum, whales' teeth, tobacco, and salt have in common? Why are they examples of money? Today, when we want to buy something, we use coins or notes (dollar bills), write a check, send an e-check, present a credit or debit card, or use a "smart card." Are all these things that we use today money? To answer these questions, we need a definition of money.

■ Definition of Money

Money
Any commodity or token that is generally accepted as a *means of payment.*

Money is any commodity or token that is generally accepted as a *means of payment.* This definition has three parts that we'll examine in turn.

A Commodity or Token

Money is always something that can be recognized and that can be divided up into small parts. So money might be an actual commodity, such as a bar of silver or gold. But it might also be a token, such as a quarter or a $10 bill. Money might also be a virtual token, such as an electronic record in a bank's database (more about this type of money later).

Generally Accepted

Money is *generally* accepted, which means that it can be used to buy *anything and everything.* Some tokens can be used to buy some things but not others. For example, a bus pass is accepted as payment for a bus ride, but you can't use your bus pass to buy toothpaste. So a bus pass is not money. In contrast, you can use a $5 bill to buy either a bus ride or toothpaste—or anything else that costs $5 or less. So a $5 bill is money.

Means of Payment

Means of payment
A method of settling a debt.

A **means of payment** is a method of settling a debt. When a payment has been made, the deal is complete. Suppose that Gus buys a car from his friend Ann. Gus doesn't have enough money to pay for the car right now, but he will have enough three months from now, when he gets paid. Ann agrees that Gus may pay for the car in three months' time. Gus buys the car with a loan from Ann and then pays off the loan. The loan isn't money. Money is what Gus uses to pay off the loan.

So what wampum, whales' teeth, tobacco, and salt have in common is that they have served as a generally accepted means of payment, and that is why they are examples of money.

■ The Functions of Money

Money performs three vital functions. It serves as a

- Medium of exchange
- Unit of account
- Store of value

Medium of Exchange

A **medium of exchange** is an object that is generally accepted in return for goods and services. Money is a medium of exchange. Without money, you would have to exchange goods and services directly for other goods and services—an exchange called **barter**. Barter requires a *double coincidence of wants*. For example, if you want a soda and have only a paperback novel to offer in exchange for it, you must find someone who is selling soda and who also wants your paperback novel. Money guarantees that there is a double coincidence of wants because people with something to sell will always accept money in exchange for it. Money acts as a lubricant that smoothes the mechanism of exchange. Money enables you to specialize in the activity in which you have a comparative advantage (see Chapter 3, pp. 72–74) instead of searching for a double coincidence of wants.

Medium of exchange
An object that is generally accepted in return for goods and services.

Barter
The direct exchange of goods and services for other goods and services, which requires a double coincidence of wants.

Unit of Account

An agreed-upon measure for stating the prices of goods and services is called a *unit of account*. To get the most out of your budget, you have to figure out whether going to a rock concert is worth its opportunity cost. But that cost is not dollars and cents. It is the number of movies, cappuccinos, ice-cream cones, or sticks of gum that you must give up to attend the concert. It's easy to do such calculations when all these goods have prices in terms of dollars and cents (see Table 11.1). If a rock concert costs $64 and a movie costs $8, you know right away that going to the concert costs you 8 movies. If a cappuccino costs $4, going to the concert costs 16 cappuccinos. You need only one calculation to figure out the opportunity cost of any pair of goods and services. For example, the opportunity cost of the rock concert is 128 sticks of gum ($64 ÷ 50¢ = 128 sticks of gum).

Now imagine how troublesome it would be if the rock concert ticket agent posted its price as 8 movies, and if the movie theater posted its price as 2 cappuccinos, and if the coffee shop posted the price of a cappuccino as 2 ice-cream cones, and if the ice-cream shop posted its price as 4 sticks of gum! Now how much running around and calculating do you have to do to figure out how much that rock concert is going to cost you in terms of the movies, cappuccino, ice cream, or sticks of gum that you must give up to attend it? You get the answer for movies right away from the sign posted by the ticket agent. For all the other goods, you're going to have to visit many different places to establish the price of each commodity in terms of another and then calculate prices in units that are relevant for your own decision. Cover up the column labeled "price in money units" in Table 11.1 and see how hard it is to figure out the number of sticks of gum it costs to attend a rock concert. It's enough to make a person swear off rock! How much simpler it is using dollars and cents.

TABLE 11.1 A UNIT OF ACCOUNT SIMPLIFIES PRICE COMPARISONS

Good	Price in money units	Price in units of another good
Rock concert	$64.00	8 movies
Movie	$8.00	2 cappuccinos
Cappuccino	$4.00	2 ice-cream cones
Ice-cream cone	$2.00	4 sticks of gum
Stick of gum	$0.50	

Store of Value

Any commodity or token that can be held and exchanged later for goods and services is called a *store of value*. Money acts as a store of value. If it did not, it would not be accepted in exchange for goods and services. The more stable the value of a commodity or token, the better it can act as a store of value and the more useful it is as money. No store of value is completely stable. The value of a physical object, such as a house, a car, or a work of art, fluctuates over time. The value of the commodities and tokens that we use as money also fluctuates, and when there is inflation, money persistently falls in value.

■ Money Today

Money in the world today is called **fiat money.** *Fiat* is a Latin word that means decree or order. Fiat money is money because the law decrees it to be so. The objects used as money have value only because of their legal status as money.

Today's fiat money consists of

- Currency
- Deposits at banks and other financial institutions

Currency

The notes (dollar bills) and coins that we use in the United States today are known as **currency.** The government declares notes to be money with the words printed on every dollar bill, "This note is legal tender for all debts, public and private."

Deposits

Deposits at banks, credit unions, savings banks, and savings and loan associations are also money. Deposits are money because they can be used to make payments. You don't need to go to the bank to get currency to make a payment. You can write a check or use your debit card to tell your bank to move some money from your account to someone else's.

Currency Inside the Banks Is Not Money

Although currency and bank deposits are money, currency *inside the banks* is *not money.* The reason is while currency is inside a bank, it isn't available as a means of payment. When you get some cash from the ATM, you convert your bank deposit into currency. You change the form of your money, but there is no change in the quantity of money that you own. Your bank deposit decreases, and your currency holding increases.

If we counted bank deposits and currency inside the banks as money, think about what would happen to the quantity of money when you get cash from the ATM. The quantity of money would appear to decrease. Your currency would increase, but both bank deposits and currency inside the banks would decrease.

You can see that counting both bank deposits and currency inside the banks as money would be double counting.

■ Official Measures of Money: M1 and M2

Figure 11.1 shows the items that make up two official measures of money. **M1** consists of currency held by individuals and businesses, traveler's checks, and checkable deposits owned by individuals and businesses. **M2** consists of M1 plus savings deposits and time deposits (less than $100,000), money market funds, and other deposits. Time deposits are deposits that can be withdrawn only after a fixed term. Money market funds are deposits that are invested in short-term securities.

Are M1 and M2 Means of Payment?

The test of whether something is money is whether it is a generally accepted means of payment. Currency passes the test. Checkable deposits also pass the test because they can be transferred from one person to another by using a debit card or writing a check. So all the components of M1 serve as means of payment.

Fiat money
Objects that are money because the law decrees or orders them to be money.

Currency
Notes (dollar bills) and coins.

M1
Currency held by individuals and businesses, traveler's checks, and checkable deposits owned by individuals and businesses.

M2
M1 plus savings deposits and small time deposits, money market funds, and other deposits.

FIGURE 11.1

Two Measures of Money: June 2013

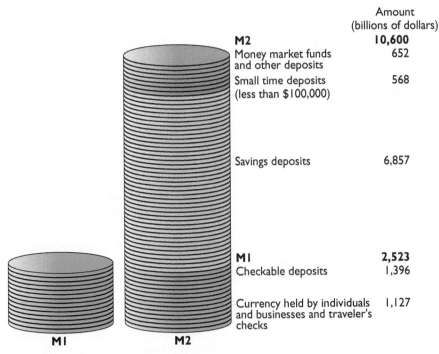

	Amount (billions of dollars)
M2	**10,600**
Money market funds and other deposits	652
Small time deposits (less than $100,000)	568
Savings deposits	6,857
M1	**2,523**
Checkable deposits	1,396
Currency held by individuals and businesses and traveler's checks	1,127

M1 Currency held by individuals and businesses and traveler's checks plus checkable deposits owned by individuals and businesses.

M2 M1 plus savings deposits plus small time deposits plus money market funds and other deposits.

SOURCE OF DATA: Federal Reserve.

Some of the savings deposits in M2 are also instantly convertible into a means of payment. You can use the ATM to get currency to pay for your groceries or gas. But other savings deposits, time deposits, and money market funds are not instantly convertible and are *not* a means of payment.

■ Checks, Credit Cards, Debit Cards, and E-Checks

In defining money and describing the things that serve as money today, we have not included checks, credit cards and debit cards, or e-checks. Aren't these things that we use when we buy something also money?

Checks

A check is not money. It is an instruction to a bank to make a payment. The easiest way to see why a check is not money is to think about how the quantity of money you own changes if you write a check. You don't suddenly have more money because you've written a check to pay a bill. Your money is your bank deposit, not the value of the checks you've written.

Credit Cards

A credit card is not money. It is a special type of ID card that gets you an instant loan. Suppose that you use your credit card to buy a textbook. You sign or enter your PIN and leave the store with your book. The book may be in your possession, but you've not yet paid for it. You've taken a loan from the bank that issued your credit card. Your credit card issuer pays the bookstore and you eventually get your credit card bill, which you pay using money.

Debit Cards

A debit card works like a paper check, only faster. And just as a check isn't money, neither is a debit card. To see why a debit card works like a check, think about what happens if you use your debit card to buy your textbook. When the sales clerk swipes your card in the bookstore, the computer in the bookstore's bank gets a message: Take $100 from your account and put it in the account of the bookstore. The transaction is done in a flash. But again, the bank deposits are the money and the debit card is the tool that causes money to move from you to the bookstore.

E-Checks

An *electronic check* (or *e-check*) is an electronic equivalent of a paper check. A group of more than 90 banks and other financial institutions have formed the Financial Services Technology Consortium to collaborate on developing the electronic check. Bank of Internet USA offers an Internet e-check system via e-mail. Like a paper check, an e-check is not money. The deposit transferred is money.

You now know that checks, credit cards and debit cards, and e-checks are not money, but one new information-age money is gradually emerging—e-cash.

■ An Embryonic New Money: E-Cash

Electronic cash (or *e-cash*) is an electronic equivalent of paper notes (dollar bills) and coins. It is an electronic currency, and for people who are willing to use it, e-cash works like other forms of money. But for e-cash to become a widely used form of money, it must evolve some of the characteristics of physical currency.

People use physical currency because it is portable, recognizable, transferable, untraceable, and anonymous and can be used to make change. The designers of e-cash aim to reproduce all of these features of notes and coins. Today's e-cash is portable, untraceable, and anonymous, but it has not yet reached the level of recognition that makes it *universally* accepted as a means of payment. E-cash doesn't yet meet the definition of money.

Like notes and coins, e-cash can be used in shops. It can also be used over the Internet. To use e-cash in a shop, the buyer uses a smart card that stores some e-cash and the shop uses a smart card reader. When a transaction is made, e-cash is transferred from the smart card directly to the shop's bank account. Users of smart cards receive their e-cash by withdrawing it from a bank account by using a special ATM or a special cell phone.

Several versions of e-cash in U.S. dollars, euros, and other currencies are available on the Internet. The most popular and widely used e-cash system is PayPal, which is owned by eBay. The most sophisticated and secure e-cash is a currency called Bitcoin, which can be used to settle debts and be traded for dollars and other currencies on the Internet.

A handy advantage of e-cash over paper notes arises when you lose your wallet. If it is stuffed with dollar bills, you're out of luck. If it contains e-cash recorded on your smart card, your bank can cancel the e-cash stored on the card and issue you replacement e-cash.

Although e-cash is not yet universally accepted, it is likely that its use will grow and that it will gradually replace physical forms of currency.

CHECKPOINT 11.1

MyEconLab Study Plan 11.1
Key Terms Quiz
Solutions

Define money and describe its functions.

Practice Problems

1. In the United States today, which of the items in List 1 are money?

2. In January 2013, currency and traveler's checks held by individuals and businesses was $1,101 billion; checkable deposits owned by individuals and businesses were $1,365 billion; savings deposits were $6,710 billion; small time deposits were $621 billion; and money market funds and other deposits were $652 billion. Calculate M1 and M2 in January 2013.

3. In July 2013, M1 was $2,549 billion; M2 was $10,710 billion; checkable deposits owned by individuals and businesses were $1,414 billion; small time deposits were $556 billion; and money market funds and other deposits were $665 billion. Calculate currency and traveler's checks held by individuals and businesses. Calculate savings deposits.

> **LIST 1**
> - Your Visa card
> - The quarters inside vending machines
> - U.S. dollar bills in your wallet
> - The check that you have just written to pay for your rent
> - The loan you took out last August to pay for your tuition

In the News

The cell phone as wallet: Will the trend catch on?
With the simple swipe of a phone—even when the battery's dead—consumers can now pay for their coffee, gas, or groceries. But as this technology becomes increasingly available, experts ask will it catch on?

Source: CTVNews.ca, September 24, 2011

As people use their cell phones to make payments, will currency disappear? How will the components of M1 change? Will debit cards disappear?

Solutions to Practice Problems

1. Money is defined as a means of payment. Only the quarters inside vending machines and U.S. dollar bills in your wallet are money.

2. M1 is $2,466 billion. M1 is the sum of currency and traveler's checks held by individuals and businesses ($1,101 billion) and checkable deposits owned by individuals and businesses ($1,365 billion).

   M2 is $10,449 billion. M2 is the sum of M1 ($2,466 billion), savings deposits ($6,710 billion), small time deposits ($621 billion), and money market funds and other deposits ($652 billion).

3. Currency and traveler's checks held by individuals and businesses is $1,135 billion. Currency and traveler's checks equals M1 ($2,549 billion) minus checkable deposits owned by individuals and businesses ($1,414 billion).

   Savings deposits are $6,940 billion. Savings deposits equals M2 ($10,710 billion) minus M1 ($2,549 billion) minus small time deposits ($556 billion) minus money market funds and other deposits ($665 billion)

Solution to In the News

Most people will probably carry less currency, but it won't disappear because currency is used in the underground economy. Most of M1 will be checkable deposits. Cell phones and debit cards will be perfect substitutes, so debit cards will probably disappear.

11.2 THE BANKING SYSTEM

The banking system consists of the Federal Reserve and the banks and other institutions that accept deposits and that provide the services that enable people and businesses to make and receive payments. Sitting at the top of the system (see Figure 11.2), the Federal Reserve (or Fed) sets the rules and regulates and influences the activities of the banks and other institutions. Three types of financial institutions accept the deposits that are part of the nation's money:

- Commercial banks
- Thrift institutions
- Money market funds

Here, we describe the functions of these institutions, and in the next section, we describe the structure and functions of the Fed.

■ Commercial Banks

A *commercial bank* is a firm that is chartered by the Comptroller of the Currency in the U.S. Treasury (or by a state agency) to accept deposits and make loans. In 2013, about 5,850 commercial banks operated in the United States, down from 13,000 a few years ago. The number of banks has shrunk because in 1997 the rules under which banks operate were changed, permitting them to open branches in every state. A wave of mergers followed this change of rules. Also, more than 130 banks failed during the financial crisis of 2008–2009.

Bank Deposits

A commercial bank accepts three broad types of deposits: checkable deposits, savings deposits, and time deposits. A bank pays a low interest rate (sometimes zero) on checkable deposits, and it pays the highest interest rate on time deposits.

■ FIGURE 11.2

The Institutions of the Banking System

The Federal Reserve regulates and influences the activities of the commercial banks, thrift institutions, and money market funds, whose deposits make up the nation's money.

EYE on the PAST
The "Invention" of Banking

It is the sixteenth century somewhere in Europe: Because gold is valuable and easy to steal, goldsmiths have well-guarded safes in which people "deposit" their gold. The goldsmiths issue gold receipts entitling owners to reclaim their "deposits" on demand.

Isabella, who has a receipt for 100 ounces of gold deposited with Samuel Goldsmith, buys some land from Henry. She can pay for the land in one of two ways: She can visit Samuel, collect her gold, and hand the gold to Henry. Or she can give Henry her gold receipt, which enables Henry to claim the 100 ounces of gold.

It is a simpler and safer transaction to use the receipt. When Henry wants to buy something, he too can pass the receipt on to someone else.

So Samuel Goldsmith's gold receipt is circulating as a means of payment. It is money!

Because the receipts circulate while the gold remains in his safe, Samuel realizes that he can lend gold receipts and charge interest for doing so. Samuel writes receipts for gold that he doesn't own, but has on deposit, and lends these receipts. Samuel is one of the first bankers.

Profit and Risk: A Balancing Act

Commercial banks try to maximize their stockholders' wealth by lending for long terms at high interest rates and borrowing from depositors and others. But lending is risky. Risky loans sometimes don't get repaid and the prices of risky securities sometimes fall. In either of these events, a bank incurs a loss that could even wipe out the stockholders' wealth. Also, when depositors see their bank incurring losses, mass withdrawals—called a run on the bank—might create a crisis. So a bank must perform a balancing act. It must be careful in the way it uses the depositors' funds and balance security for depositors and stockholders against high but risky returns. To trade off between risk and profit a bank divides its assets into four parts: reserves, liquid assets, securities, and loans.

Reserves

A bank's **reserves** consist of currency in its vaults plus the balance on its reserve account at a Federal Reserve Bank.

The currency in a bank's vaults is a reserve to meet its depositors' withdrawals. Your bank must replenish currency in its ATM every time you and your friends have raided it for cash for a midnight pizza.

A commercial bank's deposit at a Federal Reserve Bank is similar to your own bank deposit. The bank uses its reserve account at the Fed to receive and make payments to other banks and to obtain currency. The Fed requires banks to hold a minimum percentage of deposits as reserves, called the *required reserve ratio*. Banks *desired* reserves might exceed the required reserves, especially when the cost of borrowing reserves is high.

Reserves
The currency in the bank's vaults plus the balance on its reserve account at a Federal Reserve Bank.

Liquid Assets

Banks' *liquid assets* are short-term Treasury bills and overnight loans to other banks. The interest rates on liquid assets are low but these are low-risk assets. The interest rate on interbank loans, called the **federal funds rate,** is the central target of the Fed's monetary policy actions.

Federal funds rate
The interest rate on interbank loans (loans made in the federal funds market).

Securities and Loans

Securities are bonds issued by the U.S. government and by other organizations. Some bonds have low interest rates and are safe. Some bonds have high interest rates and are risky. Mortgage-backed securities are examples of risky securities.

Loans are the provision of funds to businesses and individuals. Loans earn the bank a high interest rate, but they are risky and, even when not very risky, cannot be called in before the agreed date. Banks earn the highest interest rate on unpaid credit card balances, which are loans to credit card holders.

Bank Assets and Liabilities: The Relative Magnitudes

Figure 11.3 shows the relative magnitudes of the banks' assets and liabilities—deposits and other borrowing—in 2013. After performing their profit-versus-risk balancing acts, the banks kept 18 percent of total assets in reserves (and liquid assets), 22 percent in securities, and 60 percent in loans. Checkable deposits (part of M1) were 9 percent of total funds—liabilities and net worth. Another 46 percent of total funds were savings deposits and small time deposits (part of M2).

The commercial banks' asset allocation in 2013 is not normal and is a consequence of a financial crisis in 2008 and 2009. *Eye on the U.S. Economy* on the next page contrasts normal times with the depth of the crisis.

FIGURE 11.3

Commercial Banks' Assets, Liabilities, and Net Worth   MyEconLab Animation

---

In 2013, commercial bank loans were 60 percent of total assets, securities were 22 percent, and reserves were 18 percent. Reserves were unusually large in 2013.

The banks obtained the funds allocated to these assets from checkable deposits in M1, which were 9 percent of total funds; savings deposits and small time deposits in M2 were 46 percent; other deposits were 15 percent; other borrowing was 20 percent; and bank stockholders' net worth was 11 percent.

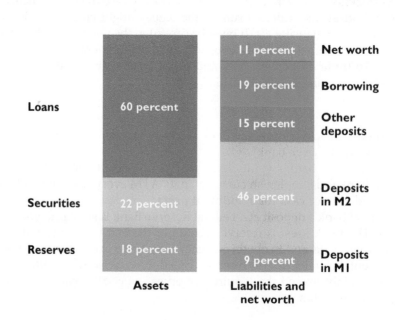

SOURCE OF DATA: Federal Reserve.

EYE on the U.S. ECONOMY
Commercial Banks Under Stress in the Financial Crisis

In normal times, bank reserves are less than 1 percent of total assets and liquid assets are less than 4 percent. Loans are 68 percent and securities 28 percent. July 2007 was such a normal time (the orange bars).

During the financial crisis that started in 2007 and intensified in September 2008, the banks took big hits as the value of their securities and loans fell.

Faced with a riskier world, the banks increased their liquid assets and reserves. In September 2009 (the blue bars), liquid assets were almost 10 percent of total assets and reserves were 8 percent.

The balancing act tipped away from risk-taking and toward security.

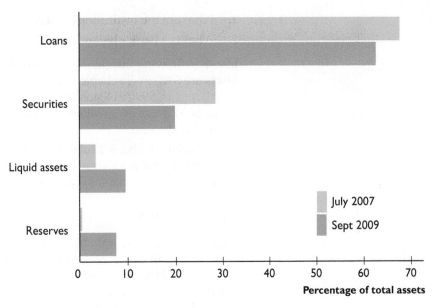

SOURCE OF DATA: Federal Reserve.

Thrift Institutions

The three types of thrift institutions are savings and loan associations, savings banks, and credit unions. A *savings and loan association (S&L)* is a financial institution that accepts checkable deposits and savings deposits and that makes personal, commercial, and home-purchase loans. A *savings bank* is a financial institution that accepts savings deposits and makes mostly consumer and home-purchase loans. The depositors own some savings banks (called mutual savings banks). A *credit union* is a financial institution owned by a social or economic group, such as a firm's employees, that accepts savings deposits and makes mostly consumer loans.

Like commercial banks, the thrift institutions hold reserves and must meet minimum reserve ratios set by the Fed.

Money Market Funds

A *money market fund* is a financial institution that obtains funds by selling shares and uses these funds to buy assets such as U.S. Treasury bills. Money market fund shares act like bank deposits. Shareholders can write checks on their money market fund accounts, but there are restrictions on most of these accounts. For example, the minimum deposit accepted might be $2,500 and the smallest check a depositor is permitted to write might be $500.

MyEconLab Study Plan 11.2
            Key Terms Quiz
               Solutions

CHECKPOINT 11.2

Describe the functions of banks.

Practice Problems

1. What are the institutions that make up the banking system?
2. What is a bank's balancing act?

Use the following information to work Problems **3** and **4**. A bank's deposits and assets are $320 in checkable deposits, $896 in savings deposits, $840 in small time deposits, $990 in loans to businesses, $400 in outstanding credit card balances, $634 in government securities, $2 in currency, and $30 in its reserve account at the Fed.

3. Calculate the bank's total deposits, deposits that are part of M1, and deposits that are part of M2.
4. Calculate the bank's loans, securities, and reserves.

In the News

Regulators close Georgia bank in 95th failure for the year
Regulators shut down Atlanta-based Georgian Bank. On July 24, 2009, Georgian Bank had $2 billion in assets and $2 billion in deposits. By September 29, 2009, Georgian Bank had lost about $2 billion in home loans and other assets.
                                                    Source: *USA Today*, September 30, 2009
Explain how Georgian Bank's balancing act failed.

Solutions to Practice Problems

1. The institutions that make up the banking system are the Fed, commercial banks, thrift institutions, and money market funds.
2. A bank makes a profit by borrowing from depositors at a low interest rate and lending at a higher interest rate. The bank must hold enough reserves to meet depositors' withdrawals. The bank's balancing act is to balance the risk of loans (profits for stockholders) against the security for depositors.
3. Total deposits are $320 + $896 + $840 = $2,056.
    Deposits that are part of M1 are checkable deposits, $320.
    Deposits that are part of M2 include all deposits, $2,056.
4. Loans are $990 + $400 = $1,390. Securities are $634.
    Reserves are $30 + $2 = $32.

Solution to In the News

In July, Georgian Bank's $2 billion of assets (home loans and securities) balanced its deposits of $2 billion. The bank expected to make a profit on its assets that exceeded the interest it paid to depositors. The financial crisis increased the risk on all financial assets. The bank was now holding assets that were more risky than it had planned. As people defaulted on their home loans and the value of securities fell, the value of Georgian Bank's assets crashed to zero. With fewer assets than deposits, regulators had no choice other than to close the bank and sell its assets and deposits. The bank failed to balance risk against profit.

11.3   THE FEDERAL RESERVE SYSTEM

The **Federal Reserve System (the Fed)** is the central bank of the United States. A central bank is a public authority that provides banking services to banks and governments and regulates financial institutions and markets. A central bank does not provide banking services to businesses and individual citizens. Its only customers are banks such as Bank of America and Citibank and the U.S. government. The Fed is organized into 12 Federal Reserve districts shown in Figure 11.4.

The Fed's main task is to regulate the interest rate and quantity of money to achieve low and predictable inflation and sustained economic expansion.

Federal Reserve System (the Fed)
The central bank of the United States.

■ The Structure of the Federal Reserve

The key elements in the structure of the Federal Reserve are

- The Chairman of the Board of Governors
- The Board of Governors
- The regional Federal Reserve Banks
- The Federal Open Market Committee

The Chairman of the Board of Governors

The Chairman of the Board of Governors is the Fed's chief executive, public face, and center of power and responsibility. When things go right, the Chairman gets the credit; when they go wrong, he gets the blame. Janet Yellen, a former University of California, Berkeley, economics professor, is the Fed's current Chair.

Fed Chair Janet Yellen

■ **FIGURE 11.4**

The Federal Reserve Districts

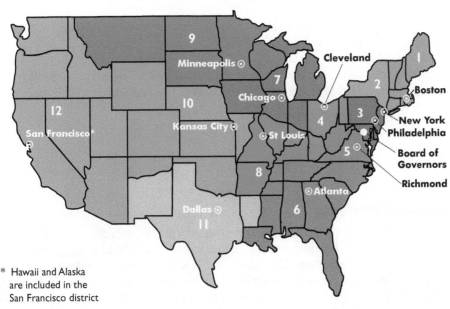

* Hawaii and Alaska are included in the San Francisco district

The nation is divided into 12 Federal Reserve districts, each having a Federal Reserve Bank. (Some of the larger districts also have branch banks.) The Board of Governors of the Federal Reserve System is located in Washington, D.C.

SOURCE: *Federal Reserve Bulletin.*

The Board of Governors

The Board of Governors has seven members (including the Chairman), who are appointed by the President of the United States and confirmed by the Senate, each for a 14-year term. The terms are staggered so that one seat on the board becomes vacant every two years. The President appoints one of the board members as Chairman for a term of four years, which is renewable.

The Regional Federal Reserve Banks

There are 12 regional Federal Reserve Banks, one for each of the 12 Federal Reserve districts shown in Figure 11.4. Each regional Federal Reserve Bank has nine directors, three of whom are appointed by the Board of Governors and six of whom are elected by the commercial banks in the Federal Reserve district. The directors of each regional Federal Reserve Bank appoint that Bank's president, and the Board of Governors approves this appointment.

The Federal Reserve Bank of New York (known as the New York Fed) occupies a special place because it implements some of the Fed's most important policy decisions.

The Federal Open Market Committee

The **Federal Open Market Committee** (FOMC) is the Fed's main policy-making committee. The FOMC consists of the following twelve members:

- The Chairman and the other six members of the Board of Governors
- The president of the Federal Reserve Bank of New York
- Four presidents of the other regional Federal Reserve Banks (on a yearly rotating basis)

The FOMC meets approximately every six weeks to review the state of the economy and to decide the actions to be carried out by the New York Fed.

■ The Fed's Policy Tools

The Fed's most important tasks are to influence the interest rate and regulate the amount of money circulating in the United States. How does the Fed perform these tasks? It does so by adjusting the reserves of the banking system. Also, by adjusting the reserves of the banking system and standing ready to make loans to banks, the Fed is able to prevent bank failures. The Fed's policy tools are:

- Required reserve ratios
- Discount rate
- Open market operations
- Extraordinary crisis measures

Required Reserve Ratios

You've seen that banks hold reserves of currency and deposits at a Federal Reserve Bank. The Fed requires the banks and thrifts to hold a minimum percentage of deposits as reserves. This minimum is known as a *required reserve ratio*. The Fed determines a required reserve ratio for each type of deposit. Currently, required reserve ratios range from zero to 3 percent on checkable deposits below a specified level to 10 percent on deposits in excess of the specified level.

Federal Open Market Committee
The Fed's main policy-making committee.

Discount Rate

The discount rate is the interest rate at which the Fed stands ready to lend reserves to commercial banks. A change in the discount rate begins with a proposal to the FOMC by at least one of the 12 Federal Reserve Banks. If the FOMC agrees that a change is required, it proposes the change to the Board of Governors for its approval.

Open Market Operations

An **open market operation** is the purchase or sale of government securities—U.S. Treasury bills and bonds—by the Federal Reserve in the open market. When the Fed conducts an open market operation, it makes a transaction with a bank or some other business but it does not transact with the federal government. The New York Fed conducts the Fed's open market operations.

Open market operation
The purchase or sale of government securities—U.S. Treasury bills and bonds—by the New York Fed in the open market.

Extraordinary Crisis Measures

The financial crisis of 2008, the slow recovery, and ongoing financial stress have brought three more tools into play. They are

- Quantitative easing (or QE)
- Credit easing
- Operation Twist

Quantitative Easing (QE) When the Fed creates bank reserves by conducting a large-scale open market purchase at a low or possibly zero federal funds rate, the action is called *quantitative easing*. There have been three episodes of quantitative easing, QE1, QE2, and QE3—see *Eye on Creating Money* on pp. 288–289.

Credit Easing When the Fed buys private securities or makes loans to financial institutions to stimulate their lending, the action is called *credit easing*.

Operation Twist When the Fed buys long-term government securities and sells short-term government securities, the action is called *Operation Twist*. The idea is to lower long-term interest rates and stimulate long-term borrowing and investment expenditure. An Operation Twist was conducted in September 2011.

◼ How the Fed's Policy Tools Work

The Fed's normal policy tools work by changing either the demand for or the supply of the monetary base, which in turn changes the interest rate. The **monetary base** is the sum of coins, Federal Reserve notes, and banks' reserves at the Fed.

Monetary base
The sum of coins, Federal Reserve notes, and banks' reserves at the Fed.

By increasing the required reserve ratio, the Fed can force the banks to hold a larger quantity of monetary base. By raising the discount rate, the Fed can make it more costly for the banks to borrow reserves—borrow monetary base. And by selling securities in the open market, the Fed can decrease the monetary base. All of these actions lead to a rise in the interest rate.

Similarly, by decreasing the required reserve ratio, the Fed can permit the banks to hold a smaller quantity of monetary base. By lowering the discount rate, the Fed can make it less costly for the banks to borrow monetary base. And by buying securities in the open market, the Fed can increase the monetary base. All of these actions lead to a decrease in the interest rate.

Open market operations are the Fed's main tool and in the next section you will learn in more detail how they work.

MyEconLab Study Plan 11.3
Key Terms Quiz
Solutions

CHECKPOINT 11.3

Describe the functions of the Federal Reserve System (the Fed).

Practice Problems

1. What is the Fed and what is the FOMC?
2. Who is the Fed's chief executive, and what are the Fed's main policy tools?
3. What is the monetary base?
4. Suppose that at the end of December 2009, the monetary base in the United States was $700 billion, Federal Reserve notes were $650 billion, and banks' reserves at the Fed were $20 billion. Calculate the quantity of coins.

In the News

Risky assets: Counting to a trillion
Prior to September 15, 2008, the start of the credit crisis, the Fed had less than $1 trillion in assets and most were safe U.S. government securities. By mid-December, 2008, the Fed's balance sheet had increased to more than $2.3 trillion. Much of the increase was in mortgage-backed securities. The massive expansion began when the Fed starting sending banks cash in exchange for risky assets.

Source: CNN Money, September 29, 2009

What are the Fed's policy tools and which policy tool did the Fed use to increase its assets to $2.3 trillion in 2008?

Solutions to Practice Problems

1. The Federal Reserve (Fed) is the U.S. central bank—a public authority that provides banking services to banks and the U.S. government and that regulates the quantity of money and the banking system. The FOMC is the Federal Open Market Committee—the Fed's main policy-making committee.

2. The Fed's chief executive is the Chair of the Board of Governors, currently Janet Yellen. The Fed's main policy tools are required reserve ratios, the discount rate, and open market operations. In unusual times, extraordinary crisis measures are an additional tool.

3. The monetary base is the sum of coins, Federal Reserve notes (dollar bills), and banks' reserves at the Fed.

4. To calculate the quantity of coins, we use the definition of the monetary base: coins plus Federal Reserve notes plus banks' reserves at the Fed.

    Quantity of coins = Monetary base − Federal Reserve notes − Banks' reserves at the Fed.

    So at the end of December 2009,

    Quantity of coins = $700 billion − $650 billion − $20 billion
    = $30 billion.

Solution to In the News

The Fed's policy tools are the required reserve ratio, discount rate, open market operations, and extraordinary crisis measures. The Fed used extraordinary crisis measures called *quantitative easing* and *credit easing*. The Fed's lending program bought risky assets of banks and increased their reserve deposits at the Fed.

11.4 REGULATING THE QUANTITY OF MONEY

Banks create money, but this doesn't mean that they have smoke-filled back rooms in which counterfeiters are busily working. Remember, most money is deposits, not currency. What banks create is deposits, and they do so by making loans.

■ Creating Deposits by Making Loans

The easiest way to see that banks create deposits is to think about what happens when Andy, who has a Visa card issued by Citibank, uses his card to buy a tank of gas from Chevron. When Andy signs the card sales slip, he takes a loan from Citibank and obligates himself to repay the loan at a later date. At the end of the business day, a Chevron clerk takes a pile of signed credit card sales slips, including Andy's, to Chevron's bank. For now, let's assume that Chevron also banks at Citibank. The bank immediately credits Chevron's account with the value of the slips (minus the bank's commission).

You can see that these transactions have created a bank deposit and a loan. Andy has increased the size of his loan (his credit card balance), and Chevron has increased the size of its bank deposit. And because deposits are money, Citibank has created money.

If, as we've just assumed, Andy and Chevron use the same bank, no further transactions take place. But the outcome is essentially the same when two banks are involved. If Chevron's bank is the Bank of America, then Citibank uses its reserves to pay the Bank of America. Citibank has an increase in loans and a decrease in reserves; the Bank of America has an increase in reserves and an increase in deposits. The banking system as a whole has an increase in loans, an increase in deposits, and no change in reserves.

EYE on YOUR LIFE
Money and Your Role in Its Creation

Imagine a world without money in which you must barter for everything you buy. What kinds of items would you have available for these trades? Would you keep some stocks of items that you know lots of people are willing to accept? Would you really be bartering, or would you be using a commodity as money? How much longer would it take you to conduct all the transactions of a normal day?

Now think about your own holdings of money today. How much money do you have in your pocket or wallet? How much do you have in the bank? How does the money you hold change over the course of a month?

Of the money you're holding, which items are part of M1 and which are part of M2? Are all the items in M2 means of payment?

Now think about the role that *you* play in creating money. Every time you charge something to your credit card, you help the bank that issued it to create money. The increase in your credit card balance is a loan from the bank to you. The bank pays the seller right away. So the seller's bank deposit and your outstanding balance increase together. Money is created.

You contribute to the currency drain that limits the ability of your bank to create money when you visit the ATM and get some cash to pay for your late-night pizza.

Of course, your transactions are a tiny part of the total. But together, you and a few million other students like you play a big role in the money creation process.

If Andy had swiped his card at an automatic payment pump, all these transactions would have occurred at the time he filled his tank, and the quantity of money would have increased by the amount of his purchase (minus the bank's commission for conducting the transactions).

Three factors limit the quantity of deposits that the banking system can create:

- The monetary base
- Desired reserves
- Desired currency holding

The Monetary Base

You've seen that the monetary base is the sum of coins, Federal Reserve notes, and banks' deposits at the Fed. The size of the monetary base limits the total quantity of money that the banking system can create because banks have a desired level of reserves and households and firms have a desired level of currency holding and both of these desired holdings of the monetary base depend on the quantity of money.

Desired Reserves

A bank's *desired* reserves are the reserves that the bank chooses to hold. The *desired reserve ratio* is the ratio of reserves to deposits that a bank wants to hold. This ratio exceeds the *required reserve ratio* by an amount that the banks determine to be prudent on the basis of their daily business requirements.

A bank's *actual reserve ratio* changes when its customers make a deposit or a withdrawal. If a bank's customer makes a deposit, reserves and deposits increase by the same amount, so the bank's reserve ratio increases. Similarly, if a bank's customer makes a withdrawal, reserves and deposits decrease by the same amount, so the bank's reserve ratio decreases.

A bank's **excess reserves** are its actual reserves minus its desired reserves. When the banking system as a whole has excess reserves, banks can create money by making new loans. When the banking system as a whole is short of reserves, banks must destroy money by decreasing the quantity of loans.

Excess reserves
A bank's actual reserves minus its desired reserves.

Desired Currency Holding

We hold our money in the form of currency and bank deposits. The proportion of money held as currency isn't constant but at any given time, people have a definite view as to how much they want to hold in each form of money.

Because households and firms want to hold some proportion of their money in the form of currency, when the total quantity of bank deposits increases, so does the quantity of currency that they want to hold.

Because desired currency holding increases when deposits increase, currency leaves the banks when loans are made and deposits increase. We call the leakage of currency from the banking system the *currency drain*. And we call the ratio of currency to deposits the *currency drain ratio*.

The greater the currency drain ratio, the smaller is the quantity of deposits and money that the banking system can create from a given amount of monetary base. The reason is that as currency drains from the banks, they are left with a smaller level of reserves (and smaller excess reserves) so they make fewer loans.

■ How Open Market Operations Change the Monetary Base

When the Fed buys securities in an open market operation, it pays for them with newly created bank reserves and money. With more reserves in the banking system, the supply of interbank loans increases, the demand for interbank loans decreases, and the federal funds rate—the interest rate in the interbank loans market—falls.

Similarly, when the Fed sells securities in an open market operation, buyers pay for the securities with bank reserves and money. With smaller reserves in the banking system, the supply of interbank loans decreases, the demand for interbank loans increases, and the federal funds rate rises. The Fed sets a target for the federal funds rate and conducts open market operations on the scale needed to hit its target.

A change in the federal funds rate is only the first stage in an adjustment process that follows an open market operation. If banks' reserves increase, the banks can increase their lending and create even more money. If banks' reserves decrease, the banks must decrease their lending, which decreases the quantity of money. We'll study the effects of open market operations in some detail, beginning with an open market purchase.

The Fed Buys Securities

Suppose the Fed buys $100 million of U.S. government securities in the open market. There are two cases to consider, depending on who sells the securities. A bank might sell some of its securities, or a person or business that is not a commercial bank—the general public—might sell. The outcome is essentially the same in the two cases. To convince you of this fact, we'll study the two cases, starting with the simpler case in which a commercial bank sells securities. (The seller will be someone who thinks the Fed is offering a good price for securities and it is profitable to make the sale.)

FOMC meeting.

A Commercial Bank Sells When the Fed buys $100 million of securities from the Manhattan Commercial Bank, two things happen:

1. The Manhattan Commercial Bank has $100 million less in securities, and the Fed has $100 million more in securities.
2. To pay for the securities, the Fed increases the Manhattan Commercial Bank's reserve account at the New York Fed by $100 million.

Figure 11.5 shows the effects of these actions on the balance sheets of the Fed and the Manhattan Commercial Bank. Ownership of the securities passes from the commercial bank to the Fed, so the bank's securities decrease by $100 million and the Fed's securities increase by $100 million, as shown by the red-to-blue arrow running from the Manhattan Commercial Bank to the Fed.

The Fed increases the Manhattan Commercial Bank's reserves by $100 million, as shown by the green arrow running from the Fed to the Manhattan Commercial Bank. This action increases the reserves of the banking system.

The commercial bank's total assets remain constant, but their composition changes. Its holdings of government securities decrease by $100 million, and its reserves increase by $100 million. The bank can use these additional reserves to make loans. When the bank makes loans, it creates deposits and the quantity of money increases.

We've just seen that when the Fed buys government securities from a bank, the bank's reserves increase. What happens if the Fed buys government securities from the public—say, from AIG, an insurance company?

FIGURE 11.5

The Fed Buys Securities from a Commercial Bank

MyEconLab Animation

Federal Reserve Bank of New York

Assets		Liabilities	
Securities	+$100 million	Reserves of Manhattan Commercial Bank	+$100 million

The Fed buys securities from a commercial bank ... ... and pays for the securities by increasing the reserves of the commercial bank

Manhattan Commercial Bank

Assets		Liabilities
Securities	−$100 million	
Reserves	+$100 million	

The Nonbank Public Sells When the Fed buys $100 million of securities from AIG, three things happen:

1. AIG has $100 million less in securities, and the Fed has $100 million more in securities.
2. The Fed pays for the securities with a check for $100 million drawn on itself, which AIG deposits in its account at the Manhattan Commercial Bank.
3. The Manhattan Commercial Bank collects payment of this check from the Fed, and the Manhattan Commercial Bank's reserves increase by $100 million.

Figure 11.6 shows the effects of these actions on the balance sheets of the Fed, AIG, and the Manhattan Commercial Bank. Ownership of the securities passes from AIG to the Fed, so AIG's securities decrease by $100 million and the Fed's securities increase by $100 million (red-to-blue arrow). The Fed pays for the securities with a check payable to AIG, which AIG deposits in the Manhattan Commercial Bank. This payment increases Manhattan's reserves by $100 million (green arrow). It also increases AIG's deposit at the Manhattan Commercial Bank by $100 million (blue arrow). This action increases the reserves of the banking system.

FIGURE 11.6

The Fed Buys Securities from the Public

MyEconLab Animation

AIG has the same total assets as before, but their composition has changed. It now has more money and fewer securities. The Manhattan Commercial Bank's reserves increase, and so do its deposits—both by $100 million. Because bank reserves and deposits have increased by the same amount, the bank has excess reserves, which it can use to make loans. When it makes loans, the quantity of money increases.

We've worked through what happens when the Fed buys government securities from either a bank or the public. When the Fed sells securities, the transactions that we've just traced operate in reverse.

The Fed Sells Securities

If the Fed sells $100 million of U.S. government securities in the open market, most likely a person or business other than a bank buys them. (A bank would buy them only if it had excess reserves and couldn't find a better use for its funds.)

When the Fed sells $100 million of securities to AIG, three things happen:

1. AIG has $100 million more in securities, and the Fed has $100 million less in securities.

2. AIG pays for the securities with a check for $100 million drawn on its deposit account at the Manhattan Commercial Bank.

3. The Fed collects payment of this check from the Manhattan Commercial Bank by decreasing its reserves by $100 million.

These actions decrease the reserves of the banking system. The Manhattan Commercial Bank is now short of reserves and must borrow in the federal funds market to meet its desired reserve ratio.

The changes in the balance sheets of the Fed and the banks that we've just described are not the end of the story about the effects of an open market operation; they are just the beginning.

■ The Multiplier Effect of an Open Market Operation

An open market purchase that increases bank reserves also increases the *monetary base* by the amount of the open market purchase. Regardless of whether the Fed buys securities from the banks or from the public, the quantity of bank reserves increases and gives the banks excess reserves that they then lend.

The following sequence of events takes place:

- An open market purchase creates excess reserves.
- Banks lend excess reserves.
- Bank deposits increase.
- The quantity of money increases.
- New money is used to make payments.
- Some of the new money is held as currency—a currency drain.
- Some of the new money remains in deposits in banks.
- Banks' desired reserves increase.
- Excess reserves decrease but remain positive.

The sequence described above repeats in a series of rounds, but each round begins with a smaller quantity of excess reserves than did the previous one. The process ends when there are no excess reserves. This situation arises when the increase in the monetary base resulting from the open market operation is willingly held—when the increase in desired reserves plus the increase in desired currency holding equals the increase in the monetary base. Figure 11.7 illustrates and summarizes the sequence of events in one round of the multiplier process.

An open market *sale* works similarly to an open market *purchase*, but the sale *decreases* the monetary base and sets off a multiplier process similar to that described in Figure 11.7. At the end of the process the quantity of money has decreased by an amount that lowers desired reserves and desired currency holding by an amount equal to the decrease in the monetary base resulting from the open market sale. (Make your own version of Figure 11.7 to trace the multiplier process when the Fed *sells* and the banks or public *buys* securities.)

The magnitude of the change in the quantity of money brought about by an open market operation is determined by the money multiplier that we now explain.

■ The Money Multiplier

The **money multiplier** is the number by which a change in the monetary base is multiplied to find the resulting change in the quantity of money. It is also the ratio of the change in the quantity of money to the change in the monetary base.

The magnitude of the money multiplier depends on the desired reserve ratio and the currency drain ratio. The smaller are these two ratios, the larger is the money multiplier. Let's explore the money multiplier in more detail.

Money multiplier
The number by which a change in the monetary base is multiplied to find the resulting change in the quantity of money.

■ FIGURE 11.7

A Round in the Multiplier Process Following an Open Market Operation
MyEconLab Animation

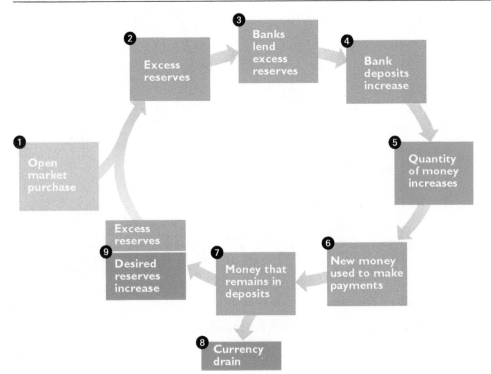

❶ An open market purchase increases bank reserves and ❷ creates excess reserves.

❸ Banks lend the excess reserves, ❹ new deposits are created, and ❺ the quantity of money increases.

❻ New money is used to make payments.

❼ Households and firms receiving payments keep some on deposit in banks and ❽ some in the form of currency—a currency drain.

❾ The increase in bank deposits increases banks' reserves but also increases banks' desired reserves.

Desired reserves increase by less than actual reserves, so the banks still have some excess reserves, but less than before. The process repeats until excess reserves have been eliminated.

To see how the desired reserve ratio and the currency drain ratio determine the size of the money multiplier, begin with two facts:

The quantity of money, M, is the sum of deposits, D, and currency, C, or $M = D + C$, and

The monetary base, MB, is the sum of reserves, R, and currency, C, or $MB = R + C$.

The money multiplier is equal to the quantity of money, M, divided by the monetary base, MB, that is:

$$\text{Money multiplier} = M/MB.$$

Because $M = D + C$ and $MB = R + C$ then:

$$\text{Money multiplier} = (D + C)/(R + C).$$

EYE on CREATING MONEY

How Does the Fed Create Money and Regulate Its Quantity?

During the Great Depression, many banks failed, bank deposits were destroyed, and the quantity of money crashed by 25 percent. Most economists believe that it was these events that turned an ordinary recession in 1929 into a deep and decade-long depression.

Former Fed Chairman Ben Bernanke is one of the economists who has studied this tragic episode in U.S. economic history, and he had no intention of witnessing a similar event on his watch.

Figure I shows what the Fed did to pump reserves into the banking system. In the fall of 2008 in an episode called QEI (see p. 279), the Fed doubled the monetary base. In 2010 and 2011, a more gradual but sustained QE2 took the monetary base to more than three times its pre-crisis level. And in 2012 and 2013, a further gradual QE3 raised the monetary base to four times its normal level.

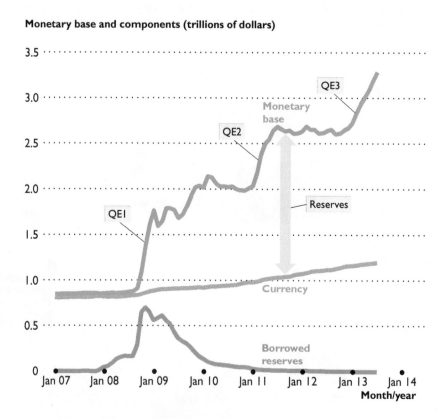

Monetary base and components (trillions of dollars)

Figure I The Monetary Base in Financial Crisis

SOURCES OF DATA: Federal Reserve and Bureau of Economic Analysis

Now divide each item on the right-hand side of the previous equation by deposits, *D*, to get:

$$\text{Money multiplier} = (1 + C/D)/(R/D + C/D)$$

Notice the $D/D = 1$; C/D is the currency drain ratio, and R/D is the desired reserves ratio.

If the currency drain ratio is 50 percent, $C/D = 0.5$; and if the desired reserve ratio is 10 percent, $R/D = 0.1$ so the money multiplier is $1.5/0.6 = 2.5$.

The larger the reserve ratio and the larger the currency drain ratio, the smaller is the money multiplier.

The reserve ratio and the currency drain ratio that determine the magnitude of the money multiplier are not constant, so neither is the money multiplier constant. You can see in *Eye on Creating Money* below that the desired reserve ratio and money multiplier changed dramatically in 2008.

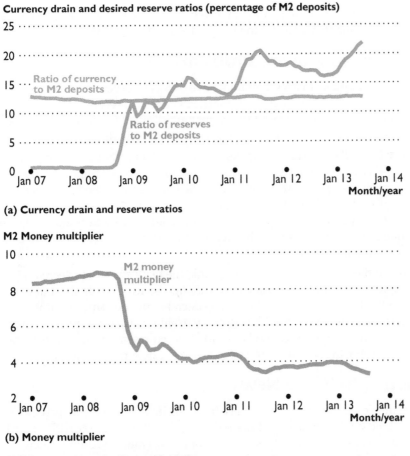

(a) Currency drain and reserve ratios

(b) Money multiplier

Figure 2 The Changing Money Multiplier

This extraordinary increase in the monetary base did not bring a similar increase in the quantity of money. Figure 2 shows the reason.

In 2008, the banks' desired reserve ratio, in part (a), increased tenfold from its normal level of 1.2 percent to 12 percent. This increase brought a crash in the money multiplier, in part (b), from a normal value of 9 to an unusually low value of 5.

The surge in the desired reserve ratio is the sole reason for the collapse in the money multiplier. You can see, in part (a), that the other influence on the multiplier, the currency drain ratio, barely changed.

The banks face an unusually high level of risk and this is the main source of the increase in the desired reserve ratio. As the risk faced by banks returns to normal, the desired reserve ratio will fall, and when this happens the Fed will decrease the monetary base or create an explosion in the quantity of money.

MyEconLab Study Plan 11.4
Key Terms Quiz
Solutions

CHECKPOINT 11.4

Explain how the banking system creates money and how the Fed controls the quantity of money.

Practice Problems

1. How do banks create new deposits by making loans, and what factors limit the amount of deposits and loans that they can create?

2. If the Fed makes an open market sale of $1 million of securities, who can buy the securities? What initial changes occur if the Fed sells to a bank?

3. If the Fed makes an open market sale of $1 million of securities, what is the process by which the quantity of money changes? What factors determine the change in the quantity of money?

In the News

Fed doubles monetary base

During the fourth quarter of 2008, the Fed doubled the monetary base but the quantity of money (M2) increased by only 5 percent.

Source: Federal Reserve

Why did M2 not increase by much more than 5 percent? What would have happened to the quantity of M2 if the Fed had kept the monetary base constant?

Solutions to Practice Problems

1. Banks can make loans when they have excess reserves. When a bank makes a loan, it creates a new deposit for the person who receives the loan. The amount of deposits created (loans made) is limited by the banks' excess reserves, its desired reserve ratio, and the currency drain ratio.

2. The Fed sells securities to banks or the public, but not the government. The initial change is a decrease in the monetary base of $1 million. Ownership of the securities passes from the Fed to the bank, and the Fed's assets decrease by $1 million. The bank pays for the securities by decreasing its reserves at the Fed by $1 million. The Fed's liabilities decrease by $1 million. The bank's total assets are unchanged, but it has $1 million less in reserves and $1 million more in securities.

3. When the Fed sells securities to a bank, the bank's reserves decrease by $1 million. The bank's deposits do not change, so the bank is short of reserves. The bank calls in loans and deposits decrease by the same amount. The desired reserve ratio and the currency drain ratio determine the decrease in the quantity of money. The larger the desired reserve ratio or the currency drain ratio, the smaller is the decrease in the quantity of money.

Solution to In the News

When the Fed increases the monetary base, M2 increases and the increase is determined by the money multiplier, $(1 + C/D)/(R/D + C/D)$, (R/D is the banks' desired reserve ratio and C/D is the currency drain ratio). M2 didn't increase by more than 5 percent because the banks increased their desired reserve ratio, R/D, which decreased the money multiplier. If the Fed had kept the monetary base unchanged, M2 would have decreased because the money multiplier decreased.

CHAPTER SUMMARY

Key Points

1. **Define money and describe its functions.**

   - Money is anything that serves as a generally accepted means of payment.
   - Money functions as a medium of exchange, unit of account, and store of value.
   - M1 consists of currency held by individuals and businesses, travelers' checks, and checkable deposits owned by individuals and businesses.
   - M2 consists of M1 plus savings deposits, small time deposits, and money market funds.

2. **Describe the functions of banks.**

   - The deposits of commercial banks and thrift institutions are money.
   - Banks borrow short term and lend long term and make a profit on the spread between the interest rates that they pay and receive.

3. **Describe the functions of the Federal Reserve System (the Fed).**

   - The Federal Reserve is the central bank of the United States.
   - The Fed influences the economy by setting the required reserve ratio for banks, by setting the discount rate, by open market operations, and by taking extraordinary measures in a financial crisis.

4. **Explain how the banking system creates money and how the Fed controls the quantity of money.**

   - Banks create money by making loans.
   - The maximum quantity of deposits the banks can create is limited by the monetary base, the banks' desired reserves, and desired currency holding.
   - When the Fed buys securities in an open market operation, it creates bank reserves. When the Fed sells securities in an open market operation, it destroys bank reserves.
   - An open market operation has a multiplier effect on the quantity of money.

Key Terms

MyEconLab Key Terms Quiz

CHAPTER CHECKPOINT

Study Plan Problems and Applications

1. What is money? Would you classify any of the items in List 1 as money?

2. What are the three functions that money performs? Which of the following items perform some but not all of these functions, and which perform all of these functions? Which of the items are money?
   - A checking account at the Bank of America
   - A dime
   - A debit card

3. Monica transfers $10,000 from her savings account at the Bank of Alaska to her money market fund. What is the immediate change in M1 and M2?

4. Terry takes $100 from his checking account and deposits the $100 in his savings account. What is the immediate change in M1 and M2?

5. Suppose that banks had deposits of $500 billion, a desired reserve ratio of 4 percent and no excess reserves. The banks had $15 billion in notes and coins. Calculate the banks' reserves at the central bank.

6. Explain the Fed's policy tools and briefly describe how each works.

7. Table 1 shows a bank's balance sheet. The bank has no excess reserves and there is no currency drain. Calculate the bank's desired reserve ratio.

8. The Fed buys $2 million of securities from AIG. If AIG's bank has a desired reserve ratio of 0.1 and there is no currency drain, calculate the bank's excess reserves as soon as the open market purchase is made, the maximum amount of loans that the banking system can make, and the maximum amount of new money that the banking system can create.

Use the following information to work Problems 9 and 10.

If the desired reserve ratio is 5 percent, the currency drain ratio is 20 percent of deposits, and the central bank makes an open market purchase of $1 million of securities, calculate the change in

9. The monetary base and the change in its components.

10. The quantity of money, and how much of the new money is currency and how much is bank deposits.

Use the following information to work Problems 11 and 12.

South Korea: Bank reserves raised

To rein in spending, the Bank of Korea raised the required reserve ratio to 7 percent from 5 percent—the first raise in almost 17 years. With higher required reserves, banks will have to cut the amount of loans they make.

Source: *The New York Times*, November 24, 2006

11. Explain why the higher required reserve ratio means that banks will have to cut the amount of loans they can make.

12. Assuming that the currency drain is zero and that the desired reserve ratio equals the required reserve ratio, calculate the change in the money multiplier that results from the increase in Korea's required reserve ratio.

13. Read *Eye on Creating Money* on pp. 288–289. By how much did the monetary base increase and why didn't M2 increase by the same percentage?

LIST 1

- Store coupons for noodles
- A $100 Amazon.com gift certificate
- Frequent flier miles
- Credit available on your Visa card
- The dollar coins that a coin collector owns

TABLE 1

Assets	Liabilities
(millions of dollars)	
Reserves at	Checkable deposits 80
the Fed 20	Savings deposits 120
Cash in vault 5	
Securities 75	
Loans 100	

Instructor Assignable Problems and Applications

MyEconLab Homework, Quiz, or Test if assigned by instructor

1. When the Fed increased the monetary base between 2008 and 2011, which component of the monetary base increased most: banks' reserves or currency? What happened to the reserves that banks borrowed from the Fed?

2. What happened to the money multiplier between 2008 and 2011? What would the money multiplier have been if the currency drain ratio had increased? What would the money multiplier have been if the banks' desired reserve ratio had not changed?

3. What are the three functions that money performs? Which of the items in List 1 perform some but not all of these functions and which of the items are money?

LIST 1

- An antique clock
- An S&L savings deposit
- Your credit card
- The coins in the Fed's museum
- Government securities

4. Naomi buys $1,000 worth of American Express travelers' checks and charges the purchase to her American Express card. What is the immediate change in M1 and M2?

5. A bank has $500 million in checkable deposits, $600 million in savings deposits, $400 million in small time deposits, $950 million in loans to businesses, $500 million in government securities, $20 million in currency, and $30 million in its reserve account at the Fed. Calculate the bank's deposits that are part of M1, deposits that are part of M2, and the bank's loans, securities, and reserves.

6. What can the Fed do to increase the quantity of money and keep the monetary base constant? Explain why the Fed would or would not
   - Change the currency drain ratio.
   - Change the required reserve ratio.
   - Change the discount rate.
   - Conduct an open market operation.

Use Table 1, which shows a bank's balance sheet, to work Problems 7 and 8. The desired reserve ratio on all deposits is 5 percent and there is no currency drain.

7. Calculate the bank's excess reserves. If the bank uses all of these excess reserves to make a loan, what is the quantity of the loan and the quantity of total deposits after the bank has made the loan?

8. If there is no currency drain, what is the quantity of loans and the quantity of total deposits when the bank has no excess reserves?

Use the following information to work Problems 9 and 10.

Inflation triggers more bank tightening
To control inflation by limiting bank loans, the People's Bank announced that it would raise the required reserve ratio for commercial banks from 21 percent to 21.5 percent.

Source: *South China Morning Post*, June 15, 2011

TABLE 1

Assets		Liabilities
(millions of dollars)		
Reserves at the Fed	25	Checkable deposits 90
Cash in vault	15	Savings deposits 110
Securities	60	
Loans	100	

9. Compare the required reserve ratio in China on June 15, 2011 and the required reserve ratio on checkable deposits in the United States today.

10. If the currency drain ratio in China and the United States is 10 percent of deposits, compare the money multipliers in the two countries.

Multiple Choice Quiz

1. A commodity or token is money if it is _____.

   A. generally accepted as means of payment
   B. a store of value
   C. used in a barter transaction
   D. completely safe as a store of value

2. Money in the United States today includes _____.

   A. currency and deposits at both banks and the Fed
   B. the currency in people's wallets, stores' tills, and the bank deposits that people and businesses own
   C. currency in ATMs and people's bank deposits
   D. the banks' reserves and bank deposits owned by individuals and businesses

3. Rick withdraws $500 from his savings account, keeps $100 as currency, and deposits $400 in his checking account.

   A. M1 increases by $400 and M2 decreases by $500.
   B. M1 does not change, but M2 decreases by $500.
   C. M1 does not change, but M2 decreases by $400.
   D. M1 increases by $500 and M2 does not change.

4. Commercial banks' assets include _____.

   A. bank deposits of individuals and businesses and bank reserves
   B. loans to individuals and businesses and government securities
   C. bank reserves and the deposits in M2
   D. government securities and borrowed funds

5. The Fed's policy tools include all the following *except* _____.

   A. required reserve ratio and open market operations
   B. quantitative easing
   C. discount rate
   D. taxing banks' deposits at the Fed

6. A commercial bank creates money when it does all the following *except* _____.

   A. decreases its excess reserves
   B. makes loans
   C. creates deposits
   D. puts cash in its ATMs

7. An open market _____ of $100 million of securities _____.

   A. purchase; increases bank reserves
   B. sale; increases bank reserves
   C. purchase; decreases the Fed's liabilities
   D. sale; increases the Fed's liabilities

8. The money multiplier _____.

   A. increases if banks increase their desired reserve ratio
   B. increases if the currency drain ratio increases
   C. is 1 if the desired reserve ratio equals the currency drain ratio
   D. decreases if banks increase their desired reserve ratio

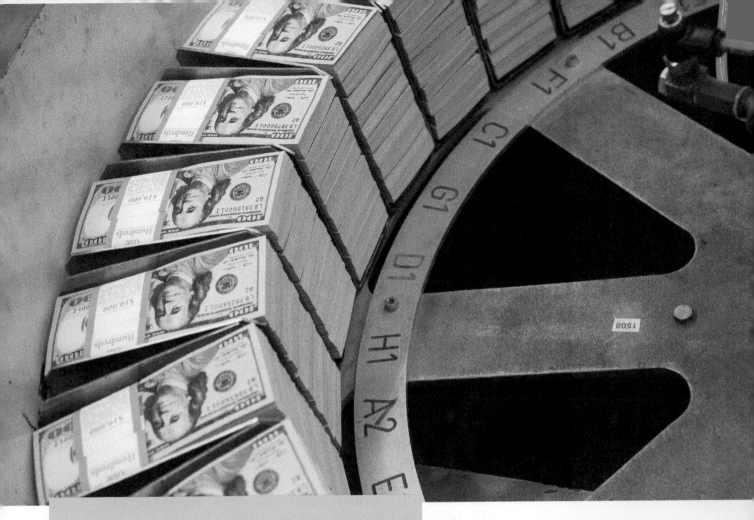

What causes inflation?

Money, Interest, and Inflation

12

When you have completed your study of this chapter, you will be able to

1 Explain what determines the demand for money and how the demand for money and the supply of money determine the *nominal* interest rate.

2 Explain how in the long run, the quantity of money determines the price level and money growth brings inflation.

3 Identify the costs of inflation and the benefits of a stable value of money.

MyEconLab Big Picture

WHERE WE ARE AND WHERE WE'RE HEADING

Before we explore the effects of money on the interest rate and the inflation rate, let's take stock of what we've learned and preview where we are heading.

■ The Real Economy

Real factors that are independent of the price level determine potential GDP and the natural unemployment rate (Chapter 8). The demand for labor and supply of labor determine the quantity of labor employed and the real wage rate at full employment. The full-employment equilibrium quantity of labor and the production function determine potential GDP. At full employment, real GDP equals potential GDP and the unemployment rate equals the natural unemployment rate.

Investment and saving along with population growth, human capital growth, and technological change determine the growth rate of real GDP (Chapter 9).

Investment and saving plans influence the demand for and supply of loanable funds, which in turn determine the real interest rate and the equilibrium amount of investment and saving (Chapter 10).

■ The Money Economy

Money consists of currency and bank deposits. Banks create deposits by making loans, and the Fed influences the quantity of money through its open market operations, which determine the monetary base and the federal funds rate—the interest rate on interbank loans (Chapter 11).

The effects of the Fed's actions and of changes in the quantity of money are complex. In the current chapter (Chapter 12), we focus on the immediate effects and on the long-run or ultimate effects of the Fed's actions.

The immediate effects are on the short-term nominal interest rate. If the Fed increases (or decreases) the quantity of money, the short-term nominal interest rate falls (or rises).

The long-run effects of the Fed's actions are on the price level and the inflation rate. In the long run, the loanable funds market determines the real interest rate and the Fed's actions determine only the price level and the inflation rate. If the Fed increases (or decreases) the quantity of money, the price level rises (or falls). And if the Fed speeds up (or slows down) the rate at which the quantity of money grows, the inflation rate increases (or decreases).

■ Real and Money Interactions and Policy

When the Fed changes the short-term nominal interest rate, other changes ripple through the economy. Expenditure plans change and real GDP, employment, unemployment, and the price level (and inflation rate) all change. In the long run, the real effects fade, leaving changes in only the price level and inflation rate. We lay the foundation for studying the ripple effects of the Fed's actions in Chapters 13–15. These chapters explain how the real and monetary factors interact and describe the short-run constraint on the Fed's choices.

Chapters 16 and 17 build on the foundation of all the preceding chapters. Chapter 16 explains how the government uses fiscal policy to sustain economic growth and stabilize output and employment. Chapter 17 explains how the Fed uses monetary policy to achieve those same goals and to control inflation.

12.1 MONEY AND THE INTEREST RATE

MyEconLab Snapshot

To understand the Fed's influence on the interest rate, we study the demand for money, the supply of money, and the forces that bring equilibrium in the market for money. We'll begin with the demand for money.

■ The Demand for Money

The amount of money that households and firms choose to hold is the **quantity of money demanded.** What determines the quantity of money demanded? The answer is the "price" of money. But what is that "price"?

Quantity of money demanded
The amount of money that households and firms choose to hold.

Two possible answers, both correct, are the value of money and the opportunity cost of holding money. The value of money is the quantity of goods and services that a dollar will buy, which is related to the *price level*. We'll explore this "price" of money when we study the long-run effects of money in the next part of this chapter. The opportunity cost of holding money is the goods and services forgone by holding money rather than some other asset.

To determine the quantity of money to hold, households and firms compare the benefit from holding money to its opportunity cost. They choose to hold the quantity that balances the benefit of holding an *additional* dollar of money against its opportunity cost. What are the benefit and opportunity cost of holding money?

Benefit of Holding Money

You've seen that money is the means of payment (Chapter 11, p. 266). The more money you hold, the easier it is for you to make payments. By holding enough money you can settle your bills at the end of each month without having to spend time and effort raising a loan or selling some other financial asset.

The marginal benefit of holding money is the change in total benefit that results from holding one more dollar as money. The marginal benefit of holding money diminishes as the quantity of money held increases. If you hold only a few dollars in money, then holding a few more dollars brings large benefits—you can buy a coffee or take a bus ride. If you hold enough money to make your normal weekly payments, then holding more dollars brings only a small benefit because you're not very likely to want to spend those extra dollars. Holding even more money brings only a small additional benefit. You barely notice the difference in the benefit of having $1,000 versus $1,001 in your bank account.

To get the most out of your assets, you hold money only up to the point at which its marginal benefit equals its opportunity cost.

Opportunity Cost of Holding Money

The opportunity cost of holding money is the interest rate forgone on an alternative asset. If you can earn 8 percent a year on a mutual fund account, then holding an additional $100 in money costs you $8 a year. Your opportunity cost of holding $100 in money is the goods and services worth $8 that you must forgo.

A fundamental principle of economics is that if the opportunity cost of something increases, people seek substitutes for it. Money is no exception. Other assets such as a mutual fund account are substitutes for money. The higher the opportunity cost of holding money—the higher the interest income forgone by not holding other assets—the smaller is the quantity of money demanded.

Opportunity Cost: *Nominal* Interest Is a *Real* Cost

The opportunity cost of holding money is the nominal interest rate. In Chapter 7 (p. 182), you learned the distinction between the *nominal* interest rate and the *real* interest rate and that

$$\text{Norminal interest rate} = \text{Real interest rate} + \text{Inflation rate.}$$

We can use this equation to find the real interest rate for a given nominal interest rate and inflation rate. For example, if the nominal interest rate on a mutual fund account is 8 percent a year and the inflation rate is 2 percent a year, the real interest rate is 6 percent a year. Why isn't the real interest rate of 6 percent a year the opportunity cost of holding money? That is, why isn't the opportunity cost of holding $100 in money only $6 worth of goods and services forgone?

The answer is that if you hold $100 in money rather than in a mutual fund, your buying power decreases by $8, not by $6. With inflation running at 2 percent a year, on each $100 that you hold as money and that earns no interest, you lose $2 worth of buying power a year. On each $100 that you put into your mutual fund account, you gain $6 worth of buying power a year. So if you hold money rather than a mutual fund, you lose the buying power of $6 plus $2, or $8—equivalent to the nominal interest rate on the mutual fund, not the real interest rate.

Because the opportunity cost of holding money is the nominal interest rate on an alternative asset,

> **Other things remaining the same, the higher the nominal interest rate, the smaller is the quantity of money demanded.**

This relationship describes the decision made by an individual or a firm about how much money to hold. It also describes money-holding decisions for the economy—the sum of the decisions of every individual and firm.

We summarize the influence of the nominal interest rate on money-holding decisions in a demand for money schedule and curve.

The Demand for Money Schedule and Curve

Demand for money
The relationship between the quantity of money demanded and the nominal interest rate, when all other influences on the amount of money that people wish to hold remain the same.

The **demand for money** is the relationship between the quantity of money demanded and the nominal interest rate, when all other influences on the amount of money that people wish to hold remain the same. We illustrate the demand for money with a demand for money schedule and a demand for money curve, such as those in Figure 12.1. If the interest rate is 5 percent a year, the quantity of money demanded is $1 trillion. The quantity of money demanded decreases to $0.98 trillion if the interest rate rises to 6 percent a year and increases to $1.02 trillion if the interest rate falls to 4 percent a year.

The demand for money curve is *MD*. When the interest rate rises, everything else remaining the same, the opportunity cost of holding money rises and the quantity of money demanded decreases—there is a movement up along the demand for money curve. When the interest rate falls, the opportunity cost of holding money falls and the quantity of money demanded increases—there is a movement down along the demand for money curve.

FIGURE 12.1

The Demand for Money

	Nominal interest rate (percent per year)	Quantity of money demanded (trillions of dollars)
A	6	0.98
B	5	1.00
C	4	1.02

The demand for money schedule is graphed as the demand for money curve, MD. Rows A, B, and C in the table correspond to points A, B, and C on the curve. The nominal interest rate is the opportunity cost of holding money.

Other things remaining the same, ❶ an increase in the nominal interest rate decreases the quantity of money demanded, and ❷ a decrease in the nominal interest rate increases the quantity of money demanded.

■ Changes in the Demand for Money

A change in the nominal interest rate brings a change in the quantity of money demanded and a movement along the demand for money curve. A change in any other influence on money holding changes the demand for money. The three main influences on the demand for money are

- The price level
- Real GDP
- Financial technology

The Price Level

The demand for money is proportional to the price level—an x percent rise in the price level brings an x percent increase in the quantity of money demanded at each nominal interest rate. The reason is that we hold money to make payments: If the price level changes, the quantity of dollars that we need to make payments changes in the same proportion.

Real GDP

The demand for money increases as real GDP increases. The reason is that when real GDP increases, expenditures and incomes increase. To make the increased expenditures and income payments, households and firms must hold larger average amounts of money.

Financial Technology

Changes in financial technology change the demand for money. Most changes in financial technology come from advances in computing and record keeping. Some advances increase the quantity of money demanded, and some decrease it.

Daily interest checking deposits and automatic transfers between checking and savings deposits enable people to earn interest on money, lower the opportunity cost of holding money, and increase the demand for money. Automatic teller machines, debit cards, and smart cards, which have made money easier to obtain and use, have increased the marginal benefit of money and increased the demand for money.

Credit cards have made it easier for people to buy goods and services on credit and pay for them when their credit card account becomes due. This development has decreased the demand for money.

A change in any of the influences on money holdings that we've just reviewed other than the interest rate changes the demand for money. A rise in the price level, an increase in real GDP, or an advance in financial technology that lowers the opportunity cost of holding money or makes money more useful increases the demand for money. A fall in the price level, a decrease in real GDP, or a technological advance that creates a substitute for money decreases the demand for money.

■ The Supply of Money

Supply of money
The relationship between the quantity of money supplied and the nominal interest rate.

The quantity of money supplied is determined by the actions of the banking system and the Fed. On any given day, the quantity of money supplied is fixed. The **supply of money** is the relationship between the quantity of money supplied and the nominal interest rate. In Figure 12.2, the quantity of money supplied is $1 trillion regardless of the nominal interest rate, so the supply of money curve is the vertical line *MS*.

■ The Nominal Interest Rate

People hold some of their financial wealth as money and some in the form of other financial assets. You have seen that the amount of wealth that people hold as money depends on the nominal interest rate that they can earn on other financial assets. Demand and supply determine the nominal interest rate. We can study the forces of demand and supply in either the market for financial assets or the market for money. Because the Fed influences the quantity of money, we focus on the market for money.

On a given day, the price level, real GDP, and the state of financial technology are fixed. Because these influences on the demand for money are fixed, the demand for money curve is given.

The interest rate is the only influence on the quantity of money demanded that is free to fluctuate. Every day, the interest rate adjusts to make the quantity of money demanded equal the quantity of money supplied—to achieve money market equilibrium.

In Figure 12.2, the demand for money curve is *MD*. The equilibrium interest rate is 5 percent a year. At any interest rate above 5 percent a year, the quantity of money demanded is less than the quantity of money supplied. At any interest rate below 5 percent a year, the quantity of money demanded exceeds the quantity of money supplied.

FIGURE 12.2

Money Market Equilibrium

MyEconLab Real-time data

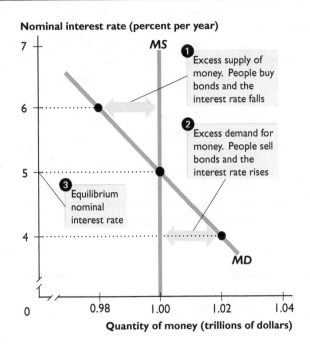

The supply of money curve is *MS*, and the demand for money curve is *MD*.

❶ If the interest rate is 6 percent a year, the quantity of money held exceeds the quantity demanded. People buy bonds, the price of a bond rises, and the interest rate falls.

❷ If the interest rate is 4 percent a year, the quantity of money held falls short of the quantity demanded. People sell bonds, the price of a bond falls, and the interest rate rises.

❸ If the interest rate is 5 percent a year, the quantity of money held equals the quantity demanded. The money market is in equilibrium.

The Interest Rate and Bond Price Move in Opposite Directions When the government issues a bond, it specifies the dollar amount of interest that it will pay each year on the bond. Suppose that the government issues a bond that pays $100 of interest a year. The interest *rate* that you receive on this bond depends on the price that you pay for it. If the price is $1,000, the interest rate is 10 percent a year—$100 is 10 percent of $1,000.

If the price of the bond *falls* to $500, the interest rate *rises* to 20 percent a year. The reason is that you still receive an interest payment of $100, but this amount is 20 percent of the $500 price of the bond. If the price of the bond *rises* to $2,000, the interest rate *falls* to 5 percent a year. Again, you still receive an interest payment of $100, but this amount is 5 percent of the $2,000 price of the bond.

Interest Rate Adjustment If the interest rate is above its equilibrium level, people would like to hold less money than they are actually holding. They try to get rid of some money by buying other financial assets such as bonds. The demand for financial assets increases, the prices of these assets rise, and the interest rate falls. The interest rate keeps falling until the quantity of money that people want to hold increases to equal the quantity of money supplied.

Conversely, when the interest rate is below its equilibrium level, people are holding less money than they would like to hold. They try to get more money by selling other financial assets. The demand for these financial assets decreases, the prices of these assets fall, and the interest rate rises. The interest rate keeps rising until the quantity of money that people want to hold decreases to equal the quantity of money supplied.

EYE on the U.S. ECONOMY
Credit Cards and Money

Today, 65 percent of U.S. households own a credit card. That's down a bit from a peak of 76 percent in 2007.

By using a credit card account to buy goods and services, it is possible to economize on money holding. Instead of holding and using money, a card holder buys with a card and then pays off the card account balance (or part of it) on her or his own pay day.

Back in 1970, only 20 percent of U.S. households had a credit card. How has the spread of credit cards affected the quantity of money that we hold?

The answer is that the quantity of M1 money has decreased as a percentage of GDP. Part (a) of the figure shows that as the ownership of credit cards expanded from 18 percent in 1970 to 76 percent in 2007, the quantity of M1 (currency plus checking deposits) fell from 20 percent of GDP to less than 10 percent.

The expansion of credit card ownership is a change in financial technology that has led to a steady decrease in the demand for money.

Part (b) of the figure shows the effects on the demand for money. Here, we graph the quantity of M1 as a percentage of GDP against the interest rate. As credit card use increased between 1970 and 2007, the demand for money decreased and the demand for money curve shifted leftward from MD_0 to MD_1.

As the interest rate fell between 2007 and 2011, the quantity of money demanded increased along the demand for money curve MD_1.

SOURCE OF DATA: Federal Reserve.

(a) Changes in the use of credit cards and money

(b) Changes in the demand for M1

■ Changing the Interest Rate

To change the interest rate, the Fed changes the quantity of money. Figure 12.3 illustrates two changes. The demand for money curve is *MD*. If the Fed increases the quantity of money to $1.02 trillion, the supply of money curve shifts rightward from MS_0 to MS_1 and the interest rate falls to 4 percent a year. If the Fed decreases the quantity of money to $0.98 trillion, the supply of money curve shifts leftward from MS_0 to MS_2 and the interest rate rises to 6 percent a year.

FIGURE 12.3

Interest Rate Changes

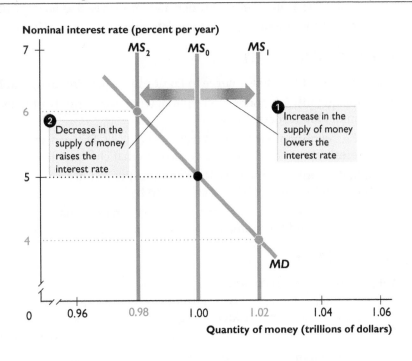

The demand for money is *MD*, and initially, the supply of money is MS_0 The interest rate is 5 percent a year.

1 If the Fed increases the quantity of money and the supply of money curve shifts rightward to MS_1, the interest rate falls to 4 percent a year.

2 If the Fed decreases the quantity of money and the supply of money curve shifts leftward to MS_2, the interest rate rises to 6 percent a year.

EYE on YOUR LIFE
Money Holding and Fed Watching

How much currency (cash) do you have in your wallet, on average? How much money do you keep in your bank account on average?

Why don't you hold a larger average bank balance by paying off a smaller part of your credit card balance than you can afford to pay?

Wouldn't it be better to keep a bit more money in the bank?

Almost certainly, that would not be a smart idea. Why? Because the opportunity cost of holding that money would be too high.

If you have an outstanding credit card balance, the interest rate on that balance is the opportunity cost of holding money.

By paying off as much of your credit card balance as you can afford, you avoid a high interest rate on the outstanding balance.

Your demand for money is sensitive to this opportunity cost.

Do you watch the Fed? Probably not, but you can learn to become an effective Fed watcher. In the process, you will become much better informed about the state of the U.S. economy and the state of the economy in your region.

To become a Fed watcher, try to get into the habit of visiting the Fed's Web site at www.federalreserve.gov. Type "Beige Book" in the Search tool and look at the latest Beige Book to see what is happening in your region.

Also, keep an eye on the FOMC calendar for the dates of interest rate announcements. On these dates, check the media for opinions on what the Fed's interest rate decision will be. After the decision is made and announced, check the Fed's explanation as to why it made its decision.

MyEconLab Study Plan 12.1
Key Terms Quiz
Solutions

CHECKPOINT 12.1

Explain what determines the demand for money and how the demand for money and the supply of money determine the *nominal* interest rate.

Practice Problems

Use the demand for money curve in Figure 1 to work Problems **1** to **3**.

1. If the quantity of money is $4 trillion, what is the supply of money and the nominal interest rate?

2. If the quantity of money is $4 trillion and real GDP increases, how will the interest rate change? Explain the process that changes the interest rate.

3. If the quantity of money is $4 trillion and the Fed decreases it to $3.9 trillion, how will the price of a bond change? Why?

4. If banks increase the interest rate they pay on deposits, how will the demand for money and the nominal interest rate in the money market change?

In the News

What to do with $50,000 now
A good strategy: Put about two-thirds of the money into bonds of developed nations and the rest into riskier emerging-market bonds.

Source: CNNMoney.com

What is the opportunity cost of holding money? If lots of people put their money into bonds, how will the demand for money and the interest rate change?

Solutions to Practice Problems

1. The supply of money is the curve *MS*. The interest rate is 4 percent a year, at the intersection of MD_1 and *MS* (Figure 2).

2. The demand for money increases, and the demand for money curve shifts from MD_1 to MD_2 (Figure 2). At an interest rate of 4 percent a year, people want to hold more money, so they sell bonds. The price of a bond falls, and the interest rate rises.

3. At 4 percent a year, people would like to hold $4 trillion. With only $3.9 trillion of money available, they sell bonds to get more money. The price of a bond falls, and the interest rate rises. The price will fall and the interest rate will rise until the quantity of money that people want to hold equals the $3.9 trillion available. The interest rate rises to 6 percent a year (Figure 3).

4. A higher interest rate on bank deposits lowers the opportunity cost of holding money, so the demand for money increases. As the demand for money increases, with no change in the supply of money, the nominal interest rate in the money market rises (as Figure 2 shows).

Solution to In the News

The opportunity cost of holding money is the interest rate forgone by not holding bonds. If people decide to buy more bonds, the demand for money decreases. The decrease in the demand for money with no change in the supply of money lowers the interest rate on bonds. (People buy more bonds so the price of a bond rises).

FIGURE 1

Nominal interest rate
(percent per year)

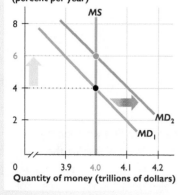

FIGURE 2

Nominal interest rate
(percent per year)

FIGURE 3

Nominal interest rate
(percent per year)

12.2   MONEY, THE PRICE LEVEL, AND INFLATION

A change in the nominal interest rate is the initial effect of a change in the quantity of money, but it is not the ultimate or long-run effect. When the interest rate changes, borrowing and lending and investment and consumption spending also change, which in turn change production and prices—change real GDP and the price level.

The details of this adjustment process are complex, and we explore them in the next two chapters. But the place where the process comes to rest—the *long-run outcome*—is easier to describe. It is crucial to understand the long-run outcome because that is where the economy is heading. We're now going to examine the long-run equilibrium in the money market.

■ The Money Market in the Long Run

The *long run* refers to the economy at full employment when real GDP equals potential GDP (Chapter 8, p. 193). Over the business cycle, real GDP fluctuates around potential GDP. But averaging over an expansion and recession and a peak and trough, real GDP equals potential GDP. That is, real GDP equals potential GDP *on average*. So another way to think about the *long run* is as a description of the economy *on average* over the business cycle.

The Long-Run Demand for Money

In the long run, equilibrium in the loanable funds market determines the real interest rate (Chapter 10, pp. 246–253). The nominal interest rate that influences money holding plans equals the real interest rate plus the inflation rate. For now, we'll consider an economy that has no inflation, so the real interest rate equals the nominal interest rate. (We'll consider inflation later in this chapter.)

With the interest rate determined by real forces in the long run, what is the variable that adjusts to make the quantity of money that people plan to hold equal the quantity of money supplied? The answer is the "price" of money. The law of demand applies to money just as it does to any other object. The lower the "price" of money, the greater is the quantity of money that people are willing to hold. What is the "price" of money? It is the *value* of money.

The Value of Money

The *value of money* is the quantity of goods and services that a unit of money will buy. It is the inverse of the *price level, P*, which equals the GDP price index divided by 100. That is,

$$\text{Value of money} = 1/P.$$

To see why, suppose that you have $100 in your wallet. If you spend that money, you can buy goods and services valued at $100. Now suppose that the price level rises by 10 percent. After the price rise, the quantity of goods and services that $100 can buy has fallen. Your $100 can now buy only $100 ÷ 1.1 or $91 of goods and services. Yesterday's $100 is worth $91 today. The price level has risen and the value of money has fallen and each percentage change is the same. The higher the value of money, the smaller is the quantity of money that people plan to hold. If it seems strange that a higher value of money makes people want to hold less money, think about how much money you would plan to hold if the price of a restaurant meal was 20 cents and the price of movie ticket was 10 cents. You would be happy to hold (say) $1 on average. But if the price of a meal is $20 and the price of a movie ticket is $10, you would want to hold $100 on average. The price level is lower and the value of money higher in the first case than in the second; and the amount of money you would plan to hold is lower in the first case than in the second.

Money Market Equilibrium in the Long Run

In the long run, money market equilibrium determines the value of money. If the quantity of money supplied exceeds the long-run quantity demanded, people go out and spend their surplus money. The quantity of goods and services available is fixed equal to potential GDP, so the extra spending forces prices upward. As the price level rises, the value of money falls.

If the quantity of money supplied is less than the long-run quantity demanded, people lower their spending to build up the quantity of money they hold. The shortage of money translates into a surplus of goods and services, so the spending cut-back forces prices downward. The price level falls and the value of money rises. When the quantity of money supplied equals the long-run quantity demanded, the price level and the value of money are at their equilibrium levels.

Figure 12.4 illustrates long-run money market equilibrium. The long-run demand for money curve is *LRMD*. Its position depends on potential GDP and the equilibrium interest rate. The supply of money is *MS*. Equilibrium occurs when the value of money is 1.

■ **FIGURE 12.4**

Long-Run Money Market Equilibrium

MyEconLab Animation

The long-run demand for money is determined by potential GDP and the equilibrium interest rate.

The *LRMD* curve shows how the quantity of money that households and firms plan to hold, in the long run, depends on the value of money (or 1/P, the inverse of the price level).

The *MS* curve shows the quantity of money supplied, which is $1 trillion.

The price level adjusts to make the value of money equal 1 and achieve long-run money market equilibrium.

■ A Change in the Quantity of Money

Suppose that starting from a long-run equilibrium, the Fed increases the quantity of money by 10 percent. In the short run, the greater quantity of money lowers the nominal interest rate. With a lower interest rate, people and businesses borrow more and spend more. But with real GDP equal to potential GDP, there are no more goods and services to buy, so when people go out and spend, prices start to rise. Eventually, a new long-run equilibrium is reached at which the price level has increased in proportion to the increase in the quantity of money. Because the quantity of money increased by 10 percent, the price level has also risen by 10 percent from 1.0 to 1.1.

Figure 12.5 illustrates this outcome. Initially, the supply of money is MS_0 and the quantity of money is $1 trillion. The Fed increases the supply of money to MS_1 and the quantity of money is now $1.1 trillion—a 10 percent increase. There is now a surplus of money and people go out and spend it. The increased spending on the same unchanged quantity of goods and services raises the price level and lowers the value of money. Eventually, the price level has increased by 10 percent from 1.0 to 1.1 and the value of money has decreased by 10 percent from 1.00 to 0.91.

You've just seen a key proposition about the quantity of money and the price level.

In the long run and other things remaining the same, a given percentage change in the quantity of money brings an equal percentage change in the price level.

FIGURE 12.5

The Long-Run Effect of a Change in the Quantity of Money

MyEconLab Animation

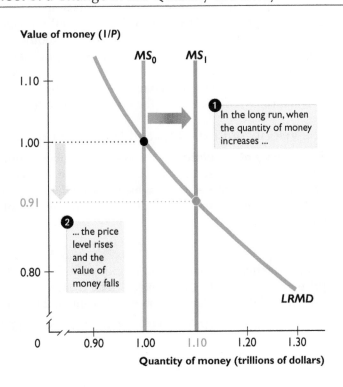

❶ The Fed increases the supply of money from MS_0 to MS_1 and the quantity of money increases from $1 trillion to $1.1 trillion, a 10 percent increase.

❷ The price level rises by 10 percent and the value of money falls by 10 percent to restore long-run money market equilibrium.

■ The Price Level in a Baby-Sitting Club

It is hard to visualize a long-run equilibrium and even harder to visualize and compare two long-run equilibrium situations like those that we've just described. An example of a simpler situation might help.

In an isolated neighborhood, there are no teenagers but lots of young children, and parents can't find any babysitters. So they form a club and sit for each other. The deal is that each time a parent sits for someone else, he or she receives a token that can be used to buy one babysitting session from another member of the club. The organizer notices that the club is inactive. Every member has a few unspent tokens, but they spend them infrequently. To make the club more active, the organizer decides to issue every member one token for each token that is currently held, so the supply of tokens doubles.

With more tokens to spend, parents start to plan more evenings out. Suddenly, the phones are ringing as parents seek babysitters. Every member of the club wants a sitter, but there are no more sitters than before. After making a few calls and finding no sitters available, anxious parents who really do need a sitter start to offer a higher price: two tokens per session. That does the trick. At the higher price, the quantity of baby-sitting services demanded decreases and the quantity supplied increases. Equilibrium is restored. Nothing real has changed, but the quantity of tokens and the price level have doubled.

Think of the equilibrium quantity of baby-sitting services as potential GDP, the quantity of tokens as the quantity of money, and the price of a baby-sitting session as the price level. You can then see how a given percentage change in the quantity of money at full employment brings an equal percentage change in the price level.

■ The Quantity Theory of Money

Quantity theory of money
The proposition that when real GDP equals potential GDP, an increase in the quantity of money brings an equal percentage increase in the price level.

The proposition that when real GDP equals potential GDP, an increase in the quantity of money brings an equal percentage increase in the price level is called the **quantity theory of money.** We've derived this proposition by looking at equilibrium in the money market in the long run. Another way of seeing the relationship between the quantity of money and the price level uses the concepts of *the velocity of circulation* and *the equation of exchange*. We're now going to explore the quantity theory. We're then going to see how ongoing money growth brings inflation and see what determines the inflation rate in the long run.

The Velocity of Circulation and Equation of Exchange

Velocity of circulation
The average number of times in a year that each dollar of money gets used to buy final goods and services.

The **velocity of circulation** is the average number of times in a year that each dollar of money gets used to buy final goods and services. The value of final goods and services is nominal GDP, which is real GDP, Y, multiplied by the price level, P. If we call the quantity of money M, then the velocity of circulation is determined by the equation:

$$V = (P \times Y) \div M.$$

In this equation, P is the GDP price index divided by 100. For example, if the GDP price index is 125, the price level is 1.25. If the price level is 1.25, real GDP is $8 trillion, and the quantity of money is $2 trillion, then the velocity of circulation is

$$V = (1.25 \times \$8 \text{ trillion}) \div \$2 \text{ trillion, or}$$

$$V = 5.$$

That is, with $2 trillion of money, each dollar gets used an average of 5 times, so $2 trillion × 5 equals $10 trillion of goods and services bought.

The **equation of exchange** states that the quantity of money, M, multiplied by the velocity of circulation, V, equals the price level P, multiplied by real GDP, Y. That is,

$$M \times V = P \times Y.$$

The equation of exchange is *always* true because it is implied by the definition of the velocity of circulation. That is, if you multiply both sides of the equation on p. 308 that defines the velocity of circulation by M, you get the equation of exchange.

Using the above numbers—a price level of 1.25, real GDP of $8 trillion, the quantity of money of $2 trillion, and the velocity of circulation of 5—you can see that

$$M \times V = \$2 \text{ trillion} \times 5 = \$10 \text{ trillion},$$

and

$$P \times Y = 1.25 \times \$8 \text{ trillion} = \$10 \text{ trillion}.$$

So,

$$M \times V = P \times Y = \$10 \text{ trillion}.$$

The Quantity Theory Prediction

We can rearrange the equation of exchange to isolate the price level on the left side. To do so, divide both sides of the equation of exchange by real GDP to obtain

$$P = (M \times V) \div Y.$$

On the left side is the price level, and on the right side are all the things that influence the price level. But this equation is still just an implication of the definition of the velocity of circulation. To turn the equation into a theory of what determines the price level, we use two other facts: (1) At full employment, real GDP equals potential GDP, which is determined only by real factors and not by the quantity of money; and (2) the velocity of circulation is relatively stable and does not change when the quantity of money changes.

So with V and Y constant, if M increases P must increase, and the percentage increase in P must equal the percentage increase in M.

We can use the above numbers to illustrate this prediction. Real GDP is $8 trillion, the quantity of money is $2 trillion, and the velocity of circulation is 5. Put these values into the equation:

$$P = (M \times V) \div Y.$$

to obtain

$$P = (\$2 \text{ trillion} \times 5) \div \$8 \text{ trillion} = 1.25.$$

Now increase the quantity of money from $2 trillion to $2.4 trillion. The percentage increase in the quantity of money is

$$(\$2.4 \text{ trilliion} - \$2 \text{ trillion}) \div \$2 \text{ trillion} \times 100 = 20 \text{ percent.}$$

Equation of exchange
An equation that states that the quantity of money multiplied by the velocity of circulation equals the price level multiplied by real GDP.

Now find the new price level. It is

$$P = (\$2.4 \text{ trillion} \times 5) \div \$8 \text{ trillion} = 1.50.$$

The price level rises from 1.25 to 1.50. The percentage increase in the price level is

$$(1.50 - 1.25) \div 1.25 \times 100 = 20 \text{ percent}.$$

When the economy is at full employment (real GDP equals potential GDP) and the velocity of circulation is stable, the price level and the quantity of money increase by the same 20 percent.

■ Inflation and the Quantity Theory of Money

The equation of exchange tells us about the price *level,* the quantity of money, the level of real GDP, and the level of the velocity of circulation. We can turn the equation into one that tells us about *rates of change* or *growth rates* of these variables. We want to make this conversion because we want to know what determines the inflation rate—the rate of change of the price level.

In rates of change or growth rates,

Money growth + Velocity growth = Inflation rate + Real GDP growth,

which means that

Inflation rate = Money growth + Velocity growth − Real GDP growth.

Constant Inflation

Figure 12.6 illustrates three cases in which the inflation rate is constant—at zero, at a low or moderate rate, and at a high or rapid rate. In each case, the velocity growth rate is 1 percent a year and the real GDP growth rate is 3 percent a year. The money growth rate is the only thing that is different across the three cases, and it is this difference that brings the different inflation rates.

If the quantity of money grows at 2 percent a year, there is no inflation. That is,

Inflation rate = 2 percent + 1 percent − 3 percent = 0 percent a year.

With the quantity of money growing at 4 percent a year, the inflation rate is 2 percent a year. That is,

Inflation rate = 4 percent + 1 percent − 3 percent = 2 percent a year.

And with the quantity of money growing at 10 percent a year, the inflation rate is 8 percent a year. That is,

Inflation rate = 10 percent + 1 percent − 3 percent = 8 percent a year.

A Change in the Inflation Rate

We've looked at three different inflation rates—zero, moderate, and rapid—with given growth rates of real GDP and velocity of circulation. We're now going to see what happens when the growth rate of money *changes.* We'll start with an increase in the money growth rate.

FIGURE 12.6

Money Growth and Inflation

MyEconLab Real-time data

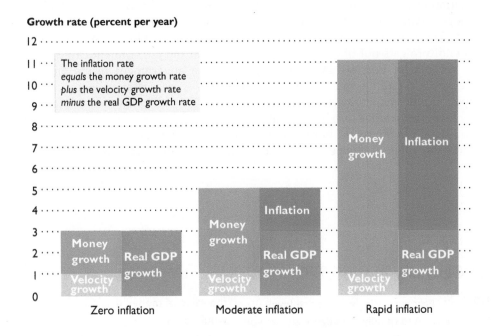

The velocity of circulation grows at 1 percent a year (the orange block), and real GDP grows at 3 percent a year (the red block). The inflation rate (green block) is determined by money growth (blue block).

If the quantity of money grows at 2 percent a year, the inflation rate is zero.

If the quantity of money grows at 4 percent a year, the inflation rate is a moderate 2 percent a year.

But if the quantity of money grows at 10 percent a year, the inflation rate is a rapid 8 percent a year.

Increase in Money Growth Rate When the money growth rate increases, the inflation rate increases slowly and there is a temporary (short-run) increase in the real GDP growth rate. The velocity of circulation increases as the inflation rate speeds up but this increase does not persist. Once the velocity has increased in response to a higher inflation rate, it remains constant at its new level. (You can see in *Eye on Inflation* on p. 313 that velocity growth has been zero for most of the past 40 years. It increased during the 1990s but decreased again during the 2000s.)

A faster inflation reduces potential GDP and slows real GDP growth (for reasons that we explore in the final section of this chapter) but for low inflation rates, these effects are small and are dominated by the main direct effect of money growth on the inflation rate. Eventually, real GDP growth slows to that of potential GDP, velocity growth returns to its long-run rate, and the inflation rate changes by the full amount of the change in the money growth rate.

Decrease in Money Growth Rate When the money growth rate decreases, the effects that we've just described work in the opposite direction.

You can see in *Eye on Inflation* (p. 313) that changes in the growth rate of real GDP and changes in velocity growth have been small in comparison to the changes in the growth rate of money and the inflation rate. So,

> In the long run and other things remaining the same, a change in the *growth rate* of the quantity of money brings an equal change in the inflation rate.

The relationship between the money growth rate and the inflation rate is at its clearest when inflation is rapid in *hyperinflation*.

■ Hyperinflation

Hyperinflation
Inflation at a rate that exceeds 50 percent *a month* (which translates to 12,875 percent per year).

When the inflation rate exceeds 50 percent *a month,* it is called **hyperinflation.** An inflation rate of 50 percent per month translates to an inflation rate of 12,875 percent per year. Hyperinflation occurs when the quantity of money grows at a rapid pace. The reason money growth sometimes becomes rapid is that government expenditure gets out of control and exceeds what the government can collect in tax revenue or borrow. In such a situation, the government prints money to finance its spending and the quantity of money increases at an extraordinarily rapid and increasing rate.

Hyperinflation is rare but not unknown (see *Eye on the Past* below). The highest inflation in the world in recent times was in the African nation of Zimbabwe, where the inflation rate peaked at 231,150,888.87 percent a year in July 2008.

EYE on the PAST
Hyperinflation in Germany in the 1920s

An international treaty signed in 1919 required Germany to pay large amounts as compensation for war damage to other countries in Europe. To meet its obligations, Germany started to print money. The quantity of money increased by 24 percent in 1921, by 220 percent in 1922, and by 43 *billion* percent in 1923!

Not surprisingly, the price level increased rapidly. The figure shows you how rapidly.

In November 1923 when the hyperinflation reached its peak, the price level was more than doubling every day. Wages were paid twice a day, and people spent their morning's wages at lunchtime to avoid the loss in the value of money that the afternoon would bring.

Hyperinflation made bank notes more valuable as fire kindling than as money. The sight of people burning Reichmarks (the name of Germany's money at that time) was a common one, as the photo shows.

SOURCE OF DATA: Phillip Cagan, "The Monetary Dynamics of Hyperinflation," in Milton Friedman (editor), *Studies in the Quantity Theory of Money,* University of Chicago Press, 1956.

EYE on INFLATION

What Causes Inflation?

According to the quantity theory of money, whether we face a future with inflation, deflation, or a stable price level depends entirely on the rate at which the Fed permits the quantity of money to grow.

But is the quantity theory correct? Does it explain our past inflation with enough accuracy to be a guide to future inflation?

The quantity theory does not predict the year-to-year changes in the inflation rate. The quantity theory does an especially bad job of explaining 2008 and 2009 because in those years, the velocity of circulation tumbled.

But on average, over a number of years, the quantity theory is a remarkably accurate predictor of the inflation rate. The figure shows that the quantity theory explains our past decade-average inflation rates.

During the 1960s, 1970s, and 1980s, the velocity of circulation (of M2) was constant. The growth rate of real GDP slowed from the fast-expanding 1960s to a more moderate pace during the 1970s and 1980s. The growth rate of the quantity of M2 increased in the 1970s and slowed in the 1980s, and the inflation rate moved in line with the changed money growth rate— exactly as predicted by the quantity theory of money.

During the 1990s, the M2 growth rate slowed again but the velocity of circulation increased. With the real GDP growth rate unchanged, the inflation rate fell.

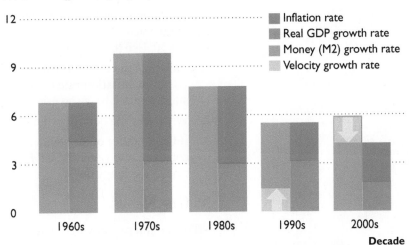

Growth rate (percent per year)

Legend:
- Inflation rate
- Real GDP growth rate
- Money (M2) growth rate
- Velocity growth rate

SOURCE OF DATA: Federal Reserve and Bureau of Economic Analysis.

The 2000s saw the M2 growth rate increase but the velocity of circulation shrank at a similar rate to that at which it had grown during the 1990s. Inflation remained close to its level in the previous decade, but real GDP growth slowed.

Aside from the small changes in velocity growth during the 1990s and 2000s, which cancelled each other out, all the decade-by-decade variation in the inflation rate has resulted from changes in the growth rate of the quantity of money.

To predict our future decade-average inflation rates, we must predict the future growth rate of money.

The Fed is able to influence the inflation rate and the money growth rate and, absent any pressures that the Fed finds impossible to resist, we can expect the Fed to do a good job of keeping inflation in check. That doesn't mean zero inflation. It means an inflation rate running at around 2 percent per year.

Will the Fed face irresistible pressure to create money too rapidly or too slowly? It is unlikely that pressure will force the Fed to shrink the quantity of money and generate deflation.

But there could be pressure in the opposite direction. Inflation is a tax. If the Fed creates money by buying government bonds, the government gets revenue just like it gets tax revenue.

With a large and long-lasting federal budget deficit, Congress might be tempted to lean on the Fed to keep interest rates down. If Congress were successful in such a move, the result would be money creation at too rapid a pace and an outbreak of inflation.

MyEconLab Study Plan 12.2
Key Terms Quiz
Solutions

 CHECKPOINT 12.2

Explain how in the long run, the quantity of money determines the price level and money growth brings inflation.

Practice Problems

In 1999, the Canadian economy was at full employment. Real GDP was $886 billion, the nominal interest rate was around 6 percent a year, the inflation rate was 2 percent a year, the price level was 1.1, and the velocity of circulation was constant at 10. Use this data to work Problems **1** and **2**.

1. Calculate the real interest rate. If the real interest rate remains unchanged when the inflation rate increases to 4 percent a year and then remains constant, explain how the nominal interest rate changes in the long run.

2. What was the quantity of money in Canada?

3. If the quantity of money grows at 10 percent a year, velocity of circulation is constant, and potential GDP grows at 3 percent a year, what is the inflation rate in the long run?

In the News

"The U.S. can pay any debt because we can always print more money."

Source: Alan Greenspan, *Meet the Press*, August 7, 2011

Explain why "always printing money" will "pay off the debt."

Solutions to Practice Problems

1. The real interest rate equals the nominal interest rate minus the inflation rate. That is, the real interest rate equals 6 percent a year minus 2 percent a year, which equals 4 percent a year. If inflation increases to 4 percent a year, then the nominal interest rate rises from 6 percent a year to 8 percent a year.

2. The quantity of money was $97.5 billion.

   Velocity of circulation (V) = Nominal GDP $(P \times Y)$ ÷ Quantity of money (M). Rewrite this equation as: $M = (P \times Y) \div V$
   $(P \times Y) = 1.1 \times \$886$ billion, or $975 billion, so $M = \$975$ billion ÷ 10, or $97.5 billion.

3. With velocity constant, velocity growth is zero. So the inflation rate in the long run equals the money growth rate minus the real GDP growth rate, which is 10 percent a year minus 3 percent a year, or 7 percent a year.

Solution to In the News

"Printing money" means the Fed increases the quantity of money by buying government bonds. This transaction doesn't "pay off the debt." It merely transfers the debt to the Fed. But at full employment and a given velocity of circulation, when the Fed increases the quantity of money, the price level rises (the quantity theory of money). The higher price level means that the real value of the government debt falls. That is how "printing money" ends up "paying off the debt."

12.3 THE COST OF INFLATION

Inflation decreases potential GDP, slows economic growth, and consumes leisure time. These outcomes occur for four reasons that we classify as the four costs of inflation:

- Tax costs
- Shoe-leather costs
- Confusion costs
- Uncertainty costs

■ Tax Costs

We've seen that inflation occurs when the quantity of money grows more rapidly than real GDP. But why would we ever want to make this happen? Why don't we keep the quantity of money growing at the same pace as real GDP grows? One part of the answer is that the government gets revenue from inflation.

Inflation Is a Tax

A government can pay its expenses with newly created money. But the things a government buys with this money aren't free. They are paid for by people and businesses in proportion to the amount of money they hold—by a tax on money holding that we call the inflation tax.

When the government spends newly created money, the quantity of money increases and, as predicted by the quantity theory, the price level rises. The inflation rate equals the growth rate of the quantity of money (other things remaining the same).

To see how the inflation tax gets paid, suppose that the Coca-Cola Company is holding $110,000 in money. The annual inflation rate is 10 percent, and the price level rises from 1.0 to 1.1. At the end of the year, Coca-Cola's money will buy only $100,000 of goods and services ($110,000 ÷ 1.1 = $100,000). The firm has lost $10,000—it has "paid" a $10,000 inflation tax.

Governments in today's world don't create new money by printing it. Money gets created when the central bank buys government bonds. In the United States, the Fed doesn't buy bonds directly from the government: it buys them in open market operations. When the Fed buys bonds, the monetary base increases and through the money multiplier, the quantity of money increases. The Fed pays its profits to the government, so the government ends up paying no interest on its bonds held by the Fed. By this process, the government prints money.

Inflation, Saving, and Investment

The income tax on interest income drives a wedge between the before-tax interest rate paid by borrowers and the after-tax interest rate received by lenders. A rise in the income tax rate increases the before-tax interest rate and decreases the after-tax interest rate. The increase in the before-tax interest rate decreases borrowing and investment, and the decrease in the after-tax interest rate decreases lending and saving.

An increase in the inflation rate increases the true tax rate on interest income, and strengthens the effect that we have just described. To see why, let's consider an example.

Suppose that the real interest rate is 4 percent a year and the income tax rate is 50 percent. With no inflation, the nominal interest rate is also 4 percent a year and the real after-tax interest rate is 2 percent a year (50 percent of 4 percent).

Now suppose the inflation rate rises to 4 percent a year, so the nominal interest rate rises to 8 percent a year. The after-tax nominal interest rate rises to 4 percent a year (50 percent of 8 percent). Subtract the 4 percent inflation rate from this amount, and you see that the after-tax real interest rate is zero! The true income tax rate has increased to 100 percent.

The fall in the after-tax real interest rate weakens the incentive to lend and save and the rise in the before-tax interest rate weakens the incentive to borrow and invest. With a fall in saving and investment, the rates of capital accumulation and real GDP growth slow down.

■ Shoe-Leather Costs

The "shoe-leather costs" of inflation are costs that arise from an increase in the velocity of circulation of money and an increase in the amount of running around that people do to try to avoid incurring losses from the falling value of money.

When money loses value at a rapid anticipated rate, it does not function well as a store of value and people try to avoid holding it. They spend their incomes as soon as they receive them, and firms pay out incomes—wages and dividends—as soon as they receive revenue from their sales. The velocity of circulation increases.

During the 1990s when inflation in Brazil was around 80 percent a year, people would end a taxi ride at the ATM closest to their destination, get some cash, pay the driver, and finish their journey on foot. The driver would deposit the cash in his bank account before looking for the next customer.

During the 1920s when inflation in Germany exceeded 50 percent a month—hyperinflation—wages were paid and spent twice in a single day!

Imagine the inconvenience of spending most of your time figuring out how to keep your money holdings close to zero.

One way of keeping money holdings low is to find other means of payment such as tokens, commodities, or even barter. All of these are less efficient than money as a means of payment. For example, in Israel during the 1980s, when inflation reached 1,000 percent a year, the U.S. dollar started to replace the increasingly worthless shekel. Consequently, people had to keep track of the exchange rate between the shekel and the dollar hour by hour and had to engage in many additional and costly transactions in the foreign exchange market.

■ Confusion Costs

We make economic decisions by comparing marginal cost and marginal benefit. Marginal cost is a real cost—an opportunity forgone. Marginal benefit is a real benefit—a willingness to forgo an opportunity. Although costs and benefits are real, we use money as our unit of account and standard of value to calculate them. Money is our measuring rod of value. Borrowers and lenders, workers and employers, all make agreements in terms of money. Inflation makes the value of money change, so it changes the units on our measuring rod.

Does it matter that our units of value keep changing? Some economists think it matters a lot. Others think it matters only a little.

Economists who think it matters a lot point to the obvious benefits of stable units of measurement in other areas of life. For example, suppose that we had not invented an accurate time-keeping technology and clocks and watches gained 5 to

15 minutes a day. Imagine the hassle you would have arriving at class on time or catching the start of the ball game. For another example, suppose that a tailor used an elastic tape measure. You would end up with a jacket that was either too tight or too loose, depending on how tightly the tape was stretched.

For a third example, recall the crash of the Mars Climate Orbiter.

> Mars Climate Orbiter...failed to achieve Mars orbit because of a navigation error....Spacecraft operating data needed for navigation were provided...in English units rather than the specified metric units. This was the direct cause of the failure. (Mars Program Independent Assessment Team Summary Report, March 14, 2000)

If rocket scientists can't make correct calculations that use just two units of measurement, what chance do ordinary people and business decision makers have of making correct calculations that involve money when its value keeps changing?

These examples of confusion and error that can arise from units of measurement don't automatically mean that a changing value of money is a big problem. But they raise the possibility that it might be.

■ Uncertainty Costs

A high inflation rate brings increased uncertainty about the long-term inflation rate. Will inflation remain high for a long time or will price stability be restored? This increased uncertainty makes long-term planning difficult and gives people a shorter-term focus. Investment falls, and so the economic growth rate slows.

But this increased uncertainty also misallocates resources. Instead of concentrating on the activities at which they have a comparative advantage, people find it more profitable to search for ways of avoiding the losses that inflation inflicts. As a result, inventive talent that might otherwise work on productive innovations works on finding ways of profiting from the inflation instead.

Uncertainty about inflation makes the economy behave a bit like a casino in which some people gain and some lose and no one can predict where the gains and losses will fall. Gains and losses occur because of unpredictable changes in the value of money. In a period of rapid, unpredictable inflation, resources get diverted from productive activities to forecasting inflation. It becomes more profitable to forecast the inflation rate correctly than to invent a new product. Doctors, lawyers, accountants, farmers—just about everyone—can make themselves better off, not by specializing in the profession for which they have been trained but by spending more of their time dabbling as amateur economists and inflation forecasters and managing their investment portfolios.

From a social perspective, this diversion of talent resulting from uncertainty about inflation is like throwing scarce resources onto the garbage heap. This waste of resources is a cost of inflation.

■ How Big Is the Cost of Inflation?

The cost of inflation depends on its rate and its predictability. The higher the inflation rate, the greater is the cost. And the more unpredictable the inflation rate, the greater is the cost. Peter Howitt of Brown University, building on work by Robert Barro of Harvard University, has estimated that if inflation is lowered from 3 percent a year to zero, the growth rate of real GDP will rise by between 0.06 and 0.09 percentage points a year. These numbers might seem small, but they are growth rates. After 30 years, real GDP would be 2.3 percent higher and the accumulated value of all the additional future output would be worth 85 percent of current GDP, or $11.7 trillion!

In hyperinflation, the costs are much greater. Hyperinflation is rare, but there have been some spectacular examples of it. Several European countries experienced hyperinflation during the 1920s after World War I and again during the 1940s after World War II. In these examples the costs of inflation were enormous.

Hyperinflation is more than just a historical curiosity. It has occurred in the recent past. In 1994, the African nation of Zaire had a hyperinflation that peaked at a monthly inflation rate of 76 percent. Also in 1994, Brazil almost reached the hyperinflation stratosphere with a monthly inflation rate of 40 percent. A cup of coffee that cost 15 cruzeiros in 1980 cost 22 billion cruzeiros in 1994. Between 1989 and 1994, Russia experienced a near hyperinflation.

The most spectacular recent hyperinflation was in Zimbabwe, which peaked at 231,150,888.87 percent per year. At that point, the monetary system collapsed, the Zimbabwe dollar was taken out of circulation and replaced by the U.S. dollar, and economic life was at a near standstill.

MyEconLab Study Plan 12.3

Solutions

 # CHECKPOINT 12.3

Identify the costs of inflation and the benefits of a stable value of money.

Practice Problems

1. Ben has $1,000 in his savings account and the bank pays an interest rate of 5 percent a year. The inflation rate is 3 percent a year. The government taxes the interest that Ben earns on his deposit at 20 percent. Calculate the after-tax nominal interest rate and the after-tax real interest rate that Ben earns.

2. **Inflation-adjusted savings bonds hit 0% rate**
    Inflation-adjusted savings bonds purchased from May through October 2009 will earn 0% for the first six months. The fixed interest rate on these bonds is 0.1% and over the previous 6 months, inflation fell at an annual rate of 5.56%. The minimum interest rate on savings bonds is set at 0%.

    Source: *USA Today*, May 5, 2009

    Are these savings bonds a better deal than cash under the mattress?

Solutions to Practice Problems

1. Ben's interest income equals 5 percent of $1,000, which is $50. The government takes $10 of his $50 of interest in tax, so the interest income Ben earns after tax is $40. The after-tax nominal interest rate is ($40 ÷ $1,000) × 100, which equals 4 percent a year.
    The after-tax real interest rate equals the after-tax nominal interest rate minus the inflation rate. The after-tax nominal interest rate is 4 percent a year. So the after-tax real interest rate equals 4 percent a year minus the inflation rate of 3 percent a year, which is 1 percent a year.

2. At 0 percent interest rate, these bonds are just as good a deal as cash under the mattress, but if inflation starts to rise as the economy recovers from recession, the nominal interest rate will exceed 0.1 percent but the real interest rate will be certain and equal 0.1 percent a year—a better deal than cash.

CHAPTER SUMMARY

Key Points

1. **Explain what determines the demand for money and how the demand for money and the supply of money determine the *nominal* interest rate.**

   - The demand for money is the relationship between the quantity of money demanded and the nominal interest rate, other things remaining the same. The higher the nominal interest rate, other things remaining the same, the smaller is the quantity of money demanded.
   - Increases in real GDP increase the demand for money. Some advances in financial technology increase the demand for money, and some advances decrease it.
   - Each day, the price level, real GDP, and financial technology are given and money market equilibrium determines the nominal interest rate.
   - To lower the interest rate, the Fed increases the supply of money. To raise the interest rate, the Fed decreases the supply of money.

2. **Explain how in the long run, the quantity of money determines the price level and money growth brings inflation.**

   - In the long run, real GDP equals potential GDP and the real interest rate is the level that makes the quantity of loanable funds demanded equal the quantity of loanable funds supplied in the global financial market.
   - The nominal interest rate in the long run equals the equilibrium real interest rate plus the inflation rate.
   - Money market equilibrium in the long run determines the price level.
   - An increase in the quantity of money, other things remaining the same, increases the price level by the same percentage.
   - The inflation rate in the long run equals the growth rate of the quantity of money minus the growth rate of potential GDP.
   - The equation of exchange and the velocity of circulation provide an alternative way of viewing the relationship between the quantity of money and the price level (and money growth and inflation).

3. **Identify the costs of inflation and the benefits of a stable value of money.**

   - Inflation has four costs: tax costs, shoe-leather costs, confusion costs, and uncertainty costs.
   - The higher the inflation rate, the greater are these four costs.

Key Terms

MyEconLab Key Terms Quiz

Demand for money, 298
Equation of exchange, 309
Hyperinflation, 312
Quantity of money demanded, 297

Quantity theory of money, 308
Supply of money, 300
Velocity of circulation, 308

CHAPTER CHECKPOINT

Study Plan Problems and Applications

1. Draw a graph to illustrate the demand for money. On the graph show the effect of an increase in real GDP and the effect of an increase in the number of families that have a credit card.

2. If the Fed makes a decision to cut the quantity of money, explain the short-run effects on the quantity of money demanded and the nominal interest rate.

3. The Fed conducts an open market purchase of securities. Explain the effects of this action on the nominal interest rate in the short run and the value of money in the long run.

In 2007, the United States was at full employment. The quantity of money was growing at 6.4 percent a year, the nominal interest rate was 4.4 percent a year, real GDP grew at 1.9 percent a year, and the inflation rate was 2.9 percent a year. Use this information to work Problems 4 and 5.

4. Calculate the real interest rate.

5. Was the velocity of circulation constant? (Hint: Use the quantity theory of money.) If velocity of circulation was not constant, how did it change and why might it have changed?

6. If the quantity of money is $3 trillion, real GDP is $10 trillion, the price level is 0.9, the real interest rate is 2 percent a year, and the nominal interest rate is 7 percent a year, calculate the velocity of circulation, the value of $M \times V$, and nominal GDP.

7. If the velocity of circulation is growing at 1 percent a year, the real interest rate is 2 percent a year, the nominal interest rate is 7 percent a year, and the growth rate of real GDP is 3 percent a year, calculate the inflation rate, the growth rate of money, and the growth rate of nominal GDP.

8. Suppose that the government passes a new law that sets a limit on the interest rate that credit card companies can charge on overdue balances. As a result, the nominal interest rate charged by credit card companies falls from 15 percent a year to 7 percent a year. If the average income tax rate is 30 percent, explain how the after-tax real interest rate on overdue credit card balances changes.

Zimbabwe inflation eases

Zimbabwe's inflation rate in July 2009 was 1 percent a month. Last year, its annual inflation rate was more than 231,000,000%, a kilo of tomatoes cost 61 billion Zimbabwe dollars, and the shelves in stores were almost empty. Now the Zimbabwean dollar has disappeared, the U.S. dollar is king, and the shelves and aisles of stores are full. Although no annual inflation rate is reported, the indication is that Zimbabwe is recovering from hyperinflation.

Source: BBC News, September 16, 2009

9. What is hyperinflation? Compare inflation in Zimbabwe in 2009 with that in Germany in 1923. Why did Germany print money in 1923 and create hyperinflation? Why is Zimbabwe printing less money today?

10. Read *Eye on Inflation* on p. 313. Why did inflation increase during the 1970s? In which decades did velocity growth break the link between money growth and inflation?

Instructor Assignable Problems and Applications

1. Explain what causes inflation. Why is it easier to predict the decade-average inflation rate than the inflation rate in a single year?

2. If the Fed doubled the quantity of money and nothing else changed, what would happen to the price level in the short run and the long run? What would happen to the inflation rate?

3. Suppose that banks launch an aggressive marketing campaign to get everyone to use debit cards for every conceivable transaction. They offer prizes to new debit card holders and introduce a charge on using a credit card. How would the demand for money and the nominal interest rate change?

4. Draw a graph of the money market to illustrate equilibrium in the short run. If the growth rate of the quantity of money increases, explain what happens to the real interest rate and the nominal interest rate in the short run.

5. The Fed conducts an open market sale of securities. Explain the effects of this action in the short run on the nominal interest rate and in the long run on the value of money and the price level.

6. What is the quantity theory of money? Define the velocity of circulation and explain how it is measured.

7. If the velocity of circulation is constant, real GDP is growing at 3 percent a year, the real interest rate is 2 percent a year, and the nominal interest rate is 7 percent a year, calculate the inflation rate, the growth rate of money, and the growth rate of nominal GDP.

8. Sara has $200 in currency and $2,000 in a bank account on which the bank pays no interest. The inflation rate is 2 percent a year. Calculate the amount of inflation tax that Sara pays in a year.

Use the following information to work Problems 9 to 12.

The Fed's $2.2 trillion fire hose
The Fed threw a lot of money at the financial crisis in 2008 to unfreeze credit markets and encourage economic activity. As part of its effort to keep the interest rate low, the Fed purchased government bonds worth $300 billion during 2009. By October, the Fed held $770 billion in government securities, nearly double its pre-crisis total. Before the crisis, the Fed held mainly government securities, which it used to control the quantity of money in the economy. Now government securities make up just 35% of the Fed's balance sheet.

Source: CNN Money, October 9, 2009

9. If government securities make up just 35 percent of the Fed's assets, calculate the Fed's total assets. What effect did the Fed's purchase of $300 billion of government bonds have on the Fed's total liabilities?

10. If the Fed purchased the government securities on the open market, explain why the purchase of $300 billion of government securities would influence the interest rate.

11. As the Fed purchased $300 billion of government securities, did the price of government securities fall or rise? Explain your answer.

12. Explain how the Fed uses its government securities to control the nominal interest rate.

MyEconLab Chapter 12 Study Plan

Multiple Choice Quiz

1. Holding money provides a benefit _____.
   A. because it is a means of payment
   B. because its opportunity cost is low
   C. which is constant no matter how much money is held
   D. because most money is in bank deposits

2. The opportunity cost of holding money _____.
   A. is determined by the inflation rate
   B. is zero because money earns no interest
   C. equals the nominal interest rate on bonds
   D. equals the real interest rate on bonds

3. The quantity of money demanded increases if _____.
   A. the supply of money increases
   B. the nominal interest rate falls
   C. banks increase the interest rate on deposits
   D. the price of a bond falls

4. If the Fed increases the quantity of money, people will be holding _____.
   A. too much money, so they buy bonds and the interest rate rises
   B. too much money, so they buy bonds and the interest rate falls
   C. the quantity of money they demand and banks will hold more money
   D. more money and will increase their demand for money

5. In the long run, money market equilibrium determines the _____.
   A. real interest rate
   B. price level
   C. nominal interest rate
   D. economic growth rate

6. If the quantity theory of money is correct and other things remain the same, an increase in the quantity of money increases _____.
   A. nominal GDP and the velocity of circulation
   B. the price level and potential GDP
   C. real GDP
   D. nominal GDP and the price level

7. In the long run with a constant velocity of circulation, the inflation rate _____.
   A. is constant and equals the money growth rate
   B. equals the money growth rate minus the growth rate of real GDP
   C. equals the growth rate of real GDP minus the growth rate of money
   D. is positive if the economic growth rate is positive

8. The costs of inflation do *not* include _____.
   A. the cost of running around to compare prices at different outlets
   B. the increased opportunity cost of holding money
   C. the tax on money held by individuals and businesses
   D. an increase in saving and investment

Why did the U.S. economy
go into recession in 2008?

Aggregate Supply and Aggregate Demand

13

When you have completed your study of this chapter,
you will be able to

CHAPTER CHECKLIST

1 Define and explain the influences on aggregate supply.

2 Define and explain the influences on aggregate demand.

3 Explain how trends and fluctuations in aggregate demand and
aggregate supply bring economic growth, inflation, and the business cycle.

MyEconLab Big Picture

13.1 AGGREGATE SUPPLY

The purpose of the aggregate supply–aggregate demand model is to explain how real GDP and the price level are determined. The model uses similar ideas to those that you encountered in Chapter 4 where you learned how the quantity and price are determined in a competitive market. But the *aggregate* supply–*aggregate* demand model (*AS-AD* model) isn't just an application of the competitive market model. Some differences arise because the *AS-AD* model is a model of an imaginary market for the total of all the final goods and services that make up real GDP. The quantity in this "market" is real GDP and the price is the price level measured by the GDP price index.

The *quantity of real GDP supplied* is the total amount of final goods and services that firms in the United States plan to produce and it depends on the quantities of

- Labor employed
- Capital, human capital, and the state of technology
- Land and natural resources
- Entrepreneurial talent

You saw in Chapter 8 that at full employment, real GDP equals *potential GDP*. The quantities of land, capital and human capital, the state of technology, and the amount of entrepreneurial talent are fixed. Labor market equilibrium determines the quantity of labor employed, which is equal to the quantity of labor demanded and the quantity of labor supplied at the equilibrium real wage rate.

Over the business cycle, real GDP fluctuates around potential GDP because the quantity of labor employed fluctuates around its full employment level. The aggregate supply–aggregate demand model explains these fluctuations.

We begin on the supply side with the basics of aggregate supply.

■ Aggregate Supply Basics

Aggregate supply
The relationship between the quantity of real GDP supplied and the price level when all other influences on production plans remain the same.

Aggregate supply is the relationship between the quantity of real GDP supplied and the price level when all other influences on production plans remain the same. This relationship can be described as follows:

Other things remaining the same, the higher the price level, the greater is the quantity of real GDP supplied, and the lower the price level, the smaller is the quantity of real GDP supplied.

Figure 13.1 illustrates aggregate supply as an aggregate supply schedule and aggregate supply curve. The aggregate supply schedule lists the quantities of real GDP supplied at each price level, and the upward-sloping *AS* curve graphs these points.

The figure also shows potential GDP: $16 trillion in the figure. When the price level is 105, the quantity of real GDP supplied is $16 trillion, which equals potential GDP (at point *C* on the *AS* curve).

Along the aggregate supply curve, the price level is the only influence on production plans that changes. A rise in the price level brings an increase in the quantity of real GDP supplied and a movement up along the aggregate supply curve; a fall in the price level brings a decrease in the quantity of real GDP supplied and a movement down along the aggregate supply curve.

FIGURE 13.1

Aggregate Supply Schedule and Aggregate Supply Curve

MyEconLab Real-time data

Price level (GDP price index, 2009 = 100)	Quantity of real GDP supplied (trillions of 2009 dollars)
E	115	17.0
D	110	16.5
C	105	16.0
B	100	15.5
A	95	15.0

The aggregate supply schedule and aggregate supply curve, AS, show the relationship between the quantity of real GDP supplied and the price level when all other influences on production plans remain the same. Each point A through E on the AS curve corresponds to the row identified by the same letter in the schedule.

❶ Potential GDP is $16 trillion, and when the price level is 105, real GDP equals potential GDP.

❷ If the price level is above 105, real GDP exceeds potential GDP.

❸ If the price level is below 105, real GDP is less than potential GDP.

Among the other influences on production plans that remain constant along the *AS* curve are

- The money wage rate
- The money prices of other resources

In contrast, along the potential GDP line, when the price level changes, the money wage rate and the money prices of other resources change by the same percentage as the change in the price level to keep the real wage rate (and other real prices) at the full-employment equilibrium level.

Why the *AS* Curve Slopes Upward

Why does the quantity of real GDP supplied increase when the price level rises and decrease when the price level falls? The answer is that a movement along the *AS* curve brings a change in the real wage rate (and changes in the real cost of other resources whose money prices are fixed). If the price level rises, the real wage rate falls, and if the price level falls, the real wage rate rises. When the real wage rate changes, firms change the quantity of labor employed and the level of production.

Think about a concrete example. A ketchup producer has a contract with its workers to pay them $20 an hour. The firm sells ketchup for $1 a bottle. The real wage rate of a ketchup bottling worker is 20 bottles of ketchup. That is, the firm must sell 20 bottles of ketchup to buy one hour of labor. Now suppose the price of ketchup falls to 50 cents a bottle. The real wage rate of a bottling worker has increased to 40 bottles—the firm must now sell 40 bottles of ketchup to buy one hour of labor.

If the price of a bottle of ketchup increased, the real wage rate of a bottling worker would fall. For example, if the price increased to $2 a bottle, the real wage rate would be 10 bottles per worker—the firm needs to sell only 10 bottles of ketchup to buy one hour of labor.

Firms respond to a change in the real wage rate by changing the quantity of labor employed and the quantity produced. For the economy as a whole, employment and real GDP change. There are three ways in which these changes occur:

- Firms change their output rate.
- Firms shut down temporarily or restart production.
- Firms go out of business or start up in business.

Change in Output Rate

To change its output rate, a firm must change the quantity of labor that it employs. It is profitable to hire more labor if the additional labor costs less than the revenue it generates. If the price level rises and the money wage rate doesn't change, an extra hour of labor that was previously unprofitable becomes profitable. So when the price level rises and the money wage rate doesn't change, the quantity of labor demanded and production increase. If the price level falls and the money wage rate doesn't change, an hour of labor that was previously profitable becomes unprofitable. So when the price level falls and the money wage rate doesn't change, the quantity of labor demanded and production decrease.

Temporary Shutdowns and Restarts

A firm that is incurring a loss might foresee a profit in the future. Such a firm might decide to shut down temporarily and lay off its workers.

The price level relative to the money wage rate influences temporary shutdown decisions. If the price level rises relative to wages, fewer firms decide to shut down temporarily; so more firms operate and the quantity of real GDP supplied increases. If the price level falls relative to wages, a larger number of firms find that they cannot earn enough revenue to pay the wage bill and so temporarily shut down. The quantity of real GDP supplied decreases.

Business Failure and Startup

People create businesses in the hope of earning a profit. When profits are squeezed or when losses arise, more firms fail, fewer new firms start up, and the number of firms decreases. When profits are generally high, fewer firms fail, more firms start up, and the number of firms increases.

The price level relative to the money wage rate influences the number of firms in business. If the price level rises relative to wages, profits increase, the number of firms in business increases, and the quantity of real GDP supplied increases. If the price level falls relative to wages, profits fall, the number of firms in business decreases, and the quantity of real GDP supplied decreases.

In a severe recession, business failure can be contagious. The failure of one firm puts pressure on both its suppliers and its customers and can bring a flood of failures and a large decrease in the quantity of real GDP supplied.

■ Changes in Aggregate Supply

Aggregate supply changes when any influence on production plans other than the price level changes. In particular, aggregate supply changes when

- Potential GDP changes.
- The money wage rate changes.
- The money prices of other resources change.

Change in Potential GDP

Anything that changes potential GDP changes aggregate supply and shifts the aggregate supply curve. Figure 13.2 illustrates such a shift. You can think of point C as an anchor point. The AS curve and potential GDP line are anchored at this point, and when potential GDP changes, aggregate supply changes along with it. When potential GDP increases from $16 trillion to $17 trillion, point C shifts to point C', and the AS curve and potential GDP line shift rightward together. The AS curve shifts from AS_0 to AS_1.

Change in Money Wage Rate

A change in the money wage rate changes aggregate supply because it changes firms' costs. The higher the money wage rate, the higher are firms' costs and the smaller is the quantity that firms are willing to supply at each price level. So an increase in the money wage rate decreases aggregate supply.

■ FIGURE 13.2

An Increase in Potential GDP

MyEconLab Real-time data

❶ An increase in potential GDP increases aggregate supply.

❷ When potential GDP increases from $16 trillion to $17 trillion, the aggregate supply curve shifts rightward from AS_0 to AS_1.

Suppose that the money wage rate is $52.50 an hour and the price level is 105. Then the real wage rate is $50 an hour ($52.50 × 100 ÷ 105 = $50)—see Chapter 7, p. 180. If the full-employment equilibrium real wage rate is $50 an hour, the economy is at full employment and real GDP equals potential GDP. In Figure 13.3, the economy is at point C on the aggregate supply curve AS_0. The money wage rate is $52.50 an hour at all points on AS_0.

Now suppose the money wage rate rises to $57.50 an hour but the full-employment equilibrium real wage rate remains at $50 an hour. Real GDP now equals potential GDP when the price level is 115, at point D on the aggregate supply curve AS_2. (If the money wage rate is $57.50 an hour and the price level is 115, the real wage rate is $57.50 × 100 ÷ 115 = $50 an hour.) The money wage rate is $57.50 an hour at all points on AS_2. The rise in the money wage rate *decreases* aggregate supply and shifts the aggregate supply curve leftward from AS_0 to AS_2.

A change in the money wage rate does not change potential GDP. The reason is that potential GDP depends only on the economy's real ability to produce and on the full-employment quantity of labor, which occurs at the equilibrium *real* wage rate. The equilibrium real wage rate can occur at any money wage rate.

Change in Money Prices of Other Resources

A change in the money prices of other resources has a similar effect on firms' production plans to a change in the money wage rate. It changes firms' costs. At each price level, firms' real costs change and the quantity that firms are willing to supply changes so aggregate supply changes.

FIGURE 13.3

A Change in the Money Wage Rate

MyEconLab Animation

A rise in the money wage rate decreases aggregate supply. The aggregate supply curve shifts leftward from AS_0 to AS_2. A rise in the money wage rate does not change potential GDP.

CHECKPOINT 13.1

MyEconLab Study Plan 13.1
Key Terms Quiz
Solutions

Define and explain the influences on aggregate supply.

Practice Problem

1. Explain the influence of each of the events in List 1 on the quantity of real GDP supplied and aggregate supply in India and use a graph to illustrate.

In the News

Eight states to hike minimum wage
The state minimum wage is will rise by up to 37 cents an hour or $770 a year for a full-time worker, in Colorado, Montana, Ohio, Oregon, and Washington. Three other states, Arizona, Florida, and Vermont, are believed to be planning similar increases.

Source: CNN Money, October 3, 2011

Explain how the rise in the minimum wage will influence aggregate supply.

LIST 1

- Fuel prices rise.
- U.S. firms move their IT and data functions to India.
- Wal-Mart and Starbucks open in India.
- Universities in India increase the number of engineering graduates.
- The money wage rate in India rises.
- The price level in India rises.

Solution to Practice Problem

1. As fuel prices rise, the quantity of real GDP supplied at the current price level decreases. The *AS* curve shifts leftward (Figure 1).

   As U.S. firms move their IT and data functions to India, real GDP supplied at the current price level increases. The *AS* curve shifts rightward (Figure 2).

   As Wal-Mart and Starbucks open, the quantity of real GDP supplied at the current price level increases. The *AS* curve shifts rightward (Figure 2).

   With more graduates, the number of skilled workers increases, and production increases at the current price level. The *AS* curve shifts rightward (Figure 2).

   As the money wage rate rises, firms' costs increase and the quantity of real GDP supplied at the current price level decreases. The *AS* curve shifts leftward (Figure 1).

   As the price level increases, other things remaining the same, businesses become more profitable and increase the quantity of real GDP supplied along the *AS* curve (Figure 3). The *AS* curve does not shift.

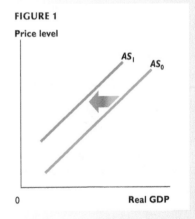
FIGURE 1

Solution to In the News

The rise in the money wage rate at the current price level increases the real wage rate and decreases aggregate supply. If the rise in the minimum wage increases the natural unemployment rate, potential GDP decreases and aggregate supply decreases further.

FIGURE 2

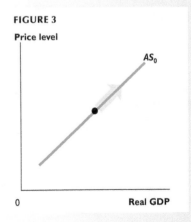
FIGURE 3

13.2 AGGREGATE DEMAND

The *quantity of real GDP demanded* (Y) is the total amount of final goods and services produced in the United States that people, businesses, governments, and foreigners plan to buy. This quantity is the sum of the real consumption expenditure (C), investment (I), government expenditure on goods and services (G), and exports (X) minus imports (M). That is,

$$Y = C + I + G + X - M.$$

Many factors influence expenditure plans. To study aggregate demand, we divide those factors into two parts: the price level and everything else. We'll first consider the influence of the price level on expenditure plans and then consider the other influences.

■ Aggregate Demand Basics

Aggregate demand
The relationship between the quantity of real GDP demanded and the price level when all other influences on expenditure plans remain the same.

Aggregate demand is the relationship between the quantity of real GDP demanded and the price level when all other influences on expenditure plans remain the same. This relationship can be described as follows:

Other things remaining the same, the higher the price level, the smaller is the quantity of real GDP demanded; and the lower the price level, the greater is the quantity of real GDP demanded.

Figure 13.4 illustrates aggregate demand by using an aggregate demand schedule and aggregate demand curve. The aggregate demand schedule lists the quantities of real GDP demanded at each price level, and the downward-sloping *AD* curve graphs these points.

Along the aggregate demand curve, the only influence on expenditure plans that changes is the price level. A rise in the price level decreases the quantity of real GDP demanded and brings a movement up along the aggregate demand curve; a fall in the price level increases the quantity of real GDP demanded and brings a movement down along the aggregate demand curve.

The price level influences the quantity of real GDP demanded because a change in the price level brings a change in

- The buying power of money
- The real interest rate
- The real prices of exports and imports

The Buying Power of Money

A rise in the price level lowers the buying power of money and decreases the quantity of real GDP demanded. To see why, think about the buying plans in two economies—Russia and Japan—where the price level has changed a lot in recent years.

Anna lives in Moscow, Russia. She has worked hard all summer and has saved 20,000 rubles (the ruble is the currency of Russia), which she plans to spend attending graduate school after she has earned her economics degree. So Anna's money holding is 20,000 rubles. Anna has a part-time job, and her income from this job pays her expenses. The price level in Russia rises by 100 percent. Anna needs 40,000 rubles to buy what 20,000 rubles once bought. To make up some of the fall in the buying power of her money, Anna slashes her spending.

FIGURE 13.4

Aggregate Demand Schedule and Aggregate Demand Curve

MyEconLab Animation

	Price level (GDP price index, 2009 = 100)	Quantity of real GDP demanded (trillions of 2009 dollars)
A	125	15.0
B	115	15.5
C	105	16.0
D	95	16.5
E	85	17.0

Price level (GDP price index, 2009 = 100)

① A rise in the price level decreases the quantity of real GDP demanded

② A fall in the price level increases the quantity of real GDP demanded

AD

Real GDP (trillions of 2009 dollars)

The aggregate demand schedule and aggregate demand curve, AD, show the relationship between the quantity of real GDP demanded and the price level when all other influences on expenditure plans remain the same. Each point A through E on the AD curve corresponds to the row identified by the same letter in the schedule.

The quantity of real GDP demanded

① decreases when the price level rises and

② increases when the price level falls.

Similarly, a fall in the price level, other things remaining the same, brings an increase in the quantity of real GDP demanded. To see why, think about the buying plans of Mika, who lives in Tokyo, Japan. She too has worked hard all summer and has saved 200,000 yen (the yen is the currency of Japan), which she plans to spend attending school next year. The price level in Japan falls by 10 percent; now Mika needs only 180,000 yen to buy what 200,000 yen once bought. With a rise in what her money buys, Mika decides to buy a DVD player.

The Real Interest Rate

When the price level rises, the real interest rate rises. You saw in Chapter 12 (p. 229) that an increase in the price level increases the amount of money that people want to hold—increases the demand for money. When the demand for money increases, the nominal interest rate rises. In the short run, the inflation rate does not change, so a rise in the nominal interest rate brings a rise in the real interest rate. Faced with a higher real interest rate, businesses and people delay plans to buy new capital and consumer durable goods and they cut back on spending. As the price level rises, the quantity of real GDP demanded decreases.

Anna and Mika Again Think about Anna and Mika again. Both of them want to buy a computer. In Moscow, a rise in the price level increases the demand for money and raises the real interest rate. At a real interest rate of 5 percent a year,

Anna was willing to borrow to buy the new computer. But at a real interest rate of 10 percent a year, she decides that the payments would be too high, so she delays buying it. The rise in the price level decreases the quantity of real GDP demanded.

In Tokyo, a fall in the price level lowers the real interest rate. At a real interest rate of 5 percent a year, Mika was willing to borrow to buy a low-performance computer. But at a real interest rate of close to zero, she decides to buy a fancier computer that costs more: The fall in the price level increases the quantity of real GDP demanded.

The Real Prices of Exports and Imports

When the U.S. price level rises and other things remain the same, the prices in other countries do not change. So a rise in the U.S. price level makes U.S.-made goods and services more expensive relative to foreign-made goods and services. This change in real prices encourages people to spend less on U.S.-made items and more on foreign-made items. For example, if the U.S. price level rises relative to the foreign price level, foreigners buy fewer U.S.-made cars (U.S. exports decrease) and Americans buy more foreign-made cars (U.S. imports increase).

Anna's and Mika's Imports In Moscow, Anna is buying some new shoes. With a sharp rise in the Russian price level, the Russian-made shoes that she planned to buy are too expensive, so she buys a less expensive pair imported from Brazil. In Tokyo, Mika is buying a DVD player. With the fall in the Japanese price level, a Sony DVD player made in Japan looks like a better buy than one made in Taiwan.

In the long run, when the price level changes by more in one country than in other countries, the exchange rate changes. The exchange rate change neutralizes the price level change, so this international price effect on buying plans is a short-run effect only. But in the short run, it is a powerful effect.

■ Changes in Aggregate Demand

A change in any factor that influences expenditure plans other than the price level brings a change in aggregate demand. When aggregate demand increases, the aggregate demand curve shifts rightward, which Figure 13.5 illustrates as the rightward shift of the AD curve from AD_0 to AD_1. When aggregate demand decreases, the aggregate demand curve shifts leftward, which Figure 13.5 illustrates as the leftward shift of the AD curve from AD_0 to AD_2. The factors that change aggregate demand are

- Expectations about the future
- Fiscal policy and monetary policy
- The state of the world economy

Expectations

An increase in expected future income increases the amount of consumption goods (especially big-ticket items such as cars) that people plan to buy now. Aggregate demand increases. An increase in expected future inflation increases aggregate demand because people decide to buy more goods and services now before their prices rise. An increase in expected future profit increases the investment that firms plan to undertake now. Aggregate demand increases.

A decrease in expected future income, future inflation, or future profit has the opposite effect and decreases aggregate demand.

FIGURE 13.5

Change in Aggregate Demand

Price level (GDP price index, 2009 = 100)

❶ Aggregate demand *increases if*

- Expected future income, inflation, or profits increase.
- The government or the Federal Reserve takes steps that increase planned expenditure.
- The exchange rate falls or the global economy expands.

❷ Aggregate demand *decreases if*

- Expected future income, inflation, or profits decrease.
- The government or the Federal Reserve takes steps that decrease planned expenditure.
- The exchange rate rises or the global economy contracts.

Fiscal Policy and Monetary Policy

We study the effects of policy actions on aggregate demand in Chapters 16 and 17. Here, we'll just briefly note that the government can use **fiscal policy**—changing taxes, transfer payments, and government expenditure on goods and services—to influence aggregate demand. The Federal Reserve can use **monetary policy**—changing the quantity of money and the interest rate—to influence aggregate demand. A tax cut or an increase in either transfer payments or government expenditure on goods and services increases aggregate demand. A cut in the interest rate or an increase in the quantity of money increases aggregate demand.

Fiscal policy
Changing taxes, transfer payments, and government expenditure on goods and services.

Monetary policy
Changing the quantity of money and the interest rate.

The World Economy

Two main influences that the world economy has on aggregate demand are the foreign exchange rate and foreign income. The foreign exchange rate is the amount of a foreign currency that you can buy with a U.S. dollar. Other things remaining the same, a rise in the foreign exchange rate decreases aggregate demand.

To see how the foreign exchange rate influences aggregate demand, suppose that $1 exchanges for 100 Japanese yen. A Fujitsu phone made in Japan costs 12,500 yen, and an equivalent Motorola phone made in the United States costs $110. In U.S. dollars, the Fujitsu phone costs $125, so people around the world buy the cheaper U.S. phone. Now suppose the exchange rate rises to 125 yen per dollar. At 125 yen per dollar, the Fujitsu phone costs $100 and is now cheaper than the Motorola phone. People will switch from the U.S. phone to the Japanese phone.

U.S. exports will decrease and U.S. imports will increase, so U.S. aggregate demand will decrease.

An increase in foreign income increases U.S. exports and increases U.S. aggregate demand. For example, an increase in income in Japan and Germany increases Japanese and German consumers' and producers' planned expenditures on U.S.-made goods and services.

■ The Aggregate Demand Multiplier

The aggregate demand multiplier is an effect that magnifies changes in expenditure plans and brings potentially large fluctuations in aggregate demand. When any influence on aggregate demand changes expenditure plans, the change in expenditure changes income; and the change in income induces a change in consumption expenditure. The increase in aggregate demand is the initial increase in expenditure plus the induced increase in consumption expenditure.

Suppose that an increase in expenditure induces an increase in consumption expenditure that is 1.5 times the initial increase in expenditure. Figure 13.6 illustrates the change in aggregate demand that occurs when investment increases by $0.4 trillion. Initially, the aggregate demand curve is AD_0. Investment then increases by $0.4 trillion ($\Delta I$) and the purple curve $AD_0 + \Delta I$ now describes aggregate spending plans at each price level. An increase in income induces an increase in consumption expenditure of $0.6 trillion, and the aggregate demand curve shifts rightward to AD_1. Chapter 14 (pp. 362–366) explains the expenditure multiplier in detail.

▦ FIGURE 13.6

The Aggregate Demand Multiplier

MyEconLab Animation

❶ An increase in investment increases aggregate demand and increases income.

❷ The increase in income induces an increase in consumption expenditure, so **❸** aggregate demand increases by more than the initial increase in investment.

CHECKPOINT 13.2

MyEconLab Study Plan 13.2
Key Terms Quiz
Solutions

Define and explain the influences on aggregate demand.

Practice Problems

1. Mexico trades with the United States. Explain the effect of each of the following events on Mexico's aggregate demand.
   - The government of Mexico cuts income taxes.
   - The United States experiences strong economic growth.
   - Mexico sets new environmental standards that require factories to upgrade their production facilities.

2. Explain the effect of each of the following events on the quantity of real GDP demanded and aggregate demand in Mexico.
   - Europe trades with Mexico and goes into a recession.
   - The price level in Mexico rises.
   - Mexico increases the quantity of money.

In the News

Durable goods orders, new-homes sales, and imports pick up

The BEA announced that demand for durable goods rose 3.4% while new-home sales rose 13.4% in the second quarter of 2013. U.S. exports increased 5.4% while U.S. imports increased 9.5%.

Source: Bureau of Economic Analysis, July 31, 2013

Explain how the items in the news clip influence U.S. aggregate demand.

Solutions to Practice Problems

1. A tax cut increases disposable income, which increases consumption expenditure, which increases aggregate demand. Strong U.S. growth increases the demand for Mexican-produced goods, which increases Mexico's aggregate demand. As factories upgrade their facilities, investment increases. Aggregate demand increases. In each case, the *AD* curve shifts rightward (Figure 1).

2. A recession in Europe decreases the demand for Mexico's exports, so aggregate demand decreases. The *AD* curve shifts leftward (Figure 2). A rise in the price level decreases the quantity of real GDP demanded along the *AD* curve, but the *AD* curve does not shift (Figure 3). An increase in the quantity of money increases aggregate demand, and the *AD* curve shifts rightward (Figure 1).

Solution to In the News

The purchase of durable goods and new homes is investment, which increased aggregate demand. The rise in U.S. imports exceeded the rise in U.S. exports, which decreased the demand for U.S.-produced goods and services and decreased U.S. aggregate demand.

FIGURE 1
Price level

0   Real GDP

FIGURE 2
Price level

0   Real GDP

FIGURE 3
Price level

0   Real GDP

13.3 EXPLAINING ECONOMIC TRENDS AND FLUCTUATIONS

The main purpose of the *AS-AD* model is to explain business cycle fluctuations in real GDP and the price level. But the model also helps our understanding of economic growth and inflation trends that we've studied in earlier chapters. The first step toward explaining economic trends and fluctuations is to combine aggregate supply and aggregate demand and determine macroeconomic equilibrium.

■ Macroeconomic Equilibrium

Macroeconomic equilibrium
When the quantity of real GDP demanded equals the quantity of real GDP supplied at the point of intersection of the *AD* curve and the *AS* curve.

Aggregate supply and aggregate demand determine real GDP and the price level. **Macroeconomic equilibrium** occurs when the quantity of real GDP demanded equals the quantity of real GDP supplied at the point of intersection of the *AD* curve and the *AS* curve. Figure 13.7 shows such an equilibrium at a price level of 105 and real GDP of $16 trillion.

To see why this position is the equilibrium, think about what happens if the price level is something other than 105. Suppose the price level is 95 and real GDP is $15 trillion (point *A* on the *AS* curve). The quantity of real GDP demanded exceeds $15 trillion, so firms are unable to meet the demand for their output. Inventories decrease, and customers clamor for goods and services. In this situation, firms increase production and raise prices. Eventually they can meet demand when real GDP is $16 trillion and the price level is 105.

Now suppose that the price level is 115 and that real GDP is $17 trillion (point *B* on the *AS* curve). The quantity of real GDP demanded is less than $17 trillion, so firms are unable to sell all their output. Unwanted inventories pile up. Firms cut production and lower prices until they can sell all their output, which occurs when real GDP is $16 trillion and the price level is 105.

■ **FIGURE 13.7**

Macroeconomic Equilibrium

Macroeconomic equilibrium occurs when the quantity of real GDP supplied on the *AS* curve equals the quantity of real GDP demanded on the *AD* curve.

❶ At a price level of 95, the quantity of real GDP supplied is $15 trillion at point *A*. The quantity of real GDP demanded exceeds the quantity supplied, so firms increase production and raise prices.

❷ At a price level of 115, the quantity of real GDP supplied is $17 trillion at point *B*. The quantity of real GDP demanded is less than the quantity supplied, so firms cut production and lower prices.

At a price level of 105, the quantity of real GDP supplied equals the quantity of real GDP demanded in macroeconomic equilibrium.

■ Three Types of Macroeconomic Equilibrium

In macroeconomic equilibrium, the economy might be at full employment or above or below full employment. Figure 13.8(a) shows these three possibilities. **Full-employment equilibrium**—when equilibrium real GDP equals potential GDP—occurs where the AD curve intersects the aggregate supply curve AS^*.

At a higher money wage rate, aggregate supply is AS_1. Real GDP is $15.5 trillion and is less than potential GDP. The economy is *below full employment* and there is a **recessionary gap**. At a lower money wage rate, aggregate supply is AS_2. In this situation, real GDP is $16.5 trillion and is greater than potential GDP. The economy is *above full employment* and there is an **inflationary gap**.

Adjustment toward Full Employment

When real GDP is below or above potential GDP, the money wage rate gradually changes to restore full employment. Figure 13.8(b) illustrates this adjustment.

In a *recessionary gap*, there is a surplus of labor and firms can hire new workers at a lower wage rate. As the money wage rate falls, the AS curve shifts from AS_1 toward AS^* and the price level falls and real GDP rises. The money wage continues to fall until real GDP equals potential GDP—full-employment equilibrium.

In an *inflationary gap*, there is a shortage of labor and firms must offer a higher wage rate to hire the labor they demand. As the money wage rate rises, the AS curve shifts from AS_2 toward AS^* and the price level rises and real GDP falls. The money wage rate continues to rise until real GDP equals potential GDP.

Full-employment equilibrium
When equilibrium real GDP equals potential GDP.

Recessionary gap
A gap that exists when potential GDP exceeds real GDP and that brings a falling price level.

Inflationary gap
A gap that exists when real GDP exceeds potential GDP and that brings a rising price level.

■ **FIGURE 13.8**

Output Gaps and Full-Employment Equilibrium   MyEconLab Real-time data

(a) Three types of macroeconomic equilibrium

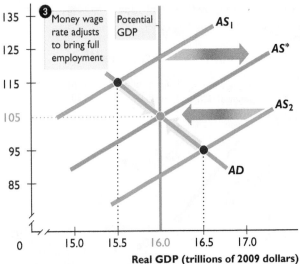

(b) Adjustment to full employment

In part (a), when equilibrium real GDP is less than potential GDP, ❶ there is a recessionary gap; when equilibrium real GDP is greater than potential GDP, ❷ there is an inflationary gap; and when equilibrium real GDP equals potential GDP, the economy is at full employment.

In part (b), when an output gap exists ❸ the money wage rate adjusts to move the economy toward full employment. With a recessionary gap, the money wage rate falls and the AS curve shifts rightward from AS_1 to AS^*. With an inflationary gap, the money wage rate rises and the AS curve shifts leftward from AS_2 to AS^*.

■ Economic Growth and Inflation Trends

Economic growth results from a growing labor force and increasing labor productivity, which together make potential GDP grow (Chapter 9, pp. 218–224). Inflation results from a growing quantity of money that outpaces the growth of potential GDP (Chapter 12, pp. 305–313).

The *AS-AD* model can be used to understand economic growth and inflation trends. In the *AS-AD* model, economic growth is increasing potential GDP—a persistent rightward shift in the potential GDP line. Inflation arises from a persistent increase in aggregate demand at a faster pace than that of the increase in potential GDP—a persistent rightward shift of the *AD* curve at a faster pace than the growth of potential GDP. *Eye on the U.S. Economy* below shows how the *AS-AD* model explains U.S. economic growth and inflation trends.

EYE on the U.S. ECONOMY
U.S. Economic Growth, Inflation, and the Business Cycle

U.S. economic growth, inflation, and the business cycle result from changes in aggregate supply and aggregate demand.

A rightward movement in the U.S. potential GDP line brings economic growth and a greater rightward movement of the U.S. *AD* curve brings inflation. Part (a) shows the shifting curves that generate growth and inflation.

Part (b) shows the history of U.S. real GDP growth and inflation from 1970 to 2013. Each dot represents the the real GDP and price level in a year—the black dot 1970 and the red dot 2013. The rightward movement of the dots is economic growth and the upward movement is a rising price level—inflation.

When the dots follow a path that is gently rising, as during the 1990s, the inflation rate is low and real GDP growth is quite rapid. When the dots follow a path that is steep, as during the 1970s, inflation is rapid and economic growth is slow.

Notice that the dots move rightward and upward in waves and occasionally

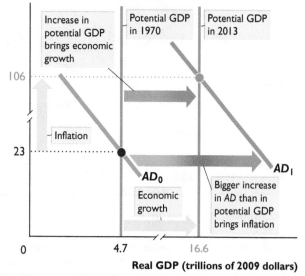

(a) Economic growth and inflation

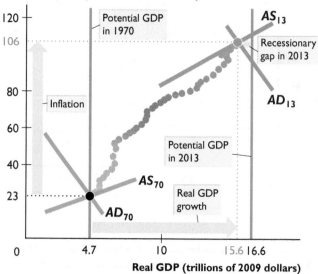

(b) U.S. economic growth and inflation

■ The Business Cycle

The business cycle results from fluctuations in aggregate supply and aggregate demand. Aggregate supply fluctuates because labor productivity grows at a variable pace, which brings fluctuations in the growth rate of potential GDP. The resulting cycle is called a **real business cycle**. But aggregate demand fluctuations are the main source of the business cycle. The key reason is that the swings in aggregate demand occur more quickly than changes in the money wage rate that change aggregate supply. The result is that the economy swings from inflationary gap to full employment to recessionary gap and back again.

Eye on the U.S. Economy below shows the most recent cycle interpreted as driven by aggregate demand fluctuations. But in the 2008–2009 recession, both aggregate demand and aggregate supply were at work as you can see on p. 348.

Real business cycle
A cycle that results from fluctuations in the pace of growth of labor productivity and potential GDP.

leftward. The pattern shows the business cycle expansions and recessions.

By comparing the dots with potential GDP, we can see that the economy was at full employment in 1970 and that the recessionary gap in 2013 was large.

Part (c) shows how changes in aggregate demand create the business cycle, and part (d) shows the most recent cycle from 2000 to 2013.

When the *AD* curve is *AD₀* in part (c), the economy is at point *A* and there is an inflationary gap. Part (d) identifies the actual gap in 2000 as *A*.

A decrease in aggregate demand to *AD₁* lowers real GDP to potential GDP and the economy moves to point *B* in parts (c) and (d).

A further decrease in aggregate demand to *AD₂* lowers real GDP to

below potential GDP and opens up a recessionary gap at point *C* in both parts (c) and (d).

In reality, *AD* rarely decreases. It increases at a slower pace than the increase in potential GDP. Also, in reality, *AS* fluctuates. But the relative positions of the *AS* and *AD* curves and the potential GDP line are like those shown in part (c).

(c) Aggregate demand fluctuations

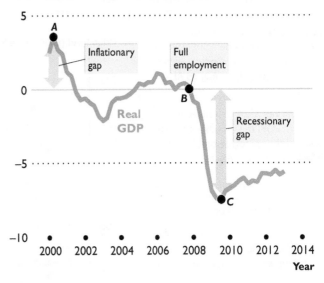

(d) The U.S. output gap

SOURCES OF DATA: Bureau of Labor Statistics, Bureau of Economic Analysis, and Congressional Budget Office.

■ Inflation Cycles

You've seen that inflation occurs if aggregate demand grows faster than potential GDP. But just as there are cycles in real GDP, there are also cycles in the inflation rate. And the two cycles are related. To study the interaction of real GDP and inflation cycles, we distinguish between two sources of inflation:

- Demand-pull inflation
- Cost-push inflation

Demand-Pull Inflation

Demand-pull inflation
Inflation that starts because aggregate demand increases.

Inflation that starts because aggregate demand increases is called **demand-pull inflation**. Demand-pull inflation can be kicked off by any of the factors that change aggregate demand but the only thing that can sustain it is growth in the quantity of money.

Figure 13.9 illustrates the process of demand-pull inflation. Potential GDP is $16 trillion. Initially, the aggregate demand curve is AD_0, the aggregate supply curve is AS_0, and real GDP equals potential GDP. Aggregate demand increases, shifting the aggregate demand curve to AD_1. Real GDP increases and the price level rises. There is now an *inflationary gap*. A shortage of labor brings a rise in the money wage rate, which shifts the aggregate supply curve to AS_1. The price level rises further and real GDP returns to potential GDP.

The quantity of money increases again, and the aggregate demand curve shifts rightward to AD_2. The price level rises further, and real GDP again exceeds potential GDP. Yet again, the money wage rate rises and decreases aggregate supply. The AS curve shifts to AS_2, and the price level rises further. As the quantity of money continues to grow, aggregate demand increases and the price level rises in an ongoing demand-pull inflation spiral.

■ FIGURE 13.9

A Demand-Pull Inflation

MyEconLab Animation

Each time the quantity of money increases, aggregate demand increases and the aggregate demand curve shifts rightward from AD_0 to AD_1 to AD_2, and so on.

Each time real GDP increases above potential GDP, the money wage rate rises and the aggregate supply curve shifts leftward from AS_0 to AS_1 to AS_2, and so on.

The price level rises from 105 to 108, 116, 120, 128, and so on.

A demand-pull inflation spiral results with real GDP fluctuating between $16 trillion and $16.5 trillion.

Cost-Push Inflation

Inflation that begins with an increase in cost is called **cost-push inflation**. The two main sources of cost increases are increases in the money wage rate and increases in the money prices of raw materials such as oil.

Cost-push inflation can be kicked off by an increase in costs but the only thing that can sustain it is growth in the quantity of money.

Figure 13.10 illustrates cost-push inflation. The aggregate demand curve is AD_0, the aggregate supply curve is AS_0, and real GDP equals potential GDP. The world price of oil rises, which decreases aggregate supply. The aggregate supply curve shifts leftward to AS_1, the price level rises, and real GDP decreases so there is a *recessionary gap*.

When real GDP decreases, unemployment rises above its natural rate and the Fed increases the quantity of money to restore full employment. Aggregate demand increases and the AD curve shifts rightward to AD_1. Real GDP returns to potential GDP but the price level rises further.

Oil producers now see the prices of everything they buy rising so they raise the price of oil again to restore its new higher relative price. The AS curve now shifts to AS_2, the price level rises again and real GDP decreases again.

If the Fed responds yet again with an increase in the quantity of money, aggregate demand increases and the AD curve shifts to AD_2. The price level rises even higher and full employment is again restored. A cost-push inflation spiral results.

The combination of a decreasing real GDP and a rising price level is called **stagflation**. You can see that stagflation poses a dilemma for the Fed. If the Fed does not respond when producers raise the oil price, the economy remains below full employment. If the Fed increases the quantity of money to restore full employment, it invites another oil price hike that will call forth yet a further increase in the quantity of money.

Cost-push inflation
An inflation that begins with an increase in cost.

Stagflation
The combination of recession (decreasing real GDP) and inflation (rising price level).

FIGURE 13.10

A Cost-Push Inflation

MyEconLab Animation

Each time a cost increase occurs, the aggregate supply curve shifts leftward from AS_0 to AS_1 to AS_2, and so on.

Each time real GDP decreases below potential GDP, the Fed increases the quantity of money and the aggregate demand curve shifts rightward from AD_0 to AD_1 to AD_2, and so on.

The price level rises from 105 to 112, 116, 124, 128, and so on.

A cost-push inflation spiral results with real GDP fluctuating between $16 trillion and $15.5 trillion.

Deflation and the Great Depression

When a financial crisis hit the United States in October 2008, many people feared a repeat of the dreadful events of the 1930s. From 1929 through 1933, the United States and most of the world experienced deflation and depression—the *Great Depression*. The price level fell by 22 percent and real GDP fell by 31 percent.

The recession of 2008–2009 turned out to be much less severe than the Great Depression. Real GDP fell by less than 4 percent and the price level continued to rise, although at a slower pace. Why was the Great Depression so bad and why was 2008–2009 so mild in comparison? You can answer these questions with what you've learned in this chapter.

During the Great Depression, banks failed and the quantity of money contracted by 25 percent. The Fed stood by and took no action to counteract the collapse of buying power, so aggregate demand also collapsed. Because the money wage rate didn't fall immediately, the decrease in aggregate demand brought a large fall in real GDP. The money wage rate and price level fell eventually, but not until employment and real GDP had shrunk to 75 percent of their 1929 levels.

In contrast, during the 2008 financial crisis, the Fed bailed out troubled financial institutions and doubled the monetary base. The quantity of money kept growing. Also, the government increased its own expenditures, which added to aggregate demand. The combined effects of continued growth in the quantity of money and increased government expenditure limited the fall in aggregate demand and prevented a large decrease in real GDP.

The challenge that now lies ahead is to unwind the monetary and fiscal stimulus as the components of private expenditure—consumption expenditure, investment, and exports—begin to increase and return to more normal levels and so bring an increase in aggregate demand. Too much stimulus will bring an inflationary gap and faster inflation. Too little stimulus will leave a recessionary gap.

You will explore these monetary and fiscal policy actions and their effects in Chapters 16 and 17.

EYE on YOUR LIFE
Using the *AS-AD* Model

Using all the knowledge that you have accumulated over the term, and by watching or reading the current news, try to figure out where the U.S. economy is in its business cycle right now.

First, can you determine if real GDP is currently above, below, or at potential GDP? Second, can you determine if real GDP is expanding or contracting in a recession?

Next, try to form a view about where the U.S. economy is heading. What do you see as the main pressures on aggregate supply and aggregate demand, and in which directions are they pushing or pulling the economy?

Do you think that real GDP will expand more quickly or more slowly over the coming months? Do you think the gap between real GDP and potential GDP will widen or narrow?

How do you expect the labor market to be affected by the changes in aggregate supply and aggregate demand that you are expecting? Do you expect the unemployment rate to rise, fall, or remain constant?

Talk to your friends in class about where they see the U.S. economy right now and where it is heading. Is there a consensus or is there a wide range of opinion?

EYE on the BUSINESS CYCLE
Why Did the U.S. Economy Go into Recession in 2008?

What causes the business cycle and what caused the 2008–2009 recession?

Business Cycle Theory

The mainstream business cycle theory is that potential GDP grows at a steady rate while aggregate demand grows at a fluctuating rate.

Because the money wage rate is slow to change, if aggregate demand grows more quickly than potential GDP, real GDP moves above potential GDP and an inflationary gap emerges. The inflation rate rises and real GDP is pulled back toward potential GDP.

If aggregate demand grows more slowly than potential GDP, real GDP moves below potential GDP and a recessionary gap emerges. The inflation rate slows. Because the money wage rate responds very slowly to the recessionary gap, real GDP does not return to potential GDP until another increase in aggregate demand occurs.

Fluctuations in investment are the main source of fluctuations in aggregate demand. Consumption expenditure responds to changes in income.

A recession can also occur if aggregate supply decreases to bring stagflation. And a recession might occur because both aggregate demand and aggregate supply decrease.

The 2008–2009 Recession

The 2008–2009 recession is an example of a recession caused by a decrease in both aggregate demand and aggregate supply. The figure illustrates these two contributing forces.

SOURCES OF DATA: Bureau of Economic Analysis and Congressional Budget Office.

At the peak in 2008, real GDP was $15 trillion and the price level was 99. In the second quarter of 2009, real GDP had fallen to $14.3 trillion and the price level had risen to 100.

The financial crisis that began in 2007 and intensified in 2008 decreased the supply of loanable funds and investment fell. In particular, construction investment collapsed.

Recession in the global economy decreased the demand for U.S. exports, so this component of aggregate demand also decreased.

The decrease in aggregate demand was moderated by a large injection of spending by the U.S. government, but this move was not enough to stop aggregate demand from decreasing.

We cannot account for the combination of a rise in the price level and a decrease in real GDP with a decrease in aggregate demand alone. Aggregate supply must also have decreased. The rise in oil prices in 2007 and a rise in the money wage rate were the two factors that brought about the decrease in aggregate supply.

MyEconLab Study Plan 13.3
Key Terms Quiz
Solutions

CHECKPOINT 13.3

Explain how trends and fluctuations in aggregate demand and aggregate supply bring economic growth, inflation, and the business cycle.

Practice Problems

The U.S. economy is at full employment when the following events occur:
* A deep recession hits the world economy.
* The world oil price rises by a large amount.
* U.S. businesses expect future profits to fall.

1. Explain the effect of each event separately on aggregate demand and aggregate supply. How will real GDP and the price level change in the short run?
2. Explain the combined effect of these events on real GDP and the price level.
3. Which event, if any, brings stagflation?

In the News

U.S. incomes fall for first time in 2 years
Consumer spending rose 0.2 percent in August, down from 0.7 percent in July. Incomes fell 0.1 percent—the first decline since October 2009. Consumer spending accounts for 70 percent of economic activity.

Source: Associated Press, September 30, 2011

Explain the effect of these events in terms of the *AS-AD* model.

Solutions to Practice Problems

1. A deep recession in the world economy decreases U.S. aggregate demand. The *AD* curve shifts leftward. In the short run, U.S. real GDP decreases and the price level falls (Figure 1). A rise in the world oil price decreases U.S. aggregate supply. The *AS* curve shifts leftward. In the short run, U.S. real GDP decreases and the price level rises (Figure 2). A fall in expected future profits decreases U.S. aggregate demand. The *AD* curve shifts leftward. In the short run, U.S. real GDP decreases and the price level falls (Figure 1).

2. All three events decrease U.S. real GDP (Figures 1 and 2). The deep world recession and the fall in expected future profits decrease the price level (Figure 1). The rise in the world oil price increases the price level (Figure 2). So the combined effect on the price level is ambiguous.

3. Stagflation is a rising price level and a decreasing real GDP together. The rise in the world oil price brings stagflation because it decreases aggregate supply, decreases real GDP, and raises the price level (Figure 2).

Solution to In the News

The news clip gives no information about aggregate supply. Consumption expenditure is 70 percent of aggregate demand, so an increase in consumption expenditure would increase aggregate demand, real GDP, and aggregate incomes. But incomes fell, so the other components of aggregate demand (investment, government expenditure, net exports) must have decreased, moving the economy down along the *AS* curve. Or aggregate supply must have decreased, moving the economy up along the *AD* curve.

FIGURE 1

Price level

Potential GDP

AS

105

100

AD_1 AD_0

0   15.5   16.0

Real GDP (trillions of 2009 dollars)

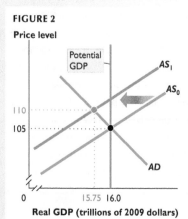

FIGURE 2

Price level

Potential GDP

AS_1

AS_0

110

105

AD

0   15.75 16.0

Real GDP (trillions of 2009 dollars)

CHAPTER SUMMARY

Key Points

1. **Define and explain the influences on aggregate supply.**

   - Aggregate supply is the relationship between the quantity of real GDP supplied and the price level when all other influences on production plans remain the same.
   - The *AS* curve slopes upward because with a given money wage rate, a rise in the price level lowers the real wage rate, increases the quantity of labor demanded, and increases the quantity of real GDP supplied.
   - A change in potential GDP, a change in the money wage rate, or a change in the money price of other resources changes aggregate supply.

2. **Define and explain the influences on aggregate demand.**

   - Aggregate demand is the relationship between the quantity of real GDP demanded and the price level when all other influences on expenditure plans remain the same.
   - The *AD* curve slopes downward because a rise in the price level decreases the buying power of money, raises the real interest rate, raises the real price of domestic goods compared with foreign goods, and decreases the quantity of real GDP demanded.
   - A change in expected future income, inflation, and profits; a change in fiscal policy and monetary policy; and a change in the foreign exchange rate and foreign real GDP all change aggregate demand—the aggregate demand curve shifts.

3. **Explain how trends and fluctuations in aggregate demand and aggregate supply bring economic growth, inflation, and the business cycle.**

   - Aggregate demand and aggregate supply determine real GDP and the price level in macroeconomic equilibrium, which can occur at full employment or above or below full employment.
   - Away from full employment, gradual changes in the money wage rate move real GDP toward potential GDP.
   - Economic growth is a persistent increase in potential GDP, and inflation occurs when aggregate demand grows at a faster rate than potential GDP.
   - Business cycles occur because aggregate demand and aggregate supply fluctuate.
   - Demand-pull and cost-push forces bring inflation and real GDP cycles.

Key Terms   MyEconLab Key Terms Quiz

Aggregate demand, 330	Fiscal policy, 333	Monetary policy, 333
Aggregate supply, 324	Full-employment equilibrium, 337	Real business cycle, 339
Cost-push inflation, 341	Inflationary gap, 337	Recessionary gap, 337
Demand-pull inflation, 340	Macroeconomic equilibrium, 336	Stagflation, 341

CHAPTER CHECKPOINT

Study Plan Problems and Applications

1. As more people in India have access to higher education, explain how potential GDP and aggregate supply will change in the long run.

2. Explain the effect of each of the following events on the quantity of U.S. real GDP demanded and the demand for U.S. real GDP:
   - The world economy goes into a strong expansion.
   - The U.S. price level rises.
   - Congress raises income taxes.

3. The United States is at full employment when the Fed cuts the quantity of money, other things remaining the same. Explain the effect of the cut in the quantity of money on aggregate demand in the short run.

4. Table 1 sets out an economy's aggregate demand and aggregate supply schedules. What is the macroeconomic equilibrium? If potential GDP is $600 billion, what is the type of macroeconomic equilibrium? Explain how real GDP and the price level will adjust in the long run.

5. Suppose that the U.S. economy has a recessionary gap and the world economy goes into an expansion. Explain the effect of the expansion on U.S. real GDP and unemployment in the short run.

6. Explain the effect of the Fed's action that increases the quantity of money on the macroeconomic equilibrium in the short run. Explain the adjustment process that returns the economy to full employment.

Use Figure 1 to work Problems 7 to 9. Initially, the economy is at point B.

7. Some events change aggregate demand from AD_0 to AD_1. Describe two possible events. What is the new equilibrium point? If potential GDP is $1 trillion, describe the type of macroeconomic equilibrium.

8. Some events change aggregate supply from AS_0 to AS_1. Describe two possible events. What is the new equilibrium point? If potential GDP is $1 trillion, does the economy have an inflationary gap, a recessionary gap, or no gap?

9. Some events change aggregate demand from AD_0 to AD_1 and aggregate supply from AS_0 to AS_1. What is the new macroeconomic equilibrium?

10. **Japan economic recovery under way as deflation eases**
    Consumer prices excluding fresh food declined 0.4 percent from a year earlier—the smallest drop since 2009. The unemployment rate unexpectedly fell to 4.9 percent from 5.1 percent—the first decrease since September. The economy will emerge from its slump "soon."

    Source: Bloomberg, January 27, 2011

    On an *AS-AD* graph show the macroeconomic equilibrium in Japan in 2010. Show why economic recovery is under way and deflation is easing.

 11. Read *Eye on the Business Cycle* on p. 343. What caused the 2008–2009 recession and how do we know that a decrease in aggregate supply played a role?

TABLE 1

Price level (GDP price index)	Real GDP demanded	Real GDP supplied
	(billions of 2009 dollars)	
90	900	600
100	850	700
110	800	800
120	750	900
130	700	1,000

FIGURE 1

Price level

Instructor Assignable Problems and Applications

MyEconLab Homework, Quiz, or Test if assigned by instructor

1. What, according to the mainstream theory of the business cycle, is the most common source of recession: a decrease in aggregate demand, a decrease in aggregate supply, or both? Which is the most likely component of aggregate demand to start a recession? How does the aggregate demand multiplier influence a recession?

2. Suppose that the United States is at full employment. Explain the effect of each of the following events on aggregate supply:
   - Union wage settlements push the money wage rate up by 10 percent.
   - The price level increases.
   - Potential GDP increases.

3. Suppose that the United States is at full employment. Then the federal government cuts taxes, and all other influences on aggregate demand remain the same. Explain the effect of the tax cut on aggregate demand in the short run.

Use the following information to work Problems 4 and 5.

Because fluctuations in the world oil price make the U.S. short-run macroeconomic equilibrium fluctuate, someone suggests that the government should vary the tax rate on oil, lowering the tax when the world oil price rises and increasing the tax when the world oil price falls, to stabilize the oil price in the U.S. market.

4. How would such an action influence aggregate demand?

5. How would such an action influence aggregate supply?

6. Table 1 sets out the aggregate demand and aggregate supply schedules in Japan. Potential GDP is 600 trillion yen. What is the short-run macroeconomic equilibrium? Does Japan have an inflationary gap or a recessionary gap and what is its magnitude?

7. Suppose that the world price of oil rises. On an *AS-AD* graph, show the effect of the world oil price rise on U.S. macroeconomic equilibrium in the short run. Explain the adjustment process that restores the economy to full employment.

8. Explain the effects of a global recession on the U.S. macroeconomic equilibrium in the short run. Explain the adjustment process that restores the economy to full employment.

Use the following information to work Problems 9 and 10.

House GOP changes course on infrastructure
House Republicans abandoned plans to slash U.S. infrastructure spending and now say they are trying to find ways to pay for a multiyear highway-construction program, which will exceed $300 billion.

Source: *The Wall Street Journal*, September 30, 2011

9. Explain the effect of the government's increased expenditure on infrastructure on U.S. aggregate demand and aggregate supply.

10. The United States in 2011 has a recessionary gap. Use the *AS-AD* model to show the effect on U.S. real GDP as the new infrastructure is completed.

TABLE 1

Price level (GDP price index)	Real GDP demanded	Real GDP supplied
	(trillions of 2005 yen)	
75	600	400
85	550	450
95	500	500
105	450	550
115	400	600
125	350	650
135	300	700

Multiple Choice Quiz

1. Aggregate supply increases when _____.
   A. the price level rises
   B. the money wage rate falls
   C. consumption increases
   D. the money price of oil increases

2. When potential GDP increases, _____.
   A. aggregate demand increases
   B. aggregate supply increases
   C. both aggregate demand and aggregate supply increase
   D. the price level rises

3. The quantity of real GDP demanded increases if _____.
   A. the buying power of money increases
   B. the money wage rate rises
   C. the price level falls
   D. the nominal interest rate falls

4. An increase in expected future income increases _____.
   A. consumption expenditure, which increases current aggregate demand
   B. investment, which increases current aggregate supply
   C. the demand for money, which decreases current aggregate demand
   D. future consumption expenditure and has no effect on current aggregate demand

5. Macroeconomic equilibrium occurs when the quantity of real GDP _____ equals the quantity of _____.
   A. demanded; real GDP supplied
   B. demanded; potential GDP
   C. supplied; potential GDP
   D. demanded; real GDP supplied and potential GDP

6. If the economy is at full employment and the Fed increases the quantity of money, _____.
   A. aggregate demand increases, a recessionary gap appears, and the money wage rate starts to rise
   B. aggregate supply increases, the price level starts to fall, and an expansion begins
   C. aggregate demand increases, an inflationary gap appears, and the money wage rate starts to rise
   D. potential GDP and aggregate supply increase together and the price level does not change

7. Over the past decade, the demand for goods produced in China has brought a sustained increase in demand for China's exports that has outstripped the growth of supply. As a result, China has experienced a _____.
   A. period of stable prices and sustained economic growth
   B. rising price level and demand-pull inflation
   C. rising price level and cost-push inflation
   D. rising price level and a falling real wage rate

How big is the government expenditure multiplier?

Aggregate Expenditure Multiplier

14

When you have completed your study of this chapter, you will be able to

1 Explain how real GDP influences expenditure plans.

2 Explain how real GDP adjusts to achieve equilibrium expenditure.

3 Explain the expenditure multiplier.

4 Derive the *AD* curve from equilibrium expenditure.

MyEconLab Big Picture

14.1 EXPENDITURE PLANS AND REAL GDP

When the government spends $1 million on a highway construction project, does that expenditure stimulate consumption expenditure in a multiplier effect? This question lies at the core of this chapter.

To answer the question, we use the *aggregate expenditure model*, a model that explains what determines the quantity of real GDP demanded and changes in that quantity *at a given price level*.

The aggregate expenditure model—also known as the *Keynesian model*—was originally designed to explain what happens in an economy in deep recession when firms can't cut their prices any further but can increase production without raising their prices, so the price level is actually fixed. The severity of the global recession of 2008–2009 gave the model a rebirth and the question of the size of the government expenditure multiplier became a hot issue.

You learned in Chapter 5 (pp. 115–117) that aggregate expenditure equals the sum of consumption expenditure, *C*, investment, *I*, government expenditure on goods and services, *G*, and net exports, *NX*. **Aggregate planned expenditure** is the sum of the spending plans of households, firms, and governments. We divide expenditure plans into autonomous expenditure and induced expenditure. *Autonomous expenditure* does not respond to changes in real GDP and *induced expenditure* does respond to changes in real GDP. We start by looking at induced expenditure and its main component, consumption expenditure.

Aggregate planned expenditure
Planned consumption expenditure plus planned investment, plus planned government expenditure, plus planned exports minus planned imports.

■ The Consumption Function

The **consumption function** is the relationship between consumption expenditure and disposable income, other things remaining the same. *Disposable income* is aggregate income—GDP—minus net taxes. (Net taxes are taxes paid to the government minus transfer payments received from the government.)

Households must either spend their disposable income on consumption or save it. A decision to spend a dollar on consumption is a decision not to save a dollar. The consumption decision and the saving decision is one decision.

Consumption function
The relationship between consumption expenditure and disposable income, other things remaining the same.

Consumption Plans

For households and the economy as a whole, as disposable income increases, planned consumption expenditure increases. But the increase in planned consumption is less than the increase in disposable income. The table in Figure 14.1 shows a consumption schedule. It lists the consumption expenditure that people plan to undertake at each level of disposable income.

Figure 14.1 shows a consumption function based on the consumption schedule. Along the consumption function, the points labeled *A* through *E* correspond to the columns of the table. For example, when disposable income is $9 trillion at point *D*, consumption expenditure is $8 trillion. Along the consumption function, as disposable income increases, consumption expenditure increases.

At point *A* on the consumption function, consumption expenditure is $2 trillion even though disposable income is zero. This consumption expenditure is called *autonomous consumption,* and it is the amount of consumption expenditure that would take place in the short run even if people had no current income. This consumption expenditure would be financed either by spending past savings or by borrowing.

FIGURE 14.1

The Consumption Function

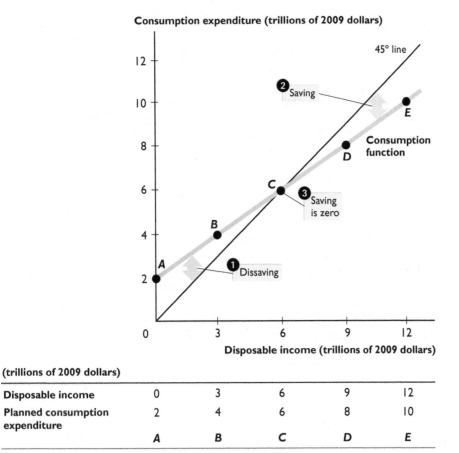

(trillions of 2009 dollars)					
Disposable income	0	3	6	9	12
Planned consumption expenditure	2	4	6	8	10
	A	*B*	*C*	*D*	*E*

The table shows consumption expenditure (and saving) plans at various levels of disposable income. The figure graphs these data as the consumption function. The figure also shows a 45° line along which consumption expenditure equals disposable income.

1 When the consumption function is above the 45° line, saving is negative (dissaving occurs).

2 When the consumption function is below the 45° line, saving is positive.

3 At the point where the consumption function intersects the 45° line, all disposable income is consumed and saving is zero.

Figure 14.1 also shows a 45° line. Because the scale on the *x*-axis measures disposable income and the scale on the *y*-axis measures consumption expenditure, and because the two scales are equal, along the 45° line consumption expenditure equals disposable income. So the 45° line serves as a reference line for comparing consumption expenditure and disposable income. Between *A* and *C*, consumption expenditure exceeds disposable income; between *C* and *E*, disposable income exceeds consumption expenditure; and at point *C*, consumption expenditure equals disposable income.

You can see saving in Figure 14.1. When consumption expenditure exceeds disposable income (and the consumption function is above the 45° line), saving is negative—called *dissaving*. When consumption expenditure is less than disposable income (the consumption function is below the 45° line), saving is positive. And when consumption expenditure equals disposable income (the consumption function intersects the 45° line), saving is zero.

When consumption expenditure exceeds disposable income, past savings are used to pay for current consumption. Such a situation cannot last forever, but it can and does occur if disposable income falls temporarily.

Marginal Propensity to Consume

Marginal propensity to consume
The fraction of a change in disposable income that is spent on consumption—the change in consumption expenditure divided by the change in disposable income that brought it about.

The **marginal propensity to consume** (*MPC*) is the fraction of a change in disposable income that is spent on consumption. It is calculated as the change in consumption expenditure divided by the change in disposable income that brought it about. That is,

$$MPC = \frac{\text{Change in consumption expenditure}}{\text{Change in disposable income}}.$$

Suppose that when disposable income increases from $6 trillion to $9 trillion, consumption expenditure increases from $6 trillion to $8 trillion. The $3 trillion increase in disposable income increases consumption expenditure by $2 trillion. Using these numbers in the formula to calculate the *MPC*,

$$MPC = \frac{\$2 \text{ trillion}}{\$3 \text{ trillion}} = 0.67.$$

The marginal propensity to consume tells us that when disposable income increases by $1, consumption expenditure increases by 67¢.

Figure 14.2 shows that the *MPC* equals the slope of the consumption function. A $3 trillion increase in disposable income from $6 trillion to $9 trillion is the base of the red triangle. The increase in consumption expenditure that results from this increase in income is $2 trillion and is the height of the triangle. The slope of the consumption function is given by the formula "slope equals rise over run" and is $2 trillion divided by $3 trillion, which equals 0.67—the *MPC*.

■ **FIGURE 14.2**

Marginal Propensity to Consume

The marginal propensity to consume, *MPC*, is equal to the change in consumption expenditure divided by the change in disposable income, other things remaining the same.

The slope of the consumption function measures the *MPC*.

In the figure:

❶ A $3 trillion change in disposable income brings

❷ a $2 trillion change in consumption expenditure, so

❸ the *MPC* equals
$2 trillion ÷ $3 trillion = 0.67.

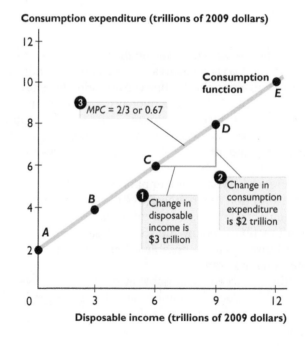

Other Influences on Consumption Expenditure

Consumption plans are influenced by many factors other than disposable income. The more important influences are

- Real interest rate
- Wealth
- Expected future income

Real Interest Rate When the real interest rate falls, consumption expenditure increases (and saving decreases) and when the real interest rate rises, consumption expenditure decreases (and saving increases).

Wealth and Expected Future Income When either wealth or expected future income decreases, consumption expenditure also decreases and when wealth or expected future income increases, consumption expenditure also increases.

Figure 14.3 shows the effects of these influences on the consumption function. When the real interest rate falls or when wealth or expected future income increases, the consumption function shifts upward from CF_0 to CF_1. Such a shift occurs during the expansion phase of the business cycle if a stock market boom increases wealth and expected future income increases.

When the real interest rate rises, or when wealth or expected future income decreases, the consumption function shifts downward from CF_0 to CF_2. Such a shift occurs during a recession if a stock market crash decreases wealth and expected future income decreases.

■ **FIGURE 14.3**

Shifts in the Consumption Function

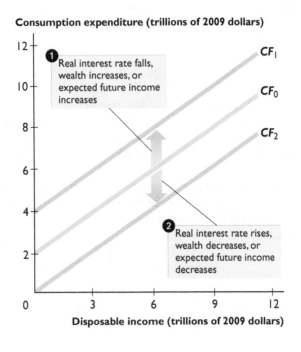

① A fall in the real interest rate or an increase in either wealth or expected future income increases consumption expenditure and shifts the consumption function upward from CF_0 to CF_1.

② A rise in the real interest rate or a decrease in either wealth or expected future income decreases consumption expenditure and shifts the consumption function downward from CF_0 to CF_2.

EYE on the U.S. ECONOMY
The U.S. Consumption Function

Each blue dot in the figure represents consumption expenditure and disposable income in the United States for a year between 1960 and 2013 (some labeled).

The lines labeled CF_{60}, and CF_{13} are estimates of the U.S. consumption function in 1960 and 2013, respectively.

The slope of these consumption functions—the marginal propensity to consume—is 0.87, which means that a $1 increase in disposable income brings an 87¢ increase in consumption expenditure.

The consumption function shifted upward from 1960 to 2013 because as economic growth brought higher expected future income and greater wealth, people chose to increase consumption expenditure from a given level of income.

During the recession of 2009, the consumption function temporarily shifted downward as a fall in house prices lowered wealth and encouraged people to save more.

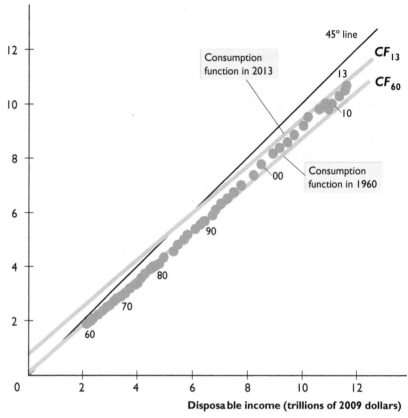

Source of data: Bureau of Economic Analysis.

■ Imports and Real GDP

Imports are the other major component of induced expenditure. Many factors influence U.S. imports, but in the short run, one factor dominates: U.S. real GDP. Other things remaining the same, an increase in U.S. real GDP brings an increase in U.S. imports. Because an increase in real GDP is also an increase in income, as incomes increase, people increase their expenditures on most goods and services. Many goods and services are imported, so as incomes increase imports increase.

The relationship between imports and real GDP is described by the **marginal propensity to import,** which is the fraction of an increase in real GDP that is spent on imports.

Marginal propensity to import
The fraction of an increase in real GDP that is spent on imports—the change in imports divided by the change in real GDP.

$$\text{Marginal propensity to import} = \frac{\text{Change in imports}}{\text{Change in real GDP}}.$$

For example, if a $1 trillion increase in real GDP increases imports by $0.2 trillion, then the marginal propensity to import is $0.2 trillion ÷ $1 trillion, which is 0.2.

CHECKPOINT 14.1

Explain how real GDP influences expenditure plans.

Practice Problems

1. Suppose that the marginal propensity to consume is 0.8. If disposable income increases by $0.5 trillion, by how much will consumption expenditure change?

2. Explain how each of the following events influences the U.S. consumption function:
   - The marginal propensity to consume decreases.
   - U.S. autonomous consumption decreases.
   - Americans expect an increase in future income.

3. Figure 1 shows the consumption function. What is the marginal propensity to consume, and what is autonomous consumption?

In the News

Personal income falls as spending rises
Personal income fell 0.1% in August, after increasing 0.1% in July, while personal spending rose just 0.2% in August, after rising 0.8% in July.

Source: CNN Money, September 30, 2011

How can consumers increase spending when personal income falls? Does the rise in consumer spending arise from a movement along the consumption function or a shift of the consumption function? Explain your answer.

Solutions to Practice Problems

1. Consumption expenditure will increase by $0.4 trillion, which is 0.8 multiplied by the change in disposable income of $0.5 trillion.

2. The marginal propensity to consume equals the slope of the consumption function. So when the marginal propensity to consume decreases, the consumption function becomes flatter.
   Autonomous consumption is the y-axis intercept of the consumption function. So when autonomous expenditure decreases, the consumption function shifts downward.
   When expected future income increases, current consumption expenditure increases and the consumption function shifts upward.

3. When disposable income increases by $100 billion, consumption expenditure increases by $80 billion. The *MPC* is $80 billion ÷ $100 billion = 0.8.
   Autonomous consumption (consumption expenditure that is independent of disposable income) equals the y-axis intercept and is $80 billion (Figure 2).

Solution to In the News

Other things remaining the same, a fall in personal income brings a fall in consumption expenditure in a movement along the consumption function. When an increase in consumption expenditure occurs at the same time that personal income decreases, the consumption function has shifted upward. Autonomous consumption expenditure has increased as households spent part of their past savings.

FIGURE 1

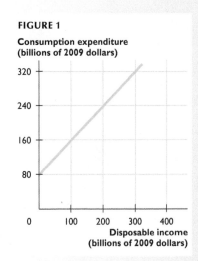

Consumption expenditure
(billions of 2009 dollars)

FIGURE 2

Consumption expenditure
(billions of 2009 dollars)

14.2 EQUILIBRIUM EXPENDITURE

You are now going to discover how, with a fixed price level, aggregate expenditure plans interact to determine real GDP. We will study the relationship between aggregate planned expenditure and real GDP; and we'll study the forces that make aggregate planned expenditure and actual expenditure equal.

But first we'll return to the distinction between *induced* expenditure and *autonomous* expenditure.

■ Induced Expenditure and Autonomous Expenditure

Aggregate planned expenditure is the sum of *induced* expenditure and *autonomous* expenditure. *Induced* expenditure equals consumption expenditure minus imports. You've seen that consumption expenditure increases when disposable income increases. But disposable income equals aggregate income—real GDP—minus net taxes. So disposable income and consumption expenditure increase when real GDP increases. You've also seen that imports increase when real GDP increases. An increase in real GDP brings a larger increase in consumption expenditure than in imports, so induced expenditure—consumption expenditure minus imports—increases as real GDP increases.

Autonomous expenditure—expenditure that does not respond directly to changes in real GDP—consists of investment, government expenditure on goods and services, exports, and autonomous consumption expenditure. These items of aggregate expenditure do change but in response to influences other than real GDP. For example, investment responds to the real interest rate and expected profit. Government expenditure on goods and services depends on the government's policy priorities. And exports depend on global demand for U.S.-produced goods and services.

We combine induced expenditure plans and autonomous expenditure to determine aggregate planned expenditure and equilibrium real GDP.

■ Aggregate Planned Expenditure and Real GDP

An aggregate expenditure schedule and an aggregate expenditure curve describe the relationship between aggregate planned expenditure and real GDP. The table in Figure 14.4 sets out an aggregate expenditure schedule. The columns are the components of aggregate expenditure, C, I, G, X, and M, and aggregate planned expenditure, AE, equals $C + I + G + X - M$.

Figure 14.4 plots an aggregate expenditure curve. The aggregate expenditure curve is the red line AE. Points A through F on that curve correspond to the rows of the table. The AE curve is a graph of aggregate planned expenditure (the last column) plotted against real GDP (the first column).

The horizontal lines in Figure 14.4 show the components of autonomous expenditure I, G, and X. The line labeled $C + I + G + X$ adds consumption expenditure to these components of autonomous expenditure. Aggregate expenditure is expenditure on U.S.-produced goods and services, but the line $C + I + G + X$ includes expenditure on imports. So the AE curve is the $C + I + G + X$ line minus imports. For example, if a student buys a Honda motorbike made in Japan, the student's expenditure is part of C, but it is not an expenditure on a U.S.-produced good. To find the expenditure on U.S.-produced goods, we subtract the value of the imported motorbike.

FIGURE 14.4

Aggregate Expenditure

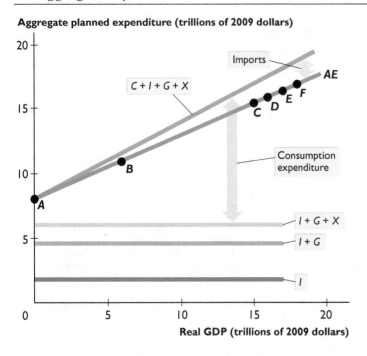

The aggregate expenditure schedule shows the relationship between aggregate planned expenditure and real GDP. For example, in row B of the table, when real GDP is $6 trillion, aggregate planned expenditure is $11.0 trillion ($5.60 + $1.75 + $2.75 + $1.50 − $0.60). As real GDP increases, aggregate planned expenditure increases.

This relationship is graphed as the aggregate expenditure curve AE. The components of aggregate expenditure that increase with real GDP are consumption expenditure and imports.

The other components—investment, government expenditure, and exports—do not vary with real GDP.

| | Real GDP (Y) | Planned expenditure | | | | | Aggregate planned expenditure (AE = C + I + G + X − M) |
		Consumption expenditure (C)	Investment (I)	Government expenditure (G)	Exports (X)	Imports (M)	
		(trillions of 2009 dollars)					
A	0	2.00	1.75	2.75	1.50	0	8.00
B	6.00	5.60	1.75	2.75	1.50	0.60	11.00
C	15.00	11.00	1.75	2.75	1.50	1.50	15.50
D	16.00	11.60	1.75	2.75	1.50	1.60	16.00
E	17.00	12.20	1.75	2.75	1.50	1.70	16.50
F	18.00	12.80	1.75	2.75	1.50	1.80	17.00

Figure 14.4 shows that aggregate planned expenditure increases as real GDP increases. But notice that for each $1 increase in real GDP, aggregate planned expenditure increases by less than $1. For example, when real GDP increases by $1 trillion, from $15 trillion in row C to $16 trillion in row D of the table, aggregate planned expenditure increases by $0.5 trillion, from $15.5 trillion to $16.0 trillion. This feature of the AE curve is important and plays a big role in determining equilibrium expenditure and the effect of a change in autonomous expenditure.

The AE curve summarizes the relationship between aggregate planned expenditure and real GDP. But what determines the point on the AE curve at which the economy operates? What determines actual aggregate expenditure?

■ Equilibrium Expenditure

Equilibrium expenditure
The level of aggregate expenditure that occurs when aggregate *planned* expenditure equals real GDP.

Equilibrium expenditure occurs when aggregate *planned* expenditure equals real GDP. In Figure 14.5(a) aggregate planned expenditure equals real GDP at all the points on the 45° line. Equilibrium occurs where the *AE* curve intersects the 45° line at point *D* with real GDP at $16 trillion. If real GDP is less than $16 trillion, aggregate planned expenditure exceeds real GDP; and if real GDP exceeds $16 trillion, aggregate planned expenditure is less than real GDP.

■ **FIGURE 14.5**

Equilibrium Expenditure

(a) Equilibrium expenditure

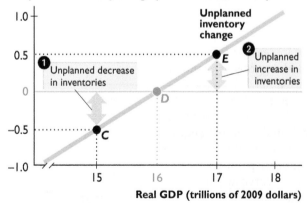

(b) Unplanned inventory change

	Real GDP	Aggregate planned expenditure	Unplanned inventory change
		(trillions of 2009 dollars)	
C	15.0	15.5	−0.5
D	16.0	16.0	0.0
E	17.0	16.5	0.5

The table shows expenditure plans and unplanned changes in inventories at different levels of real GDP. Part (a) illustrates equilibrium expenditure, and part (b) shows the unplanned inventory changes that bring changes in real GDP.

❶ When aggregate planned expenditure exceeds real GDP, an unplanned decrease in inventories occurs. Firms increase production, and real GDP increases.

❷ When real GDP exceeds aggregate planned expenditure, an unplanned increase in inventories occurs. Firms decrease production, and real GDP decreases.

❸ When aggregate planned expenditure equals real GDP, there are no unplanned inventory changes and real GDP remains at its equilibrium level.

■ Convergence to Equilibrium

At equilibrium expenditure, production plans and spending plans agree, and there is no reason for production or spending to change. But when aggregate planned expenditure and actual aggregate expenditure are unequal, production plans and spending plans are misaligned, and a process of convergence toward equilibrium expenditure occurs. Throughout this convergence process, real GDP adjusts.

What are the forces that move aggregate expenditure toward equilibrium? To answer this question, we look at a situation in which aggregate expenditure is away from equilibrium.

Convergence from Below Equilibrium

Suppose that in Figure 14.5, real GDP is $15 trillion. At this level of real GDP, actual aggregate expenditure is also $15 trillion, but aggregate planned expenditure is $15.5 trillion—point C in Figure 14.5(a). Aggregate planned expenditure exceeds actual expenditure. When people spend $15.5 trillion and firms produce goods and services worth $15 trillion, firms' inventories decrease by $0.5 trillion—point C in Figure 14.5(b). This change in inventories is *unplanned*. Because the change in inventories is part of investment, the decrease in inventories decreases actual investment. So actual investment is $0.5 trillion less than planned investment.

Real GDP doesn't remain at $15 trillion for long. Firms have inventory targets based on their sales, and when inventories fall below target, firms increase production. Firms keep increasing production as long as unplanned decreases in inventories occur.

Eventually firms will have increased production by $1 trillion, so real GDP will have increased to $16 trillion. At this real GDP, aggregate planned expenditure rises to $16 trillion—point D in Figure 14.5(a). With aggregate planned expenditure equal to actual expenditure, the unplanned change in inventories is zero and firms hold production constant. The economy has converged on equilibrium expenditure.

Convergence from Above Equilibrium

Now suppose that in Figure 14.5, real GDP is $17 trillion. Actual aggregate expenditure is also $17 trillion, but aggregate planned expenditure is $16.5 trillion—point E in Figure 14.5(a). Actual expenditure exceeds planned expenditure and firms' inventories pile up by an unwanted $0.5 trillion—point E in Figure 14.5(b).

Real GDP doesn't remain at $17 trillion. Firms now want to lower their inventories, so they decrease production.

Eventually firms will have decreased production by $1 trillion, so real GDP will have decreased to $16 trillion. At this real GDP, aggregate planned expenditure falls to $16 trillion—point D in Figure 14.5(a). With aggregate planned expenditure equal to actual expenditure, the unplanned change in inventories is zero and firms hold production constant. The economy has converged on equilibrium expenditure.

Starting from below equilibrium, unplanned decreases in inventories induce firms to increase production; starting from above equilibrium, unplanned increases in inventories induce firms to decrease production. In both cases, production is pulled toward the equilibrium level at which there are no unplanned inventory changes.

EYE on the PAST
Say's Law and Keynes' Principle of Effective Demand

During the Industrial Revolution, which began around 1760 and lasted for 70 years, technological change was rapid. People have talked about the "new economy" of the 1990s, but the 1990s was just another phase of a process that began in the truly new economy of the late 1700s. The pace of change in economic life during those years was unprecedented. Never before had old jobs been destroyed and new jobs created on such a scale. In this environment of rapid economic change, people began to wonder whether the economy could create enough jobs and a high enough level of demand to ensure that people would buy all the things that the new industrial economy could produce.

A French economist, Jean-Baptiste Say, provided the assurance that people were looking for. Born in 1767 (he was 9 years old when Adam Smith's *Wealth of Nations* was published—see Chapter 1, p. 13), Say suffered the wrath of Napoleon for his conservative call for smaller and leaner government and was the most famous economist of his era. His book *A Treatise on Political Economy (Traité d'économie politique)*, published in 1803, became the best-selling university economics textbook in both Europe and America.

In this book, Say reasoned that *supply creates its own demand*—an idea that came to be called *Say's Law*.

You've seen Say's Law at work in the full-employment economy. The real wage rate adjusts to ensure that the quantity of labor demanded equals the quantity of labor supplied and real

GDP equals potential GDP. The real interest rate adjusts to ensure that the quantity of investment that firms plan equals the quantity of saving. Because saving equals income minus consumption expenditure, the equilibrium real interest rate ensures that consumption expenditure plus investment exactly equals potential GDP.

Say's Law came under attack at various times during the nineteenth century. But it came under an onslaught during the Great Depression of the 1930s. With a quarter of the labor force unemployed and real GDP at around three quarters of potential GDP, it seemed like a stretch to argue that supply creates its own demand. But there was no simple principle or slogan with which to replace Say's Law.

In the midst of the Great Depression, in 1936, a British economist, John Maynard Keynes, provided the catch phrase that the world was looking for: *effective demand*.

Born in England in 1883, Keynes was one of the outstanding people of the twentieth century. He was a prolific writer on economic issues, represented Britain at the Versailles peace conference at the end of World War I, and played a prominent role in creating the International Monetary Fund, which monitors the global macroeconomy today.

Keynes revolutionized macroeconomic thinking by turning Say's Law on its head. In Keynes' view, supply does *not* create its own demand, and *effective demand* determines real GDP. If businesses spend less on new capital than the amount that people save,

equilibrium expenditure will be less than potential GDP. Prices and wages are sticky, and resources can become unemployed and remain unemployed indefinitely.

The aggregate expenditure model in this chapter is the modern distillation of Keynes' idea.

Jean-Baptiste Say

John Maynard Keynes

CHECKPOINT 14.2

Explain how real GDP adjusts to achieve equilibrium expenditure.

Practice Problems

Table 1 gives real GDP (Y) and its components in billions of dollars.

1. Calculate aggregate planned expenditure when real GDP is $200 billion and when real GDP is $600 billion.

2. Calculate equilibrium expenditure.

3. If real GDP is $200 billion, explain the process that moves the economy toward equilibrium expenditure.

4. If real GDP is $600 billion, explain the process that moves the economy toward equilibrium expenditure.

TABLE 1

	A	B	C	D	E	F	G
1		Y	C	I	G	X	M
2	A	100	110	50	60	60	15
3	B	200	170	50	60	60	30
4	C	300	230	50	60	60	45
5	D	400	290	50	60	60	60
6	E	500	350	50	60	60	75
7	F	600	410	50	60	60	90

In the News

Growth forecast falls as inventories shrink

Wholesalers' inventories decreased by 0.5% in the second quarter—the biggest fall since the recession. But strong wholesale sales figures and lean inventories suggests that warehouses need to be restocked to meet rising demand.

Source: *The Wall Street Journal*, July 10, 2013

Explain why a fall in inventories is associated with recession and a restocking of inventories might boost economic growth.

Solutions to Practice Problems

1. Aggregate planned expenditure equals $C + I + G + X - M$. When real GDP is $200 billion (row B of Table 1), aggregate planned expenditure is $310 billion. When real GDP is $600 billion (row F), aggregate planned expenditure is $490 billion.

2. Equilibrium expenditure occurs when aggregate planned expenditure equals real GDP. Equilibrium expenditure is $400 billion (row D of Table 1).

3. If real GDP is $200 billion, aggregate planned expenditure is $310 billion, which exceeds real GDP. Firms' inventories decrease by $110 billion. Firms' expenditure plans are not fulfilled, so they increase production to restore their inventories. Real GDP increases. As long as aggregate planned expenditure exceeds real GDP, firms increase production and real GDP increases.

4. If real GDP is $600 billion, aggregate planned expenditure is $490 billion, which is less than real GDP. Firms' inventories increase by $110 billion. Firms cut production and try to reduce their inventories. Real GDP decreases. As long as aggregate planned expenditure is less than real GDP, firms' inventories will increase. Firms will cut production as they try to reduce their inventories to their target level. Real GDP decreases.

Solution to In the News

When firms reduce their target level of inventories, planned investment falls and equilibrium expenditure and real GDP decrease—as occurred during the second quarter of 2013. When firms plan to restock their inventories, the reverse occurs. Equilibrium expenditure and real GDP increase.

Multiplier
The amount by which a change in any component of autonomous expenditure is magnified or multiplied to determine the change in equilibrium expenditure and real GDP that it generates.

14.3 EXPENDITURE MULTIPLIERS

When autonomous expenditure (investment, government expenditure, or exports) increases, aggregate expenditure and real GDP also increase. A **multiplier** determines the amount by which a change in any component of autonomous expenditure is magnified or multiplied to determine the change in equilibrium expenditure and real GDP that it generates.

■ The Basic Idea of the Multiplier

An increase in investment increases real GDP, which increases disposable income and consumption expenditure. The increase in consumption expenditure adds to the increase in investment and a multiplier determines the magnitude of the resulting increase in aggregate expenditure.

Figure 14.6 illustrates the multiplier. The initial aggregate expenditure schedule graphs as AE_0. Equilibrium expenditure and real GDP are $16 trillion. You can see this equilibrium in row B of the table and where the curve AE_0 intersects the 45° line at point B in the figure.

Suppose that investment increases by $0.5 trillion. This increase in investment increases aggregate planned expenditure by $0.5 trillion at each level of real GDP. The new AE curve is AE_1. The new equilibrium expenditure (row D') occurs where AE_1 intersects the 45° line and is $18 trillion (point D'). At this real GDP, aggregate planned expenditure equals real GDP. The increase in equilibrium expenditure ($2 trillion) is *larger* than the increase in investment ($0.5 trillion).

■ **FIGURE 14.6**

The Multiplier

Real GDP (Y)	Aggregate planned expenditure			
	Original (AE₀)		New (AE₁)	
(trillions of 2009 dollars)				
15.00	A	15.25	A'	15.75
16.00	B	16.00	B'	16.50
17.00	C	16.75	C'	17.25
18.00	D	17.50	D'	18.00
19.00	E	18.25	E'	18.75

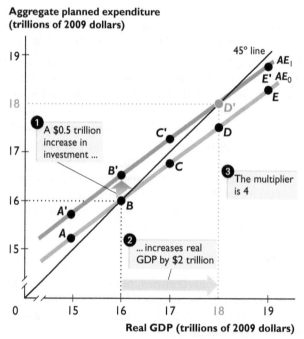

❶ A $0.5 trillion increase in investment shifts the AE curve upward by $0.5 trillion from AE_0 to AE_1.

❷ Equilibrium expenditure increases by $2 trillion from $16 trillion to $18 trillion.

❸ The increase in equilibrium expenditure is 4 times the increase in autonomous expenditure, so the multiplier is 4.

■ The Size of the Multiplier

The multiplier is the amount by which a change in autonomous expenditure is multiplied to determine the change in equilibrium expenditure that it generates. To calculate the multiplier, we divide the change in equilibrium expenditure by the change in autonomous expenditure that generated it. That is,

$$\text{Multiplier} = \frac{\text{Change in equilibrium expenditure}}{\text{Change in autonomous expenditure}}.$$

The change in equilibrium expenditure also equals the change in real GDP, which we'll call ΔY. In Figure 14.6, the change in autonomous expenditure is a change in investment, which we'll call ΔI. The multiplier is

$$\text{Multiplier} = \frac{\Delta Y}{\Delta I}.$$

In Figure 14.6, equilibrium expenditure increases by $2 trillion ($\Delta Y$ = $2 trillion) and investment increases by $0.5 trillion ($\Delta I$ = $0.5 trillion), so

$$\text{Multiplier} = \frac{\Delta Y}{\Delta I} = \frac{\$2 \text{ trillion}}{\$0.5 \text{ trillion}} = 4.$$

The multiplier is 4—real GDP changes by 4 times the change in investment.

Why is the multiplier greater than 1? It is because an increase in autonomous expenditure induces further increases in aggregate expenditure—induced expenditure increases. If the State of California spends $10 million on a new highway, aggregate expenditure and real GDP immediately increase by $10 million. Highway construction workers now have more income, and they spend part of it on cars, vacations, and other goods and services. Real GDP now increases by the initial $10 million plus the extra consumption expenditure. The producers of cars, vacations, and other goods now have increased incomes, and they in turn spend part of the increase on consumption goods and services. Additional income induces additional expenditure, which creates additional income.

■ The Multiplier and the *MPC*

Ignoring imports and income taxes, the magnitude of the multiplier depends only on the marginal propensity to consume. To see why, let's do a calculation. The change in real GDP (ΔY) equals the change in consumption expenditure (ΔC) plus the change in investment (ΔI). That is,

$$\Delta Y = \Delta C + \Delta I.$$

But with no income taxes, the change in consumption expenditure is determined by the change in real GDP and the marginal propensity to consume. It is

$$\Delta C = MPC \times \Delta Y.$$

Now substitute $MPC \times \Delta Y$ for ΔC in the previous equation:

$$\Delta Y = MPC \times \Delta Y + \Delta I.$$

Now solve for ΔY as

$$(1 - MPC) \times \Delta Y = \Delta I,$$

and rearrange the equation:

$$\Delta Y = \frac{1}{(1 - MPC)} \Delta I.$$

Finally, divide both sides of the equation by ΔI to give

$$\text{Multiplier} = \frac{\Delta Y}{\Delta I} = \frac{1}{(1 - MPC)}.$$

In Figure 14.6, the MPC is 0.75. So if we use this value of MPC,

$$\text{Multiplier} = \frac{\Delta Y}{\Delta I} = \frac{1}{(1 - 0.75)} = \frac{1}{0.25} = 4.$$

The greater the marginal propensity to consume, the larger is the multiplier. For example, with a marginal propensity to consume of 0.9, the multiplier would be 10. Let's now look at the influence of imports and income taxes.

■ The Multiplier, Imports, and Income Taxes

The size of the multiplier depends on imports and income taxes, both of which make the multiplier smaller.

When an increase in investment increases consumption and real GDP, part of the increase in expenditure is on imports, not U.S.-produced goods and services. Only expenditure on U.S.-produced goods and services increases U.S. real GDP. The larger the marginal propensity to import, the smaller is the multiplier.

When an increase in investment increases real GDP, income tax payments increase so disposable income increases by less than the increase in real GDP, which means that consumption expenditure increases by less than it would if income tax payments had not changed. The marginal tax rate determines the extent to which income tax payments change when real GDP changes. The **marginal tax rate** is the fraction of a change in real GDP that is paid in income taxes. The larger the marginal tax rate, the smaller are the changes in disposable income and real GDP that result from a given change in autonomous expenditure.

The marginal propensity to import and the marginal tax rate together with the marginal propensity to consume determine the multiplier, and their combined influence determines the slope of the AE curve. The general formula for the multiplier is

$$\text{Multiplier} = \frac{\Delta Y}{\Delta I} = \frac{1}{(1 - \text{Slope of } AE \text{ curve})}.$$

Marginal tax rate
The fraction of a change in real GDP that is paid in income taxes—the change in tax payments divided by the change in real GDP.

Figure 14.7 compares two situations. In Figure 14.7(a), there are no imports and no income taxes. The slope of the AE curve equals MPC, which is 0.75, so the multiplier is 4 (as we calculated above). In Figure 14.7(b), imports and income taxes decrease the slope of the AE curve to 0.5. In this case,

$$\text{Multiplier} = \frac{\Delta Y}{\Delta I} = \frac{1}{(1 - 0.5)} = 2.$$

Over time, the value of the multiplier changes as the marginal tax rate, the marginal propensity to consume, and the marginal propensity to import change. These ongoing changes make the multiplier hard to predict.

FIGURE 14.7

The Multiplier and the Slope of the *AE* Curve

MyEconLab Animation

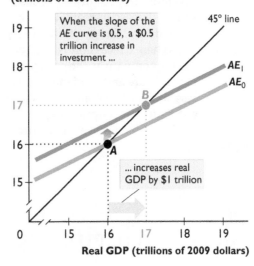

(a) Multiplier is 4

(b) Multiplier is 2

In part (a), with no imports and no income taxes, the slope of the *AE* curve equals the marginal propensity to consume, which in this example is 0.75. The multiplier is 4.

In part (b), with imports and income taxes, the slope of the *AE* curve is less than the marginal propensity to consume. In this example, the slope of the *AE* curve is 0.5 and the multiplier is 2.

EYE on YOUR LIFE
Looking for Multipliers

You can see multipliers in your daily life if you look in the right places and in the right way.

Look for an event in your home city or state that brings new economic activity. It might be a major construction project that is going on near your home or school. It might be a major sporting event that occurs infrequently and brings a large number of people to a city. Or it might be a major new business that moves into an area or expands its activity level.

What supplies do you see being delivered to the site, event, or new business? How many people do you estimate have jobs at this new activity? Where do the supplies and the workers come from?

This new economic activity sets off a multiplier process. What are the first round multiplier effects? Whose incomes are higher because of the purchase of these supplies and the expenditure of the workers hired by the project?

Where do the workers buy their coffee and lunch? Do their purchases create new jobs for students and others in local coffee shops and fast-food outlets?

Where do the workers and suppliers spend the rest of their incomes?

Now think about the second round and subsequent round effects. Where do the students hired by coffee shops spend their incomes and what additional jobs do those expenditures create?

The process goes on and on.

■ Business-Cycle Turning Points

When an expansion is triggered by an increase in autonomous expenditure, as the economy turns the corner into expansion, aggregate planned expenditure exceeds real GDP. Firms see their inventories taking an unplanned dive. To meet their inventory targets, firms increase production, and real GDP begins to increase. This initial increase in real GDP brings higher incomes, which stimulate consumption expenditure. The multiplier process kicks in, and the expansion picks up speed.

When a recession is triggered by a decrease in autonomous expenditure, as the economy turns the corner into recession, real GDP exceeds aggregate planned expenditure and unplanned inventories pile up. To cut inventories, firms produce less, and real GDP falls. This initial fall in real GDP brings lower incomes. People cut their consumption expenditure. The multiplier process reinforces the initial cut in autonomous expenditure, and the recession takes hold.

EYE on the MULTIPLIER

How Big Is the Government Expenditure Multiplier?

Christina Romer, former Chair of the President's Council of Economic Advisers, has estimated the government expenditure multiplier to be 1.6. This number led administration economists to predict that the stimulus plan that increased government expenditure would prevent the unemployment rate from rising much above 8 percent. This prediction turned out to be optimistic and one reason might be that the multiplier assumption is also too optimistic.

Robert Barro, a leading macroeconomist at Harvard University, has studied the effects of very large increases in government expenditure during wars. He finds that the multiplier is only 0.8, which means that real GDP increases by *less than* the increase in government expenditure. The reason is that some private expenditure, mainly investment, gets "crowded out" and real GDP falls.

John Taylor of Stanford University, another leading macroeconomist, agrees with Barro that the government expenditure multiplier is less than 1. He says that crowding out gets more severe as time passes, so the multiplier gets smaller after two years and smaller still after three years.

A big multiplier can occur only if there is substantial slack in the economy—when the recessionary gap is large.

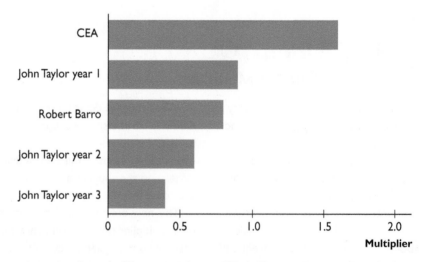

SOURCES OF DATA: Council of Economic Advisers (CEA), Christina Romer and Jared Bernstein, "The Job Impact of the American Recovery and Reinvestment Plan," January 2009; Robert J. Barro, "Government Spending Is No Free Lunch," *The Wall Street Journal*, January 22, 2009; John F. Cogan, Tobias Cwik, John B. Taylor, Volker Wieland, "New Keynesian versus Old Keynesian Government Spending Multipliers," February 2009.

CHECKPOINT 14.3

Explain the expenditure multiplier.

Practice Problems

An economy has no imports and no income taxes, *MPC* is 0.80, and real GDP is $150 billion. Businesses increase investment by $5 billion. Use this information to answer Problems 1 and 2.

1. Calculate the multiplier and the change in real GDP.

2. Calculate the new level of real GDP and explain why real GDP increases by more than $5 billion.

3. In an economy with no imports and no income taxes, an increase in autonomous expenditure of $2 trillion increases equilibrium expenditure by $8 trillion. Calculate the multiplier and the marginal propensity to consume. What happens to the multiplier if an income tax is introduced?

In the News

Keystone XL pipeline—Alberta to the Gulf of Mexico
TransCanada says building the $7 billion pipeline would put 20,000 Americans directly to work during the construction phase and add an expected 118,000 spin-off jobs. The project would also pump $20 billion into the U.S. economy.

Source: CNN Money, September 30, 2011

Explain how TransCanada's investment of $7 billion could create spin-off jobs and pump $20 billion into the U.S. economy.

Solutions to Practice Problems

1. The multiplier equals $1/(1 - MPC)$. *MPC* is 0.8, so the multiplier is 5. Real GDP increases by $25 billion. The increase in investment increases real GDP by the multiplier (5) times the change in investment ($5 billion).

2. Real GDP increases from $150 billion to $175 billion. Real GDP increases by more than $5 billion because the increase in investment induces an increase in consumption expenditure.

3. The multiplier is the increase in equilibrium expenditure ($8 trillion) divided by the increase in autonomous expenditure ($2 trillion). The multiplier is 4.
   The marginal propensity to consume is 0.75. The multiplier is $1/(1 - MPC)$. So $4 = 1/(1 - MPC)$ and *MPC* is 0.75.
   If the government introduces an income tax, the slope of the *AE* curve becomes smaller and the multiplier becomes smaller.

Solution to In the News

The investment of $7 billion will increase real GDP by more than $7 billion because the investment multiplier exceeds 1. When construction begins, new jobs are created and these workers will receive an income. They will spend part of it on consumption goods and services, which in turn will create jobs in other industries—spin-off jobs. These workers will earn an income and they will spend part of it on consumption goods and services. TransCanada says that the multiplier is $20 billion ÷ $7 billion, which is almost 3, an optimistic estimate.

14.4 THE *AD* CURVE AND EQUILIBRIUM EXPENDITURE

In this chapter, we've studied the aggregate expenditure model, in which firms change production when sales and inventories change but they don't change their prices. The aggregate expenditure model determines equilibrium expenditure and real GDP at a given price level. In Chapter 13, we studied the simultaneous determination of real GDP and the price level using the *AS-AD* model. The aggregate demand curve and equilibrium expenditure are related, and this section shows you how.

■ Deriving the *AD* Curve from Equilibrium Expenditure

The *AE* curve is the relationship between aggregate planned expenditure and real GDP when all other influences on expenditure plans remain the same. A movement along the *AE* curve arises from a change in real GDP.

The *AD* curve is the relationship between the quantity of real GDP demanded and the price level when all other influences on expenditure plans remain the same. A movement along the *AD* curve arises from a change in the price level.

Equilibrium expenditure depends on the price level. When the price level rises, other things remaining the same, aggregate planned expenditure decreases and equilibrium expenditure decreases. And when the price level falls, other things remaining the same, aggregate planned expenditure increases and equilibrium expenditure increases. The reason is that a change in the price level changes the buying power of money, the real interest rate, and the real prices of exports and imports (see Chapter 13, pp. 330–332).

When the price level rises, each of these effects decreases aggregate planned expenditure at each level of real GDP, so the *AE* curve shifts downward. A fall in the price level has the opposite effect. When the price level falls, the *AE* curve shifts upward.

Figure 14.8(a) shows the effects of a change in the price level on the *AE* curve and equilibrium expenditure. When the price level is 105, the *AE* curve is AE_0, and it intersects the 45° line at point *B*. Equilibrium expenditure is $16 trillion. If the price level rises to 125, aggregate planned expenditure decreases and the *AE* curve shifts downward to AE_1. Equilibrium expenditure decreases to $15 trillion at point *A*. If the price level falls to 85, aggregate planned expenditure increases and the *AE* curve shifts upward to AE_2. Equilibrium expenditure increases to $17 trillion at point *C*.

The changes in the price level that shift the *AE* curve and change equilibrium expenditure bring movements along the *AD* curve. Figure 14.8(b) shows these movements. At a price level of 105, the quantity of real GDP demanded is $16 trillion—point *B* on the *AD* curve. If the price level rises to 125, the quantity of real GDP demanded decreases along the *AD* curve to $15 trillion at point *A*. If the price level falls to 85, the quantity of real GDP demanded increases along the *AD* curve to $17 trillion at point *C*.

The two parts of Figure 14.8 are connected and illustrate the relationship between the *AE* curve and the *AD* curve. Each point of equilibrium expenditure corresponds to a point on the *AD* curve. The equilibrium expenditure points *A, B,* and *C* (part a) correspond to the points *A, B,* and *C* on the *AD* curve (part b).

FIGURE 14.8

Equilibrium Expenditure and Aggregate Demand

MyEconLab Animation

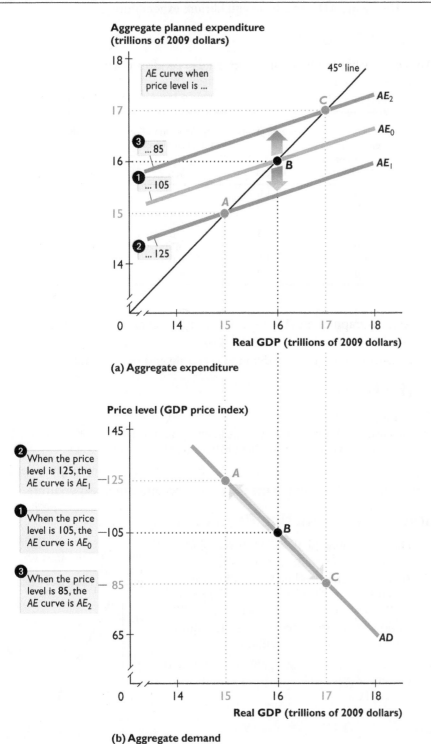

(a) Aggregate expenditure

(b) Aggregate demand

A change in the price level shifts the *AE* curve and results in a movement along the *AD* curve.

1 When the price level is 105, equilibrium expenditure is $16 trillion at point *B* on the *AE* curve *AE₀* and the quantity of real GDP demanded is $16 trillion at point *B* on the *AD* curve.

2 When the price level rises to 125, the *AE* curve shifts downward to *AE₁* and equilibrium expenditure decreases to $15 trillion at point *A*. The quantity of real GDP demanded decreases along the *AD* curve to point *A*.

3 When the price level falls to 85, the *AE* curve shifts upward to *AE₂* and equilibrium expenditure increases to $17 trillion at point *C*. The quantity of real GDP demanded increases along the *AD* curve to point *C*.

Points *A*, *B*, and *C* on the *AD* curve in part (b) correspond to the equilibrium expenditure points *A*, *B*, and *C* in part (a).

CHECKPOINT 14.4

Derive the *AD* curve from equilibrium expenditure.

Practice Problems

An economy has the following aggregate expenditure schedules:

TABLE 1

Real GDP (trillions of 2009 dollars)	Aggregate planned expenditure in trillions of 2009 dollars when the price level is		
	115	105	95
0	1.0	1.5	2.0
1.0	1.5	2.0	2.5
2.0	2.0	2.5	3.0
3.0	2.5	3.0	3.5
4.0	3.0	3.5	4.0
5.0	3.5	4.0	4.5
6.0	4.0	4.5	5.0

1. Make a graph of the *AE* curve at each price level. On the graph, mark the equilibrium expenditure at each price level.
2. Construct the aggregate demand schedule and plot the *AD* curve.

In the News

Price jump worst in 3 years
An increase in the price of essentials such as oil, food, and clothing left U.S consumers struggling with the highest inflation rate in three years.
                                    Source: CNN Money, September 26, 2011
Explain the effect of a rise in the price level on equilibrium expenditure.

Solutions to Practice Problems

1. Figure 1 shows the three *AE* curves and the three levels of equilibrium expenditure. When the price level is 95, equilibrium expenditure is $4 trillion. When the price level is 105, equilibrium expenditure is $3 trillion. When the price level is 115, equilibrium expenditure is $2 trillion.
2. Table 2 shows the aggregate demand schedule, and Figure 2 shows the aggregate demand curve.

Solution to In the News

A rise in the price level decreases consumption expenditure, which decreases aggregate planned expenditure and shifts the *AE* curve downward. Equilibrium expenditure decreases.

FIGURE 1

Aggregate planned expenditure (trillions of 2009 dollars)

TABLE 2

Price level	Real GDP demanded (trillions of 2009 dollars)
95	4
105	3
115	2

FIGURE 2

Price level (GDP price index, 2009 = 100)

CHAPTER SUMMARY

Key Points

1. **Explain how real GDP influences expenditure plans.**

   - Autonomous expenditure is the sum of the components of aggregate expenditure that real GDP does not influence directly.
   - Induced expenditure is the sum of the components of aggregate expenditure that real GDP influences.
   - Consumption expenditure varies with disposable income and real GDP and depends on the marginal propensity to consume.
   - Imports vary with real GDP and depend on the marginal propensity to import.

2. **Explain how real GDP adjusts to achieve equilibrium expenditure.**

   - Actual aggregate expenditure equals real GDP, but when aggregate planned expenditure differs from real GDP, firms have unplanned inventory changes.
   - If aggregate planned expenditure exceeds real GDP, firms increase production and real GDP increases. If real GDP exceeds aggregate planned expenditure, firms decrease production and real GDP decreases.
   - Real GDP changes until aggregate planned expenditure equals real GDP.

3. **Explain the expenditure multiplier.**

   - When autonomous expenditure changes, equilibrium expenditure changes by a larger amount: There is a multiplier.
   - The multiplier is greater than 1 because a change in autonomous expenditure changes induced expenditure.
   - The larger the marginal propensity to consume, the larger is the multiplier.
   - Income taxes and imports make the multiplier smaller.

4. **Derive the *AD* curve from equilibrium expenditure.**

   - The *AD* curve is the relationship between the quantity of real GDP demanded and the price level when all other influences on expenditure plans remain the same.
   - The quantity of real GDP demanded on the *AD* curve is the equilibrium real GDP when aggregate planned expenditure equals real GDP.

Key Terms

MyEconLab Key Terms Quiz

Aggregate planned expenditure, 350
Consumption function, 350
Equilibrium expenditure, 358
Marginal propensity to consume, 352

Marginal propensity to import, 354
Marginal tax rate, 364
Multiplier, 362

CHAPTER CHECKPOINT

Study Plan Problems and Applications

Table 1 shows disposable income and saving in an economy. Use Table 1 to answer Problems 1 and 2.

TABLE 1

Disposable income	Saving
(trillions of dollars)	
0	−5
10	−3
20	−1
30	1
40	3
50	5

1. Calculate consumption expenditure at each level of disposable income. Over what range of disposable income is there dissaving? Estimate the level of disposable income at which saving is zero.

2. Calculate the marginal propensity to consume. If wealth increases by $10 trillion, in which direction will the consumption function change?

Use Table 2 to work Problems 3, 4, and 5. Table 2 shows real GDP, Y, the components of planned expenditure, and aggregate planned expenditure (in millions of dollars) in an economy in which taxes are constant.

TABLE 2

	Planned expenditure					
Y	C	I	G	X	M	AE
0	2.0	1.75	1.0	1.25	0	6.0
2	Q	1.75	1.0	1.25	0.4	6.8
4	4.4	R	1.0	1.25	0.8	7.6
6	5.6	1.75	S	1.25	1.2	8.4
8	6.8	1.75	1.0	T	1.6	9.2
10	8.0	1.75	1.0	1.25	U	10.0
12	9.2	1.75	1.0	1.25	2.4	V

3. Find the value of Q, R, S, T, U, and V.

4. Calculate the marginal propensity to consume and the marginal propensity to import. What is equilibrium expenditure?

5. If investment crashes to $0.55 million but nothing else changes, what is equilibrium expenditure and what is the multiplier?

6. Figure 1 shows aggregate planned expenditure when the price level is 100. When the price level increases to 110, aggregate planned expenditure changes by $0.5 trillion. What is the quantity of real GDP demanded when the price level is 100 and 110?

Durable goods orders rebound in May; GDP revised up

Businesses boosted their orders for machinery 1.2%, computers 1.3%, communications equipment 3.6%, and transportation products 5.8%.

Source: Associated Press, June 24, 2011

Use this information to work Problems 7 and 8.

7. Explain the process by which an increase in planned investment at a constant price level changes equilibrium expenditure and real GDP.

8. What determines the increase in aggregate demand resulting from an increase in business investment?

9. Read *Eye on the Multiplier* on p. 366. Why do multiplier estimates differ? What conditions would be consistent with a large multiplier?

FIGURE 1

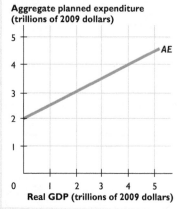

Aggregate planned expenditure (trillions of 2009 dollars)

Instructor Assignable Problems and Applications

MyEconLab Homework, Quiz, or Test if assigned by instructor

1. The output gap in the second quarter of 2009 was $0.8 trillion. How much fiscal stimulus would be required to close the output gap if the multiplier was as large as the Obama team believes? How much fiscal stimulus would be required if the multiplier was as large as Robert Barro believes?

Table 1 shows disposable income and consumption expenditure in an economy. Use Table 1 to work Problems 2 and 3.

2. Calculate saving at each level of disposable income. Over what range of disposable income does consumption expenditure exceed disposable income? Calculate autonomous consumption expenditure.

3. Calculate the marginal propensity to consume. At what level of disposable income will saving be zero? If expected future income increases, in which direction will the consumption function change?

TABLE 1

Disposable income	Consumption expenditure
(billions of dollars)	
200	350
400	500
600	650
800	800
1,000	950

Use the following information to work Problems 4 to 6.

In an economy with no exports and no imports, autonomous consumption is $1 trillion, the marginal propensity to consume is 0.8, investment is $5 trillion, and government expenditure on goods and services is $4 trillion. Taxes are $4 trillion and do not vary with real GDP.

4. If real GDP is $30 trillion, calculate disposable income, consumption expenditure, and aggregate planned expenditure. What is equilibrium expenditure?

5. If real GDP is $30 trillion, explain the process that takes the economy to equilibrium expenditure. If real GDP is $40 trillion, explain the process that takes the economy to equilibrium expenditure.

6. If investment increases by $0.5 trillion, calculate the change in equilibrium expenditure and the multiplier.

Use the following information to work Problems 7 and 8.

Figure 1 shows the aggregate demand curve in an economy. Suppose that aggregate planned expenditure increases by $0.75 trillion for each $1 trillion increase in real GDP.

7. If investment increases by $1 trillion, calculate the change in the quantity of real GDP demanded if the price level is constant at 105.

8. Compare the shift of the *AD* curve with the $1 trillion increase in investment. Explain the magnitude of the shift of the *AD* curve.

9. **Federal deficit hits record $1.42 trillion**
   The 2009 federal budget deficit of $1.42 trillion is more than three times as large as the deficit in any other single year. In September, the government spent $46.6 billion more than it collected in tax revenue. The 2008 budget deficit was $459 billion.

   Source: *USA Today*, October 16, 2009

   By how much did real GDP increase as a result of the government's additional $46.6 billion of expenditure if the multiplier is what the Obama team believed it to be?

FIGURE 1

Price level
(GDP price index, 2009 = 100)

Multiple Choice Quiz

1. The consumption function shows how an increase in _____ influences _____.
   A. income; households' aggregate planned expenditure
   B. nominal GDP; consumption expenditure
   C. disposable income; consumption expenditure
   D. consumption as a fraction of income; real GDP

2. The marginal propensity to consume tells us by how much _____ changes when _____ changes.
   A. consumption expenditure; wealth
   B. the real interest rate; planned consumption
   C. expected future income; the percentage of income spent
   D. consumption expenditure; disposable income

3. Induced expenditure includes _____.
   A. consumption expenditure, government expenditure, and exports
   B. investment, exports, and imports
   C. consumption expenditure and imports
   D. consumption expenditure, investment, and government expenditure

4. The aggregate planned expenditure curve _____ increases.
   A. slopes upward because induced expenditure increases as income
   B. is horizontal because autonomous expenditure is constant when income
   C. shifts upward if induced expenditure increases as income
   D. slopes upward because autonomous expenditure

5. If real GDP _____ planned expenditure, the economy converges to equilibrium expenditure because inventories _____ and firms increase production.
   A. exceeds ; pile up
   B. exceeds; are run down
   C. is less than; are run down
   D. is less than; pile up

6. The multiplier equals _____ divided by _____.
   A. the marginal propensity to consume; autonomous expenditure
   B. 1; (1 − Slope of the AE curve)
   C. 1; Slope of the AE curve
   D. Slope of the AE curve; the marginal propensity to consume

7. The multiplier will increase if the marginal propensity to consume _____ or the marginal tax rate _____.
   A. increases; decreases
   B. increases; increases
   C. decreases; increases
   D. decreases; decreases

8. A rise in the price level shifts the AE curve _____.
   A. upward and creates a movement up along the AD curve
   B. downward and creates a movement up along the AD curve
   C. upward and shifts the AD curve rightward
   D. downward and shifts the AD curve leftward

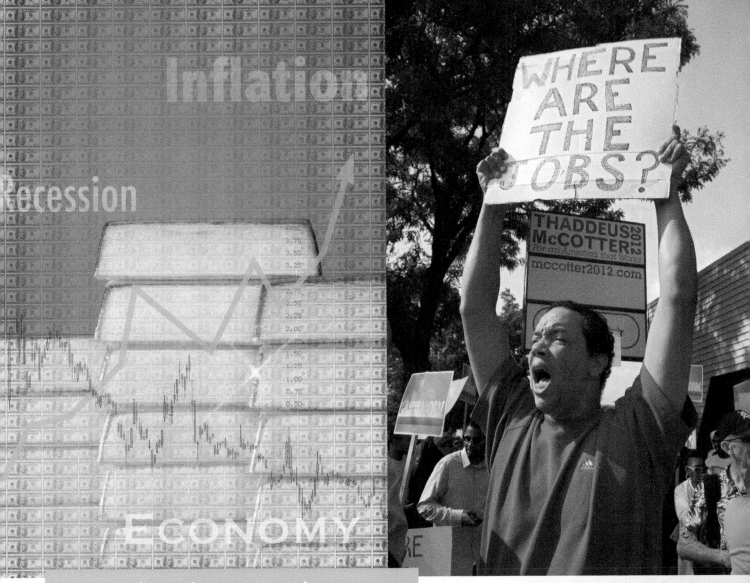

Can we have low unemployment *and* low inflation?

The Short-Run Policy Tradeoff

15

CHAPTER CHECKLIST

When you have completed your study of this chapter, you will be able to

1 Describe the short-run tradeoff between inflation and unemployment.

2 Distinguish between the short-run and the long-run Phillips curves and describe the shifting tradeoff between inflation and unemployment.

3 Explain how the Fed can influence the inflation rate and the unemployment rate.

MyEconLab Big Picture

Short-run Phillips curve
A curve that shows the relationship between the inflation rate and the unemployment rate when the natural unemployment rate and the expected inflation rate remain constant.

15.1 THE SHORT-RUN PHILLIPS CURVE

The **short-run Phillips curve** is a curve that shows the relationship between the inflation rate and the unemployment rate when the natural unemployment rate and the expected inflation rate remain constant.

Figure 15.1 illustrates the short-run Phillips curve. Here, the natural unemployment rate is 6 percent and the expected inflation rate is 3 percent a year. At full employment, the unemployment rate equals the natural unemployment rate and the inflation rate equals the expected inflation rate at point *B*. This point is the anchor point for the short-run Phillips curve.

In an expansion, the unemployment rate decreases and the inflation rate rises. For example, the economy might move to a point such as *A*, where the unemployment rate is 5 percent and the inflation rate is 4 percent a year.

In a recession, the unemployment rate increases and the inflation rate falls. For example, the economy might move to a point such as *C*, where the unemployment rate is 7 percent and the inflation rate is 2 percent a year.

The short-run Phillips curve presents a *tradeoff* between inflation and unemployment. Along a given short-run Phillips curve, a lower unemployment rate can be achieved only by paying the cost of a higher inflation rate, and a lower inflation rate can be achieved only by paying the cost of a higher unemployment rate. For example, in Figure 15.1, a decrease in the unemployment rate from 6 percent to 5 percent costs a 1-percentage-point increase in the inflation rate from 3 percent a year to 4 percent a year.

FIGURE 15.1

A Short-Run Phillips Curve

❶ If the natural unemployment rate is 6 percent, and ❷ the expected inflation rate is 3 percent a year, then ❸ point *B* is at full employment on a short-run Phillips curve.

❹ The short-run Phillips curve (*SRPC*) shows the tradeoff between inflation and unemployment at the given natural unemployment rate and expected inflation rate.

A higher unemployment rate brings a lower inflation rate, and a lower unemployment rate brings a higher inflation rate.

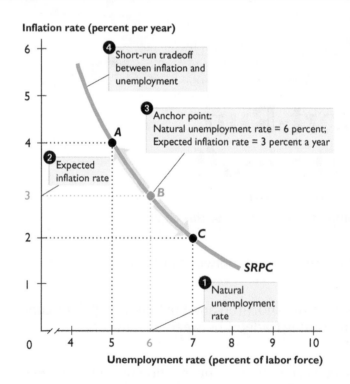

■ Aggregate Supply and the Short-Run Phillips Curve

The short-run Phillips curve is another way of looking at the upward-sloping aggregate supply curve that you learned about in Chapter 13—see pp. 324–328.

Both the short-run Phillips curve and the aggregate supply curve arise because the money wage rate is fixed in the short run.

Along an aggregate supply curve, the money wage rate is fixed. So when the price level rises, the *real wage rate* falls, and a fall in the real wage rate increases the quantity of labor employed and increases the quantity of real GDP supplied.

The events that we've just described also play out along a short-run Phillips curve. The rise in the price level means that the inflation rate has (perhaps temporarily) increased. The increase in the quantity of labor employed means a decrease in the number unemployed and a fall in the unemployment rate.

So a movement along an aggregate supply curve is equivalent to a movement along a short-run Phillips curve. Let's explore these connections between the aggregate supply curve and the short-run Phillips curve a bit more closely.

Unemployment and Real GDP

In a given period, with a fixed amount of capital and a given state of technology, real GDP depends on the quantity of labor employed. At full employment, the quantity of real GDP is *potential GDP* and the unemployment rate is the natural unemployment rate. If real GDP exceeds potential GDP, employment exceeds its full-employment level and the unemployment rate falls below the natural unemployment rate. Similarly, if real GDP is less than potential GDP, employment is less than its full-employment level and the unemployment rate rises above the natural unemployment rate.

The quantitative relationship between the unemployment rate and real GDP was first estimated by economist Arthur M. Okun and is called **Okun's Law.** Okun's Law states that for each percentage point that the unemployment rate is above (below) the natural unemployment rate, real GDP is 2 percent below (above) potential GDP. For example, if the natural unemployment rate is 6 percent and potential GDP is $10 trillion, then when the actual unemployment rate is 7 percent, real GDP is $9.8 trillion—98 percent of potential GDP, or 2 percent below potential GDP. And when the actual unemployment rate is 5 percent, real GDP is $10.2 trillion—102 percent of potential GDP, or 2 percent above potential GDP. Table 15.1 summarizes this relationship.

Inflation and the Price Level

The inflation rate is the percentage change in the price level. So starting from last period's price level, the higher the inflation rate, the higher is the current period's price level. Suppose that last year, the price level was 100. If the inflation rate is 2 percent, the price level rises to 102; if the inflation rate is 3 percent, the price level rises to 103; and if the inflation rate is 4 percent, the price level rises to 104.

With these relationships between the unemployment rate and real GDP (in Table 15.1) and between the inflation rate and the price level, we can establish the connection between the short-run Phillips curve and the aggregate supply curve. Figure 15.2 shows this connection.

First suppose that in the current year, real GDP equals potential GDP and the unemployment rate equals the natural unemployment rate. In Figure 15.2, real

Okun's Law
For each percentage point that the unemployment rate is above (below) the natural unemployment rate, real GDP is 2 percent below (above) potential GDP.

TABLE 15.1

	Unemployment rate (percent)	Real GDP (trillions of 2009 dollars)
A	5	10.2
B	6	10.0
C	7	9.8

GDP is $10 trillion and the unemployment rate is 6 percent. The economy is at point B on the short-run Phillips curve in part (a) and point B on the aggregate supply curve in part (b). The inflation rate is 3 percent a year (its expected rate) in part (a), and the price level is 103 (also its expected level) in part (b).

Next suppose that instead of being at full employment, the economy is above full employment with real GDP of $10.2 trillion at point A on the aggregate supply curve in Figure 15.2(b). In this case, the unemployment rate is 5 percent in Table 15.1 and the economy is at point A on the short-run Phillips curve in Figure 15.2(a). The inflation rate is 4 percent a year (higher than expected) in part (a), and the price level is 104 (also higher than expected) in part (b).

Finally, suppose that the economy is below full employment with real GDP of $9.8 trillion at point C on the aggregate supply curve in Figure 15.2(b). In this case, the unemployment rate is 7 percent in Table 15.1 and the economy is at point C on the short-run Phillips curve in Figure 15.2(a). The inflation rate is 2 percent a year (lower than expected) in part (a), and the price level is 102 (also lower than expected) in part (b).

FIGURE 15.2

The Short-Run Phillips Curve and the Aggregate Supply Curve

MyEconLab Animation

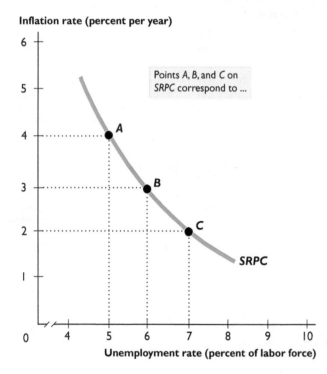

(a) The short-run Phillips curve

(b) The aggregate supply curve

Point A on the Phillips curve corresponds to point A on the aggregate supply curve: The unemployment rate is 5 percent and the inflation rate is 4 percent a year in part (a), and real GDP is $10.2 trillion and the price level is 104 in part (b).

Point B on the Phillips curve corresponds to point B on the aggregate supply curve: The unemployment rate is 6 percent and the inflation rate is 3 percent a year in part (a), and real GDP is $10 trillion and the price level is 103 in part (b).

Point C on the Phillips curve corresponds to point C on the aggregate supply curve: The unemployment rate is 7 percent and the inflation rate is 2 percent a year in part (a), and real GDP is $9.8 trillion and the price level is 102 in part (b).

■ Aggregate Demand Fluctuations

A decrease in aggregate demand that brings a movement down along the aggregate supply curve from point *B* to point *C* lowers the price level and decreases real GDP. That same decrease in aggregate demand brings a movement down along the Phillips curve from point *B* to point *C*.

Similarly, an increase in aggregate demand that brings a movement up along the aggregate supply curve from point *B* to point *A* raises the price level and increases real GDP relative to what they would have been. That same increase in aggregate demand brings a movement up along the Phillips curve from point *B* to point *A*.

EYE on the GLOBAL ECONOMY
Inflation and Unemployment

The Phillips curve is so named because New Zealand economist A. W. (Bill) Phillips discovered the relationship in about 100 years of unemployment and wage inflation data for the United Kingdom.

The figure shows data on inflation and unemployment in the United

Kingdom over most of the twentieth century—1900 to 1997. The data reveal no neat, tight tradeoff. The short-run tradeoff shifts around a great deal.

The highest inflation rate did not occur at the lowest unemployment rate, and the lowest inflation rate did

not occur at the highest unemployment rate. But the lowest unemployment rate in 1917 did bring a high inflation rate. And the highest unemployment rate during the Great Depression of the 1930s brought a gently falling price level.

A. W. (Bill) Phillips

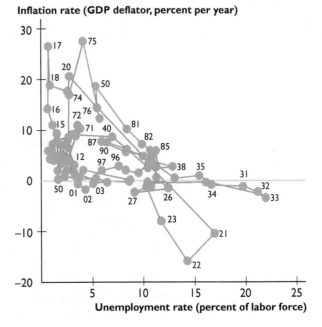

SOURCE: Michael Parkin, "Unemployment, Inflation, and Monetary Policy," *Canadian Journal of Economics*, November 1998.

EYE on the PAST
The U.S. Phillips Curve

Phillips made his discovery in 1958, two years before the election of John F. Kennedy as President of the United States. Very soon thereafter, two young American economists, Paul A. Samuelson and Robert M. Solow, both at MIT and eager to help the new Kennedy administration to pursue a low-unemployment strategy, looked for a Phillips curve in the U.S. data. The figure shows what they found: The red line joining the blue dots shows no recognizable relationship between inflation and unemployment for the 20 or so years that they studied.

Giving more weight to the 1950s experience, Samuelson and Solow proposed the Phillips curve shown in the figure. They believed that the U.S. Phillips curve provided support for the then growing view that the new Kennedy administration could pursue a low unemployment policy with only a moderate rise in the inflation rate.

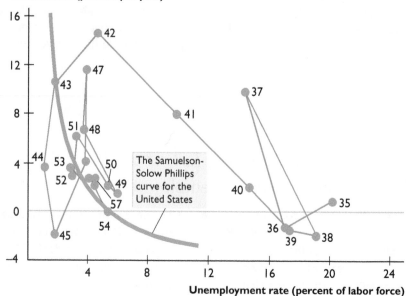

SOURCE OF DATA: Paul A. Samuelson and Robert M. Solow, "Problem of Achieving and Maintaining a Stable Price Level, Analytical Aspects of Anti-Inflation Policy." *American Economic Review*, 50(2), May 1960.

As the 1960s unfolded, the Samuelson-Solow version of the Phillips curve began to look like a permanent tradeoff between inflation and unemployment. But in the late 1960s and early 1970s, the relationship disappeared in the face of rising inflation expectations.

■ Why Bother with the Phillips Curve?

You've seen that the short-run Phillips curve is another way of looking at the aggregate supply curve. And you might be wondering, why bother with the short-run Phillips curve? Isn't the aggregate supply curve adequate for describing the short-run tradeoff?

The Phillips curve is useful for two reasons. First, it focuses directly on two policy targets: the inflation rate and the unemployment rate. Second, the aggregate supply curve shifts whenever the money wage rate or potential GDP changes. Such changes occur every day, so the aggregate supply curve is not a stable tradeoff. The short-run Phillips curve isn't a stable tradeoff either, but it is more stable than the aggregate supply curve. The short-run Phillips curve shifts only when the natural unemployment rate changes or when the expected inflation rate changes.

CHECKPOINT 15.1

MyEconLab Study Plan 15.1
Key Terms Quiz
Solutions

Describe the short-run tradeoff between inflation and unemployment.

Practice Problems

Table 1 describes five possible outcomes for 2014, depending on the level of aggregate demand in that year. Potential GDP is $10 trillion, and the natural unemployment rate is 5 percent.

1. Calculate the inflation rate for each possible outcome.
2. Use Okun's Law to find real GDP at each unemployment rate in Table 1.
3. What are the expected price level and the expected inflation rate in 2014?
4. Plot the short-run Phillips curve for 2014. Mark the points *A, B, C, D,* and *E* that correspond to the data in Table 1 and that you have calculated.
5. Plot the aggregate supply curve for 2014. Mark the points *A, B, C, D,* and *E* that correspond to the data in Table 1.

TABLE 1

	Price level (2013 = 100)	Unemployment rate (percentage)
A	102.5	9
B	105.0	6
C	106.0	5
D	107.5	4
E	110.0	3

In the News

Canada's inflation rises and unemployment falls
After two months of little change, the inflation rate rose to 3.1 percent a year in September and pushed the unemployment rate down to 7.1 percent.

> Source: TradingEconomics.com, October 7, 2011

With the expected inflation rate steady at 2.5 percent a year, did the economy move along its short-run Phillips curve? If so, how? Or did the economy move off its short-run Phillips curve?

Solutions to Practice Problems

1. The inflation rate in 2014 equals the price level in 2014 minus the price level in 2013. So for *A,* the inflation rate is 102.5 – 100, which equals 2.5 percent per year. Calculate the inflation rate at the other points in the same way.
2. Okun's Law: For each 1 percentage point the unemployment rate *U* exceeds the natural unemployment rate *U** (5 percent), real GDP is below potential GDP by 2 percent. So for *A, U* exceeds *U** by 4 percentage points, so real GDP is 8 percent below potential GDP, equal to $9.2 trillion. Calculate real GDP at the other points in the same way.
3. The expected price level is the price level at full employment—row *C.* The expected price is 106, and the expected inflation rate is 6 percent.
4. Plot the inflation rate (Solution 1) against the unemployment rate (Table 1) to get the short-run Phillips curve (Figure 1).
5. Plot the price level (Table 1) against real GDP (Solution 2) to get the aggregate supply curve (Figure 2).

Solution to In the News

With the expected inflation rate steady at 2.5 percent a year, the increase in inflation was unexpected. The Canadian economy remained on its short-run Phillips curve and moved leftward up along it as the inflation rate rose and the unemployment rate fell.

FIGURE 1

Inflation rate (percent per year)

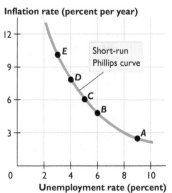

FIGURE 2

Price level (2013 = 100)

15.2 SHORT-RUN AND LONG-RUN PHILLIPS CURVES

The short-run Phillips curve shows the *tradeoff* between inflation and unemployment when the natural unemployment rate and expected inflation rate remain the same. Changes in the natural unemployment rate and the expected inflation rate change the short-run tradeoff and changes in the expected inflation rate give rise to a *long-run* Phillips curve that we'll now examine.

■ The Long-Run Phillips Curve

Long-run Phillips curve
The relationship between inflation and unemployment when the economy is at full employment. The long-run Phillips curve is a vertical line at the natural unemployment rate.

The **long-run Phillips curve** shows the relationship between inflation and unemployment when the economy is at full employment. At full employment, the unemployment rate is the *natural unemployment rate,* so on the long-run Phillips curve, there is only one possible unemployment rate: the natural unemployment rate.

In contrast, the inflation rate can take on any value at full employment. You learned in Chapter 12 (pp. 308–311) that at full employment, for a given real GDP growth rate, the greater the money growth rate, the greater is the inflation rate.

This description of the economy at full employment tells us the properties of the long-run Phillips curve: It is a vertical line located at the natural unemployment rate. In Figure 15.3, the long-run Phillips curve is *LRPC* along which the unemployment rate equals the natural unemployment rate and any inflation rate is possible.

■ FIGURE 15.3

The Long-Run Phillips Curve

The long-run Phillips curve is a vertical line at the natural unemployment rate. In the long run, there is no unemployment–inflation tradeoff.

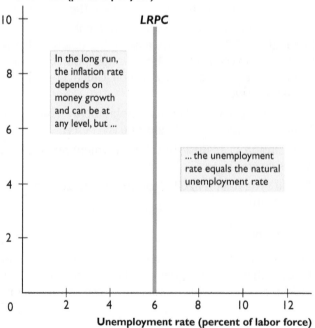

■ Expected Inflation

The **expected inflation rate** is the inflation rate that people forecast and use to set the money wage rate and other money prices. Suppose there is full employment and McDonald's servers earn $10 an hour. With no inflation, a money wage rate of $10 an hour keeps the market for servers in equilibrium. But with 10 percent inflation, a constant money wage rate means a falling real wage rate and a shortage of servers. Now, a 10 percent rise in the money wage rate to $11 is needed to keep the market for servers in equilibrium. If McDonald's and everyone else expect 10 percent inflation, the money wage rate will rise by 10 percent to prevent a labor shortage from arising.

If expectations about the inflation rate turn out to be correct, the price level rises by the 10 percent expected and the real wage rate remains constant at its full-employment equilibrium level and unemployment remains at the natural unemployment rate.

Because the actual inflation rate equals the expected inflation rate at full employment, we can interpret the long-run Phillips curve as the relationship between inflation and unemployment when the inflation rate equals the expected inflation rate.

Figure 15.4 shows short-run Phillips curves for two expected inflation rates. A short-run Phillips curve shows the tradeoff between inflation and unemployment at *a particular expected inflation rate*. When the expected inflation rate changes, the short-run Phillips curve shifts to intersect the long-run Phillips curve at the new expected inflation rate.

Expected inflation rate
The inflation rate that people forecast and use to set the money wage rate and other money prices.

■ FIGURE 15.4

Short-Run and Long-Run Phillips Curves

MyEconLab Animation

If the natural unemployment rate is 6 percent, the long-run Phillips curve is *LRPC*.

❶ If the expected inflation rate is 3 percent a year, the short-run Phillips curve is $SRPC_0$.

❷ If the expected inflation rate is 7 percent a year, the short-run Phillips curve is $SRPC_1$.

In Figure 15.4, when the expected inflation rate is 3 percent a year, the short-run Phillips curve is $SRPC_0$ and when the expected inflation rate is 7 percent a year, the short-run Phillips curve is $SRPC_1$.

■ The Natural Rate Hypothesis

Natural rate hypothesis
The proposition that when the inflation rate changes, the unemployment rate changes *temporarily* and eventually returns to the natural unemployment rate.

The **natural rate hypothesis** is the proposition that when the inflation rate changes, the unemployment rate changes *temporarily* and eventually returns to the natural unemployment rate. The temporary change in the unemployment rate occurs because the real wage rate changes, which leads to a change in the quantity of labor demanded. The unemployment rate returns to the natural rate because eventually, the money wage rate changes to catch up with the change in the price level and return the real wage rate to its full-employment level.

Figure 15.5 illustrates the natural rate hypothesis. Initially, the inflation rate is 3 percent a year and the economy is at full employment, at point A. Then the quantity of money grows more rapidly, at a rate that will generate inflation at 7 percent a year in the long run. In the short run, with a fixed money wage rate, the real wage rate falls, the quantity of labor employed increases and the unemployment rate falls. The inflation rate rises to 5 percent a year, and the economy moves from point A to point B. When the higher inflation rate is expected, the money wage rate increases. As the expected inflation rate increases from 3 percent to 7 percent a year, the short-run Phillips curve shifts upward from $SRPC_0$ to $SRPC_1$. Inflation speeds up and the unemployment rate returns to the natural unemployment rate. In Figure 15.5, the economy moves from point B to point C.

■ FIGURE 15.5

The Natural Rate Hypothesis

MyEconLab Real-time data

The inflation rate is 3 percent a year, and the economy is at full employment, at point A. Then the inflation rate increases.

In the short run, the money wage rate is fixed and the increase in the inflation rate brings a decrease in the unemployment rate—a movement along $SRPC_0$ to point B.

Eventually, the higher inflation rate is expected, the money wage rate rises, and the short-run Phillips curve shifts upward gradually to $SRPC_1$. At the higher expected inflation rate, unemployment returns to the natural unemployment rate—the natural rate hypothesis. The economy is at point C.

EYE on the PAST
A Live Test of the Natural Rate Hypothesis

The figure describes the U.S. economy from 1960 to 1971 and shows that the natural rate hypothesis describes these years well.

The natural unemployment rate was around 6 percent, so the long-run Phillips curve, *LRPC*, was located at that unemployment rate.

In 1960, the inflation rate and the expected inflation rate were around 1 percent a year. The short-run Phillips curve was $SRPC_0$.

Through 1966, the expected inflation rate remained at 1 percent a year but the actual inflation rate edged up and the unemployment rate decreased below the natural unemployment rate. The economy moved up along $SRPC_0$ from point *A* to point *B*.

Then, from 1967 to 1969, the inflation rate increased and so did the expected inflation rate. As the expected inflation rate rose. the shortrun Phillips curve shifted upward. By 1969, the economy had moved to point *C*.

By 1970, the expected inflation rate was around 5 percent a year. As the higher inflation rate came to be expected, the unemployment rate increased.

SOURCE OF DATA: Bureau of Labor Statistics and Bureau of Economic Analysis.

By 1971, the unemployment rate had returned to the natural unemployment rate, the short-run Phillips curve had shifted upward to $SRPC_1$, and the economy had moved to point *D*.

Notice the similarity between the actual events during this period and the natural rate hypothesis, which Figure 15.5 illustrates.

Edmund S. Phelps of Columbia University and Milton Friedman of the University of Chicago proposed the natural rate hypothesis and predicted these events *before* they occurred.

■ Changes in the Natural Unemployment Rate

If the natural unemployment rate changes, both the long-run Phillips curve and the short-run Phillips curve shift. When the natural unemployment rate increases, both the long-run Phillips curve and the short-run Phillips curve shift rightward; and when the natural unemployment rate decreases, both the long-run Phillips curve and the short-run Phillips curve shift leftward.

Figure 15.6 illustrates these changes. When the natural unemployment rate is 6 percent, the long-run Phillips curve is $LRPC_0$. If the expected inflation rate is 3 percent a year, the short-run Phillips curve is $SRPC_0$. A decrease in the natural

FIGURE 15.6

Changes in the Natural Unemployment Rate

The natural unemployment rate is 6 percent, and the long-run Phillips curve is $LRPC_0$. The expected inflation rate is 3 percent a year, and the short-run Phillips curve is $SRPC_0$.

A decrease in the natural unemployment rate shifts both Phillips curves leftward to $LRPC_1$ and $SRPC_1$.

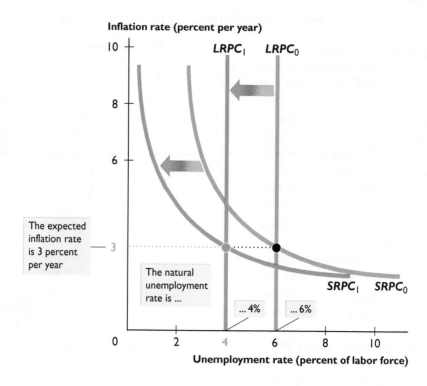

unemployment rate, with no change in the expected inflation rate, shifts both Phillips curves leftward to $LRPC_1$ and $SRPC_1$.

■ Have Changes in the Natural Unemployment Rate Changed the Tradeoff?

Changes in the natural unemployment rate have changed the tradeoff. According to the Congressional Budget Office, the natural unemployment rate increased from about 5 percent in 1950 to more than 6 percent in the mid-1970s and then decreased to 4.8 percent by 2000. It has been constant at this level through 2009.

You learned about the factors that influence the natural unemployment rate in Chapter 8 (pp. 202–207). Those factors divide into two groups: influences on job search and influences on job rationing. Job search is influenced by demographic change, unemployment compensation, and structural change. Job rationing arises from efficiency wages, the minimum wage, and union wages.

A bulge in the birth rate (known as the "baby boom") that occurred after World War II in the late 1940s and early 1950s, brought a bulge in the number of young people entering the labor force during the late 1960s and early 1970s. This bulge in the number of new entrants increased the amount of job search and increased the natural unemployment rate.

Structural change during the 1970s and 1980s, much of it a response to massive hikes in the world price of oil, also contributed to the increase in the natural unemployment rate during the 1970s and early 1980s.

EYE on the TRADEOFF

Can We Have Low Unemployment *and* Low Inflation?

In the short run, we can have low unemployment only if we permit the inflation rate to rise. And we can have low inflation only if we permit the unemployment rate to increase. In the long run, we can improve the unemployment–inflation tradeoff.

We can have low unemployment if we can lower the natural unemployment rate, but that is hard to do.

We can have low inflation if we can lower the expected inflation rate. That, too, is hard to do, but it isn't as hard as lowering the natural unemployment rate. The expected inflation rate does change frequently and sometimes by large amounts.

The years 2000–2013 show how changes in the expected inflation rate change the short-run tradeoff.

During these years, the natural unemployment rate was constant at 5 percent, so the long-run Phillips curve remained fixed at *LRPC*.

The expected inflation rate was 2.5 percent a year in 2000–2002 and the short-run Phillips curve was $SRPC_0$. The expected inflation rate then increased to 3.5 percent a year, where

it remained until 2005, and the short-run Phillips curve shifted to $SRPC_1$.

In 2006, the expected inflation rate decreased to 2.5 percent a year and the short-run Phillips curve shifted back from $SRPC_1$ to $SRPC_0$. The trade-off improved.

In 2008, both inflation and unemployment increased because the natural unemployment rate and the expected inflation rate increased. The rise and then fall in inflation in 2010–2013 suggests that the natural unemployment rate increased temporarily.

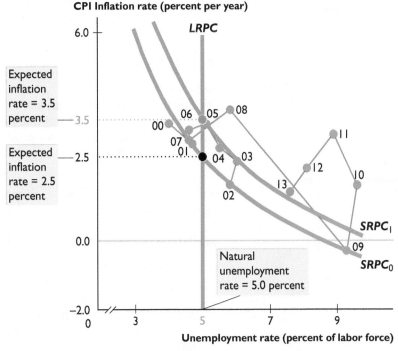

SOURCE OF DATA: Bureau of Labor Statistics and Congressional Budget Office.

As the baby boom generation approached middle age during the 1980s and 1990s, the number of new labor market entrants decreased and the natural unemployment rate decreased too. Also, during the 1990s, rapid technological change brought an increase in productivity and an increase in the demand for labor that shortened the time people spent on job search and lowered the natural unemployment rate yet further. During the 2000s, the natural unemployment rate remained steady.

The changes in the natural unemployment rate that we've just described shifted the short-run and long-run Phillips curves rightward during the 1960s and 1970s and shifted them leftward during the 1980s and 1990s.

FIGURE 1

Inflation rate (percent per year)

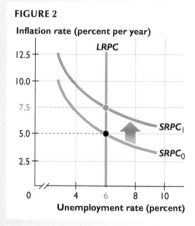

Unemployment rate (percent)

FIGURE 2

Inflation rate (percent per year)

Unemployment rate (percent)

FIGURE 3

Inflation rate (percent per year)

Unemployment rate (percent)

CHECKPOINT 15.2

Distinguish between the short-run and the long-run Phillips curves and describe the shifting tradeoff between inflation and unemployment.

Practice Problems

Figure 1 shows a short-run Phillips curve and a long-run Phillips curve.

1. Identify the curves and label them. What is the expected inflation rate and what is the natural unemployment rate?

2. If the expected inflation rate increases to 7.5 percent a year, show the new short-run and long-run Phillips curves.

3. If the natural unemployment rate increases to 8 percent, show the new short-run and long-run Phillips curves.

4. If aggregate demand starts to grow more rapidly and the inflation rate eventually hits 10 percent a year, how do unemployment and inflation change?

In the News

From the Fed's minutes

The Fed expects the unemployment rate will drop from 9.8 percent today to 9.25 percent by the end of 2010 and to 8 percent by the end of 2011. Private economists predict that the unemployment rate won't drop to a more normal 5 or 6 percent until 2013 or 2014. Inflation should stay subdued.

Source: *The New York Times*, October 14, 2009

Is the Fed predicting that the U.S. economy will move along a short-run Phillips curve or that the short-run Phillips curve will shift through 2011?

Solutions to Practice Problems

1. The long-run Phillips curve is the vertical curve, *LRPC*, and the short-run Phillips curve is the downward-sloping curve, $SRPC_0$ (Figure 2). The expected inflation rate is 5 percent a year—the inflation rate at which *LRPC* and $SRPC_0$ intersect. The natural unemployment rate is 6 percent. The *LRPC* is vertical at the natural unemployment rate.

2. The short-run Phillips curve shifts upward, but the long-run Phillips curve does not change (Figure 2).

3. Both the short-run and long-run Phillips curves shift rightward (Figure 3).

4. Figure 4 shows that as expectations change, the inflation rate rises to 10 percent a year and unemployment falls and then gradually returns to its natural rate.

FIGURE 4

Inflation rate (percent per year)

Unemployment rate (percent)

Solution to In the News

If inflation remains subdued and inflation expectations do not change, the economy is on a short-run Phillips curve at a point to the right of the *LRPC* and is predicted to move leftward up along the *SRPC* toward the *LRPC*.

15.3 INFLUENCING INFLATION AND UNEMPLOYMENT

MyEconLab Snapshot

How can the Fed influence the inflation rate and the unemployment rate and achieve low levels of both? The basic answer is that the Fed can try to lower the expected inflation rate. When the expected inflation rate is low, as it was in 2000, the tradeoff is more favorable than when the expected inflation rate is high, as it was in 1980.

■ Influencing the Expected Inflation Rate

The *expected inflation rate* is the inflation rate that people forecast and use to set the money wage rate and other money prices. To forecast the inflation rate, people use the same basic method that they use to forecast other variables that affect their lives.

Data make up the first ingredient in forecasting—data about the past behavior of the phenomenon that we want to forecast. When people lay heavy bets that the Detroit Lions will win a game, they base their forecast on the performance of the Lions and the other teams in recent games.

Science is the second ingredient in forecasting—the specific science that seeks to understand the phenomenon that we wish to forecast. If we want to know whether it is likely to rain tomorrow, we turn to the science of meteorology. Science tells people how to interpret data.

So to forecast inflation, people use data about past inflation and other relevant variables and the science of economics, which seeks to understand the forces that cause inflation.

You already know the relevant economics: the *AS-AD* model. You know that the money growth rate determines the growth of aggregate demand in the long run. And you know that the trend growth rate of real GDP is the growth rate of aggregate supply in the long run. So the trend money growth rate minus the trend real GDP growth rate determines the trend inflation rate.

The inflation rate fluctuates around its trend as the demand-pull and cost-push forces generate the business cycle. In an expansion, the inflation rate rises above trend, and in a recession, the inflation rate falls below trend as aggregate demand fluctuates to bring movements along the aggregate supply curve. And you know that the money growth rate is one of the influences on these aggregate demand fluctuations.

The Fed determines the money growth rate, so the major ingredient in a forecast of inflation is a forecast of the Fed's actions. Professional Fed watchers and economic forecasters use these ideas along with a lot of data and elaborate statistical models of the economy to forecast the inflation rate.

When all the relevant data and economic science are used to forecast inflation, the resulting forecast is called a **rational expectation**. The rational expectation of the inflation rate is a forecast based on the Fed's forecasted monetary policy along with forecasts of the other forces that influence aggregate demand and aggregate supply. But the dominant factor is the Fed's monetary policy.

Rational expectation
The forecast that results from the use of all the relevant data and economic science.

To lower the expected inflation rate, the Fed must conduct its monetary policy in a manner that creates confidence about future inflation. Chapter 17 explores some of the strategies that might achieve such an outcome. If the Fed can lower inflation expectations, it might achieve lower inflation but not a lower unemployment rate. That is constrained by the natural unemployment rate. If the Fed targets the unemployment rate, trouble lies ahead as you're now about to see.

■ Targeting the Unemployment Rate

Suppose the Fed decides that it wants to lower the unemployment rate. To do so, it speeds up the growth rate of aggregate demand by speeding up the growth rate of money and lowering interest rates. With the expected inflation rate anchored at a low level, the first effect of this action is a lower unemployment rate and a slightly higher inflation rate. But if the Fed drives the unemployment rate below the natural unemployment rate, the inflation rate will continue to rise.

As a higher inflation rate becomes expected, wages and prices start to rise more rapidly, so the actual inflation rate rises further. If the Fed keeps aggregate demand (and the quantity of money) growing fast enough, the inflation rate will keep rising and the unemployment rate will remain below the natural unemployment rate. But eventually, both inflation and unemployment will rise in a return to full employment and the natural rate of unemployment.

Figure 15.7 illustrates the sequence of changes that we've just described. The economy is below full employment with low inflation. Inflation expectations are well anchored at 3 percent per year. Unemployment is above the natural unemployment rate of 6 percent. The economy is on its short-run Phillips curve, $SRPC_0$ at point A, to the right of its long-run Phillips curve, $LRPC$.

Now the Fed speeds up the money growth rate and lowers interest rates. Aggregate demand begins to increase at a faster pace. With no change in expected inflation, money wage rates continue to rise by the same amount as before. As the unemployment rate falls and the inflation rate rises, the economy moves up along

---

■ FIGURE 15.7

Targeting the Unemployment Rate

MyEconLab Animation

The economy starts out at point *A*.

The Fed wants to lower the unemployment rate, so it makes aggregate demand grow faster and the economy slides leftward and upward along $SRPC_0$. The unemployment rate falls but the inflation rate rises.

If the Fed makes aggregate demand keep growing after the unemployment rate has fallen below the natural unemployment rate, the inflation rate keeps rising and the higher inflation becomes expected.

A rising expected inflation rate shifts the short-run Phillips curve upward toward $SRPC_1$ (red arrows). The unemployment rate remains below the natural unemployment rate throughout the adjustment to point *B*.

The unemployment rate has fallen but only temporarily, and the cost is permanently higher inflation.

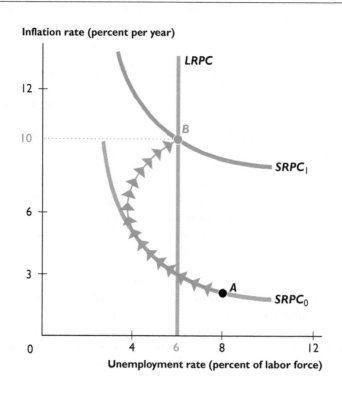

$SRPC_0$. When the expected inflation rate rises, the short-run Phillips curve shifts upward toward $SRPC_1$. The Fed's action lowers the unemployment rate but only temporarily and at the cost of permanently higher inflation. The economy follows the path of the red arrows—and unemployment remains below its natural unemployment rate until, eventually, the economy arrives at point B.

Reversing the Policy to Lower Inflation

If the inflation that results from targeting unemployment becomes unacceptably high, the only way in which low inflation can be restored is to reverse the sequence of events just described. By lowering the growth rate of aggregate demand by slowing money growth and raising interest rates, the Fed can induce a recession. The unemployment rate moves above the natural unemployment rate but inflation eventually subsides and full employment returns.

Inflation Reduction in Practice

It was back in 1981 that the Fed was last faced with a high inflation rate, and to slow it, we paid a high price. The Fed's policy action was unexpected. Money wage rates had been set too high for the path that the Fed followed. The consequence was recession—a decrease in real GDP and increased unemployment. Because it is difficult to lower the inflation rate without bringing on a recession, it is dangerous to use monetary policy to directly target unemployment. Keeping inflation low and stable is the best that monetary policy can do to keep unemployment low.

EYE on YOUR LIFE
The Short-Run Tradeoff in Your Life

The short-run tradeoff enters your life in three distinct ways:

1) It helps you to interpret and understand the current state of the U.S. economy.

2) It helps you to understand the policy decisions taken by the Fed.

3) It encourages you to take a stand on the relative weight that should be given to unemployment and inflation.

The State of the Economy

Consider the change in the U.S. unemployment rate and inflation rate over the past year. Did they change in the same direction or in opposite directions? Can you interpret the change as a movement along a short-run Phillips curve or as a shifting short-run Phillips curve? Can you think of reasons why the short-run Phillips curve might have shifted? Did the natural unemployment rate change? Did the expected inflation rate change?

Was your expected inflation rate the same as what people on the average expected?

The Fed's Recent Decisions

What has the Fed been doing to the interest rate over the past year? How do you think the changes in unemployment and inflation affected the Fed's policy decisions?

Unemployment or Inflation

You've seen that in the long run, there is no tradeoff between unemployment and inflation. But in the short run, there is a tradeoff. If the inflation rate is high, how much unemployment is worth putting up with, and for how long, to lower the inflation rate?

Economists don't agree on the answer to this question. Some say that if inflation is too high, it must be lowered quickly. Some even say that no unemployment is worth enduring to lower inflation.

What is your view? Which is worse, too much inflation or too much unemployment?

CHECKPOINT 15.3

Explain how the Fed can influence the inflation rate and the unemployment rate.

Practice Problems

Figure 1 shows the Phillips curves. Suppose that the current inflation rate is 5 percent a year and the Fed announces that it will slow the money growth rate so that inflation will fall to 2.5 percent a year.

1. If no one believes the Fed and inflation is expected to be 5 percent a year, explain how the Fed's action will affect inflation and unemployment next year.

2. If everyone believes the Fed, explain the effect of the Fed's action on inflation and unemployment next year.

3. If no one believes the Fed but the Fed keeps inflation at 2.5 percent for many years, explain the effect of the Fed's action on inflation and unemployment.

In the News

FOMC Press Release, September 21, 2011

The FOMC anticipates a slow growth in the context of price stability and substantial resource slack will keep inflation subdued for some time.

Source: Board of Governors of the Federal Reserve System

Where on the short-run Phillips curve does the Fed believe the economy to be? What is the Fed anticipating will happen to the short-run Phillips curve?

Solutions to Practice Problems

1. The inflation rate falls and the unemployment rate rises as the economy moves down along its short-run Phillips curve (see Figure 2).

2. The inflation rate falls to 2.5 percent a year, and unemployment remains at 6 percent. People believe the Fed so expected inflation falls to 2.5 percent a year. The short-run Phillips curve shifts downward to $SRPC_1$ (Figure 3).

3. Initially, inflation falls below 5 percent a year and unemployment rises above 6 percent. The longer the Fed maintains this policy, the lower the expected inflation will be and the short-run Phillips curve will shift downward. The unemployment rate will decrease. Eventually, inflation will be 2.5 percent a year when the unemployment rate returns to 6 percent (Figure 4).

Solution to In the News

With substantial resource slack, the Fed believes that the economy is at a point where the unemployment rate is above the natural rate and the inflation rate is below the expected inflation rate. The Fed anticipates that the $SRPC$ will shift downward and the inflation rate will fall.

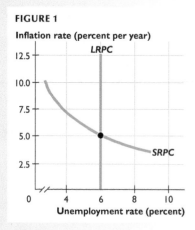

FIGURE 1

Inflation rate (percent per year)

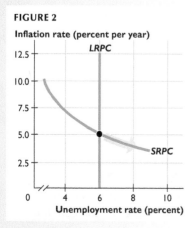

FIGURE 2

Inflation rate (percent per year)

FIGURE 3

Inflation rate (percent per year)

FIGURE 4

Inflation rate (percent per year)

CHAPTER SUMMARY

Key Points

1. Describe the short-run tradeoff between inflation and unemployment.

- The short-run Phillips curve is the downward-sloping relationship between the inflation rate and the unemployment rate when all other influences on these two variables remain the same.
- The short-run Phillips curve presents a *tradeoff* between inflation and unemployment.
- The short-run Phillips curve is another way of looking at the aggregate supply curve.

2. Distinguish between the short-run and the long-run Phillips curves and describe the shifting tradeoff between inflation and unemployment.

- The long-run Phillips curve shows the relationship between inflation and unemployment when the unemployment rate equals the natural unemployment rate and the inflation rate equals the expected inflation rate.
- The long-run Phillips curve is vertical at the *natural unemployment rate*, and there is no long-run tradeoff between unemployment and inflation.
- When the expected inflation rate changes, the short-run Phillips curve shifts to intersect the long-run Phillips curve at the new expected inflation rate.
- When the money growth rate changes, the unemployment rate changes temporarily and eventually returns to the natural unemployment rate—the natural rate hypothesis.
- Changes in the natural unemployment rate shift both the *SRPC* and the *LRPC*.

3. Explain how the Fed can influence the inflation rate and the unemployment rate.

- The rational expectation of the inflation rate is based on forecasts of the Fed's monetary policy and its influence on aggregate demand growth.
- A fall in the expected inflation rate improves the short-run tradeoff.
- Targeting the unemployment rate can only bring temporarily lower unemployment and at the cost of permanently higher inflation.

Key Terms

MyEconLab Key Terms Quiz

Expected inflation rate, 383
Long-run Phillips curve, 382
Natural rate hypothesis, 384

Okun's Law, 377
Rational expectation, 389
Short-run Phillips curve, 376

CHAPTER CHECKPOINT

Study Plan Problems and Applications

TABLE 1 DATA 2014

Price level (2013 = 100)	Real GDP (trillions of 2013 dollars)	Unemployment rate (percent)
A	102	11.0	9
B	104	11.1	7
C	106	11.2	5
D	110	11.4	3

TABLE 2 DATA 2015

Price level (2013 = 100)	Real GDP (trillions of 2013 dollars)	Unemployment rate (percent)
A	108	11.1	9
B	110	11.2	7
C	112	11.3	5
D	116	11.5	3

Table 1 describes four situations that might arise in 2014, depending on the level of aggregate demand. Table 2 describes four situations that might arise in 2015. Use Tables 1 and 2 to work Problems **1** to **4**.

1. Plot the short-run Phillips curve and aggregate supply curve for 2014 and mark the points *A, B, C,* and *D* on each curve that correspond to the data in Table 1.

2. In 2015, the outcome turned out to be row *C* of Table 1. Plot the short-run Phillips curve for 2015 and mark the points *A, B, C,* and *D* that correspond to the data in Table 2.

3. Compare the short-run Phillips curve of 2015 with that of 2014.

4. What is Okun's Law? If the natural unemployment rate is 6 percent, does this economy behave in accordance with Okun's Law?

5. Suppose that the natural unemployment rate is 7 percent in 2013 and it decreases to 6 percent in 2014 with no change in expected inflation. Explain how the short-run and long-run tradeoffs change.

6. Suppose that the natural unemployment rate is 7 percent and the expected inflation rate in 2014 is 3 percent a year. If the inflation rate is expected to rise to 5 percent a year in 2015, explain how the short-run and the long-run Phillips curves will change.

7. The inflation rate is 2 percent a year, and the quantity of money is growing at a pace that will maintain that inflation rate. The natural unemployment rate is 7 percent, and the current unemployment rate is 9 percent. In what direction will the unemployment rate change? How will the short-run Phillips curve and the long-run Phillips curve shift?

8. From 1991 until 2013, the average inflation rate in Russia was 151.48 percent per year. Explain how a history of rapid inflation might influence the short-run and long-run Phillips curves in Russia.

Use the following information to work Problems **9** to **11**.

Changing course, Australia raises interest rate
The Reserve Bank of Australia (the central bank) raised its overnight rate (equivalent to the U.S. federal funds rate) by a quarter of a percentage point, to 3.25 percent a year, amid concerns about rising inflation. The interest rate rise came earlier than many economists had expected.

Source: *The New York Times*, October 6, 2009

9. Sketch the Phillips curves if expected inflation is 2 percent a year and the natural unemployment rate is 5 percent.

10. If with the Reserve Bank's "concerns about rising inflation," people increase the expected inflation rate, explain how the short-run tradeoff will change.

11. If actual inflation had risen prior to the Reserve Bank raising the overnight rate, explain how the short-run tradeoff would change.

 12. Read *Eye on the Tradeoff* on p. 387. How can the Phillips curve account for the combination of inflation and unemployment in 2011? Do the data for that year mean that there is no tradeoff?

Instructor Assignable Problems and Applications

MyEconLab Homework, Quiz, or
Test if assigned by instructor

1. Suppose that the U.S. economy fully recovers from the 2008–2009 recession but the natural unemployment rate has risen to 8 percent and the expected inflation rate is zero. How would the short-run and long-run Phillips curves change? Would the tradeoff be more favorable or less favorable than that of 2011? Draw a graph to illustrate your answer.

2. In an economy, the natural unemployment rate is 4 percent and the expected inflation rate is 3 percent a year. Draw a graph of the short-run and long-run Phillips curves that display this information. Label each curve.

Table 1 describes four possible situations that might arise in 2015, depending on the level of aggregate demand in 2015. Table 2 describes four possible situations that might arise in 2016. Use Tables 1 and 2 to work Problems 3 and 4.

3. Plot the short-run Phillips curve and aggregate supply curve for 2015 and mark the points A, B, C, and D on each curve that correspond to the data in Table 1.

4. In 2015, the outcome turned out to be row D of Table 1. Plot the short-run Phillips curve for 2016 and mark the points A, B, C, and D that correspond to the data in Table 2.

5. Explain the relationship between the long-run Phillips curve and potential GDP and the short-run Phillips curve and the aggregate supply curve.

6. The inflation rate is 3 percent a year, and the quantity of money is growing at a pace that will maintain the inflation rate at 3 percent a year. The natural unemployment rate is 4 percent, and the current unemployment rate is 3 percent. In what direction will the unemployment rate change? How will the short-run Phillips curve and the long-run Phillips curve shift?

7. The inflation rate is 6 percent a year, the unemployment rate is 4 percent, and the economy is at full employment. The Fed announces that it intends to slow the money growth rate to keep the inflation rate at 3 percent a year for the foreseeable future. People believe the Fed. Explain how unemployment and inflation change in the short run and in the long run.

Use the following information to work Problems 8 and 9.

U.S. consumer confidence edges up
The Reuters/University of Michigan Surveys of Consumers reported a rise in September of consumer confidence that exceeded economists' expectations and a rise in expected inflation to 3.7 percent from 3.5 percent a year. Such a rise should be a concern to the Federal Reserve, which has been pumping money into the economy in an attempt to contain the recession and spur a recovery.

Source: *The New York Times*, September 16, 2011

8. Show on a graph the effect of an increase in the expected inflation rate on the Phillips curves if there is no change in the natural unemployment rate.

9. If the Fed is concerned about inflation and unexpectedly slows money growth, explain how unemployment will change in the short run and in the long run.

TABLE 1 DATA 2015

	Price level (2014 = 100)	Real GDP (trillions of 2014 dollars)	Unemployment rate (percent)
A	102	10.0	8
B	104	10.1	6
C	106	10.2	4
D	110	10.4	2

TABLE 2 DATA 2016

	Price level (2014 = 100)	Real GDP (trillions of 2014 dollars)	Unemployment rate (percent)
A	108	10.3	8
B	110	10.4	6
C	112	10.5	4
D	116	10.7	2

Multiple Choice Quiz

1. The short-run Phillips curve shows that, other things remaining the same, _____.

   A. an increase in expected inflation will lower the unemployment rate
   B. a fall in unemployment will lower the inflation rate
   C. the inflation rate rises by 1 percent when unemployment falls by 1 percent
   D. a rise in the inflation rate and a fall in the unemployment rate occur together

2. The long-run Phillips curve _____.

   A. is a horizontal curve at the expected inflation rate
   B. is a vertical curve at the natural unemployment rate
   C. slopes downward as the inflation rate falls
   D. slopes upward as the unemployment rate falls

3. The short-run Phillips curve intersects the long-run Phillips curve at _____.

   A. the expected inflation rate and the current unemployment rate
   B. the current inflation rate and the natural unemployment rate
   C. the expected inflation rate and the natural unemployment rate
   D. the current inflation rate and the current unemployment rate

4. An increase in the expected inflation rate, other things remaining the same, _____.

   A. shifts the short-run Phillips curve upward
   B. creates a movement up along the short-run Phillips curve
   C. decreases the natural unemployment rate and shifts the long-run Phillips curve leftward
   D. creates a movement up along the long-run Phillips curve with no change in the short-run Phillips curve

5. A decrease in the natural unemployment rate _____.

   A. shifts both the short-run and the long-run Phillips curves leftward
   B. shifts the short-run Phillips curve leftward but the long-run Phillips curve does not change
   C. creates a movement along the short-run Phillips curve
   D. increases the expected inflation rate and shifts the short-run Phillips curve upward

6. Suppose that the unemployment rate exceeds the natural unemployment rate and the Fed increases the money growth rate. If the Fed's action is _____.

   A. unexpected, the unemployment rate falls but the inflation rate rises
   B. unexpected, the inflation rate doesn't change but the unemployment rate falls
   C. expected, the inflation rate rises but the unemployment rate doesn't change
   D. expected, the unemployment rate doesn't change and the inflation rate equals the expected inflation rate

Fiscal Policy

**When you have completed your study of this chapter,
you will be able to**

1 Describe the federal budget process and the recent history of tax
  revenues, outlays, deficits, and debts.

2 Explain how fiscal stimulus is used to fight a recession.

3 Explain the supply-side effects of fiscal policy on employment,
  potential GDP, and the economic growth rate.

MyEconLab Big Picture

16.1 THE FEDERAL BUDGET

The federal budget is an annual statement of the tax revenues, outlays, and surplus or deficit of the government of the United States, together with the laws and regulations that authorize these revenues and outlays.

The federal budget has two purposes: to finance the activities of the federal government and to achieve macroeconomic objectives. The first purpose of the federal budget was its only purpose before the Great Depression years of the 1930s. The second purpose evolved as a response to the Great Depression and was initially based on the ideas of *Keynesian macroeconomics* (described in Chapter 8, pp. 190–191). **Fiscal policy** is the use of the federal budget to achieve the macroeconomic objectives of high and sustained economic growth and full employment.

Fiscal policy
The use of the federal budget to achieve the macroeconomic objectives of high and sustained economic growth and full employment.

■ The Institutions and Laws

The President and Congress make the budget and develop fiscal policy on a fixed annual time line and fiscal year. The U.S. fiscal year runs from October 1 to September 30 in the next calendar year. Fiscal 2015 is the fiscal year that begins on October 1, 2014.

The Roles of the President and Congress

The President *proposes* a budget to Congress each February. After Congress has passed the budget acts in September, the President either signs those acts into law or vetoes the entire budget bill. The President does not have the veto power to eliminate specific items in a budget bill and approve others—known as a line-item veto. Although the President proposes and ultimately approves the budget, the task of making the tough decisions on spending and taxes rests with Congress.

Congress begins its work on the budget with the President's proposal. The House of Representatives and the Senate develop their own budget ideas in their respective House and Senate Budget Committees. Formal conferences between the two houses eventually resolve differences of view, and a series of spending acts and an overall budget act are usually passed by both houses before the start of the fiscal year.

Figure 16.1 summarizes the budget time line and the roles of the President and Congress in the budget process.

■ Budget Balance and Debt

The government's **budget balance** is equal to tax revenues minus outlays. That is,

Budget balance
Tax revenues minus outlays.

$$\text{Budget balance} = \text{Tax revenues} - \text{Outlays.}$$

If tax revenues equal outlays, the government has a *balanced budget*. The government has a *budget surplus* if tax revenues exceed outlays. The government has a *budget deficit* if outlays exceed tax revenues.

The budget projections for the 2014 fiscal year were tax revenues of $3,000 billion, outlays of $3,627 billion, and a budget deficit of $627 billion. You can see that $3,000 billion $-$ $3,627 billion $=$ $-$627 billion.

The government budget balance is equal to government saving, which might be zero (balanced budget), positive (budget surplus), or negative (budget deficit). When the government has a budget deficit, it incurs debt. That is, the government

■ **FIGURE 16.1**

The Federal Budget Time Line for Fiscal 2015

MyEconLab Animation

```
Jan. 1, 2014 ●

Feb. 2, 2014 ●    The President submits a budget proposal to Congress.


Oct. 1, 2014 ●    Congress debates, amends, and enacts the budget.
                  The President signs the budget act into law.

                  Fiscal 2015 begins.
                  Supplementary budget laws may be passed.


                  State of the economy influences outlays,
                  tax revenues, and the budget balance.

Sept. 30, 2015 ●  Fiscal 2015 ends.

                  Accounts for Fiscal 2015 are prepared.
                  Outlays, tax revenues, and the
                  budget balance are reported.
```

The federal budget process begins with the President's proposals in February.

Congress debates and amends the President's proposals and enacts a budget before the start of the fiscal year on October 1.

The President signs the budget act into law.

Throughout the fiscal year, Congress might pass supplementary budget laws. The budget outcome is calculated after the end of the fiscal year.

borrows to finance a budget deficit. When the government has a budget surplus, it repays some of its debt. The amount of government debt outstanding—debt that has arisen from past budget deficits—is called **national debt**.

The national debt at the end of a fiscal year equals the national debt at the end of the previous fiscal year plus the budget deficit or minus the budget surplus. For example,

National debt
The amount of government debt outstanding–debt that has arisen from past budget deficits.

Debt at end of 2014 = Debt at end of 2013 + Budget deficit in 2014.

At the end of the 2013 fiscal year, national debt was $11,281 billion. With a budget deficit of $627 billion in 2014, national debt at the end of the 2014 fiscal year becomes $11,908 billion. That is, $11,281 billion + $627 billion = $11,908 billion.

A Personal Analogy

The government's budget and debt are like your budget and debt, only bigger. If you take a student loan each year to go to school, you have a budget deficit and a growing debt. After graduating, if you have a job and repay some of your loan each year, you have a budget surplus each year and a shrinking debt.

■ The Federal Budget in Fiscal 2014

Table 16.1 (next page) shows the magnitudes of the main items in the federal budget in 2014. Personal income taxes and Social Security taxes are the major sources of revenue. **Transfer payments**—Social Security benefits, Medicare and Medicaid benefits, unemployment benefits, and other cash benefits paid to individuals and firms—take the largest share of the government's financial resources. Expenditure on goods and services, which includes the government's defense and homeland security budgets, is also large.

The federal government's deficit and debt are large but they don't show the full picture: They omit a Social Security and Medicare time bomb.

Transfer payments
Social Security benefits, Medicare and Medicaid benefits, unemployment benefits, and other cash benefits.

■ **TABLE 16.1**

The Federal Budget in Fiscal 2014   MyEconLab Real-time data

The federal budget for 2014 was expected to be in a large deficit. Tax revenues of $3,000 billion were expected to be $627 billion less than outlays of $3,627 billion.

Personal income taxes are the largest revenue source and transfer payments are the largest outlay.

Item	Projections (billions of dollars)
Tax Revenues	**3,000**
Personal income taxes	1,358
Social Security taxes	1,031
Corporate income taxes	335
Indirect taxes	276
Outlays	**3,627**
Transfer payments	2,253
Expenditure on goods and services	1,152
Debt interest	222
Balance	**−627**

SOURCE OF DATA: *Budget of the United States Government, Fiscal Year 2014.*

Social Security and Medicare benefits create an $80 trillion time bomb.

■ A Social Security and Medicare Time Bomb

The age distribution of the U.S. population today is dominated by the surge in the birth rate after World War II that created what is called the "baby boom generation." There are 77 million "baby boomers" and the first of them started collecting Social Security pensions in 2008 and became eligible for Medicare benefits in 2011. By 2030, all the baby boomers will be supported by Social Security and Medicare and benefit payments will have doubled.

The government's Social Security and Medicare obligations are a debt and are just as real as the bonds that the government issues to finance its current budget deficit. How big is this debt?

In his book *Spending Beyond Our Means,* economist Jagadeesh Gokhale estimated that this debt was $91 trillion in 2012 and that it is growing by $3 trillion a year. To put the $91 trillion in perspective, note that U.S. GDP in 2012 was $16.2 trillion, so the debt is equivalent to 5.6 years of GDP.

How can the federal government meet its Social Security and Medicare obligations? In the short term, it can make workers pay more taxes. Working-age Americans will pay more than an additional $100,000 in taxes to provide benefits of almost $200,000 to the aged. In the long term, there are four alternatives:

• Raise income taxes
• Raise Social Security taxes
• Cut Social Security benefits
• Cut other federal government spending

In an earlier study, Gokhale and Frank Smetters estimated that to defuse the time bomb, income taxes would need to be raised by 69 percent, or Social Security taxes raised by 95 percent, or Social Security benefits cut by 56 percent. Even if the government stopped all other spending, including that on national defense, it would not be able to pay its bills. By combining the four measures, the pain from each could be lessened, but the pain would still be severe.

This time bomb will dominate fiscal policy decisions for many future years.

EYE on the PAST
Federal Tax Revenues, Outlays, Deficits, and Debt

In 1940, in the first year of World War II, for every dollar earned, the federal government collected 6.5 cents in taxes and spent 9.3 cents. By 1943, at the depth of the most terrible war in history, the government was spending 40 cents of every dollar earned and collecting 12 cents in taxes. The government deficit in 1943 was almost 30 percent of GDP and more than 30 percent in 1944.

The result of these enormous deficits was a mushrooming government debt. By 1946, when the debt-to-GDP ratio (debt as a percentage of GDP) peaked, the government owed more than a year's GDP.

During the 1950s and 1960s, the government's debt-to-GDP ratio tumbled as balanced budgets combined with rapid real GDP growth. By 1974, the debt-to-GDP ratio had fallen to a low of 23 percent.

Budget deficits returned during the 1980s as the defense budget swelled and some tax rates were cut. The result was a growing debt-to-GDP ratio that climbed to almost 50 percent by 1995.

Expenditure restraint combined with sustained real GDP growth lowered the debt-to-GDP ratio during the 1990s, but a surge in expenditures on defense and homeland security, further tax cuts, and a spending surge in 2009 and 2010 to fight the global financial crisis and recession, all combined to swell the debt-to-GDP ratio again. During the 2010s, the government will struggle to balance its budget.

Tax revenues and outlays (percentage of GDP)

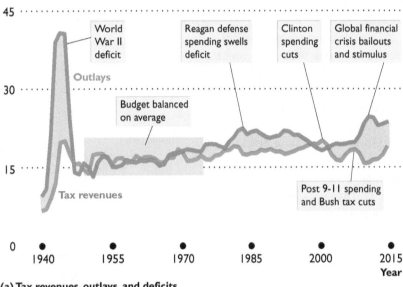

(a) Tax revenues, outlays, and deficits

Debt (percentage of GDP)

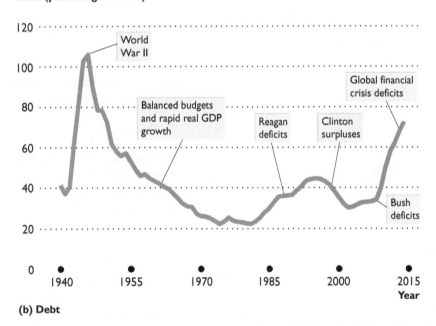

(b) Debt

Source of data: *Budget of the U.S. Government, Fiscal Year 2014*, Historical Tables, Tables 7.1 and 14.1.

EYE on the GLOBAL ECONOMY
The U.S. Budget in Global Perspective

The United States is not alone in having a government budget deficit. All the major countries share this experience. But the United States has one of the largest budget deficits as a percentage of GDP.

To compare the budget deficits across countries, we use the concept of the "general government" deficit, which combines all levels of government: federal, state, and local.

Japan, the United Kingdom, and the United States have large deficits while Australia, New Zealand, Canada, and even the Euro area have smaller deficits. The newly industrialized Asian economies have budget surpluses.

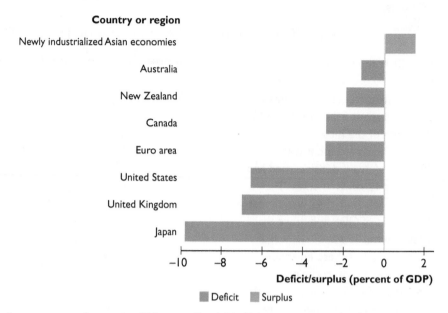

SOURCE OF DATA: International Monetary Fund, *World Economic Outlook*, April 2013.

MyEconLab Study Plan 16.1
Key Terms Quiz
Solutions

 CHECKPOINT 16.1

Describe the federal budget process and the recent history of tax revenues, outlays, deficits, and debts.

Practice Problems

1. What are the tax revenues and outlays in the federal budget, and what was the projected budget balance for Fiscal 2014?

2. In 2012 national debt was about $12 trillion. The U.S. Treasury faced a national debt limit of $16.7 trillion. If budget deficits remain constant and the debt is projected to rise by $2 trillion a year, when will the national debt limit be hit?

Solutions to Practice Problems

1. The tax revenues are personal income taxes, Social Security taxes, corporate income taxes, and indirect taxes; the outlays are transfer payments, expenditure on goods and services, and debt interest. The projected budget balance for Fiscal 2014 was a deficit of $627 billion.

2. In 2012, national debt was $12 trillion. By adding $2 trillion per year to the 2012 national debt, the limit of $16.7 trillion will be hit on (16.7 − 12)/2 years, which is during 2014.

16.2   FISCAL STIMULUS

We've described the federal budget and the institutions that make fiscal policy, and now we're going to study the *effects* of fiscal policy. In doing so, we move from describing facts to explaining theories, and the theory of fiscal policy is controversial.

■ Schools of Thought and Cracks in Today's Consensus

We described the three main schools of macroeconomic thought—*classical*, *Keynesian*, and *monetarist* macroeconomics—in Chapter 8 (see pp. 190–191). We also described today's consensus as one that takes insights from each of the schools. While there is a consensus, the slow recovery from the recession of 2008 and 2009 has placed the consensus under some stress, and cracks are emerging. Some of these cracks have become so public, with economists debating in the pages of *The New York Times*, *The Wall Street Journal*, and *The Economist*, that in discussing the theory of fiscal policy, we must explain the divergent views. The main crack is between the views of Keynesian economists and others and it is on this divide that we will focus. Before digging deeper into the details, we'll provide a quick overview of the two sides of the debate.

The Keynesian View

The Keynesian view is that *fiscal stimulus*—an increase in government outlays or a decrease in tax revenue—boosts real GDP and creates or saves jobs. The leading economists who advance this view include the 2008 Nobel Prize winner Paul Krugman (Princeton University) and President Obama's former chief economic adviser Christina Romer (University of California, Berkeley).

Keynesians say that fiscal stimulus boosts real GDP and employment by increasing aggregate demand. Further, the fiscal stimulus has a multiplier effect: A $1 increase in government outlays or decrease in tax revenue brings a greater than $1 increase in aggregate demand and real GDP.

These positive effects of fiscal stimulus, say the Keynesians, make it a vital and powerful tool in the fight against deep recession and depression.

The Mainstream View

The mainstream view is that Keynesians over-estimate the multiplier effects of fiscal stimulus and that these effects are small, short-lived, and incapable of working fast enough to be useful. Among the leading economists who advance this view are Robert J. Barro (Harvard University), the 1995 Nobel Prize winner Robert E. Lucas Jr. (University of Chicago), and John B. Taylor (Stanford University).

Mainstream economists say that government stimulus does not provide a "free lunch" and instead "crowds out" private consumption expenditure and investment. The durable results of a fiscal stimulus are bigger government, lower potential GDP, a slower real GDP growth rate, and a greater burden of government debt on future generations.

We begin our more detailed look at fiscal policy by explaining the mechanisms that Keynesians emphasize and believe operate to influence aggregate demand. Later in the chapter, we return to the mainstream view and look at supply-side and "crowding out" effects.

▪ Fiscal Policy and Aggregate Demand

A number of different fiscal policy actions might be used in an attempt to stimu-late aggregate demand. Government expenditure on goods and services, or gov-ernment transfer payments might be increased and taxes might be cut. And these changes might occur as an automatic response to the state of the economy or as a result of new spending or tax decisions by Congress. We begin with the distinc-tion between automatic and discretionary fiscal policy.

Automatic Fiscal Policy

Automatic fiscal policy
A fiscal policy action that is triggered by the state of the economy.

A fiscal policy action that is triggered by the state of the economy is called an **auto-matic fiscal policy**. For example, an increase in unemployment induces an increase in transfer payments, and a fall in incomes induces a decrease in tax revenues.

Discretionary Fiscal Policy

Discretionary fiscal policy
A fiscal policy action that is initiated by an act of Congress.

A fiscal policy action that is initiated by an act of Congress is called a **discre-tionary fiscal policy.** A discretionary fiscal policy action requires a change in a spending program or in a tax law. Increases in defense spending or cuts in the income tax rates are examples of discretionary fiscal policy.

▪ Automatic Fiscal Policy

Automatic stabilizers
Features of fiscal policy that stabilize real GDP without explicit action by the government.

Automatic fiscal policy is a consequence of tax revenues and outlays that fluc-tuate with real GDP. These features of fiscal policy are called **automatic stabiliz-ers** because they work to stabilize real GDP without explicit action by the government.

Induced Taxes

Induced taxes
Taxes that vary with real GDP.

On the revenue side of the budget, tax laws define tax *rates*, not tax *dollars*. Tax dol-lars paid depend on tax rates and incomes. But incomes vary with real GDP, so tax revenues depend on real GDP. Taxes that vary with real GDP are called **induced taxes.** When real GDP increases in an expansion, wages and profits rise, so the taxes paid on these incomes—induced taxes—rise. When real GDP decreases in a recession, wages and profits fall, so the induced taxes on these incomes fall.

Needs-Tested Spending

On the expenditure side of the budget, the government creates programs that entitle suitably qualified people and businesses to receive benefits. The spending on such programs is called *needs-tested spending,* and it results in transfer pay-ments that depend on the economic state of individual citizens and businesses. In a recession, as the unemployment rate increases, needs-tested spending on unem-ployment benefits and food stamps increases. In an expansion, the unemploy-ment rate falls and needs-tested spending decreases.

Automatic Stimulus

Because government tax revenues fall and outlays increase in a recession, the budget provides automatic stimulus that helps to shrink the recessionary gap. Similarly, because tax revenues rise and outlays decrease in a boom, the budget provides auto-matic restraint to shrink an inflationary gap.

Fluctuations in the government budget balance over the business cycle create a need to distinguish between the budget's cyclical balance and structural balance.

■ Cyclical and Structural Budget Balances

To identify the government budget deficit that arises from the business cycle, we distinguish between the budget's structural balance and its cyclical balance. The **structural surplus or deficit** is the budget balance that would occur if the economy were at full employment. That is, the structural balance is the balance that the full-employment level of real GDP would generate given the spending programs and tax laws that Congress has created. The **cyclical surplus or deficit** is the budget balance that arises purely because tax revenues and outlays are not at their full-employment levels. That is, the cyclical balance is the balance that arises because tax revenues rise and outlays fall in an inflationary gap and tax revenues fall and outlays rise in a recessionary gap. The *actual* budget balance equals the sum of the structural balance and cyclical balance. A cyclical deficit corrects itself when full employment returns, but a structural deficit requires action by Congress. *Eye on the U.S. Economy* below looks at the recent history of the U.S. structural and cyclical balances.

Structural surplus or deficit
The budget balance that would occur if the economy were at full employment.

Cyclical surplus or deficit
The budget balance that arises because tax revenues and outlays are not at their full-employment levels.

EYE on the U.S. ECONOMY
The U.S. Structural and Cyclical Budget Balances

The U.S. federal budget balance in 2013 was a deficit of $1 trillion and the recessionary gap was close to $1 trillion. With such a large recessionary gap, you would expect some of the deficit to be cyclical. But how much of the 2013 deficit was cyclical? How much was structural?

According to the Congressional Budget Office (CBO), a half of the 2013 deficit was cyclical and a half was structural. The figure shows the actual and cyclical balances as percentages of GDP from 1990 through 2013.

The structural balance equals the actual balance minus the cyclical balance. You can see that the structural deficit was small in 2007, increased in 2008, and exploded in 2009. The 2009 fiscal stimulus package created most of this structural deficit.

When full employment returns, which the CBO says will be in 2018, the cyclical deficit will vanish, but the structural deficit must be addressed by further acts of Congress. No one knows the discretionary measures that will be taken to reduce the structural deficit and this awkward fact creates uncertainty.

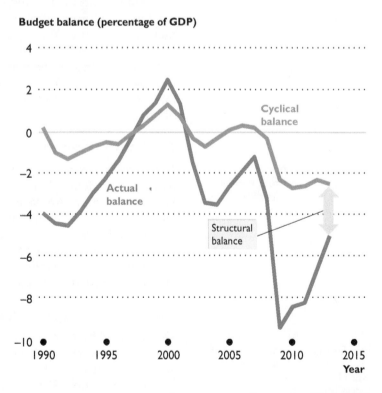

SOURCE OF DATA: Congressional Budget Office.

■ Discretionary Fiscal Policy

Discretionary fiscal policy can take the form of a change in government outlays or a change in tax revenues. And a change in government outlays can take the form of a change in expenditure on goods and services or a change in transfer payments. *Other things remaining the same*, a change in any of the items in the government budget changes aggregate demand and has a multiplier effect—aggregate demand changes by a greater amount than the initial change in the item in the government budget. These multiplier effects are similar to the ones that you studied in Chapters 13 and 14. (Other things might not remain the same, and we'll look at some possible offsetting factors after we've explained the basic Keynesian idea.)

The Government Expenditure Multiplier

Government expenditure multiplier
The effect of a change in government expenditure on goods and services on aggregate demand.

The **government expenditure multiplier** is the effect of a change in government expenditure on goods and services on aggregate demand. Government expenditure is a component of aggregate expenditure, so when government expenditure increases, aggregate demand increases. Real GDP increases and induces an increase in consumption expenditure, which brings a further increase in aggregate expenditure. A multiplier process like the one described in Chapter 14 (pp. 362–366) ensues.

The Tax Multiplier

Tax multiplier
The effect of a change in taxes on aggregate demand.

The **tax multiplier** is the magnification effect of a change in taxes on aggregate demand. A *decrease* in taxes *increases* disposable income, which increases consumption expenditure. A decrease in taxes works like an increase in government expenditure. But the magnitude of the tax multiplier is smaller than the government expenditure multiplier because a $1 tax cut generates *less than* $1 of additional expenditure. The marginal propensity to consume determines the initial increase in expenditure induced by a tax cut and the magnitude of the tax multiplier. For example, if the marginal propensity to consume is 0.75, then the initial increase in consumption expenditure induced by a $1 tax cut is only 75 cents. In this case, the tax multiplier is 0.75 times the magnitude of the government expenditure multiplier.

The Transfer Payments Multiplier

Transfer payments multiplier
The effect of a change in transfer payments on aggregate demand.

The **transfer payments multiplier** is the effect of a change in transfer payments on aggregate demand. This multiplier works like the tax multiplier but in the opposite direction. An *increase* in transfer payments *increases* disposable income, which *increases* consumption expenditure. The magnitude of the transfer payments multiplier is similar to that of the tax multiplier. Just as a $1 tax cut generates *less than* $1 of additional expenditure, so also does a $1 increase in transfer payments. Again, it is the marginal propensity to consume that determines the increase in expenditure induced by an increase in transfer payments.

The Balanced Budget Multiplier

Balanced budget multiplier
The effect on aggregate demand of a *simultaneous* change in government expenditure and taxes that leaves the budget balance unchanged.

The **balanced budget multiplier** is the magnification effect on aggregate demand of a *simultaneous* change in government expenditure and taxes that leaves the budget balance unchanged. The balanced budget multiplier is not zero. It is greater than zero because a $1 increase in government expenditure injects a dollar more into aggregate demand while a $1 tax rise (or decrease in transfer payments) takes less than $1 from aggregate demand. So when both government expenditure and taxes increase by $1, aggregate demand increases.

A Successful Fiscal Stimulus

If real GDP is below potential GDP, the government might pursue a fiscal stimulus by increasing its expenditure on goods and services, increasing transfer payments, cutting taxes, or doing some combination of all three. Figure 16.2 shows us
how these actions increase aggregate demand for a successful stimulus package.

In Figure 16.2(a), potential GDP is $16 trillion but real GDP is only $15 trillion.
The economy is at point A and there is a *recessionary gap* (see Chapter 13, p. 337).

To eliminate the recessionary gap and restore full employment, the government introduces a fiscal stimulus. An increase in government expenditure or a tax
cut increases aggregate expenditure by ΔE. If this were the only change in spending plans, the AD curve would become $AD_0 + \Delta E$ in Figure 16.2(b). But the initial
increase in government expenditure sets off a multiplier process, which increases
consumption expenditure. As the multiplier process plays out, aggregate demand
increases and the AD curve shifts rightward to AD_1.

With no change in the price level, the economy would move from the initial
point A to point B on AD_1. But the increase in aggregate demand combined with
the upward-sloping aggregate supply curve brings a rise in the price level, and the
economy moves to a new equilibrium at point C. The price level rises to 105, real
GDP increases to $16 trillion, and the economy returns to full employment.

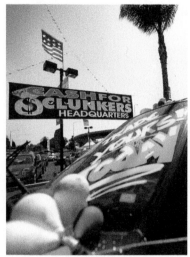

Cash for Clunkers stimulated aggre-
gate demand.

FIGURE 16.2

Fiscal Stimulus in the *AS-AD* Model   MyEconLab Real-time data

(a) Below full-employment equilibrium

(b) Full employment restored

Potential GDP is $16 trillion. At point A, real GDP is $15 trillion,
and **1** there is a $1 trillion recessionary gap. **2** An increase in
government expenditure or a tax cut increases expenditure by ΔE.

3 The multiplier increases induced expenditure. The *AD* curve
shifts rightward to AD_1, the price level rises to 105, real GDP
increases to $16 trillion, and the recessionary gap is eliminated.

■ Limitations of Discretionary Fiscal Policy

Discretionary fiscal stabilization policy looks easy. Calculate the output gap and the multiplier, and determine the direction and size of the change in government expenditure or taxes that will eliminate the gap. In reality, discretionary fiscal policy is seriously hampered by many factors, four of which are

- Law-making time lag
- Shrinking area of law-maker discretion
- Estimating potential GDP
- Economic forecasting

Law-Making Time Lag

The law-making time lag is the amount of time it takes Congress to pass the laws needed to change taxes or spending. This process takes time because each member of Congress has a different idea about what is the best tax or spending program to change, so long debates and committee meetings are needed to reconcile conflicting views. The economy might benefit from fiscal stimulation today, but by the time Congress acts, a different fiscal medicine might be needed.

Shrinking Area of Law-Maker Discretion

During the 2000s, federal spending increased faster than in any other peacetime period. This growth in spending was driven by two forces: increased security threats and an aging population.

The increased security threat resulted in a large increase in expenditure on the military and homeland security. The aging population brought a very large increase in expenditure on entitlement programs such as Medicare.

The growth of this spending has reduced the areas in which Congress can act to change either taxes or outlays. Around 80 percent of the federal budget is effectively off limits for discretionary policy action, and the remaining 20 percent of items are very hard to cut.

So even if the state of the economy calls for a change in fiscal policy, Congress's room to maneuver is severely limited.

Estimating Potential GDP

Potential GDP is not directly observed, so it must be estimated. Because it is not easy to tell whether real GDP is below, above, or at potential GDP, a discretionary fiscal action might move real GDP *away* from potential GDP instead of toward it. This problem is a serious one because too large a fiscal stimulus brings inflation and too little might bring recession.

Economic Forecasting

Fiscal policy changes take a long time to enact in Congress and yet more time to become effective. So fiscal policy must target forecasts of where the economy will be in the future. Economic forecasting has improved enormously in recent years, but it remains inexact and subject to error. So for a second reason, discretionary fiscal action might move real GDP *away* from potential GDP and create the very problems that it seeks to correct.

Further problems with discretionary fiscal policy arise from their supply-side effects that we will examine in the next section.

CHECKPOINT 16.2

Explain how fiscal stimulus is used to fight a recession.

Practice Problems

1. Classify the following items as automatic fiscal policy, discretionary fiscal policy, or not part of fiscal policy.
   - A decrease in tax revenues in a recession
   - Additional government expenditure to upgrade highways
   - An increase in the public education budget
   - A cut in infrastructure expenditure during a boom

2. Explain how aggregate demand changes when government expenditure on national defense increases by $100 billion.

3. Explain how aggregate demand changes when the government increases taxes by $100 billion.

4. Explain how aggregate demand changes when the government increases both expenditure on goods and services and taxes by $100 billion.

In the News

How to curb the deficit
Senator Evan Bayh, Democrat of Indiana, noted that Democrats want to spend more than we can afford; Republicans tend to want to cut taxes more than we can afford. So we are stuck with large deficits.

Source: *The New York Times*, October 31, 2009

What policy will change aggregate demand the most: Democrats agreeing to cut the budget outlays or Republicans agreeing to raise taxes?

Solutions to Practice Problems

1. A decrease in tax revenues in a recession is an automatic fiscal policy.
   Expenditure to upgrade highways is a discretionary fiscal policy.
   An increase in the public education budget is a discretionary fiscal policy.
   A cut in infrastructure expenditure is a discretionary fiscal policy.

2. Aggregate demand increases by more than $100 billion because government expenditure increases induced expenditure.

3. Aggregate demand decreases but by less than $100 billion because the tax increase decreases disposable income, which decreases induced expenditure.

4. An increase in government expenditure of $100 billion increases aggregate demand by more than $100 billion. An increase in taxes of $100 billion decreases aggregate demand by less than $100 billion. The increase is greater than the decrease, so together aggregate demand increases.

Solution to In the News

The effect of a cut in budget outlays on aggregate demand depends on whether the items cut are expenditure on goods and services (government expenditure multiplier) or transfer payments (transfer payments multiplier). An increase in taxes will decrease aggregate demand (tax multiplier). The magnitude of the government expenditure multiplier exceeds the other two multipliers, so a cut in government expenditure on goods and services will decrease aggregate demand the most.

16.3 THE SUPPLY SIDE: POTENTIAL GDP AND GROWTH

Supply-side effects
The effects of fiscal policy on potential GDP and the economic growth rate.

You've seen how fiscal policy can influence the output gap by changing aggregate demand and real GDP relative to potential GDP. But fiscal policy also influences potential GDP and the growth rate of potential GDP. These influences on potential GDP and economic growth arise because the government provides public goods and services that increase productivity and because taxes change the incentives that people face. These influences, called **supply-side effects**, operate more slowly than the demand-side effects emphasized by Keynesians. Supply-side effects are often ignored in times of recession when the focus is on fiscal stimulus and restoring full employment. But in the long run, the supply-side effects of fiscal policy dominate and determine potential GDP.

We'll begin an account of the supply side with a brief explanation of how full employment and potential GDP are determined in the absence of government services and taxes. Then we'll see how government services and taxes change employment and potential GDP.

■ Full Employment and Potential GDP

The quantity of labor demanded and the quantity of labor supplied depend on the real wage rate. The higher the real wage rate, other things remaining the same, the smaller is the quantity of labor demanded and the greater is the quantity of labor supplied. When the real wage rate has adjusted to make the quantity of labor demanded equal to the quantity of labor supplied, there is full employment. And when the quantity of labor is the full-employment quantity, real GDP equals potential GDP.

This brief description of how potential GDP and the full-employment quantity of labor are determined is a summary of the more detailed account in Chapter 8 (pp. 193–198).

How do taxes and the provision of government services—the elements of fiscal policy—influence employment and potential GDP?

■ Fiscal Policy, Employment, and Potential GDP

Both sides of the government budget influence potential GDP. The expenditure side provides public goods and services that enhance productivity and make labor more productive. The revenue side levies taxes that modify incentives that change the full-employment quantities of labor, as well as the amount of saving and investment.

Public Goods and Productivity

Governments provide a legal system and other infrastructure services such as roads and highways, fire-fighting and policing services, and national security, all of which increase the nation's productive potential. Today's world provides a vivid demonstration of the role that good government plays in enhancing productivity. Compare the chaos and absence of productivity in parts of the Middle East and Africa with the order and calm and the productivity they permit in the United States and other industrialized countries.

Public goods and services, financed by the government budget, increase the real GDP that a given amount of labor can produce. So the provision of public goods and services increases potential GDP.

Taxes and Incentives

A tax drives a wedge—called the **tax wedge**—between the price paid by a buyer and the price received by a seller. In the labor market, the income tax drives a wedge between the cost of labor to employers and the take-home pay of workers and decreases the equilibrium quantity of labor employed. A smaller quantity of labor produces a smaller amount of real GDP, so taxes lower potential GDP.

The income tax wedge is only a part of the tax wedge that affects labor-supply decisions. Taxes on expenditure also create a tax wedge that affects employment and potential GDP.

Taxes on consumption expenditure add to the tax wedge that lowers potential GDP. The reason is that a tax on consumption expenditure raises the prices paid for consumption goods and services and is equivalent to a cut in the real wage rate. The incentive to supply labor depends on the goods and services that an hour of labor can buy. The higher the tax on consumption expenditure, the smaller is the quantity of goods and services that an hour of labor buys and the weaker is the incentive to supply labor.

The expenditure tax rate must be added to the income tax rate to find the total tax wedge. If the income tax rate is 25 percent and the tax rate on consumption expenditure is 10 percent, a dollar earned buys only 65 cents worth of goods and services. The tax wedge is 35 percent.

Tax wedge
The gap created by a tax between what a buyer pays and what a seller receives. In the labor market, it is the gap between the before-tax wage rate and the after-tax wage rate.

EYE on the GLOBAL ECONOMY
Some Real-World Tax Wedges

Edward C. Prescott of the Arizona State University, who shared the 2004 Nobel Prize for Economic Science, has estimated the tax wedges for a number of countries. The U.S. tax wedge is a combination of consumption taxes, income taxes, and Social Security taxes.

Among the industrial countries, the U.S. tax wedge is relatively small. Prescott estimates that in France, (marginal) taxes on consumption are 33 percent and taxes on incomes are 49 percent. The estimates for the United Kingdom fall between those for France and the United States. The figure shows these components of the tax wedges in the three countries.

According to Prescott's estimates, the tax wedge has a powerful effect on

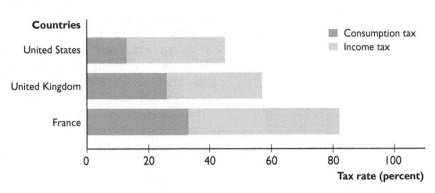

SOURCE OF DATA: Edward C. Prescott, *American Economic Review*, 2003.

employment and potential GDP. Potential GDP per person in France is lower than that of the United States, and the entire difference can be attributed to the difference in the tax wedge in the two countries.

Potential GDP per person in the United Kingdom is lower than that of the United States, and about a third of the difference arises from the different tax wedges. (The rest is due to different productivities.)

■ Fiscal Policy and Potential GDP: A Graphical Analysis

Figure 16.3 illustrates the effects of fiscal policy on potential GDP. It begins with the economy at full employment and with no income tax.

Full Employment With No Income Tax

In part (a), the demand for labor curve is *LD*, and the supply of labor curve is *LS*. The equilibrium real wage rate is $30 an hour, and 250 billion hours of labor a year are employed. The economy is at full employment. In Figure 16.3(b), the production function is *PF*. (This production function incorporates the productivity of an efficient provision of public services.) When 250 billion hours of labor are employed, real GDP—which is also potential GDP—is $16 trillion.

Let's now see how an income tax changes potential GDP.

The Effects of the Income Tax

The tax on labor income influences potential GDP by changing the full-employment quantity of labor. The income tax weakens the incentive to work and drives a wedge between the take-home wage of workers and the cost of labor to firms. The result is a smaller quantity of labor employed and a smaller potential GDP. Figure 16.3 shows this outcome.

In the labor market in part (a), the income tax has no effect on the demand for labor because the quantity of labor that firms plan to hire depends only on how productive labor is and what labor costs—the real wage rate. The demand for labor curve remains at *LD*.

But the income tax changes the supply of labor. With no income tax, the real wage rate is $30 an hour and 250 billion hours of labor a year are employed. An income tax weakens the incentive to work. Workers must pay the government part of each dollar of the before-tax wage rate, as determined by the income tax code. Workers look at the after-tax wage rate when they decide how much labor to supply. In Figure 16.3, an income tax of $15 an hour shifts the supply of labor curve leftward to *LS* + *tax*. The vertical distance between the *LS* curve and the *LS* + *tax* curve measures the $15 of income tax.

With the smaller supply of labor, the before-tax wage rate rises to $35 an hour but the after-tax wage rate falls to $20 an hour. The gap created between the before-tax wage rate and the after-tax wage rate is the *tax wedge*.

The new equilibrium quantity of labor employed is 200 billion hours a year—less than in the no-tax case. This decrease in the full-employment quantity of labor decreases potential GDP as shown in Figure 16.3(b).

Changes in the Tax Rate

A change in the income tax rate changes equilibrium employment and potential GDP. In the example that you've just worked through, the tax rate is about 43 percent—a $15 tax on a $35 wage rate. If the income tax rate is increased, the supply of labor decreases yet more and the *LS* + *tax* curve shifts farther leftward. Equilibrium employment and potential GDP decrease.

If the income tax rate is decreased, the supply of labor increases and the *LS* + *tax* curve shifts rightward. Equilibrium employment and potential GDP increase.

You can now see that a tax cut has two effects: It increases aggregate demand by boosting consumption expenditure and it increases potential GDP.

FIGURE 16.3

Fiscal Policy and Potential GDP

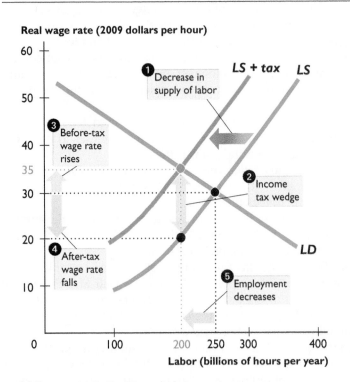

(a) Income tax in the labor market

(b) Income tax and potential GDP

In part (a), the demand for labor is *LD* and the supply of labor is *LS*. With no income tax, the equilibrium real wage rate is $30 an hour and employment is 250 billion hours. In part (b), the production function, *PF*, tells us that 250 billion hours of labor (full employment of labor) produces a potential GDP of $16 trillion.

An income tax **❶** decreases the supply of labor and creates **❷** an income tax wedge between the wage that firms pay and the wage that workers receive. **❸** The before-tax wage rate paid by employers rises and **❹** the after-tax wage rate received by workers falls. **❺** Employment decreases and **❻** potential GDP decreases.

■ Taxes, Deficits, and Economic Growth

You've just seen how taxes can change incentives in the labor market and influence potential GDP. Taxes also affect the market for financial capital, which influences the amount of saving and investment; and saving and investment in turn affect the pace of capital accumulation and the economic growth rate.

Fiscal policy influences the economic growth rate in two ways:

First, taxes drive a wedge between the interest rate paid by borrowers and the interest rate received by lenders. This wedge lowers the amount of saving and investment and slows the economic growth rate.

Second, if the government has a budget deficit, then government borrowing to finance the deficit competes with firms' borrowing to finance investment and to some degree, government borrowing "crowds out" private investment.

Let's examine these two influences on economic growth a bit more closely.

Interest Rate Tax Wedge

Lenders pay an income tax on the interest they receive from borrowers, which creates an interest rate tax wedge. The effects of this tax wedge are analogous to those of the tax wedge on labor income. But they are more serious for two reasons.

First, a tax on wages lowers the quantity of labor employed and lowers potential GDP, while a tax on interest lowers the quantity of saving and investment and slows the *growth rate of real GDP*. A tax on interest income creates a Lucas wedge (Chapter 8, p. 192)—an ever-widening gap between potential GDP and the potential GDP that might have been.

Second, the true tax rate on interest is much higher than that on wages because of the way in which inflation and taxes on interest interact. The interest rate that influences investment and saving plans is the *real after-tax interest rate*.

The *real interest rate* equals the *nominal interest rate* minus the *inflation rate* (see Chapter 7, pp. 182–183). The *after-tax real interest rate* equals the *real interest rate* minus the amount of *income tax paid on interest income*.

But the nominal interest rate, not the real interest rate, determines the amount of tax to be paid; and the higher the inflation rate, the higher is the nominal interest rate, and the higher is the true tax rate on interest income.

Here is an example. Suppose the tax rate on interest is 40 percent of the nominal interest rate. If the nominal interest rate is 4 percent a year and there is no inflation, the real interest rate is also 4 percent a year. The tax on 4 percent interest is 1.6 percent (40 percent of 4 percent), so the after-tax real interest rate is 4 percent minus 1.6 percent, which equals 2.4 percent a year.

Now suppose that the nominal interest rate is 10 percent a year and the inflation rate is 6 percent a year, so the real interest rate is still 4 percent a year. The tax on 10 percent interest is 4 percent (40 percent of 10 percent), so now the after-tax real interest rate is 4 percent minus 4 percent, which equals zero. The true tax rate in this case is not 40 percent but 100 percent!

Even modest inflation makes the true tax rate on interest income extremely high and results in a smaller equilibrium quantity of saving and investment, a slower rate of capital accumulation, and a slower growth rate of real GDP.

Deficits and Crowding Out

With no change in the government's outlays, a tax cut that increases the budget deficit brings an increase in the demand for loanable funds. (You learned about this effect of a government budget deficit in Chapter 10, pp. 256–258.) An increase in the demand for loanable funds raises the real interest rate and crowds out private investment. There is uncertainty about the magnitude of the crowding-out effect but no doubt about its presence.

You can see that this effect of an income tax cut works against the incentive effect. A lower income tax rate shrinks the tax wedge and stimulates employment, saving, and investment, but a higher budget deficit decreases investment.

■ The Supply-Side Debate

Before 1980, few economists paid attention to the supply-side effects of taxes on employment and potential GDP. Then, when Ronald Reagan took office as President, a group of supply-siders began to argue the virtues of cutting taxes. Arthur Laffer was one of them. Laffer and his supporters were not held in high esteem among mainstream economists, but they did become influential for a period. They correctly argued that tax cuts would increase employment and

EYE on FISCAL STIMULUS

Can Fiscal Stimulus End a Recession?

In February 2009, in the depths of the 2008–2009 recession, Congress passed the American Recovery and Reinvestment Act, a $787 billion fiscal stimulus package that the President signed at an economic forum in Denver.

This Act of Congress is an example of discretionary fiscal policy. Did this action by Congress contribute to ending the 2008–2009 recession and making the recession less severe than it might have been?

The Obama Administration economists are confident that the answer is yes: The stimulus package made a significant contribution to easing and ending the recession.

But many, and perhaps most, economists think that the stimulus package played a small role and that the truly big story is not discretionary fiscal policy but the role played by automatic stabilizers.

Let's take a closer look at the fiscal policy actions and their likely effects.

Discretionary Fiscal Policy

In a number of speeches, President Obama promised that fiscal stimulus would save or create 650,000 jobs by the end of the 2009 summer. In October 2009, the Administration economists declared the promise fulfilled. Fiscal stimulus had saved or created the promised 650,000 jobs.

This claim of success might be correct but it isn't startling and it isn't a huge claim. To see why, start by asking

how much GDP 650,000 people would produce. In 2009, each employed person produced $100,000 of real GDP on average. So 650,000 people would produce $65 billion of GDP.

Although the fiscal stimulus passed by Congress totalled $787 billion, by October 2009 only 20 percent of the stimulus had been spent (or taken in tax breaks). So the stimulus was about $160 billion.

If government outlays of $160 billion created $65 billion of GDP, the multiplier was 0.4 (65/160 = 0.4).

This multiplier is much smaller than the 1.6 that the Obama economists say will eventually occur. They believe, like Keynes, that the multiplier starts out small and gets larger over time as spending plans respond to rising incomes. An initial increase in expenditure increases aggregate expenditure. But the increase in aggregate expenditure generates higher incomes, which in turn induces greater consumption expenditure.

Automatic Fiscal Policy

Government revenue is sensitive to the state of the economy. When personal incomes and corporate profits fall, income tax revenues fall too. When unemployment increases, outlays on unemployment benefits and other social welfare benefits increase. These fiscal policy changes are automatic. They occur with speed and without help from Congress.

The scale of automatic fiscal policy changes depends on the depth of recession. In 2009, real GDP sank to 6 percent below potential GDP—a recessionary gap of $800 billion.

Responding to this deep recession, tax revenues crashed and transfer payments skyrocketed. The figure below shows the magnitudes as percentages of GDP. You can see that the automatic stabilizers were much bigger than the discretionary actions—six times as large. This automatic action, not the stimulus package, played the major role in limiting job losses.

SOURCES OF DATA: Budget of the United States, 2010, Bureau of Economic Analysis, and White House press releases.

increase output. But they incorrectly argued that tax cuts would increase tax revenues by enough to decrease the budget deficit. Given that U.S. tax rates are among the lowest in the industrial world, it is unlikely that tax cuts would increase tax revenues. When the Reagan administration did cut taxes, the budget deficit increased, a fact that reinforces this view.

Supply-side economics became tarnished because of its association with Laffer and came to be called "voodoo economics." But mainstream economists, including Martin Feldstein, a Harvard professor who was Reagan's chief economic adviser, recognized the power of tax cuts as incentives but took the standard view that tax cuts without spending cuts would swell the budget deficit and bring a crowding-out effect. This view is now widely accepted by economists on both sides of the political debate.

■ Combined Demand-Side and Supply-Side Effects

You've seen that a fiscal stimulus increases aggregate demand and potential GDP. What is the combined demand-side and supply-side effect? When potential GDP increases, aggregate supply also increases (see Chapter 13, p. 327). When both aggregate demand and aggregate supply increase, we know that equilibrium real GDP increases, but the price level might rise, fall, or remain the same.

Figure 16.4 illustrates this last, neutral case. A fiscal stimulus increases aggregate demand and shifts the AD curve rightward from AD_0 to AD_1. The same fiscal

■ **FIGURE 16.4**

The Combined Demand-Side and Supply-Side Effects
of a Fiscal Stimulus

MyEconLab Animation

❶ A tax cut increases disposable income, which increases aggregate demand and shifts the AD curve from AD_0 to AD_1. A tax cut also strengthens the incentives to work, save, and invest, which increases potential GDP and aggregate supply. The AS curve shifts rightward from AS_0 to AS_1.

❷ Because both aggregate demand and aggregate supply increase, real GDP increases.

The price level might rise, fall, or (as shown here) remain constant depending on which effect, the demand-side effect or the supply-side effect, is larger.

action increases aggregate supply and shifts the *AS* curve rightward from AS_0 to AS_1. In this example, the increase in aggregate supply equals the increase in aggregate demand. This combination increases real GDP and leaves the price level unchanged.

If a fiscal stimulus increases aggregate supply by more than it increases aggregate demand, real GDP would still increase but the price level would fall. (Draw a figure like Figure 16.4 to show this case.) Similarly, if the increase in aggregate supply were smaller than the increase in aggregate demand, again real GDP would increase but the price level would rise. (Draw another figure like Figure 16.4 to show this case.)

■ Long-Run Fiscal Policy Effects

The long-run consequences of fiscal policy are the most profound ones. If investment is crowded out by a large budget deficit, the economic growth rate slows and potential GDP gets ever farther below what it might have been as the Lucas wedge widens. If a large budget deficit persists so that debt increases, confidence in the value of money is eroded and inflation erupts. History provides many examples of this consequence of a fiscal stimulus that gets out of control. It is these long-run effects of fiscal policy that make it vital to keep government outlays and budget deficits under control and to have a plan for restoring a balanced budget at full employment.

EYE on YOUR LIFE
Your Views on Fiscal Policy and How Fiscal Policy Affects You

Consider the U.S. economy right now. Using all the knowledge that you have accumulated during your course and by reading or watching the current news, try to determine the macroeconomic policy issues that face the U.S. economy today.

Do we have a business-cycle problem? Does the economy have a recessionary gap or an inflationary gap, or is the economy back at full employment?

Do we have a productivity problem? Is potential GDP either too low or growing too slowly?

In light of your assessment of the current state of the U.S. economy, what type of fiscal policy would you recommend and vote for?

Are you more concerned about the provision of public services, the size of the budget deficit, or the size of the tax wedge?

If you are more concerned about the provision of public services, would your preferred package include increased spending? If so, on what programs? How would you pay for the expenditure?

If you are more concerned about the size of the budget deficit, how would you propose lowering it?

If you are more concerned about the tax wedge, would your preferred fiscal package include tax cuts? If it would, what public services would you cut to achieve lower taxes?

Consider recent changes in fiscal policy that you have seen reported in the media. What do you think these changes say about the federal government's views of the state of the economy? Do these views agree with yours?

Thinking further about the recent changes in fiscal policy: How do you expect these changes to affect you? How might your spending, saving, and labor supply decisions change?

Using your own responses to fiscal policy changes as an example, are these policy changes influencing aggregate demand, aggregate supply, or both? How do you think they will change real GDP?

MyEconLab Study Plan 16.3
Key Terms Quiz
Solutions

CHECKPOINT 16.3

Explain the supply-side effects of fiscal policy on employment, potential GDP, and the economic growth rate.

Practice Problems

1. The government cuts the income tax rate. Explain the effects of this action on the supply of labor, the demand for labor, the equilibrium level of employment, the real wage rate, and potential GDP.

2. What is the true income tax rate on interest income if the nominal interest rate is 8 percent a year, the inflation rate is 5 percent a year, and the tax rate on nominal interest is 25 percent?

3. If the government cuts its outlays but tax revenue is unchanged, explain the effects on saving, investment, the real interest rate, and the growth rate of real GDP.

In the News

The logic of cutting payroll taxes

Payroll taxes are not the only thing that stops people from working, but Obama's proposal to cut the employer portion of the payroll tax for two years by 3.1 percentage points could create a million or more jobs.

Source: *The New York Times*, September 21, 2011

Explain how the payroll tax cut will influence employment and potential GDP.

Solutions to Practice Problems

1. When the government cuts the income tax rate, the supply of labor increases but the demand for labor does not change. The equilibrium level of employment increases. The real wage rate paid by employers decreases and the real wage rate received by workers increases—the tax wedge shrinks. With increased employment, potential GDP increases.

2. The true tax is 66.67 percent. With a nominal interest rate of 8 percent a year and a tax rate of 25 percent, the tax paid is 25 percent of 8 percent, which is 2 percent. The before-tax real interest rate is 8 percent minus 5 percent, which is 3 percent a year. The true tax paid is 2 percent tax divided by 3 percent before-tax real interest, which is 66.67 percent.

3. If the government cuts outlays but tax revenue is unchanged, the budget deficit decreases or the budget surplus increases. Either way, in the loanable funds market the real interest rate falls and private saving decreases, but total saving and investment increase. With greater investment, capital grows more quickly, and so does real GDP.

Solution to In the News

The cut in payroll taxes will decrease the tax wedge and lower the cost of labor. It will increase the quantity of labor demanded and increase the quantity of labor employed. It will also increase potential GDP. When the tax cut ends after two years, employment and potential GDP will return to their previous levels (other things remaining the same).

CHAPTER SUMMARY

Key Points

1. **Describe the federal budget process and the recent history of tax revenues, outlays, deficits, and debts.**

    *   The federal budget is an annual statement of the outlays, tax revenues, and budget surplus or deficit of the government of the United States.
    *   Fiscal policy is the use of the federal budget to finance the federal government and to influence macroeconomic performance.

2. **Explain how fiscal stimulus is used to fight a recession.**

    *   Fiscal policy became controversial during the 2008–2009 recession: Keynesians advocated aggressive fiscal stimulus and others urged a more cautious approach.
    *   Fiscal policy can be either discretionary or automatic.
    *   Changes in government expenditure and changes in taxes have multiplier effects on aggregate demand and can be used to try to keep real GDP at potential GDP.
    *   In practice, law-making time lags, a shrinking area of law-maker discretion, the difficulty of estimating potential GDP, and the limitations of economic forecasting seriously hamper discretionary fiscal policy.
    *   Automatic stabilizers arise because tax revenues and outlays fluctuate with real GDP.

3. **Explain the supply-side effects of fiscal policy on employment, potential GDP, and the economic growth rate.**

    *   The provision of public goods and services increases productivity and increases potential GDP.
    *   Income taxes create a wedge between the wage rate paid by firms and received by workers and lower both employment and potential GDP.
    *   Income taxes create a wedge between the interest rate paid by firms and received by lenders and lower saving and investment and the growth rate of real GDP.
    *   A government budget deficit raises the real interest rate and crowds out some private investment, which slows real GDP growth.

Key Terms

MyEconLab Key Terms Quiz

Automatic fiscal policy, 404
Automatic stabilizers, 404
Balanced budget multiplier, 406
Budget balance, 398
Cyclical surplus or deficit, 405
Discretionary fiscal policy, 404
Fiscal policy, 398
Government expenditure multiplier, 406

Induced taxes, 404
National debt, 399
Structural surplus or deficit, 405
Supply-side effects, 410
Tax multiplier, 406
Tax wedge, 411
Transfer payments, 399
Transfer payments multiplier, 406

CHAPTER CHECKPOINT

Study Plan Problems and Applications

1. Suppose that in an economy, investment is $400 billion, saving is $400 billion, tax revenues are $500 billion, exports are $300 billion, and imports are $200 billion. Calculate government expenditure and the government's budget balance.

2. Classify the following items as automatic fiscal policy actions, discretionary fiscal policy actions, or neither.
   • An increase in expenditure on homeland security
   • An increase in unemployment benefits paid during a recession
   • Decreased expenditures on national defense during peace time
   • An increase in Medicaid expenditure brought about by a flu epidemic
   • A cut in farm subsidies

3. The U.S. economy is in recession and has a large recessionary gap. Describe what automatic fiscal policy might occur. Describe a fiscal stimulus that could be used that would not increase the budget deficit.

OilPatch is a mineral rich economy in which the government gets most of its tax revenue from oil royalties. But OilPatch has an income tax. Table 1 describes the labor market in OilPatch and Table 2 describes the economy's production function. The government introduces an income tax of $2 per hour worked. Use Tables 1 and 2 to work Problems 4 to 6.

4. What are the levels of employment and potential GDP in OilPatch, what is the real wage rate paid by employers, and what is the after-tax real wage rate received by workers?

5. If OilPatch eliminates its income tax, what then are the levels of employment and potential GDP and what is the real wage rate in OilPatch?

6. If OilPatch doubles its income tax to $4 an hour, what then are the levels of employment and potential GDP? What is the real wage rate paid by employers and the after-tax real wage rate received by workers?

7. The income tax rate on all forms of income is 40 percent and there is a tax of 10 percent on all consumption expenditure. The nominal interest rate is 7 percent a year and the inflation rate is 5 percent a year. What is the size of the tax wedge on wages and what is the true tax rate on interest?

8. **IMF reduces forecast for U.S. growth**
   The IMF expects U.S. economic growth to slow to 2% in 2012 and 2.25% in 2013. That's down from its earlier estimates of 2.15% in 2012 and 2.4% in 2013. Christine Lagarde, the IMF's managing director, said that Congress should "promptly" raise the debt ceiling and adopt strong fiscal policies.

   Source: *The New York Times*, July 3, 2012

   Explain the effects of strong fiscal stimulus if it is implemented well.

9. The Canadian Prime Minister Stephen Harper warned on November 6, 2008, that if policy makers adopt too strong a fiscal stimulus then long-term growth might be jeopardized. Explain what he meant.

 10. Read *Eye on Fiscal Stimulus* on p. 415. How big was the fiscal stimulus package of 2008–2009, how many jobs was it expected to create, and how large was the multiplier implied by that expectation? Did the stimulus work?

TABLE 1 LABOR MARKET

Real wage rate (dollars per hour)	Quantity of labor demanded	supplied
	(thousands of hours)	
10	6	2
11	5	3
12	4	4
13	3	5
14	2	6
15	1	7

TABLE 2 PRODUCTION FUNCTION

Employment (thousands of hours)	Real GDP (millions of dollars)
2	6
3	11
4	15
5	18
6	20
7	21

Instructor Assignable Problems and Applications

1. From the peak in 1929 to the Great Depression trough in 1933, government tax revenues fell by 1.9 percent of GDP and government expenditure increased by 0.3 percent. Real GDP fell by 25 percent. Compare and contrast this experience with the fiscal policy that accompanied the 2008–2009 recession. What did fiscal policy do to moderate the last recession that was largely absent during the Great Depression?

2. Suppose that the U.S. government increases its expenditure on highways and bridges by $100 billion. Explain the effect that this expenditure would have on aggregate demand and real GDP.

3. Suppose that the U.S. government increases its expenditure on highways and bridges by $100 billion. Explain the effect that this expenditure would have on needs-tested spending and the government's budget surplus.

Table 1 describes the labor market in LowTaxLand and Table 2 describes the economy's production function. LowTaxLand introduces an income tax of $1 per hour worked. Use Tables 1 and 2 to work Problems 4 to 6.

4. What are the levels of employment and potential GDP in LowTaxLand, what is the real wage rate paid by employers, and what is the after-tax real wage rate received by workers?

5. If LowTaxLand eliminates its income tax, what then are the levels of employment and potential GDP and what is the real wage rate in LowTaxLand?

6. If LowTaxLand doubles its income tax to $2 an hour, what then are the levels of employment and potential GDP? What is the real wage rate paid by employers and the after-tax real wage rate received by workers?

7. Describe the supply-side effects of a fiscal stimulus and explain how a tax cut will influence potential GDP.

8. Use an aggregate supply–aggregate demand graph to illustrate the effects on real GDP and the price level of a fiscal stimulus when the economy is in recession.

Use the following information to work Problems 9 and 10.

CBO estimates $1.3 trillion deficit for 2011

The Congressional Budget Office (CBO) predicts that the federal budget deficit hit a near-record $1.3 trillion in the just-completed fiscal year. The 2011 deficit equaled 8.6% of GDP, a slight drop from the 8.9% of GDP in 2010. It'll take some combination of new revenues and major spending cuts to get the deficit down to about 3% of GDP, the level that many analysts say is sustainable.

Source: *USA Today*, October 8, 2011

9. If the plan to reduce the deficit includes a cut in transfer payments and a rise in taxes of the same amount, how will this policy influence the budget deficit and real GDP?

10. If the plan to reduce the deficit includes an increase in taxes on the wealthy, explain how this policy might have serious supply-side consequences for both potential GDP and the growth rate of real GDP.

TABLE 1 LABOR MARKET

Real wage rate (dollars per hour)	Quantity of labor demanded	supplied
	(thousands of hours)	
10.00	18	6
10.50	15	9
11.00	12	12
11.50	9	15
12.00	6	18
12.50	3	21

TABLE 2 PRODUCTION FUNCTION

Employment (thousands of hours)	Real GDP (millions of dollars)
6	7
9	12
12	16
15	19
18	21
21	22

Multiple Choice Quiz

1. The federal government's major outlay in its budget is _____ and its major source of revenue is _____.

    A. debt interest; sales of government bonds
    B. expenditure on goods and services; taxes on goods and services
    C. Social Security and other benefits; personal income taxes
    D. subsidies to farmers; corporate taxes

2. U.S. national debt _____ when the federal government's _____.

    A. increases; outlays exceed tax revenue
    B. decreases; outlays exceed tax revenue
    C. increases; tax revenue rises faster than outlays
    D. decreases; tax revenue rises faster than outlays

3. Discretionary fiscal policy to stimulate the economy includes _____.

    A. lowering the tax rate paid by households with middle incomes
    B. raising the tax on gasoline
    C. the fall in tax revenue as the economy goes into recession
    D. the rise in tax revenue collected from businesses as their profits increase

4. Automatic fiscal policy _____.

    A. requires an action of the government
    B. is weak unless the government cuts its outlays to reduce the deficit
    C. operates as the economy moves along its business cycle
    D. reduces the deficit as the economy goes into recession

5. Needs-tested spending is _____ fiscal policy because it _____ .

    A. automatic; increases in recession and decreases in expansion
    B. discretionary; increases when tax revenue increases
    C. automatic; increases when the government's budget deficit falls
    D. discretionary; is determined by economic hardship

6. A government expenditure multiplier _____ .

    A. equals 1
    B. is less than the tax multiplier
    C. exceeds 1
    D. equals the tax multiplier

7. When the government lowers the income tax rate, _____ .

    A. employment increases and potential GDP increases
    B. employment does not change but labor productivity falls
    C. labor productivity rises and employment decreases
    D. both labor productivity and potential GDP increase

8. A tax cut increases _____ .

    A. aggregate demand but has no effect on aggregate supply
    B. aggregate demand because it increases disposable income and increases aggregate supply because it is an incentive to supply more labor
    C. aggregate demand because it increases consumption expenditure and decreases aggregate supply because labor productivity falls
    D. aggregate supply but has no effect on aggregate demand

Did the Fed save us from another Great Depression?

Monetary Policy

When you have completed your study of this chapter, you will be able to

1 Describe the objectives of U.S. monetary policy, the framework for achieving those objectives, and the Fed's monetary policy actions.

2 Explain the transmission channels through which the Fed influences real GDP and the inflation rate.

3 Explain and compare alternative monetary policy strategies.

MyEconLab Big Picture

17.1 HOW THE FED CONDUCTS MONETARY POLICY

A nation's monetary policy objectives and the framework for setting and achieving those objectives stem from the relationship between the central bank and the government. We'll describe the objectives of U.S. monetary policy and the framework and assignment of responsibility for achieving those objectives.

■ Monetary Policy Objectives

The objectives of monetary policy are ultimately political. In the United States, these objectives are set out in the mandate of the Board of Governors of the Federal Reserve System, which is defined by the Federal Reserve Act of 1913 and its subsequent amendments.

Federal Reserve Act

The Fed's mandate was most recently clarified in an amendment to the Federal Reserve Act passed by Congress in 2000, which states that

> The Board of Governors of the Federal Reserve System and the Federal Open Market Committee shall maintain long-run growth of the monetary and credit aggregates commensurate with the economy's long-run potential to increase production, so as to promote effectively the goals of maximum employment, stable prices, and moderate long-term interest rates.

This description of the Fed's monetary policy objectives has two distinct parts: a statement of goals and a prescription of the means by which to pursue the goals.

Goals: The Dual Mandate

The Fed's goals are often described as a "dual mandate" to achieve stable prices and also maximum employment.

The goal of "stable prices" doesn't mean a constant price level. Rather, it is interpreted to mean keeping the inflation rate low and predictable. Success in achieving this goal also ensures "moderate long-term interest rates."

The goal of "maximum employment" means attaining the maximum sustainable growth rate of potential GDP, keeping real GDP close to potential GDP, and keeping the unemployment rate close to the natural unemployment rate.

In the *long run*, these goals are in harmony and reinforce each other. Price stability is the key goal. It provides the best available environment for households and firms to make the saving and investment decisions that bring economic growth. So price stability encourages the maximum sustainable growth rate of potential GDP.

Price stability delivers moderate long-term interest rates because the nominal interest rate equals the real interest rate plus the inflation rate. With stable prices, the nominal interest rate is close to the real interest rate and, most of the time, this rate is likely to be moderate.

While the Fed's goals are in harmony in the long run, in the short run, the Fed faces a tradeoff. In the short run, taking an action that is designed to lower the inflation rate and achieve stable prices raises the unemployment rate and slows real GDP growth. And using monetary policy to try to lower the unemployment rate and boost real GDP growth brings the risk of a rising inflation rate. (See Chapter 15, pp. 390–391.)

Means for Achieving the Goals

The 2000 law instructs the Fed to pursue its goals by "maintain[ing] long-run growth of the monetary and credit aggregates commensurate with the economy's long-run potential to increase production." You can perhaps recognize this statement as being consistent with the quantity theory of money that you studied in Chapter 12 (see pp. 308–311). The "economy's long-run potential to increase production" is the growth rate of potential GDP. The "monetary and credit aggregates" are the quantities of money and loans. By keeping the growth rate of the quantity of money in line with the growth rate of potential GDP, the Fed is expected to be able to maintain full employment and keep the price level stable.

Prerequisite for Achieving the Goals

The financial crisis that started in the summer of 2007 and intensified in the fall of 2008 brought the problem of financial instability to the top of the Fed's agenda. The focus of policy became the single-minded pursuit of **financial stability**—of enabling financial markets and institutions to resume their normal functions of allocating capital resources and risk.

Financial stability
A situation in which financial markets and institutions function normally to allocate capital resources and risk.

The pursuit of financial stability by the Fed is not an abandonment of the mandated goals of maximum employment and stable prices. Rather, it is a prerequisite for attaining those goals. Financial instability has the potential to bring severe recession and deflation—falling prices—and undermine the attainment of the mandated goals.

To pursue its mandated monetary policy goals, the Fed must make the general concepts of maximum employment and stable prices precise and operational.

■ Operational "Maximum Employment" Goal

The Fed pays close attention to the business cycle and tries to steer a steady course between inflation and recession. To gauge the state of output and employment relative to full employment, the Fed looks at a large number of indicators that include the labor force participation rate, the unemployment rate, measures of capacity utilization, activity in the housing market, the stock market, and regional information gathered by the regional Federal Reserve Banks. All these data are summarized in the Fed's *Beige Book*.

The *output gap*—the percentage deviation of real GDP from potential GDP—summarizes the state of aggregate demand relative to potential GDP. A positive output gap—an *inflationary gap*—brings rising inflation. A negative output gap—a *recessionary gap*—results in lost output and unemployment above the natural unemployment rate. The Fed tries to minimize the output gap.

■ Operational "Stable Prices" Goal

The Fed believes that core inflation provides the best indication of whether price stability is being achieved. The *core inflation rate* is the annual percentage change in the Personal Consumption Expenditure deflator (PCE deflator) *excluding* the prices of food and fuel (see Chapter 7, pp. 175–176).

The Fed has not defined price stability but many economists regard it as meaning a core inflation rate of between 1 and 2 percent a year. Former Fed Chairman Alan Greenspan said that "price stability is best thought of as an environment in which inflation is so low and stable over time that it does not materially enter into the decisions of households and firms."

■ Responsibility for Monetary Policy

Who is responsible for monetary policy in the United States? What are the roles of the Fed, Congress, and the President?

The Role of the Fed

The Federal Reserve Act makes the Board of Governors of the Federal Reserve System and the Federal Open Market Committee (FOMC) responsible for the conduct of monetary policy. We described the composition of the FOMC in Chapter 11 (see p. 278). The FOMC makes a monetary policy decision at eight scheduled meetings a year and publishes its minutes three weeks after each meeting.

The Role of Congress

Congress plays no role in making monetary policy decisions, but the Federal Reserve Act requires the Board of Governors to report on monetary policy to Congress. The Fed makes two reports each year, one in February and another in July. These reports, along with the Fed Chairman's testimony before Congress and the minutes of the FOMC, communicate the Fed's thinking on monetary policy to lawmakers and the public.

The Role of the President

The formal role of the President of the United States is limited to appointing the members and the Chairman of the Board of Governors. But some Presidents—Richard Nixon was one—have tried to influence Fed decisions.

You now know the objectives of monetary policy and can describe the framework and assignment of responsibility for achieving those objectives. Your next task is to see how the Fed conducts its monetary policy.

■ Choosing a Policy Instrument

Monetary policy instrument
A variable that the Fed can directly control or closely target and that influences the economy in desirable ways.

Federal funds rate
The interest rate at which banks can borrow and lend reserves in the federal funds market.

To conduct its monetary policy, the Fed must select a **monetary policy instrument,** a variable that the Fed can directly control or closely target and that influences the economy in desirable ways.

As the sole issuer of the *monetary base*, the Fed is a monopoly. A monopoly can fix the quantity of its product and leave the market to determine the price; or it can fix the price of its product and leave the market to choose the quantity. The "price" of monetary base is the **federal funds rate,** the interest rate at which banks can borrow and lend reserves in the federal funds market. The Fed can target the monetary base or the federal funds rate, but not both. If the Fed wants to decrease the monetary base, the federal funds rate must rise; and if the Fed wants to raise the federal funds rate, the monetary base must decrease.

■ The Federal Funds Rate

The Fed's choice of monetary policy instrument is the federal funds rate. Given this choice, the Fed permits the monetary base and the quantity of money to find their own equilibrium values and has no preset targets for them.

Figure 17.1 shows the federal funds rate since 2000. You can see that the federal funds rate was 5.5 percent at the beginning of 2000 and during 2000 and 2001, the Fed increased the rate to 6.5 percent. The Fed raised the interest rate to this high level to lower the inflation rate.

FIGURE 17.1

The Fed's Key Monetary Policy Instrument: The Federal Funds Rate

MyEconLab Real-time data

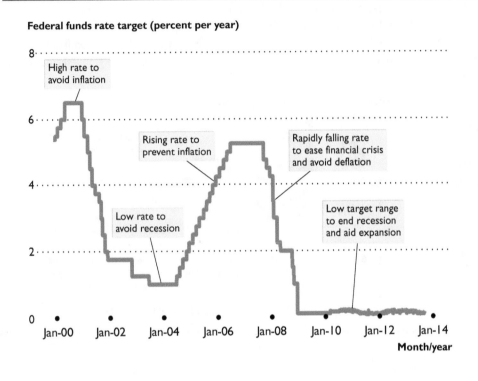

Federal funds rate target (percent per year)

High rate to avoid inflation

Rising rate to prevent inflation

Rapidly falling rate to ease financial crisis and avoid deflation

Low rate to avoid recession

Low target range to end recession and aid expansion

The Fed sets a target for the federal funds rate and then takes actions to keep the rate close to the target.

When the Fed wants to slow inflation, it raises the federal funds rate target.

When the inflation rate is below target and the Fed wants to avoid recession, it lowers the federal funds rate target.

When the Fed focused on restoring financial stability, it cut the federal funds rate target aggressively to almost zero.

SOURCE OF DATA: Board of Governors of the Federal Reserve System.

Between 2002 and 2004, the federal funds rate was set at historically low levels. The reason is that with inflation well anchored at close to 2 percent a year, the Fed was less concerned about inflation than it was about recession so it wanted to lean in the direction of avoiding recession.

From mid-2004 through early 2006, the Fed was increasingly concerned about the build-up of inflation pressures and it raised the federal funds rate target on 17 occasions to take it to 5.25 percent, a level that was held until September 2007.

When the global financial crisis began, the Fed acted cautiously in cutting the federal funds rate target. But as the crisis intensified, rate cuts became more frequent and larger, ending in December 2008 with an interest rate close to zero. The normal changes of a quarter of a percentage point (also called 25 *basis points*) were abandoned as the Fed slashed the rate, first by an unusual 50 basis points and finally, in December 2008, by an unprecedented 100 basis points. Since the end of 2008, the federal funds rate has been close to zero.

How does the Fed decide the appropriate level for the federal funds rate? And how, having made that decision, does the Fed move the federal funds rate to its target level?

■ The Fed's Decision-Making Strategy

Two alternative decision-making strategies might be used by a central bank and they are summarized as two alternative *rules*:

- Instrument rule
- Targeting rule

EYE on the U.S. ECONOMY
The Fed's Interest Rate Decisions and the Taylor Rule

John B. Taylor (Stanford University) has proposed a formula for setting the federal funds rate—the *Taylor Rule*.

If the inflation rate is 2 percent a year and there is no output gap, the Taylor Rule sets the federal funds rate to neutral at 4 percent a year.

A 1 percent deviation of the inflation rate from target and a 1 percent deviation of real GDP from potential GDP moves the federal funds rate up or down by 0.5 percent.

The Taylor Rule was derived by crunching a large amount of U.S. macroeconomic data to construct a statistical model of the economy.

The figure shows the Fed's decision and the Taylor Rule since 2000. Taylor thinks the Fed moved the interest rate too low and kept it too low for too long and then raised the interest rate too quickly and by too much. He believes the Fed's deviation from his rule contributed to the global financial crisis.

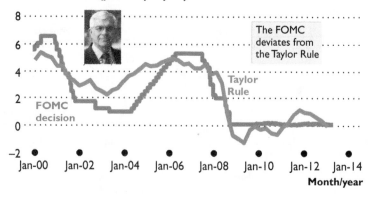

SOURCES OF DATA: Federal Reserve Board and Federal Reserve Bank of St. Louis.

Instrument Rule

Instrument rule
A decision rule for monetary policy that sets the policy instrument by a formula based on the current state of the economy.

An **instrument rule** is a decision rule for monetary policy that sets the policy instrument by a formula based on the current state of the economy. The best-known instrument rule is the *Taylor Rule*, which sets the federal funds rate by a formula that links it to the current inflation rate and current output gap. (We describe the Taylor Rule in *Eye on the U.S. Economy* above.)

To implement the Taylor Rule, the FOMC would plug the current inflation rate and output gap into the formula and calculate the level at which to set the federal funds rate. A computer would make the interest rate decision.

Targeting Rule

Targeting rule
A decision rule for monetary policy that sets the policy instrument at a level that makes the central bank's forecast of the ultimate policy goals equal to their targets.

A **targeting rule** is a decision rule for monetary policy that sets the policy instrument at a level that makes the central bank's forecast of the ultimate policy goals equal to their targets. The Fed employs such a rule. The Fed sets the federal funds rate that gets its forecasts of inflation and the output gap as close as possible to their target levels.

To implement its targeting rule, the FOMC gathers and processes a large amount of information about the economy, the way it responds to shocks, and the way it responds to policy. The FOMC then processes all these data and comes to a judgment about the best level for the federal funds rate.

The Fed does not pursue formal published targets: It has implicit targets and when the economy deviates from these targets, as it does most of the time, the Fed places relative weights on its two objectives and, constrained by the short-run tradeoff (see Chapter 15), decides how quickly to try to get inflation back on track or the economy back to full employment.

We've now described the Fed's monetary policy instrument and the FOMC's strategy for setting it. We next see what the Fed does to make the federal funds rate hit its target.

◼ Hitting the Federal Funds Rate Target

The federal funds rate is the interest rate that banks earn (or pay) when they lend (or borrow) reserves. The federal funds rate is also the opportunity cost of holding reserves. Holding a larger quantity of reserves is the alternative to lending reserves to another bank, and holding a smaller quantity of reserves is the alternative to borrowing reserves from another bank. So the quantity of reserves that banks are willing to hold varies with the federal funds rate: The higher the federal funds rate, the smaller is the quantity of reserves that the banks plan to hold.

The Fed controls the quantity of reserves supplied, and the Fed can change this quantity by conducting an open market operation. You learned in Chapter 11 (pp. 283–286) how an open market purchase increases reserves and an open market sale decreases reserves. To hit the federal funds rate target, the New York Fed conducts open market operations until the supply of reserves is at just the right quantity to hit the target federal funds rate.

Figure 17.2 illustrates this outcome in the market for bank reserves. The x-axis measures the quantity of bank reserves on deposit at the Fed, and the y-axis measures the federal funds rate. The demand for reserves—the willingness of the banks to hold reserves—is the curve labeled *RD*.

The Fed's open market operations determine the supply of reserves, which is the supply curve *RS*. To decrease reserves, the Fed conducts an open market sale. To increase reserves, the Fed conducts an open market purchase.

◼ **FIGURE 17.2**

Equilibrium in the Market for Bank Reserves   MyEconLab Real-time data

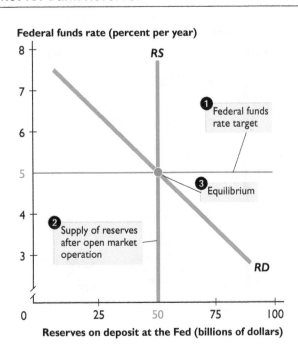

The federal funds rate (on the y-axis) is the opportunity cost of holding reserves: The higher the federal funds rate, the smaller is the quantity of reserves that banks want to hold. The demand curve for bank reserves is *RD*.

❶ The FOMC sets the federal funds rate target at 5 percent a year.

❷ The New York Fed conducts open market operations to make the quantity of reserves supplied equal to $50 billion and the supply of reserves curve is *RS*.

❸ Equilibrium in the market for bank reserves occurs at the target federal funds rate.

Equilibrium in the market for bank reserves determines the federal funds rate where the quantity of reserves demanded by the banks equals the quantity of reserves supplied by the Fed. By using open market operations, the Fed adjusts the quantity of reserves supplied to keep the federal funds rate on target.

◼ Restoring Financial Stability in a Financial Crisis

During the global financial crisis, the Fed took extraordinary steps to restore financial stability. Chapter 11 describes the tools of quantitative easing and credit easing employed by the Fed (p. 279) and *Eye on Creating Money* (pp. 288–289) shows the enormous surge in bank reserves and the monetary base brought about by "quantitative easing"—QE1—in 2008.

Figure 17.3 illustrates the Fed's QE1 action in the market for bank reserves. In normal times, the demand for reserves is RD_0 and the supply of reserves is RS_0. The federal funds rate is 5 percent and bank reserves are $50 billion.

At a time of financial instability and panic, banks' assessments of risk increase and they decide to hold more of their assets in safe, reserve deposits at the Fed. The demand for reserves increases and the demand curve becomes RD_1. If the Fed took no actions, the federal funds rate would rise, bank lending would shrink, the quantity of money would decrease, and a recession would intensify.

To avoid this outcome, the Fed's lending programs pump billions of dollars into the banks. The supply of reserves increases to RS_1, and the federal funds rate falls to zero. The banks don't start lending their increased reserves. They hang on to them. But flush with reserves, banks don't call in loans and deepen the recession. The Fed's action averted a worsening credit crisis and worsening recession.

◼ FIGURE 17.3

The Market for Bank Reserves in a Financial Crisis

MyEconLab Real-time data

In a normal time, the demand for bank reserves is RD_0 and the supply of reserves is RS_0. The federal funds rate is 5 percent per year.

In a financial crisis:

❶ The banks face increased risk and their demand for reserves increases and the demand curve shifts to RD_1.

❷ The Fed's QE1 and other actions increase the supply of reserves and the supply curve shifts to RS_1.

❸ The equilibrium federal funds rate falls to zero and the quantity of reserves explodes to $1,000 billion.

CHECKPOINT 17.1

MyEconLab Study Plan 17.1
Key Terms Quiz
Solutions

Describe the objectives of U.S. monetary policy, the framework for achieving those objectives, and the Fed's monetary policy actions.

Practice Problems

1. What are the objectives of U.S. monetary policy?
2. What is core inflation and how does it differ from total PCE inflation?
3. What is the Fed's monetary policy instrument and what influences the level at which the Fed sets it?
4. Figure 1 shows the demand curve for bank reserves, *RD*. The current quantity of reserves supplied is $20 billion. The Fed wants to set the federal funds rate at 4 percent a year. Illustrate the target on the graph and show the supply of reserves that will achieve the target. Does the Fed conduct an open market operation and if so, does it buy or sell securities?

In the News

Can Fed target jobless rate? Bernanke hints at new policy
With little notice, Bernanke seemed to buck conventional wisdom and suggest that the Fed can, and should, try to influence the long-term unemployment rate.
Source: CNBC, October 10, 2011

Explain whether trying to influence the long-term unemployment rate is consistent with the Fed's monetary policy objectives.

Solutions to Practice Problems

1. The objectives of U.S. monetary policy are to achieve stable prices (interpreted as a core inflation rate of about 2 percent per year) and maximum employment (interpreted as full employment).
2. Core inflation excludes the changes in the prices of food and fuel. The total PCE inflation rate includes the changes in all consumer prices. The core inflation rate fluctuates less than the total PCE inflation rate.
3. The federal funds rate is the Fed's monetary policy instrument and the inflation rate and output gap are two of the influences on the level at which the Fed sets the federal funds rate.
4. Figure 2 shows the market for bank reserves. With the initial quantity of reserves of $20 billion, the federal funds rate must have been 5 percent a year at point *A*. To set the federal funds rate at 4 percent a year, the Fed must conduct an open market purchase to increase the supply of reserves to *RS*. With supply *RS*, the federal funds rate equals the 4 percent target rate.

Solution to In the News

The objectives of monetary policy are maximum employment and stable prices. The maximum-employment goal means keeping the economy as close as possible to potential GDP. The stable-prices goal means keeping the inflation rate low. In 2011, the inflation rate was low but the unemployment rate and the output gap were high. By focusing on the output gap, the Fed was seeking to reestablish "maximum employment." The Fed believed that inflation would remain low, so its focus was consistent with its monetary policy objectives.

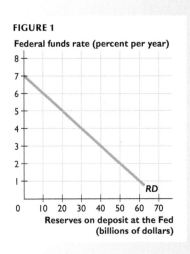
FIGURE 1
Federal funds rate (percent per year)

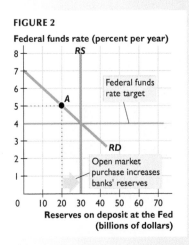
FIGURE 2
Federal funds rate (percent per year)

17.2 MONETARY POLICY TRANSMISSION

You've seen that the Fed's goal is to keep the inflation rate around 2 percent a year and to keep the output gap close to zero. You've also seen how the Fed uses its market power to set the federal funds rate at the level that is designed to achieve these objectives. We're now going to trace the events that follow a change in the federal funds rate and see how those events lead to the ultimate policy goals. We'll begin with a quick overview of the transmission process and then look a bit more closely at each step.

■ Quick Overview

When the Fed lowers the federal funds rate, other short-term interest rates and the exchange rate also fall. The quantity of money and the supply of loanable funds increase. The long-term real interest rate falls. The lower real interest rate increases consumption expenditure and investment. The lower exchange rate makes U.S. exports cheaper and imports more costly, so net exports increase. Easier bank loans reinforce the effect of lower interest rates on aggregate expenditure. Aggregate demand increases, which increases real GDP and the price level relative to what they would have been. Real GDP growth and inflation speed up.

When the Fed raises the federal funds rate, as the sequence of events that we've just reviewed plays out, the effects are in the opposite directions.

Figure 17.4 provides a schematic summary of these ripple effects for both a cut and a rise in the federal funds rate. These ripple effects stretch out over a period of between one and two years. The interest rate and exchange rate effects are immediate. The effects on money and bank loans follow in a few weeks and run for a few months. Real long-term interest rates change quickly and often in anticipation of the short-term rate changes. Spending plans change and real GDP growth changes after about one year. The inflation rate changes between one year and two years after the change in the federal funds rate. But these time lags are not entirely predictable and can be longer or shorter. We're going to look at each stage in the transmission process, starting with the interest rate effects.

■ Interest Rate Changes

The first effect of a monetary policy decision by the FOMC is a change in the federal funds rate. Other interest rates then change. These interest rate effects occur quickly and relatively predictably.

The interest rate on U.S. government 3-month Treasury bills is immediately affected by a change in the federal funds rate. A powerful *substitution effect* keeps these two rates close to each other. Banks have a choice about how to hold their short-term liquid assets and a loan to another bank is a close substitute for holding Treasury bills. If the interest rate on Treasury bills is higher than the federal funds rate, the banks increase the quantity of Treasury bills held and decrease loans to other banks. The price of a Treasury bill rises and the interest rate falls. Similarly, if the interest rate on Treasury bills is lower than the federal funds rate, the banks decrease the quantity of Treasury bills held and increase loans to other banks. The price of a Treasury bill falls, and the interest rate rises. When the interest rate on Treasury bills is close to the federal funds rate, there is no incentive for a bank to switch between making loans to other banks and holding Treasury bills. Both the Treasury bill market and the federal funds market are in equilibrium.

FIGURE 17.4

Ripple Effects of the Fed's Actions

MyEconLab Animation

The Fed changes its interest rate target and conducts open market operations to ❶ change the federal funds rate. The same day ❷ other short-term interest rates change and so does the exchange rate. A few weeks through a few months after the FOMC meeting, ❸ the quantity of money and supply of loanable funds changes, which ❹ changes the long-term real interest rate.

Up to a year after the FOMC meeting, ❺ consumption, investment, and net exports change, so ❻ aggregate demand changes. Eventually, the change in the federal funds rate has ripple effects that ❼ change real GDP and about two years after the FOMC meeting, ❽ the inflation rate changes.

Timeline (left):
- FOMC meeting
- Same day/next day
- A few weeks through a few months later
- A few weeks through a few months later
- Up to a year later
- Up to a year later
- About a year later
- About two years later

(a) The Fed tightens

❶ The Fed raises the federal funds rate

❷ Other short-term interest rates rise and the exchange rate rises

❸ The quantity of money and supply of loanable funds decrease

❹ The long-term real interest rate rises

❺ Consumption expenditure, investment, and net exports decrease

❻ Aggregate demand decreases

❼ Real GDP growth rate decreases

❽ Inflation rate decreases

(b) The Fed eases

❶ The Fed lowers the federal funds rate

❷ Other short-term interest rates fall and the exchange rate falls

❸ The quantity of money and supply of loanable funds increase

❹ The long-term real interest rate falls

❺ Consumption expenditure, investment, and net exports increase

❻ Aggregate demand increases

❼ Real GDP growth rate increases

❽ Inflation rate increases

Long-term interest rates also change, but not by as much as short-term rates. The long-term corporate bond rate, the interest rate paid on bonds issued by large corporations, is the most significant interest rate to be influenced by the federal funds rate. It is this interest rate that businesses pay on the loans that finance their purchases of new capital and that influences their investment decisions.

The long-term corporate bond rate is generally a bit higher than the short-term interest rate because long-term loans are riskier than short-term loans. To provide the incentive that brings forth a supply of long-term loans, lenders must be compensated for the additional risk. Without compensation for the additional risk, only short-term loans would be supplied.

The long-term interest rate fluctuates less than the short-term rate because it is influenced by expectations about future short-term interest rates as well as current short-term interest rates. The alternative to borrowing or lending long term is to borrow or lend using a sequence of short-term securities. If the long-term interest rate exceeds the expected average of future short-term interest rates, people will lend long term and borrow short term. The long-term interest rate will fall. And if the long-term interest rate is below the expected average of future short-term interest rates, people will borrow long term and lend short term. The long-term interest rate will rise.

These market forces keep the long-term interest rate close to the expected average of future short-term interest rates (plus a premium for the extra risk associated with long-term loans). And the expected average future short-term interest rate fluctuates less than the current short-term interest rate.

■ Exchange Rate Changes

The exchange rate responds to changes in the interest rate in the United States relative to the interest rates in other countries—the *U.S. interest rate differential*. We explain this influence in Chapter 19 (see pp. 486, 489, 491).

When the Fed raises the federal funds rate, the U.S. interest rate differential rises and, other things remaining the same, the U.S. dollar appreciates. And when the Fed lowers the federal funds rate, the U.S. interest rate differential falls and, other things remaining the same, the U.S. dollar depreciates.

Many factors other than the U.S. interest rate differential influence the exchange rate, so when the Fed changes the federal funds rate, the exchange rate does not usually change exactly as it would with other things remaining the same. So while monetary policy influences the exchange rate, many other factors also make the exchange rate change.

■ Money and Bank Loans

The quantity of money and bank loans change when the Fed changes the federal funds rate target. A rise in the federal funds rate decreases the quantity of money and bank loans; and a fall in the federal funds rate increases the quantity of money and bank loans. These changes occur for two reasons: The quantity of deposits and loans created by the banking system changes and the quantity of money demanded changes.

You've seen that to change the federal funds rate, the Fed must change the quantity of bank reserves. A change in the quantity of bank reserves changes the monetary base, which in turn changes the quantity of deposits and loans that the banking system can create. A rise in the federal funds rate decreases reserves and decreases the quantity of deposits and bank loans created; and a fall in the federal funds rate increases reserves and increases the quantity of deposits and bank loans created.

The quantity of money created by the banking system must be held by households and firms. The change in the interest rate changes the quantity of money demanded. A fall in the interest rate increases the quantity of money demanded and a rise in the interest rate decreases the quantity of money demanded.

A change in the quantity of money and the supply of bank loans directly affects consumption and investment plans. With more money and easier access to loans, consumers and firms spend more. With less money and loans harder to get, consumers and firms spend less.

■ The Long-Term Real Interest Rate

Demand and supply in the market for loanable funds determine the long-term real interest rate, which equals the long-term nominal interest rate minus the expected inflation rate. The long-term real interest rate influences expenditure decisions.

In the long run, demand and supply in the loanable funds market depend only on real forces—on saving and investment decisions. But in the short run, when the price level is not fully flexible, the supply of loanable funds is influenced by the supply of bank loans. Changes in the federal funds rate change the supply of bank loans, which changes the supply of loanable funds and changes the real interest rate in the loanable funds market.

A fall in the federal funds rate that increases the supply of bank loans increases the supply of loanable funds and lowers the equilibrium real interest rate. A rise in the federal funds rate that decreases the supply of bank loans decreases the supply of loanable funds and raises the equilibrium real interest rate.

These changes in the real interest rate, along with the other factors we've just described, change expenditure plans.

■ Expenditure Plans

The ripple effects that follow a change in the federal funds rate change three components of aggregate expenditure:

- Consumption expenditure
- Investment
- Net exports

Other things remaining the same, the lower the real interest rate, the greater is the amount of consumption expenditure and the smaller is the amount of saving.

Again, other things remaining the same, the lower the real interest rate, the greater is the amount of investment.

Finally, and again other things remaining the same, the lower the interest rate, the lower is the exchange rate and the greater are exports and the smaller are imports.

A cut in the federal funds rate increases all the components of aggregate expenditure; a rise in the federal funds rate decreases all the components of aggregate expenditure. These changes in aggregate expenditure plans change aggregate demand, which in turn changes real GDP and the inflation rate.

■ The Fed Fights Recession

We're now going to pull all the steps in the transmission story together. We'll start with inflation below target and real GDP below potential GDP. The Fed takes actions that are designed to restore full employment. Figure 17.5 shows the effects of the Fed's actions, starting in the market for bank reserves and ending in the market for real GDP.

In Figure 17.5(a), which shows the market for bank reserves, the FOMC lowers the target federal funds rate from 5 percent to 4 percent a year. To achieve the new target, the New York Fed buys securities and increases the supply of reserves in the banking system from RS_0 to RS_1.

With increased reserves, the banks create deposits by making loans and the supply of money increases. The short-term interest rate falls and the quantity of money demanded increases. In Figure 17.5(b), the supply of money increases from MS_0 to MS_1, the interest rate falls from 5 percent to 4 percent a year, and the quantity of money increases from $3 trillion to $3.1 trillion. The interest rate in the money market and the federal funds rate are kept close to each other by the powerful substitution effect described on page 852.

■ FIGURE 17.5

The Fed Fights Recession

(a) Market for bank reserves

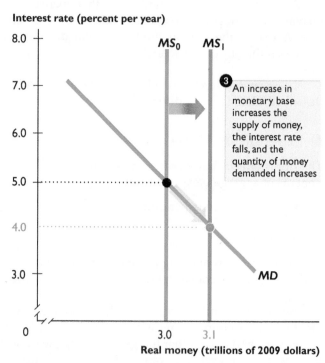

(b) Money market

❶ The FOMC lowers the federal funds rate target from 5 percent to 4 percent a year. ❷ The New York Fed buys securities in an open market operation and increases reserves from RS_0 to RS_1 to hit the new federal funds rate target.

❸ The supply of money increases from MS_0 to MS_1, the short-term interest rate falls, and the quantity of money demanded increases. The short-term interest rate and the federal funds rate change by similar amounts.

Banks create money by making loans. In the long run, an increase in the supply of bank loans is matched by a rise in the price level and the quantity of real loans is unchanged. But in the short run, with a sticky price level, an increase in the supply of bank loans increases the supply of (real) loanable funds. In Figure 17.5(c), the supply of loanable funds curve shifts rightward from SLF_0 to SLF_1. With the demand for loanable funds at DLF, the real interest rate falls from 6 percent to 5.5 percent a year.

Figure 17.5(d) shows aggregate demand and aggregate supply and the recessionary gap that triggered the Fed's action. The increase in money and loans and the decrease in the real interest rate increase aggregate planned expenditure. (Not shown in the figure, a fall in the interest rate lowers the exchange rate, which increases net exports and aggregate planned expenditure.) The increase in aggregate expenditure, ΔE, increases aggregate demand and shifts the aggregate demand curve rightward to $AD_0 + \Delta E$. A multiplier process begins. The increase in expenditure increases income, which induces an increase in consumption expenditure. Aggregate demand increases further, and the aggregate demand curve eventually shifts rightward to AD_1. The new equilibrium is at full employment but with a higher price level (and faster inflation).

MyEconLab Animation

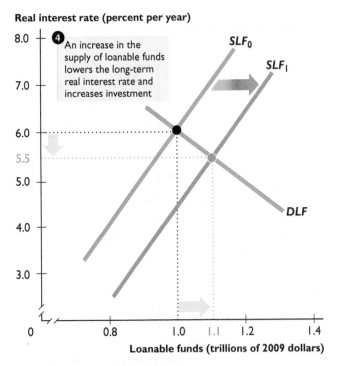

(c) Market for loanable funds

An increase in the quantity of money increases the supply of loans.
❹ An increase in the supply of bank loans increases the supply of loanable funds from SLF_0 to SLF_1 and the real interest rate falls. Investment increases.

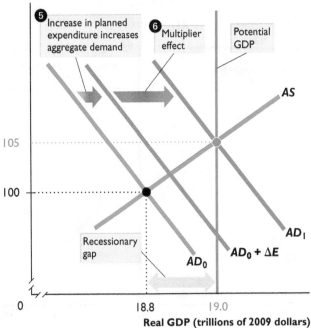

(d) Real GDP and the price level

❺ Aggregate planned expenditure increases and the aggregate demand curve shifts to $AD_0 + \Delta E$. ❻ A multiplier effect increases aggregate demand to AD_1. Real GDP increases and the price level rises (inflation speeds up).

■ The Fed Fights Inflation

If the inflation rate is too high and real GDP is above potential GDP, the Fed takes actions that are designed to lower the inflation rate and restore price stability. Figure 17.6 shows the effects of the Fed's actions starting in the market for reserves and ending in the market for real GDP.

In Figure 17.6(a), which shows the market for bank reserves, the FOMC raises the target federal funds rate from 5 percent to 6 percent a year. To achieve the new target, the New York Fed sells securities and decreases the supply of reserves in the banking system from RS_0 to RS_1.

With decreased reserves, the banks shrink deposits by decreasing loans and the supply of money decreases. The short-term interest rate rises and the quantity of money demanded decreases. In Figure 17.6(b), the supply of money decreases from MS_0 to MS_1, the interest rate rises from 5 percent to 6 percent a year, and the quantity of money decreases from $3 trillion to $2.9 trillion.

With a decrease in reserves, banks must decrease the supply of loans. The supply of (real) loanable funds decreases, and the supply of loanable funds curve shifts leftward in Figure 17.6(c) from SLF_0 to SLF_1. With the demand for loanable funds at DLF, the real interest rate rises from 6 percent to 6.5 percent a year.

■ FIGURE 17.6

The Fed Fights Inflation

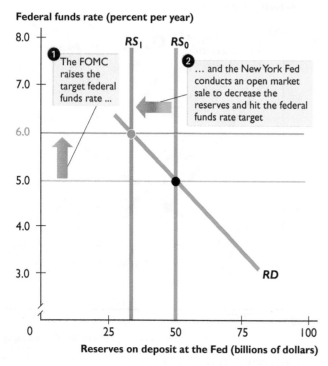

(a) Market for bank reserves

❶ The FOMC raises the federal funds rate target from 5 percent to 6 percent a year. ❷ The New York Fed sells securities in an open market operation and decreases reserves from RS_0 to RS_1 to hit the new federal funds rate target.

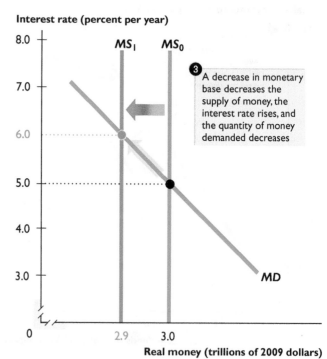

(b) Money market

❸ The supply of money decreases from MS_0 to MS_1, the short-term interest rate rises, and the quantity of money demanded decreases. The short-term interest rate and the federal funds rate change by similar amounts.

Figure 17.6(d) shows aggregate demand and aggregate supply in the market for real GDP and the inflationary gap to which the Fed is reacting. The decrease in the quantity of money and loans and the rise in the real interest rate decrease aggregate planned expenditure. The decrease in aggregate expenditure, ΔE, decreases aggregate demand and shifts the aggregate demand curve leftward to $AD_0 - \Delta E$. A multiplier process begins. The decrease in expenditure decreases income, which induces a decrease in consumption expenditure. Aggregate demand decreases further, and the aggregate demand curve eventually shifts leftward to AD_1. The economy returns to full employment. Real GDP is equal to potential GDP. The price level falls (the inflation rate slows).

In both of the examples, we have given the Fed a perfect hit at achieving full employment and keeping the price level stable. If the Fed changed aggregate demand by too little and too late, or by too much and too early, the economy would not have returned to full employment. Too little action would leave a recessionary or an inflationary gap. Too much action would overshoot the objective. If the Fed hits the brakes too hard, it pushes the economy from inflation to recession. If it stimulates too much, it turns recession into inflation.

MyEconLab Animation

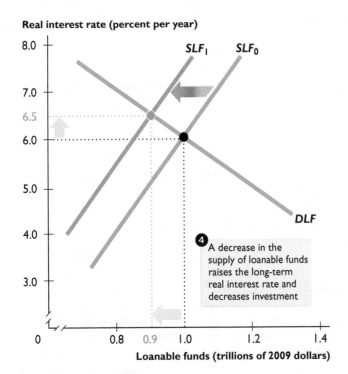

(c) Market for loanable funds

A decrease in the quantity of money decreases the supply of loans. **4** A decrease in the supply of bank loans decreases the supply of loanable funds from SLF_0 to SLF_1 and the real interest rate rises. Investment decreases.

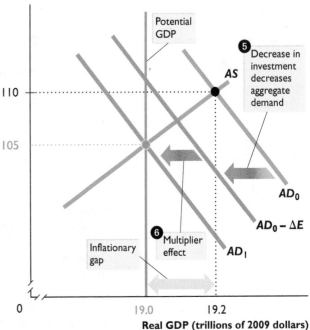

(d) Real GDP and the price level

5 Aggregate planned expenditure decreases and the aggregate demand curve shifts to $AD_0 - \Delta E$. **6** A multiplier effect decreases aggregate demand to AD_1. Real GDP decreases and the price level falls (inflation slows down).

■ Loose Links and Long and Variable Lags

The ripple effects of monetary policy that we've just analyzed with the precision of an economic model are, in reality, very hard to predict and influence.

To achieve its goals of price stability and full employment, the Fed needs a combination of good judgment and good luck. Too large an interest rate cut in an underemployed economy can bring inflation, as it did during the 1970s. And too large an interest rate rise in an inflationary economy can create unemployment, as it did in 1981 and 1991.

Loose links in the chain that runs from the federal funds rate to the ultimate policy goals make unwanted policy outcomes inevitable. And time lags that are both long and variable add to the Fed's challenges.

Loose Links from Federal Funds Rate to Spending

The long-term real interest rate that influences spending plans is linked only loosely to the federal funds rate. Also, the response of the long-term real interest rate to a change in the nominal rate depends on how inflation expectations change. The response of expenditure plans to changes in the real interest rate depends on many factors that make the response hard to predict.

Time Lags in the Adjustment Process

The Fed is especially handicapped by the fact that the monetary policy transmission process is long and drawn out. Also, the economy does not always respond in exactly the same way to a given policy change. Further, many factors other than policy are constantly changing and bringing new situations to which policy must respond.

The turmoil in credit markets and home loan markets that began during the summer of 2007 is an example of unexpected events to which monetary policy must respond. The Fed found itself facing an ongoing inflation risk but that risk was combined with a fear that a collapse of spending would bring recession.

■ A Final Reality Check

You've studied the theory of monetary policy. Does it really work in the way we've described? It does. An enormous amount of statistical research has investigated the effects of the Fed's actions on the economy and the conclusions of this research are not in doubt. When the Fed raises the federal funds rate, the economy slows for the reasons that we've described. And when the Fed cuts the federal funds rate, the economy speeds up.

The time lags in the adjustment process are not predictable, but the average time lags are known. On the average, after the Fed takes action to change the course of the economy, real GDP begins to change about one year later. The inflation rate responds with a longer time lag that averages around two years.

This long time lag between the Fed's action and a change in the inflation rate, the ultimate policy goal, makes monetary policy very difficult to implement. The state of the economy two years in the future cannot be predicted, so the Fed's actions might turn out to be exactly the opposite of what is needed to steer a steady course between recession and inflation.

You've now seen how the Fed operates and studied the effects of its actions. We close this chapter by looking at alternative approaches to monetary policy.

CHECKPOINT 17.2

Explain the transmission channels through which the Fed influences real GDP and the inflation rate.

Practice Problems

1. List the sequence of events in the transmission from a rise in the federal funds rate to a change in the inflation rate.

The economy has slipped into recession and the Fed takes actions to lessen its severity. Use this information to work Problems **2** and **3**.

2. What action does the Fed take? Illustrate the effects of the Fed's actions in the money market and the loanable funds market.

3. Explain how the Fed's actions change aggregate demand and real GDP.

In the News

Fed is open to changing bond policy
Fed policymakers signaled for the first time that they could increase or decrease stimulation of the economy in the future, but not now.

Source: *Los Angeles Times*, May 1, 2013

What are the ripple effects and time lags that the Fed must consider in deciding when to increase or decrease stimulation of the economy?

Solutions to Practice Problems

1. When the Fed raises the federal funds rate, other short-term interest rates rise and the exchange rate rises; the quantity of money and supply of loanable funds decrease and the long-term real interest rate rises; consumption, investment, and net exports decrease; aggregate demand decreases; and eventually the real GDP growth rate and the inflation rate decrease.

2. The Fed lowers the federal funds rate, which lowers the short-term interest rate, and increases the supply of money (Figure 1). The supply of loans and the supply of loanable funds increase. The real interest rate falls (Figure 2).

3. A lower real interest rate (and exchange rate) and greater quantity of money and loanable funds increase aggregate expenditure and the *AD* curve shifts to $AD_0 + \Delta E$. A multiplier effect increases aggregate demand and the *AD* curve shifts to AD_1. Real GDP increases and recession is avoided (Figure 3).

Solution to In the News

Figure 17.4 (p. 853) describes the ripple effects and the time lags. The Fed can influence interest rates quickly but it takes several months before the quantity of money and loans respond, up to a year before expenditure plans respond, and up to two years before the inflation rate responds to the interest rate actions.

FIGURE 1

FIGURE 2

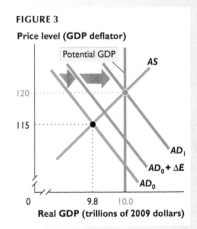

FIGURE 3

17.3 ALTERNATIVE MONETARY POLICY STRATEGIES

So far in this chapter, we've described and analyzed the Fed's method of conducting monetary policy. But the Fed does have choices among alternative monetary policy strategies. We're going to end our discussion of monetary policy by examining the alternatives and explaining why the Fed has rejected them in favor of the interest rate strategy that we've described.

You've seen that we can summarize monetary policy strategies in two broad categories: *instrument rules* and *targeting rules*.

■ Why Rules?

You might be wondering why all monetary policy strategies involve *rules*. Why doesn't the Fed pursue a **discretionary monetary policy** and just do what seems best every day, month, and year, based on its expert assessment of the current economic situation? The answer is that monetary policy must keep inflation expectations anchored close to the target inflation rate. In both financial markets and labor markets, people must make long-term commitments. These markets work best when plans are based on correctly anticipated inflation outcomes. A well-understood monetary policy rule helps to create an environment in which inflation is easier to forecast and manage.

Although rules beat discretion, there are three alternative rules that the Fed might have chosen. They are

- An inflation targeting rule
- A money targeting rule
- Nominal GDP targeting rule

■ Inflation Targeting Rule

Inflation targeting is a monetary policy strategy in which the central bank makes a public commitment to achieving an explicit inflation target and to explaining how its policy actions will achieve that target.

Of the alternatives to the Fed's current strategy, inflation targeting is the most likely to be considered. In fact, some economists see it as a small step from what the Fed currently does.

Several major central banks practice inflation targeting and have done so since the mid-1990s. The most committed inflation-targeting central banks are the Bank of England (the central bank of the United Kingdom), the Bank of Canada, the Reserve Bank of Australia, the Reserve Bank of New Zealand, the Swedish Riksbank, and the European Central Bank (the central bank of the euro countries).

Japan and the United States are the most prominent major industrial economies that do not use this monetary policy strategy. But when Ben Bernanke and Fed Governor Frederic S. Mishkin were economics professors (at Princeton University and Columbia University, respectively) they argued that inflation targeting is a sensible way in which to conduct monetary policy. And in November 2007, the Fed took a major step toward greater transparency, a central feature of inflation targeting, by publishing FOMC members' detailed forecasts of inflation, real GDP growth, and unemployment through 2010.

Inflation targets are specified in terms of a range for the CPI inflation rate. This range is typically between 1 percent and 3 percent a year, with an aim to

---

Discretionary monetary policy

A monetary policy that is based on an expert assessment of the current economic situation.

Inflation targeting

A monetary policy strategy in which the central bank makes a public commitment to achieving an explicit inflation target and to explaining how its policy actions will achieve that target.

EYE on the GLOBAL ECONOMY
Inflation Targeting Around the World

Five advanced economies and the Eurozone have inflation targets (shown by the green bars) designed to anchor inflation expectations.

In the cases where inflation targets have been achieved (orange lines), it is easier to stabilize both the inflation rate and real GDP.

In all six cases, high-quality central bank inflation reports encourage an enhanced level of public discussion about inflation and awareness of each central bank's views.

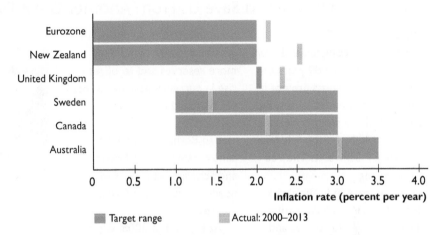

SOURCES OF DATA: National central banks and World Economic Outlook database, April 2013.

achieve an average inflation rate of 2 percent a year. Because the lags in the operation of monetary policy are long, if the inflation rate falls outside the target range, the expectation is that the central bank will move the inflation rate back on target over the next two years.

The idea of inflation targeting is to state clearly and publicly the goals of monetary policy, to establish a framework of accountability, and to keep the inflation rate low and stable while maintaining a high and stable level of employment.

There is wide agreement that inflation targeting achieves its first two goals. It's also clear that the inflation reports of inflation targeters have raised the level of discussion and understanding of the monetary policy process.

It is less clear whether inflation targeting does better than the implicit targeting that the Fed currently pursues in achieving low and stable inflation. The Fed's own record, without a formal inflation target, had been impressive until the global financial crisis called into question its neglect of a potential bubble and bust.

■ Money Targeting Rule

As long ago as 1948, Nobel Laureate Milton Friedman proposed a targeting rule for the quantity of money. Friedman's **k-percent rule** makes the quantity of money grow at a rate of k percent a year, where k equals the growth rate of potential GDP. Friedman's k-percent rule relies on a stable demand for money, which translates to a stable velocity of circulation. Friedman had examined data on money and nominal GDP and argued that the velocity of circulation of money was one of the most stable macroeconomic variables and that it could be exploited to deliver a stable price level and small business cycle fluctuations.

Friedman's idea remained just that until the 1970s, when inflation increased to more than 10 percent a year in the United States and to much higher rates in some other major countries.

k-percent rule
A monetary policy rule that makes the quantity of money grow at k percent per year, where k equals the growth rate of potential GDP.

EYE on the FED IN A CRISIS

Did the Fed Save Us From Another Great Depression?

The story of the Great Depression is complex and even today, after almost 80 years of research, economists are not in full agreement on its causes. But one part of the story is clear and it is told by Milton Friedman and Anna J. Schwartz: The Fed got it wrong.

An increase in financial risk drove the banks to increase their holdings of reserves and everyone else to lower their bank deposits and hold more currency.

Between 1929 and 1933, (Figure 1) the banks' desired reserve ratio increased from 8 percent to 12 percent and the currency drain ratio increased from 9 percent to 19 percent.

The money multiplier (Figure 2) fell from 6.5 to 3.8.

The quantity of money (Figure 3) crashed by 35 percent.

This massive contraction in the quantity of money was accompanied by a similar contraction of bank loans and by the failure of a large number of banks.

Friedman and Schwartz say that this contraction of money and bank loans and failure of banks could (and should) have been avoided by a more alert and wise Fed.

The Fed could have injected reserves into the banks to accommodate their desire for greater security by holding more reserves and to offset the rise in currency holdings as people switched out of bank deposits.

Ben Bernanke's Fed did almost exactly what Friedman and Schwartz said the Fed needed to do in the Great Depression.

At the end of 2008, when the banks faced increased financial risk, the Fed flooded them with the reserves that they wanted to hold (Figure 1).

The money multiplier fell from 9.1 in 2008 to 2.5 in 2013 (Figure 2)—much more than it had fallen between 1929 and 1933—but there was no contraction of the quantity of money (Figure 3). Rather, the quantity of M2 increased by 37.5 percent in the 5 years to August 2013, a 6.6 percent annual rate.

We can't be sure that the Fed averted a Great Depression in 2009, but we can be confident that the Fed's actions helped to limit the depth and duration of the 2008–2009 recession.

In 2013, the "dual mandate" put the Fed in a dilemma. The recovery was slow and unemployment was not falling quickly enough. The Fed's dilemma was when to stop fighting the slow recovery and start worrying about unleashing inflation.

Milton Friedman and Anna J. Schwartz, authors of A Monetary History of the United States, *who say the Fed turned an ordinary recession into the Great Depression.*

Figure 1 The Flight to Safety: Reserve and Currency Ratios Increase

Figure 2 The Collapsing Money Multiplier

Figure 3 Money Contraction Versus Growth

SOURCE OF DATA: Federal Reserve Board.

During the mid-1970s, in a bid to end the inflation, the central banks of most major countries adopted the *k*-percent rule for the growth rate of the quantity of money. The Fed, too, began to pay close attention to the growth rates of money aggregates, including M1 and M2.

Inflation rates fell during the early 1980s in the countries that had adopted a *k*-percent rule. But one by one, these countries abandoned the *k*-percent rule.

Money targeting works when the demand for money curve is stable and predictable—when the velocity of circulation is stable. But in the world of the 1980s, and possibly in the world of today, technological change in the banking system leads to large and unpredictable shifts in the demand for money curve, which make the use of monetary targeting unreliable.

With money targeting, aggregate demand fluctuates because the demand for money fluctuates. With interest rate targeting, aggregate demand is insulated from fluctuations in the demand for money (and the velocity of circulation).

■ Nominal GDP Targeting Rule

Under a **nominal GDP targeting** rule, the central bank adjusts the interest rate to achieve a given nominal GDP growth rate target. The target might be set by the government or simply adopted by the central bank. The growth rate of nominal GDP equals the growth rate of real GDP plus the inflation rate as measured by the GDP price index. The growth rate of real GDP, on average, keeps returning to its trend growth rate, so nominal GDP targeting is a version of inflation targeting. Nominal GDP targeting departs from inflation targeting by making the interest rate respond when either the inflation rate departs from its target or the real GDP growth rate departs from its long-term trend growth rate. Specifically, in a recession, monetary policy would become stimulating for two reasons: a low inflation rate and a low real GDP growth rate.

Nominal GDP targeting is an old idea that many economists have recommended, but it gained new momentum in 2011 when former Obama adviser Christina Romer joined the ranks of those supporting it.

Nominal GDP targeting
A monetary policy rule that adjusts the interest rate to achieve a target growth rate for nominal GDP.

EYE on YOUR LIFE
Your Views on Monetary Policy and How Monetary Policy Affects You

Using the knowledge that you have accumulated during your course and by reading or watching the current news, try to determine the monetary policy issues that face the U.S. economy today.

What is the greater monetary policy risk: inflation or recession? If the risk is inflation, what action do you expect the Fed to take? If the risk is

recession, what do you expect the Fed to do?

Which of these problems, inflation or recession, do you care most about? Do you want the Fed to be more cautious about inflation and keep the interest rate high, or more cautious about recession and keep the interest rate low?

When Ben Bernanke was an economics professor at Princeton, he

studied inflation targeting and found that it works well.

Do you think the United States should join the ranks of inflation targeters? Should the Fed announce an inflation target?

Watch the media for commentary on the Fed's interest rate decisions and evolving monetary policy strategy.

MyEconLab Study Plan 17.3
Key Terms Quiz
Solutions

 # CHECKPOINT 17.3

Explain and compare alternative monetary policy strategies.

Practice Problems

1. What are the three alternative monetary policy strategies that the Fed could have adopted and why is discretionary monetary policy not one of them?
2. Why does the Fed not target the quantity of money?
3. Which countries practice inflation targeting? How does this monetary policy strategy work and does it achieve a lower inflation rate?

In the News

One tool, one goal
The one-tool, one-goal rule by which central banks operated has gone. Monetary policy is now a messier business.

Source: *The Economist*, April 25, 2009

What is the tool and the goal that the news clip says is gone and what is the problem with "messy" monetary policy?

Solutions to Practice Problems

1. The Fed could have adopted three alternative monetary policy strategies: an inflation targeting rule, a *k*-percent money targeting rule, and a nominal GDP targeting rule. A rule-based monetary policy beats discretionary monetary policy because it provides a more secure anchor for inflation expectations, which in turn makes long-term contracts in labor and capital markets more efficient.
2. The Fed does not target the quantity of money because it believes that the demand for money is too unstable and fluctuations in demand would bring unwanted fluctuations in interest rates, aggregate demand, real GDP, and the inflation rate.
3. The countries that practice inflation targeting are the United Kingdom, Canada, Australia, New Zealand, Sweden, and the European countries that use the euro. Inflation targeting works by announcing a target inflation rate, setting the overnight interest rate (equivalent to the federal funds rate) to achieve the target, and publishing reports that explain how and why the central bank believes that its current policy actions will achieve its ultimate policy goals. Eurozone, New Zealand, and the United Kingdom have missed their inflation targets, but the other inflation targeters have achieved their goals.

Solution to In the News

The tool is the federal funds rate. There never has been one goal for U.S. monetary policy. The Fed's "dual mandate" is a low inflation rate and maximum employment. Even the central banks that have a formal inflation target also pay attention to the output gap and the unemployment rate. The problem with "messy" monetary policy is that it might fail to anchor inflation expectations and lead to a worsening of the short-run policy tradeoff.

CHAPTER SUMMARY

Key Points

1. **Describe the objectives of U.S. monetary policy, the framework for achieving those objectives, and the Fed's monetary policy actions.**

    *   The Federal Reserve Act requires the Fed to use monetary policy to achieve the "dual mandate" of maximum employment and stable prices.
    *   The Fed's goals can come into conflict in the short run.
    *   The Fed translates the goal of stable prices as a core inflation rate of between 1 and 2 percent a year.
    *   The Fed's monetary policy instrument is the federal funds rate.
    *   The Fed sets the federal funds rate at the level that makes its forecast of inflation and other goals equal to their targets.
    *   The Fed hits its federal funds rate target by using open market operations and in times of financial crisis by quantitative easing and credit easing.

2. **Explain the transmission channels through which the Fed influences real GDP and the inflation rate.**

    *   A change in the federal funds rate changes other interest rates, the exchange rate, the quantity of money and loans, aggregate demand, and eventually real GDP and the inflation rate.
    *   Changes in the federal funds rate change real GDP about one year later and change the inflation rate with an even longer time lag.

3. **Explain and compare alternative monetary policy strategies.**

    *   The main alternatives to setting the federal funds rate are an inflation targeting rule, a money targeting rule, or a nominal GDP targeting rule.
    *   Rules dominate discretion in monetary policy because they better enable the central bank to manage inflation expectations.

Key Terms

MyEconLab Key Terms Quiz

Discretionary monetary policy, 442
Federal funds rate, 426
Financial stability, 425
Inflation targeting, 442
Instrument rule, 428

k-percent rule, 443
Monetary policy instrument, 426
Nominal GDP targeting, 445
Targeting rule, 428

CHAPTER CHECKPOINT

Study Plan Problems and Applications

1. **Bernanke raises alarm on spending**
   Fed Chairman Ben Bernanke warned that government spending and budget deficits threaten financial stability and might be setting the scene for the next crisis.

   Source: *The Globe and Mail*, June 4, 2009

   How might a large increase in government spending and the government's budget deficit threaten financial stability and make the Fed's job harder?

   Use the following information to work Problems 2 to 4.

   Suppose that the U.S. economy is at full employment when strong economic growth in Asia increases the demand for U.S.-produced goods and services.

2. Explain how the U.S. price level and real GDP will change in the short run.

3. Explain how the U.S. price level and real GDP will change in the long run if the Fed takes monetary policy actions that are consistent with its objectives as set out in the Federal Reserve Act of 2000.

4. Explain whether the Fed faces a tradeoff in the short run.

5. What is the Fed's "dual mandate" for the conduct of monetary policy? What are the means to achieving the goals of the dual mandate?

6. What is financial stability? What actions has the Fed taken since 2007 in pursuit of financial stability? Use a graph to illustrate the effects of the Fed's actions.

   Use the following information to work Problems 7 to 9.

   Figure 1 shows the aggregate demand curve, *AD*, and the short-run aggregate supply curve, *AS*, in the economy of Artica. Potential GDP is $300 billion.

7. What are the price level and real GDP? Does Artica have an unemployment problem or an inflation problem? Why?

8. What do you predict will happen if the central bank takes no monetary policy actions? What monetary policy action would you advise the central bank to take and what do you predict will be the effect of that action?

9. Suppose that a drought decreases potential GDP in Artica to $250 billion. Explain what happens if the central bank lowers the federal funds rate. Do you recommend that the central bank lower the interest rate? Why?

10. **Departing Fed official takes shot at policies**
    "When you encourage consumption by inhibiting your interest rates from rising to their equilibrium level, you will in fact buy problems, and we have in fact bought problems," Kansas City Fed President Thomas Hoenig said in his final speech in office. The Fed has cut rates to near zero and bought more than $2 trillion in bonds to boost the economy.

    Source: Reuters, September 28, 2011

    What are some of the problems that near zero interest rates and $2 trillion of quantitative easing have created?

11. Read *Eye on the Fed in a Crisis* on p. 444. What are the key differences in monetary policy between the Great Depression and the slow recovery from the 2008–2009 recession?

FIGURE 1

Instructor Assignable Problems and Applications

MyEconLab Homework, Quiz, or Test if assigned by instructor

1. In which episode, the Great Depression or the 2008–2009 recession, did the banks' desired reserve ratio and the currency drain ratio increase by the larger amount and the money multiplier fall by the larger amount?

2. Compare and contrast the Fed's monetary policy response to the surge in desired reserves and currency holdings in the Great Depression and the 2008–2009 recession.

Use the following information to work Problems 3 to 5.

The U.S. economy is at full employment when the world price of oil begins to rise sharply. Short-run aggregate supply decreases.

3. Explain how the U.S. price level and real GDP will change in the short run.

4. Explain how the U.S. price level and real GDP will change in the long run if the Fed takes monetary policy actions that are consistent with its objectives as set out in the Federal Reserve Act of 2000.

5. Does the Fed face a tradeoff in the short run? Explain why or why not.

Use the following information to work Problems 6 to 9.

Figure 1 shows the aggregate demand curve, *AD*, and the short-run aggregate supply curve, *AS*, in the economy of Freezone. Potential GDP is $300 billion.

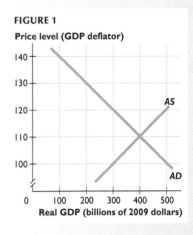

FIGURE 1

Price level (GDP deflator)

Real GDP (billions of 2009 dollars)

6. What are the price level and real GDP? Does Freezone have an unemployment problem or an inflation problem? Why?

7. What do you predict will happen in Freezone if the central bank takes no monetary policy actions? What monetary policy action would you advise the central bank to take and what do you predict will be the effect of that action?

8. What happens in Freezone if the central bank lowers the federal funds rate? Do you recommend that the central bank lower the interest rate? Why?

9. What happens in Freezone if the central bank conducts an open market sale of securities? How will the interest rate change? Do you recommend that the central bank conduct an open market sale of securities? Why?

10. Suppose that inflation is rising toward 5 percent a year, and the Fed, Congress, and the White House are discussing ways of containing inflation without damaging employment and output. The President wants to cut aggregate demand but to do so in a way that will give the best chance of keeping investment high to encourage long-term economic growth. Explain the Fed's best action for meeting the President's objectives.

Use the following information to work Problems 11 and 12.

Many ways to blow up an economy
Excessive stimulus could bring inflation in the United States in the long term, but for now, inflation is falling. Bond interest rates reflect inflation expectations that are within the Fed's long-term target levels.

Source: *Australian Financial Review*, May 9, 2009

11. Explain why inflation was falling in 2009 and how excessive stimulus could bring inflation in the long term.

12. What does it mean to say that inflation expectations are within the Fed's target levels?

Multiple Choice Quiz

1. The Fed's "dual mandate" is to achieve _____.

   A. a government budget surplus and low interest rates
   B. low inflation and maximum employment
   C. a stable quantity of money and stable prices
   D. zero unemployment and a stable means of payment

2. The Fed's operational goals include _____.

   A. a core inflation rate between 1 and 2 percent a year and an output gap as small as possible
   B. an economic growth rate of 3 percent a year and an unemployment rate equal to the natural unemployment rate
   C. a strong U.S. dollar on foreign exchange markets and a positive output gap
   D. maximum growth of stock prices and a low core inflation rate

3. The Fed's monetary policy instrument is the _____.

   A. inflation rate
   B. federal funds rate
   C. long-term interest rate
   D. monetary base

4. The Fed fights inflation by _____.

   A. lowering the federal funds rate, which lowers interest rates and decreases aggregate demand
   B. raising the federal funds rate, which raises interest rates and decreases aggregate demand
   C. decreasing the monetary base, which raises the interest rate and increases saving
   D. lowering the long-term real interest rate, which increases investment and spurs economic growth

5. To fight unemployment and close a recessionary gap, the Fed _____.

   A. stimulates aggregate demand by lowering the federal funds rate, which increases the quantity of money
   B. stimulates aggregate supply by lowering the federal funds rate, which increases potential GDP
   C. increases employment, which increases real GDP
   D. increases bank reserves, which banks use to make new loans to businesses, which increases aggregate supply

6. The Fed's choice of monetary policy strategy is _____.

   A. discretionary monetary policy
   B. the *k*-percent rule for money growth
   C. adjusting the federal funds rate to best fulfill its dual mandate
   D. setting the foreign exchange rate of the dollar

7. A monetary policy rule is _____ to discretionary monetary policy because _____.

   A. superior; discretion limits what the Fed can do in a financial crisis
   B. inferior; a rule makes it harder for people to forecast the inflation rate
   C. superior; a rule keeps inflation expectations anchored
   D. equivalent; the Fed uses its discretion to set the rule

Who wins and who loses
from globalization?

International Trade Policy

**When you have completed your study of this chapter,
you will be able to**

1 Explain how markets work with international trade and identify the gains from international trade and its winners and losers.

2 Explain the effects of international trade barriers.

3 Explain and evaluate arguments used to justify restricting international trade.

MyEconLab Big Picture

Imports
The goods and services that people and firms in one country buy from firms in other countries.

Exports
The goods and services that firms in one country sell to people and firms in other countries.

18.1 HOW GLOBAL MARKETS WORK

Because we trade with firms in other countries, the goods and services that we buy and consume are not limited by what we produce. The goods and services that we buy from firms in other countries are our **imports**; the goods and services that we sell to people and firms in other countries are our **exports**.

■ International Trade Today

Global trade today is enormous. In 2012, global exports and imports (the two numbers are the same because what one country exports another imports) were about $23 trillion, which is 31 percent of the value of global production. The United States is the world's largest international trader and accounts for 10 percent of world exports and 12 percent of world imports. Germany and China, which rank 2 and 3 behind the United States, lag by a large margin.

In 2012, total U.S. exports were $2.2 trillion, which is about 14 percent of the value of U.S. production. Total U.S. imports were $2.8 trillion, which is about 17 percent of the value of total expenditure in the United States.

The United States trades both goods and services. In 2012, exports of services were $0.6 trillion (30 percent of total exports) and imports of services were $0.4 trillion (16 percent of total imports).

Our largest exports are services such as royalties, license fees, banking, business consulting, and other private services. Our largest exports of goods are industrial and service machinery. Our largest imports are crude oil and private services. *Eye on the U.S. Economy* (p. 453) provides a bit more detail on our ten largest exports and imports.

■ What Drives International Trade?

Comparative advantage is the fundamental force that drives international trade. We defined comparative advantage in Chapter 3 (p. 71) as the ability of a person to perform an activity or produce a good or service at a lower opportunity cost than anyone else. This same idea applies to nations. We can define *national comparative advantage* as the ability of a *nation* to perform an activity or produce a good or service at a lower opportunity cost than *any other nation*.

The opportunity cost of producing a T-shirt is lower in China than in the United States, so China has a comparative advantage in producing T-shirts. The opportunity cost of producing an airplane is lower in the United States than in China, so the United States has a comparative advantage in producing airplanes.

You saw in Chapter 3 how Liz and Joe reaped gains from trade by specializing in the production of the good at which they have a comparative advantage and then trading. Both were better off. This same principle applies to trade among nations.

China has a comparative advantage at producing T-shirts and the United States has a comparative advantage at producing airplanes, so the people of both countries can gain from specialization and trade. China can buy airplanes from the United States at a lower opportunity cost than that at which it can produce them. And Americans can buy T-shirts from China for a lower opportunity cost than that at which U.S. firms can produce them. Also, through international trade, Chinese producers can get higher prices for their T-shirts and Boeing can sell airplanes for a higher price. Both countries gain from international trade.

We're going to illustrate the gains from trade that we've just described by studying demand and supply in the global markets for T-shirts and airplanes.

EYE on the U.S. ECONOMY
U.S. Exports and Imports

The blue bars in part (a) of the figure show the ten largest U.S. exports and the red bars in part (b) show the ten largest U.S. imports. Some items appear in both parts (a) and (b) because the United States exports and imports items in many of the broad categories.

Three of the top ten U.S. exports are services—private services, which includes financial, business, professional, and technical services (such as the sale of advertising by Google to

the European sportswear-maker Adidas), education (foreign students in our colleges and universities), travel (such as the expenditure on a Florida vacation by a visitor from England), and royalties and license fees (such as fees received by Hollywood movie producers on films shown abroad).

Oil is the largest U.S. import. We also import large quantities of automobiles, clothing, furniture, TVs, DVD players, computers, and industrial

machinery and equipment. Private services also feature in the ten largest imports.

Although we import a large quantity of computers, we export some too. We also export the semiconductors (computer chips) inside those imported computers. The Intel chip in a Lenovo laptop built in China and imported into the United States is an example. This chip is made in the United States and exported to China.

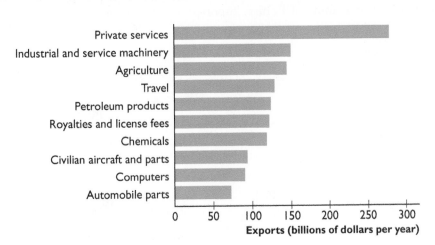

(a) The 10 largest U.S. exports

The United States exports airplanes …

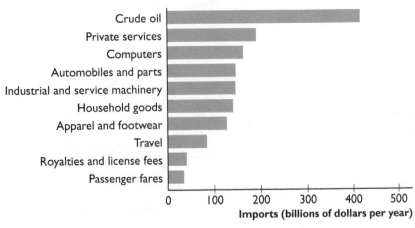

(b) The 10 largest U.S. imports

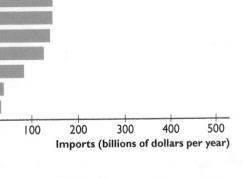

SOURCE OF DATA: Bureau of Economic Analysis.   *and imports crude oil.*

■ Why the United States Imports T-Shirts

Figure 18.1 illustrates the effects of international trade in T-shirts. The demand curve D_{US} and the supply curve S_{US} show the demand and supply in the U.S. domestic market only. The demand curve tells us the quantity of T-shirts that Americans are willing to buy at various prices. The supply curve tells us the quantity of T-shirts that U.S. garment makers are willing to sell at various prices.

Figure 18.1(a) shows what the U.S. T-shirt market would be like with no international trade. The price of a T-shirt would be $8 and 40 million T-shirts a year would be produced by U.S. garment makers and bought by U.S. consumers.

Figure 18.1(b) shows the market for T-shirts *with* international trade. Now the price of a T-shirt is determined in the world market, not the U.S. domestic market. The world price is *less than* $8 a T-shirt, which means that the rest of the world has a comparative advantage in producing T-shirts. The world price line shows the world price as $5 a T-shirt.

The U.S. demand curve, D_{US}, tells us that at $5 a T-shirt, Americans buy 60 million T-shirts a year. The U.S. supply curve, S_{US}, tells us that at $5 a T-shirt, U.S. garment makers produce 20 million T-shirts. To buy 60 million T-shirts when only 20 million are produced in the United States, we must import T-shirts from the rest of the world. The quantity of T-shirts imported is 40 million a year.

■ **FIGURE 18.1**

A Market with Imports   MyEconLab Animation

(a) Equilibrium with no international trade

(b) Equilibrium in a market with imports

With no international trade, in part (a), ❶ domestic demand and domestic supply determine ❷ the equilibrium price at $8 a T-shirt and ❸ the quantity at 40 million T-shirts a year.
With international trade, in part (b), world demand and world supply determine the world price, which is $5 per T-shirt. ❹ The domestic price falls to $5 a T-shirt. ❺ Domestic purchases increase to 60 million T-shirts a year, and ❻ domestic production decreases to 20 million T-shirts a year. ❼ 40 million T-shirts a year are imported.

Why the United States Exports Airplanes

Figure 18.2 illustrates the effects of international trade in airplanes. The demand curve D_{US} and the supply curve S_{US} show the demand and supply in the U.S. domestic market only. The demand curve tells us the quantity of airplanes that U.S. airlines are willing to buy at various prices. The supply curve tells us the quantity of airplanes that U.S. aircraft makers are willing to sell at various prices.

Figure 18.2(a) shows what the U.S. airplane market would be like with no international trade. The price of an airplane would be $100 million and 400 air-planes a year would be produced by U.S. aircraft makers and bought by U.S. airlines.

Figure 18.2(b) shows the U.S. airplane market *with* international trade. Now the price of an airplane is determined in the world market, not the U.S. domestic market. The world price is *higher than* $100 million, which means that the United States has a comparative advantage in producing airplanes. The world price line shows the world price as $150 million.

The U.S. demand curve, D_{US}, tells us that at $150 million an airplane, U.S. air-lines buy 200 airplanes a year. The U.S. supply curve, S_{US}, tells us that at $150 mil-lion an airplane, U.S. aircraft makers produce 700 airplanes a year. The quantity produced in the United States (700 a year) minus the quantity purchased by U.S. airlines (200 a year) is the quantity of U.S. exports, which is 500 airplanes a year.

FIGURE 18.2

A Market with Exports   MyEconLab Animation

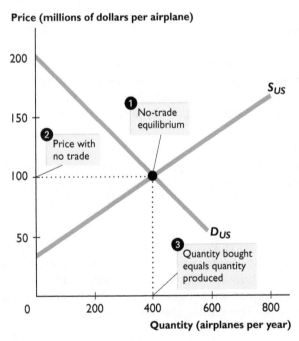

(a) Equilibrium without international trade

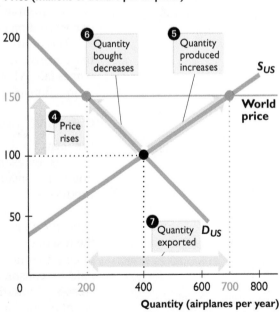

(b) Equilibrium in a market with exports

With no international trade, in part (a), ❶ domestic demand and domestic supply determine ❷ the equilibrium price at $100 mil-lion an airplane and ❸ the quantity at 400 airplanes a year. With international trade, in part (b), world demand and world sup-ply determine the world price, which is $150 million an airplane.

❹ The domestic price rises. ❺ Domestic production increases to 700 airplanes a year, ❻ domestic purchases decrease to 200 air-planes a year, and ❼ 500 airplanes a year are exported.

MyEconLab Snapshot

■ Winners, Losers, and Net Gains From Trade

International trade has winners and it has losers. It is because some people lose, that we often hear complaints about international competition. We're now going to see who wins and who loses from international trade. You will then be able to understand who complains about international competition and why. You will learn why we hear producers complaining about cheap foreign imports. You will also see why we never hear consumers of imported goods and services complaining and why we never hear exporters complaining, except when they want greater access to foreign markets.

Gains and Losses from Imports

We measure the gains and losses from imports by examining their effect on the price paid and quantity bought by domestic consumers and their effect on the price received and quantity sold by domestic producers.

Consumers Gain from Imports When a country freely imports something from the rest of the world, it is because the rest of the world has a comparative advantage at producing that item. Compared to a situation with no international trade, the price paid by the consumer falls and the quantity bought increases. It is clear that the consumer gains. The greater the fall in price and increase in quantity bought, the greater is the gain to the consumer.

Domestic Producers Lose from Imports Compared to a situation with no international trade, the price received by domestic producers of an item that is imported falls. Also, the quantity sold by these domestic producers decreases. Because domestic producers of this item sell a smaller quantity and for a lower price, producers lose from international trade. Import-competing industries shrink in the face of competition from cheaper foreign-produced imports.

The profits of firms that produce import-competing goods and services fall, these firms cut their workforce, unemployment in these industries increases, and wages fall. When these industries have a geographical concentration, such as steel production around Gary, Indiana, an entire region can suffer economic decline.

Gains and Losses from Exports

We measure the gains and losses from exports just like we measured those from imports, by examining their effect on the price paid and the quantity bought by domestic consumers and the price received and the quantity sold by domestic producers.

Domestic Consumers Lose from Exports When a country exports something to the rest of the world, it is because the country has a comparative advantage at producing that item. Compared to a situation with no international trade, the price paid by consumers rises and the quantity bought in the domestic economy decreases. Domestic consumers lose. The greater the rise in price and decrease in quantity bought, the greater is the consumers' loss.

Domestic Producers Gain from Exports Compared to a situation with no international trade, the price received by domestic producers of an item that is exported rises. Also, the quantity sold by domestic producers of this good or service increases. Because these domestic producers sell a larger quantity and for a higher

EYE on GLOBALIZATION

Who Wins and Who Loses from Globalization?

Economists generally agree that the gains from globalization vastly outweigh the losses, but there are both winners and losers.

The U.S. consumer is a big winner. Globalization has brought iPads, Wii games, Nike shoes, and a wide range of other products to our shops at ever lower prices.

The Indian (and Chinese and other Asian) worker is another big winner. Globalization has brought a wider range of more interesting jobs and higher wages.

The U.S. (and European) textile workers and furniture makers are big losers. Their jobs have disappeared and many of them have struggled to find new jobs, even when they've been willing to take a pay cut.

But one of the biggest losers is the African farmer. Blocked from global agricultural markets by trade restrictions and subsidies in the United States and Europe, globalization is leaving much of Africa on the sidelines.

The U.S. consumer ...

and Indian workers gain from globalization.

But some U.S. workers and ...

African farmers lose.

price, producers of exported goods and services gain from international trade. Export industries expand in the face of global demand for their product.

The profits of firms that produce exports rise, these firms expand their workforce, unemployment in these industries decreases and wages rise. When these industries have a geographical concentration, such as software production in Silicon Valley, an entire region can boom.

Net Gain

Export producers and import consumers gain, and export consumers and import producers lose, but the gains exceed the losses. In the case of imports, consumers gain what producers lose and then gain even more from the cheaper imports. In the case of exports, producers gain what consumers lose and then gain even more from the items exported. So international trade provides a net gain for a country.

MyEconLab Study Plan 18.1
Key Terms Quiz
Solutions

CHECKPOINT 18.1

Explain how markets work with international trade and identify the gains from international trade and its winners and losers.

Practice Problems

Before the 1980s, China did not trade internationally: It was self-sufficient. Then China began to trade internationally in, among other items, coal and shoes. The world price of coal was less than China's domestic price and the world price of shoes was higher than its domestic price.

1. Does China import or export coal? Who, in China, gains and who loses from international trade in coal? Does China gain from this trade in coal?

2. On a graph of the market for coal in China show the gains, losses, and net gain or loss from international trade in coal.

3. Does China import or export shoes? Who, in China, gains and who loses from international trade in shoes? Does China gain from this trade in shoes?

4. On a graph of the market for shoes in China, show the gains, losses, and net gain or loss from international trade in shoes.

In the News

Commodities post big drop

World commodity prices have fallen in the past six weeks. Crude oil prices dropped 7%, beef prices fell 5%, and corn prices fell 4%.

Source: *Global Commodity Watch*, June 15, 2011

The United States imports crude oil and exports beef. How do these price falls change the U.S. gains from trade in each good and the distribution of the gains?

Solutions to Practice Problems

1. The rest of the world has a comparative advantage in producing coal. China imports coal, Chinese coal users gain more than Chinese coal producers lose, so China gains from international trade in coal.

2. Figure 1 shows the market for coal in China. With international trade, the price falls, the quantity produced decreases, and the quantity bought increases. Consumers gain and producers lose.

3. China has a comparative advantage in producing shoes. China exports shoes, Chinese shoe producers gain more than Chinese shoe consumers lose, so China gains from international trade in shoes.

4. Figure 2 shows the shoe market in China. With international trade, the price rises, the quantity produced increases and the quantity bought decreases. Producers gain and consumers lose.

Solution to In the News

The United States does not have a comparative advantage in producing crude oil, so the fall in the world price increases imports and decreases U.S. production. Consumers gain and producers lose, but consumers gain more than producers lose. The United States has a comparative advantage in producing beef, so the fall in the world price decreases U.S. production. Producers lose and consumers gain, but producers lose more than consumers gain.

FIGURE 1

FIGURE 2

18.2   INTERNATIONAL TRADE RESTRICTIONS

Governments use four sets of tools to influence international trade and protect domestic industries from foreign competition. They are

- Tariffs
- Import quotas
- Other import barriers

■ Tariffs

A **tariff** is a tax that is imposed on a good when it is imported. For example, the government of India imposes a 100 percent tariff on wine imported from California. When an Indian firm imports a $10 bottle of Californian wine, it pays the Indian government a $10 import duty.

The incentive for governments to impose tariffs is strong. First, they provide revenue to the government. Second, they enable the government to satisfy the self-interest of people who earn their incomes in import-competing industries. As you will see, tariffs and other restrictions on free international trade decrease the gains from trade and are not in the social interest. Let's see how.

Tariff
A tax imposed on a good when it is imported.

EYE on the PAST
The History of U.S. Tariffs

The figure shows the average tariff rate on U.S. imports since 1930. Tariffs peaked during the 1930s when Congress passed the Smoot-Hawley Act. With other nations, the United States signed the General Agreement on Tariffs and Trade (GATT) in 1947. In a series of rounds of negotiations, GATT achieved widespread tariff cuts for the United States and many other nations. Today, the World Trade Organization (WTO) continues the work of GATT and seeks to promote unrestricted trade among all nations.

The United States is a party to many trade agreements with individual countries or regions. These include the North American Free Trade Agreement (NAFTA) and the

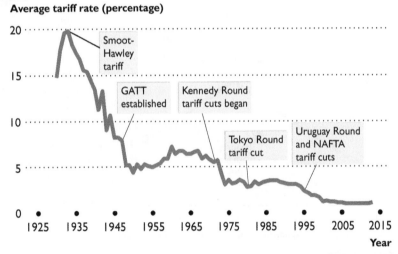

SOURCES OF DATA: The Budget for Fiscal Year 2013, Historical Tables, Table 2.5 and Bureau of Economic Analysis.

Central American Free Trade Agreement (CAFTA). These agreements have eliminated tariffs on most goods traded between the United States and the countries of North and Central America.

The Effects of a Tariff

To see the effects of a tariff, let's return to the example in which, with free international trade, the United States imports T-shirts. The T-shirts are imported and sold at the world price. Then, under pressure from U.S. garment makers, the U.S. government imposes a tariff on imported T-shirts. Buyers of T-shirts must now pay the world price plus the tariff. Several consequences follow in the market for T-shirts. Figure 18.3 illustrates these consequences.

Figure 18.3(a) is the same as Figure 18.1(b) and shows the situation with free international trade. The United States produces 20 million T-shirts and imports 40 million T-shirts a year at the world price of $5 a T-shirt.

Figure 18.3(b) shows what happens with a tariff, which is set at $2 per T-shirt. The following changes occur in the U.S. market for T-shirts:

- The price of a T-shirt in the United States rises by $2.
- The quantity of T-shirts bought in the United States decreases.
- The quantity of T-shirts produced in the United States increases.
- The quantity of T-shirts imported into the United States decreases.
- The U.S. government collects a tariff revenue.

FIGURE 18.3

The Effects of a Tariff   MyEconLab Animation

(a) Free trade

(b) Market with tariff

The world price of a T-shirt is $5. With free trade, in part (a), Americans buy 60 million T-shirts. The United States produces 20 million T-shirts and ❶ imports 40 million T-shirts.
❷ With a tariff of $2 per T-shirt in part (b), the domestic price rises to $7 a T-shirt (the world price plus the tariff). Domestic production increases, purchases decrease, and ❸ the quantity imported decreases. ❹ The U.S. government collects tariff revenue of $2 on each T-shirt imported, which is shown by the purple rectangle.

Rise in Price of a T-Shirt To buy a T-shirt, Americans must pay the world price plus the tariff, so the price of a T-shirt rises by $2 to $7. Figure 18.3(b) shows the new domestic price line, which lies $2 above the world price line.

Decrease in Purchases The higher price of a T-shirt brings a decrease in the quantity demanded, which Figure 18.3(b) shows as a movement along the demand curve from 60 million T-shirts at $5 a T-shirt to 45 million T-shirts at $7 a T-shirt.

Increase in Domestic Production The higher price of a T-shirt stimulates domestic production, which Figure 18.3(b) shows as a movement along the supply curve from 20 million T-shirts at $5 a T-shirt to 35 million T-shirts at $7 a T-shirt.

Decrease in Imports T-shirt imports decrease by 30 million from 40 million to 10 million a year. Both the decrease in purchases and the increase in domestic production contribute to this decrease in imports.

Tariff Revenue The government's tariff revenue is $20 million—$2 per T-shirt on 10 million imported T-shirts—shown by the purple rectangle.

Winners, Losers, and the Social Loss from a Tariff

A tariff on an imported good creates winners and losers. When the U.S. government imposes a tariff on an imported good,

- U.S. consumers of the good lose.
- U.S. producers of the good gain.
- U.S. consumers lose more than U.S. producers gain.

U.S. Consumers of the Good Lose Because the price of a T-shirt in the United States rises, the quantity of T-shirts demanded decreases. The combination of a higher price and smaller quantity bought makes U.S. consumers of T-shirts worse off.

U.S. Producers of the Good Gain Because the price of an imported T-shirt rises by the tariff, U.S. T-shirt producers are now able to sell their T-shirts for a higher price—the world price plus the tariff. As the price of a T-shirt rises, U.S. producers increase the quantity supplied. The combination of a higher price and a larger quantity produced increases producers' profits, so U.S. producers of T-shirts gain.

U.S. Consumers Lose More Than U.S. Producers Gain Consumers lose from the tariff for three reasons:

- They pay a higher price to domestic producers.
- They purchase a smaller quantity of the good.
- They pay tariff revenue to the government.

The tariff revenue is a loss to consumers of T-shirts but a gain to consumers of public services paid for by the tariff. The higher price paid to domestic producers pays for the higher cost of domestic production. The increased domestic production could have been obtained at lower cost as an import. Consumers lose and no one gains from the decreased quantity of T-shirts.

Let's now look at the second tool for restricting trade: quotas.

MyEconLab Snapshot

Import quota
A quantitative restriction on the import of a good that limits the maximum quantity of a good that may be imported in a given period.

■ Import Quotas

An **import quota** is a quantitative restriction on the import of a good that limits the maximum quantity of a good that may be imported in a given period. The United States imposes import quotas on many items, including sugar and steel. Quotas enable the government to satisfy the self-interest of people who earn their incomes in import-competing industries. You will see that like a tariff, a quota on imports decreases the gains from trade and is not in the social interest.

The Effects of an Import Quota

Figure 18.4 illustrates the effects. Figure 18.4(a) shows the situation with free international trade. Figure 18.4(b) shows what happens with a quota that limits imports to 10 million T-shirts a year. The U.S. supply curve of T-shirts becomes the domestic supply curve, S_{US}, plus the quantity that the quota permits to be imported. So the U.S. supply curve becomes the curve labeled $S_{US} + quota$.

The price of a T-shirt rises to $7, the quantity of T-shirts bought in the United States decreases to 45 million a year, the quantity of T-shirts produced in the United States increases to 35 million a year, and the quantity of T-shirts imported into the United States decreases to the quota quantity of 10 million a year. All these effects of a quota are identical to the effects of a $2 per T-shirt tariff, as you can check in Figure 18.3(b).

■ **FIGURE 18.4**

The Effects of an Import Quota

MyEconLab Animation

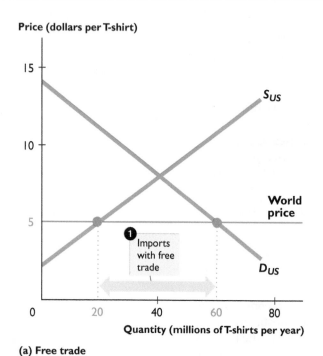

(a) Free trade

(b) Market with quota

With free trade, in part (a), Americans buy 60 million T-shirts at the world price. The United States produces 20 million T-shirts and ❶ imports 40 million T-shirts. ❷ With an import quota of 10 million

T-shirts, in part (b), the U.S. supply curve becomes $S_{US} + quota$. ❸ The price rises to $7 a T-shirt. Domestic production increases, purchases decrease, and ❹ the quantity imported decreases.

Winners, Losers, and the Social Loss from an Import Quota

An import quota creates winners and losers that are similar to those of a tariff but with an interesting difference. When the government imposes an import quota,

- U.S. consumers of the good lose.
- U.S. producers of the good gain.
- Importers of the good gain.
- Society loses.

U.S. Consumers of the Good Lose Because the price of a T-shirt in the United States rises, the quantity of T-shirts demanded decreases. The combination of a higher price and smaller quantity bought makes the consumer worse off. So the U.S. consumers lose when a quota is imposed.

U.S. Producers of the Good Gain Because the price of a T-shirt rises, U.S. T-shirt producers increase production. The combination of a higher price and larger quantity produced increases producers' profits. So the U.S. producers gain from the quota.

Importers of the Good Gain The importer is able to buy T-shirts on the world market at the world price, and sell them in the domestic market at the domestic price. Because the domestic price exceeds the world price, the importer gains.

Society Loses Society loses because the loss to consumers exceeds the gains of domestic producers and importers. Just like the social losses from a tariff, there is a social loss because part of the higher price paid to domestic producers pays the higher cost of domestic production. There is a social loss from the decreased quantity of the good bought at the higher price.

■ Other Import Barriers

Two sets of policies that influence imports are

- Health, safety, and regulation barriers
- Voluntary export restraints

Health, Safety, and Regulation Barriers

Thousands of detailed health, safety, and other regulations restrict international trade. For example, U.S. food imports are examined by the Food and Drug Administration to determine whether the food is "pure, wholesome, safe to eat, and produced under sanitary conditions." The discovery of BSE (mad cow disease) in just one U.S. cow in 2003 was enough to close down international trade in U.S. beef. The European Union bans imports of most genetically modified foods, such as U.S.-produced soybeans. Although regulations of the type we've just described are not designed to limit international trade, they have that effect.

Voluntary Export Restraints

A *voluntary export restraint* is like a quota allocated to a foreign exporter of the good. A voluntary export restraint decreases imports just like an import quota does, but the foreign exporter gets the profit from the gap between the domestic price and the world price.

MyEconLab Study Plan 18.2
Key Terms Quiz
Solutions

 CHECKPOINT 18.2

Explain the effects of international trade barriers.

Practice Problems

Before 1995, the United States imposed tariffs on goods imported from Mexico and Mexico imposed tariffs on goods imported from the United States. In 1995, Mexico joined NAFTA. U.S. tariffs on imports from Mexico and Mexican tariffs on imports from the United States are gradually being removed.

1. Explain how the price that U.S. consumers pay for goods imported from Mexico and the quantity of U.S. imports from Mexico have changed. Who, in the United States, are the winners and losers from this free trade?

2. Explain how the quantity of U.S. exports to Mexico and the U.S. government's tariff revenue from trade with Mexico have changed.

3. Suppose that this year, tomato growers in Florida lobby the U.S. government to impose an import quota on Mexican tomatoes. Explain who, in the United States, would gain and who would lose from such a quota.

In the News

Indonesians bemoan Hollywood blockbuster blackout
Four months ago Indonesia imposed an import tariff on Hollywood movies. The tariff was meant "to protect local film makers." The major Hollywood studios responded by withdrawing their films from Indonesia.

Source: *The Jakarta Post*, July 6, 2011

Explain how this tariff influences the price of seeing a movie in Indonesia, the quantity of movies produced in Indonesia, and Indonesia's gains from trade with the United States. Who, in Indonesia, gains from the tariff and who loses?

Solutions to Practice Problems

1. The price that U.S. consumers pay for goods imported from Mexico has fallen and the quantity of U.S. imports from Mexico has increased. The winners are U.S. consumers of goods imported from Mexico and the losers are U.S. producers of goods imported from Mexico.

2. The quantity of U.S. exports to Mexico has increased and the U.S. government's tariff revenue from trade with Mexico has fallen.

3. With an import quota, the price of tomatoes in the United States would rise and the quantity bought would decrease, so consumers would lose. Growers would receive a higher price and produce a larger quantity, so they would gain. Consumers would lose more than tomato growers would gain, so the U.S. society would have a net loss.

Solution to In the News

The tariff raises the price of seeing a movie in Indonesia. The production of movies in Indonesia increases, and imports of Hollywood movies fall to zero. Indonesia's gains from trade with the United States decrease. With the higher price, consumers lose. With the higher price, producers gain. The government collected zero tariff revenue.

18.3 THE CASE AGAINST PROTECTION

MyEconLab Snapshot

For as long as nations and international trade have existed, people have debated whether free international trade or protection from foreign competition is better for a country. The debate continues, but most economists believe that free trade promotes prosperity for all countries while protection reduces the potential gains from trade. We've seen the most powerful case for free trade: All countries benefit from their comparative advantage. But there is a broader range of issues in the free trade versus protection debate. Let's review these issues.

■ Three Traditional Arguments for Protection

Three traditional arguments for protection and restricting international trade are

- The national security argument
- The infant-industry argument
- The dumping argument

Let's look at each in turn.

The National Security Argument

The national security argument is that a country must protect industries that produce defense equipment and armaments and those on which the defense industries rely for their raw materials and other intermediate inputs. This argument for protection can be taken too far.

First, it is an argument for international isolation, for in a time of war, there is no industry that does not contribute to national defense. Second, if the case is made for boosting the output of a strategic industry—say aerospace—it is more efficient to achieve this outcome with a subsidy financed out of taxes than with a tariff or import quota. A subsidy would keep the industry operating at the scale that is judged appropriate, and free international trade would keep the prices faced by consumers at their world market levels.

Should producers of national security equipment be protected from international competition?

The Infant-Industry Argument

The **infant-industry argument** is that it is necessary to protect a new industry to enable it to grow into a mature industry that can compete in world markets. The argument is based on an idea called *learning-by-doing*. By working repeatedly at a task, workers become better at that task and can increase the amount they produce in a given period.

There is nothing wrong with the idea of learning-by-doing. It is a powerful engine of human capital accumulation and economic growth. Learning-by-doing can change comparative advantage. If on-the-job experience lowers the opportunity cost of producing a good, a country might develop a comparative advantage in producing that good.

But learning-by-doing does not justify protection. It is in the self-interest of firms and workers who benefit from learning-by-doing to produce the efficient quantities. If the government protected these firms to boost their production, there would be an inefficient overproduction.

The historical evidence is against the protection of infant industries. Countries in East Asia that have not given such protection have performed well. Countries that have protected infant industries, as India once did, have performed poorly.

Infant-industry argument
The argument that it is necessary to protect a new industry to enable it to grow into a mature industry that can compete in world markets.

India's protection of manufacturing industries from international competition is generally regarded as a failure.

The Dumping Argument

Dumping
When a foreign firm sells its exports at a lower price than its cost of production.

Dumping occurs when a foreign firm sells its exports at a lower price than its cost of production. You might be wondering why a firm would ever want to sell any of its output at a price below the cost of production. Wouldn't such a firm be better off either selling nothing, or, if it could do so, raising its price to at least cover its costs? Two possible reasons why a firm might sell at a price below cost and therefore engage in dumping are

- Predatory pricing
- Subsidy

China, a major producer of solar panels, is accused of dumping them on the U.S. and European markets.

Predatory Pricing A firm that engages in *predatory pricing* sets its price below cost in the hope that it can drive its competitors out of the market. If a firm in one country tries to drive out competitors in another country, it will be *dumping* its product in the foreign market. The foreign firm sells its output at a price below its cost to drive domestic firms out of business. When the domestic firms have gone, the foreign firm takes advantage of its monopoly position and charges a higher price for its product. The higher price will attract new competitors, which makes it unlikely that this strategy will be profitable. For this reason, economists are skeptical that this type of dumping occurs.

Subsidy A *subsidy* is a payment by the government to a producer. A firm that receives a subsidy is able to sell profitably for a price below cost. Subsidies are very common in almost all countries. The United States and the European Union subsidize the production of many agricultural products and dump their surpluses on the world market. This action lowers the prices that farmers in developing nations receive and weakens the incentive to expand farming in poor countries. India and Europe have been suspected of dumping steel in the United States.

Whatever its source, dumping is illegal under the rules of the WTO, NAFTA, and CAFTA and is regarded as a justification for temporary tariffs. Consequently, anti-dumping tariffs have become important in today's world.

But there are powerful reasons to resist the dumping argument for protection. First, it is virtually impossible to detect dumping because it is hard to determine a firm's costs. As a result, the test for dumping is whether a firm's export price is below its domestic price. This test is a weak one because it can be rational for a firm to charge a lower price in markets in which the quantity demanded is highly sensitive to price and a higher price in a market in which demand is less price-sensitive.

Second, it is hard to think of a good that is produced by a single firm. Even if all the domestic firms were driven out of business in some industry, it would always be possible to find several and usually many alternative foreign sources of supply and to buy at prices determined in competitive markets.

Third, if a good or service were a truly global natural monopoly, the best way to deal with it would be by regulation—just as in the case of domestic monopolies. Such regulation would require international cooperation.

The three arguments for protection that we've just examined have an element of credibility. The counterarguments are in general stronger, so these arguments do not make the case for protection. They are not the only arguments that you might encounter. There are many others, four of which we'll now examine.

■ Four Newer Arguments for Protection

Four newer and commonly made arguments for restricting international trade are that protection

- Saves jobs
- Allows us to compete with cheap foreign labor
- Brings diversity and stability
- Penalizes lax environmental standards

Saves Jobs

When Americans buy imported goods such as shoes from Brazil, U.S. workers who produce shoes lose their jobs. With no earnings and poor prospects, these workers become a drain on welfare and spend less, which creates a ripple effect of further job losses. The proposed solution is to protect U.S. jobs by banning imports of cheap foreign goods. The proposal is flawed for the following reasons.

First, free trade does cost some jobs, but it also creates other jobs. It brings about a global rationalization of labor and allocates labor resources to their highest-valued activities. Because of international trade in textiles, tens of thousands of workers in the United States have lost jobs because shoe factories and textile mills have closed. Tens of thousands of workers in other countries now have jobs because shoe factories and textile mills have opened there. And tens of thousands of U.S. workers now have better-paying jobs than as shoe makers or textile workers because other export industries have expanded and created more jobs than have been destroyed.

Second, imports create jobs. They create jobs for retailers that sell imported goods and for firms that service those goods. They also create jobs by creating incomes in the rest of the world, some of which are spent on imports of U.S.-made goods and services.

Protection saves some particular jobs, but it does so at a high cost. For example, until 2005, textile jobs in the United States were protected by import quotas imposed under an international agreement called the Multifiber Arrangement (or MFA). The U.S. International Trade Commission (ITC) estimated that because of import quotas, 72,000 jobs existed in textiles that would otherwise disappear and annual clothing expenditure in the United States was $15.9 billion ($160 per family) higher than it would be with free trade. An implication of the ITC estimate is that each textile job saved cost consumers $221,000 a year. The end of the MFA led to the destruction of a large number of textile jobs in the United States and Europe in 2005.

Few shoe factories remain in the United States and manufacturing jobs have been lost …

… but well-paid professional and service jobs have been created to replace the lost manufacturing jobs.

Allows Us to Compete with Cheap Foreign Labor

With the removal of protective tariffs in U.S. trade with Mexico, some people said that jobs would be sucked into Mexico and that the United States would not be able to compete with its southern neighbor. Let's see what's wrong with this view.

Labor costs depend on the wage rate and the quantity a worker produces. For example, if a U.S. auto worker earns $30 an hour and produces 15 units of output an hour, the average labor cost of a unit of output is $2. If a Mexican auto worker earns $3 an hour and produces 1 unit of output an hour, the average labor cost of a unit of output is $3. Other things remaining the same, the greater the output a worker produces, the higher is the worker's wage rate. High-wage workers produce a large output. Low-wage workers produce a small output.

Although high-wage U.S. workers are more productive, on the average, than lower-wage Mexican workers, there are differences across industries. U.S. labor is relatively more productive in some activities than in others. For example, the productivity of U.S. workers in producing movies, financial services, and customized computer chips is relatively higher than their productivity in the production of metals and some standardized machine parts. The activities in which U.S. workers are relatively more productive than their Mexican counterparts are those in which the United States has a comparative advantage. By engaging in free trade, increasing our production and exports of the goods and services in which we have a comparative advantage, and decreasing our production and increasing our imports of the goods and services in which our trading partners have a comparative advantage, we can make ourselves and the citizens of other countries better off.

Brings Diversity and Stability

A diversified investment portfolio is less risky than one that has all of its eggs in one basket. The same is true for an economy's production. A diversified economy fluctuates less than an economy that produces only one or two goods.

Most economies, whether the rich, advanced United States, Japan, and Europe or the developing China and Brazil, have diversified production and do not have this type of stability problem. A few economies, such as Saudi Arabia, have a comparative advantage that leads to the specialized production of only one good. But even these economies can stabilize their income and consumption by investing in a wide range of production activities in other countries.

Penalizes Lax Environmental Standards

A new argument for protection is that many poorer countries, such as Mexico, do not have the same environmental standards that we have, and because they are willing to pollute and we are not, we cannot compete with them without tariffs. If these countries want free trade with the richer and "greener" countries, then they must raise their environmental standards.

This argument for trade restrictions is not entirely convincing. A poor country is less able than a rich one to devote resources to achieving high environmental standards. If free trade helps a poor country to become richer, then it will also help that country to develop the means to improve its environment. But there probably is a case for using the negotiation of free trade agreements such as NAFTA and CAFTA to hold member countries to higher environmental standards. There is an especially large payoff from using such bargaining to try to avoid irreversible damage to resources such as tropical rainforests.

So the four common arguments that we've just considered do not provide overwhelming support for protection. They all have flaws and leave the case for free international trade a strong one.

■ Why Is International Trade Restricted?

Why, despite all the arguments against protection, is international trade restricted? One reason that applies to developing nations is that the tariff is a convenient source of government revenue, but this reason does not apply to the United States where the government has access to income taxes and sales taxes.

Political support for international trade restrictions in the United States and most other developed countries arises from rent seeking. **Rent seeking** is lobbying and other political activity that seeks to capture the gains from trade. You've seen that free trade benefits consumers but shrinks the producer surplus of firms that compete in markets with imports.

The winners from free trade are the millions of consumers of low-cost imports, but the benefit per individual consumer is small. The losers from free trade are the producers of import-competing items. Compared to the millions of consumers, there are only a few thousand producers.

Now think about imposing a tariff on clothing. Millions of consumers will bear the cost in the form of a higher price and a smaller quantity and a few thousand garment makers and their employees will share the gain arising from the higher price and larger quantity.

Because the gain from a tariff is large, producers have a strong incentive to incur the expense of lobbying *for* a tariff and *against* free trade. On the other hand, because each consumer's loss is small, consumers have little incentive to organize and incur the expense of lobbying *for* free trade. The gain from free trade for any one person is too small for that person to spend much time or money on a political organization to lobby for free trade. The loss from free trade will be seen as being so great by those bearing that loss that they will find it profitable to join a political organization to prevent free trade. Each group weighs benefits against costs and chooses the best action for themselves, but the anti-free-trade group will undertake more political lobbying than will the pro-free-trade group.

Rent seeking
Lobbying and other political activity that aims to capture the gains from trade.

EYE on YOUR LIFE
International Trade

International trade plays an extraordinarily large role in your life in three broad ways. It affects you as a

- Consumer
- Producer
- Voter

As a *consumer*, you benefit from the availability of a wide range of low-cost, high-quality goods and services that are produced in other countries.

Look closely at the labels on the items you buy. Where was your computer made? Where were your shirt and your shoes made? Where are the fruits and vegetables that you buy, especially in winter, grown?

The answers to all these questions are most likely Asia, Mexico, or South America. A few items were produced in Europe, Canada, and the United States.

As a *producer* (or as a potential producer if you don't yet have a job), you benefit from huge global markets for U.S. products. Your job prospects would be much dimmer if the firm for which you work didn't have global markets in which to sell its products.

People who work in the aircraft industry, for example, benefit from the huge global market for large passenger jets. Airlines from Canada to China are buying Boeing 777 aircraft as fast as they can be pushed out of the production line.

Even if you were to become a college professor, you would benefit from international trade in education services when your school admits foreign students.

As a *voter*, you have a big stake in the politics of free trade versus protection. As a buyer, your self-interest is hurt by tariffs and quotas on imported goods. Each time you buy a $20 sweater, you contribute $5 to the government in tariff revenue. But as a worker, your self-interest might be hurt by offshoring and by freer access to U.S. markets for foreign producers.

So as you decide how to vote, you must figure out what trade policy serves your self-interest and what best serves the social interest.

MyEconLab Study Plan 18.3
Key Terms Quiz
Solutions

 CHECKPOINT 18.3

Explain and evaluate arguments used to justify restricting international trade.

Practice Problems

1. Japan grows rice and sets an import quota on rice. California rice growers would like to export more rice to Japan. What are Japan's arguments for restricting imports of Californian rice? Are these arguments correct? Who loses from this restriction in trade?

2. The United States produces steel and, from time to time, has limited imports of steel from Europe. What argument has the United States used to justify this quota? Who wins from this restriction? Who loses?

3. The United States maintains an import quota on sugar. What is the argument for this import quota? Is this argument flawed? If so, explain why.

In the News

Indonesians bemoan Hollywood blockbuster blackout
The Indonesian import tariff on Hollywood movies was meant "to protect local film makers," but major Hollywood studios withdrew their films.

Source: *The Jakarta Post,* July 6, 2011

What argument is Indonesia using against free trade with the United States? What is wrong with Indonesia's argument?

Solutions to Practice Problems

1. The main arguments are that Japanese rice is a better quality rice and that the quota limits competition faced by Japanese farmers. The arguments are not correct. If Japanese consumers do not like the quality of Californian rice, they will not buy it. The quota limits competition and allows Japanese farmers to use their land less efficiently. The big losers are the Japanese consumers who pay about three times the U.S. price for rice.

2. The U.S. argument is that European producers dump steel on the U.S. market. With an import quota, U.S. steel producers will face less competition and U.S. jobs will be saved. Workers in the steel industry and owners of steel companies will win at the expense of U.S. buyers of steel.

3. The argument is that the import quota protects the jobs of U.S. workers. The argument is flawed because the United States does not have a comparative advantage in producing sugar and so an import quota allows the U.S. sugar industry to be inefficient. With free international trade in sugar, the U.S. sugar industry would exist but it would be much smaller and more efficient.

Solution to In the News

Indonesia is using the infant-industry argument: Protection is needed to allow its movie industry to mature and, through learning-by-doing, Indonesia will develop a comparative advantage in movie production. What's wrong with this argument is that protected industries generally perform poorly and the country does not develop the comparative advantage.

CHAPTER SUMMARY

Key Points

1. **Explain how markets work with international trade and identify the gains from international trade and its winners and losers.**

   - Comparative advantage drives international trade.
   - When the world price of a good is lower than the price that balances domestic demand and supply, a country gains by decreasing production and importing the good.
   - When the world price of a good is higher than the price that balances domestic demand and supply, a country gains by increasing production and exporting the good.
   - Compared to a no-trade situation, in a market with imports, consumers gain and producers lose, but the gains exceed the losses.
   - Compared to a no-trade situation, in a market with exports, producers gain and consumers lose, but the gains exceed the losses.

2. **Explain the effects of international trade barriers.**

   - Countries restrict international trade by imposing tariffs, import quotas, and other import barriers.
   - Trade restrictions raise the domestic price of imported goods, lower the quantity imported, decrease consumer surplus, increase producer surplus, and create a deadweight loss.

3. **Explain and evaluate arguments used to justify restricting international trade.**

   - The arguments that protection is necessary for national security, for infant industries, and to prevent dumping are weak.
   - Arguments that protection saves jobs, allows us to compete with cheap foreign labor, makes the economy diversified and stable, and is needed to penalize lax environmental standards are flawed.
   - Trade is restricted because protection brings small losses to a large number of people and large gains to a small number of people.

Key Terms

MyEconLab Key Terms Quiz

Dumping, 466
Exports, 452
Import quota, 462
Imports, 452

Infant-industry argument, 465
Rent seeking, 469
Tariff, 459

CHAPTER CHECKPOINT

Study Plan Problems and Applications

Use Figures 1 and 2 to work Problems 1 to 4. Figure 1 and Figure 2 show the markets for shoes if there is no trade between the United States and Brazil.

1. Which country has a comparative advantage in producing shoes? With international trade, explain which country would export shoes and how the price of shoes in the importing country and the quantity produced by the importing country would change. Explain which country gains from this trade.

2. The world price of a pair of shoes is $20. Explain how consumers and producers in the United States gain or lose as a result of international trade. On the graph, show the change in U.S. purchases, production, and the price of a pair of shoes.

3. The world price of a pair of shoes is $20. Explain how consumers and producers in Brazil gain or lose as a result of international trade. Show the change in Brazil's purchases, production, and the price of a pair of shoes.

4. Who in the United States loses from free trade in shoes with Brazil? Explain.

Use the following information to work Problems 5 to 7.

5. The supply of roses in the United States is made up of U.S.-grown roses and imported roses. Draw a graph to illustrate the U.S. rose market with free international trade. On your graph, mark the price of roses and the quantities of roses bought, produced, and imported into the United States.

6. Who in the United States loses from this trade in roses and would lobby for a restriction on the quantity of imported roses? Suppose that the U.S. government put a tariff on rose imports. Show on your graph the effect of the tariff on U.S. consumers and U.S. producers. Show the government's tariff revenue.

7. Suppose that the U.S. government puts an import quota on roses. Show on your graph the effect on the quantity bought by U.S. consumers, the quantity produced by U.S. rose growers, and the quantity imported.

Use the following information to work Problems 8 to 10.

U.S. expands China paper anti-dumping tariff
The United States raised the tariff on glossy paper imports from China to 99.65 percent, as a result of complaints by NewPage Corp. of Dayton, Ohio. Imports from China increased 166 percent from 2005 to 2006. This glossy paper is used in art books, high-end magazines, and textbooks.

Source: *Reuters*, May 30, 2007

8. Explain who, in the United States, gains and who loses from this tariff on paper. How do you expect the prices of magazines and textbooks to change?

9. What is dumping? Who in the United States loses from China's dumping of glossy paper?

10. Explain what an anti-dumping tariff is. What argument might NewPage Corp. have used to get the government to raise the tariff to 99.65 percent?

 11. Read *Eye on Globalization* on p. 457 and draw two graphs to show how U.S. consumers gain from iPads manufactured in China and why Chinese workers also gain.

FIGURE 1 U.S. SHOE MARKET

Quantity (millions of pairs per year)

FIGURE 2 BRAZIL'S SHOE MARKET

Quantity (millions of pairs per year)

Instructor Assignable Problems and Applications

MyEconLab Homework, Quiz, or Test if assigned by instructor

Use the following information to work Problems 1 and 2.

The future of U.S.–India relations

In May 2009, Secretary of State Hillary Clinton gave a major speech covering all the issues in U.S.–India relations. On economic and trade relations she noted that India maintains significant barriers to U.S. trade. The United States also maintains barriers against Indian imports such as textiles. Mrs. Clinton, President Obama, and Anand Sharma, the Indian Minister of Commerce and Industry, say they want to dismantle these trade barriers.

Source: www.state.gov

1. Explain who in the United States would gain and who might lose from dismantling trade barriers between the United States and India.

2. Draw a graph of the U.S. market for textiles and show how removing a tariff would change the quantities produced, bought, and imported. Explain why the gains exceed the losses.

3. The United States exports wheat. Draw a graph to illustrate the U.S. wheat market if there is free international trade in wheat. On your graph, mark the price of wheat and the quantities bought, produced, and exported by the United States.

4. Suppose that the world price of sugar is 20 cents a pound, Brazil does not trade internationally, and the equilibrium price of sugar in Brazil is 10 cents a pound. Brazil then begins to trade internationally.
   • How does the price of sugar in Brazil change? Do Brazilians buy more or less sugar? Do Brazilian sugar growers produce more or less sugar?
   • Does Brazil export or import sugar and why?

5. The United States exports services and imports coffee. Why does the United States gain from exporting services and importing coffee? How do economists measure the net gain from this international trade?

Use Figure 1 and the following information to work Problems 6 to 8.

Figure 1 shows the car market in Mexico when Mexico places no restriction on the quantity of cars imported. The world price of a car is $10,000.

6. If the government of Mexico introduces a $2,000 tariff on car imports, what will be the price of a car in Mexico, the quantity of cars produced in Mexico, the quantity imported into Mexico, and the government's tariff revenue?

7. If the government of Mexico introduces an import quota of 4 million cars a year, what will be the price of a car in Mexico, the quantity of cars produced in Mexico, and the quantity imported?

8. What argument might be used to encourage the government of Mexico to introduce a $2,000 tariff on car imports from the United States? Who will gain and who will lose as a result of Mexico's tariff?

9. In the 1950s, Ford and General Motors established a small car-producing industry in Australia and argued for a high tariff on car imports. The tariff has remained through the years. Until 2000, the tariff was 22.5 percent. What might have been Ford's and General Motors' argument for the high tariff? Is the tariff the best way to achieve the goals of the argument?

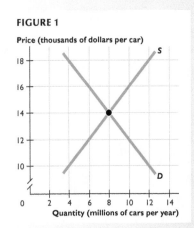

FIGURE 1

Price (thousands of dollars per car)

Multiple Choice Quiz

1. The fundamental force driving international trade is comparative _____.

    A. advantage: a country exports those goods that have high prices
    B. abundance: the country that produces more than it needs exports the good
    C. advantage: the country with the lower opportunity cost of production exports the good
    D. cost: a country trades with other countries that produce cheaper goods

2. A country will export wheat if, with no international trade, _____.

    A. it produces a surplus of wheat
    B. its opportunity cost of producing wheat is below the world price
    C. its domestic price of wheat exceeds the world price
    D. other countries have a shortage of wheat

3. With free trade between the United States and Canada, the United States exports tomatoes and Canada exports maple syrup. U.S. consumers _____.

    A. of tomatoes gain and Canadian consumers of maple syrup lose
    B. of both tomatoes and maple syrup gain more than either producer
    C. of maple syrup gain more than U.S. producers of maple syrup lose
    D. of tomatoes gain more than U.S. producers of tomatoes lose

4. With free trade between China and the United States, the winners are _____ and the losers are _____.

    A. U.S. consumers of U.S. imports; U.S. producers of the U.S. import good
    B. China's consumers of China's imports; China's producers of its export good
    C. U.S. producers of the U.S. export good; U.S. consumers of U.S. imports
    D. China's consumers of China's export good; China's producers of its imported good

5. The U.S. tariff on paper _____ the U.S. price of paper, _____ U.S. production of paper and _____the U.S. gains from trade.

    A. raises; increases; increases
    B. doesn't change; increases; increases
    C. doesn't change; doesn't change; decreases
    D. raises; increases; decreases

6. If Korea imposes an import quota on U.S. oranges, losers include Korean _____ of oranges and U.S. _____ of oranges.

    A. consumers; consumers
    B. consumers; producers
    C. producers; consumers
    D. producers; producers

7. The people who support restricted international trade say that _____.

    A. protection saves jobs, in both the U.S. and foreign economies
    B. U.S. firms won't be able to compete with low-wage foreign labor if trade is free
    C. outsourcing sends jobs abroad, which brings diversification and makes our economy more stable
    D. protection is needed to enable U.S. firms to produce the things at which they have a comparative advantage

Why does our dollar fluctuate?

International Finance

CHAPTER CHECKLIST

When you have completed your study of this chapter,
you will be able to

1 Describe a country's balance of payments accounts and explain what determines the amount of international borrowing and lending.

2 Explain how the exchange rate is determined and why it fluctuates.   MyEconLab Big Picture

19.1 FINANCING INTERNATIONAL TRADE

When Apple, Inc. imports iPods manufactured in Taiwan, it pays for them using Taiwanese dollars. When a French construction company buys an earthmover from Caterpillar, Inc., it uses U.S. dollars. Whenever we buy things from another country, we pay in the currency of that country. It doesn't make any difference what the item being traded is; it might be a consumption good or a service or a capital good, a building, or even a firm.

We're going to study the markets in which different types of currency are bought and sold. But first we're going to look at the scale of international trading and borrowing and lending and at the way in which we keep our records of these transactions. These records are called the balance of payments accounts.

■ Balance of Payments Accounts

Balance of payments accounts
The accounts in which a nation records its international trading, borrowing, and lending.

A country's **balance of payments accounts** record its international trading, borrowing, and lending. There are in fact three balance of payments accounts:

- Current account
- Capital and financial account
- Official settlements account

Current account
Record of receipts from the sale of goods and services to other countries (exports), minus payments for goods and services bought from other countries (imports), plus the net amount of interest and transfers received from and paid to other countries.

The **current account** records receipts from the sale of goods and services to other countries (exports), minus payments for goods and services bought from other countries (imports), plus the net amount of interest and transfers (such as foreign aid payments) received from and paid to other countries. The **capital and financial account** records foreign investment in the United States minus U.S. investment abroad. The **official settlements account** records the change in U.S. official reserves. **U.S. official reserves** are the government's holdings of foreign currency. If U.S. official reserves increase, the official settlements account balance is negative. The reason is that holding foreign money is like investing abroad and U.S. investment abroad is a minus item in the capital and financial account. (And if official reserves decrease, the official settlements account balance is positive.)

Capital and financial account
Record of foreign investment in the United States minus U.S. investment abroad.

Official settlements account
Record of the change in U.S. official reserves.

U.S. official reserves
The government's holdings of foreign currency.

The sum of the balances on the three accounts always equals zero. That is, to pay for our current account deficit, we must either borrow more from abroad than we lend abroad or use our official reserves to cover the shortfall.

Table 19.1 shows the U.S. balance of payments accounts in 2012. Items in the current account and capital and financial account that provide foreign currency to the United States have a plus sign; items that cost the United States foreign currency have a minus sign. The table shows that in 2012, U.S. imports exceeded U.S. exports and the current account deficit was $440 billion. To pay for imports that exceeded the value of our exports we borrowed from the rest of the world. The capital and financial account tells us by how much. We borrowed $544 billion (foreign investment in the United States) and made $98 billion of loans to the rest of the world (U.S. investment abroad). Other net foreign borrowing of $4 billion and a statistical discrepancy of –$6 billion made our capital account balance $444 billion. Our official reserves increased by $4 billion and are shown in Table 19.1 as a negative $4 billion, a convention that makes the three accounts sum to zero.

You might better understand the balance of payments accounts and the way in which they are linked if you think about the income and expenditure, borrowing and lending, and bank account of an individual.

EYE on the U.S. ECONOMY
The U.S. Balance of Payments

The numbers in Table 19.1 provide a snapshot of the U.S. balance of payments in 2012. This figure puts this snapshot into perspective by showing how the balance of payments evolved from 1980 to 2012.

A current account deficit emerged during the 1980s but briefly disappeared with a near-zero balance in the recession of the early 1990s. As the economy resumed its expansion during the 1990s, the current account deficit increased and kept on increasing until 2006.

As economic growth slowed and the economy went into recession, imports shrank and so did the current account deficit.

The capital and financial account balance is almost a mirror image of the current account balance and the reason is that the official settlements

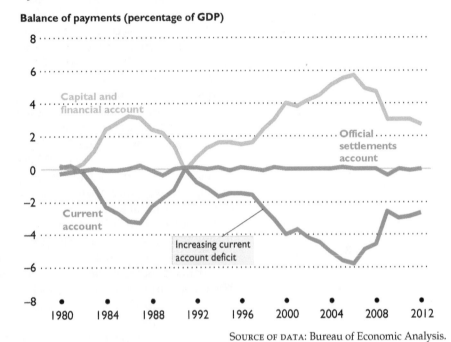

Balance of payments (percentage of GDP)

SOURCE OF DATA: Bureau of Economic Analysis.

balance—the change in foreign exchange reserves—is very small in

comparison with the balances on the other two accounts.

TABLE 19.1
The U.S. Balance of Payments Accounts in 2012

MyEconLab Real-time data

	(billions of dollars)	
Current account		The three balance of payments accounts are the current account, the capital and financial account, and the official settlements account.
Exports of goods and services	+2,211	
Imports of goods and services	−2,745	
Net interest	+224	
Net transfers	−130	
Current account balance	**−440**	
		The sum of the balances on the three accounts is always zero. That is, the official settlements account balance always equals the negative of the sum of the current account balance and the capital and financial account balance.
Capital and financial account		
Foreign investment in the United States	+544	
U.S. investment abroad	−98	
Other net foreign investment in the United States	+4	
Statistical discrepancy	−6	
Capital and financial account balance	**+444**	
Official settlements account		
Official settlements account balance	**−4**	

SOURCE OF DATA: Bureau of Economic Analysis.

Personal Analogy

You have a set of personal balance of payments accounts that parallel those of a nation. You have a current account, a capital account, and a settlements account.

Your current account records your income from supplying the services of factors of production and your expenditure on goods and services. Consider, for example, Joanne. She worked in 2013 and earned an income of $25,000. Joanne has $10,000 worth of investments that earned her interest of $1,000. Joanne's current account shows an income of $26,000. Joanne spent $18,000 buying goods and services for consumption. She also bought a new apartment, which cost her $60,000. So Joanne's total expenditure was $78,000. The difference between her expenditure and her income is $52,000 ($78,000 minus $26,000).

To pay for expenditure of $52,000 in excess of her income, Joanne has to use her bank account or take a loan. Suppose that Joanne took a mortgage of $50,000 to help buy her apartment. This mortgage was the only borrowing that Joanne did, so her capital and financial account surplus was $50,000. With a current account deficit of $52,000 and a capital and financial account surplus of $50,000, Joanne is still $2,000 short. She got that $2,000 from her own bank account. Her cash holdings decreased by $2,000. Joanne's settlements balance was $2,000.

Joanne's income from her work is like a country's income from its exports. Her income from her investments is like a country's interest from foreigners. Her purchases of goods and services, including her purchase of an apartment, are like a country's imports. Joanne's mortgage—borrowing from someone else—is like a country's borrowing from the rest of the world. The change in Joanne's bank account is like the change in a country's official reserves.

Check that the sum of Joanne's balances is zero. Her current account balance is −$52,000, her capital and financial account balance is +$50,000, and her settlements account balance is +$2,000, so the sum of the three balances is zero.

■ Borrowers and Lenders, Debtors and Creditors

Net borrower
A country that is borrowing more from the rest of the world than it is lending to the rest of the world.

Net lender
A country that is lending more to the rest of the world than it is borrowing from the rest of the world.

A country that is borrowing more from the rest of the world than it is lending to the rest of the world is called a **net borrower**. Similarly, a **net lender** is a country that is lending more to the rest of the world than it is borrowing from it.

The United States is a net borrower, but it is a relative newcomer to the ranks of net borrower nations. Throughout the 1960s and most of the 1970s, the United States was a net lender. It had a surplus on its current account and a deficit on its capital and financial account. It was not until 1983 that the United States became a significant net borrower. Between 1983 and 1987, U.S. borrowing increased each year. Then it decreased and was briefly zero in 1991. From 1991 through 2006, U.S. borrowing increased, but after 2006 it decreased. The average net foreign borrowing by the United States between 1983 and 2012 was $306 billion a year.

Most countries are net borrowers like the United States. But a small number of countries, including China and oil-rich Saudi Arabia, are net lenders.

Debtor nation
A country that during its entire history has borrowed more from the rest of the world than it has lent to the rest of the world.

Creditor nation
A country that during its entire history has invested more in the rest of the world than other countries have invested in it.

A net borrower might be reducing its net assets held in the rest of the world, or it might be going deeper into debt. A nation's total stock of foreign investment determines whether the nation is a debtor or creditor. A **debtor nation** is a country that during its entire history has borrowed more from the rest of the world than it has lent to the rest of the world. A debtor nation has a stock of outstanding debt to the rest of the world that exceeds the stock of its own claims on the rest of the world. A **creditor nation** is a country that during its entire history has invested more in the rest of the world than other countries have invested in it.

Flows and Stocks

At the heart of the distinction between a net borrower and a net lender on the one hand and between a debtor nation and a creditor nation on the other hand is the distinction between flows and stocks, which you have encountered many times in your study of macroeconomics. Borrowing and lending are flows—amounts borrowed or lent per unit of time. Debts are stocks—amounts owed at a point in time. The flow of borrowing and lending changes the stock of debt.

The United States was a debtor nation through the nineteenth century as we borrowed from Europe to finance our westward expansion, railroads, and industrialization. The United States paid off its debt and became a creditor nation for most of the twentieth century. But following a string of current account deficits, the United States became a debtor nation again in 1989.

Since 1989, the total stock of U.S. borrowing from the rest of the world has exceeded U.S. lending to the rest of the world. The largest debtor nations are the capital-hungry developing countries (as the United States was during the nineteenth century). The international debt of these countries grew from less than a third to more than a half of their gross domestic product during the 1980s and created what is called the "Third World debt crisis."

Should we be concerned that the United States is a net borrower? The answer to this question depends mainly on what the net borrower is doing with the borrowed money. If the borrowed money is financing investment that in turn is generating economic growth and higher income, then the borrowing is not a problem. If the borrowed money is being used to finance consumption, then higher interest payments are being incurred, and consequently, consumption will eventually have to be reduced. In this case, the more the borrowing and the longer it goes on, the greater is the reduction in consumption that will eventually be necessary. We'll see below whether the United States is borrowing for investment or consumption.

■ Current Account Balance

What determines a country's current account balance and net foreign borrowing? You've seen in Table 19.1 that exports of goods and services (X) and imports of goods and services (M) are the largest items in the current account. We call exports minus imports net exports (NX). So net exports is the main component of the current account. We can define the current account balance (CAB) as

$$CAB = NX + \text{Net interest and transfers from abroad.}$$

Fluctuations in net exports are the main source of fluctuations in the current account balance. Net interest and transfers from abroad are small and have trends, but they do not fluctuate much. So we can study the current account balance by looking at what determines net exports.

■ Net Exports

The government budget and private saving and investment determine net exports. To see how they determine net exports, we need to recall some of the things that we learned about the national income accounts in Chapter 21. Table 19.2 will refresh your memory and summarize some calculations.

Part (a) of Table 19.2 lists the national income variables with their symbols. Part (b) defines three balances. *Net exports* are exports of goods and services minus imports of goods and services.

Private sector balance
Saving minus investment.

The **private sector balance** is saving minus investment. If saving exceeds investment, a private sector surplus is lent to other sectors. If investment exceeds saving, borrowing from other sectors finances a private sector deficit.

Government sector balance
Net taxes minus government expenditure on goods and services.

The **government sector balance** is equal to net taxes minus government expenditure on goods and services. If that number is positive, a government sector surplus is lent to other sectors; if that number is negative, borrowing from other sectors must finance a government deficit. The government sector is the sum of the federal, state, and local governments.

Part (b) also shows the values of these balances for the United States in 2012. As you can see, net exports were −$547 billion, a deficit. The private sector saved $3,435 billion and invested $2,475 billion, so it had a surplus of $960 billion. The government sector's revenue from net taxes was $1,660 billion, and its expenditure was $3,167 billion, so the government sector balance was −$1,507 billion, a deficit.

Part (c) of Table 19.2 shows the relationship among the three balances.

TABLE 19.2

Net Exports, the Government Budget, Saving, and Investment

		Symbols and equations	United States in 2012 (billions of dollars)
Net exports equals exports minus imports.	**(a) Variables**		
	Exports	X	2,196
The private sector balance equals saving minus investment.	Imports	M	2,743
	Investment	I	2,475
	Saving	S	3,435
The government sector balance equals net taxes minus government	Government expenditure	G	3,167
expenditure on goods and services.	Net taxes	NT	1,660
	(b) Balances		
These three balances are related:	Net exports	$X - M$	$2,196 - 2,743 = -547$
Net exports equals the sum of the	Private sector balance	$S - I$	$3,435 - 2,475 = 960$
private sector and government	Government sector balance	$NT - G$	$1,660 - 3,167 = -1,507$
sector balances.			
	(c) Relation among balances		
	National accounts	$Y = C + I + G + X - M = C + S + NT$	
	Rearranging:	$X - M = S - I + NT - G$	
	Net exports	$X - M$	−547
	Equals:		
	Private sector balance	$S - I$	960
	Plus:		
	Government sector balance	$NT - G$	−1,507

SOURCE OF DATA: Bureau of Economic Analysis, 2013. (The *National Income and Product Accounts* measures of exports and imports are slightly different from the Balance of Payments Accounts measures in Table 19.1 on p. 477. The government sector includes state and local governments.)

From the national income accounts, we know that real GDP, Y, is the sum of consumption expenditure, C; investment, I; government expenditure on goods and services, G; and net exports, $X - M$. Real GDP also equals the sum of consumption expenditure, C, saving, S, and net taxes, NT. Rearranging these equations tells us that net exports equals $(S - I)$, the private sector balance, plus $(NT - G)$, the government sector balance. That is,

$$\text{Net exports} = (S - I) + (NT - G).$$

Should we be concerned that the United States is a net borrower? The answer is probably not. Our international borrowing finances the purchase of new capital goods. In 2012, businesses spent $2,475 billion on new buildings, plant, and equipment. Governments spent $619 billion on defense equipment and public structures. All these purchases added to the nation's capital, and much of it increased productivity. Governments also purchased education and health care services, which increased human capital.

Our international borrowing is financing private and public investment, not consumption.

EYE on the GLOBAL ECONOMY
Current Account Balances Around the World

The U.S. current account deficit in 2012 is the major international payments deficit. No other country has a deficit remotely similar to that of the United States.

For every deficit, there must be a corresponding surplus. The figure shows that the U.S. deficit is reflected in a large number of surpluses spread around the world. No single country has a surplus to match the U.S. deficit.

But China, other advanced economies, and Japan have surpluses that in total equal the U.S. deficit.

The oil-exporting countries of the Middle East and the newly industrialized Asian economies also have surpluses.

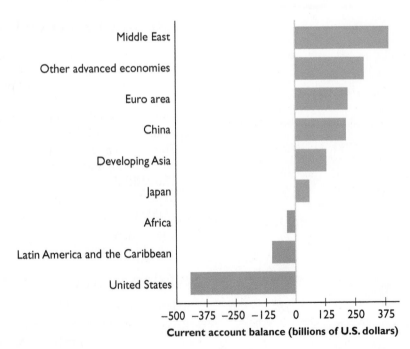

SOURCE OF DATA: International Monetary Fund, *World Economic Outlook*, April 2013.

MyEconLab Study Plan 19.1
Key Terms Quiz
Solutions

 # CHECKPOINT 19.1

Describe a country's balance of payments accounts and explain what determines the amount of international borrowing and lending.

Practice Problems

Use the following information about the United States to work Problems 1 and 2.

Imports of goods and services: $2,000 billion; interest paid to the rest of the world: $500 billion; interest received from the rest of the world: $400 billion; decrease in U.S. official reserves: $10 billion; government sector balance: $200 billion; saving: $1,800 billion; investment: $2,000 billion; net transfers: zero.

1. Calculate the current account balance, the capital and financial account balance, the official settlements account balance, and exports of goods and services.

2. Is the United States a debtor or a creditor nation?

In the News

Something has got to give
As the recovery takes hold, the U.S. government must reduce its expenditure to trim its huge budget deficit. To keep aggregate demand growing, consumption, investment, or exports must grow. U.S. consumers are burdened with debt, U.S. firms have unused capital, so exports must grow.

Source: USA Today, September 3, 2009

Explain why a cut in government expenditure to trim the budget deficit with no change in net taxes will require exports to grow.

Solutions to Practice Problems

1. The current account balance equals net exports plus net interest from abroad (−$100 billion) plus net transfers (zero). Net exports equal the government sector balance ($200 billion) plus the private sector balance. The private sector balance equals saving ($1,800 billion) minus investment ($2,000 billion), which is −$200 billion So net exports are zero, and the current account balance is −$100 billion.
    The capital and financial account balance is the negative of the sum of the current account and official settlements account balances, which is $90 billion.
    The official settlements account balance is a *surplus* of $10 billion.
    Exports equal net exports (zero) plus imports ($2,000 billion), which equals $2,000 billion.

2. The United States is a debtor nation because it pays more in interest to the rest of the world than it receives in interest from the rest of the world.

Solution to In the News

The link between the government sector balance and the private sector balance is given by the equation: $(X − M) = (S − I) + (NT − G)$. Rewrite the equation as $(G − NT) = (S − I) − (X − M)$. A cut in the budget deficit will decrease the left side of the equation. An increase in consumption or an increase in I decreases $(S − I)$ and makes the right side of the equation decrease. If $(S − I)$ does not change, then to make the right side of the equation decrease, X must increase.

19.2   THE EXCHANGE RATE

MyEconLab Snapshot

When we buy foreign goods or invest in another country, we pay using that country's currency. When foreigners buy U.S.-made goods or invest in the United States, they pay in U.S. dollars. We get foreign currency and foreigners get U.S. dollars in the foreign exchange market. The **foreign exchange market** is the market in which the currency of one country is exchanged for the currency of another. The foreign exchange market is not a place like a downtown flea market or produce market. It is made up of thousands of people: importers and exporters, banks, and specialist traders of foreign exchange, called foreign exchange brokers. The foreign exchange market opens on Monday morning in Hong Kong, which is still Sunday evening in New York. As the day advances, markets open in Singapore, Tokyo, Bahrain, Frankfurt, London, New York, Chicago, and San Francisco. As the U.S. West Coast markets close, Hong Kong is only an hour away from opening for the next business day. Dealers around the world are in continual contact, and on a typical day in 2013, more than $4 trillion changed hands.

Foreign exchange market
The market in which the currency of one country is exchanged for the currency of another.

The price at which one currency exchanges for another is called a **foreign exchange rate**. For example, in August 2013, one U.S. dollar bought 75 euro cents. The exchange rate was 0.75 euros per dollar. We can also express the exchange rate in terms of dollars per euro, which in August 2013 was $1.33 per euro. Figure 19.1 shows the history of the U.S. dollar exchange rate against the euro since 1999 in terms of euros per dollar.

Foreign exchange rate
The price at which one currency exchanges for another.

Currency appreciation is the rise in the value of one currency in terms of another currency. For example, when the dollar rose from 86 euro cents in 1999 to 1.17 euros in 2000, the dollar appreciated by 36 percent.

Currency appreciation
The rise in the value of one currency in terms of another currency.

■ FIGURE 19.1

The U.S. Dollar Exchange Rate Against the Euro

MyEconLab Real-time data

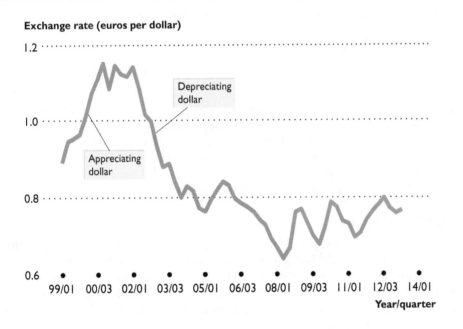

From 1999 to 2000, the value of the dollar rose against the euro—the dollar *appreciated*. From 2002 to 2008, the value of the dollar fell against the euro—the dollar *depreciated*. The overall fall was from a high of 1.17 euros per dollar in 2000 to a low of 0.63 euros per dollar in 2008.

Since 2008, through the turmoil of global financial crisis and repeated financial and political crises in Europe, the dollar and the euro have fluctuated between around 0.70 and 0.80 euros per dollar.

SOURCE OF DATA: Board of Governors of the Federal Reserve System.

Currency depreciation
The fall in the value of one currency in terms of another currency.

Currency depreciation is the fall in the value of one currency in terms of another currency. For example, when the dollar fell from 1.17 euros in 2000 to 0.63 euros in 2008, the dollar depreciated by 46 percent. Why does the U.S. dollar fluctuate in value? Why does it sometimes depreciate and sometimes appreciate?

The exchange rate is a price. And like all prices, demand and supply determine the exchange rate. So to understand the forces that determine the exchange rate, we need to study demand and supply in the foreign exchange market. We'll begin by looking at the demand side of the market.

◼ Demand in the Foreign Exchange Market

The quantity of U.S. dollars that traders plan to buy in the foreign exchange market during a given time period depends on many factors, but the main ones are

- The exchange rate
- Interest rates in the United States and other countries
- The expected future exchange rate

Let's look first at the relationship between the quantity of dollars demanded in the foreign exchange market and the exchange rate.

◼ The Law of Demand for Foreign Exchange

People do not buy dollars because they enjoy them. The demand for dollars is a *derived demand*. People demand dollars so that they can buy U.S.-made goods and services (U.S. exports). They also demand dollars so that they can buy U.S. assets such as bank accounts, bonds, stocks, businesses, and real estate. Nevertheless, the law of demand applies to dollars just as it does to anything else that people value.

Other things remaining the same, the higher the exchange rate, the smaller is the quantity of dollars demanded. For example, if the price of the U.S. dollar rises from 0.70 euros to 0.80 euros but nothing else changes, the quantity of U.S. dollars that people plan to buy decreases. Why does the exchange rate influence the quantity of dollars demanded? There are two separate reasons, and they are related to the two sources of the derived demand for dollars. They are

- Exports effect
- Expected profit effect

Exports Effect

The larger the value of U.S. exports, the larger is the quantity of dollars demanded. But the value of U.S. exports depends on the exchange rate. For example, if the exchange rate falls from 0.70 euros to 0.60 euros per U.S. dollar, other things remaining the same, the cheaper are U.S.-made goods and services to people in Europe, the more the United States exports, and the greater is the quantity of U.S. dollars demanded to pay for those exports.

Expected Profit Effect

The larger the expected profit from holding dollars, the greater is the quantity of dollars demanded in the foreign exchange market. But expected profit depends on today's exchange rate and the expected future exchange rate. For a given expected future exchange rate, the lower the exchange rate today, the larger is the expected profit from holding dollars and the greater is the quantity of dollars demanded in the foreign exchange market.

FIGURE 19.2

The Demand for Dollars

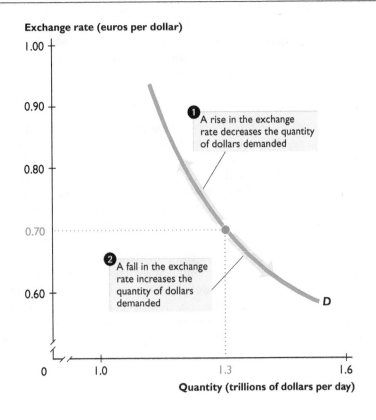

Other things remaining the same, the quantity of dollars that people plan to buy depends on the exchange rate.

❶ If the exchange rate rises, the quantity of dollars demanded decreases and there is a movement up along the demand curve for dollars.

❷ If the exchange rate falls, the quantity of dollars demanded increases and there is a movement down along the demand curve for dollars.

To understand this effect, suppose that you think the dollar will be worth 0.80 euros by the end of the month. If a dollar costs 0.75 euros today, you buy dollars. But a person who thinks that the dollar will be worth 0.75 euros at the end of the month does not buy dollars. Now suppose that today's exchange rate falls to 0.65 euros per dollar. More people think that they can profit from buying dollars, so the quantity of dollars demanded today increases.

Figure 19.2 shows the demand curve for U.S. dollars in the foreign exchange market. For the two reasons we've just reviewed, when the foreign exchange rate rises, other things remaining the same, the quantity of dollars demanded decreases and there is a movement up along the demand curve, as shown by the arrow. When the exchange rate falls, other things remaining the same, the quantity of dollars demanded increases and there is a movement down along the demand curve, as shown by the arrow.

■ **Changes in the Demand for Dollars**

A change in any other influence on the quantity of U.S. dollars that people plan to buy in the foreign exchange market brings a change in the demand for dollars. These other influences are

- Interest rates in the United States and other countries
- The expected future exchange rate

U.S. interest rate differential
The U.S. interest rate minus the foreign interest rate.

Interest Rates in the United States and Other Countries

If you can borrow in another country and lend in the United States at a higher interest rate, you will make a profit. What matters is not the level of foreign and U.S. interest rates, but the gap between them. This gap, the U.S. interest rate minus the foreign interest rate, is called the **U.S. interest rate differential**. The larger the U.S. interest rate differential, the greater is the demand for U.S. assets and the greater is the demand for dollars.

The Expected Future Exchange Rate

Suppose you are the finance manager of the German auto maker BMW. The exchange rate is 0.70 euros per dollar, and you expect that by the end of the month, it will be 0.80 euros per dollar. You spend 700,000 euros today and buy $1,000,000. At the end of the month, the dollar equals 0.80 euros, as you predicted, and you sell the $1,000,000. You get 800,000 euros. You've made a profit of 100,000 euros. The higher the expected future exchange rate, the greater is the expected profit and the greater is the demand for dollars today.

Figure 19.3 summarizes the influences on the demand for dollars. A rise in the U.S. interest rate differential or a rise in the expected future exchange rate increases the demand for dollars today and shifts the demand curve rightward from D_0 to D_1. A fall in the U.S. interest rate differential or a fall in the expected future exchange rate decreases the demand for dollars today and shifts the demand curve leftward from D_0 to D_2.

FIGURE 19.3

Changes in the Demand for Dollars

MyEconLab Animation

1 The demand for dollars increases if:

- The U.S. interest rate differential increases.
- The expected future exchange rate rises.

2 The demand for dollars decreases if:

- The U.S. interest rate differential decreases.
- The expected future exchange rate falls.

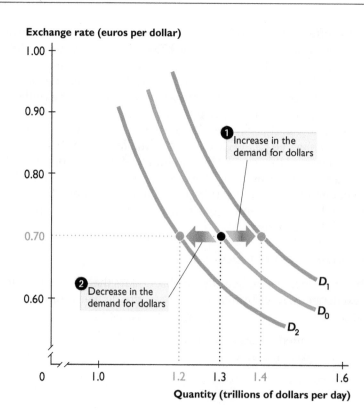

■ Supply in the Foreign Exchange Market

The quantity of U.S. dollars that traders plan to sell in the foreign exchange market during a given time period depends on many factors, but the main ones are

- The exchange rate
- Interest rates in the United States and other countries
- The expected future exchange rate

Does this list of factors seem familiar? It should: It is the same list as that for demand. The demand side and the supply side of the foreign exchange market are influenced by all the same factors. But the ways in which these three factors influence supply are the opposite of the ways in which they influence demand.

Let's look first at the relationship between the quantity of dollars supplied in the foreign exchange market and the exchange rate.

■ The Law of Supply of Foreign Exchange

Traders supply U.S. dollars in the foreign exchange market when people and businesses buy other currencies. They buy other currencies so that they can buy foreign-made goods and services (U.S. imports). Traders also supply dollars and buy foreign currencies so that people and businesses can buy foreign assets such as bank accounts, bonds, stocks, businesses, and real estate. The law of supply applies to dollars just as it does to anything else that people plan to sell.

Other things remaining the same, the higher the exchange rate, the greater is the quantity of dollars supplied in the foreign exchange market. For example, if the price of the U.S. dollar rises from 0.70 euros to 0.80 euros but nothing else changes, the quantity of U.S. dollars that people plan to sell in the foreign exchange market increases. Why does the exchange rate influence the quantity of dollars supplied?

There are two reasons, and they parallel the two reasons on the demand side of the market. They are

- Imports effect
- Expected profit effect

Imports Effect

The larger the value of U.S. imports, the larger is the quantity of foreign currency demanded to pay for these imports. And when people buy foreign currency, they supply dollars. So the larger the value of U.S. imports, the greater is the quantity of dollars supplied in the foreign exchange market. But the value of U.S. imports depends on the exchange rate. The higher the exchange rate, other things remaining the same, the cheaper are foreign-made goods and services to Americans. So the more the United States imports, the greater is the quantity of U.S. dollars supplied in the foreign exchange market to pay for these imports.

Expected Profit Effect

The larger the expected profit from holding a foreign currency, the greater is the quantity of that currency demanded and the greater is the quantity of dollars supplied in the foreign exchange market. But the expected profit depends on today's exchange rate and the expected future exchange rate. For a given expected future exchange rate, the higher the exchange rate today, the larger is the expected profit from selling dollars and the greater is the quantity of dollars supplied in the foreign exchange market.

FIGURE 19.4

The Supply of Dollars

MyEconLab Animation

Other things remaining the same, the quantity of dollars that people plan to sell depends on the exchange rate.

1 If the exchange rate rises, the quantity of dollars supplied increases and there is a movement up along the supply curve of dollars.

2 If the exchange rate falls, the quantity of dollars supplied decreases and there is a movement down along the supply curve of dollars.

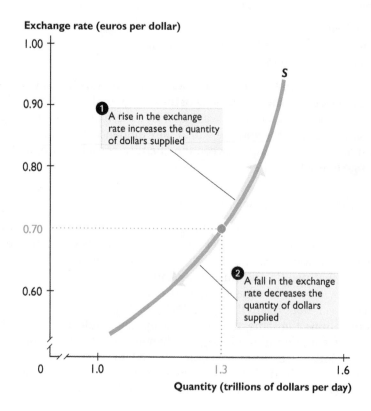

For the two reasons we've just reviewed, other things remaining the same, when the exchange rate rises, the quantity of dollars supplied increases, and when the exchange rate falls, the quantity of dollars supplied decreases. Figure 19.4 shows the supply curve of U.S. dollars in the foreign exchange market. In this figure, when the exchange rate rises, other things remaining the same, there is an increase in the quantity of dollars supplied and a movement up along the supply curve, as shown by the arrow. When the exchange rate falls, other things remaining the same, there is a decrease in the quantity of dollars supplied and a movement down along the supply curve, as shown by the arrow.

■ Changes in the Supply of Dollars

A change in any other influence on the quantity of U.S. dollars that people plan to sell in the foreign exchange market brings a change in the supply of dollars, and the supply curve of dollars shifts. Supply either increases or decreases. These other influences on supply parallel the other influences on demand but have exactly the opposite effects. These influences are

- Interest rates in the United States and other countries
- The expected future exchange rate

Interest Rates in the United States and Other Countries

The larger the U.S. interest rate differential, the smaller is the demand for foreign assets and the smaller is the supply of dollars in the foreign exchange market.

The Expected Future Exchange Rate

Other things remaining the same, the higher the expected future exchange rate, the smaller is the supply of dollars. To see why, suppose that the dollar is trading at 0.70 euros per dollar today and you think that by the end of the month, the dollar will trade at 0.80 euros per dollar. You were planning on selling dollars today, but you decide to hold off and wait until the end of the month. If you supply dollars today, you get only 0.70 euros per dollar. But at the end of the month, if the dollar is worth 0.80 euros as you predict, you'll get 0.80 euros for each dollar you supply. You'll make a profit of 0.10 euros per dollar. So the higher the expected future exchange rate, other things remaining the same, the smaller is the expected profit from selling U.S. dollars and the smaller is the supply of dollars today.

Figure 19.5 summarizes the influences on the supply of dollars. A rise in the U.S. interest rate differential or the expected future exchange rate decreases the supply of dollars today and shifts the supply curve leftward from S_0 to S_1. A fall in the U.S. interest rate differential or the expected future exchange rate increases the supply of dollars today and shifts the supply curve rightward from S_0 to S_2.

FIGURE 19.5

Changes in the Supply of Dollars

MyEconLab Animation

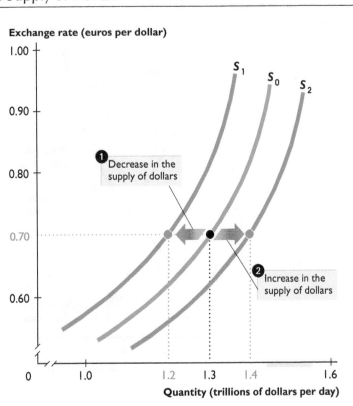

1. The supply of dollars increases if:
   - The U.S. interest rate differential decreases.
   - The expected future exchange rate falls.

2. The supply of dollars decreases if:
   - The U.S. interest rate differential increases.
   - The expected future exchange rate rises.

■ Market Equilibrium

Demand and supply in the foreign exchange market determine the exchange rate. Just as in all the other markets you've studied, the price (the exchange rate) acts as a regulator. If the exchange rate is too high, there is a surplus—the quantity supplied exceeds the quantity demanded. If the exchange rate is too low, there is a shortage—the quantity supplied is less than the quantity demanded. At the equilibrium exchange rate, there is neither a shortage nor a surplus. The quantity supplied equals the quantity demanded.

Figure 19.6 illustrates market equilibrium. The demand for dollars is *D*, and the supply of dollars is *S*. The equilibrium exchange rate is 0.70 euros per dollar. At this exchange rate, the quantity demanded equals the quantity supplied and is $1.3 trillion a day. If the exchange rate is above 0.70 euros, for example, 0.80 euros per dollar, there is a surplus of dollars and the exchange rate falls. If the exchange rate is below 0.70 euros, for example, 0.60 euros per dollar, there is a shortage of dollars and the exchange rate rises.

The foreign exchange market is constantly pulled to its equilibrium by the forces of supply and demand. Foreign exchange dealers are constantly looking for the best price they can get. If they are selling, they want the highest price available. If they are buying, they want the lowest price available. Information flows from dealer to dealer through the worldwide computer network, and the price adjusts second by second to keep buying plans and selling plans in balance. That is, price adjusts second by second to keep the market at its equilibrium.

■ FIGURE 19.6

Equilibrium Exchange Rate

MyEconLab Animation

The demand curve for dollars is *D*, and the supply curve is *S*.

❶ If the exchange rate is 0.80 euros per dollar, there is a surplus of dollars and the exchange rate falls.

❷ If the exchange rate is 0.60 euros per dollar, there is a shortage of dollars and the exchange rate rises.

❸ If the exchange rate is 0.70 euros per dollar, there is neither a shortage nor a surplus of dollars and the exchange rate remains constant. The market is in equilibrium.

EYE on the DOLLAR

Why Does Our Dollar Fluctuate?

Our dollar fluctuates: Sometimes its value rises and sometimes it falls. Let's see what makes our dollar fluctuate by looking at two episodes in its bouncing life.

A Rising Dollar: 1999–2000

The dollar appreciated against the euro when it rose from 0.86 euros per dollar in 1999 to 1.17 euros per dollar in 2000. Figure 1 explains why this happened.

In 1999, the demand and supply curves were those labeled D_{99} and S_{99}. The equilibrium exchange rate was 0.86 euros per dollar—where the quantity of dollars supplied equaled the quantity of dollars demanded.

During the next two years, the U.S. economy expanded faster than the European economy. Interest rates in

Europe were 2 percentage points lower than in the United States, and the euro was expected to depreciate and the dollar was expected to appreciate.

With a positive U.S. interest rate differential and an expected dollar appreciation, the demand for dollars increased and the supply of dollars decreased. The demand curve shifted from D_{99} to D_{00} and the supply curve shifted from S_{99} to S_{00}. These two reinforcing shifts made the exchange rate rise to 1.17 euros per dollar.

A Falling Dollar: 2001–2008

Between 2001 and 2008, the dollar fell from 1.17 euros to 0.63 euros per dollar. Figure 2 explains this fall.

In 2001, the demand and supply curves were those labeled D_{01} and

S_{01}. The exchange rate was 1.17 euros per dollar. During the next few years, U.S. economic growth slipped below the European growth rate, European inflation fell, interest rates in Europe exceeded those in the United States, and the U.S. current account deficit continued to increase.

Under these conditions, currency traders expected the exchange rate to fall. The demand for dollars decreased and the supply of dollars increased. The demand curve shifted leftward to D_{08} and the supply curve shifted rightward to S_{08}. The exchange rate fell to 0.63 euros per dollar.

Since 2008, our dollar has fluctuated around a slightly rising trend. No one knows whether that trend will continue, or whether our dollar will start to sink again.

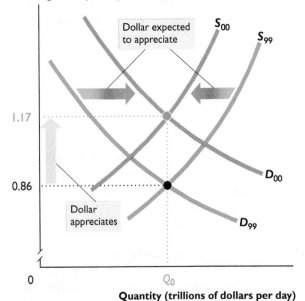

Figure 1 1999 to 2000

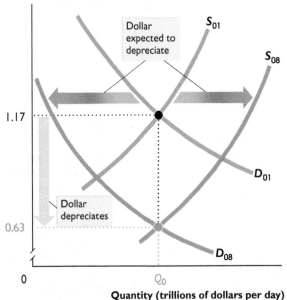

Figure 2 2001 to 2008

Why Exchange Rates Are Volatile

You've seen that sometimes the dollar depreciates and at other times it appreciates. The exchange rates of other currencies are similarly volatile. The Japanese yen, Canadian dollar, and Mexican peso along with most currencies swing between appreciation and depreciation. Yet the quantity of dollars (and other currencies) traded in the foreign exchange market each day barely changes. Why?

A large part of the answer is that everyone in the foreign exchange market is potentially either a buyer or a seller—a demander or a supplier. Each has a price above which he or she will sell and below which he or she will buy.

This fact about the participants in the foreign exchange market means that supply and demand are not independent. The same shocks to the market that change the demand for a currency also change its supply. Demand and supply change in *opposite directions*, and the result is large price changes and small quantity changes.

The two key influences that change both demand and supply in the foreign exchange market are the interest rate differential and the expected future exchange rate.

A rise in the U.S. interest rate differential *increases* the *demand* for U.S. dollars in the foreign exchange market and *decreases* the *supply*. A rise in the expected future exchange rate also increases the demand for U.S. dollars and decreases the supply.

These common influences that change demand and supply in *opposite directions* bring changes in the exchange rate and little change in the quantities of currencies traded. They can bring cumulative movements in the exchange rate or frequent changes of direction—volatility.

MyEconLab Snapshot

◼ Exchange Rate Expectations

The changes in the exchange rate that we've just considered occur in part because the exchange rate is expected to change. This explanation sounds a bit like a self-fulfilling forecast. What makes expectations change? The answer is new information about the deeper forces that influence the value of money. There are two such forces:

- Purchasing power parity
- Interest rate parity

◼ Purchasing Power Parity

Money is worth what it will buy. But two kinds of money, U.S. dollars and Canadian dollars, for example, might buy different amounts of goods and services. Suppose a Big Mac costs $4 (Canadian) in Toronto and $3 (U.S.) in New York. If the Canadian dollar exchange rate is $1.33 Canadian per U.S. dollar, the two monies have the same value. You can buy a Big Mac in either Toronto or New York for either $4 Canadian or $3 U.S.

Purchasing power parity
Equal value of money—a situation in which money buys the same amount of goods and services in different currencies.

The situation we've just described is called **purchasing power parity**, which means equal value of money. If purchasing power parity does not prevail, some powerful forces go to work. To understand these forces, suppose that the price of a Big Mac in New York rises to $4 U.S., but in Toronto the price remains at $4 Canadian. Suppose the exchange rate remains at $1.33 Canadian per U.S. dollar. In this case, a Big Mac in Toronto still costs $4 Canadian or $3 U.S. But in New

EYE on the GLOBAL ECONOMY
Purchasing Power Parity

Purchasing power parity (PPP) is a long-run phenomenon. In the short run, deviations from PPP can be large.

The figure shows the range of deviations from PPP in August 2013. At that time, the Swiss franc was overvalued by 60 percent and the Norwegian krone was overvalued by 50 percent. An overvalued currency is one that, according to PPP, will depreciate at some point in the future.

The most undervalued currencies in August 2013 were the Turkish lira and South African rand. An undervalued currency is one that, according to PPP, will appreciate at some time in the future.

PPP theory predicts that a currency might depreciate or appreciate but not *when* it will depreciate or appreciate.

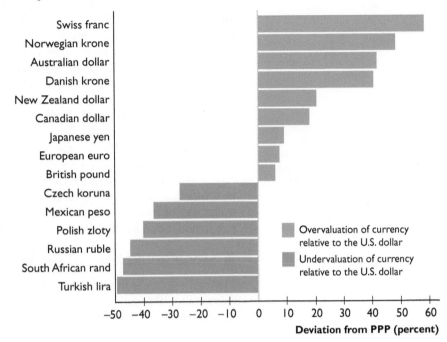

SOURCE OF DATA: PACIFIC FX Service, University of British Columbia, August 26, 2013.

York, it costs $4 U.S. or $5.32 Canadian. Money buys more in Canada than in the United States. Money is not of equal value in both countries.

If all (or most) prices have increased in the United States and not increased in Canada, then people will generally expect that the U.S. dollar exchange rate is going to fall. The demand for U.S. dollars decreases, and the supply of U.S. dollars increases. The U.S. dollar exchange rate falls, as expected. If the U.S. dollar falls to $1.00 Canadian and there are no further price changes, purchasing power parity is restored. A Big Mac now costs $4 in either U.S. dollars or Canadian dollars in both New York and Toronto.

If prices increase in Canada and other countries but remain constant in the United States, then people will generally expect that the value of the U.S. dollar in the foreign exchange market is too low and that the U.S. dollar exchange rate will rise. The demand for U.S. dollars increases, and the supply of U.S. dollars decreases. The U.S. dollar exchange rate rises, as expected.

Ultimately, the value of money is determined by prices. So the deeper forces that influence the exchange rate have tentacles that spread throughout the economy. If prices in the United States rise faster than those in other countries, the exchange rate falls. And if prices in the United States rise more slowly than those in other countries, the exchange rate rises.

Interest Rate Parity

Suppose a Canadian dollar bank deposit in a Toronto bank earns 5 percent a year and a U.S. dollar bank deposit in a New York bank earns 3 percent a year. Why does anyone deposit money in New York? Why doesn't all the money flow to Toronto? The answer is: Because of exchange rate expectations. Suppose people expect the Canadian dollar to depreciate by 2 percent a year. This 2 percent depreciation must be subtracted from the 5 percent interest to obtain the net return of 3 percent a year that an American can earn by depositing funds in a Toronto bank. The two returns are equal. This situation is one of **interest rate parity**—equal interest rates when exchange rate changes are taken into account.

Interest rate parity always prevails. Funds move to get the highest return available. If interest rate parity did not hold because the Canadian dollar had too high a value in the foreign exchange market, the expected return in Toronto would be lower than in New York. In seconds, traders would sell the Canadian dollar, its exchange rate would fall, and the expected return from lending in Toronto would rise to equal that in New York.

■ Monetary Policy and the Exchange Rate

Monetary policy influences the interest rate (see Chapter 12, pp. 300–303), so monetary policy also influences the interest rate differential and the exchange rate. If the Fed increases the U.S. interest rate and other central banks keep interest rates in other countries unchanged, the value of the U.S. dollar rises in the foreign exchange market. If other central banks increase their interest rates and the Fed keeps the U.S. interest rate unchanged, the value of the U.S. dollar falls in the foreign exchange market. So exchange rates fluctuate in response to changes and expected changes in monetary policy in the United States and around the world.

■ Pegging the Exchange Rate

Some central banks try to avoid exchange rate fluctuations by pegging the value of their currency against another currency. Suppose the Fed wanted to keep the dollar at 0.70 euros per dollar. If the exchange rate rose above 0.70 euros, the Fed would sell dollars and if it fell below 0.70 euros, the Fed would buy dollars.

Figure 19.7 illustrates foreign exchange market intervention. The supply of dollars is S, and initially, the demand for dollars is D_0. The equilibrium exchange rate is 0.70 euros per dollar, which is also the Fed's target—the horizontal red line.

If the demand for dollars increases to D_1, the Fed increases the supply of dollars—sells dollars—and prevents the exchange rate from rising. If the demand for dollars decreases to D_2, the Fed decreases the supply of dollars—buys dollars—and prevents the exchange rate from falling.

When the Fed buys dollars, it uses its reserves of euros; when the Fed sells dollars, it takes euros in exchange and its reserves of euros increase. As long as the demand for dollars fluctuates around and on average remains at D_0, the Fed's reserves of euros fluctuate but neither run dry nor persistently increase.

But if the demand for dollars decreased permanently to D_2, the Fed would have to buy dollars and sell euros every day to maintain the exchange rate at 0.70 euros per dollar. The Fed would soon run out of euros, and when it did, the dollar would sink. If the demand for dollars increased permanently to D_1, the Fed would have to sell dollars and buy euros every day. The Fed would be piling up unwanted euros and at some point would let the dollar rise.

Interest rate parity
Equal interest rates—a situation in which the interest rate in one currency equals the interest rate in another currency when exchange rate changes are taken into account.

■ **FIGURE 19.7**

Foreign Exchange Market Intervention

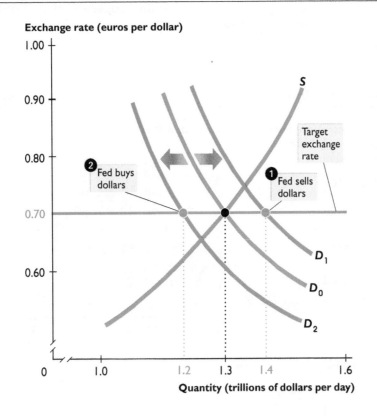

Initially, the demand for dollars is D_0, the supply of dollars is S, and the exchange rate is 0.70 euros per dollar. The Fed can intervene in the foreign exchange market to keep the exchange rate close to its target rate (0.70 euros per dollar in this example).

❶ If demand increases from D_0 to D_1, the Fed sells dollars to increase the supply of dollars and maintain the exchange rate.

❷ If demand decreases from D_0 to D_2, the Fed buys dollars to decrease the supply of dollars and maintain the exchange rate.

Persistent intervention on one side of the market cannot be sustained.

■ The People's Bank of China in the Foreign Exchange Market

Although the Fed could peg the value of the dollar, it chooses not to do so. But China's central bank, the People's Bank of China, does intervene to peg the value of its currency—the yuan. *Eye on the Global Economy* on p. 497 shows the result of this intervention.

During much of the period that the yuan has been pegged to the U.S. dollar, China has piled up U.S. dollar reserves. Figure 19.8(a) shows the numbers. During 2007 to 2009, China's reserves increased by more than $1 trillion.

Figure 19.8(b), which shows the market for U.S. dollars priced in terms of the yuan, explains why China's reserves increased. The demand curve D and supply curve S intersect at 5 yuan per dollar. If the People's Bank of China took no actions in the foreign exchange market, this exchange rate would be the equilibrium rate. (This particular value is only an example. No one knows what the yuan-dollar exchange rate would be with no intervention.)

By intervening in the market and buying U.S. dollars, the People's Bank can peg the yuan at 6.10 yuan per dollar. But to do so, it must keep holding the dollars that it buys. In Figure 19.8(b), the People's Bank buys $76 billion (the actual quantity that the People's Bank bought in 2012).

Only by allowing the yuan to appreciate can China stop accumulating dollars. Since July 2005, the People's Bank has been permitting the yuan to rise in value.

But China continues to intervene in the foreign exchange market to manage the rate of appreciation of the yuan. The scale of intervention fell sharply in 2012 and eventually, when China's foreign exchange market becomes more accustomed to a floating yuan, it is possible that the People's Bank will end its intervention so that the value of the yuan is determined by market forces.

FIGURE 19.8

China's Foreign Exchange Market Intervention

China has been piling up reserves of U.S. dollars since 2000. During 2007 through 2011, the build-up of reserves was very large. Part (a) shows the numbers.

Part (b) shows the market for the U.S. dollar in terms of the Chinese yuan. Note that a higher exchange rate (yuan per dollar) means a lower value of the yuan and a higher value of the dollar. The yuan appreciates when the number of yuan per dollar decreases.

❶ With demand curve D and supply curve S, the equilibrium exchange rate is 5 yuan per dollar. (The actual equilibrium value is not known, and the value assumed is only an example.)

❷ In 2012, the People's Bank of China had a target exchange rate of 6.10 yuan per dollar. At this exchange rate, the yuan is *undervalued.*

❸ To keep the exchange rate pegged at its target level, the People's Bank of China must buy U.S. dollars in exchange for yuan, and China's reserves of U.S. dollars pile up.

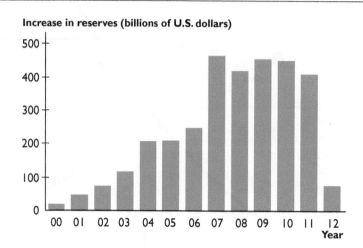

(a) Increase in U.S. dollar reserves

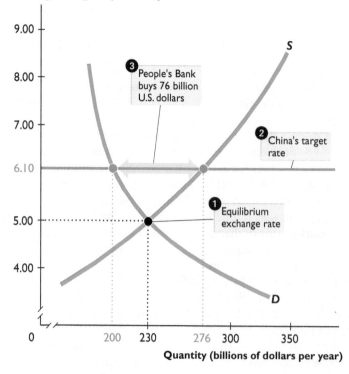

(b) Managing the yuan

SOURCE OF DATA: The People's Bank of China.

EYE on the GLOBAL ECONOMY
The Managed Yuan

The Chinese central bank, the People's Bank of China, pegged the value of the yuan in terms of the U.S. dollar for more than 10 years. The figure shows the value of the yuan (yuan per U.S. dollar) from the early 1990s to 2013.

The yuan was devalued in January 1994. It appreciated a bit during 1994 and 1995. But it was then pegged at 8.28 yuan per U.S. dollar, a value that the People's Bank of China maintained for more than 10 years. In July 2005, the yuan began a managed float—a managed appreciation of the yuan. Then, in July 2008, the exchange rate was again pegged, this time at 6.8 yuan per dollar. Since early 2010, the yuan has been floating again.

SOURCE OF DATA: PACIFIC FX Service, University of British Columbia.

EYE on YOUR LIFE
Your Foreign Exchange Transactions

If you plan to go to Europe for a vacation next summer, you will need some euros. What is the best way to get euros?

You could just take your ATM/debit card or credit card and use an ATM in Europe. You'll get euros from the cash machine, and your bank account in the United States will get charged for the cash you obtain.

When you get euros, the number of euros you request is multiplied by the exchange rate to determine how many dollars to take from your bank account.

You have just made a transaction in the foreign exchange market. You have exchanged dollars for euros.

The exchange rate that you paid was probably costly. Your bank took a commission for helping you get euros. Some banks charge as much as 5 percent. Check in advance. It might be better to buy euros from your bank before you leave on your trip.

Another question has possibly occurred to you: How many euros will your budget buy next summer? Should

you get the euros now at a price that is certain or would it be better to wait until closer to your travel date and take a chance on the value of the dollar then?

No one can answer this question. But you can buy euros today at a fixed price for delivery at a later date. (This transaction is made in a market called the forward exchange market.) Again, though, you'll end up paying a big commission for the service.

MyEconLab Study Plan 19.2
            Key Terms Quiz
              Solutions

 CHECKPOINT 19.2

Explain how the exchange rate is determined and why it fluctuates.

Practice Problems

Suppose that yesterday, the U.S. dollar was trading in the foreign exchange market at 100 yen per dollar. Today, the U.S. dollar is trading at 105 yen per dollar.

1.   Which currency appreciated and which depreciated today?
2.   List the events that could have caused today's change in the value of the U.S. dollar in the foreign exchange market. Did the events on your list change the demand for U.S. dollars, the supply of U.S. dollars, or both the demand for and supply of U.S. dollars?
3.   If the Fed had tried to stabilize the exchange rate at 100 yen per dollar, what action would it have taken? How would U.S. official reserves have changed?

In the News

Dollar up vs euro and yen after Fed signals higher interest rate
The dollar rose against the euro and yen buoyed by the appeal of higher short-term rates after the Fed chose not to increase the money supply.

Source: Reuters, September 20, 2011

1.   Did the dollar appreciate or depreciate against the euro and the Japanese yen? Did the euro and the yen appreciate or depreciate against the dollar?
2.   What actions in the foreign exchange market raised the foreign exchange value of the dollar?

Solutions to Practice Problems

1.   Because the price of the U.S. dollar is a larger number of yen, the U.S. dollar has appreciated. The yen has depreciated because it buys fewer dollars.
2.   The main events might be an increase in the U.S. interest rate, a decrease in the Japanese interest rate, or a rise in the expected future exchange rate of the U.S. dollar.

     The events listed change both the demand for and supply of U.S. dollars. The events increase the demand for and decrease the supply of U.S. dollars.
3.   To stabilize the exchange rate, the Fed would have sold U.S. dollars to increase the supply of dollars in the foreign exchange market. When the Fed sells U.S. dollars, it buys foreign currency. U.S. official reserves would have increased.

Solutions to In the News

1.   Because the dollar buys more euros, the euro has depreciated and the dollar has appreciated. Because the dollar buys more yen, the dollar appreciated against the yen and the yen depreciated against the dollar.
2.   As the Fed signaled that short-term interest rates would rise, the U.S. interest rate differential increased and the demand for U.S. dollars increased and the supply of U.S. dollars decreased. The increase in demand and decrease in supply raises the value of the U.S. dollar in the foreign exchange market.

CHAPTER SUMMARY

Key Points

1. **Describe a country's balance of payments accounts and explain what determines the amount of international borrowing and lending.**

   - Foreign currency is used to finance international trade and the purchase of foreign assets.
   - A country's balance of payments accounts record its international transactions.
   - Historically, the United States has been a net lender to the rest of the world, but in 1983 that situation changed and the United States became a net borrower. In 1989 the United States became a debtor nation.
   - Net exports are equal to the private sector balance plus the government sector balance.

2. **Explain how the exchange rate is determined and why it fluctuates.**

   - Foreign currency is obtained in exchange for domestic currency in the foreign exchange market.
   - The exchange rate is determined by demand and supply in the foreign exchange market.
   - The lower the exchange rate, the greater is the quantity of dollars demanded. A change in the exchange rate brings a movement along the demand curve for dollars.
   - Changes in the expected future exchange rate and the U.S. interest rate differential change the demand for dollars and shift the demand curve.
   - The lower the exchange rate, the smaller is the quantity of dollars supplied. A change in the exchange rate brings a movement along the supply curve of dollars.
   - Changes in the expected future exchange rate and the U.S. interest rate differential change the supply of dollars and shift the supply curve.
   - Fluctuations in the exchange rate occur because fluctuations in the demand for and supply of dollars are not independent.
   - A central bank can intervene in the foreign exchange market to smooth fluctuations in the exchange rate.

Key Terms

MyEconLab Key Terms Quiz

Balance of payments accounts, 476
Capital and financial account, 476
Creditor nation, 478
Currency appreciation, 483
Currency depreciation, 484
Current account, 476

Debtor nation, 478
Foreign exchange market, 483
Foreign exchange rate, 483
Government sector balance, 480
Interest rate parity, 494
Net borrower, 478

Net lender, 478
Official settlements account, 476
Private sector balance, 480
Purchasing power parity, 492
U.S. interest rate differential, 486
U.S. official reserves, 476

CHAPTER CHECKPOINT

Study Plan Problems and Applications

TABLE 1

Item	(billions of dollars)
Imports	150
Exports of goods and services	50
Net interest	–10
Net transfers	35
Foreign investment in Antarctica	125
Antarctica's investment abroad	55

Table 1 gives some data that describe the economy of Antarctica in 2050. Use Table 1 to answer Problems 1 and 2.

1. Calculate Antarctica's current account balance, capital and financial account balance, and the increase in Antarctica's official reserves.

2. Is Antarctica a debtor nation or a creditor nation? Are its international assets increasing or decreasing? Is Antarctica borrowing to finance investment or consumption? Explain.

3. **U.S. trade deficit grows**
   The Commerce Department report said that exports of goods and services were $187.1 billion, while imports were $232.1 billion.

   Source: *The New York Times*, July 3, 2013

   Explain how the United States pays for its net export deficit.

4. The U.S. dollar depreciates. Explain which of the following events could have caused the depreciation and why.

   • The Fed intervened in the foreign exchange market. Did the Fed buy or sell U.S. dollars?
   • People began to expect that the U.S. dollar would depreciate.
   • The U.S. interest rate differential increased.
   • Foreign investment in the United States increased.

Suppose that the inflation rate is lower in Japan than it is in the United States, and that the difference in the inflation rates persists for some years. Use this information to answer Problems 5 to 7.

5. Will the U.S. dollar appreciate or depreciate against the yen and will purchasing power parity be violated? Why or why not?

6. Will U.S. interest rates be higher or lower than Japanese interest rates and will interest rate parity hold? Why or why not?

7. Explain how the expected future exchange rate will change.

8. Suppose that the U.K. pound is trading at 1.82 U.S. dollars per U.K. pound and at this exchange rate purchasing power parity holds. The U.S. interest rate is 2 percent a year and the U.K. interest rate is 4 percent a year. Calculate the U.S. interest rate differential. What is the U.K. pound expected to be worth in terms of U.S. dollars one year from now?

9. **Aussie dollar hit by interest rate talk**
   The Australian dollar fell against the U.S. dollar to its lowest value in the past two weeks. CPI inflation was reported to be generally as expected, but not strong enough to justify expectations for an aggressive interest rate rise by Australia's central bank next week.

   Source: Reuters, October 28, 2009

   Explain why the expected rise of the Australian interest rate with no change in the U.S. interest rate lowered the current value of the Australian dollar against the U.S. dollar.

 10. Read *Eye on the Dollar* on p. 491. When and why did the dollar rise against the euro and when and why did it fall?

Instructor Assignable Problems and Applications

MyEconLab Homework, Quiz, or Test if assigned by instructor

1. If the European Central Bank starts to raise its policy interest rate before the Fed starts to raise the federal funds rate target, what do you predict will happen to the dollar/euro exchange rate? Illustrate your answer with an appropriate graphical analysis.

2. Table 1 gives some data that describe the economy of Atlantis in 2020. Calculate the current account balance, the capital and financial account balance, the government sector balance, and the private sector balance.

3. The U.S. dollar appreciates, and U.S. official reserves increase. Explain which of the following events might have caused these changes to occur and why.
   - The Fed intervened in the foreign exchange market and sold U.S. dollars.
   - The Fed conducted an open market operation and sold U.S. bonds.
   - People began to expect that the U.S. dollar would appreciate.
   - The U.S. interest rate differential narrowed.

TABLE 1

Item	(billions of dollars)
Government expenditure	200
Saving	100
Increase in official reserves of Atlantis	5
Net foreign investment in Atlantis	50
Net taxes	150
Investment	125

4. Which of the following events might have caused the euro to appreciate and why?
   - The European Central Bank sold euros in the foreign exchange market.
   - The Fed intervened in the foreign exchange market and bought U.S. dollars.
   - The EU interest rate differential increased.
   - Profits increased in Europe, and U.S. investment in Europe surged.

Use the following information to work Problems 5 and 6.

Suppose that the euro keeps appreciating against the U.S. dollar. The Fed decides to stop the euro from appreciating (stop the U.S. dollar from depreciating) and intervenes in the foreign exchange market.

5. What actions might the Fed take in the foreign exchange market? Could these actions persist in the long run? Would the Fed's actions prevent interest rate parity from being achieved? Why or why not?

6. Are there any other actions that the Fed could take to raise the foreign exchange value of the dollar? Explain your answer.

Use the following information to work Problems 7 and 8.

In July 2011, the exchange rate between the U.S. dollar and the Brazilian real was 1.6 real per dollar. In the same month, the price of a Big Mac was 9.36 real in Sao Paulo and $4.00 in New York. Brazil's interest rate was 12 percent per year and the U.S. interest rate was 1 percent per year.

Sources: Pacific Exchange Rate Service and *The Economist*

7. Does purchasing power parity (PPP) hold between Brazil and the United States? If not, does PPP predict that the real will appreciate or depreciate against the U.S. dollar?

8. Does interest rate parity hold between Brazil and the United States? If interest rate parity does hold, what is the expected rate of appreciation or depreciation of the Brazilian real against the U.S. dollar? If the Fed raised the interest rate while the Brazilian interest rate remained at 12 percent a year, how would the expected appreciation or depreciation of the real change?

Multiple Choice Quiz

1. The current account balance equals _____.

    A. exports minus imports plus net interest and net transfers
    B. net exports plus net foreign investment in the United States
    C. the capital and financial account balance minus the official settlements account balance
    D. net exports plus the official settlements balance

2. China's official reserves have ballooned, fueled by strong foreign investment and large trade surpluses. China is a net _____ and a _____ nation.

    A. lender; debtor
    B. borrower; debtor
    C. lender; creditor
    D. borrower; creditor

3. Net exports equal the _____.

    A. private sector balance plus the government sector balance
    B. private sector balance minus the government sector balance
    C. government sector balance minus the private sector balance
    D. private sector balance plus the government's budget deficit

4. A net exports deficit will become a surplus if _____.

    A. the government budget deficit is turned into a surplus and the private sector has a surplus
    B. the private sector surplus adjusts to equal the government sector deficit
    C. private saving and government saving exceed private investment
    D. the country appreciates its currency

5. The quantity of U.S. dollars demanded in the foreign exchange market increases if _____.

    A. the value of U.S. imports increases
    B. traders expect the future exchange rate to rise
    C. the U.S. interest rate rises relative to those in other countries
    D. the U.S. dollar depreciates against other currencies

6. The supply of U.S. dollars in the foreign exchange market increases if _____.

    A. the value of U.S. imports increases
    B. the U.S. interest rate differential decreases
    C. the U.S. dollar depreciates against other currencies
    D. the U.S. dollar is expected to appreciate against other currencies in the future

7. Purchasing power parity _____.

    A. holds if the price of a good is the same number of euros, pounds, or dollars
    B. means that the value of the euro, the pound, and the dollar are equal
    C. always holds because exchange rates adjust automatically
    D. implies that international trade is competitive

8. To keep the yuan-U.S. dollar exchange rate constant, _____.

    A. the Fed agrees not to sell U.S. dollars in the foreign exchange market
    B. the People's Bank of China buys U.S. dollars
    C. the Fed and the People's Bank agree on the value of the exchange rate
    D. the Fed does not buy yuan in the foreign exchange market

Glossary

Absolute advantage When one person (or nation) is more productive than another—needs fewer inputs or takes less time to produce a good or perform a production task. (p. 71)

Aggregate demand The relationship between the quantity of real GDP demanded and the price level when all other influences on expenditure plans remain the same. (p. 330)

Aggregate planned expenditure Planned consumption expenditure plus planned investment plus planned government expenditure plus planned exports minus planned imports. (p. 350)

Aggregate supply The relationship between the quantity of real GDP supplied and the price level when all other influences on production plans remain the same. (p. 324)

Automatic fiscal policy A fiscal policy action that is triggered by the state of the economy. (p. 404)

Automatic stabilizers Features of fiscal policy that stabilize real GDP without explicit action by the government. (p. 404)

Balance of payments accounts The accounts in which a nation records its international trading, borrowing, and lending. (p. 476)

Balanced budget multiplier The magnification effect on aggregate demand of a *simultaneous* change in government expenditure and taxes that leaves the budget balanced unchanged. (p. 406)

Barter The direct exchange of goods and services for other goods and services, which requires a double coincidence of wants. (p. 267)

Benefit The benefit of something is the gain or pleasure that it brings, measured by what you are willing to give up to get it. (p. 9)

Bond A promise to pay specified sums of money on specified dates. (p. 242)

Budget balance Tax revenues minus outlays. (p. 398)

Business cycle A periodic but irregular up-and-down movement of total production and other measures of economic activity. (p. 128)

Capital Tools, instruments, machines, buildings, and other items that have been produced in the past and that businesses now use to produce goods and services.
(pp. 35, 240)

Capital and financial account Record of foreign investment in the United States minus U.S. investment abroad. (p. 476)

Capital goods Goods bought by businesses and governments to increase productive resources to use over future periods to produce other goods. (p. 32)

Chained-dollar real GDP The measure of real GDP calculated by the Bureau of Economic Analysis. (p. 139)

Change in demand A change in the quantity that people plan to buy when any influence on buying plans other than the price of the good changes. (p. 85)

Change in the quantity demanded A change in the quantity of a good that people plan to buy that results from a change in the price of the good with all other influences on buying plans remaining the same. (p. 85)

Change in the quantity supplied A change in the quantity of a good that suppliers plan to sell that results from a change in the price of the good with all other influences on selling plans remaining the same. (p. 90)

Change in supply A change in the quantity that suppliers plan to sell when any influence on selling plans other than the price of the good changes. (p. 90)

Circular flow model A model of the economy that shows the circular flow of expenditures and incomes that result from decision makers' choices and the way those choices interact to determine what, how, and for whom goods and services are produced. (p. 46)

Classical growth theory The theory that the clash between an exploding population and limited resources will eventually bring economic growth to an end. (p. 226)

Classical macroeconomics The view that the market economy works well, that aggregate fluctuations are a natural consequence of an expanding economy, and that government intervention cannot improve the efficiency of the market economy. (p. 190)

Comparative advantage The ability of a person to perform an activity or produce a good or service at a lower opportunity cost than anyone else. (p. 71)

Complement A good that is consumed with another good. (p. 85)

Complement in production A good that is produced along with another good. (p. 90)

Consumer Price Index A measure of the average of the prices paid by urban consumers for a fixed market basket of consumption goods and services. (p. 166)

Consumption expenditure The expenditure by households on consumption goods and services. (p. 115)

Consumption function The relationship between consumption expenditure and disposable income, other things remaining the same. (p. 350)

Consumption goods and services Goods and services that individuals and governments buy and use in the current period. (p. 32)

Core inflation rate The annual percentage change in the PCE price index excluding the prices of food and energy. (p. 175)

Cost of living index A measure of the change in the amount of money that people need to spend to achieve a given standard of living. (p. 172)

Cost-push inflation An inflation that begins with an increase in costs. (p. 341)

Creditor nation A country that during its entire history has invested more in the rest of the world than other countries have invested in it. (p. 478)

Cross-section graph A graph that shows the values of an economic variable for different groups in a population at a point in time. (p. 22)

Crowding-out effect The tendency for a government budget deficit to raise the real interest rate and decrease investment. (p. 258)

Currency Notes (dollar bills) and coins. (p. 268)

Currency appreciation The rise in the value of one currency in terms of another currency. (p. 483)

Currency depreciation The fall in the value of one currency in terms of another currency. (p. 484)

Current account Record of receipts from the sale of goods and services to other countries (exports), minus payments for goods and services bought from other countries (imports), plus the net amount of interest and transfers received from and paid to other countries. (p. 476)

Cyclical surplus or deficit The budget balance that arises because revenues and outlays are not at their full-employment levels. (p. 405)

Cyclical unemployment The fluctuating unemployment over the business cycle that increases during a recession and decreases during an expansion. (p. 156)

Debtor nation A country that during its entire history has borrowed more from the rest of the world than it has lent to the rest of the world. (p. 478)

Deflation A situation in which the price level is *falling* and the inflation rate is *negative*. (p. 169)

Demand The relationship between the quantity demanded and the price of a good when all other influences on buying plans remain the same. (p. 83)

Demand curve A graph of the relationship between the quantity demanded of a good and its price when all the other influences on buying plans remain the same. (p. 84)

Demand for labor The relationship between the quantity of labor demanded and the real wage rate when all other influences on firms' hiring plans remain the same. (p. 195)

Demand for loanable funds The relationship between the quantity of loanable funds demanded and the real interest rate when all other influences on borrowing plans remain the same. (p. 247)

Demand for money The relationship between the quantity of money demanded and the nominal interest rate, when all other influences on the amount of money that people wish to hold remain the same. (p. 298)

Demand-pull inflation An inflation that starts because aggregate demand increases. (p. 340)

Demand schedule A list of the quantities demanded at each different price when all the other influences on buying plans remain the same. (p. 84)

Depreciation The decrease in the value of capital that results from its use and from obsolescence. (p. 122)

Diminishing returns The tendency for each additional hour of labor employed to produce a successively smaller additional amount of real GDP. (p. 194)

Direct relationship A relationship between two variables that move in the same direction. (p. 24)

Discouraged worker A marginally attached worker who has not made specific efforts to find a job within the past four weeks because previous unsuccessful attempts to find a job were discouraging. (p. 146)

Discretionary fiscal policy A fiscal policy action that is initiated by an act of Congress. (p. 404)

Discretionary monetary policy Monetary policy that is based on expert assessment of the current economic situation. (p. 442)

Dumping When a foreign firm sells its exports at a lower price than its cost of production. (p. 466)

Economic freedom A condition in which people are able to make personal choices, their private property is protected by the rule of law, and they are free to buy and sell in markets. (p. 230)

Economic growth The sustained expansion of production possibilities. (pp. 68, 214)

Economic growth rate The annual percentage change of real GDP. (p. 214)

Economic model A description of the economy or part of the economy that includes only those features assumed necessary to explain the observed facts. (p. 12)

Economics The social science that studies the choices that individuals, businesses, government, and entire societies make as they cope with *scarcity*, the influences on those choices, and the arrangements that coordinate them. (p. 2)

Efficiency wage A real wage rate that is set above the full-employment equilibrium wage rate to induce greater work effort. (p. 205)

Entrepreneurship The human resource that organizes labor, land, and capital to produce goods and services. (p. 36)

Equation of exchange An equation that states that the quantity of money multiplied by the velocity of circulation equals the price level multiplied by real GDP. (p. 309)

Equilibrium expenditure The level of aggregate expenditure that occurs when aggregate *planned* expenditure equals real GDP. (p. 358)

Equilibrium price The price at which the quantity demanded equals the quantity supplied. (p. 94)

Equilibrium quantity The quantity bought and sold at the equilibrium price. (p. 94)

Excess reserves A bank's actual reserves minus its desired reserves. (p. 282)

Expected inflation rate The inflation rate that people forecast and use to set the money wage rate and other money prices. (p. 383)

Exports The goods and services that firms in one country sell to people and firms in other countries. (p. 452)

Exports of goods and services Items that firms in the United States produce and sell to the rest of the world. (p. 116)

Factor markets Markets in which the services of factors of production are bought and sold. (p. 46)

Factors of production The productive resources that are used to produce goods and services—land, labor, capital, and entrepreneurship. (p. 34)

Federal funds rate The interest rate at which banks can borrow and lend reserves (interbank loans) in the federal funds market. (pp. 274, 426)

Federal Open Market Committee The Fed's main policy-making committee. (p. 278)

Federal Reserve System (the Fed) The central bank of the United States. (p. 277)

Fiat money Objects that are money because the law decrees or orders them to be money. (p. 268)

Final good or service A good or service that is produced for its final user and not as a component of another good or service. (p. 114)

Financial institution A firm that operates on both sides of the market for financial capital: It borrows in one market and lends in another. (p. 243)

Financial stability A situation in which financial markets and institutions function normally to allocate capital resources and risk. (p. 425)

Firms The institutions that organize the production of goods and services. (p. 46)

Fiscal policy Changing taxes, transfer payments, and government expenditure on goods and services. (p. 333) The use of the federal budget to achieve the macroeconomic objectives of high and sustained economic growth and full employment. (p. 398)

Foreign exchange market The market in which the currency of one country is exchanged for the currency of another. (p. 483)

Foreign exchange rate The price at which one currency exchanges for another. (p. 483)

Frictional unemployment The unemployment that arises from normal labor turnover—from people entering and leaving the labor force, from quitting jobs to find better ones, and from the ongoing creation and destruction of jobs. (p. 155)

Full employment When there is no cyclical unemployment or, equivalently, when all the unemployment is frictional or structural. (p. 156)

Full-employment equilibrium When equilibrium real GDP equals potential GDP. (p. 337)

Full-time workers People who usually work 35 hours or more a week. (p. 147)

GDP price index An average of the current prices of all the goods and services included in GDP expressed as a percentage of base-year prices. (p. 175)

Goods and services The objects (goods) and the actions (services) that people value and produce to satisfy human wants. (p. 3)

Goods markets Markets in which goods and services are bought and sold. (p. 46)

Government expenditure multiplier The effect of a change in government expenditure on goods and services on aggregate demand. (p. 406)

Government expenditure on goods and services The expenditure by all levels of government on goods and services. (p. 116)

Government sector balance Net taxes minus government expenditure on goods and services. (p. 480)

Great Depression A period of high unemployment, low incomes, and extreme economic hardship that lasted from 1929 to 1939. (p. 149)

Gross domestic product (GDP) The market value of all the final goods and services produced within a country in a given time period. (p. 114)

Gross investment The total amount spent on new capital goods. (p. 240)

Households Individuals or groups of people living together. (p. 46)

Human capital The knowledge and skill that people obtain from education, on-the-job training, and work experience. (p. 35)

Hyperinflation Inflation at a rate that exceeds 50 percent a *month* (which translate to 12,875 percent a year). (p. 312)

Import quota A quantitative restriction on the import of a good that limits the maximum quantity of a good that may be imported in a given period. (p. 462)

Imports The goods and services that people and firms in one country buy from firms in other. (p. 452)

Imports of goods and services Items that households, firms, and governments in the United States buy from the rest of the world. (p. 116)

Incentive A reward or a penalty—a "carrot" or a "stick"—that encourages or discourages an action. (p. 11)

Induced taxes Taxes that vary with real GDP. (p. 404)

Infant-industry argument The argument that it is necessary to protect a new industry to enable it to grow into a mature industry that can compete in world markets. (p. 465)

Inferior good A good for which demand decreases when income increases and demand increases when income decreases. (p. 85)

Inflationary gap A gap that exists when real GDP exceeds potential GDP and that brings a rising price level. (p. 337)

Inflation rate The percentage change in the price level from one year to the next. (p. 169)

Inflation targeting A monetary policy strategy in which the

central bank makes a public commitment to achieving an explicit inflation target and to explaining how its policy actions will achieve that target. (p. 442)

Instrument rule A decision rule for monetary policy that sets the policy instrument by a formula based on the current state of the economy. (p. 428)

Interest Income paid for the use of capital. (p. 37)

Interest rate parity Equal interest rates—a situation in which the interest rate in one currency equals the interest rate in another currency when exchange rate changes are taken into account. (p. 494)

Intermediate good or service A good or service that is used as a component of a final good or service. (p. 114)

Inverse relationship A relationship between two variables that move in opposite directions. (p. 25)

Investment The purchase of new *capital goods*—tools, instruments, machines, buildings, and additions to inventories. (p. 115)

Job rationing A situation that arises when the real wage rate is above the full-employment equilibrium level. (p. 204)

Job search The activity of looking for an acceptable vacant job. (p. 203)

Keynesian macroeconomics The view that the market economy is inherently unstable and needs active government intervention to achieve full employment and sustained economic growth. (p. 190)

k-percent rule A monetary policy rule that makes the quantity of money grow at *k* percent per year, where *k* equals the growth rate of potential GDP. (p. 443)

Labor The work time and work effort that people devote to producing goods and services. (p. 35)

Labor force The number of people employed plus the number unemployed. (p. 144)

Labor force participation rate The percentage of the working-age population who are members of the labor force. (p. 146)

Labor productivity The quantity of real GDP produced by one hour of labor. (p. 218)

Land The "gifts of nature," or *natural resources*, that we use to produce goods and services. (p. 34)

Law of demand Other things remaining the same, if the price of a good rises, the quantity demanded of that good decreases; and if the price of a good falls, the quantity demanded of that good increases. (p. 83)

Law of diminishing marginal returns If the quantity of capital is small, an increase in capital brings a large increase in production; and if the quantity of capital is large, an increase in capital brings a small increase in production. (p. 219)

Law of market forces When there is a surplus, the price falls; when there is a4shortage, the price rises. (p. 94)

Law of supply Other things remaining the same, if the price of a good rises, the quantity supplied of that good increases; and if the price of a good falls, the quantity supplied of that good decreases. (p. 88)

Linear relationship A relationship that graphs as a straight line. (p. 24)

Loanable funds market The aggregate of all the individual financial markets. (p. 246)

Long-run Phillips curve The vertical line that shows the relationship between inflation and unemployment when the economy is at full employment. (p. 382)

Loss Income earned by an entrepreneur for running a business when that income is negative. (p. 37)

M1 Currency held by individuals and firms, traveler's checks, and checkable deposits owned by individuals and businesses. (p. 268)

M2 M1 plus savings deposits and small time deposits, money market funds, and other deposits. (p. 268)

Macroeconomic equilibrium When the quantity of real GDP demanded equals the quantity of real GDP supplied at the point of intersection of the *AD* curve and the *AS* curve. (p. 336)

Macroeconomics The study of the aggregate (or total) effects on the national economy and the global economy of the choices that individuals, businesses, and governments make. (p. 3)

Margin A choice on the margin is a choice that is made by comparing *all* the relevant alternatives systematically and incrementally. (p. 10)

Marginal benefit The benefit that arises from a one-unit increase in an activity. The marginal benefit of something is measured by what you *are willing to* give up to get *one additional* unit of it. (p. 10)

Marginal cost The opportunity cost that arises from a one-unit increase in an activity. The marginal cost of something is what

you *must* give up to get one additional unit of it. (p. 10)

Marginal propensity to consume The fraction of a change in disposable income that is spent on consumption—the change in consumption expenditure divided by the change in disposable income that brought it about. (p. 352)

Marginal propensity to import The fraction of an increase in real GDP that is spent on imports—the change in imports divided by the change in real GDP. (p. 354)

Marginal tax rate The fraction of a change in real GDP that is paid in income taxes—the change in tax payments divided by the change in real GDP. (p. 364)

Marginally attached worker A person who does not have a job, is available and willing to work, has not made specific efforts to find a job within the previous four weeks, but has looked for work sometime in the recent past. (p. 146)

Market Any arrangement that brings buyers and sellers together and enables them to get information and do business with each other. (p. 46)

Market equilibrium When the quantity demanded equals the quantity supplied—buyers' and sellers' plans are in balance. (p. 94)

Means of payment A method of settling a debt. (p. 266)

Medium of exchange An object that is generally accepted in return for goods and services. (p. 267)

Microeconomics The study of the choices that individuals and businesses make and the way these choices interact and are influenced by governments. (p. 2)

Minimum wage law A government regulation that makes hiring labor services for less than a specified wage illegal. (pp. 103, 205)

Monetarist macroeconomics The view that the market economy works well, that aggregate fluctuations are the natural consequence of an expanding economy, but that fluctuations in the quantity of money generate the business cycle. (p. 191)

Monetary base The sum of coins, Federal Reserve notes, and banks' reserves at the Fed. (p. 279)

Monetary policy Changing the quantity of money and the interest rate. (p. 333)

Monetary policy instrument A variable that the Fed can directly control or closely target and that influences the economy in desirable ways. (p. 426)

Money Any commodity or token that is generally accepted as a means of payment. (p. 266)

Money multiplier The number by which a change in the monetary base is multiplied to find the resulting change in the quantity of money. (p. 287)

Multiplier The amount by which a change in any component of autonomous expenditure is magnified or multiplied to determine the change that it generates in equilibrium expenditure and real GDP. (p. 362)

National debt The amount of government debt outstanding—the debt that has arisen from past budget deficits. (p. 399)

Natural rate hypothesis The proposition that when the inflation rate changes, the unemployment rate changes *temporarily* and eventually returns to the natural unemployment rate. (p. 384)

Natural unemployment rate The unemployment rate when the economy is at full employment. (p. 156)

Negative relationship A relationship between two variables that move in opposite directions. (p. 25)

Net borrower A country that is borrowing more from the rest of the world than it is lending to the rest of the world. (p. 478)

Net exports of goods and services The value of exports of goods and services minus the value of imports of goods and services. (p. 116)

Net investment The change in the quantity of capital—equals gross investment minus depreciation. (p. 240)

Net lender A country that is lending more to the rest of the world than it is borrowing from the rest of the world. (p. 478)

Net taxes Taxes paid minus cash benefits received from governments. (p. 116)

Net worth The total market value of what a financial institution has lent minus the market value of what it has borrowed. (p. 244)

New growth theory The theory that our unlimited wants will lead us to ever greater productivity and perpetual economic growth. (p. 226)

Nominal GDP The value of the final goods and services produced in a given year expressed in terms of the prices of that same year. (p. 124)

Nominal GDP targeting A monetary policy rule that adjusts the interest rate to achieve a target growth rate for nominal GDP. (p. 445)

Nominal interest rate The dollar amount of interest expressed as a percentage of the amount loaned. (p. 182)

Nominal wage rate The average hourly wage rate measured in *current* dollars. (p. 180)

Normal good A good for which demand increases when income increases and demand decreases when income decreases. (p. 85)

Official settlements account Record of the change in U.S. official reserves. (p. 476)

Okun's Law For each percentage point that the unemployment rate is above the natural unemployment rate, real GDP is 2 percent below potential GDP. (p. 377)

Open market operation The purchase or sale of government securities—U.S. Treasury bills and bonds—by the New York Fed in the open market. (p. 279)

Opportunity cost The opportunity cost of something is the best thing you *must* give up to get it. (p. 8)

Output gap Real GDP minus potential GDP expressed as a percentage of potential GDP. (p. 158)

Part time for economic reasons People who work 1 to 34 hours per week but are looking for full-time work and cannot find it because of unfavorable business conditions. (p. 147)

Part-time workers People who usually work less than 35 hours a week. (p. 147)

PCE price index An average of the current prices of the goods and services included in the consumption expenditure component of GDP expressed as a percentage of base-year prices. (p. 175)

Physical capital The tools, instruments, machines, buildings, and other items that have been produced in the past and that are used to produce goods and services. (p. 240)

Positive relationship A relationship between two variables that move in the same direction. (p. 24)

Potential GDP The value of real GDP when all the economy's factors of production—labor, capital, land, and entrepreneurial ability—are fully employed. (pp. 127, 158, 193)

Price cap A government regulation that places an *upper* limit on the price at which a particular good, service, or factor of production may be traded. (p. 105)

Price ceiling A government regulation that places an *upper* limit on the price at which a particular good, service, or factor of production may be traded. (p. 105)

Price floor A government regulation that places a *lower* limit on the price at which a particular good, service, or factor of production may be traded. (p. 103)

Private sector balance Saving minus investment. (p. 480)

Production efficiency A situation in which the economy is getting all that it can from its resources and cannot produce more of one good or service without producing less of something else. (p. 60)

Production function A relationship that shows the maximum quantity of real GDP that can be produced as the quantity of labor employed changes and all other influences on production remain the same. (p. 194)

Production possibilities frontier The boundary between the combinations of goods and services that can be produced and the combinations that cannot be produced, given the available factors of production and the state of technology. (p. 58)

Profit Income earned by an entrepreneur for running a business. (p. 37)

Productivity curve The relationship that shows how real GDP per hour of labor changes as the quantity of capital per hour of labor changes. (p. 220)

Property rights Social arrangements that govern the protection of private property—legally established titles to the ownership, use, and disposal of factors of production and goods and services that are enforceable in the courts. (p. 230)

Purchasing power parity Equal value of money—a situation in which money buys the same amount of goods and services in different currencies. (p. 492)

Quantity demanded The amount of any good, service, or resource that people are willing and able to buy during a specified period at a specified price. (p. 83)

Quantity of labor demanded The total labor hours that all the firms in the economy plan to hire during a given time period at a given real wage rate. (p. 195)

Quantity of labor supplied The number of labor hours that all the households in the economy plan to work during a given time period at a given real wage rate. (p. 197)

Quantity of money demanded The amount of money that households and firms choose to hold. (p. 297)

Quantity supplied The amount of any good, service, or resource that people are willing and able to sell during a specified period at a specified price. (p. 88)

Quantity theory of money The proposition that when real GDP equals potential GDP, an increase in the quantity of money brings an equal percentage increase in the price level. (p. 308)

Rational choice A choice that uses the available resources to best achieve the objective of the person making the choice. (p. 9)

Rational expectation The forecast resulting from use of all the relevant data and economic science. (p. 389)

Real business cycle A cycle that results from fluctuations in the pace of growth of labor productivity and potential GDP. (p. 339)

Real GDP The value of the final goods and services produced in a given year expressed in terms of the prices in a *base year*. (p. 124)

Real interest rate The goods and services forgone in interest expressed as a percentage of the amount loaned and calculated as the nominal interest rate minus the inflation rate. (p. 182)

Real wage rate The average hourly wage rate measured in the dollars of a given reference base year. (p. 180)

Recession A period during which real GDP decreases for at least two successive quarters; or defined by the NBER as "a period of significant decline in total output, income, employment, and trade, usually lasting from six months to a year, and marked by contractions in many sectors of the economy." (p. 128)

Recessionary gap A gap that exists when potential GDP exceeds real GDP and that brings a falling price level. (p. 337)

Reference base period A period for which the CPI is defined to equal 100. Currently, the reference base period is 1982–1984. (p. 166)

Rent Income paid for the use of land (p. 37)

Rent seeking Lobbying and other political activity that aims to capture the gains from trade. The act of obtaining special treatment by the government to create economic profit or divert consumer surplus or producer surplus away from others. (p. 469)

Reserves The currency in the bank's vaults plus the balance on its reserve account at a Federal Reserve Bank. (p. 273)

Rule of 70 The number of years it takes for the level of any variable to double is approximately 70 divided by the annual percentage growth rate of the variable. (p. 215)

Saving The amount of income that is not paid in net taxes or spent on consumption goods and services. (p. 116)

Scarcity The condition that arises because wants exceed the ability of resources to satisfy them. (p. 2)

Scatter diagram A graph of the value of one variable against the value of another variable. (p. 22)

Self-interest The choices that are best for the individual who makes them. (p. 4)

Short-run Phillips curve A curve that shows the relationship between the inflation rate and the unemployment rate when the natural unemployment rate and the expected inflation rate remain constant. (p. 376)

Slope The change in the value of the variable measured on the y-axis divided by the change in the value of the variable measured on the x-axis. (p. 27)

Social interest The choices that are best for society as a whole. (p. 4)

Stagflation A combination of recession (falling real GDP) and inflation (rising price level). (p. 341)

Stock A certificate of ownership and claim to the profits that a firm makes. (p. 242)

Structural surplus or deficit The budget balance that would occur if the economy were at full employment. (p. 405)

Structural unemployment The unemployment that arises when changes in technology or international competition change the skills needed to perform jobs or change the locations of jobs. (p. 155)

Substitute A good that can be consumed in place of another good. (p. 85)

Substitute in production A good that can be produced in place of another good. (p. 90)

Supply The relationship between the quantity supplied and the price of a good when all other influences on selling plans remain the same. (p. 88)

Supply curve A graph of the relationship between the quantity supplied of a good and its price when all the other influences on selling plans remain the same. (p. 89)

Supply of labor The relationship between the quantity of labor supplied and the real wage rate when all other influences on work plans remain the same. (p. 197)

Supply of loanable funds The relationship between the quantity of loanable funds supplied and the real interest rate when all other influences on lending plans remain the same. (p. 249)

Supply of money The relationship between the quantity of money supplied and the nominal interest rate. (p. 300)

Supply schedule A list of the quantities supplied at each different price when all the other influences on selling plans remain the same. (p. 89)

Supply-side effects The effects of fiscal policy on potential GDP and the economic growth rate (p. 410)

Tariff A tax imposed on a good when it is imported. (p. 459)

Targeting rule A decision rule for monetary policy that sets the policy instrument at a level that makes the central bank's forecast of the ultimate policy goals equal to their targets. (p. 428)

Tax multiplier The effect of a change in taxes on aggregate demand. (p. 406)

Tax wedge The gap created by a tax between what a buyer pays and what a seller receives. In the labor market, it is the gap between the before-tax wage rate and the after-tax wage rate. (p. 411)

Time-series graph A graph that measures time on the x-axis and the variable or variables in which we are interested on the y-axis. (p. 22)

Tradeoff An exchange—giving up one thing to get something else. (pp. 8, 61)

Transfer payments Social Security benefits, Medicare and Medicaid benefits, unemployment benefits, and other cash benefits. (p. 399)

Transfer payments multiplier The effect of a change in transfer payments on aggregate demand. (p. 406)

Trend A general tendency for the value of a variable to rise or fall over time. (p. 22)

Unemployment rate The percentage of the people in the labor force who are unemployed. (p. 145)

Union wage A wage rate that results from collective bargaining between a labor union and a firm. (p. 205)

U.S. interest rate differential The U.S. interest rate minus the foreign interest rate. (p. 486)

U.S. official reserves The government's holdings of foreign currency. (p. 476)

Velocity of circulation The average number of times in a year that each dollar of money gets used to buy final goods and services. (p. 308)

Wages Income paid for the services of labor. (p. 37)

Wealth The value of all the things that people own. (p. 240)

Working-age population The total number of people aged 16 years and over who are not in jail, hospital, or some other form of institutional care or in the U.S. Armed Forces. (p. 144)

Index

unemployment benefits and, 203
wages and, 205–206

Kahn, Lawrence M., 151
Kennedy, John F., 380
Kershaw, Clayton, 15
Keynes, John Maynard, 190, 360
Keynesian macroeconomics, 190, 350
full employment and, 190–191
goods and services in, 190–191
Keynesian view, 403
k-percent rule, 443
Kremer, Michael, 216
Krugman, Paul, 191, 403
Kydland, Finn E., 190

Labor, 35. *See also* Demand for labor;
Quantity of labor
division of, 13
in factors of production, 35
specialization of, 71
supply of, 197–198
in United States, 35, 58
United States' productivity
growth in, 224
Labor force, 144
categories of, 145
participation of, 198
unemployment rate in, 145
Labor force participation rate, 146
Labor markets
activity and status in, 158
demand for labor in, 195–196
equilibrium of, 198–199, 324
income tax influencing, 412
indicators in, 144–147
participation rate in, 151
supply of labor in, 197–198
unemployment rate in, 149–150
Labor productivity, 218
growth in, 222–223, 224
physical capital and, 218–222
United States growth in, 224
Laffer, Arthur, 414, 416
Land, 34
Law-maker discretion, 408
Law-making time lag, 408
Law of demand, 83, 84, 96–97,
484–485
**Law of diminishing marginal
returns, 219–220**
Law of market forces, 94

Law of supply, 88, 487–488
Leisure time, 131, 198
Lenders, 478–479
Life expectancy, 132
Linear relationships, 24
Liquid assets, 274
Loanable funds market, 246
circular flows in, 246
demand in, 246–248
equilibrium in, 252–253
in financial crisis, 254
financial markets grouped with,
246
government budget deficit in,
257–258
government budget surplus in,
256–257
government involved in, 256–258
savings and, 258
supply changes in, 251
supply in, 249–250, 259
Loans
by banks, 274
deposits by making, 281–282
market for, 241–242
Local governments, 48
Long run
demand for money in, 305
full employment in, 305–306
money market in, 305–306
Long-run fiscal policy, 417
Long-run Phillips curve, 382–387
Long-term interest rates, 434
Long-term real interest rates, 435, 440
Loss, 37
Lucas, Robert E., 192, 403
Lucas wedge, 192

M1, 268–269
M2, 268–269
Macroeconomic equilibrium, 336, 337
Macroeconomics, 3
classical, 190–191
Keynesian, 190–191, 350
monetarist, 191
nominal and real values in, 179
Mainstream economic view, 403
Malthusian theory, 226
Margin, 10
Marginal benefits, 10, 11
Marginal cost, 10
Marginally attached workers, 146

Marginal propensity to consume,
352–353, 363–364
Marginal propensity to import, 354
Marginal returns, 219
Marginal tax rate, 364
Market(s), 46. *See also* Factor markets;
Financial markets; Foreign
exchange market; Labor
markets; Loanable funds
market
bond, 242
buyers and sellers in, 230–231
with circular flow, 46
for college education, 101
competitive, 82
economic freedom and, 230–231
emerging, 39
exports of, 455
for financial capital, 241–242
for goods, 46
imports of, 454
loan, 241–242
money, 275, 301, 305–306
price cap in, 107
stock, 242
Market demand, 85
Market equilibrium, 94
in bank reserves, 429
foreign exchange and, 490
in international finance, 490–492
law of market forces and, 94–95
price influencing, 94–95
quantity of labor and, 324
Market forces, law of, 94–95
Market price, 121
Maximum employment, 424–425
Maximum/minimum points, 26
Means of payment, 266
Medicaid, 14, 48, 399
Medicare, 14, 48, 399–400
Medium of exchange, 267
MFA. *See* Multifiber Arrangement
Microeconomics, 2
Microsoft, 36
Mill, John Stuart, 190
Minimum wage
federal, 207
price floor and, 103–104
unemployment created by, 104
in United States, 105, 207
Minimum wage law, 103, 205
Mishkin, Frederic S., 442

Photo Credits

Chapter 1: p. 1: Kali9/Getty Images; p. 2: © The New Yorker Collection 1985 Frank Modell from Cartoonbank. com. All rights reserved. p. 3 top: Owen Franken/Alamy; p. 3 bottom: Andia/Alamy; p. 4: Wavebreak Media/Thinkstock; p. 5 top: Qi Qi Jx/AP Images; p. 5 bottom: Christian Prandl/Imagebroker/Alamy; p. 6 top: Stockbyte/Getty Images; p. 6 bottom: Manuel Balce Ceneta/AP Images; p. 8: Jeff Greenberg/Alamy; p. 9: David R. Frazier/Alamy; p. 11 left: Yuri Arcurs/Shutterstock; p. 11 right: Ron Buskirk/Alamy; p. 13: Classic Image/Alamy; p. 15: European Pressphoto Agency (EPA)/Alamy.

Chapter 2: p. 31: Keith Draycott/FlickrVision/Getty Images; p. 33 first: David Joel/Getty Images; p. 33 second: Monkey Business Images/Shutterstock; p. 33 third: Justaa/Fotolia; p. 33 fourth: Joe Sohm/VisionsofAmerica/Getty Images; p. 36 top left: Stockbyte/Getty Images; p. 36 top right: Jean Shweitzer/Shutterstock; p. 36 bottom left: Ryan McVay/Getty Images; p. 36 bottom right: Rob Melnychuk/Getty Images; p. 41: Acestock/Alamy; p. 43 top left: Dave and Les Jacobs/Blend Images/Corbis; p. 43 top right: Design Pics/Ron Nickel/Getty Images; p. 43 middle left: Muzaffer Akarca/Getty Images; p. 43 middle right: Peter Stuckings/Getty Images; p. 43 bottom left: Panorama/Alamy; p. 43 bottom right: Keren Su/Alamy.

Chapter 3: p. 57: Derrell McCain/Alamy; p. 70: Steve Vidler/SuperStock; p. 71 top: Jim West/Alamy; p. 71 bottom: Irin-k/Shutterstock; p. 72 top: Pearson Education, Inc.; p. 72 bottom: Jack Hollingsworth/Corbis.

Chapter 4: p. 81: Danny Moloshok/Reuters; p. 82 left: Ocean/Corbis; p. 82 middle: Howard Grey/Getty Images;

p. 82 right: Pearson Education, Inc.; p. 99: Elenathewise/Fotolia.

Chapter 5: p. 113: Jim West/Alamy; p. 120: Tony Freeman/PhotoEdit, Inc.

Chapter 6: p. 143: Justin Sullivan/Getty Images; p. 144: Don Emmert/AFP/Getty Images; p. 147: U.S. Census Bureau; p. 155 top: WavebreakmediaMicro/Fotolia; p. 155 bottom: ClassicStock/Alamy.

Chapter 7: p. 165: Jeff Greenberg/Alamy; p. 172: Nenetus/Shutterstock; p. 173 top: Mary Altaffer/AP Images; p. 173 middle: Hurst Photo/Shutterstock; p. 173 bottom: David Paul Morris/Getty Images; p. 178: Igor Golovnov/Alamy.

Chapter 8: p. 189 left: John Burke/Getty Images; p. 189 right: Yellow Dog Productions/Getty Images; p. 207: Foodcollection/Alamy.

Chapter 9: p. 213: Alex Segre/Alamy; p. 219 left: Mucha Josef/Alamy; p. 219 right: Rick Dalton/Ag/Alamy; p. 221 top: Culver Pictures, Inc./SuperStock; p. 221 bottom: Caro/Alamy; p. 224 top left: Michael Ochs Archives/Getty Images; p. 224 top right: Lowell Georgia/Denver Post via Getty Images; p. 224 middle left: Tom McHugh/Getty Images; p. 224 middle right: Tony Korody/Time & Life Pictures/Getty Images; p. 224 bottom left: Justin Sullivan/Getty Images; p. 224 bottom right: Science & Society Picture Library/Getty Images.

Chapter 10: p. 239 left: Robert Clay/Alamy; p. 239 right: Fotolia; p. 254 top: Ken Howard/Alamy; p. 254 bottom: Bloomberg/Getty Images.

Chapter 11: p. 265: Feng Yu/Fotolia; p. 270: Courtesy of Bitcoin; p. 273: Masterpics/Alamy; p. 277: Charles

Dharapak/AP Images; p. 283: Federal Reserve.

Chapter 12: p. 295: Kristoffer Tripplaar/Alamy; p. 312: Bettmann/Corbis.

Chapter 13: p. 323 left: Stock Connection Distribution/Alamy; p. 323 right: Kurhan/Fotolia.

Chapter 14: p. 349 left: Justin Sullivan/Getty Images; p. 349 right: Sean Gallup/Getty Images; p. 360 top: SPL/Science Source/Photo Researchers, Inc.; p. 360 bottom: Charles Phelps Cushing/ClassicStock/Alamy.

Chapter 15: p. 375 left: B.A.E., Inc./Alamy; p. 375 right: Jim West/Alamy.

Chapter 16: p. 397: Pool/Getty Images; p. 400: Dennis Hallinan/Alamy; p. 407: Gabriel Bouys/AFP/Getty Images/Newscom.

Chapter 17: p. 423: Sandra Baker/Alamy; p. 444 left: Chuck Nacke/Alamy; p. 444 right: Gary Spector Photography.

Chapter 18: p. 451: Peter Parks/AFP/Getty Images; p. 453 top: John Froschauer/AP Images; p. 453 bottom: Anna Sheveleva/Shutterstock; p. 457 top left: Chris O'Meara/AP Images; p. 457 top right: Joerg Boethling/Alamy; p. 457 bottom left: Sokolovsky/Shutterstock; p. 457 bottom right: Shawn Baldwin/Bloomberg via Getty Images; p. 465 top: Paulo M.F. Pires/Fotolia; p. 465 bottom: Kumar A. Mahesh/AP Images; p. 466: ArtisticPhoto/Shutterstock; p. 467 top: Richard Graulich/The Palm Beach Post/ZUMA Press/Alamy; p. 467 bottom: Gregg Vignal/Alamy.

Chapter 19: p. 475: Image_/Alamy.

Macroeconomic Data

These macroeconomic data series show some of the trends in GDP and its components, the price level, and other variables that provide information about changes in the standard of living and the cost of living—the central questions of macroeconomics. You will find these data in a spreadsheet that you can download from your MyEconLab Web site.

		NATIONAL INCOME AND PRODUCT ACCOUNTS	1967	1968	1969	1970	1971	1972	1973	1974	1975	1976
		EXPENDITURE APPROACH										
the sum of	1	Personal consumption expenditure	507	557	605	648	701	769	851	932	1,033	1,150
	2	Gross private domestic investment	143	157	174	170	197	228	267	275	257	323
	3	Government expenditure	208	227	240	254	269	288	306	343	383	406
	4	Exports	44	48	52	60	63	71	95	127	139	150
less	5	Imports	40	47	51	56	62	74	91	128	123	151
equals	6	Gross domestic product	862	943	1,020	1,076	1,168	1,282	1,429	1,549	1,689	1,878
		INCOME APPROACH										
	7	Compensation of employees	483	532	586	625	667	734	815	890	950	1,051
plus	8	Net operating surplus	208	222	228	222	247	280	317	323	357	405
equals	9	Net domestic product at factor cost	691	754	814	847	914	1,013	1,132	1,214	1,307	1,457
plus	10	Indirect taxes less subsidies	64	72	79	87	96	101	112	122	131	141
	11	Depreciation (capital consumption)	104	113	125	137	149	161	178	206	238	259
equals	12	GDP (income approach)	858	939	1,018	1,071	1,158	1,275	1,423	1,541	1,676	1,857
plus	13	Statistical discrepancy	3	3	2	5	10	7	6	7	13	21
equals	14	GDP (expenditure approach)	862	943	1,020	1,076	1,168	1,282	1,429	1,549	1,689	1,878
	15	Real GDP (billions of 2009 dollars)	4,351	4,565	4,708	4,718	4,873	5,129	5,418	5,390	5,380	5,669
	16	Real GDP growth rate (percent per year)	2.7	4.9	3.1	0.2	3.3	5.2	5.6	−0.5	−0.2	5.4
		OTHER DATA										
	17	Population (millions)	199	201	203	205	208	210	212	214	216	218
	18	Labor force (millions)	77	79	81	83	84	87	89	92	94	96
	19	Employment (millions)	74	76	78	79	79	82	85	87	86	89
	20	Unemployment (millions)	3	3	3	4	5	5	4	5	8	7
	21	Labor force participation rate (percent of working–age population)	59.6	59.6	60.1	60.4	60.2	60.4	60.8	61.3	61.2	61.6
	22	Unemployment rate (percent of labor force)	3.8	3.6	3.5	5.0	6.0	5.6	4.9	5.6	8.5	7.7
	23	Real GDP per person (2009 dollars per year)	21,893	22,739	23,222	23,003	23,463	24,432	25,565	25,200	24,907	25,996
	24	Growth rate of real GDP per person (percent per year)	1.6	3.9	2.1	−0.9	2.0	4.1	4.6	−1.4	−1.2	4.4
	25	Quantity of money (M2, billions of dollars)	504	545	579	602	674	758	832	881	964	1,087
	26	GDP deflator (2009 = 100)	19.8	20.6	21.7	22.8	24.0	25.0	26.4	28.7	31.4	33.1
	27	GDP deflator inflation rate (percent per year)	2.9	4.3	4.9	5.3	5.1	4.3	5.5	9.0	9.3	5.5
	28	Consumer price index (1982–1984 = 100)	33.4	34.8	36.7	38.8	40.5	41.8	44.4	49.3	53.8	56.9
	29	CPI inflation rate (percent per year)	2.8	4.2	5.4	5.9	4.2	3.3	6.3	11.0	9.1	5.8
	30	Current account balance (billions of dollars)	3	1	0	2	−1	−6	7	2	18	4

1977	1978	1979	1980	1981	1982	1983	1984	1985	1986	1987	1988	1989
1,277	1,426	1,590	1,755	1,938	2,074	2,287	2,498	2,723	2,898	3,092	3,347	3,593
397	478	540	530	631	581	638	820	830	849	892	937	1,000
436	477	526	591	655	710	766	825	908	975	1,031	1,078	1,152
159	187	230	281	305	283	277	302	303	321	364	445	504
182	212	253	294	318	303	329	405	417	453	509	554	591
2,086	2,357	2,632	2,863	3,211	3,345	3,638	4,041	4,347	4,590	4,870	5,253	5,658
1,169	1,320	1,481	1,626	1,795	1,895	2,014	2,218	2,389	2,546	2,726	2,951	3,144
457	526	564	576	670	684	767	921	983	987	1,059	1,175	1,242
1,626	1,846	2,045	2,202	2,465	2,578	2,782	3,139	3,372	3,533	3,785	4,126	4,386
153	162	172	191	224	226	242	269	287	299	317	345	372
288	325	371	426	485	534	561	594	637	682	728	782	836
2,067	2,334	2,587	2,819	3,174	3,338	3,584	4,002	4,296	4,513	4,830	5,253	5,594
19	23	45	44	37	7	54	39	51	77	41	–1	64
2,086	2,357	2,632	2,862	3,211	3,345	3,638	4,041	4,347	4,590	4,870	5,253	5,658
5,931	6,260	6,459	6,443	6,611	6,484	6,785	7,277	7,586	7,852	8,124	8,465	8,777
4.6	5.6	3.2	–0.2	2.6	–1.9	4.6	7.3	4.2	3.5	3.5	4.2	3.7
220	223	225	228	230	232	234	236	239	241	243	245	247
99	102	105	107	109	110	112	114	115	118	120	122	124
92	96	99	99	100	100	101	105	107	110	112	115	117
7	6	6	8	8	11	11	9	8	8	7	7	7
62.2	63.2	63.7	63.8	63.9	64.0	64.0	64.4	64.8	65.2	65.6	65.9	66.4
7.1	6.1	5.9	7.2	7.6	9.7	9.6	7.5	7.2	7.0	6.2	5.5	5.3
26,922	28,120	28,694	28,295	28,741	27,923	28,953	30,784	31,805	32,624	33,453	34,544	35,479
3.6	4.5	2.0	–1.4	1.6	–2.8	3.7	6.3	3.3	2.6	2.5	3.3	2.7
1,221	1,322	1,426	1,540	1,679	1,831	2,055	2,219	2,417	2,614	2,784	2,934	3,056
35.2	37.6	40.8	44.4	48.6	51.6	53.6	55.5	57.3	58.5	59.9	62.0	64.5
6.2	7.0	8.3	9.0	9.3	6.2	3.9	3.5	3.2	2.0	2.6	3.5	3.9
60.6	65.2	72.6	82.4	90.9	96.5	99.6	103.9	107.6	109.7	113.6	118.3	123.9
6.5	7.6	11.3	13.5	10.4	6.2	3.2	4.4	3.5	1.9	3.6	4.1	4.8
–14	–15	–0	2	5	–6	–39	–94	–118	–147	–161	–121	–99

Macroeconomic Data

These macroeconomic data series show some of the trends in GDP and its components, the price level, and other variables that provide information about changes in the standard of living and the cost of living—the central questions of macroeconomics. You will find these data in a spreadsheet that you can download from your MyEconLab Web site.

		NATIONAL INCOME AND PRODUCT ACCOUNTS	1990	1991	1992	1993	1994	1995	1996	1997	1998	1999
		EXPENDITURE APPROACH										
the sum of	1	Personal consumption expenditure	3,826	3,960	4,216	4,471	4,741	4,984	5,268	5,561	5,903	6,317
	2	Gross private domestic investment	994	944	1,013	1,107	1,257	1,318	1,432	1,596	1,735	1,884
	3	Government expenditure	1,238	1,298	1,345	1,366	1,404	1,452	1,496	1,554	1,614	1,726
	4	Exports	552	595	633	655	721	813	868	954	953	989
less	5	Imports	630	624	668	720	813	903	964	1,056	1,116	1,251
equals	6	Gross domestic product	5,980	6,174	6,539	6,879	7,309	7,664	8,100	8,609	9,089	9,666
		INCOME APPROACH										
	7	Compensation of employees	3,345	3,455	3,674	3,824	4,014	4,207	4,426	4,719	5,082	5,418
plus	8	Net operating surplus	1,258	1,270	1,341	1,432	1,590	1,721	1,896	2,059	2,154	2,251
equals	9	Net domestic product at factor cost	4,603	4,725	5,015	5,256	5,604	5,928	6,322	6,779	7,236	7,669
	10	Indirect taxes less subsidies	398	430	453	466	513	523	546	578	603	628
plus	11	Depreciation (capital consumption)	887	931	960	1,004	1,056	1,123	1,176	1,240	1,310	1,401
equals	12	GDP (income approach)	5,888	6,086	6,428	6,726	7,172	7,574	8,044	8,596	9,149	9,698
plus	13	Statistical discrepancy	91	88	111	152	137	91	57	12	–60	–32
equals	14	GDP (expenditure approach)	5,980	6,174	6,539	6,879	7,309	7,664	8,100	8,609	9,089	9,666
	15	Real GDP (billions of 2009 dollars)	8,945	8,939	9,257	9,511	9,895	10,164	10,550	11,023	11,513	12,071
	16	Real GDP growth rate (percent per year)	1.9	–0.1	3.6	2.7	4.0	2.7	3.8	4.5	4.4	4.8
		OTHER DATA										
	17	Population (millions)	250	254	257	260	263	267	270	273	276	279
	18	Labor force (millions)	126	126	128	129	131	132	134	136	138	139
	19	Employment (millions)	119	118	118	120	123	125	127	130	131	134
	20	Unemployment (millions)	7	9	10	9	8	7	7	7	6	6
	21	Labor force participation rate (percent of working-age population)	66.5	66.2	66.4	66.3	66.6	66.6	66.8	67.1	67.1	67.1
	22	Unemployment rate (percent of labor force)	5.6	6.9	7.5	6.9	6.1	5.6	5.4	4.9	4.5	4.2
	23	Real GDP per person (2009 dollars per year)	35,756	35,258	36,029	36,540	37,557	38,125	39,114	40,383	41,692	43,216
	24	Growth rate of real GDP per person (percent per year)	0.8	–1.4	2.2	1.4	2.8	1.5	2.6	3.2	3.2	3.7
	25	Quantity of money (M2, billions of dollars)	3,224	3,342	3,403	3,438	3,482	3,553	3,724	3,910	4,190	4,497
	26	GDP deflator (2009 = 100)	66.8	69.1	70.6	72.3	73.9	75.4	76.8	78.1	78.9	80.1
	27	GDP deflator inflation rate (percent per year)	3.7	3.3	2.3	2.4	2.1	2.1	1.8	1.7	1.1	1.4
	28	Consumer price index (1982–1984 = 100)	130.7	136.2	140.3	144.5	148.2	152.4	156.9	160.5	163.0	166.6
	29	CPI inflation rate (percent per year)	5.4	4.2	3.0	3.0	2.6	2.8	2.9	2.3	1.5	2.2
	30	Current account balance (billions of dollars)	–79	3	–52	–85	–122	–114	–125	–141	–215	–301

2000	2001	2002	2003	2004	2005	2006	2007	2008	2009	2010	2011	2012
6,802	7,107	7,385	7,764	8,258	8,790	9,298	9,744	10,006	9,843	10,202	10,712	11,150
2,034	1,929	1,925	2,028	2,277	2,527	2,681	2,644	2,425	1,878	2,101	2,232	2,475
1,834	1,959	2,095	2,221	2,357	2,494	2,642	2,802	3,003	3,089	3,174	3,159	3,167
1,094	1,029	1,005	1,043	1,183	1,310	1,479	1,666	1,843	1,584	1,844	2,101	2,196
1,474	1,398	1,430	1,544	1,798	2,026	2,241	2,376	2,556	1,976	2,362	2,670	2,743
10,290	10,625	10,980	11,512	12,277	13,095	13,858	14,480	14,720	14,418	14,958	15,534	16,245
5,863	6,054	6,150	6,373	6,749	7,098	7,514	7,909	8,090	7,796	7,975	8,287	8,620
2,344	2,410	2,517	2,665	2,886	3,176	3,483	3,307	3,179	3,214	3,557	3,811	4,033
8,207	8,464	8,667	9,038	9,634	10,274	10,997	11,216	11,269	11,010	11,532	12,098	12,653
663	669	721	759	818	874	940	980	989	968	1,001	1,037	1,066
1,514	1,604	1,662	1,727	1,832	1,982	2,136	2,264	2,363	2,368	2,382	2,453	2,543
10,384	10,737	11,050	11,524	12,284	13,129	14,073	14,460	14,621	14,346	14,915	15,588	16,262
−95	−112	−70	−12	−7	−34	−215	20	99	72	43	−54	−17
10,290	10,625	10,980	11,512	12,277	13,095	13,858	14,480	14,720	14,418	14,958	15,534	16,245
12,565	12,684	12,910	13,270	13,774	14,236	14,615	14,877	14,834	14,418	14,779	15,052	15,471
4.1	0.9	1.8	2.8	3.8	3.4	2.7	1.8	−0.3	−2.8	2.5	1.8	2.8
282	285	288	291	293	296	299	302	305	307	310	312	314
143	144	145	147	147	149	151	153	154	154	154	154	155
137	137	136	138	139	142	144	146	145	140	139	140	142
6	7	8	9	8	8	7	7	9	14	15	14	12
67.1	66.8	66.6	66.2	66.0	66.0	66.2	66.0	66.0	65.4	64.7	64.1	63.7
4.0	4.7	5.8	6.0	5.5	5.1	4.6	4.6	5.8	9.3	9.6	8.9	8.1
44,495	44,472	44,832	45,660	46,968	48,094	48,910	49,311	48,708	46,927	47,710	48,239	49,226
3.0	−0.1	0.8	1.8	2.9	2.4	1.7	0.8	−1.2	−3.7	1.7	1.1	2.0
4,769	5,179	5,562	5,950	6,237	6,506	6,847	7,269	7,765	8,386	8,594	9,222	10,011
81.9	83.8	85.1	86.8	89.1	92.0	94.8	97.3	99.2	100.0	101.2	103.2	105.0
2.3	2.3	1.5	2.0	2.7	3.2	3.1	2.7	2.0	0.8	1.2	2.0	1.7
172.2	177.0	179.9	184.0	188.9	195.3	201.6	207.3	215.3	214.6	218.1	224.9	229.6
3.4	2.8	1.6	2.3	2.7	3.4	3.2	2.9	3.8	−0.3	1.6	3.1	2.1
−416	−397	−458	−519	−629	−740	−798	−713	−681	−382	−449	−458	−440